Accelerated 7

Copyright © 2020 by Houghton Mifflin Harcourt Publishing Company

All rights reserved. No part of this work may be reproduced or transmitted in any form or by any means, electronic or mechanical, including photocopying or recording, or by any information storage or retrieval system, without the prior written permission of the copyright owner unless such copying is expressly permitted by federal copyright law. Requests for permission to make copies of any part of the work should be submitted through our Permissions website at https://customercare.hmhco.com/contactus/Permissions.html or mailed to Houghton Mifflin Harcourt Publishing Company, Attn: Rights Compliance and Analysis, 9400 Southpark Center Loop, Orlando, Florida 32819-8647.

Common Core State Standards © Copyright 2010. National Governors Association Center for Best Practices and Council of Chief State School Officers. All rights reserved.

This product is not sponsored or endorsed by the Common Core State Standards Initiative of the National Governors Association Center for Best Practices and the Council of Chief State School Officers.

Currency and Coins Photos courtesy of United States Mint, Bureau of Engraving and Houghton Mifflin Harcourt

Printed in the U.S.A.

ISBN 978-0-358-11605-9

9 10 0607 28 27 26 25 24 23

4500868021 .21

If you have received these materials as examination copies free of charge, Houghton Mifflin Harcourt Publishing Company retains title to the materials and they may not be resold. Resale of examination copies is strictly prohibited.

Possession of this publication in print format does not entitle users to convert this publication, or any portion of it, into electronic format.

Dear Students and Families,

Welcome to *Into Math*, Accelerated 7! In this program, you will develop skills and make sense of mathematics by solving real-world problems, using hands-on tools and strategies, and collaborating with your classmates.

With the support of your teacher and by engaging with meaningful practice you will learn to persevere when solving problems. *Into Math* will not only help you deepen your understanding of mathematics, but also build your confidence as a learner of mathematics.

Even more exciting, you will write all your ideas and solutions right in your book. In your *Into Math* book, writing and drawing on the pages will help you think deeply about what you are learning, help you truly understand math, and most important, you will become a confident user of mathematics!

**Sincerely,
The Authors**

Authors

Edward B. Burger, PhD
President, Southwestern University
Georgetown, Texas

Matthew R. Larson, PhD
Past-President, National Council
of Teachers of Mathematics
Lincoln Public Schools
Lincoln, Nebraska

Juli K. Dixon, PhD
Professor, Mathematics Education
University of Central Florida
Orlando, Florida

Steven J. Leinwand
Principal Research Analyst
American Institutes for Research
Washington, DC

Timothy D. Kanold, PhD
Mathematics Educator
Chicago, Illinois

Consultants

English Language Development Consultant

Harold Asturias
Director, Center for Mathematics
Excellence and Equity
Lawrence Hall of Science, University of California
Berkeley, California

Program Consultant

David Dockterman, EdD
Lecturer, Harvard Graduate School of Education
Cambridge, Massachusetts

Blended Learning Consultant

Weston Kiercshneck
Senior Fellow
International Center for Leadership in Education
Littleton, Colorado

STEM Consultants

Michael A. DiSpezio
Global Educator
North Falmouth, Massachusetts

Marjorie Frank
Science Writer and
Content-Area Reading Specialist
Brooklyn, New York

Bernadine Okoro
Access and Equity and
STEM Learning Advocate and Consultant
Washington, DC

Cary I. Sneider, PhD
Associate Research Professor
Portland State University
Portland, Oregon

Unit 1: Ratios and Proportional Reasoning

Unit Opener 1

MODULE 1 Identify and Represent Proportional Relationships

Module Opener 3

Are You Ready? 4

Lesson 1 Explore Relationships 5

Lesson 2 Recognize Proportional Relationships in Tables 11

Lesson 3 Compute Unit Rates Involving Complex Fractions 19

Lesson 4 Recognize Proportional Relationships in Graphs 27

Lesson 5 Use Proportional Relationships to Solve Rate Problems 35

Lesson 6 Practice Proportional Reasoning with Scale Drawings 43

Module Review 51

● Build Conceptual Understanding   ● Connect Concepts and Skills   ● Apply and Practice

MODULE 2 Proportional Reasoning with Percents

Module Opener 53

Are You Ready? 54

Lesson 1 Percent Change 55

Lesson 2 Markups and Discounts 61

Lesson 3 Taxes and Gratuities 67

Lesson 4 Commissions and Fees 73

Lesson 5 Simple Interest 79

Module Review 85

Unit 2 Number Systems and Operations

Unit Opener 87

MODULE 3 Understand Addition and Subtraction of Rational Numbers

Module Opener 89

Are You Ready? 90

Lesson 1 Add or Subtract a Positive Integer on a Number Line 91

Lesson 2 Add or Subtract a Negative Integer on a Number Line 97

Lesson 3 Use a Number Line to Add and Subtract Rational Numbers 105

Module Review 113

Build Conceptual Understanding   Connect Concepts and Skills   Apply and Practice

vii

MODULE 4 Fluency with Rational Number Operations

Module Opener **115**

Are You Ready? **116**

Lesson 1 Compute Sums of Rational Numbers **117**

Lesson 2 Compute Differences of Rational Numbers **125**

Lesson 3 Understand and Compute Products and Quotients of Rational Numbers **133**

Lesson 4 Write Rational Numbers as Decimals............ **141**

Lesson 5 Multiply and Divide Rational Numbers in Context **149**

Module Review **155**

MODULE 5 Applying Properties to Operations

Module Opener **157**

Are You Ready? **158**

Lesson 1 Apply Properties to Multi-Step Problems with Rational Numbers **159**

Lesson 2 Solve Multi-Step Problems with Rational Numbers in Context.. **167**

Lesson 3 Add, Subtract, Factor, and Expand Algebraic Expressions **175**

Module Review **183**

○ Build Conceptual Understanding   ○ Connect Concepts and Skills   ○ Apply and Practice

Unit 3
Equations and Inequalities in One Variable

Unit Opener 185

MODULE 6 Solve Linear Equations

Module Opener **187**

Are You Ready? **188**

Lesson 1 Write Two-Step Equations for Situations **189**

Lesson 2 Apply Two-Step Equations to Solve
Real-World Problems **195**

Lesson 3 Solve Multi-Step Linear Equations **201**

Lesson 4 Examine Special Cases **209**

Lesson 5 Apply Linear Equations **215**

Module Review **223**

● Build Conceptual Understanding   ● Connect Concepts and Skills   ● Apply and Practice

ix

MODULE 7 Solve Problems Using Inequalities

Module Opener **225**

Are You Ready? **226**

Lesson 1 Understand and Apply Properties to Solve
One-Step Inequalities **227**

Lesson 2 Write Two-Step Inequalities for Situations **235**

Lesson 3 Apply Two-Step Inequalities to Solve Problems **241**

Module Review **247**

Build Conceptual Understanding   Connect Concepts and Skills   Apply and Practice

Unit 4
Transform and Construct Geometric Figures

Unit Opener 249

MODULE 8 Transformations and Congruence

Module Opener	**251**
Are You Ready?	**252**
Lesson 1 Investigate Transformations	**253**
Lesson 2 Explore Translations	**259**
Lesson 3 Explore Reflections	**267**
Lesson 4 Explore Rotations	**275**
Lesson 5 Understand and Recognize Congruent Figures	**283**
Module Review	**291**

● Build Conceptual Understanding   ● Connect Concepts and Skills   ● Apply and Practice

MODULE 9 Draw and Analyze Two-Dimensional Figures

Module Opener 293

Are You Ready? 294

Lesson 1 Draw Shapes with Given Conditions 295

Lesson 2 Draw and Construct Triangles Given Side Lengths 301

Lesson 3 Draw and Construct Triangles Given Angle Measures 309

Lesson 4 Draw and Analyze Shapes to Solve Problems 315

Module Review 321

MODULE 10 Transformations and Similarity

Module Opener 323

Are You Ready? 324

Lesson 1 Investigate Reductions and Enlargements 325

Lesson 2 Explore Dilations 333

Lesson 3 Understand and Recognize Similar Figures 341

Module Review 349

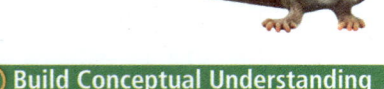  

Unit 5: Similarity, Slope, and Linear Relationships

Unit Opener 351

MODULE 11 Angle Relationships

Module Opener	353
Are You Ready?	354
Lesson 1 Develop Angle Relationships for Triangles	355
Lesson 2 Investigate Angle-Angle Similarity	363
Lesson 3 Explore Parallel Lines Cut by a Transversal	371
Module Review	379

MODULE 12 Linear Relationships

Module Opener	381
Are You Ready?	382
Lesson 1 Explain Slope with Similar Triangles	383
Lesson 2 Derive $y = mx$	389
Lesson 3 Derive and Interpret $y = mx + b$	395
Lesson 4 Describe and Sketch Nonlinear Relationships	401
Module Review	409

Build Conceptual Understanding   Connect Concepts and Skills   Apply and Practice

Unit 6: Applications of Real Numbers and Exponents

Unit Opener 411

MODULE 13 Real Numbers

Module Opener	413
Are You Ready?	414
Lesson 1 Understand Rational and Irrational Numbers	415
Lesson 2 Investigate Roots	421
Lesson 3 Order Real Numbers	429
Module Review	435

MODULE 14 The Pythagorean Theorem

Module Opener	437
Are You Ready?	438
Lesson 1 Prove the Pythagorean Theorem and Its Converse	439
Lesson 2 Apply the Pythagorean Theorem	445
Lesson 3 Apply the Pythagorean Theorem in the Coordinate Plane	453
Module Review	459

● Build Conceptual Understanding   ● Connect Concepts and Skills   ● Apply and Practice

MODULE 15 Exponents and Scientific Notation

Module Opener 461

Are You Ready? 462

Lesson 1 Know and Apply Properties of Exponents 463

Lesson 2 Understand Scientific Notation 471

Lesson 3 Compute with Scientific Notation 479

Module Review 485

Build Conceptual Understanding   Connect Concepts and Skills   Apply and Practice

Unit 7　Area and Volume

Unit Opener 487

MODULE 16　Analyze Figures to Find Circumference and Area

Module Opener **489**

Are You Ready? **490**

Lesson 1　Derive and Apply Formulas for Circumference **491**

Lesson 2　Derive and Apply a Formula
　　　　　　for the Area of a Circle **497**

Lesson 3　Areas of Composite Figures **503**

Module Review **509**

Build Conceptual Understanding　　Connect Concepts and Skills　　Apply and Practice

MODULE 17 Cross Sections, Surface Area, and Volume

Module Opener **511**

Are You Ready? **512**

Lesson 1 Describe and Analyze Cross Sections of Solids **513**

Lesson 2 Derive and Apply Formulas for Surface Areas of Cubes and Right Prisms **519**

Lesson 3 Derive and Apply a Formula for the Volume of a Right Prism **525**

Lesson 4 Find Volume of Cylinders **531**

Lesson 5 Find Volume of Cones and Spheres **537**

Lesson 6 Solve Multi-Step Problems with Surface Area and Volume **545**

Module Review **551**

● Build Conceptual Understanding   ● Connect Concepts and Skills   ● Apply and Practice

xvii

Unit 8 Data Analysis and Sampling

Unit Opener 553

MODULE 18 Proportional Reasoning with Samples

Module Opener **555**

Are You Ready? **556**

Lesson 1 Understand Representative Samples **557**

Lesson 2 Make Inferences from a Random Sample **563**

Lesson 3 Make Inferences from Repeated Random Samples . . . **571**

Module Review **577**

MODULE 19 Use Statistics and Graphs to Compare Data

Module Opener **579**

Are You Ready? **580**

Lesson 1 Compare Center and Spread of Data Displayed in Dot Plots **581**

Lesson 2 Compare Center and Spread of Data Displayed in Box Plots **587**

Lesson 3 Compare Means Using Mean Absolute Deviation and Repeated Sampling **593**

Module Review **599**

Build Conceptual Understanding　　Connect Concepts and Skills　　Apply and Practice

Unit 9 Probability

Unit Opener 601

MODULE 20 Understand and Apply Experimental Probability

Module Opener 603

Are You Ready? 604

Lesson 1 Understand Probability of an Event 605

Lesson 2 Find Experimental Probability of Simple Events 611

Lesson 3 Find Experimental Probability of Compound Events 619

Lesson 4 Use Experimental Probability and Proportional Reasoning to Make Predictions 627

Module Review 633

● Build Conceptual Understanding   ● Connect Concepts and Skills   ● Apply and Practice

xix

MODULE 21 Understand and Apply Theoretical Probability

Module Opener **635**

Are You Ready? **636**

○ **Lesson 1** Find Theoretical Probability of Simple Events **637**

○ **Lesson 2** Find Theoretical Probability of Compound Events **645**

○ **Lesson 3** Use Theoretical Probability and Proportional Reasoning to Make Predictions **653**

○ **Lesson 4** Conduct Simulations **659**

Module Review **665**

○ Build Conceptual Understanding   ○ Connect Concepts and Skills   ○ Apply and Practice

Interactive Standards

My Progress on Mathematics Standards

The lessons in your *Into Math* book provide instruction for Mathematics Standards for an Accelerated 7 course. You can use the following pages to reflect on your learning and record your progress through the standards.

As you learn new concepts, reflect on this learning. Consider inserting a checkmark if you understand the concepts or inserting a question mark if you have questions or need help.

	Student Edition Lessons	My Progress
Domain: RATIOS & PROPORTIONAL RELATIONSHIPS		
Cluster: Analyze proportional relationships and use them to solve real-world and mathematical problems.		
Compute unit rates associated with ratios of fractions, including ratios of lengths, areas and other quantities measured in like or different units.	1.3, 1.6	
Recognize and represent proportional relationships between quantities.	1.1 *See also below.*	
• Decide whether two quantities are in a proportional relationship, e.g., by testing for equivalent ratios in a table or graphing on a coordinate plane and observing whether the graph is a straight line through the origin.	1.2, 1.4	
• Identify the constant of proportionality (unit rate) in tables, graphs, equations, diagrams, and verbal descriptions of proportional relationships.	1.1, 1.2, 1.4, 1.5	
• Represent proportional relationships by equations.	1.2	
• Explain what a point (*x*, *y*) on the graph of a proportional relationship means in terms of the situation, with special attention to the points (0, 0) and (1, *r*) where *r* is the unit rate.	1.4	
Use proportional relationships to solve multistep ratio and percent problems.	1.5, 1.6, 2.1, 2.2, 2.3, 2.4, 2.5	

Mathematics Standards **xxi**

Interactive Standards

Domain: THE NUMBER SYSTEM		
Cluster: Apply and extend previous understandings of operations with fractions to add, subtract, multiply, and divide rational numbers.		
Apply and extend previous understandings of addition and subtraction to add and subtract rational numbers; represent addition and subtraction on a horizontal or vertical number line diagram.	3.1, 3.2, 3.3, 4.1, 4.2 See also below.	
• Describe situations in which opposite quantities combine to make 0.	3.3	
• Understand $p + q$ as the number located a distance $|q|$ from p, in the positive or negative direction depending on whether q is positive or negative. Show that a number and its opposite have a sum of 0 (are additive inverses). Interpret sums of rational numbers by describing real-world contexts.	3.1, 3.2, 3.3, 4.1	
• Understand subtraction of rational numbers as adding the additive inverse, $p - q = p + (-q)$. Show that the distance between two rational numbers on the number line is the absolute value of their difference, and apply this principle in real-world contexts.	4.1, 4.2	
• Apply properties of operations as strategies to add and subtract rational numbers.	5.1	
Apply and extend previous understandings of multiplication and division and of fractions to multiply and divide rational numbers.	See below.	
• Understand that multiplication is extended from fractions to rational numbers by requiring that operations continue to satisfy the properties of operations, particularly the distributive property, leading to products such as $(-1)(-1) = 1$ and the rules for multiplying signed numbers. Interpret products of rational numbers by describing real-world contexts.	4.3, 4.5	
• Understand that integers can be divided, provided that the divisor is not zero, and every quotient of integers (with non-zero divisor) is a rational number. If p and q are integers, then $-\left(\frac{p}{q}\right) = \frac{(-p)}{q} = \frac{p}{(-q)}$. Interpret quotients of rational numbers by describing real-world contexts.	4.3, 4.4	

xxii Mathematics Standards

Interactive Standards

• Apply properties of operations as strategies to multiply and divide rational numbers.	4.3, 5.1	
• Convert a rational number to a decimal using long division; know that the decimal form of a rational number terminates in 0s or eventually repeats.	4.4	
Solve real-world and mathematical problems involving the four operations with rational numbers.	4.1, 4.2, 4.3, 4.5, 5.1, 5.2	

Cluster: Know that there are numbers that are not rational, and approximate them by rational numbers.

Know that numbers that are not rational are called irrational. Understand informally that every number has a decimal expansion; for rational numbers show that the decimal expansion repeats eventually, and convert a decimal expansion which repeats eventually into a rational number.	13.1	
Use rational approximations of irrational numbers to compare the size of irrational numbers, locate them approximately on a number line diagram, and estimate the value of expressions (e.g., π^2).	13.3	

Domain: EXPRESSIONS & EQUATIONS

Cluster: Use properties of operations to generate equivalent expressions.

Apply properties of operations as strategies to add, subtract, factor, and expand linear expressions with rational coefficients.	5.3	
Understand that rewriting an expression in different forms in a problem context can shed light on the problem and how the quantities in it are related.	2.2, 5.3	

Cluster: Solve real-life and mathematical problems using numerical and algebraic expressions and equations.

Solve multi-step real-life and mathematical problems posed with positive and negative rational numbers in any form (whole numbers, fractions, and decimals), using tools strategically. Apply properties of operations to calculate with numbers in any form; convert between forms as appropriate; and assess the reasonableness of answers using mental computation and estimation strategies.	5.2, 6.2, 16.1, 16.2, 16.3, 17.2, 17.3, 17.4, 17.5, 17.6, 20.4, 21.3	

Interactive Standards

Use variables to represent quantities in a real-world or mathematical problem, and construct simple equations and inequalities to solve problems by reasoning about the quantities.	6.1, 7.2 See also below.	
• Solve word problems leading to equations of the form $px + q = r$ and $p(x + q) = r$, where p, q, and r are specific rational numbers. Solve equations of these forms fluently. Compare an algebraic solution to an arithmetic solution, identifying the sequence of the operations used in each approach.	6.2, 6.5	
• Solve word problems leading to inequalities of the form $px + q > r$ or $px + q < r$, where p, q, and r are specific rational numbers. Graph the solution set of the inequality and interpret it in the context of the problem.	7.1, 7.3	
Cluster: Work with radicals and integer exponents.		
Know and apply the properties of integer exponents to generate equivalent numerical expressions.	15.1	
Use square root and cube root symbols to represent solutions to equations of the form $x^2 = p$ and $x^3 = p$, where p is a positive rational number. Evaluate square roots of small perfect squares and cube roots of small perfect cubes. Know that $\sqrt{2}$ is irrational.	13.2	
Use numbers expressed in the form of a single digit times an integer power of 10 to estimate very large or very small quantities, and to express how many times as much one is than the other.	15.2	
Perform operations with numbers expressed in scientific notation, including problems where both decimal and scientific notation are used. Use scientific notation and choose units of appropriate size for measurements of very large or very small quantities (e.g., use millimeters per year for seafloor spreading). Interpret scientific notation that has been generated by technology.	15.3	
Cluster: Understand the connections between proportional relationships, lines, and linear equations.		
Graph proportional relationships, interpreting the unit rate as the slope of the graph. Compare two different proportional relationships represented in different ways.	1.4, 1.5, 12.2	

Interactive Standards

Use similar triangles to explain why the slope m is the same between any two distinct points on a non-vertical line in the coordinate plane; derive the equation $y = mx$ for a line through the origin and the equation $y = mx + b$ for a line intercepting the vertical axis at b.	12.1, 12.2, 12.3	
Cluster: Analyze and solve linear equations and pairs of simultaneous linear equations.		
Solve linear equations in one variable.	6.3, 6.4, 6.5 See also below.	
• Give examples of linear equations in one variable with one solution, infinitely many solutions, or no solutions. Show which of these possibilities is the case by successively transforming the given equation into simpler forms, until an equivalent equation of the form $x = a$, $a = a$, or $a = b$ results (where a and b are different numbers).	6.4, 6.5	
• Solve linear equations with rational number coefficients, including equations whose solutions require expanding expressions using the distributive property and collecting like terms.	6.3, 6.4	
Domain: FUNCTIONS		
Cluster: Use functions to model relationships between quantities.		
Describe qualitatively the functional relationship between two quantities by analyzing a graph (e.g., where the function is increasing or decreasing, linear or nonlinear). Sketch a graph that exhibits the qualitative features of a function that has been described verbally.	12.4	
Domain: GEOMETRY		
Cluster: Draw, construct, and describe geometrical figures and describe the relationships between them.		
Solve problems involving scale drawings of geometric figures, including computing actual lengths and areas from a scale drawing and reproducing a scale drawing at a different scale.	1.6	
Draw (freehand, with ruler and protractor, and with technology) geometric shapes with given conditions. Focus on constructing triangles from three measures of angles or sides, noticing when the conditions determine a unique triangle, more than one triangle, or no triangle.	9.1, 9.2, 9.3, 9.4	

Interactive Standards

Describe the two-dimensional figures that result from slicing three-dimensional figures, as in plane sections of right rectangular prisms and right rectangular pyramids.	17.1	
Cluster: Solve real-life and mathematical problems involving angle measure, area, surface area, and volume.		
Know the formulas for the area and circumference of a circle and use them to solve problems; give an informal derivation of the relationship between the circumference and area of a circle.	16.1, 16.2	
Use facts about supplementary, complementary, vertical, and adjacent angles in a multi-step problem to write and solve simple equations for an unknown angle in a figure.	6.5	
Solve real-world and mathematical problems involving area, volume and surface area of two- and three-dimensional objects composed of triangles, quadrilaterals, polygons, cubes, and right prisms.	16.3, 17.2, 17.3, 17.6	
Cluster: Understand congruence and similarity using physical models, transparencies, or geometry software.		
Verify experimentally the properties of rotations, reflections, and translations:	8.1, 8.2, 8.3, 8.4 See also below.	
• Lines are taken to lines, and line segments to line segments of the same length.	8.1, 8.2, 8.3, 8.4	
• Angles are taken to angles of the same measure.	8.1, 8.2, 8.3, 8.4	
• Parallel lines are taken to parallel lines.	8.1, 8.2, 8.3, 8.4	
Understand that a two-dimensional figure is congruent to another if the second can be obtained from the first by a sequence of rotations, reflections, and translations; given two congruent figures, describe a sequence that exhibits the congruence between them.	8.5	
Describe the effect of dilations, translations, rotations, and reflections on two-dimensional figures using coordinates.	8.5, 10.1, 10.2	
Understand that a two-dimensional figure is similar to another if the second can be obtained from the first by a sequence of rotations, reflections, translations, and dilations; given two similar two-dimensional figures, describe a sequence that exhibits the similarity between them.	10.3	

Interactive Standards

Use informal arguments to establish facts about the angle sum and exterior angle of triangles, about the angles created when parallel lines are cut by a transversal, and the angle-angle criterion for similarity of triangles.	11.1, 11.2, 11.3	
Cluster: Understand and apply the Pythagorean Theorem.		
Explain a proof of the Pythagorean Theorem and its converse.	14.1	
Apply the Pythagorean Theorem to determine unknown side lengths in right triangles in real-world and mathematical problems in two and three dimensions.	14.2	
Apply the Pythagorean Theorem to find the distance between two points in a coordinate system.	14.3	
Cluster: Solve real-world and mathematical problems involving volume of cylinders, cones, and spheres.		
Know the formulas for the volumes of cones, cylinders, and spheres and use them to solve real-world and mathematical problems.	17.4, 17.5, 17.6	
Domain: STATISTICS & PROBABILITY		
Cluster: Use random sampling to draw inferences about a population.		
Understand that statistics can be used to gain information about a population by examining a sample of the population; generalizations about a population from a sample are valid only if the sample is representative of that population. Understand that random sampling tends to produce representative samples and support valid inferences.	18.1	
Use data from a random sample to draw inferences about a population with an unknown characteristic of interest. Generate multiple samples (or simulated samples) of the same size to gauge the variation in estimates or predictions.	18.2, 18.3	
Cluster: Draw informal comparative inferences about two populations.		
Informally assess the degree of visual overlap of two numerical data distributions with similar variabilities, measuring the difference between the centers by expressing it as a multiple of a measure of variability.	19.1, 19.2, 19.3	
Use measures of center and measures of variability for numerical data from random samples to draw informal comparative inferences about two populations.	19.1, 19.2, 19.3	

Mathematics Standards **xxvii**

Interactive Standards

Cluster: Investigate chance processes and develop, use, and evaluate probability models.		
Understand that the probability of a chance event is a number between 0 and 1 that expresses the likelihood of the event occurring. Larger numbers indicate greater likelihood. A probability near 0 indicates an unlikely event, a probability around $\frac{1}{2}$ indicates an event that is neither unlikely nor likely, and a probability near 1 indicates a likely event.	20.1	
Approximate the probability of a chance event by collecting data on the chance process that produces it and observing its long-run relative frequency, and predict the approximate relative frequency given the probability.	20.2, 20.4, 21.1, 21.3	
Develop a probability model and use it to find probabilities of events. Compare probabilities from a model to observed frequencies; if the agreement is not good, explain possible sources of the discrepancy.	See below.	
• Develop a uniform probability model by assigning equal probability to all outcomes, and use the model to determine probabilities of events.	21.1, 21.3	
• Develop a probability model (which may not be uniform) by observing frequencies in data generated from a chance process.	20.2	
Find probabilities of compound events using organized lists, tables, tree diagrams, and simulation.	See below.	
• Understand that, just as with simple events, the probability of a compound event is the fraction of outcomes in the sample space for which the compound event occurs.	20.3, 21.2	
• Represent sample spaces for compound events using methods such as organized lists, tables and tree diagrams. For an event described in everyday language (e.g., "rolling double sixes"), identify the outcomes in the sample space which compose the event.	20.3, 21.2	
• Design and use a simulation to generate frequencies for compound events.	20.3, 21.4	

Unit 1: Ratios and Proportional Reasoning

Astronomer

Michael E. Brown is a professor of planetary astronomy at the California Institute of Technology and the author of the book *How I Killed Pluto and Why It Had It Coming*. Brown and his team discovered a number of objects in our solar system farther away than Neptune. One of these objects, the dwarf planet Eris, is more massive than Pluto (shown above). This discovery resulted in The International Astronomical Union demoting Pluto to a dwarf planet.

STEM Task:

We often use ratios to describe scale models. If a model rocket has a scale 1 inch = 12 feet, that means for every part of the model that measures 1 inch the corresponding part of the rocket measures 12 feet. Use this scale to calculate the height of a rocket if the model is 26 inches tall. Explain your reasoning.

Learning Mindset
Perseverance Collects and Tries Multiple Strategies

Perseverance is the ability to stick with a task, even if it is difficult. Have you ever noticed that you are able to manage your time on tasks better than before or that you are able to identify study skills that are effective for you? Those are signs that your ability to persevere is growing. Here are some tips for helping you persevere through difficult tasks.

- Get rid of distractions, like your cell phone, while you are working. Your brain is less effective when you attempt to multi-task. All human brains are! That's because multi-tasking isn't really doing two things at once. Your brain is actually shifting attention between the activities, and that slows you down. It can also make the quality of your work decrease.

- Divide complex tasks into smaller steps. This helps you focus your efforts. It also makes it easier to spot mistakes.

- Even if your effort is unsuccessful, look at what you can learn from each attempt and adjust your strategy.

- Check for a fixed-mindset voice in your head telling you that you're not good with certain content or with certain tasks. Activate your growth-mindset voice telling you that you can learn more about the content and get better at the tasks.

Reflect

Q What are some strategies you used to manage your time while working on the STEM Task?

Q How have you kept yourself on task in the past? What is your plan for improving your ability to stay focused as you face math challenges?

Module 1

Identify and Represent Proportional Relationships

WHICH RATIO DOES NOT BELONG?

Express each ratio of apples to oranges shown below in words and as a fraction. Share with a partner or a small group.

A.

B.

C.

Apples	Oranges
8	18
32	72
56	126

D. A grocer displays 4 dozen apples 9 dozen oranges

 Turn and Talk

- Explain how the ratios are related and how they are different.
- Which ratio does not belong? Explain why.

Are You Ready?

Complete these problems to review prior concepts and skills you will need for this module.

Solve One-Step Equations

Solve the equation.

1. $8x = 56$ _____
2. $4a = 23$ _____

Ordered Pairs on the Coordinate Plane

Write the ordered pair for each point.

3. A _____
4. B _____

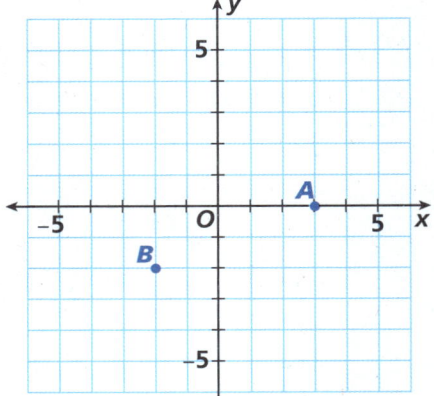

Plot and label the ordered pairs on the graph.

Point	(x, y)
5. C	(−3, 2)
6. D	(1, −2)

Divide Fractions and Mixed Numbers

Divide.

7. $\frac{3}{4} \div \frac{3}{5}$ _____
8. $7\frac{1}{2} \div \frac{5}{8}$ _____
9. $\frac{3}{8} \div \frac{1}{2}$ _____

Ratio Language

10. Jasper has a jar of marbles. Complete the table to show the ratios of marbles.

blue:red	
blue:yellow	
red:blue	
yellow:red	

Build Conceptual Understanding

Lesson 1

Name _____

Explore Relationships

I Can recognize when relationships presented in tables, diagrams, and verbal descriptions can be represented by a constant unit rate.

Spark Your Learning

These salsas are made for a competition.

On Fire!
2 tablespoons peppers; 5 tablespoons tomatoes

Blazin'
4 tablespoons peppers; 12 tablespoons tomatoes

Kickin'
6 tablespoons peppers; 15 tablespoons tomatoes

Feel the Burn
3 tablespoons peppers; 6 tablespoons tomatoes

If peppers and tomatoes are the only ingredients in the salsas and the names are based on taste, which two salsas should have the same name? Show your work and explain.

 Turn and Talk Using the ratios described in the salsa recipes, describe which recipe is most hot and which recipe is most mild.

Module 1 • Lesson 1

5

Build Understanding

1 The table shows how many ounces of salsa you get when buying small jars of salsa.

Small jars of salsa	4	8	12	16	
Ounces of salsa	32	64	96		

A. Describe a pattern you see in the rows of the table.

B. Describe a pattern you see in the columns of the table.

C. Use your patterns to extend the table.

D. You previously learned that a unit rate is a rate in which the second quantity in the comparison is one unit, such as 4 ounces per 1 serving. Describe the relationship between ounces of salsa and small jars of salsa using a unit rate.

E. The diagram shows how many ounces of salsa you get when buying medium jars of salsa. Describe the relationship using a unit rate.

48 ounces

Turn and Talk Is the relationship represented in the table the same as the relationship represented in the diagram in Part E? Why or why not?

2 The tables show the prices and weights of avocados.

Avocados	Price
1	$1.25
2	$2.50
3	$3.75
4	$5.00
5	$6.25

Avocados	Weight
1	7 oz
2	13 oz
3	20 oz
4	26 oz
5	34 oz

An avocado is classified as a fruit, and in particular, as a one-seeded berry.

A. Can the relationship between the price and the number of avocados be described with a constant rate? Explain.

_____
_____
_____

B. Can the relationship between the weight and the number of avocados be described with a constant rate? Explain.

_____
_____
_____

Check Understanding

1. A 2-pound package of hamburger costs $7.00, and you pay $10.50 for a 3-pound package of hamburger. Complete the table. Then decide whether it makes sense to use a constant rate to describe the relationship. Explain.

Weight (lb)	2	3	4	5
Cost ($)	7.00		14.00	17.50

_____
_____

2. The table shows the total costs of different numbers of tickets. Decide whether it makes sense to use a constant rate to describe the relationship. Explain.

Number of tickets	6	8	10	14	25
Total cost ($)	34.50	44.00	52.50	73.50	131.25

_____
_____

Module 1 • Lesson 1

On Your Own

3. **Reason** Flo measures the amount of water her high pressure sprayer uses and finds that it uses 20 gallons of water in 4 minutes and 30 gallons in 6 minutes. Complete the table. Then decide whether it makes sense to use a constant rate to describe the relationship. Explain.

Time (min)	2	4		10	18
Water (gal)	10		30	50	90

_____

_____

_____

For Problems 4–5, use the given information.

Ken rode his bike on Monday and Tuesday. Each table shows the distance that he was from home at various times.

Monday	
Time (min)	Distance (km)
20	5
40	10
60	12
80	14
100	16

Tuesday	
Time (min)	Distance (km)
20	4
40	8
60	12
80	16
100	20

4. Can the relationship in Monday's table be described by a constant unit rate? Explain.

_____

5. Can the relationship in Tuesday's table be described by a constant unit rate? Explain.

_____

 I'm in a Learning Mindset!

What can I apply from previous work with ratios and rates to recognize when a relationship between two quantities can be described by a constant unit rate?

_____

_____

Name _____

Explore Relationships

LESSON 1.1
More Practice/ Homework

ONLINE Video Tutorials and Interactive Examples

1. The amount of money Chaz earned for walking dogs is given in the table. Can the relationship be described by a constant rate? Explain.

Dogs walked	6	8	11
Money earned ($)	112.50	150.00	206.25

_____
_____

2. **STEM** The diagram shows the structure of a molecule of sulfur dioxide. The ratio of oxygen atoms to sulfur atoms in sulfur dioxide is always the same. How many oxygen atoms (O) are there when there are 6 sulfur atoms (S)? Explain how you got your answer.

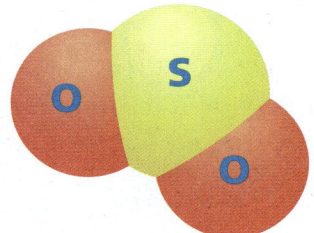

_____
_____
_____

3. **Reason** Three different sizes of sports–drink mix are shown with their prices. Can the relationship between price and volume (in grams) be described by a constant rate? Explain.

_____
_____

For Problems 4–5, use the values in the table.

Servings of cereal	Cups of cereal	Cups of milk
16	12	4
24	18	6

4. Can the relationship between cups of milk and cups of cereal be described by a constant ratio? Why or why not?

_____
_____

5. Can the relationship between cups of cereal and servings of cereal be described by a constant rate? Why or why not?

_____
_____

Module 1 • Lesson 1

Test Prep

6. Jane is saving to buy a cell phone. She is given a $100 gift to start and saves $35 a month from her allowance. So after 1 month, Jane has saved $135. Does it make sense to represent the relationship between the amount saved and the number of months with one constant rate? Why or why not? Explain your answer.

_____

_____

_____

_____

7. Raj is mixing different colors of paint. The table shows the amount of each color paint Raj uses for each mixture.

Raj's Paint Mixtures		
Mixture	Red (ounces)	Blue (ounces)
1	2	1
2	7	3.5
3	4.5	2
4	5.5	2.5

Select the two mixtures that will produce the same color.

(A) mixtures 1 and 2

(B) mixtures 3 and 4

(C) mixtures 1 and 3

(D) mixtures 2 and 4

Spiral Review

8. At 1:00 p.m., a diver's elevation is −30 feet relative to sea level. At 2:00 p.m., the diver's elevation is −45 feet. At which time is the diver farther from sea level?

_____

9. A share of stock costs $83.60. The next day, the price increases $15.35. The following day, the price decreases $4.75. What is the final price?

_____

Connect Concepts and Skills

Lesson 2

Name _____

Recognize Proportional Relationships in Tables

I Can identify proportional relationships in tables and equations, identify the constant of proportionality, and write the associated equation.

Spark Your Learning

For which tables can you predict the cost of 100 units of the item? Explain why you can make that prediction for some of the tables and not for others. For the tables that let you predict the cost of 100 units, find the cost.

Peanut butter (oz)	Total cost ($)
8	3
16	4
40	6

Binder clips	Total cost ($)
12	2
36	5
50	6

Trail mix (lb)	Total cost ($)
2	6
8	24
12	36

Shower sponges	Total cost ($)
4	8
8	16
10	20

 Turn and Talk What characteristic of the table allows you to predict the cost of any number of items?

Build Understanding

1 Maxine walks dogs to earn extra money. The table of values shows the proportional relationship between the number of dogs Maxine walks and the amount of money she earns.

Dogs walked	2	4	6
Amount ($)	7	14	21

Connect to Vocabulary

Two quantities have a **proportional relationship** if the **ratio** of one quantity to the other is a constant. In a proportional relationship, the constant unit rate is called the **constant of proportionality** and is usually represented by the letter k.

A. Show that the ratio of dogs walked to amount earned is a constant ratio.

_____

B. Show that the ratio of amount earned to dogs walked is a constant ratio.

_____

C. What is the unit rate of dogs walked per dollar earned? Does it make sense? Explain.

_____
_____

D. What is the unit rate of dollars earned per dog walked? Does it make sense? Explain.

_____
_____

E. What is the constant of proportionality k in this situation?

_____

F. Describe what the unit rate k represents in this situation.

_____
_____

 **Turn and Talk** In a table of values that represents a proportional relationship, how can you find the constant of proportionality?

Step It Out

2 Two relationships are represented in the tables. Which table shows a proportional relationship, and which does not? Explain.

Table 1

Windows washed, x	3	6	7
Amount earned ($), y	36	72	84

Table 2

Windows washed, x	4	5	8
Amount earned ($), y	48	55	64

Table 1

The ratios $\frac{\text{amount earned (\$), } y}{\text{windows, } x}$ are:

$\frac{36}{\square} = \square$ $\frac{\square}{6} = \square$ $\frac{\square}{7} = \square$

The ratios $\frac{y}{x}$ are / are not equivalent. Therefore, the relationship shown in this table is / is not proportional.

Table 2

The ratios $\frac{\text{amount earned (\$), } y}{\text{windows, } x}$ are:

$\frac{48}{\square} = \square$ $\frac{\square}{5} = \square$ $\frac{\square}{8} = \square$

The ratios $\frac{y}{x}$ are / are not equivalent. Therefore, the relationship shown in this table is / is not proportional.

3 The number of students whom Malcolm tutors is proportional to the amount earned. The calendar shows Malcolm's earnings from tutoring in one week.

Tutoring Schedule

Mon	Tue	Wed	Thu	Fri
Clive Bray Jen Haley $120	Justice Krissy Eve Nolan Armond Landree $180	Rance Kimee Yuri $90	Molly Rick Sharona Mikay Paco $150	Janis $30

A. Complete the table.

Number of students, x		3		5	
Amount earned ($), y	30		120		180

B. Find the constant of proportionality k.

$k = \frac{y}{x} = \frac{\square}{\square} = \square$

C. The **equation** for a proportional relationship is $y = kx$, where k is the constant of proportionality. Find k and write an equation for this proportional relationship.

$k = \frac{y}{x} = \frac{120}{\square} = \square$

$y = \square \, x$

Module 1 • Lesson 2

4 The equation $y = 12x$ represents the number of inches y in x feet.

A. The equation $y = 12x$ ⬚ does / does not ⬚ represent a proportional relationship. If so, what is the constant of proportionality? How do you know?

_____

_____

B. Use the equation to complete the table of values for the relationship between inches and feet.

Feet, x	0	1	2			5
Inches, y				36	48	

Turn and Talk When would it be better to use an equation to represent a proportional relationship? When would it be better to use a table?

Check Understanding

1. There are 4 quarters in $1.00.

   A. Make a table of values to represent this relationship.

Dollars, x				
Quarters, y				

   B. Is this a proportional relationship? If so, identify k and explain what it represents. If not, explain why not.

   _____

   C. Write an equation for the situation. _____

2. The equation $y = 7x$ gives the cost y of x pounds of chicken at the grocery store. Complete the table for the given weights of chicken.

Weight (lb), x	1	2	5	8
Cost ($), y				

3. Is the relationship in the table proportional? If it is, write its equation.

x	1	2	3	4
y	5	10	15	20

On Your Own

4. **Model with Mathematics** Reanna is making a scrapbook which holds 14 photos on each 2-page spread. Make a table of values to represent this relationship. Write an equation for the situation.

2-page spreads, x					
Photos, y					

Tell whether each table represents a proportional relationship. If it does, identify the constant of proportionality.

5.
x	3	7	9
y	63	147	189

6.
x	14	15	16
y	21	22.5	15

7. Determine whether the table represents a proportional relationship. If it does, find the constant of proportionality and use it to write an equation to represent the table of values.

x	1	2	3	4	5
y	7	14	21	28	35

8. The equation $y = 8x$ gives the number of slices y in x pizzas. Make a table of values using the equation. Identify the constant of proportionality. Then complete each sentence.

Pizzas, x					
Slices, y					

There are _____ slices in 3 pizzas.

There are 16 slices in _____ pizzas.

9. **Reason** The table shows the relationship between the number of workers painting apartments in an apartment building and the number of days it takes to paint all 50 apartments. Determine whether the relationship is proportional. Explain your reasoning.

Workers, x	5	10	15	20	25
Duration of job (days), y	60	30	20	15	12

Module 1 • Lesson 2

Model with Mathematics For Problems 10–12, use the description of a proportional relationship to make a table. Then identify the constant of proportionality, and write an equation for the situation.

10. A 2-cup serving of chicken noodle soup has 1.5 ounces of noodles.

Cups of soup, x	Ounces of noodles, y

_____

11. Rick is exercising at a constant pace.

Time (min), x	Steps, y

_____

126 steps every 3 minutes

12. Colin is preparing equal-sized care packages. He placed 34 items in 2 care packages he made.

Packages, x				
Items, y				

_____

13. The equation $y = 100x$ gives the number of centimeters y in x meters. Make a table of values using the equation. Identify the constant of proportionality. Then complete each sentence.

Meters, x				
Centimeters, y				

k = _____ ; There are _____ centimeters in 3 meters. There are 200 centimeters in _____ meters.

I'm in a Learning Mindset!

What strategies do I use to decide if a relationship displayed in a table is proportional? How do I know when I am finished?

_____
_____

Recognize Proportional Relationships in Tables

LESSON 1.2 More Practice/Homework

Tell whether each table represents a proportional relationship. If it does, identify the constant of proportionality.

1.
x	2	5	7
y	18	45	63

2.
x	3	4	5
y	42	60	80

3. **Math on the Spot** Determine whether the table represents a proportional relationship. If it does, find the constant of proportionality and use it to write an equation to represent the table of values.

Number of lawns, x	1	2	3	4
Amount earned ($), y	24	48	72	96

4. The equation $y = 6x$ gives the cost y of x of the tickets shown. Make a table of values. Identify the constant of proportionality. Then complete each sentence.

Tickets, x					
Cost ($), y					

It costs _____ for 5 tickets.

It costs $24 for _____ tickets.

(MP) Model with Mathematics Use the description of a proportional relationship in each table. Identify the constant of proportionality, then write an equation to represent the situation in the table.

5. Alison earned $24 by stocking shelves at the grocery store for 3 hours.

Time (h), x	1	2	3	6
Total pay ($), y	8	16	24	48

6. Each cooler holds 18 water bottles.

Coolers, x	1	2	4	7
Water bottles, y	18	36	72	126

Module 1 • Lesson 2

Test Prep

7. Which table represents a proportional relationship?

Table 1			
Carrots (lb)	2	3	4
Number of carrots	23	33	43

Table 2			
Deli meat (lb)	2	3	4
Total cost ($)	23	34.50	46

_____

8. Use the proportional relationship in the table.

A. Write an equation for the relationship.

Milk (gal), x	2	4	8
Servings, y	32	64	128

_____

B. There are 4 quarts in a gallon and 4 cups in a quart. How many cups are in one serving? _____

C. There are 8 fluid ounces in a cup. How many fluid ounces are in one serving? _____

9. What is the meaning of the constant of proportionality in this situation?

Rocking chairs, x	2	3	5
Time to build (h), y	48	72	120

_____

10. Describe a method for determining whether a table represents a proportional relationship.

_____

_____

_____

11. Kevin uses $\frac{2}{3}$ cup of flour to make 2 servings of biscuits. How many cups of flour are there per serving? How many cups of flour should Kevin use to make 7 servings?

Ⓐ $\frac{1}{3}$ cup; $2\frac{1}{3}$ cups
Ⓑ $\frac{2}{3}$ cup; $2\frac{1}{3}$ cups
Ⓒ $\frac{2}{3}$ cup; $4\frac{2}{3}$ cups
Ⓓ $1\frac{1}{3}$ cups; $4\frac{2}{3}$ cups

Spiral Review

12. Donya ran a 3k race at a constant speed in 21 minutes 30 seconds. At this speed, how long does it take her to run 1k?

_____

13. It costs $20 for 4 play tickets and $35 for 7 play tickets. Is cost per ticket constant? Why or why not?

_____

Connect Concepts and Skills

Lesson 3

Name _____

Compute Unit Rates Involving Complex Fractions

I Can compute unit rates associated with ratios of fractions.

Spark Your Learning

Rick and Tina hiked at different constant rates. Rick hiked $\frac{1}{2}$ mile every 15 minutes, or $\frac{1}{4}$ hour. It took Tina 10 minutes to hike $\frac{1}{4}$ mile. Find the distance each hiked in 1 hour.

Rick

Tina

Turn and Talk How can you use the distance they each hiked in 1 hour to write a ratio for the distance they each would hike in 2 hours?

Module 1 • Lesson 3   19

Build Understanding

1 Jessie loves to go hiking on rustic trails through trees and along rivers. One day in 20 minutes of hiking, she hiked 1 mile. If Jessie hiked at a constant rate, what would that rate be?

A. Write Jessie's hiking rate in all the ways you can think of from the information given.

B. Complete the statements below to show how to write Jessie's hiking rate as a unit rate in miles per hour.

$$\frac{1 \text{ mile}}{20 \text{ minutes}} = \frac{1 \text{ mile}}{\frac{1}{3} \text{ hour}} = \frac{1 \text{ mile} \times \square}{\frac{1}{3} \text{ hour} \times \square} = \frac{\square \text{ miles}}{1 \text{ hour}}$$

You have to multiply $\frac{1}{3}$ hour by _____ to make the second quantity in the unit rate _____ hour, so multiply the first quantity by _____ as well.

C. Amiya prefers hiking on more hilly trails. One time Amiya reached the mile marker pictured in 20 minutes hiking at a steady pace. Show how to find the unit rate in minutes per mile.

$$\frac{20 \text{ min}}{\boxed{} \text{ mi}} =$$

$\frac{1}{2}$ mile

Turn and Talk Compare the rates "minutes per mile" and "miles per minute." Give an example of each rate.

Step It Out

2 A recipe says to use $\frac{2}{3}$ cup of milk to make $\frac{4}{5}$ serving of pudding. How many cups of milk are in 1 serving?

A. Recall that **reciprocals** are two numbers whose product is 1. Explain how reciprocals are used to find the unit rate.

$$\frac{\frac{2}{3} \text{ cup of milk}}{\frac{4}{5} \text{ serving of pudding}} \quad \frac{\frac{2}{3} \times \frac{5}{4}}{\frac{4}{5} \times \frac{5}{4}} = \frac{\frac{5}{6}}{1}, \text{ or } \frac{5}{6} \text{ cup of milk per serving}$$

_____

_____

B. How can you use division to find this unit rate?

_____

 Turn and Talk How can you find the number of servings of pudding for every cup of milk?

3 Jaylan makes limeade using $\frac{3}{4}$ cup of water for every $\frac{1}{5}$ cup of lime juice. Rene's limeade recipe is different. He uses $\frac{2}{3}$ cup of water for every $\frac{1}{6}$ cup of lime juice. Whose limeade has a weaker flavor?

A. What do you need to know to solve this problem?

_____

B. Compute the unit rate of water to lime juice in each limeade.

Jaylan $\dfrac{\frac{3}{4} \text{ cup water}}{\frac{1}{5} \text{ cup lime juice}}$ 	Rene $\dfrac{\frac{2}{3} \text{ cup water}}{\frac{1}{6} \text{ cup lime juice}}$

$\frac{3}{4} \div \frac{1}{5} = \dfrac{\square}{4} \times \dfrac{\square}{1}$ 	 $\frac{2}{3} \div \frac{1}{6} = \dfrac{2}{\square} \times \dfrac{6}{\square}$

$= \dfrac{\square}{\square}$, or $\square$ 	 $= \dfrac{\square}{\square}$, or $\square$

$\square$ c water / 1 c lime juice 	 $\square$ c water / 1 c lime juice

C. Whose limeade has a weaker flavor? Explain.

_____

_____

Module 1 • Lesson 3

4. The moon has a weaker gravitational pull than Earth, so objects weigh less on the moon. For example, Jaxon weighs $30\frac{5}{6}$ pounds on the moon and 185 pounds on Earth. Viola weighs 135 pounds on Earth and $22\frac{1}{2}$ pounds on the moon.

A. Show that the relationship between weight on the moon and weight on Earth is proportional.

Jaxon: $\dfrac{30\frac{5}{6}}{\boxed{}} = 30\frac{5}{6} \div \boxed{} =$ _____

Viola: $\dfrac{\boxed{}}{135} = \boxed{} \div 135 =$ _____

The constant of proportionality for $\dfrac{\text{moon weight (lb)}}{\text{Earth weight (lb)}}$ is _____.

B. Let x represent the weight on Earth. Let y represent the weight on the moon. Write an equation for the proportional relationship. Use it to find the weight of a 20-pound dog on the moon.

The equation is _____.

On the moon, the dog would weigh about _____ pounds.

Turn and Talk What would a dog that weighs 12 pounds on the moon weigh on Earth?

Check Understanding

1. A faucet leaks $\frac{5}{8}$ quart of water in 15 minutes. How many quarts does the faucet leak per hour?

   _____

2. Toni ran $\frac{4}{5}$ mile in $\frac{1}{5}$ hour. Write an equation for the distance in miles y that she ran in x hours if she ran at a constant rate.

   _____

3. Write $\frac{3}{4}$ cup per $\frac{1}{2}$ serving as a unit rate.

   _____

4. Write $2\frac{1}{4}$ miles in $\frac{3}{4}$ hour as a unit rate.

   _____

Name _____

On Your Own

5. **Health and Fitness** Jorge measured his heart rate after jogging. He counted 11 beats during a 6-second interval. What was the unit rate for Jorge's heart rate in beats per minute? _____

6. Chen bikes $2\frac{1}{2}$ miles in $\frac{5}{12}$ hour. What is Chen's unit rate in miles per hour?
   _____

7. Amal can run $\frac{1}{8}$ mile in $1\frac{1}{2}$ minutes.

   A. If he can maintain that pace, how long will it take him to run 1 mile?
   _____

   B. How long would it would take Amal to run 3 miles at that pace?
   _____

   C. Naomi can run $\frac{1}{4}$ mile in 2 minutes. Does Amal or Naomi run faster? How do you know?
   _____
   _____

8. **Open Ended** When both quantities in a rate are fractions, what strategy do you use to write the rate as a unit rate?
   _____
   _____

9. **(MP) Reason** What is the ratio of dried fruit to sunflower seeds in the granola recipe? If you need to triple the recipe, will the ratio change? Explain.
   _____
   _____

Granola

2 cups old-fashioned oats
2/3 cup raw nuts
1/8 cup sunflower seeds
1/2 cup dried fruit, chopped
3 tablespoons honey
2 tablespoons sunflower oil
1/2 teaspoon vanilla
1/8 teaspoon salt

Preheat oven to 300 °F. Combine and mix ingredients in a bowl. Spread on baking sheet. Bake for 10 minutes. Cool. Store in closed container in the refrigerator.

Module 1 • Lesson 3

10. The table shows the numbers of packages of peanut butter crackers y that can be made using various amounts of peanut butter x.

Peanut butter (tbsp)	$\frac{1}{2}$	$\frac{5}{8}$	$\frac{3}{4}$	$\frac{7}{8}$
Cracker packages	2	$2\frac{1}{2}$	3	$3\frac{1}{2}$

A. Show that the relationship is proportional.

B. Write an equation to represent the relationship, and find the amount of peanut butter used to make 25 cracker packages.

11. The relationship between adult dog weight x in pounds and the daily recommended amount of dog food y in cups is proportional.

Dog weight (lb)	10	40	50	100
Dog food (cups)	$\frac{1}{6}$	$\frac{2}{3}$	$\frac{5}{6}$	$1\frac{2}{3}$

Write an equation for the relationship. How much dog food is recommended for a 25-pound adult dog?

For Exercises 12–15, find each unit rate.

12. $\frac{5}{8}$ mile in $\frac{1}{4}$ hour

13. $68 for $8\frac{1}{2}$ hours

14. $1\frac{1}{4}$ cup of flour per $\frac{1}{8}$ cup of butter

15. $2\frac{1}{2}$ miles in $\frac{3}{4}$ hour

 I'm in a Learning Mindset!

What did I learn from peers when they shared their strategies with me for writing a unit rate?

Name _____

**LESSON 1.3
More Practice/
Homework**

Compute Unit Rates Involving Complex Fractions

ONLINE Video Tutorials and Interactive Examples

1. **STEM** Density is a unit rate measured in units of mass per unit of volume. The mass of a garnet is 5.7 grams. The volume is 1.5 cubic centimeters (cm^3). What is the density of the garnet?

   _____

2. **Math on the Spot** Jen and Kamlee are walking to school. After 20 minutes, Jen has walked $\frac{4}{5}$ mile. After 25 minutes, Kamlee has walked $\frac{5}{6}$ mile. Find their speeds in miles per hour. Who is walking faster?

   _____

3. **(MP) Reason** Maria and Franco are mixing sports drinks for a track meet. Maria uses $\frac{2}{3}$ cup of powdered mix for every 2 gallons of water. Franco uses $1\frac{1}{4}$ cups of powdered mix for every 5 gallons of water. Whose sports drink is stronger? Explain how you found your answer.

   _____
   _____
   _____

4. **(MP) Model with Mathematics** Serena estimates that she can paint 60 square feet of wall space every half-hour. Write an equation for the relationship with time in hours as the independent variable. Can Serena paint 400 square feet of wall space in 3.5 hours? Why or why not?

   _____

5. Cheri paid $6.50 for the bunch of grapes with the weight shown on the scale. What was the price per pound?

   _____

Find the unit rate.

6. $\frac{1}{4}$ kilometer in $\frac{1}{3}$ hour

7. $\frac{7}{8}$ square foot in $\frac{1}{4}$ hour

8. $6.50 for $3\frac{1}{4}$ pounds of grapes

9. $49.50 for $5\frac{1}{2}$ hours

10. 247 heart beats in $6\frac{1}{2}$ minutes

11. $8\frac{1}{2}$ miles in $\frac{1}{2}$ hour

Module 1 • Lesson 3

25

Test Prep

12. Select all the rates equivalent to the rate $\frac{3}{4}$ cup per pound.

- (A) $\frac{3}{8}$ cup per $\frac{1}{2}$ pound
- (B) $\frac{1}{4}$ cup per $\frac{1}{2}$ pound
- (C) 3 cups for every 2 pounds
- (D) $1\frac{1}{2}$ cups for every 2 pounds
- (E) 0.1875 cup for every 0.25 pound

13. Jordan cooked a $16\frac{1}{5}$-pound turkey in $5\frac{2}{5}$ hours. How many minutes per pound did it take to cook the turkey? Express your answer as a unit rate.

_____

14. Mr. March sells popcorn at his theater. He uses $3\frac{3}{4}$ cups of unpopped corn to make 15 bags of popped corn. Write an equation for the number of bags of popcorn b that can be made with c cups of unpopped corn.

_____

15. Lucia uses 3 ounces of pasta to make $\frac{3}{4}$ serving of pasta. How many ounces of pasta are there per serving? How many ounces of pasta should Lucia use to make 5 servings?

- (A) 3 ounces; 15 ounces
- (B) 4 ounces; 20 ounces
- (C) 6 ounces; 30 ounces
- (D) 9 ounces; 40 ounces

Spiral Review

16. John left school with $8.43. He found a quarter on his way home and then stopped to buy an apple for $0.89. How much money did he have when he got home?

$ _____

17. Arian is making bracelets. For each bracelet, it takes $\frac{1}{10}$ hour to pick out materials and $\frac{1}{4}$ hour to braid it together. How many bracelets can Arian make in 5 hours?

_____

18. For a game, 3 people are chosen in the first round. Each of those people chooses 3 people in the second round, and so on. How many people are chosen in the sixth round?

_____

Connect Concepts and Skills

Lesson 4

Name _____

Recognize Proportional Relationships in Graphs

I Can decide whether a relationship shown in a graph is proportional and explain the connection between the constant of proportionality and the point (1, *r*) on the graph.

Spark Your Learning

Jake makes custom-painted sneakers. He makes 6 pairs in 4 hours. On a graph of this proportional relationship, what point would represent 6 pairs in 4 hours? Justify your answer with a description or model.

 **Turn and Talk** How did you decide which axis represents which variable? Explain.

Module 1 • Lesson 4   **27**

Build Understanding

1 The table shows the proportional relationship between pairs of sneakers Jake makes to sell at a craft fair and the revenue from selling them.

Pairs of sneakers, x	0	1	2	3	4	5
Revenue ($), y	0	40	80	120	160	200

A. How do the data in the table show a proportional relationship? How do you know?

_____

B. Write the data in the table as ordered pairs and graph them.

_____

C. Do the points all lie along a straight line? _____

D. Does the graph pass through the origin? _____

 **Turn and Talk** Describe the characteristics of the graph of a proportional relationship.

2 Maya sells homemade spice mixes in different sizes at the craft fair. The graph shows the proportional relationship between teaspoons of cumin and teaspoons of chili powder in one recipe.

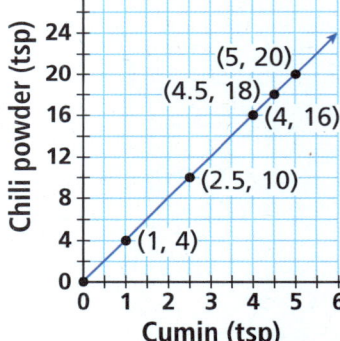

A. What does the origin represent?

_____
_____

B. What are the coordinates of the point at $x = 1$, and what do they represent?

_____
_____

C. Explain why the graph shows a proportional relationship.

_____
_____

D. Why is the graph a solid line?

_____
_____

Step It Out

3 Parker sells lemonade at the craft fair. The relationship between the number of servings and cups of water used is shown.

Servings, x	2	3	6	8
Water (c), y	1	$1\frac{1}{2}$	3	4

A. Graph the relationship, and tell whether it is a proportional relationship. Explain how you know.

B. The graph of the line should be ⬚ solid / dashed ⬚ because x and y can be any nonnegative numbers.

C. What is the constant of proportionality? Write an equation for the relationship.

4 Angel was in charge of ordering graphic T-shirts for the craft fair. The graph shows the relationship between the number of boxes of T-shirts Angel ordered x and the total number of T-shirts y.

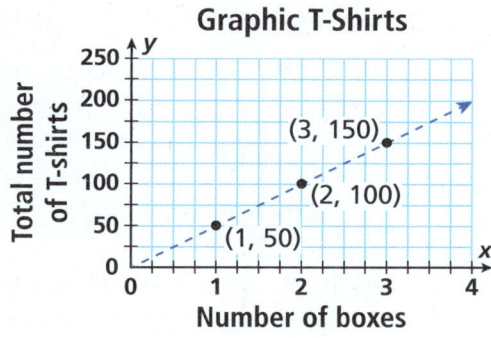

A. Is the relationship in the graph a proportional relationship? Explain how you know.

B. What is the constant of proportionality? How do you know based on the graph?

C. Write an equation to represent the relationship.

D. Why is the graph dashed rather than solid?

Module 1 • Lesson 4   29

5 Alonso pays a fee of $4 plus a percentage of his sales to participate in the crafts fair. The table shows the amount Alonso pays in relationship to his sales.

Sales ($), x	10.00	20.00	35.00	45.00	50.00
Fee ($), y	4.50	5.00	5.75	6.25	6.50

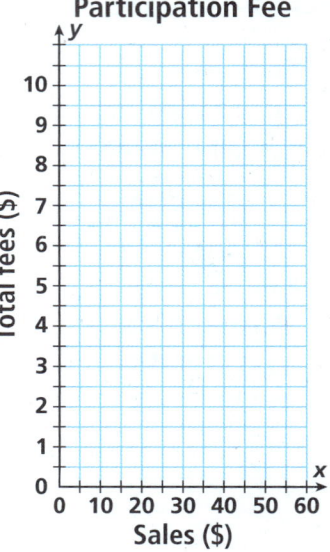

A. Graph the relationship.

B. What does the point (0, 4.00) represent?

_____

_____

C. Is the ratio of $\frac{y}{x}$ constant? Justify your answer.

_____

_____

D. Is the relationship between the total fees and the amount of sales a proportional relationship? Explain.

_____

Check Understanding

1. Amber works at the doggy daycare after school.

A. Use the information in the photograph to complete the table and make a graph of the data.

Time (h), x	0	1	2	3		5
Amount earned ($), y	0				32	

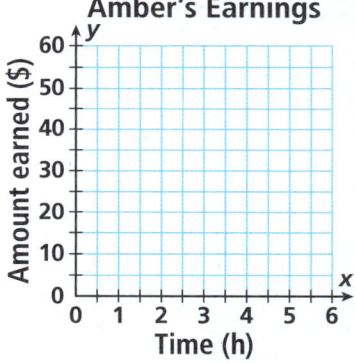

B. Is the relationship between the amount Amber earns and the number of hours a proportional relationship? Explain.

_____

_____

C. What point represents the constant of proportionality?

_____

D. What is the ratio $\frac{y}{x}$ for each point on the graph?

_____

30

On Your Own

2. **Model with Mathematics** The table shows the amounts of cherries (in cups c) used to bake pies.

Make a graph of the data. Tell whether the relationship between the amounts of cherries and the number of pies is a proportional relationship. Explain. If the relationship is proportional, write an equation for the relationship.

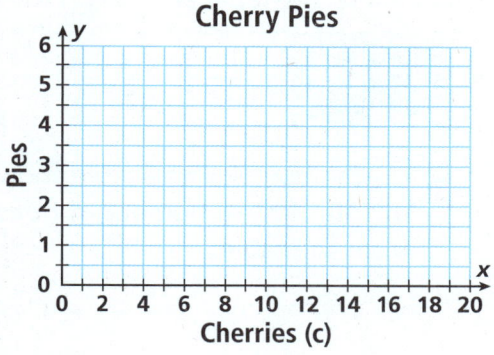

Cherry Pies

Cherries (c), x	4	8	12	16
Pies, y	1	2	3	4

_____

_____

_____

3. The graph shows the distance x Yazmin jogs and the amount of time y that it takes her.

A. What is the meaning of the point (1, 16) on the graph?

_____

_____

_____

B. Does the graph show a proportional relationship? If so, what is the constant of proportionality k? What is the equation of the graph? Explain your reasoning.

_____

_____

_____

C. **Open Ended** Describe how the graph would be different if Yazmin's jogging rate were a different constant.

_____

_____

_____

_____

Module 1 • Lesson 4

4. **Model with Mathematics** Henry goes to the town fair. Use the prices on the photograph to complete the table and graph the data.

Rides, x	1	2	3	4
Cost ($), y	16	22		34

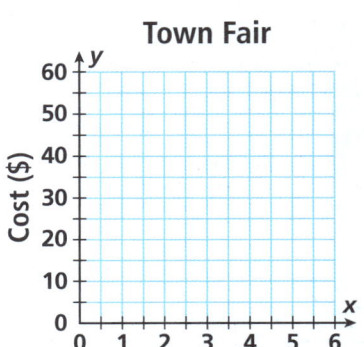

$10 entry fee and $6 per ride

A. Do the points in the table show a constant ratio of total cost to number of rides? Give an example from the table.

_____

_____

B. Does the graph show a proportional relationship? Why or why not?

_____

_____

_____

Town Fair

Tell whether the graph shows a proportional relationship. Explain.

5. **Book Boxes**

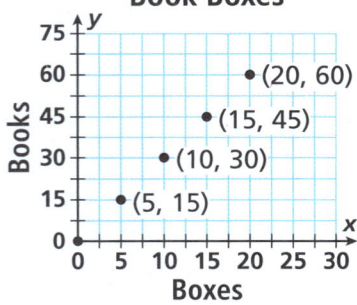

6. **Rental Costs**

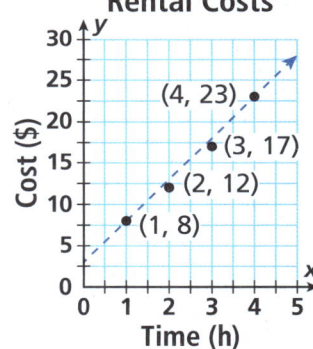

_____

_____

_____

_____

_____

_____

I'm in a Learning Mindset!

How can I make the process of writing a proportional relationship for a graph more efficient?

_____

_____

Name _____

Recognize Proportional Relationships in Graphs

**LESSON 1.4
More Practice/
Homework**

1. The graph shows the area y that can be covered by a given amount of paint x when using a paint sprayer.

   A. Does the graph show a proportional relationship? Explain.

   _____
   _____
   _____

   B. Using the point (3, 45), find the constant of proportionality k and write an equation that describes the proportional relationship.

   _____

   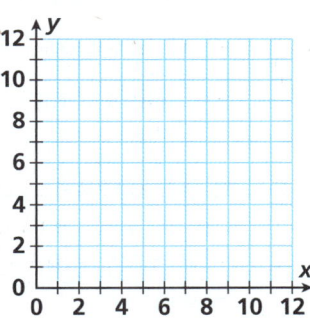

   Paint Usage

2. **Construct Arguments** Graph the data from the table.

x	2	4	6	8	10
y	4	6	8	10	12

   Does the graph show the relationship is a proportional relationship? Does the relationship have a constant of proportionality? Justify your answer using any two points from the table.

   _____
   _____
   _____
   _____

3. **Open Ended** Think of a proportional relationship you may see in your daily life. Make a table of data and graph the data. Explain how you know that the data show a proportional relationship.

Module 1 • Lesson 4   33

Test Prep

4. The table shows the costs of books at the library book sale. Select all the ordered pairs that would be on the graph of this relationship.

Books, x	2	4	6	8	10
Cost ($), y	5	10	15	20	25

   Ⓐ (3, 7.5)
   Ⓑ (12, 33)
   Ⓒ (9, 22.5)
   Ⓓ (11, 27)
   Ⓔ (5, 12.5)

   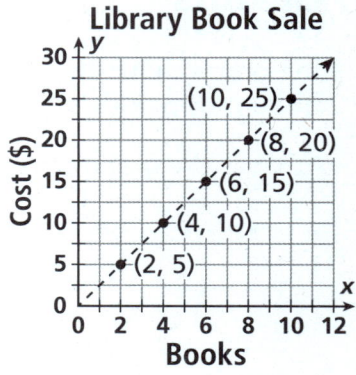
   Library Book Sale

5. Sonia plays a computer game and completes puzzles during levels of the game. The data are shown in the graph.

   What does the point (1, 3) on the graph represent?

   Ⓐ Sonia completes 1 puzzle every 3 levels.
   Ⓑ Sonia completes 3 puzzles on each level.
   Ⓒ Sonia completes 1 puzzle on level 3.
   Ⓓ Sonia completes puzzles 1 to 3.

   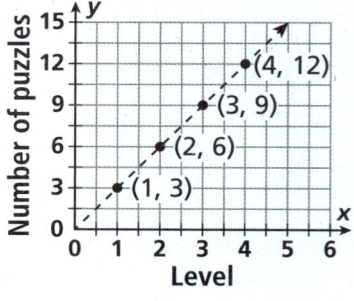
   Computer Game Puzzles

Spiral Review

6. There are 12 girls and 14 boys in class today. What is the ratio of girls to boys?

7. A bakery charges $14.00 for 4 croissant sandwiches. What is the unit rate?

8. The table shows how many pages Andy reads. Does Andy read at a constant rate? Explain.

Time (min), x	10	20	30	40	50
Pages, y	4	9	10	15	20

Apply and Practice

Lesson 5

Use Proportional Relationships to Solve Rate Problems

I Can identify the constant of proportionality and write an equation for a proportional relationship presented in various forms and use them to solve multi-step ratio problems.

Step it Out

1 The bar diagram shows how many inches a garden snail travels over time. At this rate, how many feet would the snail travel in 0.75 hour?

A. What is the unit rate in inches per second? Use conversion factors to convert the unit rate to feet per hour.

$$\frac{\boxed{} \text{ in.}}{1 \text{ s}} \times \frac{\boxed{} \text{ s}}{1 \text{ min}} \times \frac{\boxed{} \text{ min}}{1 \text{ h}} = \frac{1{,}584 \text{ in.}}{1 \text{ h}} \times \frac{1 \text{ ft}}{\boxed{} \text{ in.}} = \frac{132 \text{ ft}}{1 \text{ h}}$$

B. Write an equation for the number of feet y the snail travels in x hours, and use it to solve the problem.

$y = kx$

$y = \underline{} \, x$

$y = \underline{} \, (\underline{}) = 99$ feet in 0.75 hour

C. What is the unit rate in miles per hour? Write an equation for the number of miles y the garden snail travels in x hours. (5,280 ft = 1 mi)

$$\frac{\boxed{} \text{ ft}}{1 \text{ h}} = \frac{0.025 \text{ mi}}{1 \text{ h}} \qquad y = \underline{} \, x$$

 **Turn and Talk** Explain how you converted the unit rate to miles per hour.

2 The graph shows the number of gallons of water used over time in one lane of a car wash. At this rate, how much water would be used if the lane were used continuously from 8:00 a.m. to noon?

Water Use

A. What is the unit rate in gallons per minute? Use conversion factors to convert the unit rate to gallons per hour.

$$\frac{\boxed{}\ \text{gal}}{1\ \text{min}} \times \frac{\boxed{}\ \text{min}}{1\ \text{h}} = \frac{\boxed{}\ \text{gal}}{1\ \text{h}}$$

B. Write an equation for the number of gallons of water y used in x hours, and use it to solve the problem.

$y = kx$

$y = \underline{}\ x$

$y = \underline{}\ (\underline{}) = 1{,}200$ gallons

C. How much water would be used during the hours of 7:30 a.m. to 3:45 p.m.?

$y = \underline{}\ x$

$y = \underline{}\ (\underline{}) = 2{,}475$ gallons

Turn and Talk In Parts B and C, how did you find the number to put in the parentheses?

3 The graph shows Michaela's earnings over time. Marcus's hourly rate is represented in the table. Who has a greater rate of pay, and how much more than the other will that person earn in 40 hours of work?

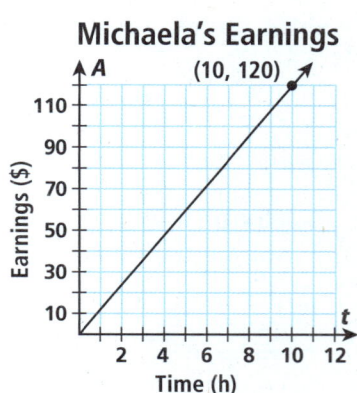

Michaela's Earnings

Marcus's Earnings				
Time (h)	2	4	5	
Earnings ($)	19.00			57.00	76.00

A. Complete the table, write an equation, and graph Marcus's earnings A over time t.

$k = \dfrac{19}{2} = \underline{} \qquad A = \underline{}$

36

Name _____

B. Use the graph to determine who is earning a greater rate of pay. Explain how you know.

_____
_____

C. What information do you still need in order to solve the problem? Solve the problem and show your work.

I still need: _____

Michaela

$\dfrac{\boxed{}}{10} = k$, or $k =$ _____

$A = kt$

$A =$ _____ t

$A =$ _____ (_____) = $480

Marcus

$A = kt$

$A =$ _____ t

$A =$ _____ (_____) = _____

_____
_____

 **Turn and Talk** What happens to the difference in their earnings over time?

Check Understanding

1. Solve the problems using the diagrams.

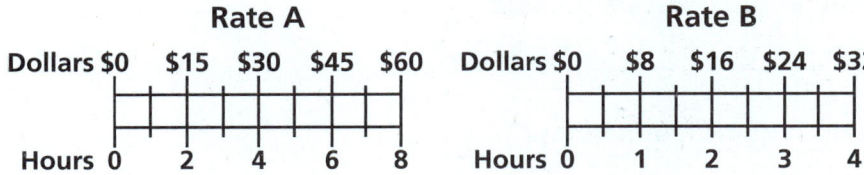

A. Write an equation for the number of dollars y earned from working x hours for each rate.

_____

B. What is the difference between total dollars earned from 40 hours of work for these rates? Show your work.

_____

Module 1 • Lesson 5   37

On Your Own

2. Use the diagram of distance traveled at a constant rate.

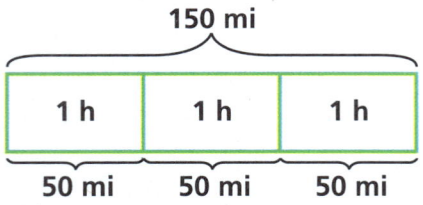

A. What is the unit rate? _____

B. Convert the rate to feet per minute. _____

C. Convert the rate to inches per second.
_____

3. **Model with Mathematics** The graph shows the number of cubic feet of water used over time at a water park that is open during the hours in the table. At this rate, how many cubic feet of water would be used at the water park on a Sunday?

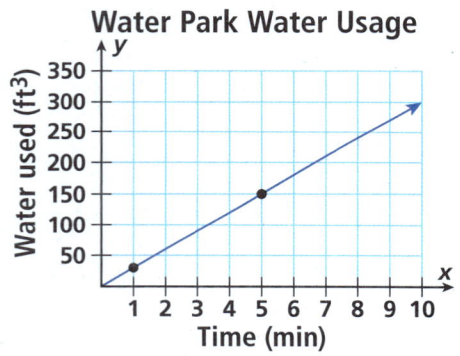

Water Park Hours of Operation	
Days	Hours
Monday to Thursday	11:00 a.m. to 7:30 p.m.
Friday and Saturday	11:00 a.m. to 9:00 p.m.
Sunday	12:00 p.m. to 6:00 p.m.

A. What is the unit rate in cubic feet per minute?
_____

B. What is the unit rate in cubic feet per hour?
_____

C. Write an equation for the number of cubic feet of water y used in x hours, and use it to solve the problem.
_____

D. How many cubic feet of water would be used at the water park on a Tuesday?
_____

4. **Model with Mathematics** The distance Dan jogged over time is shown in the graph. Pattie's constant jogging speed is represented in the table. Who has a faster jogging speed? How much more distance will that jogger have traveled with a total of 22 hours jogging?

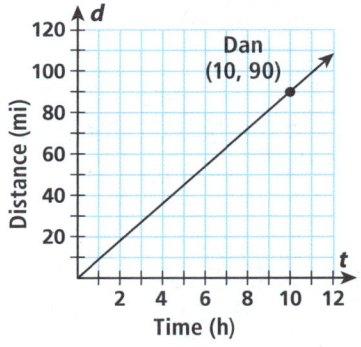

Dan

Time (h)	Distance (mi)
2	12
3	
5	
	42
	60

Pattie

A. Use the table to find Pattie's jogging speed k. Complete the table.

_____

B. Write an equation for the distance in miles d that Pattie jogs in t hours. Graph the equation on the grid with Dan's graph.

_____

C. Solve the problem and show your work.

Module 1 • Lesson 5

5. A cheetah, the world's fastest land animal, cannot maintain its top speed for very long. This bar diagram shows a cheetah's top speed, in feet per minute. Suppose a racecar is driven at the cheetah's top speed. How many miles would it travel in 3 hours?

A. What is the unit rate in feet per hour?

B. What is the unit rate in miles per hour, to the nearest tenth?

C. Write an equation for the number of miles y that the racecar travels in x hours, and use it to solve the problem.

6. Rhoni reads at a rate of 75 pages per hour. The number of pages Rie reads over time is shown in the table.

Time (h)	3	5	9	10
Pages	195	325	585	650

A. Who has a greater rate of reading?

B. At these rates, what is the difference in the number of pages they will read in 4 hours?

C. How long will it take each student to read a book with 780 pages? Show your work.

Use Proportional Relationships to Solve Rate Problems

LESSON 1.5 More Practice/Homework

Give each rate in miles per hour. Round to the nearest tenth.

1. Dev jogs $8\frac{1}{2}$ miles in $1\frac{1}{2}$ hours.

   _____

2. Caroline walks $9\frac{1}{2}$ inches per second.

   _____

3. Dhruv jogs 8 feet per second.

   _____

4. Rachel jogs 20 feet in 3 seconds.

   _____

5. A bald eagle flies 43.2 meters in 3 seconds. The graph shows the distance a typical peregrine falcon flies over time. At these rates, what is the difference in the distances flown by these two birds after 3 hours of flight? Show your work.

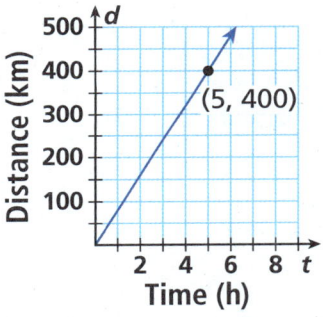

6. Two water tanks are leaking. Tank A has leaked $\frac{1}{16}$ of a gallon in $\frac{1}{12}$ minute, and Tank B has leaked $\frac{3}{80}$ of a gallon in $\frac{1}{30}$ minute. Which tank is leaking faster?

   _____

7. **(MP) Model with Mathematics** Write an equation for each boat-rental company that gives the cost in dollars y of renting a kayak for x hours. What is the difference in cost between the company that charges the most and the one that charges the least for 4 hours? Show your work.

   Company B The cost y of renting a kayak for x hours is $9.00 for each half hour.

   Company C The cost y of renting a kayak is $14.25 per hour.

Company A	
Hours	Total cost ($)
2	$33.00
3	$49.50
4	$66.00
5	$82.50

Module 1 • Lesson 5

Test Prep

8. James walked at a constant rate for 3 hours as shown in the graph. Jaycee walked 14.5 miles in 3 hours at a constant rate. Who walked farther, and how much farther? Explain.

_____

_____

_____

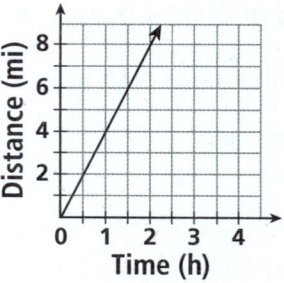

9. A squirrel can run a short distance at a rate of $4\frac{3}{4}$ miles in 15 minutes. A fox can run a short distance at a rate of 21 miles in half an hour. Which is faster, and how much faster in miles per hour?

    Ⓐ the squirrel; 23 miles per hour

    Ⓑ the fox; 23 miles per hour

    Ⓒ the squirrel; 2 miles per hour

    Ⓓ the fox; 2 miles per hour

10. Joelle can read 3 pages in 4 minutes, 4.5 pages in 6 minutes, and 6 pages in 8 minutes. Paxton can read 3 times as fast as Joelle. Which is the equation for the number of pages y that Paxton can read in x minutes?

    Ⓐ $y = \frac{9}{4}x$ Ⓒ $y = \frac{3}{4}x$

    Ⓑ $y = \frac{6}{5}x$ Ⓓ $y = \frac{1}{4}x$

Spiral Review

Compare. Write < or >.

11. -3 _____ -15

12. $-\frac{5}{8}$ _____ $-\frac{1}{4}$

13. List the numbers in order from least to greatest.

    $-2, 8, -15, -5, 3, 1$

    _____

Graph each number on the number line. Then use your number line to find the absolute value of each number.

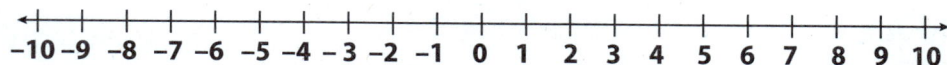

14. 2 _____

15. -8 _____

16. -5 _____

Apply and Practice
Lesson 6

Practice Proportional Reasoning with Scale Drawings

I Can make scale drawings and use them to find actual dimensions.

Step It Out

> **Connect to Vocabulary**
> A **scale** is a ratio between two sets of measurements.
> A **scale drawing** is a proportional two-dimensional drawing of an object.

The scale on a scale drawing can be shown in the same unit or in different units.

1 Mario's school is building a basketball court from the scale drawing.

Drawing length (in.)	Actual length (ft)
0.6	12
2.1	42

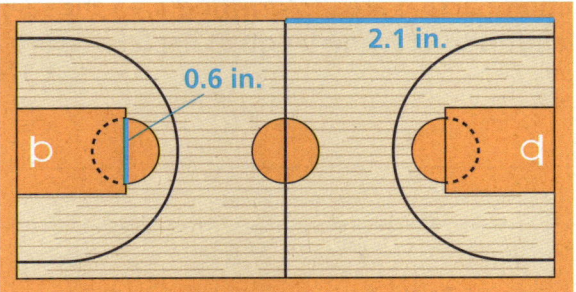

A. The table shows some lengths from the drawing and the corresponding lengths on the actual court. How can you tell this is a scale drawing?

_____

_____

B. What is the scale of the drawing in inches to feet? _____

C. Write an equation for the proportional relationship between the actual length in feet x and the drawing length in inches y. _____

D. Use your equation from Part C to find the actual length represented by a scale drawing length of 1.5 inches, and to find the scale drawing length that represents an actual length of 70 feet.

$\boxed{} = \frac{1}{20}x$, so $x = \boxed{}$

1.5 inches represents an actual length of $\boxed{}$ feet.

$y = \frac{1}{20} \boxed{} = \boxed{}$

70 feet represents a drawing length of $\boxed{}$ inches.

Module 1 • Lesson 6

2 What is the relationship between area in the scale drawing and area on the actual basketball court?

A. Show how to find the area of the court in the scale drawing.

_____

B. Show how to find the length and width of the actual court.

_____

C. What is the area of the actual basketball court? Show your work.

_____

D. Is the ratio of actual area to drawing area the same as the ratio of actual lengths to drawing lengths? Explain.

_____

_____

_____

Turn and Talk Is there a relationship between the scale for area and the scale for length? If so, describe the relationship.

3 Mario's school is also planning to make a rectangular garden 60 feet wide by 70 feet long. On the grid provided, make a scale drawing of the rectangular garden using the scale given.

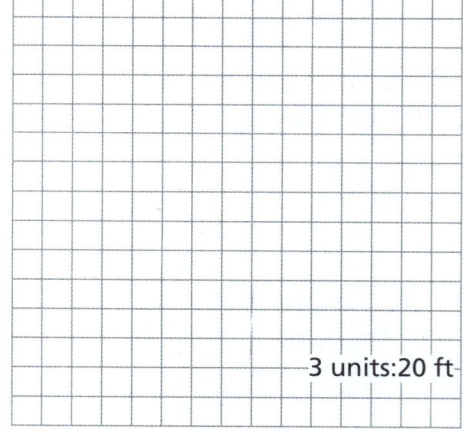

A. Write an equation for the actual length y based on a drawing length x.

_____

_____

B. Use the equation you wrote in Part A to find the scale drawing lengths. Then make the scale drawing.

_____

_____

Turn and Talk How could you write an equation for the drawing length y based on an actual length x?

Name _____

4 Mario's school is also planning a smaller rectangular area as a sitting spot. A scale drawing of the sitting spot is shown. Redraw the sitting spot on the grid at a scale of $\frac{1 \text{ grid unit}}{4 \text{ feet}}$.

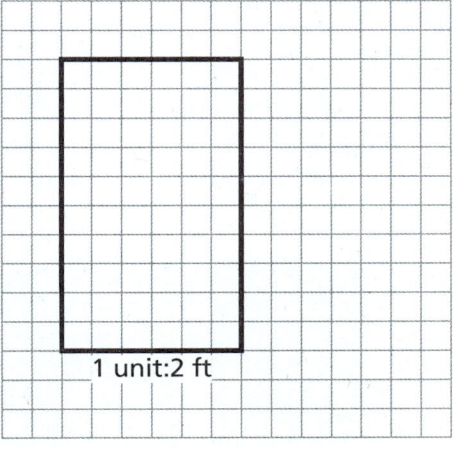

1 unit:2 ft

A. Write and simplify the ratio of the new scale to the original scale.

$$\frac{\text{new scale}}{\text{original scale}} = \frac{\boxed{}}{\frac{1 \text{ grid unit}}{2 \text{ ft}}} = \boxed{}$$

B. Each side of the new drawing will be longer / shorter than the corresponding side of the original drawing.

C. Draw the rectangle for the new scale.

Turn and Talk What is another way you could have found the dimensions of your new scale drawing?

Check Understanding

1. The dimensions of an Olympic swimming pool are shown. A scale drawing of the swimming pool has dimensions of 50 centimeters by 100 centimeters and a diagonal that is about 112 centimeters long.

   A. What is the scale of the drawing in centimeters to meters? _____

   B. What is the actual length of the diagonal of the pool? _____

   25 m

   50 m

2. A different scale drawing of the same Olympic pool uses a scale of $\frac{5 \text{ cm}}{1 \text{ m}}$. What are the dimensions of the drawing? _____

Module 1 • Lesson 6   45

On Your Own

3. **Use Structure** Veronica's town is building a tennis court using the scale drawing below. Find the scale between the drawing and the actual court. Then use the scale to show how a given length on the drawing represents a length on the tennis court, and how a given length on the tennis court is represented in the drawing.

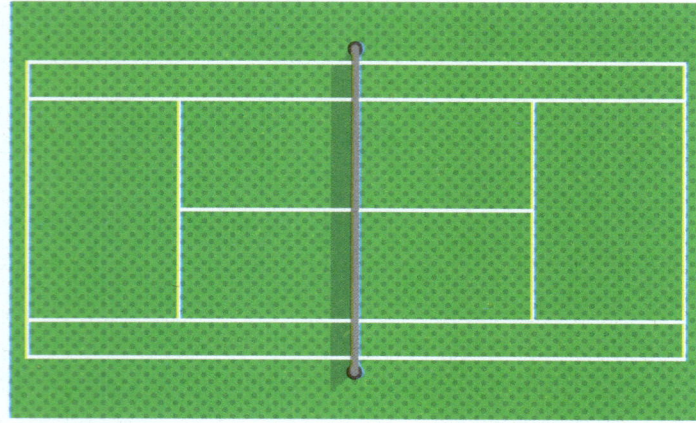

A. The table shows some lengths in the drawing and the corresponding lengths on the actual court. Explain how you can tell from the table that the drawing is a scale drawing.

Drawing length (in.)	Actual length (ft)
2	10
3	15
5	25
10	50

B. What is the ratio between the actual length and the drawing length as a unit rate?

C. Write an equation for the proportional relationship between the drawing lengths and the court lengths, where x is length in the drawing in inches and y is length on the court in feet.

D. Use your equation from Part C to find the actual length represented by a scale drawing length of 3.5 inches.

E. Use your equation from Part C to find the scale drawing length that represents an actual length of 40 feet.

4. What is the relationship between area in the scale drawing and area on the actual tennis court?

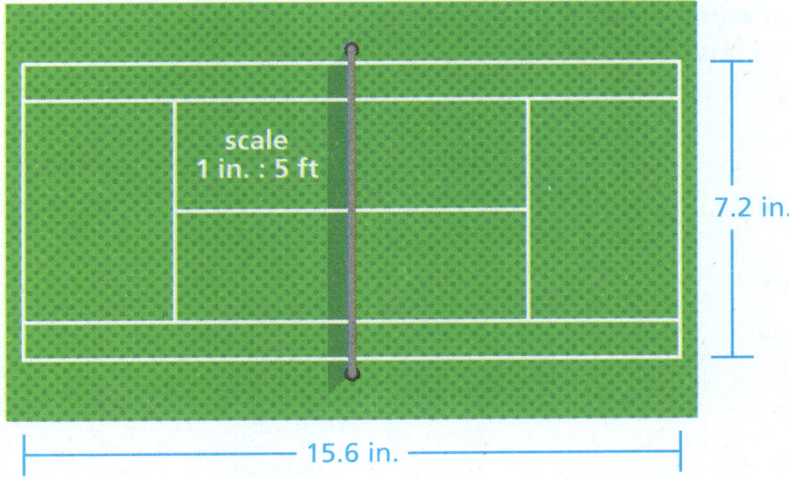

A. Show how to find the area of the scale drawing of the tennis court.

B. Show how to find the length and width of the actual court.

C. Show how to find the area of the actual tennis court.

D. **Attend to Precision** What is the ratio of the area of the actual court to the area of the drawing (as a unit rate)? Is it the same as the ratio of the length of the actual court to the length of the drawing? How do you know?

Module 1 • Lesson 6

5. The students in Suzanne's school are painting a rectangular mural outside the building that will be 15 feet by 45 feet.

   A. Write the unit rate for the proportional relationship between lengths on the mural y and lengths in the scale drawing x.

   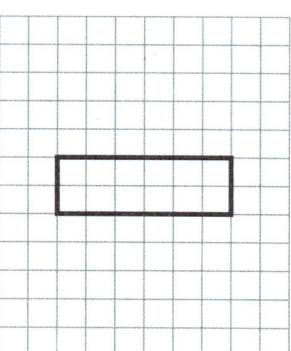

   _____

   B. **(MP) Model with Mathematics** Write an equation that relates x and y. Then estimate the length of the diagonal of the mural.

   _____

6. The students at Suzanne's school are also going to paint a smaller mural inside the building. A scale drawing of the mural is shown on the grid.

   A. Redraw the inside mural on the grid using a scale of 1 unit:1 foot.

   B. How many grid units are there for every 3 feet of mural in the original scale? How many grid units are there for every 3 feet of mural in the new scale?

   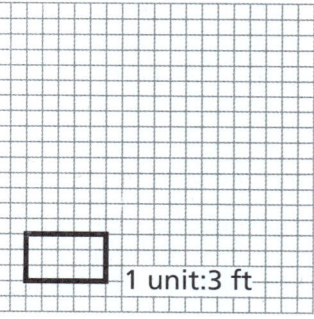

   _____

   C. What is the length of your scale drawing compared to the length of the original scale drawing?

   $$\frac{\text{your scale}}{\text{given scale}} = \frac{\boxed{}}{\frac{1 \text{ grid unit}}{3 \text{ feet}}} = \frac{\boxed{}}{\boxed{}} = \boxed{} \text{ times as long}$$

   D. How does the area of your drawing compare to the original area?

   _____

48

Name _____

Practice Proportional Reasoning with Scale Drawings

LESSON 1.6
More Practice/ Homework

 ONLINE Video Tutorials and Interactive Examples

1. **MP** **Model with Mathematics** Martine's town is building a volleyball court based on a scale drawing that is 40 centimeters by 80 centimeters and uses the scale 1 cm:22.5 cm.

   A. Write an equation for the proportional relationship between drawing court lengths x in centimeters and court lengths y in centimeters.

   _____

   B. What are the length and width in meters of the actual court? Show your work.

   _____
   _____

   C. Write the ratio of the area of the actual court to the area of the court in the scale drawing.

   _____

2. The students in Roberto's school are painting a mural that will be 8 feet by 15 feet. First they make a scale drawing of the mural with a scale of 2 feet:5 feet.

   A. Write an equation for the proportional relationship between drawing mural lengths x in feet and mural lengths y in feet.

   _____

   B. What are the length and width of the scale drawing in feet? Show your work.

   _____
   _____

   C. **Open Ended** Choose a different scale and use it to make a scale drawing of the mural that will fit on a piece of graph paper.

   _____

3. **Geography** A map has a scale of 1 in.:10 mi. Find the distance on the map between two cities that lie 147 miles apart. Show your work.

   _____
   _____

Module 1 • Lesson 6   49

Test Prep

4. Ricardo draws a scale model of the floor plan of his house. His house is 60 feet long and 40 feet wide. He uses the scale $\frac{1 \text{ inch}}{4 \text{ feet}}$ to draw his model. Which statements are true? Select all that apply.

   Ⓐ The equation $\ell = \frac{1}{4}(60)$ can be used to find the length of the scale model.

   Ⓑ The equation $w = (4)(40)$ can be used to find the width of the scale model.

   Ⓒ The width of the scale model is 10 inches.

   Ⓓ The length of the scale model is 240 inches.

   Ⓔ The scale means that 1 inch in the model represents 4 feet in the house.

5. A scale drawing of an elephant shows the animal as 6 inches high and 10.8 inches long. The scale used for the drawing was 3 in.:5 ft. What are the height and length of the actual elephant?

   Height: _____ feet   Length: _____ feet

6. Town planners are planning a 500-foot by 700-foot parking lot by making a scale drawing that is 90 inches by 126 inches. What is the scale of inches in the drawing to inches in the actual object?

   Ⓐ 3:200   Ⓑ 1:300   Ⓒ 2:30   Ⓓ 1:200

Spiral Review

7. A machine produces parts at a steady rate of 160 parts in 8 hours. Complete the table for this relationship.

Hours	2		5	8
Parts		60		160

8. The table shows possible numbers of basketball teams in a league and the number of jerseys needed for the number of teams.

   A. Graph the relationship between the number of teams in the league and the number of jerseys needed.

   B. Is the relationship between the number of teams and the number of jerseys proportional? Explain.

Teams, x	Jerseys, y
3	36
4	48
5	60
6	72
7	84
8	96

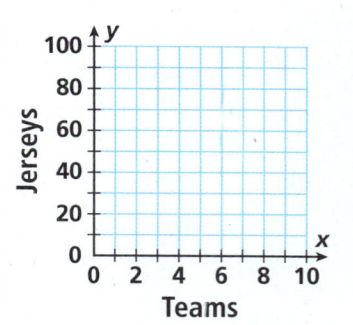

Module 1 Review

Vocabulary

Choose the correct term from the Vocabulary box.

> **Vocabulary**
> constant of proportionality
> proportional relationship
> ratio
> scale
> scale drawing
> unit rate

1. the quantity k in a relationship described by an equation of the form $y = kx$

   _____

2. a rate in which the second quantity is one unit

   _____

3. a relationship between two quantities in which the rate of change or the ratio of one quantity to the other is constant

   _____

Concepts and Skills

4. Which ratio is equivalent to the scale 3 in.:1 ft?

   Ⓐ $\dfrac{\frac{1}{4} \text{ in.}}{\frac{2}{3} \text{ ft}}$ Ⓑ $\dfrac{2 \text{ in.}}{\frac{2}{3} \text{ ft}}$ Ⓒ $\dfrac{4 \text{ in.}}{\frac{5}{6} \text{ ft}}$ Ⓓ $\dfrac{5 \text{ in.}}{6 \text{ ft}}$

5. **MP Use Tools** A news radio program has 3 commercial breaks per half-hour of programming. What is the unit rate of commercials to hours of programming? State what strategy and tool you will use to answer the question, explain your choice, and then find the answer.

   _____

   _____

6. A recipe calls for 2 cups of sugar for $\frac{1}{4}$ cup of butter. What is the unit rate for sugar to butter? _____

7. Jana and Jenn are training to run a race. Jana runs 3 miles in $\frac{1}{3}$ hour. Jenn runs 5 miles in $\frac{3}{4}$ hour. Who runs faster, and what is the unit rate of her speed in minutes per mile? _____

8. A scale drawing of a rectangular mural has the dimensions 2 inches by 3 inches. The scale is 0.5 inches:5 feet. Find the actual dimensions of the mural. Then find the dimensions of another scale drawing with the scale 0.25 inches:10 feet. _____

Module 1

9. Which of the following tables represents data that have a proportional relationship?

A.
x	y
0	0
1	1.5
3	3.5
6	6.5
8	8.5

B.
x	y
0	0
1	1.5
3	4.5
6	9.0
8	12.0

C.
x	y
0	0.5
1	1
3	3
6	6
8	8

D.
x	y
0	0
1	0.5
3	1.5
6	3
8	5

Write an equation of the form $y = kx$ for the relationship shown in the graph or table.

10.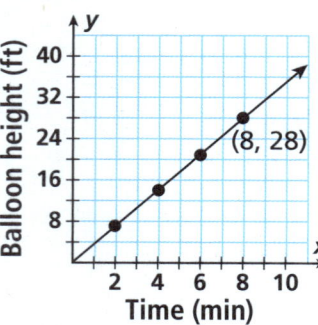

11.
x	y
6	45
10	75
12	90

_____

12. Use the graph from Problem 10. What is the value of r at the point with coordinates (1, r)? What does this point mean in terms of the proportional relationship shown in the graph?

_____

_____

13. A store sells beans for 80¢ per pound.

   A. Graph the proportional relationship that gives the cost y in dollars of buying x pounds of beans.

   B. Write an equation of the form $y = kx$ to represent this relationship.

   _____

   C. A farmers' market sells organic locally grown beans for $1.25 per pound. How much more would it cost to buy 3 pounds of beans at the farmers' market than at the store?

   _____

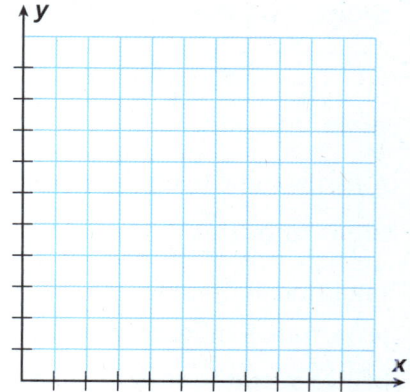

52

Module 2

Proportional Reasoning with Percents

THE CASE OF THE MISSING DIAGRAM

The Bounceville Table Tennis Club holds a 50-game tournament each year.

The shaded portion of each diagram represents the games won by a table tennis team during the tournament.

Write a sentence for each diagram that describes the percent of the whole that is shown. The first one is done for you.

A. Team Dachshunds: 10% of 50 is 5.

B. Team Ferrets _____

C. Team Tigers _____

D. Team Honey Badgers _____
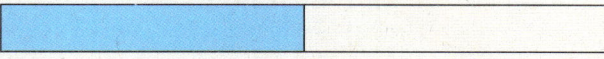

 **Turn and Talk**

What diagram do you think is missing from the sequence of figures above? Explain your reasoning using a diagram.

Module 2   53

Are You Ready?

Complete these problems to review prior concepts and skills you will need for this module.

Multiply Decimals by Whole Numbers

Find each product.

1. 0.3(12) _____
2. 0.75(68) _____
3. 1.25(40) _____

Find a Percent or a Whole

Solve each problem.

4. What is 60% of 120? _____
5. Find 8% of 65. _____
6. 50% of what number is 27? _____
7. 63% of what number is 252? _____
8. Carl scored 35% of his basketball team's 40 points during a game. How many points did Carl score?

   _____

Use Ratio and Rate Reasoning

Solve each problem.

9. The ratio of fish to snails in an aquarium is 3 to 2. There are 18 fish in the aquarium. How many snails are in the aquarium?

   _____

10. Irina ran 0.25 mile in 2 minutes. At this rate, how many minutes will it take her to run 2 miles?

    _____

11. A painter mixes gray paint by using 1 gallon of black paint for every 7 gallons of white paint. How much black paint and how much white paint will the painter need to mix 20 gallons of gray paint?

    _____

    _____

Apply and Practice
Lesson 1

Name _____

Percent Change

I Can solve multi-step problems involving percent change.

Step It Out

1 When a quantity increases or decreases, you can use number sense and proportional reasoning to compare the amount of change to the original amount.

> **Connect to Vocabulary**
>
> **Percent increase** is an amount of increase expressed as a percent of the original amount.
> **Percent decrease** is an amount of decrease expressed as a percent of the original amount.

A. Janis earns $7.00 per hour at Pizza King. After 6 months, her salary increases to $7.70 per hour. What is the percent increase in her hourly rate of pay?

The original amount is $_____. The new amount is $_____. The amount of change is $_____.

Write the ratio of the amount of change to the original amount as a percent. This is the **percent change**. Note that the original amount is 10 times the amount of change.

$$\frac{\text{amount of change}}{\text{original amount}} = \frac{0.7}{7} = \frac{1}{\square} = \underline{\hspace{1cm}} = \underline{\hspace{1cm}}\%$$

B. Pizza King decides to decrease the price of a large pizza as shown on their sign. What is the percent decrease in the cost of a large pizza?

The original amount is $_____. The new amount is $_____. The amount of change is $_____.

$$\frac{\text{amount of change}}{\text{original amount}} = \frac{4}{16}$$
$$= \frac{1}{\square}$$
$$= \underline{\hspace{1cm}}$$
$$= \underline{\hspace{1cm}}\%$$

 **Turn and Talk** How can you use number sense to write $\frac{1}{8}$ as a percent?

Module 2 • Lesson 1   55

2 A population of cheetahs has decreased 30% over the last 18 years. If there were originally about 12,000 cheetahs, how many cheetahs are there now?

A. Find the change in the number of cheetahs. Write the percent as a decimal.

Percent of decrease × Original amount = Decrease

_____ × _____ = _____

B. How many cheetahs are there now?

_____ − _____ = _____, so there are about _____ cheetahs now.

 Turn and Talk What is another way to determine how many cheetahs there are now?

3 A machine cuts lumber into 8-foot planks. Company regulations allow the lengths to vary by $\frac{1}{2}$%, that is to increase or decrease by up to $\frac{1}{2}$%. Find the range of values allowed by the company's regulations.

A. How do you express $\frac{1}{2}$% as a decimal?

☐ ÷ 100 = ☐

B. What are the lengths of the shortest and the longest allowable planks?

Shortest: ☐ − (☐ × 8) = ☐ feet

Longest: ☐ + (☐ × 8) = ☐ feet

The range of allowable lengths is ☐ feet to ☐ feet.

Check Understanding

1. Peggy earned $20 for each lawn she mowed last summer. This summer, she raised her price to $23 per lawn. What is the percent increase?

   _____

2. Robert is inspecting a shipment of 22-inch pipes. The lengths of the pipes may vary by 1%. What is the range of allowable lengths of the pipes?

   _____

3. When Bart bought his car, it averaged 28 miles per gallon of gas. Now, the car's average miles per gallon has decreased by 14%. What is the car's average miles per gallon now? Round your answer to the nearest mile per gallon.

   _____

Name _____

On Your Own

4. The population of deer in a protected area is 225. If the population increases at a rate of 24% per year, how many deer will be in the area next year?

   _____

5. There are 75 students enrolled in a camp. The day before the camp begins 8% of the students cancel. How many students actually attend the camp?

   _____

6. Two years ago, a car was valued at $24,000. This year, the value of the car is $23,160. What was the percent decrease in the value of the car?

   _____

7. **MP Use Structure** Mr. Milton had $1,200 in his savings account at the beginning of the year. If his account has a balance of $1,230 at the end of the year, what is the percent increase of his balance?

   _____

8. Last year, 140 people in a community had cell phones. This year the number of people in the community with cell phones has increased by 65%.

   A. What is the change in the number of people who have cell phones?

   _____

   B. How many people in the community have cell phones this year?

   _____

9. A library has 300 feet of shelves for books. The library will increase the number of feet of shelves by 18%.

   A. How many feet of shelves are being added?

   _____

   B. **MP Reason** The library plans to add 1,000 books to its collection. If the library can fit 15 books on each foot of shelving, will the library have enough room on the new shelves for all the new books? Explain.

   _____

   _____

Module 2 • Lesson 1

10. Last year, 360 students walked to school each day. This year the number of students who walk to school decreased by 25%. What is the change in the number of students who walk to school each day? How many students walk to school each day this year?

_____

Find each percent change. State whether it is an increase or decrease.

11. From 50 to 22

_____

12. From 50 to 43

_____

13. From 20 to 35

_____

14. From 112 to 140

_____

15. **(MP) Attend to Precision** A display for rolls of tape indicates that each roll contains 150 yards of tape. If the actual length of tape can vary by 2.5% of that amount, what is the range for the length of tape on a roll?

_____

16. **(MP) Attend to Precision** An airline states that a flight between two cities takes 2.5 hours. The airline also says that the actual flying time can change by up to 15% of that amount. What are the shortest and longest times for the airplane flight? Round your answers to the nearest tenth of an hour.

_____

Find the range of allowable values based on the given information. Round to the nearest tenth.

17. 15; can vary by 2%

_____

18. 24; can vary by 3.5%

_____

19. The *percent error* of a measurement tells how close the measurement is to the actual value. Dani ran four times around the track, which is 1,600 meters. Her GPS watch recorded the distance as 1,592 meters.

   A. To find the percent error, first find the absolute value of the difference between the distance recorded on Dani's watch and the actual distance.

_____

   B. Now express the difference from Part A as a percent of the actual value. This is the percent error.

_____

   C. When Cam ran 800 meters, his watch recorded the distance as 810 meters. What is the percent error?

_____

Name _____

Percent Change

LESSON 2.1 More Practice/ Homework

1. Five years ago, a typical 70" TV cost about $2,400. Now a similar TV costs approximately $1,680. What is the percent decrease in TV price?

2. **Financial Literacy** Antoine made $33,284 last year. He received a 4.5% annual raise. What will his new salary be for the coming year?

3. **STEM** A scientist observes and counts the bacteria in a culture as 155. Later the scientist counts again and finds that the number has increased by 40%. How many bacteria are there now?

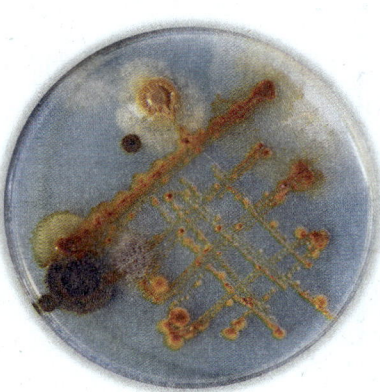

4. The number of veggie burgers sold at a restaurant in Houston, Texas, went from 425 in April to 357 in May. What was the percent decrease of the number of veggie burgers sold from April to May?

5. **Attend to Precision** A warehouse worker fills 150 orders per day on average. From day to day, the number of orders varies by 2%. What is the range of the number of orders the worker fills each day?

6. Find the percent change from 96 to 93. State whether it is an increase or decrease.

7. Find the percent change from 32 to 60. State whether it is an increase or decrease.

8. **Attend to Precision** Find the range of allowable values based on a measure of 130 inches if the values can vary by 1.4%.

Module 2 • Lesson 1

Test Prep

9. A collector bought a rare coin for $30. The coin is now valued at $37.50.

Select all the true statements.

Ⓐ The scenario represents a percent increase.

Ⓑ The scenario represents a percent decrease.

Ⓒ The percent of change was 20%.

Ⓓ The percent of change was 25%.

Ⓔ The percent of change was 75%.

10. A coffee machine dispenses 8-ounce cups of coffee automatically. The amount of coffee may vary by 3%. What are the least and greatest number of ounces the coffee machine will dispense?

Least number: _____ ounces

Greatest number: _____ ounces

11. A German shepherd puppy weighed 25 pounds at 4 months old and 31 pounds at 5 months old. What is the percent increase or decrease?

Ⓐ 35% decrease

Ⓑ 35% increase

Ⓒ 24% decrease

Ⓓ 24% increase

12. The butterfly population at Glen Arbor Farms was 250 last year. This year there are 100 butterflies. What is the percent increase or decrease?

Ⓐ 50% decrease

Ⓑ 50% increase

Ⓒ 60% decrease

Ⓓ 60% increase

Spiral Review

13. There is a proportional relationship between time in hours and time in days.

A. What is the constant of proportionality?

_____

B. What equation describes this relationship?

_____

14. Kate walks 3.5 kilometers along a hiking trail. How far does Kate walk in meters?

_____

Markups and Discounts

I Can calculate markups, markdowns, and retail prices and write equations for markup and markdown situations.

Step It Out

1 Music Enterprise buys digital downloads of music albums for $5.00. The markup rate is 30%. How much will you pay if you want to buy the latest album of your favorite artist, not including tax?

Connect to Vocabulary

Markup is the amount of increase in a price. The markup rate is similar to percent increase but more specific to selling items.
Retail price is the amount an item is sold for after a company adds the markup.
Markdown is the amount of decrease in a price.

A. Calculate the amount of the markup. Show your work.

☐ × 5 = ☐

The markup amount is $_____.

B. Calculate the retail price, which is the price you will pay.

$5.00 + $☐ = $☐

C. Express the ratio of the retail price to the cost of the download as a percent. How does this percent relate to the markup rate?

☐/☐ = ☐ or ☐ %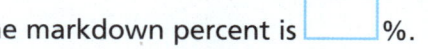

D. What is another way you could find the percent of the original amount that the retail price represents?

original amount + markup = retail

100% + ☐% = ☐%

After New Year's Day, Music Enterprise marks down their albums as shown in their ad. How much will the album cost after this markdown?

E. The retail price is $☐. The markdown percent is ☐%.

F. Find the amount of the markdown.

☐ × $6.50 = $☐

G. Calculate the album price after the markdown. Is this cost reasonable? Explain.

_____

_____

Turn and Talk Would the final price be $5 if there were a markdown of 30% and then a markup of 30%? Explain.

Module 2 • Lesson 2

2 You can also use equations to solve problems involving markups, markdowns, and discounts.

Penelope buys bracelets in bulk to sell at her store. She uses a markup rate of 125% which is added to the bracelet cost. What is the retail price of a bracelet with an original cost of $8?

A. The markup rate is _____. The equation $y = $ _____ x gives the markup amount y in dollars for the bracelets in terms of the original amount x in dollars.

B. Use the equation to find the markup amount for a bracelet with an original cost of $8.

$y = $ ☐ $\times$ $☐ = $☐

C. Calculate the retail price of the bracelet.

$8 + $☐ = $☐

D. The markup amount is _____x. An equation for the retail price y in dollars in terms of the original amount x in dollars is

$y = $ _____$x + $ _____$x = $ _____x.

3 Penelope marked down the price of necklaces in her store as shown.

A. Calculate what percent the sale price is of the retail price.

$\dfrac{\text{sale price}}{\text{retail price}} = \dfrac{\$\,☐}{\$\,☐} = ☐ = ☐\%$

B. What is an equation in the form $y = kx$ that relates the sale price to the retail price x?

_____

 Turn and Talk Discuss how you find the markup and markdown amounts. Which concept did you find more challenging to understand, and why?

Check Understanding

1. A grocery store buys organic apples for $0.75 per apple. The grocery store marks up the cost of each apple by 18%. To the nearest cent, how much will one organic apple cost at the grocery store?

_____

2. A store is selling all toaster ovens at 15% off. Write an equation in the form of $y = kx$ to represent the sale price y in dollars of a toaster with a retail price of x dollars. Then find the amount Jill paid for a toaster with a retail price of $40.

_____

Name _____

On Your Own

3. A hobby store marks up remote-controlled cars 20%. The original cost was $35. What is the retail price to purchase a remote-controlled car at the hobby store?

   _____

4. Organic hot dogs at the grocery store cost $2.00 each. At a major league baseball game, an organic hot dog costs $6.50. By what percent are the organic hot dogs marked up?

   _____

5. **Financial Literacy** The Bakers want to sell their house for $145,500. After 2 months, the Bakers decided to mark down the price of their house 8% to sell more quickly. How much are the Bakers selling their house for now?

   _____

6. (MP) **Reason** What is the retail price of a pair of shoes if there is a 10% discount and the sale price is $76.50?

   _____

7. A convenience store sells prepaid mobile phones. It purchases them for $12 each and uses a markup rate of 250%.

   A. (MP) **Model with Mathematics** The markup rate is the constant of proportionality in the equation $y = kx$. Write an equation that can be used to find the amount of markup on the cost x of a phone.

   _____

   B. Use the equation to calculate the markup amount. What is the retail price of a phone?

   _____

   C. Next week the store is going to reduce the price to $31.50. Calculate what percent the sale price is of the retail price. Show your work.

   _____

   D. (MP) **Model with Mathematics** Based on your answer to Part C, what is an equation in the form $y = kx$ that relates the sale price to the retail price x?

   _____

Module 2 • Lesson 2   63

For Problems 8–9, find the new price for the markup or discount given. Round to the nearest cent if necessary.

8. $3.00 marked up 72%

9. $125.49 discounted 30%

10. The thrift store is selling their old DVDs. When the DVDs first came out, they sold for $19. They have now been marked down as shown. What is the sale price of a DVD?

11. **(MP) Attend to Precision** A manufacturer makes hand-woven scarves for $10 and then ships them to retail boutiques around the country. The boutiques sell the scarves for $25. What percent markup do the boutiques charge their customers?

12. **(MP) Model with Mathematics** Melissa makes apple pies and sells them with a markup of 78%. Write an equation representing the retail price y of Melissa's apple pies in terms of the original cost x.

13. All of last year's car models were marked down 40%. Tracy wants to buy a car that now costs $18,000. What was the retail price of the car?

14. A video game store buys used games and marks them up 25% for resale.

   A. **(MP) Model with Mathematics** If the store pays x dollars for a used game, the expression $x + 0.25x$ gives the price the store charges for the game. Simplify this expression.

   B. Complete this statement: Increasing a quantity by 25% is the same as multiplying the quantity by _____.

15. For a sale, a video game store discounts the prices of all games by 8%.

   A. **(MP) Model with Mathematics** If p is the retail price of a game, write two expressions that each represent the sale price.

   B. Complete this sentence: Decreasing a quantity by 8% is the same as multiplying the quantity by _____.

Name _____

Markups and Discounts

**LESSON 2.2
More Practice/
Homework**

ONLINE Video Tutorials and Interactive Examples

1. **(MP) Attend to Precision** A local nonprofit organization is selling popcorn to raise money for hurricane relief. The organization paid $4 per bag for the popcorn and sold it for $5 per bag. What was the percent markup on each bag of popcorn?

   _____

2. A high school decided to buy new uniforms for the girls and boys basketball teams. They plan to buy 35 uniforms with a total retail cost of $1,235. The store offers discounts based on the number of items the school buys, as shown. What will the discounted price be for the high school?

   _____

   BASKETBALL UNIFORM GROUP DISCOUNTS
   - 10% off — Buy 10–24 items, Get 10% off, Use code: 10
   - 15% off — Buy 25–49 items, Get 15% off, Use code: 15
   - 20% off — Buy 50+ items, Get 20% off, Use code: 20

3. Professor Burger bought a DVD player with an original price of $150 that was reduced by 20%. What was the reduced price?

   _____

For Problems 4–7, find the new price for the markup, markdown, or discount given. Round to the nearest cent if necessary.

4. $6.25 marked up 25%

   _____

5. $13.50 discounted 75%

   _____

6. $112 marked down 40%

   _____

7. $220 marked up 60%

   _____

8. **Open Ended** Describe a real-life situation involving markup, markdown, or discount that the equation $y = x + 0.4x$ could represent.

   _____

   _____

9. A local jewelry store sells class rings. The store engraves a name and date on the ring and sells it using a markup rate of 340%. Write an equation that can be used to find the amount of markup on the cost of a ring.

   _____

Module 2 • Lesson 2

65

Test Prep

10. Nate just started working at a clothing store. He receives a 40% discount on any item, once a month. This month Nate decided to buy a jacket with a retail price of $74.99. How much did Nate pay for his jacket?

- Ⓐ $29.99
- Ⓑ $34.99
- Ⓒ $44.99
- Ⓓ $104.99

11. Which equation shows that marking up the original price p of an item by 35% is equivalent to multiplying the original price by 1.35?

- Ⓐ $p + 1.35p = 2.35p$
- Ⓑ $p + 0.35p = 1.35p$
- Ⓒ $p - 1.35p = -0.35p$
- Ⓓ $2.35p - p = 1.35p$

12. Write an equation that represents a discount of 18% on a retail price of $55. Let p represent the new price.

_____

13. Brooke needs a new computer. On Friday, the computer was $200. On Saturday, the price of the computer was $149. Determine if there was a markup or markdown and by what percent.

- Ⓐ markup; 25.5%
- Ⓑ markup; 34.5%
- Ⓒ markdown; 25.5%
- Ⓓ markdown; 34.5%

Spiral Review

14. Determine whether the cost of grapes is proportional to the number of pounds.

Grapes (lb)	1	2	3	4
Cost ($)	3	6	9	12

_____

15. Find the range of allowable masses for a ball bearing with an expected mass of 250 grams for which values are allowed to vary by 5%.

_____

Apply and Practice
Lesson 3

Taxes and Gratuities

I Can find taxes, gratuities, and total costs by writing and using equations of the form $y = kx$, and assess the reasonableness of results.

> **Connect to Vocabulary**
>
> A **gratuity** is a percent that is given or paid in addition to the price of a service. It is also referred to as a **tip**.
>
> **Sales tax** is a percent that is added to the price of goods or services.

Step It Out

1 Jeremy paid a barber $15 for a haircut. He also paid 15% as a tip. What is the total amount that Jeremy paid?

A. What percent of the cost did Jeremy pay the barber, including the tip? _____

B. Calculate the total cost of the haircut, including the tip. Show your work. _____

2 Kelsey and Jamal went to lunch on Saturday. Their lunch cost $17.60, they gave the waiter a 15% gratuity, and they were charged a 5% sales tax rate. No tax is charged on the gratuity. What was the total cost of the lunch?

A. Write an equation in the form $y = kx$ to find the amount of the gratuity y in dollars on an amount of x dollars.

$y =$ _____ x

Use the equation to find the gratuity.

$y =$ _____ × 17.60 = _____

The gratuity was $_____.

B. Write an equation in the form $y = kx$ to find the tax y in dollars on an amount of x dollars.

$y =$ _____ x

Use the equation to find the tax on Kelsey and Jamal's bill.

$y =$ _____ × 17.60 = _____

The tax was $_____.

C. Find the total cost of the lunch.

$17.60 + $_____ + $_____ = $_____.

Haircuts $15

Turn and Talk Round up the cost of the meal before tax and tip. Explain how to use mental math to estimate a tip of at least 15% rounded to the nearest dollar.

Module 2 • Lesson 3   67

3 Nolan buys office supplies for his home business. Nolan paid a total of $210, which included a sales tax rate of 5%. What was the cost of the supplies before tax was added?

A. What was the total cost of the office supplies including sales tax in terms of the original cost x? Express the answer using a percent and using a decimal.

_____

B. Write an equation in the form $y = kx$ to find the cost y in dollars including sales tax for items with a cost of x dollars without the sales tax.

$y =$ _____ x

C. Use the equation to find the cost of Nolan's office supplies without the tax.

$210 =$ _____ x

_____ $= x$

The cost of the office supplies without the sales tax was $_____.

D. Does your answer seem reasonable? Explain.

_____
_____

 **Turn and Talk** Explain another way you could have justified in Part D the reasonableness of your answer to Part C.

Check Understanding

1. Ella buys a computer for $785. Her local tax rate is 7%. How much does Ella pay for the computer, including tax?

_____

2. Kim works as a DJ and earns $1,250 to play music for 6 hours at a wedding reception. At the end of the night, she gets an 18% tip. How much in total did she earn?

_____

3. Adrian shops for school clothes and spends a total of $93.42. If the local tax rate is 8%, how much was the cost without tax?

_____

On Your Own

4. The amount that a charter boat captain charges a group to go deep-sea fishing is shown. If the group tips the captain 17%, what is the total amount that the captain receives for the fishing trip?

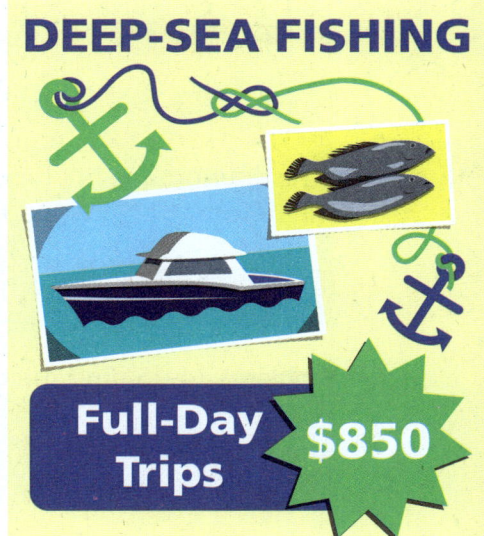

5. (MP) **Reason** The school secretary orders a new printer and pays $310.30 after tax. The tax rate is 7%. What was the original price of the printer?

For Problems 6–7, find the total amount given the original price and tax rate. Round to the nearest cent if necessary.

6. $15.25, 7%

7. $31.69, 6%

8. Miguel buys a car for $14,999. The tax rate is 6%. What is the total purchase price of the car?

9. The music boosters have their year-end banquet at a hotel that charges $750. The president of the boosters tips the banquet team 20%. What is the total amount spent?

10. (MP) **Model with Mathematics** A family used a professional decorator to help furnish their new home. The decorator selected $1,580 worth of furnishings. In addition to paying for the purchases, the family paid 4.5% tax on the purchases. The decorator's fee was 12% of the purchases, not including the tax.

A. Write an equation in the form of $y = kx$ to represent the decorator's fee. Then use the equation to calculate the amount of that fee. Round to the hundredths place if necessary.

B. Write an equation in the form of $y = kx$ to represent the tax. Then use the equation to calculate the amount of tax. Round to the hundredths place if necessary.

C. What is the total cost that the family paid? Show your work.

Module 2 • Lesson 3   69

For Problems 11–12, find the total amount given the original price and tip rate. Round to the nearest cent if necessary.

11. $22.22, 10%

12. $41.32, 15%

13. (MP) **Use Structure** A group of friends receives a dinner bill of $287.50 at a restaurant. The bill includes a 15% tip for the server. How much was the bill before the tip was added? Explain how you found your answer.

For Problems 14–15, find the original price given the total amount and tip rate.

14. $51.84, 20%

15. $38.35, 18%

16. Jayme buys the painting shown for his apartment. The tax rate is 6.5%. How much did Jayme spend? Round to the nearest cent if necessary.

17. A business traveler buys a round-trip plane ticket for $629. The tax rate is 7.5%. How much was the cost after tax? Round to the nearest cent if necessary.

For Problems 18–19, find the tax amount given the original price and tax rate. Round to the nearest cent if necessary.

18. $58.73, 6.5%

19. $73.81, 7.5%

20. Three coworkers buy a baby shower gift for $60. The local tax rate is 6%. How much was the tax?

For Problems 21–22, find an equation for the total amount y after the given rate of increase is added to the original amount x.

21. 20%

22. 8.5%

23. (MP) **Model with Mathematics** The cost x of the Sennet family's meal at a restaurant is $172.65, and they tip 20%. Write and use an equation to find the total cost y of the dinner.

Name _____

Taxes and Gratuities

**LESSON 2.3
More Practice/
Homework**

ONLINE Video Tutorials and Interactive Examples

1. Beau buys a skateboard with a price tag of $82.50 not including tax. The tax rate is 8%. How much does he pay, including tax?

2. Professor Burger orders flowers to be delivered to his mother. The flowers cost $59.95, not including tax. If there is a 6% sales tax, what is the total cost of the flowers to the nearest cent?

3. Monty takes a cab to work and pays a fare of $12.75. He tips the driver 20% and the tax rate is 8%. How much does he spend on the trip?

4. **(MP) Reason** Mary Jo takes her son to get a haircut at the barbershop. The total cost of the haircut is $12.60, including a 20% tip. How much was the haircut before the tip?

5. Derek and Jeannine buy a car for a total price, including tax, of $19,795. The price of the car without tax was $18,500. What is the tax rate?

For Problems 6–7, find the total amount given the original price and tax or tip rate. Round to the nearest cent if necessary.

6. $123.28, 7.5%

7. $156.67, 6%

For Problems 8–9, find the total amount given the original price, tax rate, and tip rate. Round to the nearest cent if necessary.

8. $90.34, 3.5%, 20%

9. $101.33, 6.7%, 18%

For Problems 10–11, find the original price given the total amount and tax or tip rate.

10. $128,500, 5.5%

11. $307.32, 20%

Module 2 • Lesson 3

Test Prep

12. Match the amounts and tip or tax rates in the first column to the total cost with the tip or tax included in the second column.

$123.01, 7.5% •   • $1,336.66

$52.48, 6.5%   •   • $57.86

$1,261, 6%   •   • $258.19

$224.51, 15%   •   • $132.24

$48.22, 20%   •   • $55.89

13. Brett plays an acoustic guitar at an event for $500. At the end of the event, the sponsor tips him 20%. How much does Brett make at this event?

_____

14. Carmine buys a canoe priced at $478. He pays a total, including tax, of $509.07. What was the tax rate?

Ⓐ 6%

Ⓑ 6.5%

Ⓒ 7%

Ⓓ 7.5%

15. Kenton buys a tool box, drill set, and socket set. He spends a total of $564.45 after tax, and the tax rate is 6%. What was the total cost before tax?

Ⓐ $540.04

Ⓑ $537.50

Ⓒ $534.99

Ⓓ $532.50

Spiral Review

16. An 8-ounce cup of juice costs $1.20. A 12-ounce cup of the same juice costs $1.44. Can the relationship between cost and ounces of juice be described by a constant rate? Explain.

_____

_____

17. Last year, 320 students were members of Pine Hill Middle School clubs. This year, there was a 20% increase in members. How many students are members this year?

_____

Apply and Practice
Lesson 4

Name _____

Commissions and Fees

I Can calculate commissions, fees, and total earnings and assess the reasonableness of my results.

Step It Out

1.75% commission

1 ▶ Harlan is a real estate agent whose total annual earnings are the sum of his annual salary and the commission shown. Last year, Harlan sold 10 homes that totaled $2,500,000 in sales. How much commission did Harlan earn?

   A. The amount of Harlan's sales for the year is $_____.

   Harlan will receive _____% of his sales as his commission amount.

   B. Calculate Harlan's commission.

   $_____ × _____ = $_____

   C. How do you know your answer is reasonable?

   _____
   _____
   _____

> **Connect to Vocabulary**
>
> A **commission** is a fee a person earns for sales or services. It is often a percent of an amount of sales. The person may or may not also earn a salary.

2 ▶ A **fee** is a payment to someone for a service. Fees can be paid as a fixed amount or as a percent of an amount.

Yuan is an insurance salesman who makes a base monthly salary of $1,500 with a commission of 1% of the value of each policy he sells. In addition, each time his client makes an investment transaction, Yuan receives a $5.00 service fee.

This month, Yuan sells one policy valued at $50,000 and his client makes 4 investment transactions. How much does Yuan earn this month?

Base Salary + Commission Amount + Earnings from Fees = Total Earnings

1,500 + 50,000(_____) + 5(_____) = total earnings

1,500 + _____ + _____ = _____

Yuan's total earnings this month are $_____.

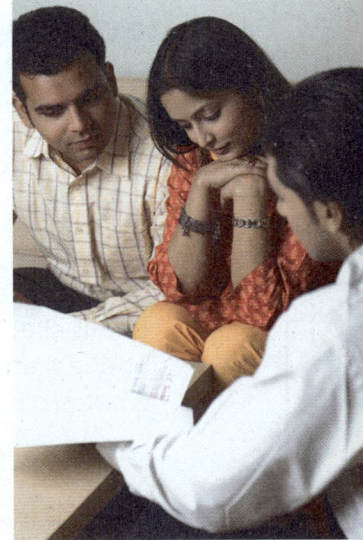

Turn and Talk How do the payments vary for the people described in this lesson so far?

Module 2 • Lesson 4

3. A loan officer makes a base salary of $22,500 per year, with a commission of 0.4% of the amount of the loans he processes. He also gets a service fee of $1.75 on every loan preapproval application he processes. Assume the loan officer processes an average of $100,000 in loans and completes 8 preapproval applications each week. How much will he earn this year?

- ✓ $22,500 base salary
- ✓ 0.4% commission
- ✓ $1.75 service fee

A. The total amount of the loans he processes this year is 52 × $_____ = $_____.

B. The total commission the loan officer earns is 0.004 × $_____ = $_____.

C. The total number of preapproval applications he processes this year is 8 × _____ = _____.

D. The total of the fees he earns for preapproval applications this year is $1.75 × _____ = $_____.

E. Find the loan officer's total earnings this year.

_____

Turn and Talk How are the amounts earned in Tasks 1, 2, and 3 different, and how are they the same?

Check Understanding

1. Anna sells computer software and makes a salary of $50,000 annually and 6.5% commission on total sales. If Anna sells $3 million in computer software this year, how much does she make?

_____

2. Dirk is a broker who earns a salary of $41,000 annually, 3.5% commission on his clients' investments of $2.4 million, and a fee of $5.25 on each online transaction. If Dirk processes 1,250 online transactions this year, what are his annual earnings?

_____

3. Brenton is a phone sales specialist who makes $33,000 per year plus an $8 fee for each sale he makes. If Brenton makes 15 sales per week, what are his annual earnings?

_____

Name _____

On Your Own

4. A literary agent makes $30,000 a year plus 13% commission on the sales of her clients' books to publishers. The agent sold 4 books for $175,000 each for her clients this year. Find her total earnings.

_____

5. An insurance agent earns a base salary of $28,000, a commission of 2% of sales, and receives an additional fee of $9.00 for each sale of an investment policy. The agent had total sales of $75,000 and 6 investment policies this month. Find the commission and fees earned.

_____

6. Find the commission based on total sales of $98,000 and a commission of 1.5%.

_____

7. Find the total fees: Applications: 48, Fee: $2.95 per application.

_____

8. Find the total earnings based on the given information.
Base Salary: $42,000; Total Sales: $175,000; Commission: 4%

_____

9. Financial Literacy A stockbroker earns $53,000 annually plus 0.8% of his clients' total investment portfolios. If his clients' investments total $1.2 million, what is his commission this year?

_____

10. (MP) **Reason** A home sold for $286,000. The amount the homeowner received, before taxes and closing costs, was the selling price minus the commission to the real estate agent, which was 6%. How much commission did the real estate agent earn on the sale? How do you know your answer is reasonable?

_____
_____
_____
_____

Module 2 • Lesson 4

11. **Construct Arguments** An oil painting was sold at an auction house for $6,550. The buyer agrees to pay that price plus a commission called the buyer's premium. For the painting, the rate for the buyer's premium was 25%. Calculate the amount of the commission. How do you know your answer is reasonable?

12. A golf equipment salesperson earns a base salary plus commission on golf equipment sold as shown. If the salesperson sells $78,000 worth of equipment in a year, what is the total annual salary earned?

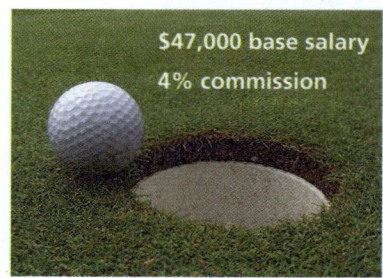

$47,000 base salary
4% commission

13. Irma works for a service that delivers groceries and pet supplies. She earns a base monthly salary of $1,900. In addition, she gets a commission of 1.8% of the cost of each grocery order, and she also gets a delivery fee of $11 for each delivery of pet supplies.

   A. How is calculating Irma's total monthly earnings different from calculating earnings based on salary and commission?

   B. **Attend to Precision** Last month Irma's deliveries consisted of $33,600 in groceries, and she made 140 deliveries of pet supplies. What are Irma's total earnings for the month?

   Next year the delivery service is going to change the way it pays its delivery drivers. Irma will make a base monthly salary of $2,750. She will also earn a commission of 2.1% of the cost of groceries and a commission of 10.2% of the cost of pet supplies.

   C. How will next year's pay structure differ from this year's pay structure?

   D. Suppose Irma's deliveries during a month next year consist of $35,100 in groceries and $1,080 in pet supplies. How much will her earnings be that month?

Name _____

Commissions and Fees

**LESSON 2.4
More Practice/
Homework**

1. Maryanne sells cruise vacations. She makes a base salary of $2,500 per month plus 5% of the cost of each vacation. This month she sold $80,000 in cruises. What are her total monthly wages?

   _____

2. **Use Structure** A realtor sells 3 houses this month for a total of $825,000, and each buyer uses her company to process their loan. She earns a base pay of $2,600 each month plus 1.5% of her total house sales. She also gets a fee of $12 for each loan she gets serviced through her company. What are her total earnings for the month?

   _____

3. A pharmaceutical sales representative gets paid $50,000 annually plus 3.5% commission on total sales. This year he sold $420,000 in pharmaceuticals. What are his annual total earnings?

   _____

4. **Open Ended** Write and solve a problem about base pay and commission. Show your work.

   _____
   _____
   _____

For Problems 5–8, find the requested information based on the given facts.

5. Total Sales: $55,000; Commission: 3.5%; determine commission.

   _____

6. Transactions: 175; Fee: $2.75 per transaction; determine total fees.

   _____

7. Base: $54,300; Total Sales: $950,000; Commission: 2.75%; determine total earnings.

   _____

8. Base: $48,000; Commission: 9% of $256,000; Transactions: 325; Fee: $7.25 per transaction; determine total earnings.

   _____

Test Prep

For Problems 9 and 10, mark all the statements that are true.

9. Marcus works for base pay: $25,000, commission: 2%, and fees: $3.75 per transaction.
   - (A) Commission on $50,000 is $1,000.
   - (B) Commission on $35,000 is $800.
   - (C) Fees for 25 transactions are $93.75.
   - (D) Total earnings for $75,000 in sales and 10 transactions are $1,537.50.
   - (E) Total earnings for $75,000 in sales and 10 transactions are $26,537.50.

10. Maddy works for base pay: $37,555 and commission: 5.5%.
    - (A) Commission on $155,000 is $852.50.
    - (B) Commission on $155,000 is $8,525.
    - (C) Total earnings for $85,000 in sales are $42,230.
    - (D) Total earnings for $45,000 in sales are $40,300.
    - (E) Total earnings for $115,000 in sales are $43,880.

11. Veronica sells Internet ads over the phone. She is paid $12 per hour plus $15 for every ad she sells. She works 4 hours a day 5 days a week and sells on average 13 ads per day. What are her average weekly earnings?

12. A trampoline salesman makes $25,000 annually plus 6% commission on his total sales. If he sold $40,000 worth of trampolines this year, what are his total earnings?

Spiral Review

13. Haley scored 93 on her first math test and 86 on her second test. What is her percent decrease from Test 1 to Test 2 to the nearest tenth?

14. It takes Camden 45 minutes to complete $\frac{1}{5}$ of his art project. How many hours will it take him to complete the whole project if he works at the same rate?

15. Maggie eats at a restaurant and gets a bill for $23.50. She wants to leave a 20% gratuity. What is Maggie's total cost?

Apply and Practice
Lesson 5

Simple Interest

I Can calculate simple interest and the total value of an account after any period of time. I understand and can apply the equation $I = Prt$.

Step It Out

1 ▶ Big Money Bank loans $12,000 to Carlotta. This initial amount borrowed is called the **principal**.

At the end of 8 years, Carlotta has to repay the loan to the bank at a rate of 5.5% simple interest per year. What is the total amount of interest she will have to pay on her loan?

> **Connect to Vocabulary**
>
> **Simple interest** is a fixed percent of the principal. It is calculated using the formula $I = Prt$, where P represents the principal, r the rate of interest, and t the time.

A. Find the amount of simple interest I that Carlotta owes after one year by finding 5.5% of $12,000.

$I = \boxed{} \times 12{,}000 = \boxed{}$

Carlotta owes $ _____ in interest after one year.

B. Calculate the total interest Carlotta owes for the 8 years of the loan.

Interest for one year × 8 years = Interest for 8 years

_____ × 8 = _____

Over 8 years Carlotta will pay _____ in simple interest on her loan.

2 ▶ Melanie deposits $8,200 in a bank account paying 4.4% simple interest. How much is in her account after 5 years and 6 months?

A. Use the equation $I = Prt$ to find the amount of interest Melanie earns after 5.5 years.

$I = (8{,}200)(_____)(_____) = \$ _____$

B. The total amount of money in Melanie's account after 5 years and 6 months will be $P + I$: her original principal P plus the interest earned I.

P   +   I   =   account total

8,200 + _____ = _____

Melanie's account will contain $ _____ after 5 years and 6 months.

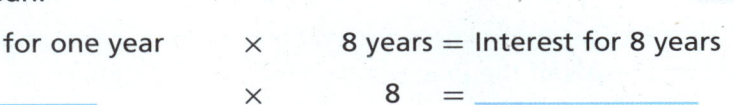

Turn and Talk Which of the following changes would increase Melanie's balance the most: increasing the time to 10 years, increasing the interest rate to 6.5%, or increasing the principal to $9,000.00? Explain.

Module 2 • Lesson 5

3 Gregory borrowed money to buy a used car, which he paid back at the end of the loan period. It cost him $10,650 to repay the loan. How many years was the loan period?

- $7,500 loan
- annual simple interest rate of 6%

A. P + I = Total repayment

7,500 + _____ = _____

Gregory paid a total of _____ in interest.

B. To find the loan period t, solve $I = Prt$ for t.

I = P × r × t

_____ = 7,500 × _____ × t

_____ = 450 × t

$\dfrac{\Box}{\Box}$ = t

$\Box$ = t

The loan period was _____ years.

 **Turn and Talk** Suppose you know the amount of a loan, the amount repaid, and the number of years of the loan period. How could you find the interest rate?

Check Understanding

1. Arisia puts $500 into a savings account with an annual simple interest rate of 4.5%.

   A. How much interest does she earn per year?

   B. If the interest rate stays the same, how much interest will Arisia's account earn after 15 years?

   C. If the interest rate stays the same, how much money will be in Arisia's account after 20 years?

   D. If the savings account pays 5% simple interest, how much interest will Arisia earn on her $500 principal over 20 years?

On Your Own

2. **Financial Literacy** Marcus borrows $3,000 from his local credit union, to be repaid with 3.5% annual simple interest at the end of 4 years. What are the principal, interest rate, and time in this situation?

Principal	☐
Interest rate	$\dfrac{\square}{100} = \square$
Time	☐ years

3. Inez opens a savings account with $2,400. The account pays her 2.4% annual simple interest.

   A. Find the amount of interest that the account will earn per year.

   _____

   B. Calculate the total interest Inez would earn in 10 years.

   _____

4. Barry opens a savings account after seeing the ad shown. He deposits $1,300.

   Savings accounts over $1,000 earn 2.2% annual interest.

   A. (MP) **Model with Mathematics** Write an equation that relates the amount of time t in years that Barry holds his account to the amount of simple interest I that Barry earns.

   _____

   B. How much interest does Barry earn in 7 years?

   _____

5. Avram borrows $14,500 at 5.4% annual simple interest to open up a small business. He must pay back the borrowed money and interest at the end of 9 years.

   A. How much interest will Avram have to pay on the loan?

   _____

   B. How much money will Avram have to repay in all?

   _____

Module 2 • Lesson 5   81

Use the information for Problems 6 and 7.

Financial Literacy Regina is buying a new car. She sees two advertisements for the same car at different prices from different dealerships. Both dealers are offering a simple-interest loan for the price of the car.

Ad A
$24,200
6.5% interest
XX years

Ad B
$XXXX
5.3% interest
9 years

6. Regina calculates that to buy the car in Ad A, the loan would ultimately cost her $41,503. After how many years is the loan in Ad A to be paid back?

   _____

7. Regina calculates that to buy the car in Ad B, the loan would ultimately cost her $38,402. What is the price of the car offered in Ad B?

   _____

8. **(MP) Model with Mathematics** Write an equation to find the simple interest rate when $450,000 earns $31,500 interest in 2 years.

   _____

9. **(MP) Use Structure** A savings account pays an annual simple interest rate of 1.5%.

   A. How much interest would you earn in 1 year on $2,000?

   _____

   B. What would be the balance in your account after 5 years?

   _____

   C. How long would it take to earn $500 or more in interest?

   _____

10. **(MP) Use Structure** It costs $36,736 to repay a loan of $20,500 at 6.6% annual simple interest.

    A. How much interest would you pay each year?

    _____

    B. After how many years must you repay the loan?

    _____

82

Name _____

Simple Interest

LESSON 2.5 More Practice/Homework

1. **Financial Literacy** Rena's grandfather opened a savings account as a college fund for her. His initial deposit and the yearly simple interest rate are shown. How much will Rena have in the account after 2 years and 6 months?

2. (MP) **Use Structure** If you deposit $5,000 in a savings account, you will earn 6.5% simple interest over the first 10 years.

   A. How much interest will the account earn over this period?
   _____

   B. How much will be in the account after the 10-year period?
   _____

   C. At the Town Savings Bank, you will earn $2,950 in simple interest on a $5,000 deposit over the first 10 years. What rate of interest does that bank pay?
   _____

3. (MP) **Use Structure** Dream Loan Bank offers loans. Carrie borrows $10,500 to help start a business. The loan must be repaid at 4.5% annual simple interest after 10 years. How much money will Carrie have to pay back?
   _____

4. **Financial Literacy** Kevin is going to open a savings account with $4,000.

   Bank A offers an account that will pay 6% annual simple interest for 6 years.

   Bank B offers an account that will pay 7% annual simple interest for 3 years. After the 3 years, Kevin would have to transfer all his money to a regular account that will pay 5% annual simple interest on the *new* transferred principal. Which offer will leave Kevin with more money after 6 years? Explain.

Module 2 • Lesson 5   83

Test Prep

5. Delilah deposits $8,255 in an account that pays 4.2% simple interest. How much money will be in her account after 8 years?

    Ⓐ $2,773.69
    Ⓑ $11,028.68
    Ⓒ $12,254.66
    Ⓓ $27,736.80

6. Edgar takes out a loan of $5,540, to be repaid after 7 years at 8.5% simple interest. How much interest will Edgar have to pay on the loan?

    Ⓐ $470.90
    Ⓑ $3,296.30
    Ⓒ $3,775.60
    Ⓓ $8,836.30

7. Gregoria borrowed $2,450, to be paid back at 3.5% annual simple interest. She repays $3,221.75. How many years was the loan period?

Spiral Review

For Problems 8 and 9, use the number line.

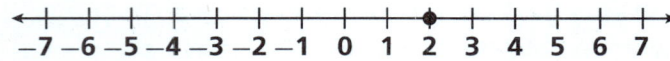

8. What number is 3 units to the right of 2 on the number line?

9. What number is 3 units to the left of 2?

10. Bianca had a weekly allowance of $8.50 two years ago. Last year, her weekly allowance was $9.75. This year, Bianca's weekly allowance is $12.00. Does it make sense to represent the relationship between the amount of her allowance and the year with a constant rate? Why or why not? Explain your answer.

Module 2 Review

Vocabulary

Choose the correct term from the Vocabulary box.

Vocabulary
- commission
- gratuity
- markdown
- principal
- sales tax

1. the amount by which a price is reduced so that an item will sell:
   _____

2. an amount of money that is deposited or borrowed and that earns or is charged interest:
   _____

3. an amount of money given as a tip to someone who has performed a service:
   _____

4. an amount paid to an employee that represents a percent of the employee's sales:
   _____

Concepts and Skills

5. **Use Tools** All sweaters at a store are on sale at the same percent discount. A sweater that is regularly priced at $32.00 is on sale for $25.60. What is the sale price of a sweater regularly priced at $28.00? State what strategy and tool you will use to answer the question, explain your choice, and then find the answer.

   _____
   _____

6. The depth of water d in a swimming pool increases and decreases by 3% over a one-month period. Match each verbal description of the greatest and least water depths with all equivalent expressions.

	0.97d	1.03d	$d - 0.03$	$d + 0.03d$	$(1 - 0.03)d$
d increased by 3%	☐	☐	☐	☐	☐
d decreased by 3%	☐	☐	☐	☐	☐

7. Phillip wants to buy a baseball cap. Sales tax in his city is 8%. Select the prices of all caps Phillip could buy for less than or equal to $20 once sales tax is added.

   (A) $18.18   (B) $18.50   (C) $18.68   (D) $19.00   (E) $19.90

8. Amy and two of her friends eat lunch at a restaurant. Their bill comes to $27.63. They decide to split the bill equally. Amy wants to leave a 20% tip for her portion. What is the total amount Amy should pay, including tip? Round to the nearest cent. $ _____

9. Mr. Bauer deposits $600 in an account that earns simple interest at an annual rate of 2%. Use three of the numbers from the box at right to complete an expression that represents the amount, in dollars, that will be in Mr. Bauer's account after 3 years.

   _____ (1 + _____ · _____)

   | 0.02 |
   | 0.2 |
   | 2 |
   | 3 |
   | 100 |
   | 600 |

10. A salesperson earns $8 per hour plus 6% commission on her sales. In a week when she worked 40 hours, her total earnings were $692. What was the amount of her sales for the week? $ _____

11. The owner of an art supply store buys tubes of magenta oil paint for $10.80 and marks up the cost by 110% to determine the retail price. The tubes of paint do not sell well, so the owner marks down the retail price by 20%. To the nearest cent, what is the marked-down price of a tube of magenta oil paint?

    (A) $9.50   (B) $11.88   (C) $18.14   (D) $22.68

12. A ticket company charges a service fee of 5% of the ticket price for each ticket to a concert. Use this information to complete the table.

Ticket Price ($)	Service Fee ($)	Total Cost with Service Fee ($)
19.00		
	1.40	
		47.25

13. For a scale to pass inspection, the scale's reading can vary by at most 0.1% from the actual mass of an object on the scale. A test mass has an exact mass of 250.00 grams. In what range must the scale's reading be for the scale to pass inspection?

    _____

14. This year, 17,884 people attended a basketball team's first game, and 17,150 people attended its second game. What is the percent decrease from the first game to the second game in the number of people who attended? Round to the nearest tenth of a percent.

    _____ %

Unit 2
Number Systems and Operations

Film Director

Michelle Dougherty and Daniel Hinerfeld are film directors. In 2016, they directed and produced *Sonic Sea*, a film about the negative impact of ocean noise on whales and other marine life. In 2017, *Sonic Sea* won two Emmy awards, including Outstanding Nature Documentary.

STEM Task:

Scientists use an underwater robot to collect specimens from five sea shelves located below the ocean's surface. The shelves are located at depths of 82.25 meters, 106 meters, 79.8 meters, 131.04 meters, and 90.7 meters. Order these depths from shallowest to deepest. What is the vertical distance from the shallowest shelf to the deepest shelf? Explain.

Learning Mindset
Strategic Help-Seeking Identifies Need for Help

Strategic help-seeking is more than just asking for help with a task. It means recognizing when you need help and knowing where to find it. Strategic help-seekers look for help that promotes their learning and understanding, not just for help that gives them the answer. Here are some ideas to think about when it comes to getting help.

- Do you need help? Avoid the habit of always asking for help right away—giving yourself a chance to struggle with a task is a great way to learn. On the other hand, if you've been struggling for some time and cannot move forward, that is a sign you may need some help.

- Where can you find help? Think about people, tools, references, and other resources.

- What help do you need? You have a better chance of getting the help you need if you can clearly communicate what you need assistance with. It may be useful to write down a question or sentence about what is challenging you or holding you back. Be as specific as you can.

Reflect

Q How do you know when you need help with a task?

Q What resources did you use to help you understand and complete the STEM Task?

Module 3
Understand Addition and Subtraction of Rational Numbers

What's the Pattern?

Five explorers are each at different elevations in a cave. The rational numbers given show their elevations in kilometers. The signs of the numbers indicate the elevation above (+) or below (−) ground level.

Plot each rational number on the number line next to it.

A. $-1\frac{3}{5}$

B. $-\frac{9}{10}$

C. $-\frac{1}{5}$

D. $\frac{1}{2}$

E. $1\frac{1}{5}$

Turn and Talk

What pattern is formed by the five elevations? Explain your reasoning.

Module 3   89

Are You Ready?

Complete these problems to review prior concepts and skills you will need for this module.

Add and Subtract Fractions and Decimals

Find the sum or difference.

1. $\frac{2}{5} + \frac{1}{2}$ _____ **2.** $\frac{5}{6} + \frac{1}{3}$ _____ **3.** $2\frac{3}{4} - 1\frac{5}{6}$ _____

Opposites and Absolute Value

Complete the table by describing the opposite of the given situation and representing it with a positive or negative number.

	Quantity	Opposite Quantity
4.	A football team gains 6 yards on a play. Number: +6	
5.	A penguin is $2\frac{1}{2}$ feet below sea level. Number: $-2\frac{1}{2}$	
6.	Marci deposits $38 into her bank account. Number: +38	

Rational Numbers on a Number Line

For Problems 7–14, use the given number line.

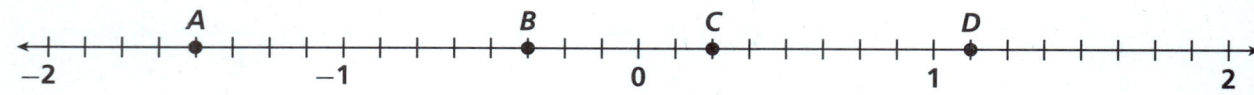

Write the rational number for each point on the number line.

7. A _____   **8.** B _____   **9.** C _____   **10.** D _____

Plot and label each number on the number line.

11. $\frac{7}{8}$ **12.** $-1\frac{5}{8}$ **13.** $-\frac{3}{4}$ **14.** $1\frac{3}{4}$

Build Conceptual Understanding
Lesson 1

Name _____

Add or Subtract a Positive Integer on a Number Line

I Can use a number line to add and subtract positive integers.

Spark Your Learning

John has an account balance of $20. He receives his weekly paycheck for work at his part-time job in the amount of $110. He can't find a bike he wants, so he buys some comic books for $40. Then John finds his dream bike with a price tag of $80. If he buys the bike now, what will his account balance be?

Turn and Talk What happens when you subtract a greater positive number from a lesser positive number?

Module 3 • Lesson 1

Build Understanding

1 Use the thermometer as a number line to answer the following questions.

Monday

A. On Monday morning, it was 35 °F outside. Plot this on the thermometer.

B. By afternoon, the temperature rose 20 **degrees**.

What distance will you move on the thermometer? _____

In which direction will you move? _____

C. What was the temperature Monday afternoon? _____
Show the change in temperature on the thermometer.

D. Tuesday's high temperature was 25 °F. The temperature dropped by 30 °F overnight. What direction on the number line is this?

_____

Show this on the number line. What is the resulting temperature?

_____

E. Explain why Tuesday's temperature drop resulted in a negative temperature.

_____
_____
_____

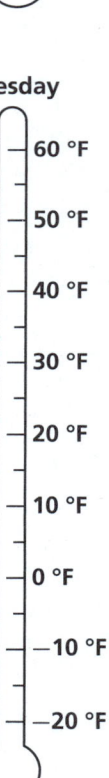

Turn and Talk Is it possible to start with a positive temperature and then have a rise in temperature which leads to a negative temperature? Explain.

92

Name _____

2 Use a number line to answer the following questions.

A. Thursday's low temperature was −5 °F. The temperature rose 20 degrees by mid-afternoon. At what point do you start on the number line?

_____

What distance do you move? _____

In which direction do you move? _____

Show this on the number line. What is the temperature Thursday afternoon? _____

B. The temperature is −15 °F and it rises by 5 degrees. Find the resulting temperature using the number line. _____

C. The temperature is −20 °F and it drops by 10 degrees. Find the resulting temperature using the number line. _____

D. Explain why the temperatures from Parts B and C are both negative, even though one is the result of an increase in temperature and one is the result of a decrease in temperature.

_____

_____

_____

E. The temperature is −10 °F and it increases by 15 degrees. Then, later in the day, it decreases by 20 degrees. Find the resulting temperature using the number line. _____

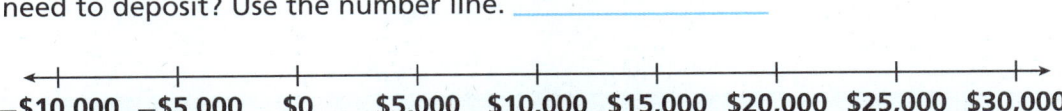

Check Understanding

1. A business has $25,000 in its bank account. In order to build an addition onto their office, it will cost $30,000. If they write a check, they will need to deposit money before the check clears. What minimum amount do they need to deposit? Use the number line. _____

Turn and Talk How can you predict whether the sum of a positive and a negative number will be positive or negative by comparing the two numbers?

Module 3 • Lesson 1

On Your Own

2. A scuba diver starts at a point 300 feet below sea level. She descends another 200 feet. Where is she in relation to sea level now? Use the number line. _____

3. **Use Tools** Use the number line for Parts A and B.

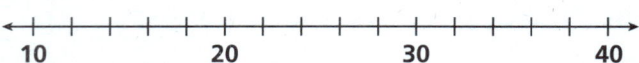

A. It is first down in the football game, your team has the ball at your 25-yard marker, and the play is a successful run for 6 yards. Where does the ball end up? Where is the ball relative to where it started?

_____

B. On second down, your quarterback drops back to pass but is sacked for a 10-yard loss. Where does the ball end up?

_____

C. **Reason** Review the actions covered in Parts A and B. Over these two plays, has your team gained or lost total ground? How much? Explain using an addition statement.

_____

4. What is the result of subtracting 35 from 25? Use the number line. _____

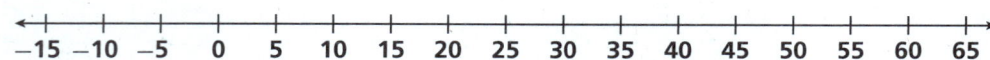

Use the number line for Problems 5–8.

5. What is the result of 20 plus 30 minus 60?

6. What is the result of −10 plus 30?

7. What is the result of 70 minus 50 plus 20?

8. What is the result of 20 minus 50?

 I'm in a Learning Mindset!

How did I apply prior knowledge to subtracting positive integers?

_____

Name _____

LESSON 3.1
More Practice/ Homework

Add or Subtract a Positive Integer on a Number Line

ONLINE Video Tutorials and Interactive Examples

1. You have a beaker of water that is currently at 70 °F. You add some ice to lower the temperature by 15 degrees. What temperature do you want the water to go down to?

   _____

2. **STEM** A chemical reaction is *endothermic* if it absorbs heat from its surroundings and thereby lowers the temperature. It is *exothermic* if it gives off heat to its surroundings. In her chemistry class, Lily is given a salt (ammonium nitrate) and a beaker of water at 60 °F. She dissolves the salt in the water and sees that the temperature of the solution is now 50 °F. Did the temperature of the solution go up or go down? By how many degrees? What kind of reaction has occurred? Use the thermometer provided.

   _____
   _____
   _____
   _____

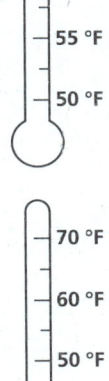

3. The low temperature on a given day is −2 °F. During the day, the temperature rises by 6 degrees. Show the movement on the number line and give the result.

   _____

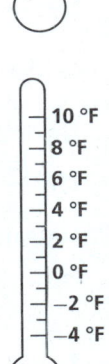

4. On another day, The high temperature is 20 °F. Overnight a storm comes in and the temperature drops 25 degrees. During the following day the temperature continues to decrease another 5 degrees. Show the movement on the number line and give the final result.

   _____

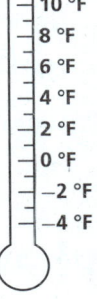

5. **(MP) Reason** Can you subtract a positive integer from a positive integer and get a negative result? Explain your answer.

   _____
   _____
   _____
   _____

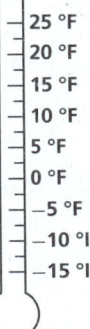

Module 3 • Lesson 1

Test Prep

6. The goal of a game is to be the first person to get to 30 points. Players select cards from a red bin and green bin. A card from the red bin must be added and a card from the green bin must be subtracted. On Cameron's first 3 turns he draws a 20 from the red bin, a 30 from the red bin and 15 from the green bin. What is Cameron's current score? Show your work on the number line _____

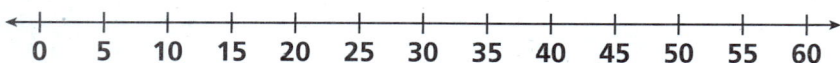

7. The water in a lake is 4 feet above its usual level. Then the level of the lake drops 7 feet. If 0 represents its usual level, which number line shows the final level in feet of the water in the lake?

(A)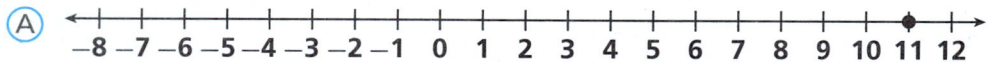

(B)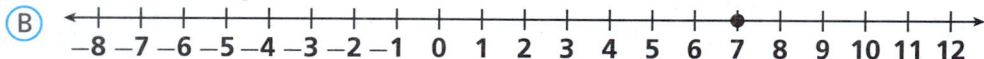

(C)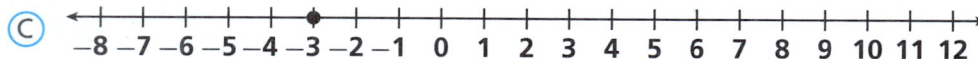

(D)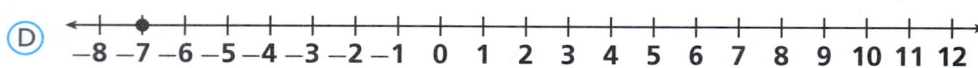

Circle the word that best completes the sentence.

8. Donna subtracts a positive number from a greater positive number. The resulting difference will be positive / negative.

9. Devon subtracts a positive number from a lesser positive number. The resulting difference will be positive / negative.

Spiral Review

10. Find the sum.
    $1.208 + 6.45 = $ _____

11. Raoul makes shell necklaces to sell at a craft fair. The supplies for each necklace cost $3.75. Raoul sells the necklaces for $11.25. How much does Raoul earn from each necklace he sells? _____

12. Neveah goes out to dinner at a restaurant with 4 friends. The bill for dinner is $57.25, including the tip. If they split the bill evenly, how much does each person owe? _____

Add or Subtract a Negative Integer on a Number Line

I Can use a number line to add and subtract negative integers.

Spark Your Learning

The scores of three contestants on a game show are shown. The final question is worth 50 points. A correct answer adds 50 points to a contestant's score. An incorrect answer deducts 50 points.

Show the possible final scores for each contestant. What circumstances are necessary for each contestant to win?

Turn and Talk How can you add a number to each score to show a loss?

Build Understanding

1 The table shows the scores of three contestants on a game show.

Game Show Scores		
Latrell	Mayumi	Scott
8	6	3

A. Latrell spins a wheel to find out how many points he adds to his score. The wheel stops on "−5 points." Use the number line to add −5 points to Latrell's score. Then complete the equation.

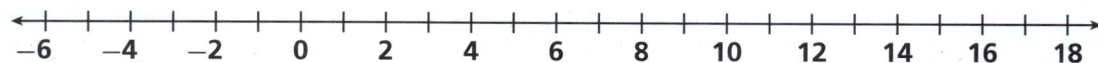

$8 + (-5) =$ _____

B. Mayumi spins the wheel next. The wheel stops on "−11 points." Use the number line to add −11 points to her score. Complete the equation.

$6 + (-11) =$ _____

C. How do Latrell's and Mayumi's final scores compare to their starting scores? Explain why this is reasonable.

_____

_____

_____

D. Because Scott started with the lowest score, he plays a penalty round. In the penalty round, the wheel determines the number of points that are *subtracted* from a player's score. The result of Scott's spin is shown. Use the number line to subtract −7 points from Scott's score. (Hint: To subtract a negative integer you move to the right.) Then complete the equation.

Penalty Round
Subtract:

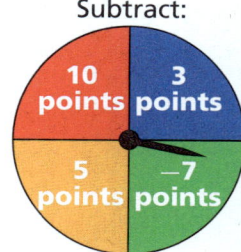

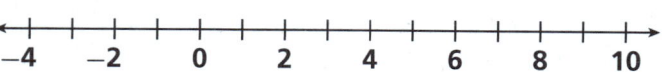

$3 - (-7) =$ _____

 **Turn and Talk** Is it possible to subtract a loss from a positive number and result in a negative number? Why or why not?

Name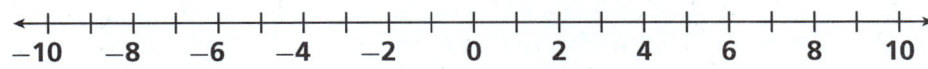

2 The table shows the scores of three contestants on a game show.

Game Show Scores		
Natalie	Gina	Tyler
−2	−6	−6

A. Natalie spins a wheel to find out how many points she adds to her score. The wheel stops on "−6 points." Use the number line to add −6 points to Natalie's score. Then complete the equation.

$-2 + (-6) =$ _____

B. Gina and Tyler both started with the lowest score, so they each play a penalty round. In the penalty round, the wheel determines the number of points that are *subtracted* from a player's score. The result of Gina's spin is shown. Use the number line to find Gina's score. Then complete the equation.

Penalty Round
Subtract:
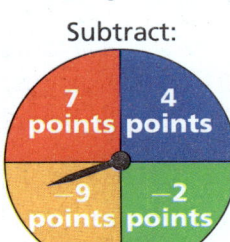

$-6 - (-9) =$ _____

C. Explain which direction to move on the number line when you subtract a negative integer.

_____

_____

_____

D. The result of Tyler's spin is shown. Use the number line to find Tyler's score. Then complete the equation.

Penalty Round
Subtract:
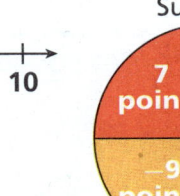

$-6 - (-2) =$ _____

Turn and Talk Is it possible to add a loss to a negative number and result in a positive number? Why or why not?

Module 3 • Lesson 2

3 Jackson and Flora both have bank accounts, and they use credit cards. Use the number line to determine if they can pay off their credit card bills.

A. Jackson has $20 in his account. He uses a credit card to spend $30 on a coat and $10 on a movie. Jackson then deposits $50 into his account. How much will Jackson have left after he pays the credit card bill? Use the number line.

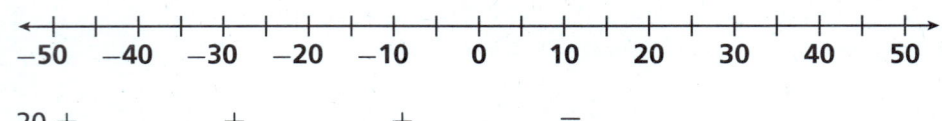

20 + _____ + _____ + _____ = _____

Can Jackson pay his credit card bill? Explain.

_____

_____

B. Flora starts with $10 in her account. She uses a credit card to spend $20 on a gift, $40 on some shoes, and then returns a $30 appliance for a refund to be applied to her card. Use the number line to show these transactions.

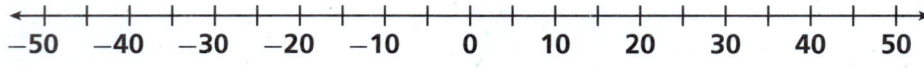

10 − _____ − _____ − _____ = _____

Can Flora pay her credit card bill? Explain.

_____

_____

Check Understanding

Use the number lines to find the answers. Then complete the equations.

1. Jessica starts at an elevation of 40 feet. She descends 60 feet. What is her new elevation in feet?

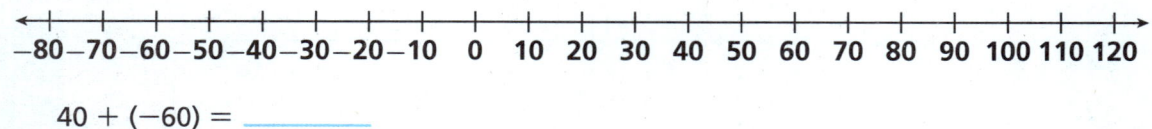

40 + (−60) = _____

2. A contestant on a game show has a score of −4. After spinning the wheel, −2 is subtracted from her score. What is her new score?

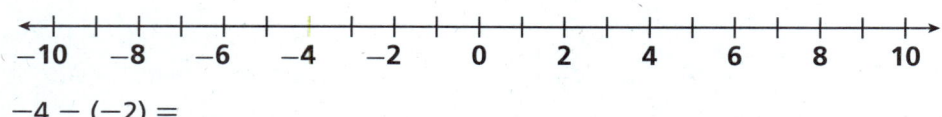

−4 − (−2) = _____

On Your Own

3. **Use Tools** Denny has a balance of $7 on his transit card. Each train ride debits $3, which is the same as adding −$3 to the card. Use the number line to add −$3 to Denny's balance. Then complete the equation.

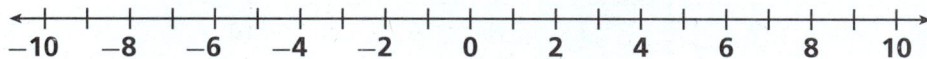

$7 + (−$3) = _____

Use Tools Three friends are playing a board game. The table shows their current scores. Each player draws two cards. The first card says "add" or "subtract." The second card says a number of points. Use a number line and complete the equation to find each player's final score.

Player	Score
Andrew	−4
Saleema	−3
Cassie	−9

4. Andrew's cards say "add" and "−4 points."

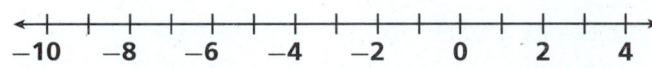 $-4 + (-4) = $ _____

5. Saleema's cards say "subtract" and "−7 points."

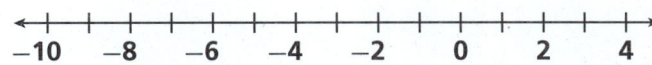 $-3 - (-7) = $ _____

6. Cassie's cards say "subtract" and "−8 points."

   $-9 - (-8) = $ _____

7. **Use Tools** Tomas and a friend are hiking in Death Valley National Park in California. They start at an elevation of −10 meters. During the hike they ascend 30 meters, then descend 40 meters, and then descend another 20 meters. Use the number line and complete the equation to find their final elevation.

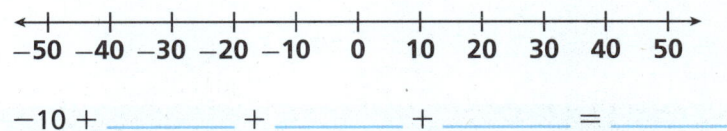

−10 + _____ + _____ + _____ = _____

Final elevation: _____

In the United States, the lowest point of elevation is found in Death Valley in California.

Module 3 • Lesson 2   101

8. **Use Tools** The temperature at midnight is −7 °F. Before noon, the temperature decreases by 2 °F, then increases by 5 °F, and then increases by 4 °F. Use the number line and complete the equation to find the temperature at noon.

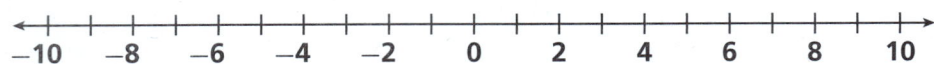

−7 °F − _____ + _____ + _____ = _____   Temperature at noon: _____

9. **Critique Reasoning** Leah said that when you add two negative integers the result must be negative. Do you agree or disagree? Use a number line to help explain your answer.

10. **Open Ended** Write a story problem for the number line shown. Provide the answer to the problem.

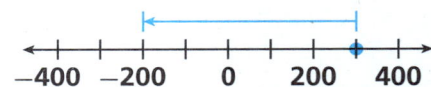

11. **STEM** The freezing point of seawater is −2 °C. The freezing point of nitric acid is −42 °C. How much greater is the freezing point of seawater than the freezing point of nitric acid?

For Problems 12–17, use a number line to add or subtract.

12. 7 − (−3) = _____   13. −20 + (−30) = _____   14. −1 + (−6) = _____

15. 5 − (−4) = _____   16. −8 − (−5) = _____   17. 5 + (−5) = _____

I'm in a Learning Mindset!

What strategies do I have for subtracting negative integers?

Add or Subtract a Negative Integer on a Number Line

LESSON 3.2 More Practice/ Homework

1. **Use Tools** Brad has 8 points during a trivia game. He answers a question incorrectly and −12 points are added to his score. Use the number line to add −12 points to Brad's score. Then complete the equation to show his final score.

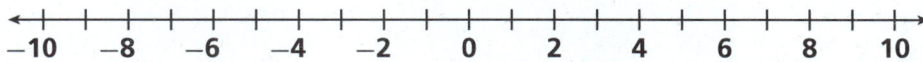

   $8 + (-12) = $ _____

2. **Math on the Spot** A dolphin is swimming 3 feet below sea level. It dives down 9 feet to catch some fish. Then it swims 4 feet up toward the surface with its catch. What is the dolphin's final elevation relative to sea level?

   _____

3. **Use Tools** Dario is scuba diving. He is currently at an elevation of −20 feet. He descends 20 feet. What is his elevation in relation to the other diver shown? Use the number line and complete the equation to find his relative elevation.

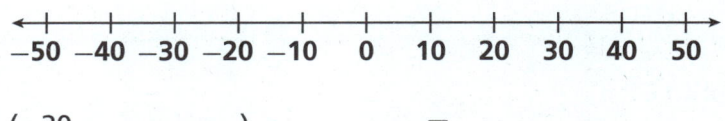

   $(-20 - $ _____ $) - $ _____ $= $ _____

   Relative elevation: _____

4. **Use Tools** Latisha has $40 in her checking account. She makes a withdrawal of $20 and then writes a check for $40. Then she deposits $30. Use the number line and complete the equation to find her final balance.

   ```
   ←—+—+—+—+—+—+—+—+—+—+—+—+—+—+→
     −30 −20 −10  0  10 20 30 40 50 60 70 80 90 100
   ```

   $40 + _____ + _____ + _____ = _____

   Final balance: _____

For Problems 5–10, use a number line to add or subtract.

5. $2 - (-4) = $ _____

6. $-2 + (-7) = $ _____

7. $-10 + (-60) = $ _____

8. $3 - (-1) = $ _____

9. $-7 - (-7) = $ _____

10. $2 + (-9) = $ _____

Test Prep

11. Elena wants to use a number line to find the difference $5 - (-7)$. Which is the best description of how she should do this?

- Ⓐ Start at −7 and move 5 units right.
- Ⓑ Start at −7 and move 5 units left.
- Ⓒ Start at 5 and move 7 units right.
- Ⓓ Start at 5 and move 7 units left.

12. Which sum or difference can you evaluate using the number line model shown?

- Ⓐ $-3 - (-2)$
- Ⓑ $-3 - 2$
- Ⓒ $-1 + 3$
- Ⓓ $-1 - (-3)$

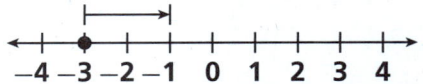

13. Aaron is playing a board game and has a score of 20 points. He spins a spinner to see how many points will be added to his score. The spinner lands on "−50 points." Find Aaron's final score. Show your work.

14. Which sum or difference is equal to 0?

- Ⓐ $-7 - 7$
- Ⓑ $4 - (-4)$
- Ⓒ $-1 + (-1)$
- Ⓓ $6 + (-6)$

Spiral Review

15. At a restaurant, Brianna and Naomi each order an appetizer for $6.50 and an entree for $9.75. The sales tax is $0.98 and they leave a tip of $5.85. How much did Brianna and Naomi spend in all?

_____

16. Colton has a balance of $6 on his transit card. He takes several bus rides over the weekend for a total cost of $9. Use the number line to subtract $9 from Colton's balance. Then complete the equation.

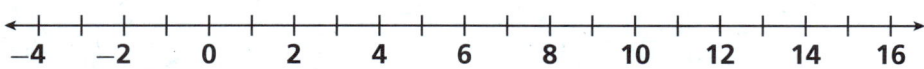

$6 − $9 = _____

Lesson 3

Use a Number Line to Add and Subtract Rational Numbers

I Can use a number line to add and subtract rational numbers.

Spark Your Learning

When a person owes money on a credit card, the credit card holder can think of it as a negative balance.

Devin has a balance of −$9.50 on a credit card. Which two items can he purchase without his balance going below −$15.00? Find all the pairs of items Devin can purchase.

Dinner rolls
$0.50

Pizza dough
$3.00

Cinnamon bread
$4.50

Turn and Talk If the cinnamon bread was on sale for $2.00, could he purchase all three items? Explain.

Module 3 • Lesson 3

Build Understanding

1 An underwater camera is dropped from a helicopter flying $4\frac{1}{2}$ feet over the water. The camera has an elevation change of −8 feet. Where is the camera now in relation to the surface of the water?

A. The number line represents distance from sea level.

What do positive numbers represent?

_____

What do negative numbers represent?

_____

What does 0 represent?

_____

B. On the number line, draw an arrow representing the camera's change in elevation. Where is the camera after the change in elevation of −8 feet from the helicopter?

$4\frac{1}{2} + (-8) =$ _____

C. Later, the camera is at $-5\frac{1}{2}$ feet and has an elevation change of +3 feet. What is the camera's final elevation in relation to the surface?

On the number line a line would start at _____ and go _____ 3 units. Draw an arrow representing the camera's change in elevation.

$-5\frac{1}{2} + 3 =$ _____

D. Now the camera is at $-5\frac{1}{2}$ feet again, and it sinks $2\frac{1}{2}$ feet. What is the camera's final elevation in relation to the surface? Use the number line to show your work.

$-5\frac{1}{2} + \left(-2\frac{1}{2}\right) =$ _____

Turn and Talk If the camera is at −2.5 feet and undergoes a change of elevation of 0 feet, where will the camera be then? Will it be at the surface?

Step It Out

2 Carmela is playing with a ball.

A. The ball is on a platform 2.3 meters above the ground, then the ball falls to the ground. Use the number line to represent the change in height of the ball.

   Begin at _____ to represent the height of the ball on the platform, then show the decrease in height.

B. Complete the equation to represent the situation in Part A.

   2.3 − _____ = _____

C. The ball fell into a pit 1.5 feet below ground level. Carmela grabs the ball and puts it back on ground level.

   Begin at _____ to represent the height of the ball in the pit, then show the increase in height on the number line.

D. Complete the equation to represent the situation in Part C.

   −1.5 + _____ = _____

E. Carmela stands on the ground and kicks the ball 4.5 meters up into the air. It falls down and goes in another pit that is 3.5 meters deep.

   Use the number line to show the changes in the height of the ball.
   Begin at _____ to represent the height of the ball on the ground, and show the increase followed by the decrease.

F. Complete the equation to represent the situation in Part E.

   _____ + 4.5 − _____ = −3.5

G. Using the number line model in Parts C and D as an example, explain the **Addition Property of Opposites** which states that the sum of a number and its **opposite** equals zero. Another name for opposite is **additive inverse**.

   _____
   _____
   _____
   _____

 **Turn and Talk** How can you interpret the model in Parts A and B as a sum to show that the sum of a number and its opposite is 0?

Module 3 • Lesson 3

3 Describe each situation in words.

A. Margarita has $50 in her bank account. What transaction would result in an account balance of $0?

B. The temperature is 15 °F. What change in temperature would result in the temperature being 0 °F?

C. A kite is 25 feet in the air. What needs to happen to the kite in order for it to be at ground level?

D. Describe a situation in which opposite quantities combine to make 0.

Check Understanding

1. From an elevation of 2.5 feet above a lake's surface a bird dives 4 feet to catch a fish. How far below the surface is the fish?

   A. Represent this situation on the number line shown.

   B. Evaluate the expression.

   $2.5 - 4 =$ _____

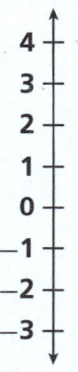

2. Pietro used a number line to subtract $-\frac{1}{8} - \left(-\frac{1}{4}\right)$. The figure shows the arrow he drew to represent the subtraction. Is he getting the right result? Explain.

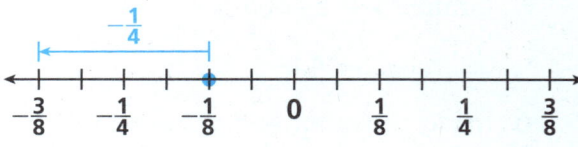

3. The overnight low temperature is −3 °F. By morning, the temperature increases by 13 degrees. Draw an arrow on the thermometer to represent this situation, and find the morning temperature.

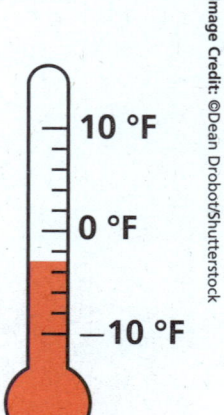

4. Mr. Anderson has a credit card balance of −$80.23 at the end of the month. Use Mr. Anderson's credit card balance to describe a situation in which opposite quantities combine to make 0.

Name _____

On Your Own

MP Use Tools The temperature in Mittenville is changing. Use the thermometer to help solve each problem.

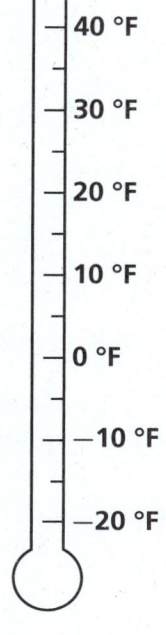

5. In the morning, the temperature is −5 °F. The temperature increases by 13 °F, then decreases by 5 °F. Write an equation to show the new temperature.

   _____

6. The high temperature for the day is 28 °F. The record high for the day was 54 °F. What is the difference in temperatures?

   _____

7. The high temperature for the day is 28 °F. The record low for the day was −12 °F. What is the difference in temperatures?

   _____

8. This morning the temperature was −5 °F. How much must the temperature change to reach 0 °F?

   _____

9. **MP Reason** Evan added $\left(-2\frac{1}{2}\right) + 4$ and got $6\frac{1}{2}$. Draw arrows on the number line to represent the problem. Then explain Evan's error.

   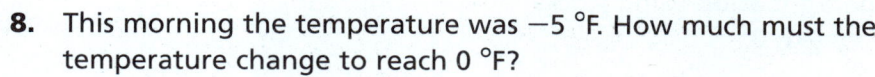

   _____
   _____

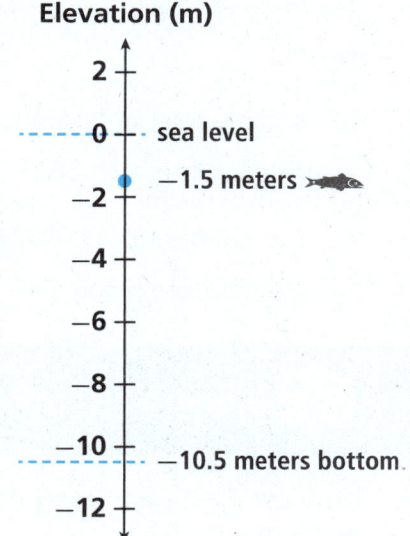

10. The number line shows the elevation of the bottom of a harbor and the elevation of a fish swimming close to the surface.

    A. What change in elevation is necessary for the fish to reach bottom?

    _____

    B. Once the fish reaches the bottom, what change in elevation will bring it back up to the surface?

    _____

Module 3 • Lesson 3

11. **Financial Literacy** Stock in Boomer Branding, Inc. started the week at $26.50 per share. During the week the following changes in the share price were registered:

    (+$2.75), (+$3.00), (−$8.25), (+$1.50), (−$6.75)

    A. Show the changes on the number line.

    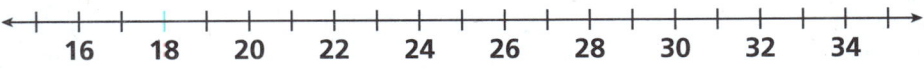

    B. What was the price per share at the end of the week? _____

    C. **Open Ended** Describe a situation using stocks in which opposite quantities combine to make 0.

    _____
    _____
    _____

For Problems 12–15, find rational numbers to complete each equation. Use the number line to help.

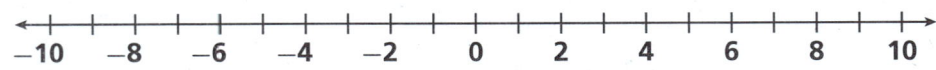

12. _____ + (− _____) = −8.75

13. _____ − _____ = $-1\frac{3}{4}$

14. (− _____) + (− _____) = −19.25

15. _____ + _____ = 0

16. A bank account has a balance of $135. What transaction would result in an account balance of $0? _____

17. The temperature is −7 °F. What change in temperature would result in the temperature being 0 °F? _____

 I'm in a Learning Mindset!

How can I help my peers describe situations in which opposites combine to make 0?

_____

Name _____

Use a Number Line to Add and Subtract Rational Numbers

LESSON 3.3
More Practice/Homework

ONLINE Video Tutorials and Interactive Examples

1. **MP Use Tools** Caleb rode his bike $3\frac{1}{2}$ miles in the morning. Then he rode his bike another $2\frac{1}{2}$ miles in the afternoon. How many miles did Caleb ride altogether? Draw an arrow on the number line to show how to find the answer, then write the answer.

   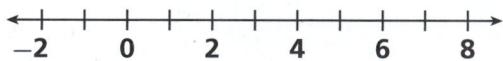

2. **MP Critique Reasoning** Jasmine evaluated the expression $10 - (-3)$ and says it is equal to 7. Is she right? If not, what was her mistake?

   _____

3. On a number line, what other number is the same distance from -2.8 as -7.2?

   _____

4. A number line is drawn left to right with integers spaced 1 centimeter apart. An ant crawls onto the number line at $+2$. It then crawls 3.5 centimeters left, 4.8 centimeters right, and 7.9 centimeters left.

   A. Where is the ant on the number line now? _____

   B. How far is it from its original position? _____

   C. What is the total distance the ant crawled along the number line? _____

   D. **Open Ended** Describe a situation in which the ant crawls in a way that results in opposite quantities combining to make 0.

   _____
   _____
   _____

For Problems 5–6, draw arrows on the number line to show the operations indicated and fill in the answer.

5. $0.5 + (-1.5) - (-5.5) =$ _____

6. $-1\frac{1}{2} - \left(+3\frac{1}{2}\right) - \left(-\frac{5}{8}\right) =$ _____

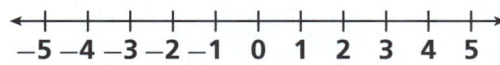
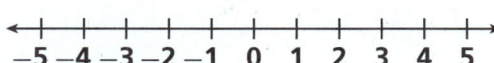

Module 3 • Lesson 3   111

Test Prep

7. If the temperature was 0 °C and then there was a temperature change of +5 °C, what temperature change would return the temperature to 0 °C?

- Ⓐ −10 °C
- Ⓑ −5 °C
- Ⓒ 0 °C
- Ⓓ 5 °C

8. Find the sum.
$-\frac{1}{8} + \frac{1}{8} + \frac{5}{8}$

- Ⓐ $\frac{1}{8}$
- Ⓑ $\frac{3}{8}$
- Ⓒ $\frac{5}{8}$
- Ⓓ $\frac{7}{8}$

9. Which set of operations corresponds to the arrows shown on the number line?

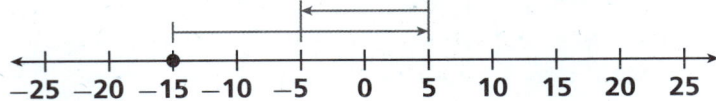

- Ⓐ −15 − (+20) + (−10)
- Ⓑ −15 + (+20) − (−10)
- Ⓒ −15 − (+20) − (+10)
- Ⓓ −15 − (−20) + (−10)

Spiral Review

10. A box of cereal contains 14.25 ounces. One serving is equal to 1.5 ounces. How many servings are in the box?

11. In an inspection, a bag of rice that was supposed to contain 5 kilograms was found to contain 4.8 kilograms. How many kilograms need to be added to the bag?

12. Mrs. Hernandez deposits $45.50 from every paycheck into a savings account. If she receives 26 paychecks in one year, how much will she deposit in one year?

Module 3 Review

Vocabulary

For each number, select the terms that apply to it.

		Positive integer	Negative integer	Rational number
1.	23	☐	☐	☐
2.	$-\frac{3}{10}$	☐	☐	☐
3.	1.4	☐	☐	☐
4.	−7	☐	☐	☐

Concepts and Skills

5. **MP Use Tools** Name two numbers that are 7 units from 3. State what strategy and tool you will use to answer the question, explain your choice, and then find the answer.

   _____

   _____

6. A school, a bookstore, and a park are on the same straight street. The bookstore (B) is 2.25 miles from the school (S). The park (P) is 1.75 miles from the school. What is the distance from the park to the bookstore?

   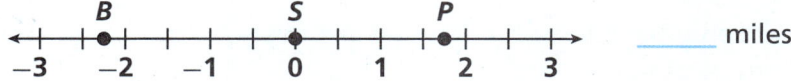 _____ miles

7. Paolo is using number lines to find the value of the expression $\frac{1}{6} + \frac{2}{3} + \left(-1\frac{1}{3}\right)$.

   A. Paolo's first two steps are shown. Draw an arrow on the number line provided to show the last step.

Step 1: Start at $\frac{1}{6}$.	number line from −1 to 1 with point near $\frac{1}{6}$
Step 2: Add $\frac{2}{3}$.	number line showing arrow from $\frac{1}{6}$ to $\frac{5}{6}$
Last step: Add $\left(-1\frac{1}{3}\right)$.	number line from −1 to 1

   B. What is the value of the expression $\frac{1}{6} + \frac{2}{3} + \left(-1\frac{1}{3}\right)$? _____

8. A number line is shown. Eric knows that *n* is the opposite of *m*. Which statement about *m* and *n* is true?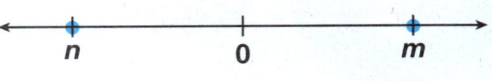

    Ⓐ $m = n$ Ⓑ $m = -(-n)$ Ⓒ $m + n = 0$ Ⓓ $m - n = 0$

9. The difference $a - b$ is equal to *c*. The number line shows *a* and *b*. Select all statements about *c* that are true.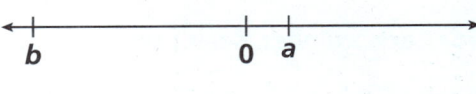

    Ⓐ $c < 0$　　　　　Ⓓ *c* is closer to 0 than *a*.
    Ⓑ $c = 0$　　　　　Ⓔ *c* is the same distance from 0 as *a*.
    Ⓒ $c > 0$　　　　　Ⓕ *c* is farther from 0 than *a*.

10. On a quiz show, Anabel started with 0 points. She gained 10 points on her first turn and lost 10 points on her second turn. What is her combined score after her first two turns? Use addition of integers to explain your reasoning.

    _____
    _____
    _____

11. An equation is shown, where $s > 0$ and $t < 0$.

    $$r - s = t$$

    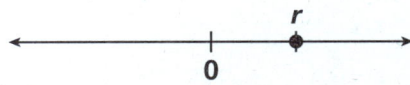

    Plot and label two points on the number line to show possible locations of *s* and *t*.

12. Ivy's hair has grown $\frac{5}{8}$ inch since her last haircut in May. At her next haircut in June, she has $1\frac{1}{2}$ inches of hair cut off.

    A. Which expressions represent the total change, in inches, in the length of Ivy's hair since her haircut in May? Select all that apply.

    Ⓐ $\frac{5}{8} - 1\frac{1}{2}$　　　　Ⓓ $-1\frac{1}{2} - \frac{5}{8}$

    Ⓑ $\frac{5}{8} + \left(-1\frac{1}{2}\right)$　　Ⓔ $1\frac{1}{2} - \frac{5}{8}$

    Ⓒ $\frac{5}{8} + 1\frac{1}{2}$

    B. Plot a point on the number line to represent the total change, in inches, in the length of Ivy's hair since her haircut in May.

    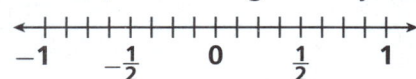

Module 4

Fluency with Rational Number Operations

Can You Find the Mystery Number?

You are the new investigator for the Math Detective Agency. Your first case depends on finding a mystery number. Follow these steps.

A. Find each sum or difference.

$-7 + 9 =$ _____ $-5 - (-4) =$ _____

$-\frac{4}{5} - \frac{4}{5} =$ _____ $-\frac{1}{10} + \frac{3}{5} =$ _____

$-1 + 1\frac{1}{10} =$ _____ $-\frac{1}{5} - \frac{1}{2} =$ _____

B. Plot and label each sum or difference from Part A on the number line.

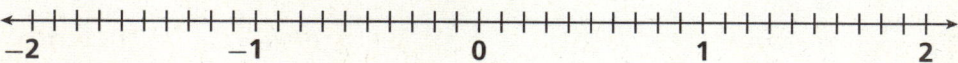

 **Turn and Talk**

The mystery number is the distance between the two closest points that you plotted. What is the mystery number? Explain how you found it.

115

Are You Ready?

Complete these problems to review prior concepts and skills you will need for this module.

Write and Interpret Numerical Expressions

Write a numerical expression to express the calculation. Do not simplify the expression.

1. The comic books in Cora's favorite series regularly cost $2.99. Today, they are on sale for $0.50 off the regular price. Cora subtracts $0.50 from $2.99 and multiplies the result by 4 to find the cost of 4 comic books at the sale price.

   _____

Add Fractions and Decimals

Find each sum.

2. $8.04 + 4.15$ _____

3. $\frac{5}{6} + \frac{2}{3}$ _____

Multiply with Decimals

Find each product.

4. 1.68×2.5 _____

5. 0.45×0.08 _____

Divide Fractions and Mixed Numbers

Find each quotient.

6. $3 \div \frac{1}{5}$ _____

7. $\frac{7}{8} \div \frac{1}{2}$ _____

8. $3\frac{2}{3} \div \frac{3}{5}$ _____

9. One serving of rice is equal to $\frac{3}{4}$ cup. Gerardo makes 4 cups of rice. How many servings of rice did Gerardo make?

   _____

Connect Concepts and Skills

Lesson 1

Name _____

Compute Sums of Rational Numbers

I Can compute sums of rational numbers with the same or different signs, and for real-world problems, I can interpret the results.

Spark Your Learning

A research submarine was stationed 700 feet below sea level. It ascends 250 feet every hour. If the submarine continues to ascend at the same rate, when will the submarine be at the surface?

Turn and Talk How can you express the position of the submarine as an integer to show that the submarine is below sea level? Explain.

Module 4 • Lesson 1   117

Build Understanding

1 ▸ A submarine descends to 800 feet below sea level. Then it descends another 200 feet. What is the submarine's final elevation? First use a number line to find out. Then use **absolute value** to solve the same problem without a number line.

A. Write an addition expression, and use the number line to determine the final elevation of the submarine.

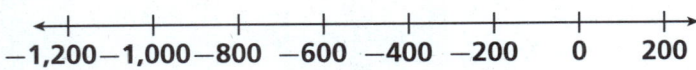

_____

B. Recall that the absolute value of a number is the number's distance from 0 on the number line. For example, the absolute value of −4 is 4 because −4 is 4 units from 0.

Because the arrows you drew for −800 and −200 in Part A both point in the same direction, you can find the submarine's final distance from 0 by adding the absolute values of these numbers.

|−800| + |−200| = ☐ + ☐ = ☐

C. How does the sum of the absolute values compare to the sum of −800 and −200?

_____

D. How can you use the sum of absolute values in Part B to find the final elevation—that is, to find the sum of −800 and −200?

_____
_____

E. Find −100 + (−300) by first adding the absolute values. Use the number line in Part A to check your answer.

|−100| + |−300| = ☐ + ☐ = ☐ , so −100 + (−300) = ☐.

F. Complete the rule for adding rational numbers with the same signs:

_____ the absolute values of the numbers and use the _____ of the addends.

 Turn and Talk Use a number line to explain why adding two rational numbers with the same sign will always result in a sum that has the same sign as the addends.

Name _____

2 The temperature in the morning in Sioux City, Iowa, is shown. By the afternoon, the temperature had risen 25 °F. What was the temperature in the afternoon? First use a number line to find out. Then use absolute value to solve the same problem without a number line.

A. Write an addition expression and use the number line to determine the temperature in the afternoon.

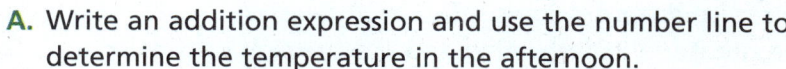

The temperature in the afternoon is _____ °F.

B. Use absolute value to find the distance of the final temperature from 0. Because the first number moves you left on the number line and the second number moves you right, subtract the lesser absolute value from the greater absolute value. How does the result compare to the sum in Part A?

_____
_____

C. On another day, the temperature was 30 °F but a severe ice storm caused a temperature drop of 35 °F. Write an addition expression and use the number line to determine the temperature after the ice storm.

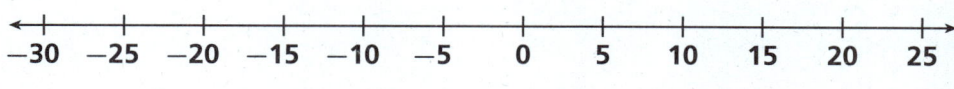

The temperature after the ice storm was _____ °F.

D. Use absolute value to find the distance of the final temperature from 0. Because the first number moves you right on the number line and the second number moves you left, subtract the lesser absolute value from the greater absolute value. How does the result compare to the sum in Part C?

_____
_____

E. Complete the rule for adding rational numbers with different signs:

_____ the lesser absolute value from the greater absolute value and use the sign of the addend with the _____ absolute value.

Module 4 • Lesson 1

Step It Out

Here are the rules for adding rational numbers:
- To add rational numbers with the same sign, add their absolute values and use the sign of the addends.
- To add rational numbers with different signs, subtract the lesser absolute value from the greater absolute value and use the sign of the addend with the greater absolute value.

3 The water level of a river decreased by $\frac{1}{5}$ foot on Monday and increased by $\frac{3}{10}$ foot on Tuesday.

A. Write an addition expression for the number of feet gained or lost.

B. Use the rules above to find and interpret the sum of your expression in Part A.

C. Explain why your answer is reasonable.

D. Use the Commutative Property of Addition to show that the result is the same if the two changes happened in reverse order.

E. The water level of a canal decreased by 4.8 meters and then decreased by another 3.5 meters. Write an addition expression for the number of meters gained or lost.

F. Use the rules above to find and interpret the sum of your expression in Part E.

Check Understanding

1. A football player averages 16.4 yards in his first game. During his second game, his average changes by −2.3 yards. Write and evaluate an addition expression to find the player's new average.

2. Evaluate $-7\frac{1}{3} + \left(-\frac{2}{5}\right)$.

On Your Own

3. Belle's dad lends her $10. Then Belle borrows another $15 from him. Write and evaluate an expression that shows the change in the amount of money Belle's dad has.

_____

4. The changes in the elevation of a plane while it was flying are shown. Write and evaluate an expression that shows the plane's final elevation compared to its altitude before the first descent.

_____

Descends 1,500 ft

Ascends 900 ft

5. In the stock market, changes in value used to be indicated by fractions, which represented portions of $1. If a stock had a value of $11.50, write and evaluate an addition expression to find how much the stock is worth after an increase of $\frac{1}{4}$.

_____

6. Jayvon has 33.6 points in a competition. He loses 5.5 points. Write and evaluate an addition expression to determine Jayvon's current score.

_____

For 7–12, find each sum.

7. $-7 + 10$

8. $-42 + (-6)$

9. $-\frac{5}{7} + \left(-\frac{3}{14}\right)$

10. $-21.6 + (-5.6)$

11. $12\frac{2}{3} + \left(-9\frac{1}{6}\right)$

12. $-15.23 + 6.23$

Module 4 • Lesson 1

13. **Reason** Blake's journey on the elevators of his building is shown. Write and evaluate an expression that shows Blake's location compared to his starting point.

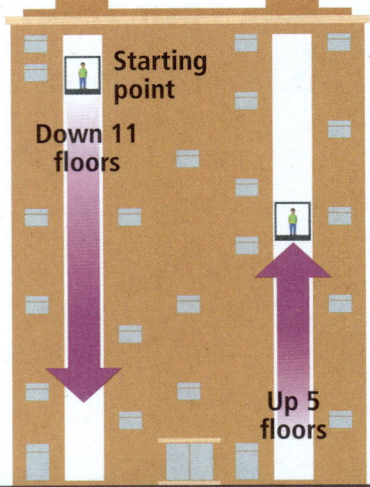

_____

14. Seth earned $76.50 and spent $42.95. Write and evaluate an expression that shows how much money Seth has left.

_____

_____

15. Brock rides his bike $22\frac{1}{8}$ miles to the nature preserve. On his way home, after $16\frac{1}{5}$ miles, he stops for lunch. How far is Brock from home? Write and evaluate an addition expression to solve the problem. Show your work.

_____

_____

For 16–21, find each sum.

16. $\frac{3}{8} + \left(-\frac{1}{2}\right)$

17. $4 + (-50)$

18. $-9.36 + 4.48$

19. $-6\frac{3}{8} + \left(-5\frac{3}{4}\right)$

20. $36.7 + (-36.7)$

21. $13.97 + (-4.71)$

22. **Financial Literacy** A bank account had a balance of $1,184.57. Then the customer withdrew $455.75. Write and evaluate an addition expression showing the new account balance.

_____

_____

I'm in a Learning Mindset!

What can I do to check my understanding when I solve problems in which I add rational numbers?

_____

_____

Compute Sums of Rational Numbers

LESSON 4.1 More Practice/ Homework

Video Tutorials and Interactive Examples

1. **Use Structure** Joni climbed $75\frac{1}{2}$ feet up a hill and then rappelled down $92\frac{1}{4}$ feet into a valley.

   A. Write an addition expression to represent the situation.

   _____

   B. Evaluate the expression to determine how far Joni was from where she started.

   _____

2. **Model with Mathematics** The temperature at 8:00 a.m. on a winter day was −2 °F. By noon, the temperature had increased by 28 °F. Write and evaluate an expression to find the temperature at noon.

   _____

3. **Math on the Spot** Andrea's income from a lemonade stand was $28. Supply expenses were $9. Write and evaluate an expression to find Andrea's profit or loss.

   _____

   _____

For Problems 4–12, find each sum.

4. $14 + 8$

5. $20 + (-5)$

6. $-19 + 2$

7. $27.81 + (-13.97)$

8. $-3\frac{2}{3} + 14\frac{2}{3}$

9. $-5\frac{2}{7} + (-2\frac{1}{5})$

10. $100 + (-26)$

11. $-22.8 + 22.8$

12. $15 + (-3\frac{7}{9})$

13. Leandra bought two shirts for a total of $46.72. She returned one of the shirts for a refund of $24.61. Write and evaluate an addition expression to show what Leandra paid for the shirt she kept.

_____

Module 4 • Lesson 1

Test Prep

14. Melissa has $37.25 and spends $15.65. Which expression represents this situation?

- Ⓐ 37.25 + 15.65
- Ⓑ −37.25 + (−15.65)
- Ⓒ −37.25 + 15.65
- Ⓓ 37.25 + (−15.65)

15. A rock climber descends $22\frac{1}{2}$ feet into a small canyon. The climber then climbs up $7\frac{1}{2}$ feet. What is his final position relative to where he started?

- Ⓐ 30 ft
- Ⓑ 15 ft
- Ⓒ −15 ft
- Ⓓ −30 ft

16. Write and evaluate an expression for the following number line.

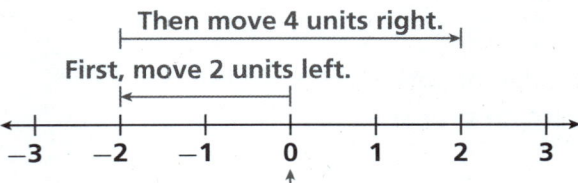

Spiral Review

17. Lauren plots the rational numbers shown below on a number line. Which of the numbers is farthest left on the number line?

$-1.4 \quad 2\frac{2}{3} \quad -0.99 \quad -2\frac{1}{3} \quad \frac{99}{100}$

18. Pablo has a piece of ribbon that is $41\frac{1}{4}$ feet long. As part of an art project, he wants to cut the ribbon into smaller pieces that are each $3\frac{3}{4}$ feet long. How many smaller pieces of ribbon can he make?

19. Jamal buys 3.45 kilograms of tomatoes to make sauce. The tomatoes cost $2.75 per kilogram. What is the cost of the tomatoes? Round your answer to the nearest cent.

Connect Concepts and Skills

Lesson 2

Name _____

Compute Differences of Rational Numbers

I Can compute differences of rational numbers with the same or different signs, and for real-world problems, I can interpret the results.

Spark Your Learning

Evan and Laura are playing a video game. Their scores are shown. By how many points is Laura winning the game? Show your thinking.

Scores
Evan   −30
Laura   80

Turn and Talk Write an addition expression that can be used to solve the problem. Does order matter in this problem? Why or why not?

Module 4 • Lesson 2

Build Understanding

1 The afternoon temperature was 20 °F. It went down by 30 °F by evening.

A. Write a subtraction expression, and use the number line to determine what the temperature was by evening.

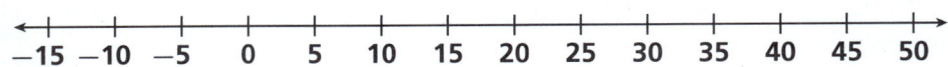

_____

By evening the temperature was _____ °F.

B. What is the sign of the number you subtracted? What direction did you move on the number line to subtract? _____

C. Look at your number line movement for subtracting a positive number, and complete the equivalent addition expression.

$20 - 30 = 20 + ($ ☐ $)$

D. Complete the conjecture: To subtract a positive rational number, add its _____.

2 Jenny borrows $20 from Bill. Jenny is now in debt to Bill. Her debt can be represented as −20 dollars. Bill tells Jenny to ignore $12 of that loan.

A. The expression $-20 - (-12)$ represents this situation. Use the number line to determine the amount of money Jenny still owes Bill.

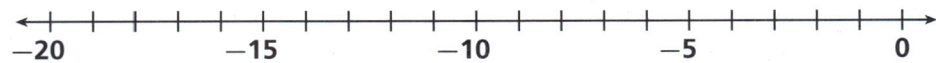

Write Jenny's debt to Bill as a negative number. _____ dollars

B. What is the sign of the number you subtracted? What direction did you move on the number line to subtract? _____

C. Look at your number line movement for subtracting a negative number, and complete the equivalent addition expression.

$-20 - (-12) = -20 +$ ☐

 Turn and Talk Why do subtracting 30 and adding −30 give the same result? Is the same true for every integer?

Name _____

3 A scuba diver jumps in the water and continues to descend until reaching −10.75 feet. How far did the diver descend?

The diver is 4.5 ft above the water's surface.

A. Use the number line to find the distance the diver descended. Explain how you got your answer.

_____
_____
_____
_____
_____

B. Write and evaluate a subtraction expression to find the distance the diver traveled, starting from the diver's elevation of 4.5 feet above sea level.

_____

C. Now write and evaluate an expression to find the difference between the diver's ending point and starting point.

_____

D. How are your answers to Parts B and C alike, and how are they different? Are they equal or opposites?

_____
_____

E. Distance is always expressed as a positive number because it does not indicate direction. When you subtract to find the distance between two locations, how can you make sure that your result is always positive?

_____
_____

Turn and Talk How can you use subtraction and absolute value to find the distance between any two numbers on a number line?

Module 4 • Lesson 2

Step It Out

To subtract a positive or negative rational number, add its opposite.

4 ▸ Rewrite the subtraction as addition. Then evaluate.

A. $3.2 - 6.8 = 3.2 +$ ☐ $=$ ☐

B. $5\frac{1}{3} - \left(-4\frac{1}{2}\right) = 5\frac{1}{3} +$ ☐ $=$ ☐

C. $-8.42 - 7.3 = -8.42 +$ ☐ $=$ ☐

D. $-6\frac{2}{5} - \left(-6\frac{2}{5}\right) = -6\frac{2}{5} +$ ☐ $=$ ☐

E. Complete each statement.

After rewriting subtraction as addition, a statement that adds two negative numbers results in a _____ number.

After rewriting subtraction as addition, a statement that adds two positive numbers results in a _____ number.

After rewriting subtraction as addition, a statement that adds opposites results in _____.

Check Understanding

1. Elise had a credit card balance of −$120. She made a payment of $70. Write and evaluate a subtraction expression to find her new balance.

   _____

   _____

2. Use subtraction and absolute value to find the distance between the numbers −7.3 and 2.1 on a number line.

   _____

3. Rewrite the subtraction expression as an addition expression. Then evaluate.

   A. $7\frac{2}{7} - \left(-15\frac{2}{7}\right) =$ ☐ $+$ ☐ $=$ ☐

   B. $-14\frac{1}{6} - 4 =$ ☐ $+$ ☐ $=$ ☐

4. How do you subtract a rational number from another rational number without using a number line? Give an example.

   _____

   _____

Name _____

On Your Own

5. The temperature is 2 °F and drops to −15 °F overnight. Write and evaluate a subtraction expression to determine the change in temperature.

   _____

   _____

6. A submarine descended 500 feet below sea level. It then descended another 275 feet. Write and evaluate a subtraction expression to determine the new position of the submarine relative to sea level.

   _____

7. **(MP) Reason** Ingvar is playing a video game that takes away points for losing treasures. His current score is shown. Then he loses treasure worth 27.7 points.

   A. Write and evaluate a subtraction expression to find Ingvar's new score.

   _____

   B. Is your answer reasonable? Why?

   _____

   _____

   _____

Ingvar's current score is −56.2.

8. Malik earns an average of $4\frac{1}{2}$ points on his daily homework quizzes. Near the end of the quarter, his average decreases by $\frac{3}{4}$ point. Write and evaluate a subtraction expression to find his current quiz grade average.

   _____

9. **Financial Literacy** Miss Aliyah's checking account balance is $15.50. She withdraws $5.37. Write and evaluate a subtraction expression to find the new balance.

   _____

For Problems 10–13, find the distance in units between the numbers on a number line.

10. $\frac{5}{8}$ and $\frac{1}{4}$

11. −12 and 14

12. $1\frac{1}{2}$ and $-2\frac{5}{6}$

13. −5.75 and −6.42

Module 4 • Lesson 2

14. The West High football team gained 7 yards but then lost 15 yards. Write and evaluate a subtraction expression to determine the total change in yardage.

_____

15. Financial Literacy Amy had a $9.78 monthly fee for music streaming due when she received her paycheck. After paying for the music streaming service, she had $65.02 remaining from her paycheck. Write and evaluate a subtraction expression to determine the original value of Amy's paycheck.

_____

16. At the beginning of a game, April had a score of −150 points. April played for another 20 minutes, and her final score was −355 points. Write and evaluate a subtraction expression to determine the change of her score from the beginning of the game to the end of the game.

_____

_____

For Problems 17–24, write each subtraction expression as an equivalent addition expression and evaluate it.

17. $41.7 - 41.7$

_____

18. $36 - 48$

_____

19. $-13\frac{1}{4} - \left(-10\frac{3}{4}\right)$

_____

20. $-33\frac{5}{8} - 7\frac{1}{2}$

_____

21. $21.85 - 6.03$

_____

22. $-9 - (-13.11)$

_____

23. $0 - (-5)$

_____

24. $1.9 - 1.9$

_____

 I'm in a Learning Mindset!

What did I learn by discussing strategies for subtracting rational numbers with my peers?

_____

Compute Differences of Rational Numbers

LESSON 4.2 More Practice/Homework

1. Wednesday morning, the temperature was −12 °F. By the afternoon, the temperature was 23 °F. Write and evaluate a subtraction expression to determine the number of degrees of change in temperature between the morning and the afternoon.

2. **STEM** Scientists are studying the effects of increased temperature, which causes bleaching on coral reefs. A scientist dives at two different reefs, one located 34.5 feet below sea level and one at 26.25 feet below sea level. Represent the position of each reef as a rational number. Then use subtraction and absolute value to find the vertical distance between the reefs.

Coral reef that has been affected by bleaching

Coral reef that has not been affected by bleaching

3. Savana walks $3\frac{1}{3}$ miles to a park. On her way home, she stops at Ray's house after $1\frac{2}{3}$ miles to pick up a book. Write and evaluate a subtraction expression to find how much farther Savana must walk to get home.

4. Joseph removes $\frac{5}{8}$ gallon of white paint from a can. Then he adds $\frac{5}{8}$ gallon of blue paint to the can. Write and evaluate an addition expression to find the overall increase or decrease in the amount of paint in the can.

For Problems 5–8, evaluate the expression.

5. $\frac{1}{4} - \left(-\frac{1}{6}\right)$

6. $-4\frac{1}{2} - 2\frac{3}{4}$

7. $-233.2 - 25.8$

8. $27.81 - (-13.97)$

Test Prep

9. Maya's bank account had $55.29. She wrote a check for $42. Which expression represents the situation?

- Ⓐ 55.29 + 42
- Ⓑ −42 − 55.29
- Ⓒ 55.29 − 42
- Ⓓ 42 − 55.29

10. George had a score of 25 points in a game. During the rest of the game, he lost 59 points. What score did George have at the end?

- Ⓐ 34 points
- Ⓑ −34 points
- Ⓒ 84 points
- Ⓓ −84 points

11. The highest elevation in California is 14,505 feet, and the lowest elevation is −282 feet. Write and evaluate an expression to determine the distance between the lowest and highest elevations.

12. Evaluate $-13\frac{1}{2} - \left(-17\frac{1}{2}\right)$.

- Ⓐ −31
- Ⓑ −4
- Ⓒ 4
- Ⓓ 31

13. Evaluate 23 − (−9).

Spiral Review

14. What is the value of |−6.8|?

15. On Friday, Lakesha jogs 3.21 miles. On Saturday, she jogs 3.75 miles. On Sunday, she jogs 1.94 miles. What is the total distance she jogs over the three days?

16. Alex wants to model −4 + (−3) on a number line. He starts at −4. What should he do next to find the sum?

Connect Concepts and Skills

Lesson **3**

Name _____

Understand and Compute Products and Quotients of Rational Numbers

I Can apply the rules for multiplying and dividing rational numbers.

Spark Your Learning

Arnot wins a $50 gift card for a virtual reality arcade. If he does not use the card for a whole year, the balance on the card will be reduced by $5 each month that it continues to go unused. What will be the change in the value of the card if Arnot doesn't use it for 18 months?

 **Turn and Talk** Did you use the same method as your partner? If not, explain your reasoning to make sure both methods are correct.

Module 4 • Lesson 3

Build Understanding

1. Jordan is scuba diving and stops each time she descends 15 feet to take a photo. Starting at the surface, she does this 4 times. What is her overall change in elevation?

A. Write an addition equation to represent the overall change in elevation.

_____

B. Adding ☐ units ☐ times can be written as

the multiplication expression ☐(☐).

C. How should your answer in Part A compare to the value of the multiplication expression? Explain your reasoning.

_____

D. We want the Commutative Property of Multiplication to hold for all rational numbers. So if $(4)(-15) = -60$, then $(-15)(4) =$ ☐.

E. Complete the last column in the table indicating the sign of the product pq.

F. Write a rule for multiplication of rational numbers with different signs.

The product of two rational numbers with different signs is a | positive / negative | number.

Products of Rational Numbers		
Sign of factor p	Sign of factor q	Sign of product pq
+	−	
−	+	

G. We want the Distributive Property to hold for all rational numbers. Use your rule from Part F to show that the Distributive Property holds for $3(6 + (-4))$. Then determine what the value of $(-3)(-4)$ must be for the Distributive Property to hold for $-3(6 + (-4))$.

$3(6 + (-4)) \stackrel{?}{=} 3(6) + 3(\boxed{})$ $-3(6 + (-4)) = (-3)(6) + (-3)(-4)$

$\quad\quad 3(2) \stackrel{?}{=} 18 + (\boxed{})$ $\quad\quad -3(2) = -18 + \boxed{}$

$\quad\quad\quad\quad 6 = \boxed{}$ $\quad\quad\quad\quad -6 = -6$

This means that $(-3)(-4) = \boxed{}$.

H. Complete the table.

I. Write a rule for multiplication of rational numbers with the same sign.

The product of two rational numbers with the same sign is a | positive / negative | number.

Products of Rational Numbers		
Sign of factor p	Sign of factor q	Sign of product pq
+	+	
−	−	

Name _____

2 You can use what you know about multiplying signed numbers to figure out the rules for dividing signed numbers.

A. Use the fact that division and multiplication are **inverse operations** to complete the number statements in the table.

Multiplication	Related division
2 × 4 = 8	8 ÷ ☐ = 4 and 8 ÷ 4 = ☐
−2 × 4 = −8	−8 ÷ ☐ = 4 and −8 ÷ 4 = ☐
2 × (−4) = −8	−8 ÷ ☐ = −4 and −8 ÷ (−4) = ☐
−2 × (−4) = 8	8 ÷ ☐ = −4 and 8 ÷ (☐) = −2

B. Use your results from Part A to complete the table.

C. Complete the rules for division of rational numbers.
- The quotient of two rational numbers with different signs is a _____ number.
- The quotient of two rational numbers with the same sign is a _____ number.

Quotients of Rational Numbers

Sign of dividend p	Sign of divisor q	Sign of quotient $\frac{p}{q}$
+	−	
−	+	
+	+	
−	−	

3 You can multiply pairs of factors to find the product of three or more rational numbers.

A. Complete the table.

	Product	Number of negative factors	Sign of product
(−3)(4)(7)			
(−5)(−5)(2)(6)			
(−1)(−3)(−10)			
(3)(−2)(−1)(−2)(−3)			

B. What relationship do you see between the number of negative factors and the sign of the corresponding product?

_____
_____

 Turn and Talk How do the rules you learned previously for multiplying two numbers with the same sign and two numbers with different signs support your answer to Part B?

Module 4 • Lesson 3   135

Step It Out

4 Find each product or quotient.

A. $\left(-\frac{1}{3}\right)(-7)(-9) = \left(\boxed{}\right)\left(-\frac{1}{3}\right)(-9)$

$= \left(\boxed{}\right)\left[\left(-\frac{1}{3}\right)(-9)\right]$

$= \left(\boxed{}\right)(3)$

$= -21$

B. $-135 \div 15$

This is a quotient of two rational numbers with different signs, so the quotient is a positive / negative number.

$-135 \div 15 = \boxed{}$

C. $-\frac{3}{4} \div \left(-\frac{5}{4}\right)$

This is a quotient of two rational numbers with the same sign, so the quotient is a positive / negative number.

$-\frac{3}{4} \div \left(-\frac{5}{4}\right) = -\frac{3}{4} \times \left(\boxed{}\right) = \boxed{}$

Check Understanding

1. Jared writes a multiplication expression with eight rational factors. Half of the factors are positive and half are negative. Is the product positive or negative? Why?

   _____

2. The expression $(8)(-1.5)$ represents the change in a scuba diver's elevation in meters after 8 minutes. Find the change in elevation.

   _____

Find each product or quotient.

3. $-1 \div (-0.25)$ _____

4. $(10)(-3)\left(-\frac{4}{5}\right)\left(-\frac{5}{6}\right)$ _____

5. Compare the rules for finding the signs of products and quotients.

   _____

   _____

   _____

Name _____

On Your Own

MP Model with Mathematics In Problems 6–7, model the situation with a multiplication expression and an addition expression involving negative numbers. Then evaluate.

6. Every day that Annabelle takes the train to work, she uses an app to charge the parking fee shown to her credit card. What will be her card balance for commuter parking if she parks and takes the train to work 10 times?

   _____
   _____
   _____

7. Alejandro makes $100 donations to five of his favorite charities every December. He pays for the donations by check. What is the change in his checking account balance after making these donations?

   _____
   _____

For Problems 8–13, identify the sign of the product or quotient. Do not evaluate.

8. $253 \times (-185)$

9. -59×819

10. $-1,200 \times (-490)$

11. $1,242 \div (-18)$

12. $-1,890 \div (-15)$

13. $-18,175 \div 125$

14. DeMarcus multiplies all of the integers from -10 to -1, including -10 and -1. Should his answer be positive or negative? Explain your thinking.

   _____
   _____
   _____

For Problems 15–23, find each product or quotient.

15. $(-4)(-8)(-5)$

16. $(-4)(-2)(5)(3)$

17. $-270 \div (-3)$

18. $(0.2)(50)(-0.9)$

19. $(0.1)(-0.2)(10)(-10)$

20. $14.7 \div (-3.5)$

21. $\left(-\frac{1}{3}\right)\left(\frac{3}{5}\right)\left(-\frac{5}{7}\right)$

22. $\left(\frac{2}{7}\right)\left(\frac{14}{15}\right)\left(-\frac{1}{2}\right)$

23. $-\frac{3}{2} \div \frac{1}{4}$

Module 4 • Lesson 3

24. **Construct Arguments** Complete each step to show that $(-1)(-1) = 1$.

$(-1)(0) = \boxed{}$ — Multiplication Property of Zero

$(-1)(-1 + 1) = 0$ — Addition Property of Opposites

$(-1)(-1) + (-1)(1) = 0$ — _____

$(-1)(-1) + \boxed{} = 0$ — Identity Property of Multiplication

$(-1)(-1) + (-1) + \boxed{} = 0 + \boxed{}$ — Addition Property of Equality

$(-1)(-1) + (-1 + 1) = 0 + 1$ — _____

$(-1)(-1) + \boxed{} = 0 + 1$ — Addition Property of Opposites

$(-1)(-1) = \boxed{}$ — Identity Property of Addition

25. The value of a collectible baseball card decreased as shown.

Value decreased by $12 in 6 months.

A. **Use Tools** To find the average monthly change in the value of the card, use the number line to find $-12 \div 6$.

```
◄—┼—┼—┼—┼—┼—┼—┼—┼—┼—┼—┼—►
 -16 -14 -12 -10 -8  -6  -4  -2   0   2   4
```

$-12 \div 6 =$ _____

B. **Construct Arguments** What is the sign (positive or negative) of the quotient? Explain why this makes sense in the context of the problem.

_____

_____

26. **Open Ended** Write a different division problem involving negative numbers that can be solved using the number line given in Problem 25.

_____

I'm in a Learning Mindset!

How can I use my understanding of rational number multiplication to help support my understanding of rational number division?

_____

_____

Understand and Compute Products and Quotients of Rational Numbers

LESSON 4.3 More Practice/Homework

ONLINE Video Tutorials and Interactive Examples

MP Model with Mathematics For Problems 1 and 2, model the situation with a multiplication expression and an addition expression involving negative numbers. Then evaluate.

1. After a gymnastics competition, the coaches reviewed all the gymnasts' scores to identify areas for improvement. A missed landing on an aerial cartwheel deducts 2 points from the score. The coaches found that aerial cartwheels were missed 5 times across the competition. How did these missed landings affect the scores overall?

   _____
   _____
   _____

2. The temperature fell by 3°F every hour during a 6-hour period. What was the overall change in temperature during the 6-hour period?

   _____
   _____

For Problems 3–5, identify the sign of the product. Do not evaluate.

3. $-819 \times (-324)$

4. $-1{,}201 \times 54$

5. $10{,}005 \times (-84)$

   _____   _____   _____

6. **MP Critique Reasoning** Dario said that if the dividend and divisor have the same sign, then the quotient also has that same sign. Do you agree or disagree? Explain.

   _____
   _____

7. **MP Use Structure** Explain how you can use the fact that multiplication and division are inverse operations to help you determine whether the quotient $-10 \div (-5)$ is positive or negative.

   _____
   _____

For Problems 8–11, find each product or quotient.

8. $(3)(5)(-3)(-2)(10)(-1)$

9. $-4300 \div (-100)$

10. $\left(\dfrac{2}{3}\right)\left(-\dfrac{9}{8}\right)\left(-\dfrac{4}{5}\right)(-1)$

11. $-3\dfrac{1}{2} \div \dfrac{3}{4}$

Test Prep

12. Which quotients are negative? Select all that apply.

- (A) $\frac{-52}{13}$
- (B) $14 \div (-2)$
- (C) $-36 \div (-9)$
- (D) $\frac{-20}{-5}$
- (E) $-27 \div 3$
- (F) $\frac{7}{-1}$

13. Marley's bank charges a $3 service fee each time money is withdrawn from another bank's ATM. Marley is traveling and must withdraw money from another bank's ATM 4 times. Which expressions model the change in the balance of her account due to the service fees? Select all that apply.

- (A) $-3 + (-3) + (-3) + (-3)$
- (B) $-4 + (-4) + (-4)$
- (C) $4 \times (-3)$
- (D) $-4 \times (-3)$
- (E) 3×4

14. An equation is shown.

$a \times b = c$

Which statement is true?

- (A) If $a > 0$ and $b > 0$, then $c < 0$.
- (B) If $a > 0$ and $b < 0$, then $c < 0$.
- (C) If $a < 0$ and $b > 0$, then $c > 0$.
- (D) If $a < 0$ and $b < 0$, then $c < 0$.

Spiral Review

15. Miguel takes $50 to the mall. He buys a flannel shirt for $18.99 and a hat for $12.49. On his way home, he stops at the bank and withdraws $25. How much money does Miguel have now?

_____

16. Callie bought 4 pies from a bakery for a holiday dinner. The total cost was $75.80. If each pie cost the same, how much did one pie cost?

_____

17. The temperature at 6:00 a.m. on a winter day is $-6\,°F$. The temperature rises by $7\,°F$ by noon. Use the number line to represent the situation. Then complete the equation.

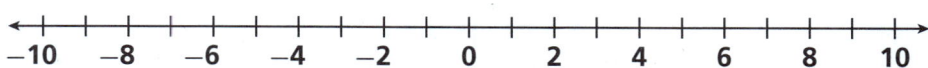

$-6\,°F + 7\,°F = $ _____ $°F$

Connect Concepts and Skills

Lesson 4

Name _____

Write Rational Numbers as Decimals

I Can show that a number is rational by writing it as a ratio of integers, and I can convert a rational number to a decimal. I can show that $-\left(\frac{p}{q}\right) = \frac{(-p)}{q} = \frac{p}{(-q)}$ for specific values of p and q.

Spark Your Learning

Hayley is buying herbs. She wants to buy $\frac{5}{6}$ ounce of basil. The scale she is using to weigh the basil displays the weight as a decimal. How will she know when the display on the scale is correct to the tenths place? Explain your reasoning.

 **Turn and Talk** What do you think the digit in the hundredths place of the display will be? Explain your reasoning.

Module 4 • Lesson 4   141

Build Understanding

1 ▶ Hayley wants to buy the amounts of herbs shown. How can you convert these fractions to decimals?

$\frac{3}{4}$ oz oregano, $\frac{2}{3}$ oz thyme

A. You can use **equivalent fractions** to convert a fraction to a decimal. Does that method work well for these fractions? Why or why not?

_____

_____

_____

_____

B. You can also use long division to convert a fraction to a decimal, because $\frac{a}{b} = a \div b$ for all fractions $\frac{a}{b}$.

Think about dividing 3 ounces into 4 equal parts as shown. How many tenths and hundredths will there be in each part?

```
    0.75
 4)3.00
  -28
    20
   -20
     0
```

_____

_____

C. How can you use the decimal form of $\frac{3}{4}$ ounce to find what Hayley will pay for basil that costs $5.80 per ounce?

_____

D. Use long division to find the decimal equivalent of $\frac{2}{3}$ ounce to the thousandths place. Do not round.

_____

```
      0. □ □ □
   3)2. □ □ □
      -□
       □
      -□
       □
      -□
       □
```

E. Describe the pattern in the quotient. Will the pattern continue if you write a zero in the ten-thousandths place and continue dividing? Why or why not?

_____

_____

_____

_____

 **Turn and Talk** Can the number 20 be divided evenly by 3? What does your answer imply about the quotient in Part E? Explain.

Step It Out

2 Every quotient of integers is a **rational number**, provided that the divisor is not zero. A rational number can be written as a fraction in which the numerator and the denominator are integers. The decimal form of a rational number either *terminates* (ends) or *repeats*.

Examples: terminating decimal: $\frac{3}{4} = 0.75$

repeating decimal: $\frac{2}{3} = 0.666...$, or $0.\overline{6}$

The bar over the 6 means that it repeats forever.

```
      2. □ □
      ─────
   6) 1 7. 0 □ □
      −1 2
      ─────
          5 0
        − □
        ─────
          2 0
        − □
        ─────
          2 0
        − □
        ─────
             2
```

A. Suppose Hayley wants to buy $2\frac{5}{6}$ ounces of basil. Complete the statement to show that $2\frac{5}{6}$ is a rational number.

$2\frac{5}{6} = \frac{\Box}{6}$, and _____ and _____ are integers.

B. Complete the long division shown to write $2\frac{5}{6}$ as a decimal. Then complete the statement.

$2\frac{5}{6} =$ _____, which is a terminating / repeating decimal.

3 Use the rules you've learned for dividing negative numbers.

A. Find each quotient. Then complete the statement.

$\frac{15}{-3} =$ _____ ÷ _____ = _____

$\frac{-15}{3} =$ _____ ÷ _____ = _____

$-\left(\frac{15}{3}\right) =$ _____

The rational numbers $\frac{15}{-3}$, $\frac{-15}{3}$, and $-\left(\frac{15}{3}\right)$ are / are not equivalent.

B. If p and q are rational numbers and q is not zero, what is true about $\frac{-p}{q}$, $\frac{p}{-q}$, and $-\left(\frac{p}{q}\right)$? _____

C. The value of a share of stock decreased by $15 in 3 days. If it decreased the same amount each day, which expression in Part A best represents the daily change in the stock's value? Explain.

_____

Turn and Talk Is the number $-2\frac{5}{6}$ a rational number? Why or why not?

Module 4 • Lesson 4   143

4 What are some different ways you can express the rational number $\frac{100}{-11}$?

A. Express the rational number as a fraction in different ways.

$$\frac{100}{-11} = \frac{\boxed{}}{\boxed{}} = -\frac{\boxed{}}{\boxed{}}$$

B. Express the rational number as a mixed number.

$$\frac{100}{-11} = -9\frac{\boxed{}}{\boxed{}}$$

C. Complete the division to express the rational number as a decimal.

$$\frac{100}{-11} = \underline{}$$

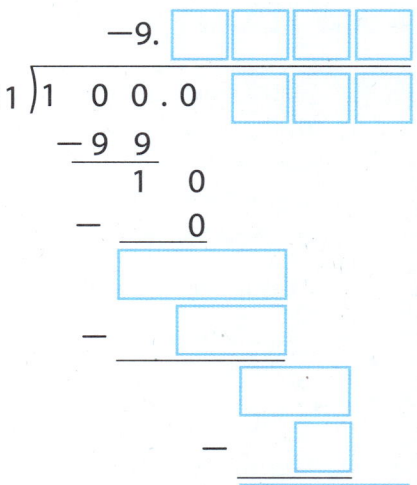

> **Turn and Talk** Predict the decimal value of the rational number $\frac{-200}{11}$. Explain your reasoning.

Check Understanding

1. Eloise needs $3\frac{5}{8}$ yards of fabric to make a costume.

   A. Show that the amount of fabric is a rational number.

   B. Write the amount of fabric as a decimal.

2. A. Write the mixed number $-5\frac{4}{9}$ as a fraction in three different ways. Then write it as a decimal.

   B. Explain why $-5\frac{4}{9}$ is a rational number.

3. The temperature outside dropped 27 degrees over a period of 3 hours. Find the quotient $-27 \div 3$, and explain what it means in this context.

On Your Own

4. Rafael is buying $1\frac{3}{8}$ pounds of salad at a salad bar that charges the amount shown.

   A. Show that the amount of salad is a rational number.

   _____

   B. Write the amount of salad as a decimal.

   _____

   C. What will Rafael pay for the salad?

   _____

5. Mariana drives for $\frac{9}{20}$ hour at a constant speed of 52 miles per hour.

   A. Write the amount of time Mariana drives as a decimal.

   _____

   B. What is the total distance Mariana drives?

   _____

6. Write the rational number $\frac{-55}{99}$ in at least four different ways.

   _____

7. **Use Repeated Reasoning** Use the table shown.

   A. Convert each fraction in the table to a decimal. Describe a pattern in the results.

   _____
   _____

Fraction	Decimal
$\frac{1}{8}$	
$\frac{2}{8}$	
$\frac{3}{8}$	

   B. Does this pattern continue? Why or why not?

   _____
   _____
   _____

8. **Use Structure** Michelle has to find the decimal equivalent of $15\frac{1}{8}$. How can she do this without first writing the mixed number as a fraction?

   _____
   _____

Module 4 • Lesson 4

9. The value of a gift card to a rock climbing gym decreased by $34 after 4 equal charges to the card. Jamar represented this as $\frac{-34}{4}$. Write the rational number as a decimal and explain what it means in this context.

10. **(MP) Reason** Are all integers rational numbers? Explain.

For Problems 11–16, convert each number to a decimal.

11. $\frac{5}{8}$ _____ 12. $\frac{5}{16}$ _____

13. $\frac{7}{9}$ _____ 14. $1\frac{1}{6}$ _____

15. $10\frac{4}{11}$ _____ 16. $7\frac{3}{11}$ _____

For Problems 17–18, write two fractions equivalent to the given fraction.

17. $\frac{-3}{5}$ _____ 18. $-\left(\frac{7}{10}\right)$ _____

19. Explain why $-7\frac{3}{5}$ is a rational number.

Write each rational number as a decimal.

20. $\frac{-69}{-11}$ _____ 21. $\frac{60}{-8}$ _____

22. **Open Ended** Write two rational numbers that can be converted to terminating decimals and two that can be converted to repeating decimals.

 I'm in a **Learning Mindset!**

How effective was using long division to write a rational number as a decimal? What questions do I still have?

146

Name _____

LESSON 4.4
More Practice/ Homework

Write Rational Numbers as Decimals

1. Sean is buying $\frac{9}{16}$ pound of tea at a teashop. The cost of the tea is shown.

   A. Write the amount of tea as a decimal.

   _____

   B. What will Sean pay for the tea?

   _____

For Problems 2–3, convert each number to a decimal.

2. $\frac{1}{3}$

3. $4\frac{7}{8}$

4. Write two fractions that are equivalent to $\frac{50}{-17}$. Then explain why it is a rational number.

   _____

   _____

For Problems 5–8, write each rational number as a decimal.

5. $\frac{42}{-70}$

6. $\frac{-56}{800}$

7. $\frac{-27}{5}$

8. $\frac{35}{-3}$

9. **Use Repeated Reasoning** Use the table shown.

   A. Convert each fraction in the table to a decimal. Describe a pattern in the results.

   _____

   _____

Fraction	Decimal
$\frac{1}{9}$	
$\frac{2}{9}$	
$\frac{3}{9}$	

   B. Does this pattern continue? Why or why not?

   _____

   _____

   _____

Module 4 • Lesson 4   147

Test Prep

10. Which of the following are equivalent to $-\left(\dfrac{a}{b}\right)$? Select all that apply.

- Ⓐ $\dfrac{a}{b}$
- Ⓑ $\dfrac{-a}{-b}$
- Ⓒ $\dfrac{-a}{b}$
- Ⓓ $\dfrac{a}{-b}$
- Ⓔ $-\left(\dfrac{a}{-b}\right)$

11. Match each fraction to its integer value.

$\dfrac{-64}{8}$ •   • -8

$\dfrac{-48}{-6}$ •   • -6

$\dfrac{-36}{-6}$ •   • 6

$\dfrac{24}{-4}$ •   • 8

Spiral Review

12. Use the number line to show how to find the given difference. Then write an equivalent addition expression.

$1 - 6 =$ _____

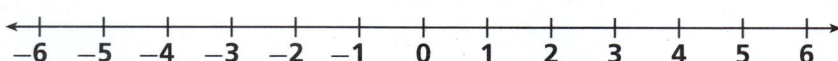

13. In 2016, the price of a stock decreased by $11. In 2017, the price decreased by $13. Write a sum of two integers that represents the overall change in the price of the stock for the two years. Then find the sum and explain what it tells you about the price of the stock.

14. Audra has a subscription to a news site. To pay for the subscription, $8 is automatically deducted from her checking account once per month.

A. Write a product of three or more integers that represents the change in Audra's account after three years.

B. What integer represents the change in Audra's account after three years?

Apply and Practice
Lesson 5

Name _____

Multiply and Divide Rational Numbers in Context

I Can solve word problems that require multiplying and dividing rational numbers.

Step It Out

1 Dashon is flying a hot air balloon at an altitude of 570 meters. He releases air from the balloon in order to change the altitude by −2.5 meters every second for 4 seconds. What is the new altitude of the balloon?

A. Write and use a model to find the change in altitude.

Change in altitude	=	Number of seconds	×	Change per second
	=	☐	×	☐
	=	☐		

The altitude changes by _____ meters.

B. Write and use a model to find the new altitude.

New altitude	=	Original altitude	+	Change in altitude
	=	☐	+	☐
	=	☐		

The new altitude is _____ meters.

C. Use a number line to show that your answer is reasonable.

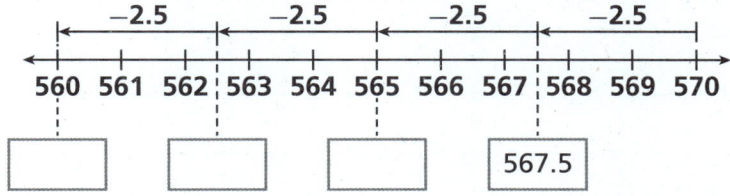

Turn and Talk Write and solve your own multiplication problem based on this situation.

Module 4 • Lesson 5   **149**

2 In $4\frac{1}{2}$ minutes, a scuba diver swims from the surface to an elevation of −85 feet, swimming at a constant speed. Later, she swims upward 5 feet following a fish. Finally, she takes $10\frac{2}{3}$ minutes to ascend to the surface, swimming at a constant speed.

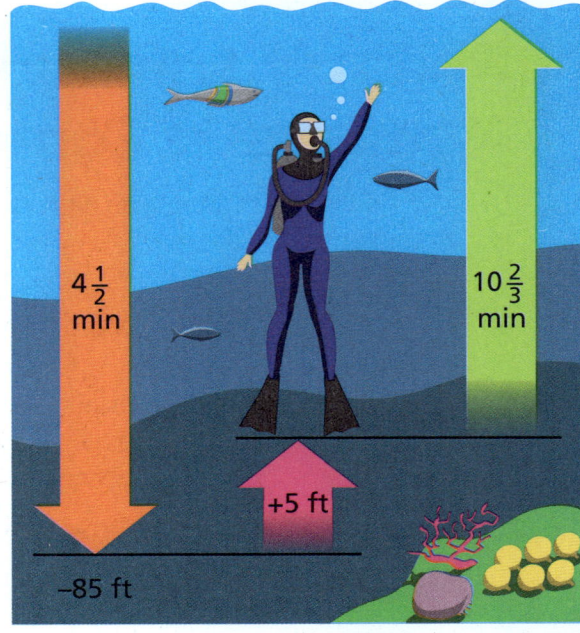

A. Write and use a model to find how many feet her elevation changes every minute during her descent.

$$\frac{\text{Change in elevation}}{\text{Number of minutes}} = \frac{\boxed{} \text{ feet}}{4\frac{1}{2} \text{ minutes}} = \boxed{} \div \frac{9}{2}$$

$$= \boxed{} \times \frac{\boxed{}}{\boxed{}}$$

$$= \boxed{}$$

Her elevation changes by about _____ feet every minute.

B. How do you know that your answer is reasonable?

_____

_____

Turn and Talk What is the scuba diver's change in elevation in feet per minute during her final ascent? Explain.

Check Understanding

1. If the scuba diver in Task 2 originally swam $-12\frac{1}{2}$ feet every minute for $4\frac{1}{2}$ minutes, how would this change the situation?

_____

_____

2. Susan has $\frac{3}{4}$ cup of raisins and she is dividing it into $\frac{3}{8}$ cup servings. Complete the following. What does the answer represent?

$$\frac{\frac{3}{4}}{\frac{3}{8}} = \boxed{} \div \frac{3}{8} = \boxed{} \times \boxed{} = \boxed{}$$

_____

150

Name _____

On Your Own

3. **STEM** Air temperature changes as you move away from Earth's surface. Under certain conditions in Earth's lower atmosphere, the temperature changes with increase in elevation as shown. Use this relationship to solve each problem.

   Temperature change: about −18.8 °F for each mile increase in elevation

   A. Find and interpret the change in temperature for an increase in elevation of 0.2 mile.

   _____
   _____

   B. Find and interpret the change in temperature for a decrease in elevation of 0.2 mile.

   _____
   _____

   C. How are your answers to Parts A and B related?
   _____

4. A butterfly is flying $8\frac{3}{4}$ feet above the ground. It descends at a steady speed to a spot $6\frac{1}{4}$ feet above the ground in $1\frac{2}{3}$ minutes. What is the butterfly's change in elevation each minute?

   _____

5. One scuba diver's elevation changed by $-15\frac{5}{8}$ feet every minute. This was $1\frac{1}{4}$ times as fast as the elevation of a second diver changed. How much did the second diver's elevation change every minute? Show your work.

   _____
   _____

6. **Open Ended** Write a real-world problem based on one of the contexts in the lesson that can be solved using multiplication or division of negative fractions or decimals.

   _____
   _____
   _____

Module 4 • Lesson 5

7. Carl has $3\frac{1}{2}$ cups of blueberries. He is storing them in containers that each hold $\frac{2}{3}$ cup. How many containers can he fill? Find the answer and interpret the result.

___

___

___

8. Mrs. Anderson writes a check for $10.50 to each of her four nieces. What will be the total change in Mrs. Anderson's checking account balance after all four checks are cashed?

___

___

___

9. The denominator of a fraction is $\frac{-3}{4}$. The numerator is $\frac{1}{4}$ more than the denominator. Identify the fraction. Then show that it is a rational number.

For Problems 10–15, find each quotient.

10. $\dfrac{\frac{7}{10}}{\frac{-1}{5}}$ _____

11. $\dfrac{-\frac{5}{6}}{\frac{-6}{7}}$ _____

12. $\dfrac{\frac{252}{4}}{\frac{3}{-8}}$ _____

13. $\dfrac{2.8}{-4}$ _____

14. $-\dfrac{5.5}{0.5}$ _____

15. $\dfrac{0.72}{-0.9}$ _____

I'm in a Learning Mindset!

What questions can I ask my teacher to help me understand how to set up a problem that involves division?

___

___

Multiply and Divide Rational Numbers in Context

LESSON 4.5 More Practice/ Homework

1. **Math on the Spot** Sarah drove her police car at a constant speed down a mountain. Her elevation decreased by 200 feet over a 10-minute period. What was the change in elevation during the first minute?

2. A submarine descends $\frac{1}{120}$ mile every minute. Write a product of three or more rational numbers to represent the change in the submarine's elevation after 3 hours. Then find the value of the product, and explain what it represents.

3. **Financial Literacy** Tanisha takes a dance class that is priced as shown. The charge appears as negative on her account balance until she makes her monthly payment.

    $12.50 per class

    A. Show how to find the balance of Tanisha's account for dance classes during a 4-week period in which she attends 3 classes per week.

    B. **Reason** Suppose the balance on Tanisha's account for a 2-week period is −$100. If Tanisha attended at least 1 dance class per week, how many classes could she have attended each week? Explain your reasoning.

    C. Evaluate the expression $-112.50 \div (-12.50)$ and interpret what it could mean in this context.

For Problems 4–6, find each quotient.

4. $\dfrac{\frac{-5}{8}}{\frac{15}{16}}$ _____

5. $\dfrac{\frac{-2}{3}}{\frac{4}{-9}}$ _____

6. $\dfrac{\frac{24}{7}}{\frac{-6}{35}}$ _____

Module 4 • Lesson 5   153

Test Prep

7. Salton Sea Beach in California has an elevation of about −230 feet. This is about 11.5 times the elevation of Indio, California. What is the elevation of Indio, California?

about _____ feet

8. During a winter cold spell, the temperature change was −1.2 °F per hour for a period of 4.5 hours. Which expressions can be used to find the overall change in temperature during that time period?

Ⓐ 4.5 ÷ (−1.2) degrees Fahrenheit

Ⓑ 4.5 × (−1.2) degrees Fahrenheit

Ⓒ 4.5 − (−1.2) degrees Fahrenheit

Ⓓ (−1.2) + (−1.2) + (−1.2) + (−1.2) degrees Fahrenheit

Ⓔ 4(−1.2) + (0.5)(−1.2) degrees Fahrenheit

9. Which expression is equivalent to $\dfrac{-\frac{5}{6}}{\frac{10}{3}}$?

Ⓐ $-\dfrac{5}{6} \div \dfrac{3}{10}$

Ⓑ $-\dfrac{5}{6} \div \dfrac{10}{3}$

Ⓒ $-\dfrac{5}{6} \times \dfrac{10}{3}$

Ⓓ $-\dfrac{6}{5} \times \dfrac{3}{10}$

Spiral Review

10. What is the difference when −2 is subtracted from 2?

_____

11. Complete the number line diagram. What addition problem does the diagram represent?

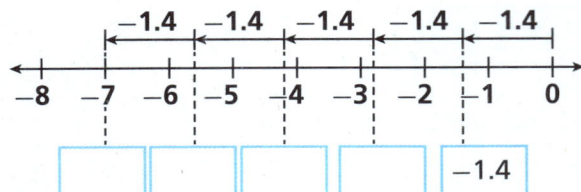

_____

Module 4 Review

Vocabulary

Choose the correct term from the Vocabulary box.

Vocabulary
absolute value
opposite

1. The number −4 is the _____ of 4.

2. The _____ of a number always represents the distance of that number from zero on a number line.

3. Complete the Venn diagram by writing at least three numbers in each oval as examples of the types of numbers described.

4. When subtracting two numbers, you add the _____ of the number being subtracted.

Concepts and Skills

MP Use Tools Find the value of each expression. State what strategy and tool you will use to answer the questions, explain your choice, and then find the answers.

5. $10 + (-6)$

6. $-1 + (-7)$

7. $3 - 8\frac{2}{3}$

8. $-2.7 - 1.8$

9. $5\frac{1}{5} \div \left(-2\frac{4}{15}\right)$

10. $(-0.4)(-3.8)$

11. Let $p \cdot q = r$, where $p < 0$.

   A. Assume $r > 0$. Plot a point on the number line to identify a possible location for q.

   B. Assume $r < 0$. Plot a point on the number line to identify a possible location for q.

Module 4   155

12. The depth of water in a swimming pool decreases by $\frac{1}{8}$ inch per day due to evaporation. No water is added to the pool for a 2-week period. What is the total change in the depth of the water during this time period?

    Ⓐ $-1\frac{3}{4}$ inches

    Ⓑ $-\frac{1}{4}$ inch

    Ⓒ $\frac{1}{16}$ inch

    Ⓓ $1\frac{1}{2}$ inches

13. Which expression is equivalent to $-\left(\frac{2}{5}\right)$?

    Ⓐ $-\frac{(-2)}{5}$

    Ⓑ $-\frac{2}{(-5)}$

    Ⓒ $\frac{-2}{-5}$

    Ⓓ $\frac{2}{-5}$

14. Which decimal is equivalent to $\frac{5}{9}$?

    Ⓐ $0.\overline{5}$

    Ⓑ 0.6

    Ⓒ 1.8

    Ⓓ 5.9

15. Tressa has 57.9 points in a competition. She loses 8.6 points. Write and evaluate an addition expression to determine Tressa's current score.

16. Oliver walks on his treadmill for $\frac{7}{10}$ hour at a constant speed of 3 miles per hour. Write the amount of time Oliver walks as a decimal. What is the total distance Oliver walks?

17. The temperature is 5 °F and drops to −2 °F overnight. Write and evaluate a subtraction expression to determine the change in temperature.

18. Mr. Weber writes a check for $28.75 to each of her six favorite charities. What will be the total change in Mr. Weber's checking account balance after all six checks are cashed?

Module 5

Applying Properties to Operations

Property Giveaways

A new company purchased tote bags and travel cups with its company logo to give away at a charity event. The new company purchased x tote bags for $12 each plus a one-time $15 shipping charge. The new company purchased x travel cups for $8 each. How much did the new company spend on tote bag and travel cup giveaways?

A. Complete the table that shows the costs of purchasing the tote bags and travel cups.

Item	Cost per Item ($)	Shipping Cost ($)	Total Cost ($)
tote bag	12	15	
travel cup			8x

B. List the properties used to simplify the expression to find the cost of purchasing the tote bags and travel cups.

Expression	Reason
$(12x + 15) + 8x$	Cost of purchasing x hand bags and x cupholders
$12x + (15 + 8x)$	
$12x + (8x + 15)$	
$(12x + 8x) + 15$	
$x(12 + 8) + 15$	
$x(20) + 15$	Add.
$20x + 15$	Multiply.

 Turn and Talk

Explain how you know when the Associative Property of Addition, Commutative Property of Addition, and the Distributive Property were used to simplify the expression that represents the cost of purchasing the tote bags and travel cups.

Are You Ready?

Complete these problems to review prior concepts and skills you will need for this module.

Write and Interpret Numerical Expressions

Write a numerical expression from the verbal expression.

1. the sum of eight and the quotient of six and three _____

2. the difference of ten and four, all divided by two _____

3. three times the sum of thirteen and five _____

4. seven times the quotient of twelve and six _____

Order of Operations

Evaluate each expression.

5. $12 + 2 - 4^2 \div 8$ _____

6. $80 \div 4 + 2 \times (9 - 5)^2$ _____

7. $8 \times 6 - 3^2$ _____

8. $(4 \times 5 + 2^2) \div (3 \times 4)$ _____

Apply Properties of Operations

Identify the property illustrated by each equation.

9. $5.3 + 3.5 = 3.5 + 5.3$

   _____

10. $9(mn) = (9m)n$

    _____

11. The length, in inches, of a rectangular garden is represented by the expression $x + 4$. The width is 8 inches. The area of the garden can be found by multiplying the length by the width. Use the Distributive Property to write two equivalent expressions for the area of the garden.

    _____

    _____

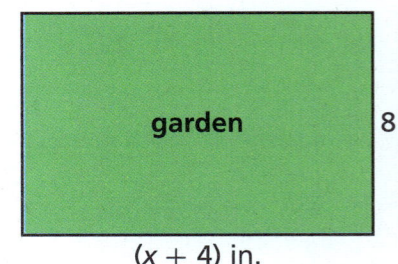

garden — 8 in. — $(x + 4)$ in.

Apply and Practice
Lesson 1

Apply Properties to Multi-Step Problems with Rational Numbers

I Can apply properties of operations to evaluate multi-step expressions with positive and negative rational numbers.

Step It Out

1 Andy usually skates for about 6 hours per week. On Monday, he spent $1\frac{1}{5}$ hours skating; on Wednesday, he spent $2\frac{3}{5}$ hours skating; and on Thursday, he spent $1\frac{5}{6}$ hours skating. Andy wrote the following expression to find the number of hours he spent skating. He grouped Wednesday and Thursday together because those were his best days, without thinking too much about what would be easiest to add.

$1\frac{1}{5} + \left(2\frac{3}{5} + 1\frac{5}{6}\right)$

A. Rewrite the expression to make it simpler to add.

$\left(\square + 2\frac{3}{5}\right) + \square$

B. What property is demonstrated by rewriting the expression?

_____

C. Regrouping makes the problem simpler because it associates two mixed numbers with _____.

D. To add the numbers in parentheses,

Add the whole numbers: $1 + \square = \square$

Add the like fractions: $\frac{1}{5} + \square = \square$

Combine the results: _____

E. Use your result from Part D to finish evaluating the expression.

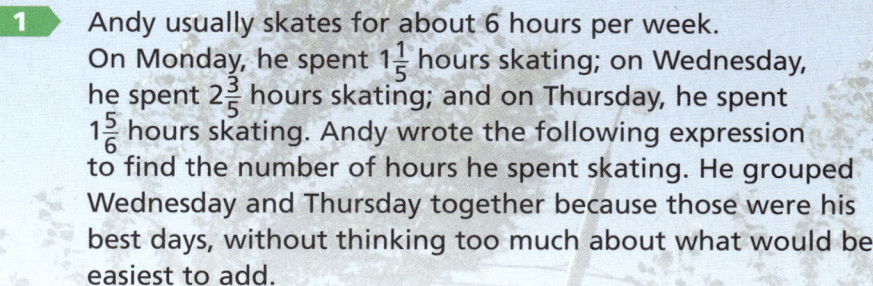

$3\frac{4}{5} + \square = \frac{\square}{5} + \frac{11}{6} = \frac{114}{\square} + \frac{55}{\square} = \frac{\square}{30} = \square$

Turn and Talk Is there another way to solve this problem? Explain.

Module 5 • Lesson 1

2 Rae goes scuba diving in the lake, starting at the water's surface. Her change in elevation in the lake is described. She:

- descends 15.5 feet and takes some pictures of fish;
- ascends $8\frac{1}{5}$ feet to explore another area;
- descends 1.6 feet to capture video while following a fish;
- descends 20.4 feet to find some feeding bass; and finally,
- ascends 15.5 feet to take more pictures.

How far does Rae have left to ascend before reaching the surface?

A. Write an expression involving addition and subtraction to represent Rae's change in elevation from the water's surface.

_____

B. Write your expression from Part A as an addition expression.

_____

C. Rewrite the expression to make it simpler to find the sum by first adding opposites.

_____

D. What properties of operations did you use to rewrite your expression in Part C?

_____
_____

E. Add the opposites in your expression in Part C, and write the resulting expression.

_____

F. Evaluate your expression in Part E to find Rae's elevation relative to the water's surface. Identify the property used in the second line.

$8\frac{1}{5}$ + ☐ + ☐

= $8\frac{1}{5}$ + ☐   _____ Property

= 8.2 + ☐

= ☐

Rae needs to ascend ☐ feet to reach the water's surface.

Turn and Talk How are the properties of addition used to evaluate the expression in Task 2?

3 A dot symbol in an expression indicates multiplication. Use properties to evaluate $\frac{4}{7}\left(-\frac{3}{5}\right) \cdot \frac{5}{3}\left(-\frac{9}{10} - \frac{3}{10}\right)$.

$\frac{4}{7}\left[\left(-\frac{\square}{\square}\right) \cdot \frac{\square}{\square}\right]\left(-\frac{9}{10} - \frac{3}{10}\right)$ _____ Property of Multiplication

$= \frac{4}{7} \cdot \left(\square\right)\left(-\frac{9}{10} - \frac{3}{10}\right)$ Inverse Property of Multiplication

$= \square \left(-\frac{9}{10} - \frac{3}{10}\right)$ Identity Property of Multiplication

$= \square \left(\square\right)$ Subtraction

$= \square$ Multiplication

4 Max has 6 ounces of white paint. He gives $\frac{1}{3}$ of the paint to a friend. He uses the rest to paint model cars. The amount he uses is shown. Write and evaluate an expression to find the number of cars Max can paint.

Paint Required: 0.02 oz for each car

$\left[6 - \left(\square\right) \cdot 6\right] \div \square$

$= \dfrac{6 - \square}{\square} = \dfrac{\square}{\square} = \square$ cars

Check Understanding

1. Soojin is flying his drone. First the drone ascends to an altitude of $20\frac{2}{3}$ feet. Then it descends $7\frac{3}{4}$ feet. Finally, it ascends $5\frac{3}{4}$ feet. Write and evaluate an addition expression to determine the drone's current altitude.

_____

2. Suresh has 4 coupon books, each with 6 coupons. He keeps $\frac{1}{3}$ of the coupons and gives the rest away. Fifty percent of those he keeps are for the movie theater. Write and evaluate an expression to show how many movie theater coupons he has.

_____

3. Explain how to use properties to evaluate the expression mentally.
$-\frac{3}{21} \cdot \frac{3}{5} \cdot 7 \cdot 15$

_____

_____

Module 5 • Lesson 1   161

On Your Own

4. **Use Structure** Dena cuts wood for a treehouse. She has five pieces of wood left over with the following lengths in centimeters: 12.7, $26\frac{3}{10}$, $15\frac{4}{5}$, $21\frac{1}{4}$, and 19.2.

   A. Write and evaluate an expression to find the total length of wood left over.

   _____

   B. Dena wants to make a birdhouse with the leftover wood. She needs $105\frac{3}{5}$ centimeters of wood for the birdhouse. Write and evaluate an expression to determine how much more wood she will need.

   _____

5. **Use Repeated Reasoning** The table shows the highest and lowest elevations in four states.

   A. Write and evaluate an expression to find the difference in elevation in each state.

   _____

   _____

   _____

State	Highest elevation (ft)	Lowest elevation (ft)
Louisiana (LA)	535	−8
California (CA)	14,505	−282
Indiana (IN)	1,257	320
Florida (FL)	345	0

   B. Roger says the difference between the lowest elevation in California and the lowest elevation in Louisiana is 290 feet. Determine if his answer is reasonable.

   _____

6. The high temperatures for a 4-day holiday weekend were:
   −2.6 °F, 16.7 °F, −3.4 °F, 6.1 °F
   Use properties of addition to help you find the sum.

   _____

   _____

For Problems 7–12, evaluate each expression.

7. $2.6 + (-3.7 - (-1.5))$

8. $-15 - 2\frac{3}{4} - 1.7 - \left(-2\frac{2}{5}\right)$

9. $-1\frac{1}{5} + 2.9 - \left(-3\frac{3}{8}\right)$

10. $2\frac{3}{4} + (-8.34) + \left(-7\frac{3}{10}\right)$

11. $-11.5 + 15\frac{2}{5} - 10.1$

12. $5\frac{1}{4} - (-3.55) + \left(-3\frac{2}{5}\right)$

Name _____

13. **Model with Mathematics** Liu Tse is 6 years older than four times the age of her daughter, Lan. Lan will be 9 years old in 3 years.

   A. Write and evaluate an expression that shows Lan's age.
   _____

   B. Use Lan's age to write and evaluate the expression for Liu Tse's age.
   _____

14. **Reason** Ella has $\frac{1}{3}$ as many trading cards as Kip. Adira has 3 more than half of the number of cards that Kip has. Kip has 18 cards.

   A. Write an expression for the total number of cards the group has.
   _____

   B. Evaluate the expression.
   _____

15. Tamir bought $2\frac{1}{2}$ pounds of fish at $5.50 per pound, and two bananas at the price shown.

   A. Write an expression to show how much change he received from a $20 bill.

   Bananas: $0.45 each
   _____

   B. Evaluate the expression to show his change.
   _____

Module 5 • Lesson 1

16. Tre earns $16 per hour. An expression for the amount of money she earned in one week is $16(3\frac{1}{2}) + 16(2\frac{1}{4}) + 16(5\frac{3}{4}) + 16(4\frac{1}{2})$. Rewrite the expression so that it only has one multiplication operation, and then evaluate the expression.

_____

Earns $16 per hour

17. **(MP) Attend to Precision** Erin has 10 bags of cherries. These are the weights of the bags in pounds: $2\frac{1}{2}, 2\frac{3}{4}, 2\frac{1}{2}, 2\frac{1}{4}, 1\frac{1}{4}, 2\frac{1}{2}, 2\frac{1}{2}, 1\frac{1}{4}, 2\frac{1}{4}, 2\frac{1}{4}$. She wants to redistribute the cherries so that each bag weighs the same. Write an expression to find the weight of each bag after she does this. Evaluate the expression.

18. Rewrite the expression $6 \cdot (-\frac{1}{3}) + 2(\frac{1}{2}) - 2(\frac{3}{4})$ using the Distributive Property. Then evaluate the expression.

$6 \cdot (-\frac{1}{3}) + 2(\frac{\square}{\square} - \frac{\square}{\square}) = \square$

19. Evaluate the expression $[0.75 \cdot (-12)] - (-6 \div \frac{2}{3})$. _____

20. Rewrite the expression $-\frac{1}{4} \cdot 3\frac{1}{3} \cdot 8 \cdot (-1\frac{1}{5})$ using the Commutative Property of Multiplication. Then evaluate the expression.

21. Rewrite the expression $\frac{1}{2} \cdot 33 \cdot \frac{1}{11}$ using the Associative Property of Multiplication. Evaluate the expression.

_____

22. What property was used to rewrite the expression below? What is the sum?

$-5.5 + 10.63 + (-3.7) = -5.5 + (-3.7) + 10.63$

Name _____

Apply Properties to Multi-Step Problems with Rational Numbers

LESSON 5.1
More Practice/ Homework

ONLINE Video Tutorials and Interactive Examples

1. Brian is adding the lengths of wood posts that he has left from building a pen for his chickens. The lengths are $3\frac{2}{3}$, $2\frac{1}{4}$, and $2\frac{1}{3}$ feet. Brian began with 20 feet of wood. Write and evaluate an expression to determine how much wood he used for the pen.

   _____

2. At dinner time, the temperature outside was −13.9 °F. The temperature decreased by 12.8 °F overnight. Write and evaluate an expression to determine the temperature in the morning.

   _____

3. Evaluate the expression. Identify the property used in each step.

   $\frac{3}{4} + \left(-\frac{3}{8}\right) + \left(-\frac{1}{4}\right) = \left(-\frac{3}{8}\right) + \frac{3}{4} + \left(-\frac{1}{4}\right)$ _____ Property of Addition

   $= -\frac{3}{8} + \left[\frac{3}{4} + \left(-\frac{1}{4}\right)\right]$ _____ Property of Addition

   $= \boxed{}$

4. **Model with Mathematics** Mr. Chung's math class is 1 hour long. Today, he spent 6 minutes taking attendance and collecting homework. Then he spent 18 minutes teaching. After that, the class worked on 4 problems. For each problem, the class spent 3 minutes working and 6 minutes discussing the answer. Write and evaluate an expression to find how much class time was left after this.

   _____

5. **Math on the Spot** Sophia uses $3\frac{3}{4}$ cups of flour for each loaf of bread she makes. She has a 10-pound bag of flour that cost $8.79 and contains 152 quarter-cup servings. How many loaves can Sophia make if she uses all the flour? How much does the flour for one loaf cost?

   _____
   _____

6. Evaluate $5 - 44 \cdot (-0.75) - 18 \div \frac{2}{3} \cdot 0.8 + \left(-\frac{4}{5}\right)$.

   _____

7. The sum of 7 and 2.6 is multiplied by 9. Then this product is divided by the result of 4 − 2.8. Add parentheses to the expression, $9 \cdot 7 + 2.6 \div 4 - 2.8$, to show the correct order for the calculations described.

   _____

Module 5 • Lesson 1   **165**

Test Prep

8. While Jackie was in Hawaii, she dove for shells. One afternoon she dove 7.8 feet. Her next two dives were each $2\frac{1}{8}$ feet deeper than the dive before it. What were the elevations relative to sea level of her second and third dives?

_____

_____

9. Which expression has a value of 7?

   Ⓐ $4 + 0.5 \times 8 - 2$

   Ⓑ $(4 + 0.5) \times 8 - 2$

   Ⓒ $4 + 0.5 \times (8 - 2)$

   Ⓓ $(4 + 0.5) \times (8 - 2)$

10. Chandra bought twice as many plants as Marvin. Kira bought $\frac{1}{3}$ as many plants as Chandra. Marvin bought 6 plants. Write an expression that shows the total number of plants purchased. Who bought the most plants?

_____

11. This morning, the temperature was $13\frac{1}{2}$ °F. During the day, the temperature increased by 5.6 °F. At night, the temperature decreased by 23.8 °F. What was the temperature after it decreased?

    Ⓐ 18.2 °F

    Ⓑ 4.7 °F

    Ⓒ −4.7 °F

    Ⓓ −18.2 °F

12. Simplify the expression: $-7\frac{7}{8} + 3.7 - (-15.9)$.

_____

Spiral Review

13. Overnight, the temperature decreased by $17\frac{1}{2}$ °F. If the temperature began at −3.6 °F, what is the current temperature?

_____

14. Pauline plots the numbers $4\frac{1}{3}$ and $-5\frac{1}{8}$ on a number line. Explain how she can use the number line to determine which number is greater. Then write an inequality to compare the numbers.

_____

_____

Apply and Practice
Lesson 2

Name _____

Solve Multi-Step Problems with Rational Numbers in Context

I Can solve multi-step problems that involve rational numbers in different forms and multiple operations.

Step It Out

1 Sandi is one of 4 friends who will go to the park together 3 times this year. She says they will save about $200 if they buy the season pass. Use estimation to determine whether her statement is reasonable.

A. Estimate the cost of 4 season passes.

$ [ ] · 4 = $ [ ]

Season pass: $249.99
Day pass: $82.99

B. Overestimate the cost of 4 day passes for 3 days. Use the Distributive Property to make calculations easier.

4 day passes:

$ [ ] · 4 = ([ ] + [ ])4 = [ ] + [ ] = $ [ ]

4 day passes for 3 days:

$ [ ] · 3 = ([ ] + [ ])3 = [ ] + [ ] = $ [ ]

C. Sandi's estimation of saving about $200 is / is not reasonable. Explain.

_____
_____
_____

Turn and Talk If the 4 friends visited the park 4 times, would season passes save them money? Explain.

2 Estimate $-3.8 \cdot \frac{14}{5} - \frac{117}{20}$ using integers. Tell whether your estimate is an underestimate or an overestimate. Explain.

$-3.8 \cdot \frac{14}{5} - \frac{117}{20} \approx$ [ ] · [ ] − [ ] ≈ [ ]

_____
_____
_____
_____

Module 5 • Lesson 2   167

3 Charise collects antique salt and pepper shakers. She bought 3 sets of cactus salt and pepper shakers. The value of each set at the time of purchase is shown.

During the next 5 years, Charise tracked the value of the salt and pepper shakers on an auction website. The annual changes in the value of each set are shown in the table. What is the total value of the 3 sets of salt and pepper shakers at the end of the 5-year period?

A. What was the total value of the 3 sets of salt and pepper shakers at the beginning of the 5-year period?

3 × $ ☐ = $ ☐

Year	Change in value ($)
1	2.52
2	−1.40
3	−5.65
4	0.80
5	1.75

B. What is the total change in the value of one set of salt and pepper shakers over the 5-year period? How did you find your answer?

_____

_____

C. Did the value of a set of salt and pepper shakers increase or decrease during the 5-year period? Explain how you know.

_____

D. In Part B you found the total change in the value of one set of salt and pepper shakers. What is the total change, in dollars, in the value of all 3 sets of shakers?

3 × ☐ = ☐

E. What is the total value of the 3 sets of salt and pepper shakers at the end of the 5-year period? Explain how you found your answer.

_____

_____

_____

_____

 Turn and Talk A student said you can solve this problem by finding the total change in the value of one set of shakers, adding the total change to $56.28, and then multiplying the result by 3. Does this method work? Explain.

168

Name _____

4. Suppose the aquarium shown developed a leak at the bottom corner and lost water at an average rate of $6\frac{3}{4}$ fluid ounces per minute. How many hours, to the nearest tenth, would it take for the aquarium to be empty?

20-gallon tank

A. There are 128 fluid ounces in 1 gallon. How many fluid ounces of water are in the tank?

_____ · _____ = _____

There are _____ fluid ounces in the tank.

B. Find the number of minutes, to the nearest tenth, that it takes for the aquarium to empty.

_____ ÷ $6\frac{3}{4}$ = 2,560 ÷ _____ ≈ _____ minutes

C. What remaining work do you need to do to solve the problem? Solve the problem and show your work.

_____
_____
_____

D. Explain how you can check your answer for reasonableness.

_____
_____
_____
_____

Check Understanding

1. A block of clay contains twenty 4-ounce portions of clay. A ceramics teacher wants to use the block to make as many spheres of clay as possible, each weighing $\frac{2}{5}$ pound. How many spheres can she make?

_____

2. A laptop computer costs $356.75 when it is new. The value of the computer is expected to change by −$35.50 per year during the first 3 years. What is the expected value of the computer after 3 years? Is your answer reasonable? Use estimation to show why.

_____
_____

Module 5 • Lesson 2

On Your Own

3. Luis is hiking at a park. He sees the sign shown and decides to hike to Wandering Twin Lake. Luis knows that he can hike at an average rate of $\frac{1}{3}$ mile in 6 minutes.

    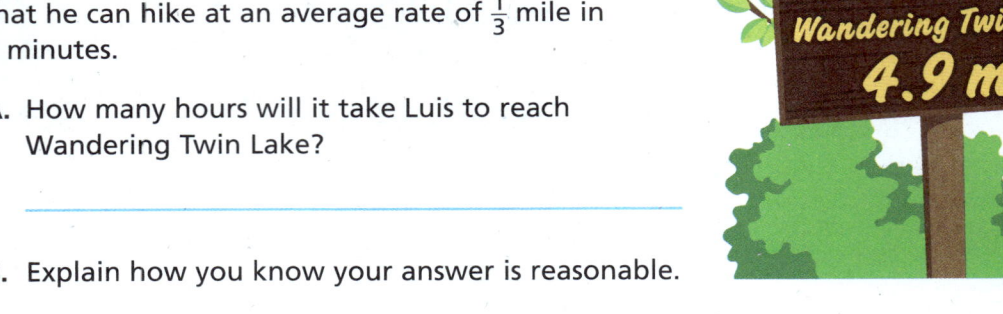

    A. How many hours will it take Luis to reach Wandering Twin Lake?

    B. Explain how you know your answer is reasonable.

4. **Financial Literacy** Mr. Liling bought 10 shares of stock in QJZ Software at the beginning of 2016 for $198.58 per share. The table shows how the value of the stock changed during 2016 and during 2017.

    A. What was the total value of Mr. Liling's shares at the end of 2016?

QJZ Software	
Year	Change in stock price
2016	−$9.73
2017	+$19.36

    B. What was the total value of Mr. Liling's shares at the end of 2017?

    C. Explain how you know your answers are reasonable.

5. According to Denise's recipe, each batch of granola requires 1.75 cups of shelled sunflower seeds. She has 3 bags of shelled sunflower seeds that each contain eleven $\frac{1}{4}$-cup servings. What is the maximum number of batches of granola that Denise can make with the sunflower seeds?

Name _____

6. A desert tour includes 305 people traveling by van. Each van can transport 18 people.

   A. Estimate the number of vans needed.

   _____

   B. **Construct Arguments** Is your answer an overestimate or an underestimate? In this situation, would it be better to overestimate or underestimate? Explain your choice.

   _____
   _____
   _____

7. **Critique Reasoning** A bag of dry pet food costs the pet store $18.66. A case of canned food costs $11.43. The owner puts in an order for 27 bags of dry food and 34 cases of canned food. The owner thinks he owes $1,835.49.

   A. Estimate the total amount of the order.

   _____

   B. Is the owner's total reasonable? Explain your answer.

   _____

8. **STEM** Sound travels about 1,125.33 feet in a second. An engineer detects the sound of an explosion from a test site 8 seconds after the blast.

   A. To find the distance the engineer was from the blast, you can multiply the speed of sound, 1,125.33 feet per second, by 8 seconds. Estimate this distance in feet and then in miles.

   _____
   _____

   You can use the speed of sound to calculate the distance away from a visible loud object.

   B. If the engineer wants to find the exact spot of the blast, should she use an estimate or an exact answer? Explain your choice.

   _____
   _____
   _____

Module 5 • Lesson 2

9. Gianna is taking a walking tour in her city. The entire tour is $10\frac{1}{10}$ kilometers long. According to an app on her phone, Gianna's average walking rate is 1.6 meters per second.

   A. How many meters does Gianna walk each hour?

   B. How many kilometers does Gianna walk each hour?

   C. About how long will it take Gianna to complete the walking tour? Express your answer in hours and minutes.

   D. (MP) **Construct Arguments** Explain how you know your answer is reasonable.

10. **Open Ended** A container of oatmeal costs $3.79 and contains about 17 servings of the size shown. Write a word problem involving the serving size, the number of servings per container, and the price of the oatmeal.

    Serving size: $\frac{1}{4}$ cup uncooked

11. (MP) **Attend to Precision** A snail is moving along a path that is 4 meters long. The snail moves $3\frac{3}{10}$ inches each minute.

    A. Find the length of the path to the nearest inch. (*Hint:* 1 in. = 2.54 cm)

    B. To the nearest minute, how long does it take the snail to reach the end of the path?

172

Name _____

Solve Multi-Step Problems with Rational Numbers in Context

LESSON 5.2
More Practice/ Homework

ONLINE Video Tutorials and Interactive Examples

1. Students sold 342 tickets to the school carnival for $11.75 each. Nine tickets were refunded. Estimate the amount of money that the school took in. Is your estimate an overestimate or underestimate?

   _____
   _____

2. **(MP) Use Tools** A bobsled team is practicing runs on a track. Their first run takes 4.85 minutes. On each of the next two runs, the team's time changes by −0.27 minute compared to the previous time.

   A. What was the team's time on their final run?

   _____

   B. Explain how you can check your answer for reasonableness.

   _____
   _____
   _____
   _____

3. Calvin maintains a 55-gallon artificial pond. He fills the pond with a hose at an average rate of $9\frac{3}{16}$ quarts per minute.

   A. How long, to the nearest tenth of a minute, does it take to fill the pond?

   _____

   B. Explain how you can check your answer for reasonableness.

   _____
   _____
   _____

4. Estimate $210 \div 5.2 \cdot 9\frac{3}{4} + (-205)$. Is 188.75 a reasonable answer? Explain your answer.

   _____
   _____

Module 5 • Lesson 2

Test Prep

5. A new mobile device has a value of $256.25. Its value changes by −$57.65 each year for the next two years. What is the value of the phone after two years?
   - (A) $140.93
   - (B) $198.60
   - (C) $140.95
   - (D) $83.30

6. Khalid has 2 bags of cornmeal that each contain 25 servings. One serving is $\frac{3}{4}$ cup. Khalid is making muffins that require 2.5 cups of cornmeal per batch. What is the maximum number of batches of muffins that Khalid can make using the cornmeal?
   - (A) 7
   - (B) 15
   - (C) 18
   - (D) 37

7. A $2\frac{1}{2}$-quart container of juice develops a leak and loses 3.3 fluid ounces of juice each minute. Which is the best estimate of the time it takes until the container is empty?
   - (A) 0.75 minute
   - (B) 8 minutes
   - (C) 24 minutes
   - (D) 80 minutes

8. Laura jogs at an average rate of 5.6 miles per hour for $2\frac{1}{10}$ hours. Priya jogs the same distance but takes $1\frac{3}{5}$ hours. Write an expression you can use to find Priya's average rate, using a decimal value or an operation symbol (+, −, ×, ÷) to fill in each box.

   5.6 × ☐ ☐ ☐

Spiral Review

9. Nicolas and Jerome are scuba diving. Nicolas is at an elevation of −25 feet compared to the surface of the water. Jerome is at an elevation of −32 feet. Which diver is closer to the surface of the water? How much closer is he compared to the other diver?

   _____

10. The temperature at noon on a winter day was 2 °F. By 6 p.m., the temperature had dropped to −9 °F. Write a subtraction expression you can use to find the change in temperature. Then evaluate the expression.

    _____

11. A bottle contains 0.78 liter of medicine. Each dose is supposed to be 0.02 liter. How many doses are in the bottle?

    _____

Apply and Practice
Lesson 3

Add, Subtract, Factor, and Expand Algebraic Expressions

I Can add, subtract, factor, and expand algebraic expressions with rational coefficients, and apply these skills to real-world problems.

Step It Out

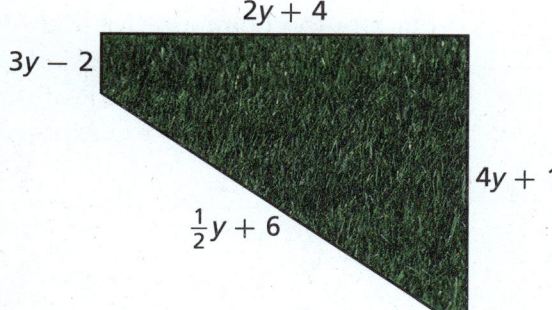

1 A yard is shaped like a quadrilateral.

A. Write an expression that shows the perimeter of the yard as the sum of its side lengths.

$(2y + 4) +$ ☐ $+ \left(\frac{1}{2}y + 6\right) +$ ☐

B. How can you identify like terms in an expression?

_____

C. Remove the parentheses and rewrite the expression as a sum of eight terms.

$2y + 4 +$ ☐ $+$ ☐ $+ \frac{1}{2}y + 6 +$ ☐ $+$ ☐

D. Use the Commutative Property to rearrange the addends so that all the y-terms are together and all the integer terms are together.

$2y +$ ☐ $+ \frac{1}{2}y +$ ☐ $+$ ☐ $+$ ☐ $+$ ☐ $+ (-2)$

E. How can the Associative Property of Addition be applied to simplify this expression? Explain.

_____
_____
_____

F. Simplify the expression by combining like terms.

☐ $+$ ☐

Turn and Talk What is the advantage of the expression in Part A? What is the advantage of the expression in Part F?

Module 5 • Lesson 3   175

2 A path in a park forms the shape of an **equilateral triangle** with the side length shown.

A. Write an expression that represents the length of the triangular path as a sum of the lengths of the three sides.

[ ] + [ ] + [ ]

B. Use the Commutative and Associative Properties of Addition to reorder and group like terms in your expression from Part A. Then combine like terms to simplify the expression.

$(7.2d + \boxed{} + \boxed{}) +$
$((-4) + \boxed{} + \boxed{}) = \boxed{}$

C. Write an expression for the length of the path using the factor 3 and the length of one side.

$3(\boxed{})$

D. Use the Distributive Property to *expand* the expression from Part C, and then simplify it.

$3(\boxed{}) = 3(\boxed{}) - 3(\boxed{}) = \boxed{}$

Turn and Talk How do your results from Parts B and C show that the two expressions you wrote for the path's length are equivalent?

3 Another path in the park goes around a square playground. The length of the entire path can be represented by the expression $20x + 8$.

A. Divide by 4 to find an expression that represents the length of each side of the square.

$\frac{20x+8}{4} = \frac{\boxed{}}{4} + \frac{8}{4}$
$= \boxed{} + \boxed{}$

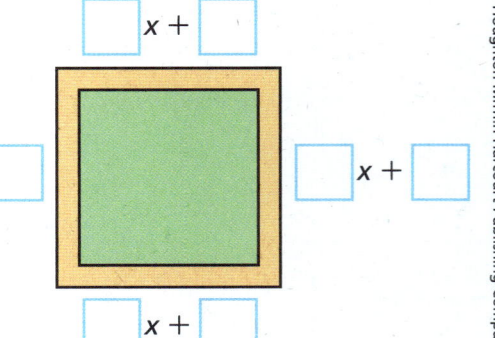

B. Complete the expressions for the side lengths the diagram.

C. Complete the equivalent expression for the length of the path, $20x + 8$.

$20x + 8 = 4(\boxed{})$

Name _____

4 ▶ Apply what you have learned about adding, subtracting, factoring, and expanding algebraic expressions to rewrite the following expressions.

A. Simplify $(-t - 5) + (-2t + 3)$.

$(-t - 5) + (-2t + 3)$

$= -t + \Box + \Box + 3$ Rewrite as the sum of terms.

$= \Box t + \Box$ Combine like terms.

$= \Box - \Box$ Combine like terms.

B. Simplify $(7 + 3d) - (5d - 5)$.

$(7 + 3d) - (5d - 5)$

$= 7 + \Box + \Box + \Box$ Rewrite as the sum of terms.

$= \Box d + \Box$ Combine like terms.

C. Factor $30x - 5$ using the greatest common factor (GCF).

$30x - 5$

$= \Box \left(6x - \Box\right)$ The GCF is 5.

D. Expand $-7(3x + 1)$.

$-7(3x + 1)$

$= -7\left(\Box\right) + (-7)\left(\Box\right)$ Use the Distributive Property.

$= \Box - \Box$ Simplify.

Check Understanding

1. A playground is shaped like a pentagon with side lengths of x, $(2x + 3)$, $4x$, $(3x - 2)$, and $(2x + 4)$. Write an expression to represent the perimeter of the playground. Then, use the Commutative and Associative Properties to simplify the expression by combining like terms.

   _____

   _____

2. Use the Distributive Property to expand the expression $3(3x + 6)$. Then simplify the expression.

   _____

3. Factor $24x - 20$ using the GCF.

   _____

Module 5 • Lesson 3

On Your Own

4. Recall that a regular polygon has sides that are all equal in length and angles that all have the same measure. A regular decagon has side lengths as shown.

   A. **Model with Mathematics** Write an expression for the perimeter of the regular decagon as a product of the number of sides and one side length. Explain.

   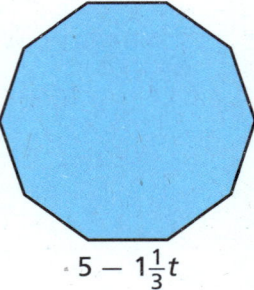
   $5 - 1\frac{1}{3}t$

   _____

   _____

   _____

   B. Use the Distributive Property to expand the expression from Part A. Then simplify.

   _____

5. Factor $14f + 21$ using the GCF.

   _____

6. **Model with Mathematics** A pentagon has these side lengths: $(12 + 4x)$, $(10 + 8x)$, $(15 + 3x)$, $(9 + 2x)$, and $(14 + 3x)$.

   Write a simplified expression that represents the perimeter of the pentagon. Use the Distributive Property to factor the expression.

For Problems 7–8, factor the expressions using 3 as one factor.

7. $3x - 30$

8. $3x + 15$

For Problems 9–10, simplify the expressions using properties of operations.

9. $(4x - 7.2) + (-5.3x - 8)$

10. $(t - 1) - (-7t + 2)$

For Problems 11–12, expand the expressions using the Distributive Property. Then simplify the expressions.

11. $4(7x + 3)$

12. $9(3y - 5)$

13. Emilio buys liter bottles of shampoo when the store has the promotion shown. Write an expression in two different ways to represent the total cost of 3 liters of shampoo.

_____

14. A plumber charges a customer a one-time service fee of $79, $62 per hour for labor, and a surcharge of $15 per hour due to the call being an emergency. Write an expression in two different ways that represents the total charges for the plumber.

_____

Buy 2 liters, get $1 off 3rd liter.

15. **MP Reason** Gavin uses x yards of material to make quilts. A customer requests 3 such quilts plus 5 additional quilts that are twice as large as his normal pattern.

  A. Write an expression in two different ways that represents the total yards of material needed for the customer's quilts.

  _____

  B. What information does each expression from Part A give you?

  _____
  _____
  _____
  _____

16. Maribelle works two part-time jobs to pay for college. She works 8 hours each week tutoring and 10 hours each week in the dining hall. She gets paid the same wage at each job. She is also provided $50 per week for expenses. Maribelle writes this expression, $18w + 50$, where w represents her hourly wage, to represent her total weekly income. Write another expression equivalent to Maribelle's.

_____

For Problems 17–20, decide whether the expressions are equivalent. Circle Yes or No.

17. $3n + 4n + 1 + 2n - 3$ and $9n - 2$

  Yes   No

18. $0.85b - 0.2b$ and $0.65b$

  Yes   No

19. $13x - 7x + 4$ and $20x + 4$

  Yes   No

20. $26 - 0.9y + 0.32y - 4$ and $22 - 0.58y$

  Yes   No

Module 5 • Lesson 3

21. **Model with Mathematics** The width of a rectangle is shown. The length is twice the width. Write an expression for the perimeter that shows each side length. Simplify the expression.

$5 - \frac{1}{4}x$

22. **Model with Mathematics** Katelyn drew a pentagon. The side lengths are $(6.7t + 4.3)$, $(-t + 11)$, $(4.8t + 3)$, $(9.7t - 0.4)$, and $(8.6t - 0.2)$.

   A. Write an expression for the perimeter. Group the like terms with variables and then group the constants. Then combine like terms to simplify.

   B. What two properties allowed you to reorder and regroup the terms?

For Problems 23–24, simplify the expressions using properties of operations.

23. $\left(-6s - 7\frac{2}{5}\right) + (-6s + 6)$

24. $5(y - 7) - (2y + 9)$

For Problems 25–26, expand and simplify the expressions using properties of operations.

25. $8(3x - 7)$

26. $14(3b + 2)$

For Problems 27–28, simplify using properties of operations and then factor the expressions using the GCF.

27. $(10p + 10) + (8p - 1)$

28. $(2g + 2) - (-4g - 7)$

29. Wesley wrote the following equivalent expressions for the perimeter of a rectangular garden plot.

    $2(7x) + 2(3x)$ $14x + 6x$ $20x$

    Which expression gives the most information about the dimensions of the rectangle? Explain.

Name _____

LESSON 5.3
More Practice/ Homework

Add, Subtract, Factor, and Expand Algebraic Expressions

ONLINE
Video Tutorials and Interactive Examples

1. **(MP) Model with Mathematics** Write a simplified expression that represents the perimeter of a quadrilateral with side lengths $\left(2\frac{1}{4}t - 5\right)$, $(4t + 3)$, $\left(\frac{1}{2}t - 1\right)$, and $(3t + 2)$.

   _____

2. **(MP) Reason** The length of a rectangle is represented by $4 + 6x$. The width is half the length. What expression represents the perimeter of the rectangle? Explain your reasoning.

   _____
   _____
   _____

3. **(MP) Model with Mathematics** A regular octagon has a perimeter represented by the expression shown. Write an expression to represent the length of one side of the octagon.

   _____

   Perimeter = $48y - 40$

4. **Math on the Spot** Simplify the expressions using properties of operations.

   A. $5(x - 4) + 2x$

   B. $18t - 3 - 5t + 8$

   _____ _____

   C. $7.5 + 5f + 16.2 + 2f$

   D. $-8(1 + x) + 7x$

   _____ _____

   E. $7\frac{1}{3}t - \left(10\frac{2}{3}t - 6\right)$

   F. $(-r - 5) - (-2r - 4)$

   _____ _____

For problems 5–6, expand and simplify the expressions using properties of operations.

5. $7(11c + 3)$

   _____

6. $6(7y - 8)$

   _____

Module 5 • Lesson 3

Test Prep

7. A square has a perimeter represented by the expression $8.8s - 20$. Write an expression to represent the length of one side of the square.

8. Simplify $-5(7 + x) + 2\frac{5}{6}x$.

9. Which expression is equivalent to $9y + 2(1 - 5y)$?
- Ⓐ $4y + 2$
- Ⓑ $19y + 2$
- Ⓒ $y + 2$
- Ⓓ $-y + 2$

10. A pentagon has side lengths of $(x + 3)$, $(2x - 4)$, $(4x + 5)$, $(3x - 1)$, and x. Which simplified expression represents the pentagon's perimeter?
- Ⓐ $11x - 3$
- Ⓑ $24x + 60$
- Ⓒ $11x + 3$
- Ⓓ $-9x + 3$

11. Leon orders sheets of metal for an art class he teaches. He needs 12 sheets for his Tuesday night class and 8 sheets for his Thursday night class. There is also a $7.95 delivery fee. Select all the expressions that represent the total cost of Leon's order, if x is the cost of one sheet.
- Ⓐ $12x + 8x$
- Ⓑ $12x + 8x + 7.95$
- Ⓒ $20x + 7.95$
- Ⓓ $12x + 8x - 7.95$
- Ⓔ $12x + 8x + 7.95x$

Spiral Review

12. Jovan is 15 years old. His sister is 6 years older than $\frac{1}{3}$ his age. How old is Jovan's sister?

13. Steven finds the product of all the integers from -99 to -90, including -99 and -90. Should his answer be positive or negative? Explain.

Module 5 Review

Vocabulary

Complete the following to review your vocabulary for this module.

> **Vocabulary**
> equilateral triangle
> greatest common factor
> regular polygon
> quadrilateral

1. The number 6 is the _____ of 18 and 24.

2. A closed plane figure with straight sides all with the same length and angles all with the same measure is a _____.

3. A(n) _____ is a closed plane figure with 4 straight sides.

4. A(n) _____ is a closed plane figure with 3 straight sides with the same length.

Concepts and Skills

MP Use Tools Evaluate each expression. State what strategy and tool you will use to answer the questions, and explain your choice.

5. $3.8 + (-2.4 - (-1.9))$ _____

6. $-12 - 4\frac{3}{5} - 2.5 - \left(-3\frac{1}{4}\right)$ _____

7. $-3\frac{1}{8} + 3.6 - \left(-2\frac{2}{5}\right)$ _____

8. $4\frac{3}{4} + (-4.28) + \left(-5\frac{7}{10}\right)$ _____

_____

_____

Factor the expressions using 5 as one factor.

9. $5x - 35$ _____

10. $5x + 20$ _____

Simplify the expressions using properties of operations.

11. $(3x - 3.6) + (-3.4x - 9)$

12. $(m + 2) - (-3m + 7)$

Expand the expressions using the Distributive Property. Then simplify the expressions.

13. $8(3x - 6)$

14. $6(4y + 9)$

Module 5   183

15. An aquarium can hold 3,744 cubic inches of water. Ben fills the aquarium $\frac{9}{10}$ full of water. Water weighs about 0.036 pound per cubic inch. Which estimate of the weight of the water in the aquarium is closest to the exact value?

- (A) 2 pounds
- (B) 120 pounds
- (C) 165 pounds
- (D) 3,370 pounds

16. Simplify $(y - 2) - (-6y + 1)$.

- (A) $7y - 1$
- (B) $7y - 3$
- (C) $-5y - 1$
- (D) $-5y - 3$

17. Which expressions are equivalent to $8(2s + 6)$? Select all that apply.

- (A) $16s + 6$
- (B) $16s + 48$
- (C) $10s + 48$
- (D) $4(4s + 12)$
- (E) $2(4s + 1) + 4(2s + 1)$

18. A rectangular backyard has a length of 68 feet and a width of $40\frac{1}{2}$ feet. The owner wants to plant $\frac{3}{4}$ of the yard with grass seed. The directions say to plant 1.5 pounds of seed for every 1,000 square feet of area. To the nearest tenth of a pound, how much grass seed will the owner need to plant?

_____ pounds

19. Kyle plans to make 15 turkey burger patties, each weighing $\frac{1}{4}$ pound, for a cookout. At the store, ground turkey meat is priced at $3.66 per pound. If Kyle orders the exact amount of meat he needs, how much will it cost, rounded to the nearest cent?

$ _____

20. A triangle has these side lengths:

$(7 + x)$, $(6 + x)$, and $(5 + 4x)$.

Write a simplified expression that represents the perimeter of the triangle.

_____

21. A bag of plums costs $3 per pound, and a bag of oranges costs $2 per pound. If Cammie buys the same number of pounds of plums and oranges, what expression could she write to find the total amount she will spend?

_____

Unit 3

Equations and Inequalities in One Variable

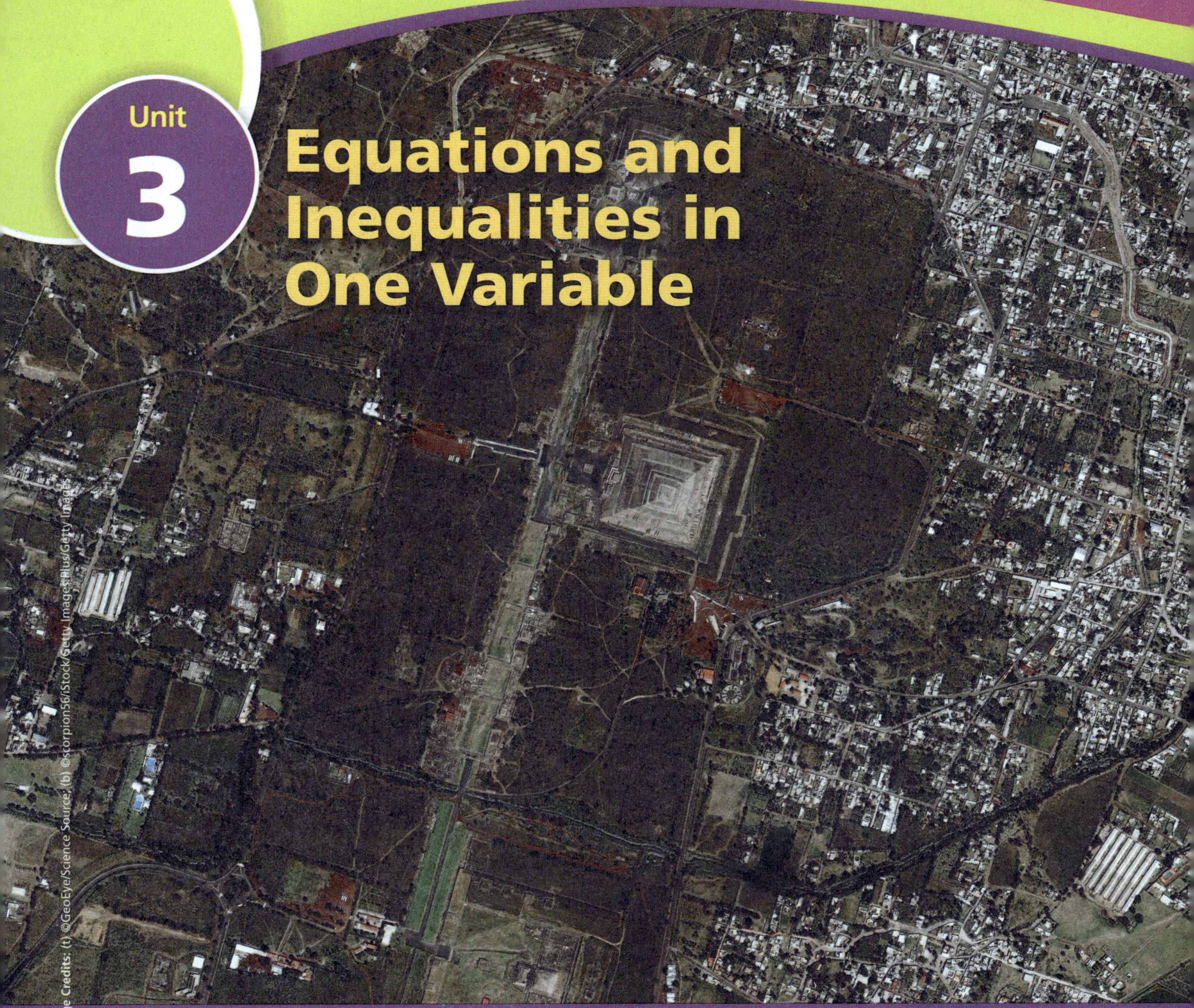

Archaeologist

STEM POWERING INGENUITY

An archaeologist collects and analyzes data about past civilizations in order to learn about human life and cultures. Sarah Parcak is a space archaeologist who uses satellite images to identify ancient sites. Her wish is "for us to discover the millions of unknown archaeological sites across the globe" and to "find and protect the world's heritage."

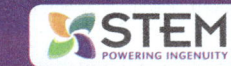

STEM Task:

Volunteers often help archaeologists at excavation sites. At one excavation site, there can be no more than 8 volunteers for every field guide. If a total of 50 people are working at the site, what is the greatest possible number of volunteers? Explain your thinking.

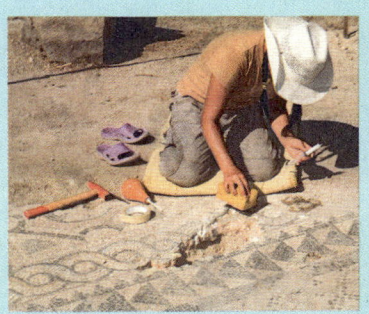

Learning Mindset
Resilience Identifies Obstacles

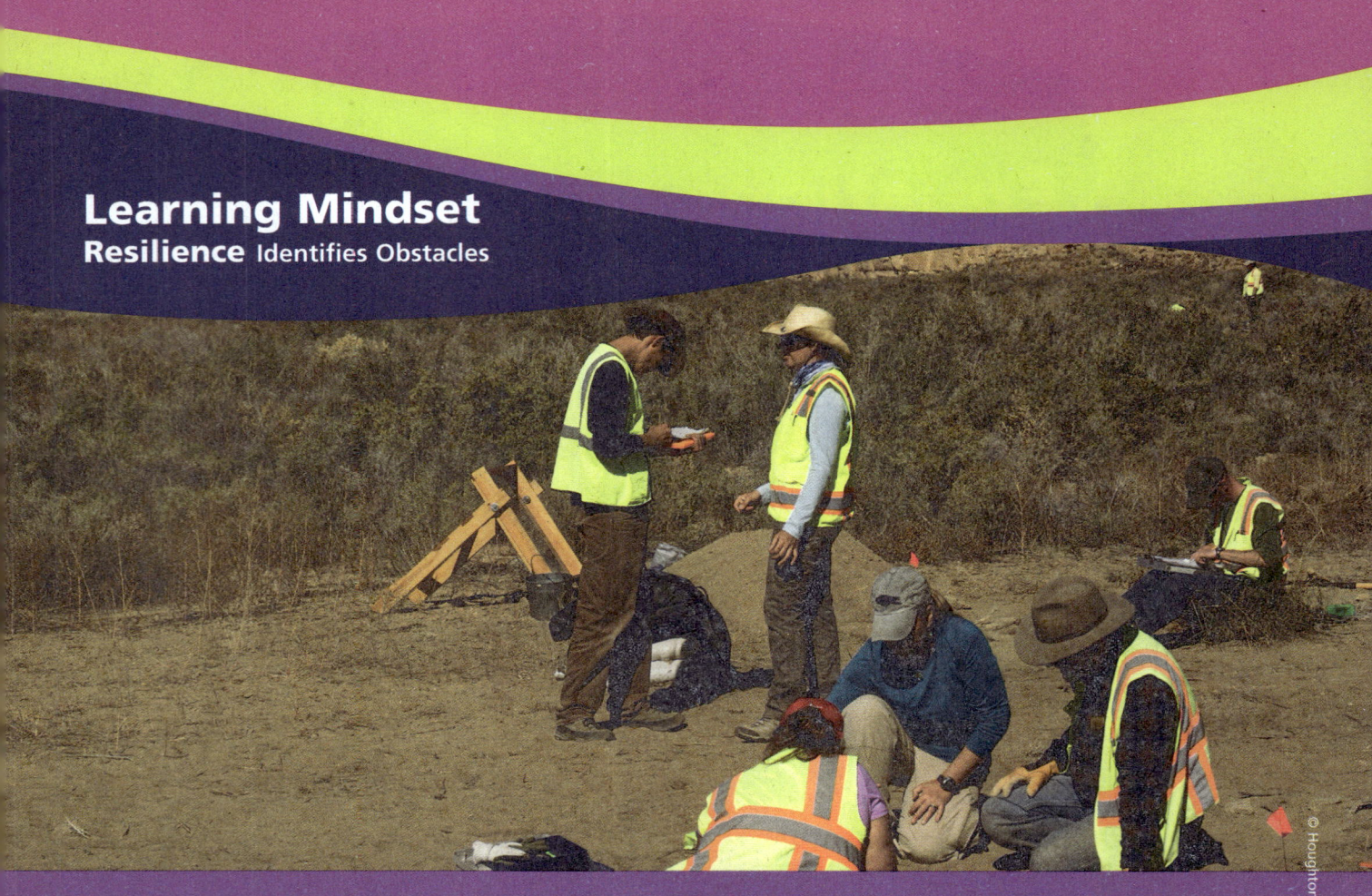

Resilience is the ability to recover from a setback. Everyone encounters challenges or obstacles at some point. Resilience allows you to overcome them and continue moving forward. Next time you run into some difficulty completing a task or reaching a goal, try following these steps.

- Identify the problem or obstacle. What is holding you back from moving ahead?

- Develop a list of ideas for overcoming the obstacle. Visualize strategies you can apply to the problem and ways you can break the problem down into smaller steps. If you're still not sure what to do, think about where you can look for help.

- Choose an idea from your list and give it a try.

- Did you successfully overcome the obstacle? If not, try a different approach. And if that one does not work, try another one. Ask for help if you need it, but don't give up.

Reflect

Q What challenges or problems did you encounter as you worked on the STEM Task? How did you address them?

Q Have you given up in the past when you encountered an obstacle or difficulty? What can you do to improve your resilience?

Module 6

Solve Linear Equations

BALANCE Mystery

Jada has set up several balance mysteries for her friends. She has made stacks of 1, 2, or 3 blocks and hidden some blocks in cups. She is challenging her friends to figure out how many blocks are in each cup. If more than one cup is on a balance, there is an equal number of blocks in each cup. The cups are light enough that their mass does not impact the balance.

Write and solve an equation for each balance.

A.

B.

C.

D.

 **Turn and Talk**

Darius says, "Balances A and D are both solved with the same operation." What pattern did Darius notice? Explain.

Are You Ready?

Complete these problems to review prior concepts and skills you will need for this module.

Solve One-Step Equations

Solve the equation.

1. $c + 27 = 68$ _____
2. $t - 1.5 = 7.9$ _____
3. $\frac{a}{3} = 21$ _____
4. $r + \frac{3}{4} = \frac{7}{8}$ _____
5. $4.2x = 25.2$ _____
6. $15b = 75$ _____

7. All tickets to a play have the same cost. A group bought 6 tickets and paid a total of $99.

   A. Write a multiplication equation that can be used to determine the cost c in dollars for each ticket.

   _____

   B. Solve the equation and tell what the solution represents.

   _____

8. It costs $0.80 to download a song from an online music store. Maxine has $6.00 to spend on songs. The equation $0.80s = 6.00$ can be used to determine the number of songs s that she can afford to download. Solve the equation, and interpret the solution.

   _____

Apply Properties of Operations

Use the given property to write an equivalent expression.

9. Commutative Property of Addition

   $4(3x + 10)$ _____

10. Associative Property of Addition

    $(16 + 4n) + 2n$ _____

11. Distributive Property

    $2(a - b)$ _____

12. Associative Property of Multiplication

    $\frac{1}{4}(12p)$ _____

Build Conceptual Understanding

Lesson 1

Name _____

Write Two-Step Equations for Situations

I Can write two-step equations for various situations.

Spark Your Learning

Write an equation to represent each scenario.

Scenario 1: The cook at Sam's Diner made 19 quiches today. This is 1 more than 3 times the number of quiches he made yesterday. How many quiches did he make yesterday?

Scenario 2: Javier buys four dozen eggs. He saves $1.50 by using a coupon. The total he pays is $8.50. What was the cost of a dozen eggs without the coupon?

Scenario 3: Lina ate $\frac{1}{4}$ of a quiche for lunch. Her two sisters split another piece equally. The three ate a total of $\frac{7}{12}$ of the quiche. What fraction of the quiche did each of Lina's sisters eat?

A quiche is a pastry crust, like a pie crust, filled with a mixture of eggs and milk or cream with any variety of other ingredients, as desired.

 **Turn and Talk** Choose one of the equations you wrote. Make up another scenario that the equation could represent.

Module 6 • Lesson 1

189

Build Understanding

1 ▶ The perimeter of an isosceles triangle is 60 feet. The base is 12 feet long. Write an equation that could be used to find the lengths of the congruent sides.

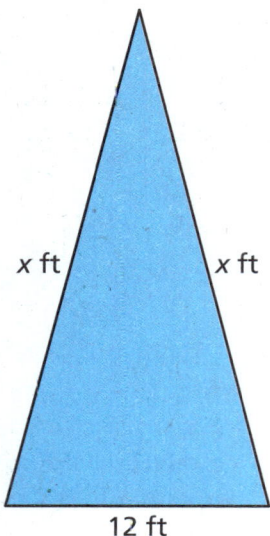

A. Write an **expression** for the perimeter (in feet) of the isosceles triangle. Use the variable x to stand for the unknown information.

☐ + ☐ + ☐

B. Combine any **like terms** in the expression.

☐ + ☐

C. What is the value of the expression you wrote?

_____

D. Use your answers from Parts B and C to write an equation that can be used to find the length of each of the two equal sides.

_____

E. How would your equation change if the perimeter were 80 feet?

_____

F. What would your equation be if the perimeter were 80 feet and the base were 10 feet long?

_____

Turn and Talk How is an equation like an expression? How is it different?

Name _____

2 Chelsea buys a shirt and shoes at the store with the coupon shown. The price of the shirt before the discount is $22, and her total discount is $18.55. Write an equation to find the price of the shoes before the discount.

50% off entire purchase

A. What information are you trying to find? How can a variable help determine that information?

_____
_____
_____

B. Write an equation that can be used to find the unknown information. Use x as the variable.

_____

C. What does each side of the equation represent?

_____
_____
_____
_____

D. What does the variable x represent?

_____

 Turn and Talk Write a basic two-step equation, then have a partner make a real-world scenario that fits the equation.

Check Understanding

1. Each time Cheryl runs, she runs 3 miles. She rides her bike only on Saturdays and always for 10 miles. She exercises the same amount each week. She rides and runs for a total of 22 miles in a week. Write an equation that can be used to find out how many times Cheryl goes running each week.

_____

2. Mrs. Wu uses a 25% off coupon to buy 1 adult ticket and 1 child ticket to a movie. She pays a total of $9.00. A child ticket without the coupon costs $4.00. Write an equation that can be used to find the cost of an adult ticket without the coupon.

_____

Module 6 • Lesson 1

On Your Own

Model with Mathematics For Problems 3–8, write an equation to represent the situation.

3. Carl is making the kite shown. It has a perimeter of 120 inches. The two longer sides of the kite are the same length. Write an equation that could be used to find the length of each of the longer sides.

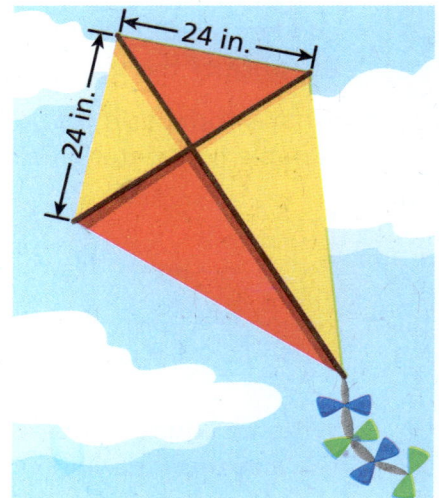

4. Mrs. Malia bought a laptop with a 10% discount. She also bought a mouse for $13.99 and spent a total of $621.49 before taxes. Write an equation to find the original cost of the laptop.

5. Paolo is using his grandmother's breakfast bar recipe. He always doubles the amount of yogurt and oats. The recipe calls for $2\frac{1}{2}$ cups of yogurt. The total amount of yogurt and oats after doubling is $6\frac{1}{3}$ cups. Write an equation to find the original amount of oats in the recipe.

6. A square has side lengths as shown in the picture and a perimeter of 54.8 centimeters. Write an equation to find the value of x.

$x + 3$

7. Ms. Emlyn buys a hat and gloves with a coupon for 30% off her entire purchase. The gloves cost $35 before the discount. Her bill before tax is $44.80. Write an equation to find the original cost of the hat.

8. Bo's sister Anna is $\frac{3}{4}$ his age minus 1 year. She is 11 years old. Write an equation to find Bo's age.

I'm in a Learning Mindset!

What barriers do I perceive to writing two-step equations for situations?

Name _____

Write Two-Step Equations for Situations

LESSON 6.1 More Practice/ Homework

Model with Mathematics For Problems 1–4, write an equation to represent the situation.

1. Pierce is making a rectangular frame for a photo collage that has a perimeter of 72.2 inches. The length of the frame is 20.3 inches. Write an equation to find the width of the frame.

2. Kendra is 3 times her daughter's age plus 7 years. Kendra is 49 years old. Write an equation to find her daughter's age.

3. Mitchell orders a plain turkey sandwich and a drink for lunch. The drink is $2.95. Instead he is served the super sandwich with lettuce, tomato, and mayonnaise. The restaurant manager takes 15% off the price of the sandwich. Write an equation to determine the original price of Mitchell's sandwich if his new bill is $8.86.

4. Bianca and Meredith are sisters. Meredith's height is $\frac{2}{3}$ of Bianca's height plus 32 inches. Meredith is 60 inches tall. Write an equation to find Bianca's height in inches.

5. **Health and Fitness** Tyler does squats and pushups. He wants to increase the number of each type of exercise by 20% by the end of the month. He currently does 25 pushups. If Tyler meets his goal, he will do a total of 13 more squats and pushups than he does now. Write an equation to show how many squats Tyler does now.

6. **Model with Mathematics** An equilateral triangle has side lengths that measure $x + 4$ inches. The perimeter of the triangle is 18.6 inches. Write an equation to find the value of x.

7. **Model with Mathematics** Ms. Lynette earns $19.50 an hour when she works overtime. She worked overtime twice this week. One day she worked 3 hours of overtime. Her total overtime pay for the week is $146.25. Write an equation to find the number of overtime hours she worked on the second day.

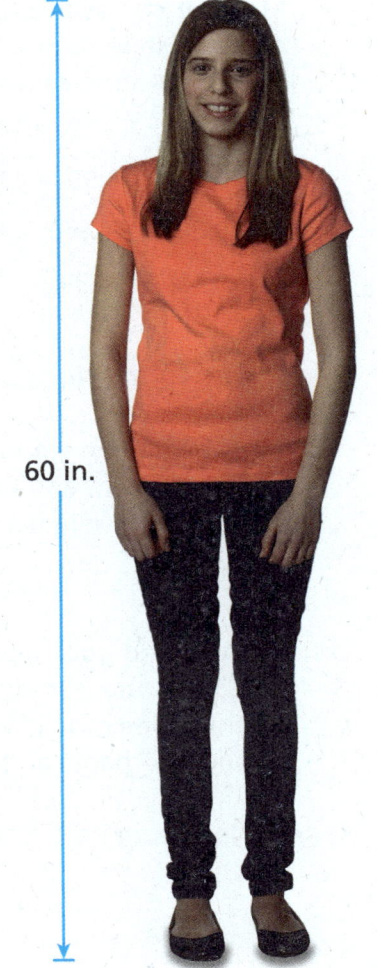

60 in.

Module 6 • Lesson 1

Test Prep

8. A parallelogram has a perimeter of $50\frac{1}{2}$ inches. The two longer sides of the parallelogram are each $16\frac{1}{4}$ inches. Write an equation to find the length of each of the shorter sides.

_____

9. A baby usually gains 10% of its birth weight plus 2 pounds in the first six weeks after birth. One baby gained 2.8 pounds during this time. Write an equation to estimate the baby's birth weight.

_____

10. A rhombus has sides of length $x + 6$ inches and a perimeter of 49 inches. Which equation represents this situation?

Ⓐ $4x + 6 = 49$

Ⓑ $4(x + 6) = 49$

Ⓒ $x + 6 = 49$

Ⓓ $x + 24 = 49$

11. Mrs. Owens has a coupon for 40% off a pair of shoes. She pays $111.79 for a pair of shoes and a dress after using the coupon. The dress costs $64.99. Which equation can be solved for x, the retail price of the shoes?

Ⓐ $0.6x + 64.99 = 111.79$

Ⓑ $0.4x + 64.99 = 111.79$

Ⓒ $0.6(x + 64.99) = 111.79$

Ⓓ $0.4(x + 64.99) = 111.79$

Spiral Review

12. Sarah began the school week with $2.60 in her lunch account. She deposited $20 on Monday, and then spent $4.75 each day that week for lunch. What was the balance in her lunch account at the end of the day on Friday?

_____

13. Mr. Alvarado goes shopping at the mall with $70. He buys a pair of pants for $33.76 and a shirt for $29.52. He also returns a hat he bought the previous week for $19.67. How much money does Mr. Alvarado have after he buys the pants and shirt and returns the hat?

_____

Connect Concepts and Skills

Lesson 2

Name _____

Apply Two-Step Equations to Solve Real-World Problems

I Can apply two-step equations to solve a variety of problems.

Spark Your Learning

A diagram of the rectangular sitting area in a botanical garden is shown. What is the length of the sitting area in the garden?

Perimeter = 60 ft   10 ft

Turn and Talk Describe how you figured this out. Did you use a formula? Explain.

Module 6 • Lesson 2

195

Build Understanding

1. Lucy installs a towel bar $10\frac{3}{4}$ inches long in the center of a door $29\frac{1}{2}$ inches wide. How far is each end of the bar from the nearer edge of the door?

A. Estimate the distance from each end of the towel bar to the nearer edge of the door. Explain your reasoning.

_____

_____

_____

_____

B. Calculate the exact distance from each end of the towel bar to the nearer edge of the door. Is your answer reasonable? Explain.

C. Let x be the distance from each end of the bar to the nearer edge of the door. Write an equation of the form $px + q = r$ that you can use to find x.

_____

D. To solve for x, you perform the same operations on each side of the equation until x is by itself on one side. What operation should you perform first on your equation from Part C? What new equation do you get?

> **Connect to Vocabulary**
>
> A **solution of an equation** is a number that makes the equation true when substituted for the variable (such as x).

_____

E. What operation should you perform next on your equation from Part D? What is the solution of the equation?

_____

Turn and Talk Compare the steps used to solve the equation you wrote in part C with the steps used to calculate the distance in part B.

Name _____

Step It Out

2 Tracy's fitness goal is shown on her planner. To meet her goal, she will need a total of 8 pushups more than her current daily total of morning and evening pushups. Tracy has been doing 25 pushups in the evening. How many pushups has she been doing in the morning?

Weekly Planner GOAL: 20% improvement on pushups

	Mon.	Tues.	Wed.	Thurs.	Fri.
AM	Pushups ✓		Pushups ✓		Pushups ✓
PM	Pushups ✓	Pushups ✓	Pushups ✓		Pushups ✓

A. Let x represent the number of pushups Tracy does in the morning. Write an expression for the current daily total of pushups.

$x + \boxed{}$

B. Write an expression for Tracy's desired increase in pushups.

$\boxed{}(x + \boxed{})$

C. Write and solve an equation to find her current number of morning pushups.

$0.2(x + \boxed{}) = \boxed{}$

$0.2x + \boxed{} = \boxed{}$ _____ Property

$\underline{} \underline{-\boxed{} \quad -\boxed{}}$ _____ Property of Equality

$0.2x = \boxed{}$

$\dfrac{0.2x}{\boxed{}} = \dfrac{3}{\boxed{}}$ _____ Property of Equality

$x = \boxed{}$

D. Check your solution.

$0.2(x + 25) = 8$

$0.2(\boxed{} + 25) = \boxed{}$ ✓

Check Understanding

1. Cookie Castle sells 8-inch cookies for $3 each plus a flat $5 delivery fee. Zach has $14 to spend on cookies. Write and solve an equation to determine how many cookies Zach can buy and have delivered.

_____

2. Mr. Muñoz has a coupon for 15% off his entire purchase. He buys binoculars for $105 and boots. He spends a total of $170 before tax. Write and solve an equation to find how much the boots cost before the discount.

_____

Module 6 • Lesson 2

On Your Own

3. **Model with Mathematics** Geoff works at a warehouse, earning $17.50 per hour plus a $200 one-time hiring bonus. In Geoff's first week, his pay including the bonus was $637.50.

   A. Write and evaluate a numerical expression to find how many hours Geoff worked his first week. Explain your thinking.

   _____
   _____
   _____
   _____

   B. Write and solve an equation of the form $px + q = r$ to find the number of hours x that Geoff worked his first week. Compare your solution with your answer from part A.

   _____
   _____

4. **Model with Mathematics** Mr. Burns takes a one-day trip and rents a car at the rate shown. The car rental costs $68.25. Write and solve an equation to find how many miles he traveled.

   _____

5. **Attend to Precision** A regular hexagon has sides of length $x + 5$ inches and a perimeter of 72 inches. Write and solve an equation to find x. How long is a side?

   _____

For Problems 6–9, solve each equation. Check your solution.

6. $-3(n + 5) = 12$

7. $-9h - 15 = 93$

8. $\frac{z}{5} + 3 = -35$

9. $3\left(y + \frac{2}{5}\right) = -\frac{1}{5}$

I'm in a Learning Mindset!

How do I keep myself motivated to solve problems with two-step equations?

_____

Name _____

LESSON 6.2
More Practice/ Homework

Apply Two-Step Equations to Solve Real-World Problems

ONLINE
Video Tutorials and Interactive Examples

1. **MP Model with Mathematics** Julie wants to buy tulip bulbs to plant. Each bulb costs $0.50. There is a one-time $4.50 shipping cost. She has $22 to spend. Write and solve an equation to determine how many bulbs Julie can buy and have shipped.

2. **Math on the Spot** The total charge for a yearly Internet DVD rental membership is $231. A registration fee of $15 is paid up front, and the rest is paid monthly. How much do new members pay each month? Explain.

3. **MP Attend to Precision** Bev is making peanut butter–banana bread. She always doubles the amount of nuts and peanut butter chips. The total amount of chips and nuts after doubling is $4\frac{1}{2}$ cups. Write and solve an equation to find the original amount of nuts in the recipe.

$1\frac{1}{2}$ c peanut butter chips
? c nuts
3 very ripe bananas

4. Dirk sold 7 more than 2 times as many gym memberships this month than last month. This month he sold 43 memberships. Write and solve an equation to find the number of memberships Dirk sold last month.

For Problems 5–8, solve each equation. Check your solution.

5. $3 = 0.2m - 7$

6. $1.3z + 1.5 = 5.4$

7. $-3(t + 6) = 0$

8. $-8(1 - g) = 56$

9. **Open Ended** Write a two-step equation that involves multiplication and subtraction, includes a negative coefficient, and has a solution of $x = 7$.

10. **Open Ended** Write a two-step equation that involves division and addition and has a solution of $x = -25$.

Module 6 • Lesson 2

199

Test Prep

11. Leo started working for a new company that paid him $25 per hour with a hiring bonus of $100. During the first two weeks, he was paid $1,200, which included the bonus. How many hours did he work during the first two weeks?

Ⓐ 40

Ⓑ 44

Ⓒ 48

Ⓓ 52

12. To convert to degrees Fahrenheit, use the formula $F = \frac{9}{5}C + 32$, where C is the temperature in degrees Celsius. From the choices below, which is the first step to solve for the Celsius temperature if the Fahrenheit temperature is 70 °F?

Ⓐ Add 32 to both sides.

Ⓑ Subtract 32 from both sides.

Ⓒ Divide both sides by $\frac{5}{9}$.

Ⓓ Multiply both sides by $\frac{9}{5}$.

13. Fred earns $16.50 an hour for overtime. He worked overtime on Monday and Thursday this week. On Monday, he worked 4 hours of overtime. His total overtime pay for the week was $123.75. Write and solve an equation to find the number of overtime hours Fred worked on Thursday.

_____

14. Solve $\frac{1}{2}m - 5 = 23$.

Ⓐ 13.5

Ⓑ 27

Ⓒ 33

Ⓓ 56

Spiral Review

15. Apples at the farmers' market cost $2.50 for 5 apples or $0.70 for 1 apple. Which is the better buy if you want 5 apples? Explain.

_____

16. Mr. Spencer drives 200 miles in 5 hours. What is his unit rate?

_____

Lesson 3: Solve Multi-Step Linear Equations

I Can solve linear equations with integer and rational number coefficients.

Spark Your Learning

Jordan buys 2 new jerseys and a glove for softball. She pays the price shown for the glove and gives the clerk two fifty-dollar bills to pay the exact amount. How much does Jordan pay for each jersey? Write and solve an equation.

What would the equation and solution be if Jordan gives the clerk a single hundred-dollar bill? How are the equations alike or different? How is the process of solving the equations alike or different?

$44

Turn and Talk Is there another equation that will solve the same problem? Explain.

Build Understanding

1 A batting machine uses an automatic baseball feeder. During baseball practice the feeder is $\frac{1}{6}$ full. An attendant fills it with 15 baseballs so that the feeder is now $\frac{2}{3}$ full. How many baseballs does the feeder hold when full?

A. Write an equation to represent the problem.

$\frac{1}{6}x + \boxed{} = \boxed{} x$

B. In order to **isolate the variable**, all terms containing *x* need to be on one side of the equation. How can you isolate the variable in the equation? What is the resulting equation before simplifying?

_____

_____

C. Solve the equation for *x*.

D. Look back at the original equation. How could you use the least **common denominator** of the fractions to rewrite the equation with integer coefficients? A **coefficient** is the number multiplied by the variable.

_____

E. Use your answer from part D to rewrite the equation. What is the new equation? Solve this new equation. Do you get the same solution?

This is an example of a linear equation with only one solution.

Turn and Talk Which equation did you prefer to work with? Why?

Step It Out

2 Lanie and Jen buy the same number of books at the used book sale. Lanie buys paperback books and Jen buys hardcover books. Lanie spends $1.50 less than Jen. Solve the equation to find the number of books each of them buys.

$$1.2n - 1.5 = 0.45n$$

$$1.2n = 0.45n + \boxed{}$$

$$1.2n - \boxed{} = \boxed{}$$

$$\boxed{} = \boxed{}$$

$$n = \boxed{}$$

A. Look at the decimals in the equation and think about how you could rewrite the equation with integer coefficients. What is the least **multiple** of 10 you could multiply each term by to eliminate all the decimals?

_____

B. Multiply each term of the original equation by your answer from part A to eliminate all the decimals. Solve the equation.

$$1.2n - 1.5 = 0.45n$$

$$\boxed{}(1.2n) - \boxed{}(1.5) = \boxed{}(0.45n)$$

$$\boxed{}n - \boxed{} = \boxed{}n$$

$$\boxed{}n = \boxed{}$$

$$n = \boxed{}$$

C. Do you get the same solution?

_____

D. Which equation was easier to solve? Why?

_____

_____

 **Turn and Talk** How is solving an equation that involves fractions similar to solving an equation with decimals? What methods can you use to solve each type of equation?

Module 6 • Lesson 3

3 Jackie has a coupon for $8 off the price of a jacket. Then the clerk takes 25% off the discounted price, so she saves an additional $10. Determine the original price of the jacket.

A. Write an equation using the **Distributive Property**, which states that for all real numbers a, b, and c, $a(b + c) = ab + ac$, and $a(b - c) = ab - ac$. Convert the percentage to a fraction. Solve the equation.

$$\tfrac{1}{4}(p - 8) = 10$$

$$\frac{\square}{\square}p - \square = 10$$

$$\frac{\square}{\square}p = \square$$

$$p = \square$$

B. Write the original equation, eliminate the fractions, and solve.

$$\tfrac{1}{4}(p - 8) = 10$$
$$4\left[\tfrac{1}{4}(p - 8)\right] = 4(10)$$
$$p - \square = \square$$
$$p = \square$$

4 Solve the equation $4(2.5x + 2) - x = 26.9$.

A. Use the Distributive Property to write an equivalent equation.

_____

B. Combine like terms and solve.

_____

Check Understanding

1. Anna spent $2.75 at the school store. She bought two erasers and some pencils. How many pencils did she buy? Write and solve an equation.

_____

2. Solve the equation. Check your solution.

$$\tfrac{1}{5}(n - 10) = 6 - 3\tfrac{1}{2}$$

_____

204

Name _____

On Your Own

3. Three people participated in a free throw shooting contest. Glenna made x shots, Val made $2x - 10$ shots, and Kim made $x + 10$ shots. If a total of 180 shots were made, how many did each person make? Write and solve an equation.

_____

4. **Reason** Jamie solved the equation $\frac{2}{3}x + 4 = 2 + \frac{1}{2}x$. Is his solution correct? Explain.

$\frac{2}{3}x + 4 = 2 + \frac{1}{2}x$

$6\left(\frac{2}{3}x + 4\right) = 6\left(2 + \frac{1}{2}x\right)$

$4x + 24 = 12 + x$

$3x + 24 = 12$

$3x = -12$

$x = -4$

_____

5. Karinne hit 4 more home runs than half the number of home runs Lu hit. Together they hit 10 home runs. Let x represent the number of home runs Lu hit.

A. Write an equation to represent the situation.

_____

B. Solve for x.

_____

C. How many home runs did Lu hit?

_____

D. How many home runs did Karinne hit?

_____

E. How can you check your answer?

_____

Module 6 • Lesson 3

6. **Construct Arguments** Max and Corey solve the same equation but they use different methods. Which method would you use? Explain your answer.

Max
$$x + \frac{x}{4} = 14 - \frac{x}{2}$$
$$4\left(x + \frac{x}{4}\right) = 4\left(14 - \frac{x}{2}\right)$$
$$4x + x = 56 - 2x$$
$$5x + 2x = 56$$
$$7x = 56$$
$$x = 8$$

Corey
$$x + \frac{x}{4} = 14 - \frac{x}{2}$$
$$x + \frac{x}{4} + \frac{x}{2} = 14$$
$$\frac{4x}{4} + \frac{x}{4} + \frac{2x}{4} = 14$$
$$\frac{7x}{4} = 14$$
$$7x = 56$$
$$x = 8$$

7. What is the first step to solve the equation $0.3n - 15 = 0.2n - 5$?

Solve each equation. Check your solution.

8. $3(x - 2) + 6 = 5(x + 4)$

9. $2.2(4p + 2) = 13.2$

10. $\frac{m + 3}{2} = m - 5$

11. $2(11t + 1.5t) = 12 - 5t$

12. $\frac{7}{8}m - \frac{1}{2} = \frac{3}{16}m + 5$

13. $9(n + 1) = 2(n - 1)$

14. $\frac{4}{5}x - 3 = \frac{3}{10}x + 7$

15. $-4(-5 - b) = \frac{1}{3}(b + 16)$

16. $3.6w = 2(0.8w + 12)$

I'm in a Learning Mindset!

What about solving multi-step linear equations triggers a fixed-mindset voice in my head?

Solve Multi-Step Linear Equations

LESSON 6.3 More Practice/Homework

1. Elsie is planting a rectangular section of grass.

   If the perimeter of the rectangle is 96 feet, what are the length and width of the rectangular section?

   _____

2. **Math on the Spot** Solve each equation.

   A. $3n + 1 = 19$ **B.** $21 = -2p - 5$

3. **(MP) Reason** What step would you perform first to solve the following equation? Explain your reasoning.

   $\frac{1}{4}(12 - 8x) = \frac{2}{3}(6x)$

   _____

   _____

4. Heather has a family phone plan. The monthly payment for each phone is $22.91 per month plus a monthly line fee of $20 per phone. The cost of the family data and text for a family plan is $70 per month, and her monthly bill is $241.64. Write and solve an equation to find how many phones are on the plan.

   _____

Solve each equation. Check your solution.

5. $a + 3(a - 1) = 3(2 + 1)$ 6. $5y - 3(2 - y) = 10$

7. $1.2x - 2 = 7 + 0.9x$ 8. $-k + 4(k + 1) = 2k$

9. $4\left(\frac{x}{6} + 5\right) = 2x + 10$ 10. $3w + \frac{w}{2} + 1 = 10 - w$

Module 6 • Lesson 3

Test Prep

11. Which could be the first step in solving the equation $0.05x + 3 - 0.02x = 4$?

- Ⓐ Add 3 to each side of the equation.
- Ⓑ Divide each side of the equation by 100.
- Ⓒ Multiply each side of the equation by 100.
- Ⓓ Subtract $0.02x$ from each side of the equation.

12. Solve the equation. Check your solution.
$\frac{3}{2}(x + 6) = 16 + \frac{1}{2}(x - 24)$

$x = \boxed{}$

13. Laurie earns $7.50 per hour at the fruit stand plus an extra $2.00 per hour on Sundays. One week in August, she worked on Sunday, Monday, and Wednesday. She worked the same number of hours on Monday and on Wednesday. On Sunday she worked 4 hours. If she earned a total of $83.00 for the week, how many hours did Laurie work on Monday? Write and solve an equation.

_____

14. Which equation has the solution $x = 8$?

- Ⓐ $x + 2x - 4 = \frac{1}{4}(3x + 4)$
- Ⓑ $x + \frac{1}{2}(x + 8) = 4(1 + 3)$
- Ⓒ $2(x - 4) = \frac{1}{4}(1 + 3) + x$
- Ⓓ $x + 4(1 + 3) = \frac{1}{2}(2x + 4)$

15. Each year Rolando saves 8% of his income. This year he saved $3,000 and his salary was $2,000 less than in the previous year. What was his salary in the previous year? Write and solve an equation.

_____

Spiral Review

16. The perimeter of a square is given by the expression $28x + 12$. Use the Distributive Property to factor the expression. What does your answer show?

_____

_____

17. A bowling ball travels 60 feet at an average speed of $26\frac{2}{5}$ feet per second from a bowler's hand to the first pin it strikes. For how many seconds does the bowling ball travel? Explain how you know your answer is reasonable.

_____

_____

Examine Special Cases

I Can recognize and solve linear equations that have no solution, one solution, or infinitely many solutions.

Spark Your Learning

Leah and Mai are taking a card-making class. The teacher has 4 packs of blank cards and an additional 8 cards. Leah buys 4 packs of cards that each come with an additional 3 free cards in the pack. Mai buys 4 packs of cards that each come with an additional 2 free cards in the pack.

How many cards would need to be in each pack of cards so that the teacher has the same number of cards as Leah? as Mai?

Leah and Teacher	Mai and Teacher
$4(x + 3) = 4x + 8$	$4(x + 2) = 4x + 8$

What do you notice when you solve each equation? What do you think this means?

Turn and Talk What do you think it means when an equation simplifies to a false statement? Why?

Module 6 • Lesson 4 209

Build Understanding

You know that to solve an equation means to find the values for the variable that make a true statement. Sometimes an equation may have **no solution** or may have **infinitely many solutions**.

Just like a detective, you can gather clues to help you discover what will happen in each equation. Then you can record your clues in a table.

Solution	Meaning	Number of solutions
$x = a$	Only one value of x makes the equation true.	1

1 Solve the equation $2\left(\frac{x}{8} + 3\right) = 7 + \frac{1}{4}x$.

A. What do you notice about the final equation?

_____

B. Substitute several different values for x into the original equation. Simplify. Explain what happens.

_____

_____

C. How many solutions does the equation have? Use what you have discovered to fill in the table.

Solution	Meaning	Number of solutions
$a = b$, where $a \neq b$		

Turn and Talk How can you write an equation with a variable x that uses addition on both sides of the equation and is never true?

Step It Out

2. Solve the equation $x + 8 = 2(0.5x + 4)$.

$x + 8 = 2(0.5x + 4)$

$x + 8 = \boxed{} + \boxed{}$

$x + 8 - x = \boxed{} + \boxed{} - x$

$8 = \boxed{}$

A. Substitute several different values for x into the original equation. Simplify. Explain what happens.

_____
_____
_____

B. How many solutions does the equation have? Use what you have discovered to fill in the table.

Solution	Meaning	Number of solutions
$a = a$ or $x = x$		

 **Turn and Talk** What do you notice about equations that have no solution and equations that have infinitely many solutions? How are they alike or different?

Check Understanding

1. Brynne simplifies an equation and gets $2 = 3$. What does this tell you about the equation?

_____
_____

2. Simplify the equation and tell whether the equation has one solution, no solution, or infinitely many solutions.

   $9(x + 5) = 20 + 9x + 25$

_____
_____

Module 6 • Lesson 4

On Your Own

3. Lilly starts hiking along a trail at 3 miles per hour. Dave starts hiking the same trail from the same starting point at 3.5 miles per hour. If Lilly walked 2 miles before Dave started hiking, will he catch up to her? Write an equation to represent the situation and determine how many solutions the equation has.

_____

4. Maria pays a yearly fee of $3 to her swimming club and $2 per lesson. Carmen pays a yearly fee of $5 and $2 per lesson. After how many lessons will Maria and Carmen have paid the same amount? Write an equation and explain your answer.

_____
_____
_____

5. **(MP) Construct Arguments** Alex says that $3.2x - 5 = 3.2(x - 5)$ has infinitely many solutions. Is Alex correct? Explain why or why not.

_____
_____

6. **Open Ended** Write an equation that has infinitely many solutions. Prove that your equation is correct.

_____

For Problems 7–8, solve each equation. Tell whether each equation has one solution, no solution, or infinitely many solutions. If there is only one solution, find it.

7. $\frac{1}{2}x + 3 - \frac{1}{4}x = 3 + \frac{1}{4}x$

_____

8. $5.4x + 12 = 2(2.7x - 9)$

_____

I'm in a Learning Mindset!

What strategy did I use to overcome barriers to writing an equation that has infinitely many solutions?

_____
_____

Name _____

Examine Special Cases

LESSON 6.4
More Practice/ Homework

ONLINE Video Tutorials and Interactive Examples

1. Denis orders a large pizza for $16.50 plus $2 for each topping. Sheng orders a medium pizza for $13.25 plus $2 for each topping. Can they both pay the same total amount if they get the same number of toppings? Write an equation and explain.

   _____
   _____
   _____

2. **Health and Fitness** Shara scored 34 points in the basketball game last night. She scored six 3-point baskets, and the rest were 2-point baskets. Write an equation to determine how many 2-point baskets Shara scored. Determine how many solutions the equation has.

   _____
   _____

3. (MP) **Construct Arguments** Blake says that $4(x - 1) = 12 - 4x$ has zero solutions. Is Blake correct? Explain why or why not.

   _____

Complete each equation so that it has one solution.

4. $-2(z + 3) - z =$ _____ $- 4(z + 2)$

5. $\frac{1}{4}x - 4(2) = -\frac{1}{2}\left(\frac{1}{2}x +$ _____ $\right)$

Complete each equation so that it has infinitely many solutions.

6. $\frac{3}{4} + x = 2x - x +$ _____

7. $2h - 3(3 - h) +$ _____ $= 5h - 8$

Complete each equation so that it has no solution.

8. $6x + 5 = 3 +$ _____

9. $-k +$ _____ $(k + 1) = 2k$

For Problems 10–12, determine whether each equation has one solution, no solution, or infinitely many solutions. If there is only one solution, find it.

10. **Math on the Spot**

    A. $x + 8x + 4 = 9x + 4$

    B. $4(y + 5) = y - 10 + 3y$

11. $3.2(x - 1) = 2.2x + 1$

12. $3m - 2 = 25 - 6m$

Module 6 • Lesson 4

Test Prep

13. What missing value would make the equation have infinitely many solutions?

$2(3 + 4x) = 8x + \square$

- Ⓐ 1.5
- Ⓑ 3
- Ⓒ 6
- Ⓓ 6x

14. How many solutions does the following equation have? If there is only one solution, find it.

$3 + \frac{4}{5}x = \frac{9}{10}x$

_____

15. Complete the equation so that it has no solution.

$10.5x - 4 = 5 + \square$

16. Complete the equation so that it has the solution $c = 4$.

$5\left(2c - \square\right) = 2(c + 11)$

17. How many solutions does the following equation have? If there is only one solution, find it.

$2x + 8 = 2(x + 3)$

- Ⓐ one solution; $x = -5$
- Ⓑ one solution; $x = 5$
- Ⓒ no solution
- Ⓓ infinitely many solutions

Spiral Review

18. A parking garage charges the rates shown. Write an equation that can be used to find the number of hours h a car parked if the total bill was $47.50.

First hour	$12.50
Each hour after the first hour	$8.75 per hour

_____

19. The height of a giraffe when it was born was 1.5 meters. By the giraffe's first birthday, its height had increased by 80%. The giraffe's height on its second birthday was 40% greater than a year before.

A. What was the giraffe's height on its first birthday? Show your work.

_____

B. What was the giraffe's height on its second birthday? Show your work.

_____

Apply and Practice
Lesson 5

Name _____

Apply Linear Equations

I Can solve equations and interpret solutions in context.

Step It Out

1. A student service club is raising money through a "Loose Change" competition among the grades. Jenaya brings in 20 coins, all of which are nickels and dimes, that have a total value of $1.30 to put in her grade's bucket.

The equation $5(20 - d) + 10d = 130$ can be solved to determine the number of dimes in Jenaya's donation. How many dimes did Jenaya place in the bucket?

A. Apply the Distributive Property to the left side of the equation.

☐ − ☐ + $10d = 130$

B. Combine like terms.

☐ + ☐ = 130

C. Solve the equation for d.

100 ☐ + $5d = 130$ ☐

☐ = ☐

$\dfrac{☐}{☐} = \dfrac{☐}{☐}$

$d =$ ☐

D. How many dimes does Jenaya place in the bucket? Write a sentence.

_____

E. What if Jenaya brought 10 nickels and some dimes with a total value of $1.30? How many dimes does Jenaya place in the bucket? Explain.

_____

Turn and Talk Which variable or expression represents the number of dimes? Which variable or expression represents the number of nickels? Explain your reasoning.

Module 6 • Lesson 5

You previously learned that a right angle measures 90°. In this lesson, you will also work with pairs of angles called complementary angles and supplementary angles.

2 Use the diagram for Parts A–D.

Connect to Vocabulary

Two angles whose measures have a sum of 90° are called **complementary angles**.
Two angles whose measures have a sum of 180° are called **supplementary angles**.

A. Name a pair of complementary angles.

∠ _____ and ∠ _____

B. Name a pair of supplementary angles.

∠ _____ and ∠ _____

C. If the measure of ∠CBD is equal to $(5x)°$ and the measure of ∠DBE is 40°, write an equation involving x. Then solve it.

☐ + ☐ = ☐

$x =$ ☐

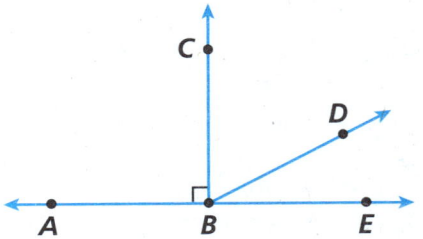

D. What is the measure of ∠CBD? _____

3 Use the figure for Parts A–E.

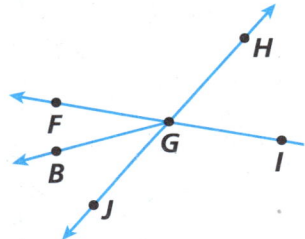

Connect to Vocabulary

Vertical angles are opposite congruent angles formed by intersecting lines.

A. Name two pairs of vertical angles.

∠ _____ and ∠ _____

∠ _____ and ∠ _____

B. Vertical angles $\boxed{\text{are / are not}}$ congruent.

C. Given ∠FGH measures $(6x - 24)°$ and ∠JGI measures 96°, write an equation that can be used to determine the value of x. Solve for x.

☐ = ☐ and $x =$ ☐

D. Name a pair of adjacent angles.

∠ _____ and ∠ _____

E. Given m∠FGJ = 84°, m∠FGB = $(4x)°$, and m∠JGB = $(5x + 3)°$, write an equation that can be used to determine the value of x. Solve for x.

☐ + ☐ = ☐ and $x =$ ☐

Connect to Vocabulary

Adjacent angles are two angles in the same plane with a common vertex and a common side, but no common interior points.

Name _____

4 ▶ Pam and Rachel buy books at the bookstore where Rachel works. Each uses a coupon. After her coupon is applied, Rachel pays only 75% of the resulting price. How many books could each purchase and spend the same amount for the same number of books?

Pam: I bought books for $4.00 each and used a $5.00 off coupon.

A. Complete the equation to represent Rachel and Pam buying *x* books each and paying the same amount.

☐ = 0.75 (☐)

B. Solve the equation.

x = ☐

C. Is it possible for Pam and Rachel to purchase *x* books and pay the same amount? Explain.

_____
_____

Rachel: I bought books where I work for $8.00 each and used a $4.00 off coupon.

D. What does the solution to the equation tell you about the situation?

_____
_____

Turn and Talk How would the solution be different if Rachel did not have a coupon?

Check Understanding

1. The equation $x + (75.3 - x) = 75.3$ represents the sum of the measures of two angles. How many possible combinations of angle measures satisfy the equation?

_____

2. Two bicyclists on a 75-mile trail ride toward each other. One begins at the 45-mile marker. The other begins at the end of the trail. The expressions shown represent each cyclist's distance from the parking lot.

   A. Write an equation to represent the bicyclists' meeting after *x* hours.

   _____

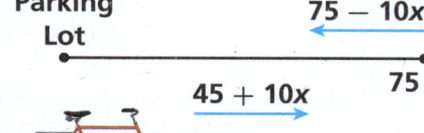

Parking Lot

$75 - 10x$ ←

$45 + 10x$ →

75 mi

   B. After how many hours do the bicyclists meet?

   _____

   C. How far away are the bicyclists from the parking lot when they meet?

   _____

Module 6 • Lesson 5   217

On Your Own

3. James rides down an elevator that starts at a height of 120 feet. Brianne runs up the stairs from the ground floor.

   Use the equation $120 - 2.5t = 1.5t$ to represent when James and Brianne are at the same height after t seconds.

   A. Solve the equation.

   B. What does the solution represent about James and Brianne's locations?

   C. What is their height above the ground floor when they are at the same height at the same time? Explain.

4. The expression $100 - 2.5x$ represents the balance of Grace's account after x days. The expression $100 + 2.5(5 - x)$ represents the balance of Tim's account after x days. After how many days do the accounts have the same balance?

5. Josh is 3 years older than Lynette. The sum of their ages is 49. Write expressions for Josh's age and Lynette's age, and use the expressions to write an equation relating their ages. Use the equation to determine Josh's age and Lynette's age.

6. $\angle A$ is complementary to $\angle B$. The measure of $\angle A$ is $(8x + 12)°$. The measure of $\angle B$ is half the measure of $\angle A$. Write an equation that can be used to determine the value of x. Then solve for x.

7. **Open Ended** A business *breaks even* when its production costs are equal to its revenue. The expression $120 + 4x$ represents the cost of producing x items. Decide on a selling price for each item, and write an expression for the revenue generated by selling x items. How many items would you need to sell at your chosen price to break even? Write an equation and solve it.

8. **STEM** A scientist conducts an experiment with two trees over many years. To the shorter tree, he applies a fertilizer, and to the taller tree, he does not. The shorter tree grows at an average rate of 8 inches per year. The taller tree grows at an average rate of 6 inches per year.

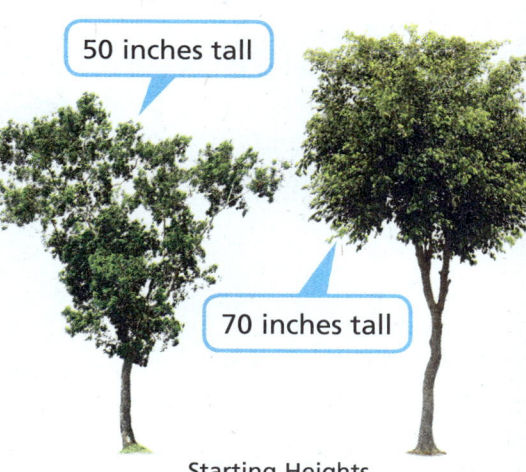

Starting Heights

A. Complete the equation to represent the trees having the same height after t years:

$50 + 8t = $ ☐

B. After how many years will the heights of the two trees be equal?
_____

C. What will the height of the trees be when they are the same height?
_____

For Problems 9 and 10, consider an angle with a measure of $(2x + 11)°$.

9. What is the measure of an angle that is vertical to the given angle?
_____

10. Write an expression to represent the measure of an angle supplementary to the given angle.
_____

11. **Critique Reasoning** Ethan said $5x - 20 = 5(x - 20)$ has infinitely many solutions. Is he correct? Explain.
_____
_____
_____
_____

12. Abigail wants to find three consecutive even integers whose sum is four times the smallest of those integers. She lets n represent the smallest integer, then writes this equation: $n + (n + 2) + (n + 4) = 4n$.

A. Solve the equation.
_____

B. What are the three integers?
_____

13. Every year Aiden uses income from his job to pay for 75% of his college tuition. Next year's tuition will be $720 more than this year's, and Aiden will pay $2400. How much is this year's tuition?
_____

Module 6 • Lesson 5   219

14. **Model with Mathematics** For Pool A, the water level is dropping 0.5 inch per minute. For Pool B, the water level increases 0.5 inch per minute. Starting water levels are shown. When will the pools have the same water level? Write an equation and solve.

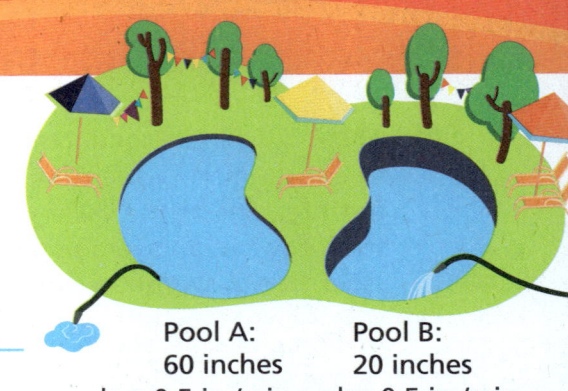

Pool A: 60 inches less 0.5 in./min

Pool B: 20 inches plus 0.5 in./min

_____

_____

15. The diagram shows a right angle. What does x equal? What are the angle measures?

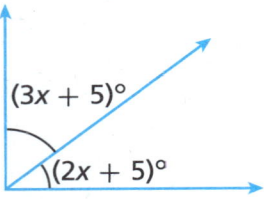

_____

16. Determine whether each equation has one solution, no solution, or infinitely many solutions.

	No solution	One solution	Infinitely many solutions
$4x + 17 = 4(x + 9) - 12$	☐	☐	☐
$3.5 + 7.2x + 3.2x = x$	☐	☐	☐
$9x - 7x + 3x - 16 = 2x + 22 - x$	☐	☐	☐
$\frac{1}{2}x - x + 7 = \frac{1}{2}(14 - x)$	☐	☐	☐

17. **STEM** A rocket blasts off at a 90° angle from Earth. A second rocket launches at a different angle as shown in the diagram.

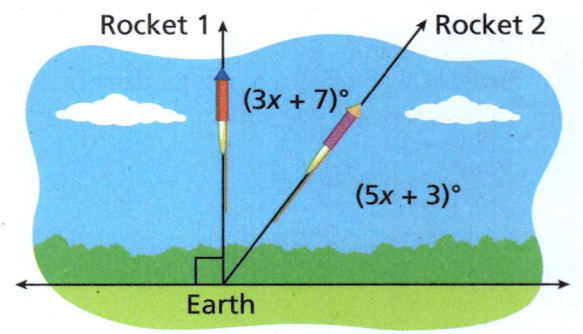

A. Write an equation that can be used to determine the value of x.

_____

B. What is the value of x?

_____

C. What is the measure of the angle of the second rocket launch in relation to Earth?

_____

220

Name _____

LESSON 6.5
More Practice/ Homework

Apply Linear Equations

1. The expression 0.9(2x + 5) represents how much Stacy pays for x games of bowling at Lively Lanes. The expression 4.50 + 1.80x represents how much Parker pays for x games of bowling at Bowling and More. For how many games of bowling would they pay the same amount?

   _____

2. **(MP) Reason** Janesa has 24 coins in her pocket worth exactly $1.00. She tells her younger brother Jackson that he can have the coins if he correctly guesses how many of each coin she has. She gives him the hint that there are only nickels and pennies.

   A. Complete the equation that represents the total value of the nickels and p pennies:

   $5() + p = 100$

   B. How many pennies does Janesa have in her pocket? _____

   C. What is the total value of the pennies? _____

   D. What is the total value of the nickels? _____

   E. What should Jackson guess to get his sister's coins?

   _____

3. **Math on the Spot** Flex Gym charges a membership fee of $150.00 plus $40.50 per month to join the gym. A rival gym, Able Gym, charges a membership fee of $120.00 plus $46.75 per month. Find the number of months for which you would pay the same total fee to both gyms.

   _____

4. **(MP) Attend to Precision** Ms. Baumgartner draws a pair of supplementary angles and tells the class that the angle measures are $(4x + 30)°$ and $(2x + 6)°$.

   A. Write an equation to determine the value of x. Solve for x.

   _____

   B. What does the larger angle measure? What does the smaller angle measure?

   _____

Module 6 • Lesson 5   221

Test Prep

5. Consider adjacent angles that measure $(2x + 45)°$ and $(3x + 55)°$. The sum of the measures of these two angles is 135°.

  A. Write and solve an equation to find the value of x.

  _____

  B. Using the value of x, what is the angle measure represented by the expression $(2x + 45)°$? _____

Use the information to answer Problems 6–7.

Riley is comparing cell phone plans. The table shows four options Riley is considering. The gigabytes of data used each month is represented by g.

Plan	Monthly fee	Charge per gigabyte of data	Total monthly cost ($)
1	$60	$5	$60 + 5g$
2	$40	$10	$40 + 10g$
3	$80	$0	80
4	$50	$5	$50 + 5g$

6. Which two plans will never cost the same amount for any amount of data?

  Ⓐ Plans 1 and 3   Ⓒ Plans 3 and 2
  Ⓑ Plans 2 and 4   Ⓓ Plans 4 and 1

7. Which plan should Riley get if he only uses 3 gigabytes of data each month?

  Ⓐ Plan 1   Ⓒ Plan 3
  Ⓑ Plan 2   Ⓓ Plan 4

Spiral Review

8. How many solutions does the equation $9 + 4(3 + 7n) = 3(8n + 7) + 4n$ have?

  _____

9. A kerosene lamp burns $\frac{1}{10}$ ounce of oil every 12 minutes. At this rate, how many ounces of oil does the lamp burn per hour?

  _____

10. The water in a rain barrel weighs 187.48 kilograms. The weight decreases by 22.69 kilograms as some of the water evaporates. Then it increases by 4.62 kilograms as the result of a storm. How much does the water weigh now?

  _____

Module 6 Review

Vocabulary

Choose the correct term from the Vocabulary box.

> **Vocabulary**
> adjacent angles
> complementary angles
> supplementary angles
> vertical angles

1. a pair of angles with measures that add to 90° _____

2. a pair of angles with measures that add to 180° _____

3. a pair of opposite angles formed by two intersecting lines _____

4. a pair of angles that share a vertex and a ray but have no interior points in common _____

5. Underline the like terms in the equation in the box. $-2x + 4 = 15x$

6. Which equation demonstrates the Distributive Property?
   - Ⓐ $3(n - 2) = 3n - 6$
   - Ⓑ $8(n + 7) = 8(7 + n)$
   - Ⓒ $(n + 4) + 10 = n + 14$
   - Ⓓ $12 + 3(n - 4) = 3(n - 4) + 12$

Concepts and Skills

7. **MP Use Tools** The box shows how Andrew attempted to solve the equation $\frac{1}{3}(n + 6) = -10$. His work contains at least one error. Which statements about Andrew's work are true?

   List the step(s) with an error and find the correct solution. State what strategy and tool you will use to answer the question, explain your choice, and then find the answer.

   > $\frac{1}{3}(n + 6) = -10$
   > Step 1: $\frac{1}{3}n + \frac{1}{3}(6) = -10$
   > Step 2: $\frac{1}{3}n + 2 = -10$
   > Step 3: $\frac{1}{3}n = -12$
   > Step 4: $n = -4$

   _____
   _____

Solve each equation.

8. $-\frac{1}{2}d + \frac{5}{8} = \frac{3}{8}d - \frac{11}{16}$

   $d =$ _____

9. $0.4(p - 5) = 0.6p + 2$

   $p =$ _____

10. Select whether each equation has no solution, one solution, or infinitely many solutions.

	No solution	One solution	Infinitely many solutions
$2.5(n + 4) = n + 1.5n - 7$	☐	☐	☐
$2.5(n + 4) = 2n + 0.5n + 10$	☐	☐	☐
$2.5(n + 4) = 2.5n + 0.5n$	☐	☐	☐

Determine the measure in degrees of the angle indicated with an arc.

11.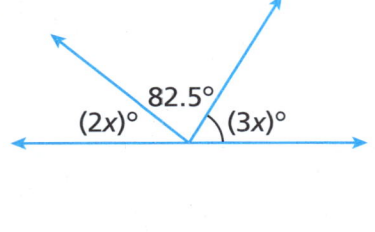

_____

12.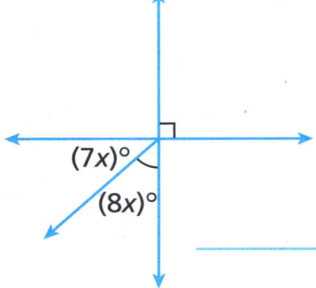

_____

13. Use numbers from the box to complete the equation so that it has no solution.

> 2.5   3   5.5   9   12   15

$3x + 2.5 = 12x - \boxed{}x + \boxed{}$

14. A rancher uses 280 feet of fencing to build a rectangular corral for a horse. The length of the corral is 2.5 times the width. What is the area of the corral?

Ⓐ 112 square feet
Ⓑ 700 square feet
Ⓒ 4,000 square feet
Ⓓ 16,000 square feet

15. Two hikers walk on a trail in the direction of increasing mile marker numbers. Mandy starts at mile marker 1 and hikes at a rate of 2.5 miles per hour. At the same time, Rita starts at mile marker 2 and hikes at a rate of 3 miles per hour. The equation $2.5h + 1 = 3h + 2$ represents the number of hours h it will take Mandy to catch up with Rita.

A. What is the solution of the equation?

$h =$ _____

B. What does the solution of the equation indicate in this situation?

_____

_____

_____

Module 7

Solve Problems Using Inequalities

The Suspect is Over There!

I believe the suspect is greater than or equal to four-fifths.

In your work with the Math Detective Agency, you have been asked to locate an integer suspect using witness reports given as inequalities. For example, the report $x \geq \frac{4}{5}$ means that the witness believes the suspect is greater than or equal to four-fifths.

Summarize each report by graphing the inequality on the number line.

A. $x \geq \frac{4}{5}$

B. $y < 6$

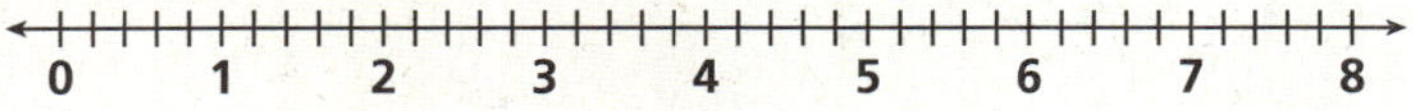

C. $n \leq 2.8$

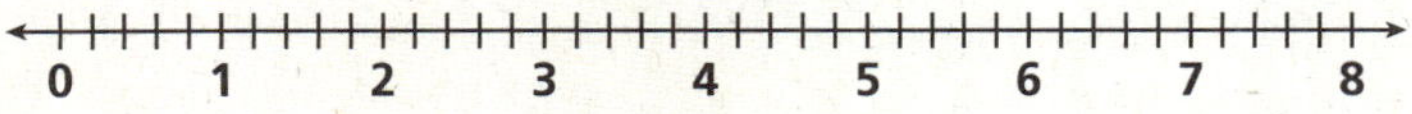

D. $p > \frac{8}{5}$

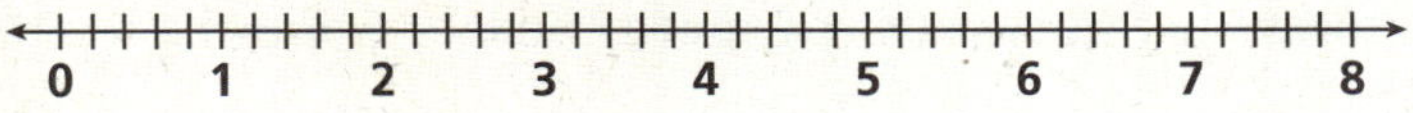

🗨️ **Turn and Talk**

If all the witness reports are correct, do you have enough information to determine which integer is the suspect? Explain.

Are You Ready?

Complete these problems to review prior concepts and skills you will need for this module.

Compare Rational Numbers

Compare. Write < or >.

1. -7 ☐ -3
2. 0 ☐ -1
3. $\frac{1}{3}$ ☐ $-\frac{3}{4}$
4. -2.10 ☐ -2.19
5. $-7\frac{2}{5}$ ☐ $5\frac{1}{2}$
6. $-\frac{2}{5}$ ☐ -0.35

Interpret, Write, and Graph Inequalities

For each inequality, circle the values in the box that can be substituted for the variable to make the inequality true.

7. $x + 2.4 < 8.6$

   | 0 | 2.4 | 5.7 | 8.5 | 9.1 |

8. $\frac{1}{3}n > \frac{2}{5}$

   | $\frac{3}{4}$ | 1 | $\frac{6}{5}$ | $\frac{4}{3}$ | 2 |

Write an inequality to represent each situation.

9. The temperature t in a freezer must be at most -10 °F.

   _____

10. A person's weight w must be more than 110 pounds for the person to donate blood to a blood bank.

    _____

Graph each inequality.

11. $x < 16$

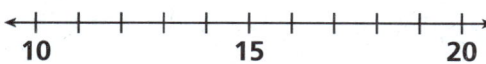

12. $n > 5.2$

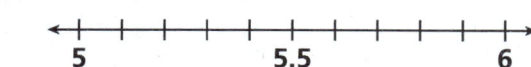

Lesson 1

Understand and Apply Properties to Solve One-Step Inequalities

I Can write and solve one-step inequalities.

Spark Your Learning

Suppose the lowest elevation to which the submarine shown has been tested is −490 meters. If it is currently at an elevation of −125 meters, how many meters more can it dive without going below the lowest elevation tested?

Elevation = −125 m

Turn and Talk Can the submarine dive 200 meters more without going below the lowest elevation tested? 400 meters more? How do you know?

Module 7 • Lesson 1 — 227

Build Understanding

Recall that an equation is a mathematical sentence showing that two quantities are equal, or equivalent. Likewise, an **inequality** is a mathematical sentence showing that two quantities are not equivalent. The meanings of the inequality symbols are shown in the table.

> **Connect to Vocabulary**
>
> The **solution of an inequality** is a value or values that makes an inequality true.

Greater than	>	Greater than or equal to	≥
Less than	<	Less than or equal to	≤

The **number line** shows $x \leq 365$. Note the closed circle represents "or equal to" in the inequality to indicate the inclusion of 365.

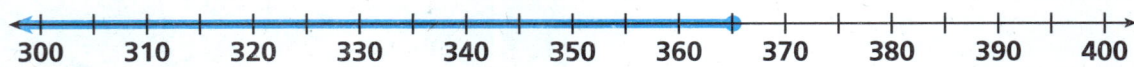

1. A submarine is at sea level, and it descends with a **rate of change** of -10 feet per second.

   A. Write an inequality to represent the time t it takes the submarine to reach an elevation of -140 feet or deeper from sea level.

   _____

   B. Write three values for t that will make the inequality from Part A true. Substitute each value in the inequality to check. Then describe the set of numbers that can make the inequality true.

   _____

   _____

   C. Solve the inequality from Part A by writing a simple inequality that describes all of the numbers that will make the inequality true. Write an inequality symbol in the first box and a number in the second box.

   D. Graph the inequality from Part C. Can the submarine reach an elevation of -140 feet or deeper in less than 14 seconds? Explain.

   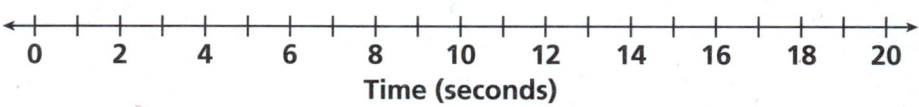
   Time (seconds)

   _____

   E. How are solving $-10t = -140$ and $-10t \leq -140$ alike? How are they different?

   _____

   _____

Name _____

Step It Out

2 During the spring rains, the water level in a lake rises. Although the lake has a dam, when the water reaches the top of the dam, water will begin flowing over the top of the dam.

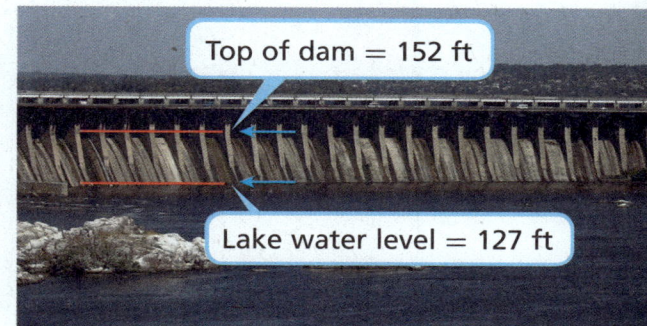
Top of dam = 152 ft
Lake water level = 127 ft

A. Write an inequality that expresses how much more the lake can rise r so that the water does not flow over the top of the dam.

_____

B. Write three values for r that will make the inequality from Part A true. Then write and graph a simple inequality that describes all of the numbers that will make the inequality true.

_____

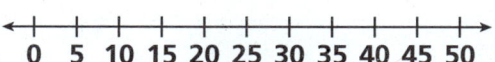
0 5 10 15 20 25 30 35 40 45 50

> **Turn and Talk** How are solving $127 + r \leq 152$ and solving $127 + r = 152$ alike, and how are they different?

3 The properties of equality you used when solving equations hold true for inequalities, with one exception. When you multiply or divide by a negative number, you must reverse the inequality symbol. Apply properties of inequalities to solve each inequality.

A.
$$m - 0.3 > 1.45$$
$$\underline{+ \boxed{} \qquad + \boxed{}}$$
$$m > \boxed{}$$

B.
$$3.5n \leq 7$$
$$\frac{3.5n}{\boxed{}} \leq \frac{7}{\boxed{}}$$
$$n \leq \boxed{}$$

C.
$$-2 \geq b + \frac{1}{8}$$
$$\underline{- \boxed{} \qquad - \boxed{}}$$
$$\boxed{} \geq b$$
$$b \leq \boxed{}$$

D.
$$-\frac{1}{2}y < 6$$
$$\boxed{} \cdot -\frac{1}{2}y > \boxed{} \cdot 6$$
$$y > \boxed{}$$

E.
$$-x < -4$$
$$\boxed{} \cdot -x > \boxed{} \cdot -4$$
$$x > \boxed{}$$

F.
$$\frac{-2a}{3} > 6$$
$$-\frac{2}{3}a > \boxed{}$$
$$\boxed{} \cdot -\frac{2}{3}a < \boxed{} \cdot \boxed{}$$
$$a < \boxed{}$$

Module 7 • Lesson 1

4 ▶ Leila is designing a rectangular table. What is the range of values for *x* if the area of the table shown is to be 12 square feet or less?

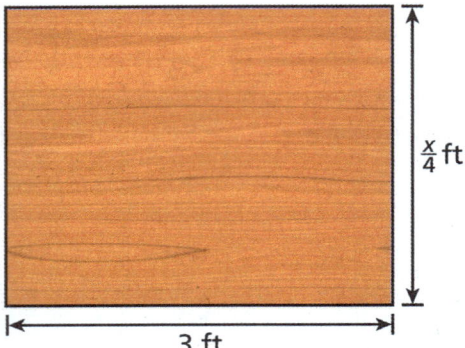

A. What is the inequality using the formula for the area of a rectangle?

_____

B. Solve the inequality for *x*.

_____

C. Give the range of values for *x* that are reasonable in the context of this problem and justify your answer. Graph the solution.

_____

_____

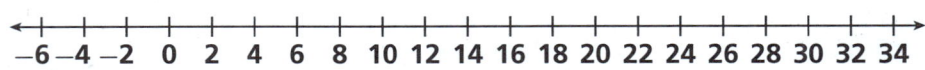

Turn and Talk What is the longest the unknown side of the table can be? Explain.

Check Understanding

1. The veterinarian told Hector that his 8-inch puppy would get no taller than 24 inches. Write and solve an inequality to find how much more his puppy, shown here, may grow.

_____

_____

For Problems 2–3, solve the inequality. Graph the solution.

2. $\frac{-2x}{3} \leq 2$

_____

3. $x - 2 > -6$

_____

230

On Your Own

For Problems 4–5, use the given information.

Mr. Berg is designing a room addition to his home and wants a rectangular window with area that is more than 12 square feet but not more than 24 square feet. Mr. Berg knows he wants the window to be 4 feet wide.

4. **(MP) Model with Mathematics** Write and solve an inequality to find the length x that will guarantee that the window is not too small. Explain.

   _____
   _____
   _____

5. **(MP) Model with Mathematics** Write and solve an inequality to find the length x that will guarantee that the window is not too large. Explain.

   _____
   _____
   _____

6. **(MP) Use Structure** Emir is solving the inequality $-\frac{2}{3}x < 18$. What steps should he follow to find the solution?

   _____
   _____

For Problems 7–10, solve the inequality. Graph the solution.

7. $10 \leq x + 7$ _____

   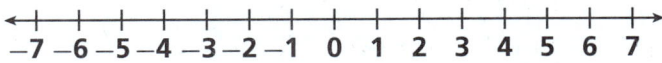

8. $-x \geq -5$ _____

   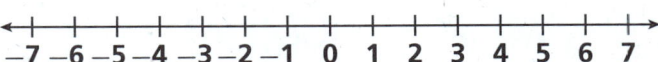

9. $\frac{3x}{5} > -6$ _____

   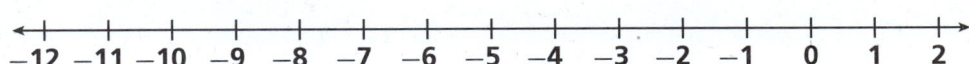

10. $2 < -\frac{x}{3}$ _____

    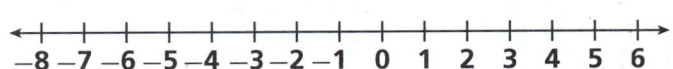

For Problems 11–13, use the given information.

Three friends are shopping at the garage sale shown.

11. **(MP) Attend to Precision** Ming has $24. Write and solve an inequality for the number of shorts she can buy. Interpret the solution in the context of the problem.

_____

Garage Sale
Pants $8
Shirts $6
Shorts $4
Belts $3

12. **(MP) Attend to Precision** Camille can buy up to 5 shirts. How much money could she have?

_____

13. **(MP) Construct Arguments** Juanita has $24. Can she buy 5 shirts? Explain your answer.

_____

14. **(MP) Model with Mathematics** Rudo has a target of at least $150 in pledges for a walkathon. He currently has $65 in pledges. Write and solve an inequality for the amount p Rudo has left to raise.

_____

For Problems 15–17, solve the inequality. Graph the solution.

15. $x - 2.5 > 8.7$ _____

⟵|+++++++++++++++++++++++++++⟶
  6   7   8   9   10 11 12

16. $1.8x \leq 13.5$ _____

⟵|+++++++++++++++++++++++++++⟶
  4   5   6   7   8   9   10

17. $x + 1\frac{3}{5} < -2$ _____

⟵|+++++++++++++++++++++++++++⟶
 −5 −4 −3 −2 −1   0   1

I'm in a Learning Mindset!

What part of solving one-step inequalities elicits a fixed-mindset voice in my head?

_____

_____

Understand and Apply Properties to Solve One-Step Inequalities

LESSON 7.1 More Practice/ Homework

1. **MP Model with Mathematics** Cara is designing the rectangular patio shown. She wants the area of the patio to be larger than 72 square feet but no greater than 156 square feet.

   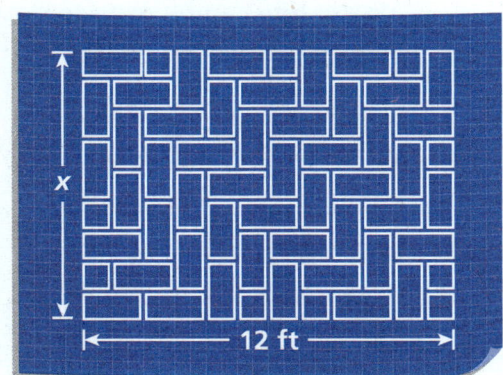

   A. Write and solve an inequality representing a length that meets the requirement for the minimum area.

   _____

   B. Write and solve an inequality representing a length that meets the requirement for the maximum area.

   _____

   C. Describe the possible lengths for the unknown side.

   _____

2. **Math on the Spot** Solve the inequality. Graph the solution.

   A. $-4x < 12$ _____

   ← −10 −9 −8 −7 −6 −5 −4 −3 −2 −1 0 1 2 3 4 5 6 7 8 9 10 →

   B. $-1 \geq \dfrac{w}{-4}$ _____

   ← −10 −9 −8 −7 −6 −5 −4 −3 −2 −1 0 1 2 3 4 5 6 7 8 9 10 →

3. **STEM** In the science lab, Will is testing the freezing point of a substance, which should be −24 °C. He is changing the temperature at a rate of −3 °C per minute, starting at 0 °C. Write and solve an inequality for the time t before the temperature reaches the freezing point.

   _____

4. **MP Model with Mathematics** Tania has already saved $25.75. She needs at least $53.88 to buy a set of headphones. Write and solve an inequality that shows how much more she needs to save to buy headphones.

   _____

Module 7 • Lesson 1

Test Prep

5. Chan is in a running club and needs to run at least 500 miles in a year to earn the gold level of achievement. He is presently at 220 miles. Which inequality can be used to determine the additional number of miles he can run and earn gold?

Ⓐ $x + 220 < 500$

Ⓑ $x + 220 \geq 500$

Ⓒ $x + 500 > 220$

Ⓓ $x + 500 \leq 220$

6. Select the number line that represents the solution of the inequality $7 - x \geq 4$.

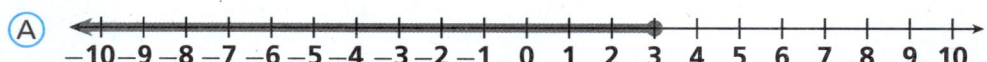

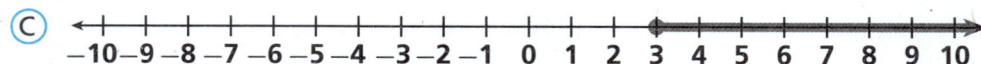

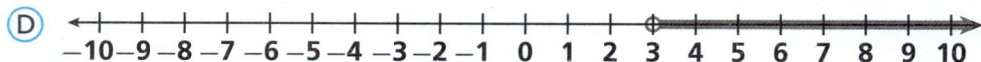

7. Shawna earns $12.75 per hour. How many hours does she need to work to earn $102 or more?

at least / at most / less than / more than _____ hours

Spiral Review

8. Francisco bought 2 theater tickets online. The total charge was $35 with an online booking charge of $5. If x is the price of the ticket, write an equation to solve for the ticket price.

_____

9. Solve for x.

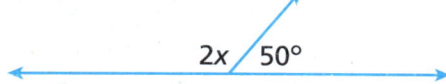

_____

10. The perimeter of the table shown is 16 feet. Write an equation in the form $px + q = r$ to solve for x.

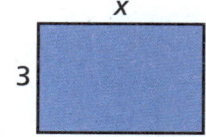

_____

234

Connect Concepts and Skills

Lesson 2

Write Two-Step Inequalities for Situations

I Can write two-step inequalities to solve problems.

Spark Your Learning

A small business owner is planning to upgrade the computer system. A new system will cost $1,200, but the total cost can be more with installation. The owner has saved $300 and will continue to save $30 from profits each day for the new system. How many days will it take the business owner to save enough money to purchase the new computer system?

Select the inequality that represents this situation. Describe what each part of the inequality represents.

$300 + 30x \geq 1,200$ $300 + 30x \leq 1,200$

$300 + 30x < 1,200$ $300 + 30x > 1,200$

Turn and Talk Describe a situation that could be represented by changing the direction of the inequality symbol in the inequality above. Explain.

Module 7 • Lesson 2   **235**

Build Understanding

As you have learned, a one-step inequality involves one operation. For example, $x + 1 > 3$ is a one-step inequality. In this example, 4, 40, and 4,000,000 are all solutions because they make the inequality true when substituted for x, but 1 is not a solution because it does not make the inequality true when substituted for x.

A two-step inequality involves two operations.

1 Caitlyn wants to buy sheets of trumpet music at the price shown. She has only $25, and she first needs to pay back $5 to her friend. How many sheets can Caitlyn buy?

Trumpet Music
$3 per sheet

A. Describe how this problem represents an inequality situation.

_____

_____

B. Describe the part of this situation that is a variable quantity.

_____

C. What are all the costs that Caitlyn's money will cover?

_____

D. Write an expression to represent all the costs that Caitlyn's money will cover.

_____

E. Write an inequality for this situation.

_____

F. State a possible solution for this inequality.

_____

G. State a value for the variable that would NOT be a possible solution for this inequality.

_____

 **Turn and Talk** If Caitlyn wanted more than $4 left over, how would you change the inequality? Explain.

Step It Out

2 Kyle's family is renting a boat at a lake. The rental company initially charges $50 for the boat plus the hourly fee shown. The family plans to spend no more than $250 on the boat rental.

A. What are the values in the problem that cannot change?

_____

_____

B. What value in the problem can vary? How can this be represented?

_____

_____

C. Write an inequality for how many hours the family can rent the boat.

_____

3 An office manager wants to buy headsets that cost $12 each. The budget allows $155, but the manager wants to leave more than $20 for an emergency. How many headsets can the manager buy?

A. Write an inequality for how many headsets the manager can buy while staying within the limits.

_____

B. Explain why the inequality does or does not include *equal to* as part of the inequality symbol.

_____

_____

Check Understanding

1. Gloria is saving for the scooter shown. She has $63 already. She earns $7 each week for doing chores around the house. How many weeks will it take for Gloria to save at least enough money to buy the scooter? Write an inequality to represent the situation. Do not solve the inequality.

_____

2. Suppose Mario either wants to earn *no more than $500* or *more than $500* to afford his phone. How would the inequalities be different based on these two phrases?

_____

Module 7 • Lesson 2

On Your Own

3. **Model with Mathematics** Saleem is saving for a fish tank that costs $140. He has $20 and earns $23 per day at a part-time job. What is an inequality he can write to find the number of days he has to work to have at least $140?

4. **Open Ended** Consider the inequality $3x + 7 \geq 25$. Write a word problem that this inequality could represent.

For Problems 5–6, indicate whether each value of x is a *solution* or is *not a solution* of the inequality $33x + 55 > 17$.

5. $x = -2$

6. $x = 0$

7. **Model with Mathematics** The vet says that George's cat Milo has to lose weight, so George is going to portion out Milo's meals and stop giving Milo table scraps. If Milo loses 0.25 pound every week, write an inequality for how many weeks it will take Milo to drop below 18 pounds.

22 lb

Model with Mathematics For Problems 8–9, write an inequality based on the statement.

8. Twice a number plus four is at most twelve.

9. Three less than a quarter of a number is less than six.

I'm in a Learning Mindset!

Do I recognize any obstacles to understanding two-step inequalities? Can those obstacles be changed? Why or why not?

Name _____

Write Two-Step Inequalities for Situations

**LESSON 7.2
More Practice/
Homework**

ONLINE Video Tutorials and Interactive Examples

1. **Music** Jason has already rapped a 40-word intro to a song and continues to rap 5 words per second. Write an inequality to represent how many more seconds t Jason will rap for the total song including the intro to be at least 500 words.

   _____

2. **(MP) Construct Arguments** A team can spend no more than $300 on shirts. The team has already spent $80. How many shirts for $15 each can the team still buy?

   A. Write an inequality that represents the situation. _____

   B. Explain why you chose the inequality sign.

   _____

   C. Without solving, explain how you know that 20 is not a solution.

   _____
   _____

3. **(MP) Model with Mathematics** Felicia spends $50 on materials to make jewelry, and she plans on selling the pieces for $7 each. A friend donates $5 to get her started. Write an inequality for the number of pieces of jewelry Felicia can sell and make a profit.

   _____

4. **Open Ended** Write a real-world problem that could be represented by $5x + 30 \geq 90$.

   _____
   _____
   _____

5. Write the inequality in words: $2n - 10 > 22$.

   _____

6. **(MP) Model with Mathematics** Rania is playing with her friend Arun, and they are setting up dominoes across the room. Each domino is 2 inches long. They have already placed 10 dominoes end to end. The room is 10 feet long and they want to know how many more dominoes they can set up before they reach all the way across the room. Write an inequality that models this situation.

   _____

Module 7 • Lesson 2   239

Test Prep

7. A small plane can carry a maximum of 1,200 pounds of people and luggage. The people on the plane have a combined weight of 800 pounds. Each bag weighs 75 pounds. Write an inequality for the number of bags b that can be taken on board.

   _____

8. Select an inequality that represents *3 less than 5 times a number is no more than 63*.

   (A) $5n - 3 \geq 63$ (C) $5n - 3 \leq 63$
   (B) $5n \geq 63 - 3$ (D) $5n \leq 63 - 3$

9. Match the words with the inequality.

   $4n - 4 > 10$ •   • 4 times a number is greater than 10.

   $4n + 4 < 10$ •   • 4 less than 4 times a number is greater than 10.

   $4n > 10$ •   • 4 less than 4 times a number is no more than 10.

   $4n - 4 \geq 10$ •   • The sum of 4 and 4 times a number is less than 10.

   $4n + 4 \geq 10$ •   • The sum of 4 and 4 times a number is at least 10.

   $4n - 4 \leq 10$ •   • 4 less than 4 times a number is 10 or more.

10. Olivia's class is having a bake sale, and their goal is to raise at least $500. So far they have raised $210. If the items are all $5 each, which inequality represents how many more items they need to sell to meet their goal?

    (A) $5b + 210 \geq 500$ (C) $b + 500 \geq 210$
    (B) $5b \geq 500 + 210$ (D) $5b + 210 \leq 500$

Spiral Review

11. Max had d dollars and spent $31 but has at least $15 left. Write and solve an inequality to find d.

    _____

12. Write a simplified expression for the perimeter of the polygon shown.

    _____

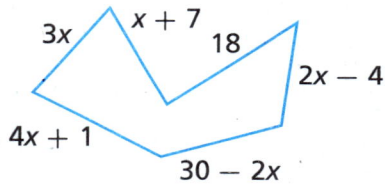

Apply and Practice

Lesson 3

Name _____

Apply Two-Step Inequalities to Solve Problems

I Can write and solve two-step inequalities to solve problems.

Step It Out

1 ▶ A study found that twice the number of deer in Maple Park is at least 20 more than the number of deer in Smith Park. The study found that there are 50 deer in Smith Park.

A. Write an expression to represent the difference between twice the number of deer in Maple Park and the number of deer in Smith Park. Use x for the number of deer in Maple Park.

_____

B. What do you know is true about this difference?

The difference is _____ than or equal to _____.

C. Write and solve an inequality to determine the possible number of deer in Maple Park.

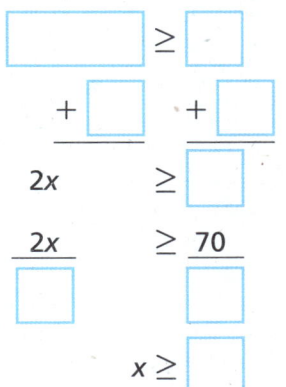

D. Graph the solution of the inequality. Do all the values make sense? Explain.

```
←—+—+—+—+—+—+—+—+—+—+—→
  30 31 32 33 34 35 36 37 38 39 40
```

_____

E. What does the solution of the inequality represent in the problem?

In _____ Park, there are _____ deer.

 **Turn and Talk** Can you write the inequality for this situation differently and still find the same solution? Explain.

Module 7 • Lesson 3   **241**

2 Rosina and Asia collect stamps. The number of stamps Rosina has is 7 more than 3 times the number of stamps Asia has. Rosina has fewer than 85 stamps. How many stamps can Asia have?

A. Write and solve an inequality to find the number of stamps Asia has in her collection.

$$3x + \boxed{} < \boxed{}$$
$$\underline{-\boxed{} \quad -\boxed{}}$$
$$3x \quad < \quad 78$$

$$\frac{3x}{\boxed{}} < \frac{78}{\boxed{}}$$

$$x < \boxed{}$$

B. Graph the solution of the inequality. Which values make sense for the situation? What does the solution of the inequality represent in the problem?

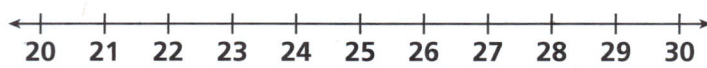

_____

_____

3 Solve and graph the inequality: $-3b - 2 \leq 13$.

$$-3b - 2 \leq 13$$
$$\underline{+\boxed{} \quad +\boxed{}}$$
$$-3b \quad \leq \quad \boxed{}$$

$$\frac{-3b}{\boxed{}} \geq \frac{15}{\boxed{}}$$

$$b \geq \boxed{}$$

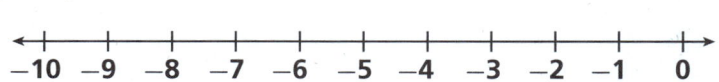

Check Understanding

1. Solve the inequality $-7m + 4 < -45$. Graph the solution.

_____

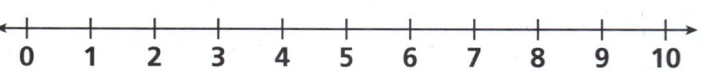

2. The number of students using the cafeteria's healthy lunch line can be found by solving $\frac{1}{2}s - 51 \leq 20$. How many students use this lunch line?

_____

Name _____

On Your Own

3. **MP Attend to Precision** A warehouse has 2,100 tables packaged in boxes. The daily shipment is shown. After how many days will there be fewer than 1,500 tables in the warehouse?

   25 tables shipped daily

   A. Write and solve an inequality for this situation.

   _____

   B. Graph the solution of the inequality.

   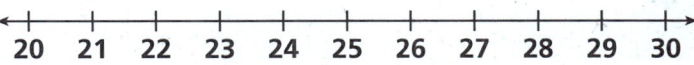

   C. Do all the values make sense? What does the solution of the inequality represent in this context?

   _____
   _____

4. **MP Attend to Precision** Zachary and Dovante deliver packages. Dovante delivers 9 less than 4 times the number of packages Zachary delivers in one day. Dovante delivers no more than 11 packages in one day.

   A. Write and solve an inequality to find the number of packages Zachary delivers each day. Graph the solution of the inequality.

   _____

   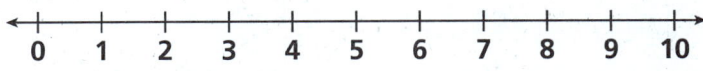

   B. Do all the values make sense? What does the solution of the inequality represent in this context?

   _____

For Problems 5–8, solve the inequality. Graph the solution.

5. $6x - 11 > 67$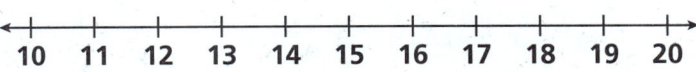

   _____

6. $3w + 1 \geq 19$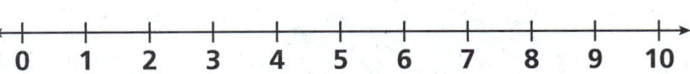

   _____

7. $-13d + 6 \leq 45$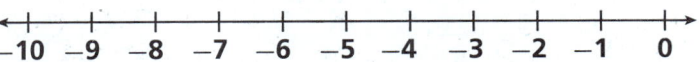

   _____

8. $-8n - 4 < -60$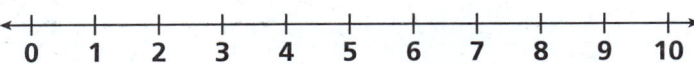

   _____

9. Felipe is distributing discount coupons for a concert. He starts with 25 coupons. He gives 2 coupons to each person he sees. He will leave to get more coupons after he has fewer than 4 coupons left. How many people will Felipe give coupons to before he leaves to get more?

   A. **Model with Mathematics** What is an inequality for this situation? What is the solution?

   _____

   B. **Attend to Precision** What does the solution of the inequality mean in this context? Explain.

   _____
   _____

10. Alicia is mixing paint. She has a bucket that contains $5\frac{1}{2}$ pints of paint. She adds $\frac{1}{4}$-pint containers of paint to the bucket until she has at most $8\frac{3}{4}$ pints of paint in the bucket. How many containers of paint can she add to the bucket?

   _____

11. **Open Ended** Write a two-step inequality whose solution is represented by the number line.

   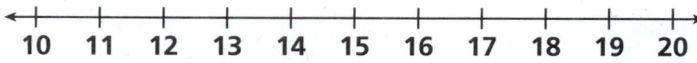

For Problems 12–17, solve the inequality. Graph the solution.

12. $-5y + 47 > -13$

13. $18 - 4z \geq 26$

14. $8g + 30 < -2$

15. $\frac{2}{3}t - \frac{1}{6} \leq \frac{5}{6}$

16. $-\frac{1}{10}a - \frac{2}{5} > \frac{3}{10}$

17. $2\frac{2}{3}b + 8 \geq 0$

244

Apply Two-Step Inequalities to Solve Problems

LESSON 7.3 More Practice/Homework

Solve the inequality. Graph the solution.

1. $5x + 13 \leq 48$

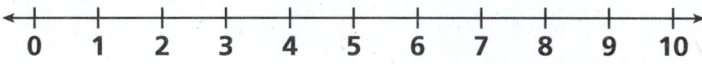

2. $16 - 7v < 2$

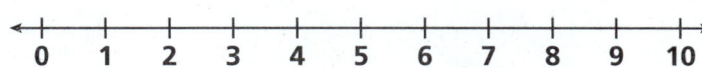

3. $9r - \frac{3}{5} > 3\frac{9}{10}$

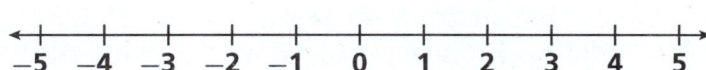

4. $-8c + 13 \geq 47$

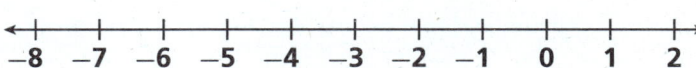

5. **Math on the Spot** Members of the drama club plan to present its annual spring musical. They have $1,262.50 left from fundraising, but they estimate that the entire production will cost $1,600.00. How many tickets at the price shown must they sell to at least break even?

Tickets: $6.75 each

6. **(MP) Model with Mathematics** Jenna has a collection of trading cards. She started her collection with 175 cards. She buys packs of cards that contain 15 cards each. Write and solve an inequality to determine how many packs of cards Jenna buys so that she will have over 400 cards in her collection.

   A. What is an inequality that represents this situation? What is the solution?

   B. How many packs of cards does Jenna buy?

7. **(MP) Model with Mathematics** Drew and Larry are working together on a jigsaw puzzle. Drew places 11 less than 3 times the number of pieces that Larry places. Drew places at least 10 pieces. How many pieces does Larry place?

Module 7 • Lesson 3

Test Prep

8. Dwight and Walt are building model cars. Dwight builds 7 fewer models than 4 times the number Walt builds. Dwight builds at most 9 models. Which inequality could be used to find the number of models Walt builds?

Ⓐ $4m - 7 < 9$

Ⓑ $4m - 7 \leq 9$

Ⓒ $4m - 7 > 9$

Ⓓ $4m - 7 \geq 9$

9. A truck rental company rents a truck for a one-time fee of $25 plus $1.50 per mile traveled. Kelly has $80 she can spend on the rental truck. What is the greatest number of miles that she can travel?

_____

10. Ricardo measured the temperature in the morning. The temperature was −6 °C. The temperature is increasing $1\frac{1}{2}$ °C every hour. After how many hours will the temperature be at least 2 °C? Select the best answer.

Ⓐ more than $2\frac{1}{3}$ hours

Ⓑ $5\frac{1}{3}$ hours or more

Ⓒ less than 4 hours

Ⓓ less than $1\frac{1}{3}$ hours

Spiral Review

11. A football team earns 6 points for a touchdown and 3 points for a field goal. In one game, a team scored a touchdown and some field goals. The total points the team scored is 18 points. Write an equation that can be used to find the number of field goals the team scored.

_____

12. Ben can buy 5 notebooks for $6.75 at Store A or 3 notebooks for $4.50 at Store B. Which store offers the better value?

_____

Module 7 Review

Name _____

Vocabulary

1. Complete the graphic organizer for the vocabulary term *solution of an inequality*.

Definition in your own words	Facts/characteristics
Example	Non-example

(Center: Solution of an Inequality)

Concepts and Skills

2. **Use Tools** Water is pumped out of a 500-gallon tank at a rate of 2.5 gallons per second. The inequality $500 - 2.5t < 100$ can be used to determine the time t, in seconds, after which there will be less than 100 gallons of water remaining in the tank. Solve the inequality, then state what the solution represents. State what strategy and tool you will use to answer the question, explain your choice, and then find the answer.

_____

_____

3. Faith wants to run at least 7 miles this week. She already has run $2\frac{1}{2}$ miles. She plans to run an equal distance on each of the last 3 days of this week. Write and solve an inequality to represent this situation, where d represents the distance in miles that Faith must run on each of the last 3 days to reach her goal. Graph the solution set on the number line.

_____

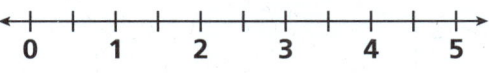

4. An airplane can carry a maximum of 36,600 pounds of cargo, passengers, and luggage. On the plane's next flight, it will carry 7,320 pounds of cargo. If each passenger with luggage weighs 220 pounds, what is the greatest number of passengers the plane can carry on its next flight?

   (A) 44 passengers
   (B) 133 passengers
   (C) 166 passengers
   (D) 199 passengers

5. At midnight, the outdoor temperature is 2 °C. The temperature is expected to drop by 0.5 °C per hour for the rest of the night. Select all inequalities that can be used to determine the number of hours h after midnight at which the temperature will be below 0 °C.

   (A) $0.5h < 2$
   (B) $0.5h > 2$
   (C) $0.5h - 2 < 0$
   (D) $0.5h + 2 < 0$
   (E) $2 - 0.5h < 0$
   (F) $2h - 0.5 < 0$

6. Winnie made headbands to sell at the school craft fair. She spent a total of $22.50 on expenses, and she plans to sell the headbands for $5 each. She wants to earn at least $50 in profit. Write and solve an inequality to represent this situation, where h represents the number of headbands Winnie needs to sell to make a profit of at least $50. Then state what the solution represents.

   _____

   _____

7. Marcus is ordering supplies online for his dog. He plans to order a collar for $6.76 and some bags of treats for $4.80 each. The total for his order must be more than $25 to qualify for free shipping.

   A. Write an inequality that Marcus can use to determine the number of bags of treats t he must order to get free shipping.

   _____

   B. Marcus says that the minimum number of bags of treats he needs to order to get free shipping is 3. Do you agree? Explain your reasoning.

   _____

   _____

   _____

8. Sarah begins the week with $21.55. A school lunch costs $2.75. How many school lunches can she buy and still have at least $10 left at the end of the week? Write and solve an inequality that Sarah can use to determine the number of lunches n that she can buy.

   _____

Unit 4
Transform and Construct Geometric Figures

Puzzle Designer

A puzzle designer combines creativity and imagination with logical reasoning to produce challenging and entertaining puzzles. From three-dimensional puzzles to jigsaw puzzles to mazes to crossword puzzles, puzzle designers have something to intrigue just about everyone.

STEM Task:

Starting with 12 toothpicks arranged as shown each time, perform each task:

- Remove 4 toothpicks to form exactly 1 square.
- Remove 4 toothpicks to form exactly 2 squares.
- Move 3 toothpicks to form exactly 3 squares.

Learning Mindset
Challenge-Seeking Builds Confidence

Have you ever been asked to do something that you didn't know how to do? This happens to everyone at one time or another. Sometimes, people back away from a challenge because they are afraid of making a mistake. But taking on a challenge can be a rewarding growth experience. Here are two suggestions that can help you overcome a challenge when your confidence is fading.

- Build your confidence by trying simpler versions of the task. Think of levels in a video game. Succeeding at simpler levels give you confidence that you can complete the next levels.

- Don't give up. Remember, you are learning and growing through this process. If you got it right on the first try, it wasn't very challenging. A positive attitude will make this and future challenges easier to meet.

Reflect

Q Did you feel confident as you worked on the STEM Task?

Q How does self-confidence affect your ability to successfully complete tasks or meet challenges?

Module 8

Transformations and Congruence

TREASURE Hunt

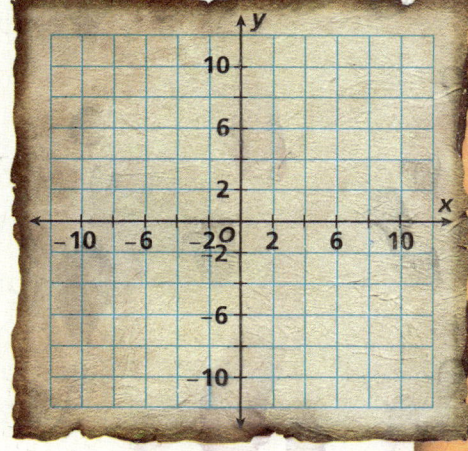

A treasure is on a remote island represented by the coordinate plane.

Graph the following polygons.

A. ABCD with A(1, 6), B(7, 6), C(7, −5), D(−4, −5)

B. FGHJ with F(−1, 3), G(6, 3), H(6, −4), J(−1, −4)

C. KLMN with K(−6, −3), L(3, −3), M(0, −9), N(−9, −9)

D. STUV with S(−9, 2), T(−3, 2), U(−3, −6), V(−9, −6)

E. Clues: The treasure is at a point with integer coordinates. The treasure is buried inside a trapezoid that is not a parallelogram, outside any squares or rectangles, and inside a parallelogram.

Where is the treasure buried? Explain how you know.

_____
_____
_____
_____

 **Turn and Talk**

How did you use the clues to find the treasure?

Are You Ready?

Complete these problems to review prior concepts and skills you will need for this module.

Polygons in the Coordinate Plane

Draw each polygon in the coordinate plane.

1. Triangle *ABC* has vertices *A*(−4, 3), *B*(3, 1), and *C*(1, −3).

2. Quadrilateral *FGHJ* has vertices *F*(−2, −3), *G*(−2, 4), *H*(1, 4), and *J*(5, −3).

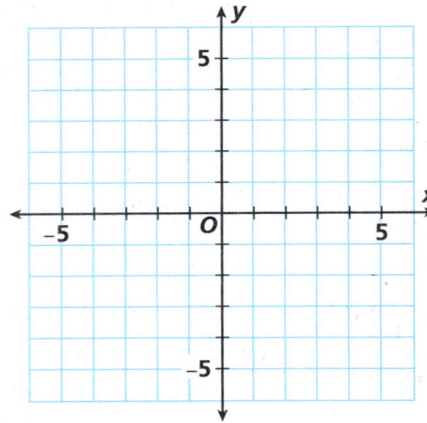
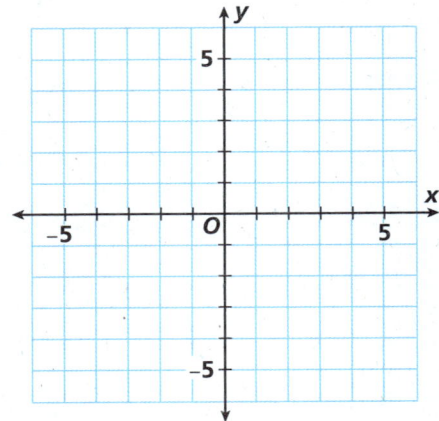

Draw Shapes with Given Conditions

Use a ruler and protractor to draw a quadrilateral that matches each description. Label the sides or angles described.

3. a square with a side length of 2 centimeters

4. a parallelogram with two angles that measure 65° and two angles that measure 115°

Use a ruler and protractor to draw a triangle that matches each description. Label the sides or angles described.

5. a right triangle with sides that measure 3 centimeters, 4 centimeters, and 5 centimeters

6. a triangle with two angles measuring 70° and the side between them measuring 3 centimeters

Build Conceptual Understanding

Lesson 1

Name _____

Investigate Transformations

I Can describe what happens to the sides and angles of a figure when it is transformed.

Spark Your Learning

Rachel is tiling a rectangular floor using triangles. Draw a triangle and cut it out. Move the triangle in different ways, and trace those shapes to draw a rectangular pattern using triangular tiles. Experiment with different shapes of triangles and different ways of moving the triangle to tile the whole floor with no gaps or overlapping tiles.

 **Turn and Talk** Describe multiple ways you could move the original triangle to tile the floor.

Module 8 • Lesson 1 253

Build Understanding

> **Connect to Vocabulary**
> A **transformation** is a change in the position of a figure.

1 On graph paper, draw a quadrilateral that has exactly one pair of parallel sides. Remember, parallel sides are sides that would not intersect even if extended indefinitely. Cut out the shape and trace it in the center of the box.

A. Slide the quadrilateral to a new location in the box and trace it. Describe the direction and length you slid the shape.

_____

B. Use a ruler to measure the sides of each quadrilateral. Use a protractor to measure the angles of the original shape and the new shape. What has happened to the lengths of the sides, the measures of the angles, and the relationship between the parallel sides of the two shapes?

_____
_____
_____

C. When you slid the shape, did anything change besides its position?

_____

D. Draw a horizontal line near, but outside, your second quadrilateral. Flip the second quadrilateral in Part A over the horizontal line and trace it in the box as your third shape. Measure the lengths of the sides and the angles of both quadrilaterals. How have the relationships between the sides and angles of the original shape changed or stayed the same compared to the flipped shape?

_____
_____

Turn and Talk Describe a way to move the third quadrilateral back to the original location of the first quadrilateral.

Name _____

2 ▶ On graph paper, draw a polygon that has at least six sides and one pair of parallel lines. Cut out the shape and trace it in the center of the box.

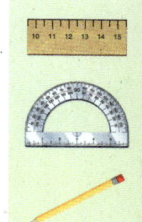

A. Place the tip of your pencil on the center of the shape and turn the shape. Trace the shape in its new location.

B. How do the sides and angles of the original polygon compare to the polygon you drew after turning the original?

_____
_____
_____

C. Based on your work in Tasks 1 and 2, what do you think stays the same and what changes when you slide, flip, or turn a shape?

_____
_____
_____

Check Understanding

1. Darby hung a kite on the wall. Then she slid the kite higher on the wall to a better position. What is true about the size and shape of her kite? Explain what happened to the side lengths and angle measures after she made the move.

_____
_____
_____

2. Marlon cuts a label in the shape of a capital letter V. He turns the label one-quarter turn clockwise to place it on a package. Which way is the open part of the V facing after the turn?

_____
_____

3. Rachel tells Jonah that she can turn a square, but he won't be able to tell that it was turned after she is finished. How can she do this?

_____
_____

Module 8 • Lesson 1   255

On Your Own

4. **MP Reason** Is Figure B a transformation of Figure A? Why or why not?

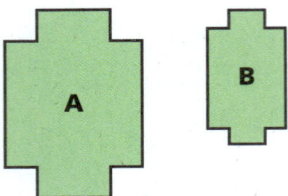

_____
_____
_____

5. **MP Reason** Is Figure Y a transformation of Figure X? Why or why not?

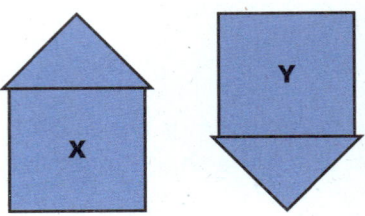

_____
_____
_____

6. Bailey has a sheet of plywood with four right angles. She saws off one of the angles and turns the plywood one-half turn clockwise. How many right angles are there on the plywood now?

_____

7. Margot draws a shape with one pair of parallel lines that are four centimeters apart. She then flips the shape across a horizontal line. How many pairs of parallel lines are on the flipped shape? How far apart are the parallel lines on the flipped shape? How do you know?

_____
_____

8. Complete the drawing of the parallelogram after a slide to the right.

9. **Open Ended** Perform a transformation on the shape. Draw the result and describe the transformation you performed.

_____

I'm in a Learning Mindset!

Did I have confidence in my answer to Problem 9? What specific evidence do I have that I performed a transformation correctly?

_____
_____

Name _____

LESSON 8.1
More Practice/ Homework

Investigate Transformations

1. **Social Studies** Nautical flags are used by ships for signaling. Flipping a flag vertically can be a sign of distress. The flag representing the number 7 is shown. Where is the yellow side if the flag is flipped vertically? Explain.

   _____

   _____

   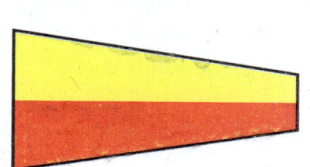

2. A quadrilateral has a pair of vertical parallel sides on the left and right of the figure. Ryan turns the quadrilateral one-half turn clockwise. Where are the parallel sides on the turned figure?

   _____

3. Does each pair of shapes show a flip, slide, or turn? If so, identify which.

   A.

   B.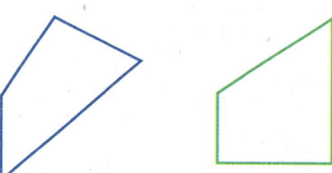

4. **Attend to Precision** Complete the drawing of the shape slid to the right.

   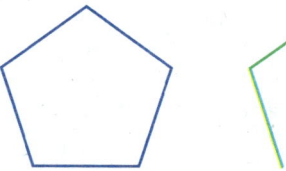

5. **STEM** A biologist is studying leaves with *line symmetry*. Complete the biologist's sketch of the leaf by flipping the shape across the vertical line.

   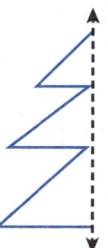

6. **Attend to Precision** Complete the drawing of the shape after it has been turned.

   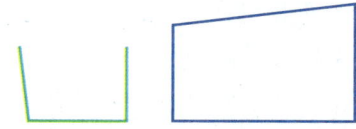

Test Prep

Use the information to answer Problems 7–9.

Daniel is babysitting his little sister. He makes her a sandwich and then uses a cookie cutter to cut the sandwich into the shape of a rhombus. Then he flips the sandwich over.

7. What shape is the flipped sandwich? _____

8. Determine the number of pairs of parallel sides for the flipped sandwich.
   _____ pairs of parallel sides

9. Are the side lengths of the flipped sandwich longer, shorter, or the same size as the side lengths of the unflipped sandwich?
   _____

10. Select the description of the transformation of the given figure.

		Slide	Flip	Turn
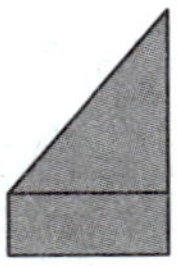 (figure)	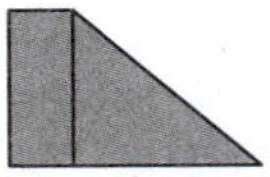 (figure)	☐	☐	☐
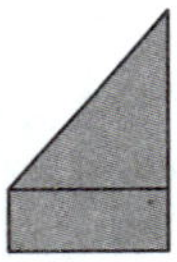 (figure)	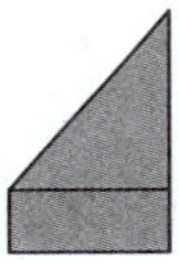 (figure)	☐	☐	☐
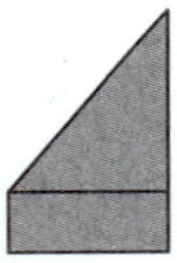 (figure)	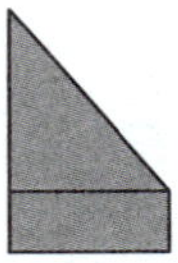 (figure)	☐	☐	☐

Spiral Review

11. A store sells a bicycle tube for $21.00 and a tire patch kit for $9.00. The tax rate is 7%. How much would it cost to purchase both?
    _____

12. Tell whether the following relationship is a proportional relationship. Explain why or why not. If it is, identify the unit rate.

Time (min)	3	5	8	10
Words Typed	120	200	320	400

258

Connect Concepts and Skills

Lesson 2

Name _____

Explore Translations

I Can translate figures, describe the translations using words and mapping notation, and determine an algebraic rule for translating a figure on a coordinate plane.

Spark Your Learning

The objective of chess is for one player's pieces to capture the other player's king. Each chess piece moves according to special rules.

Piece	Movement
♟ ♙	Pawns can move forward 2 squares on the first move and 1 square thereafter. They can also move diagonally to capture another piece.
♞ ♘	Knights can move 2 squares horizontally and 1 square vertically, or 2 squares vertically and 1 square horizontally.

Which move(s) will get any piece to land on a yellow, a blue, or a red dot? Two of the dots?

 **Turn and Talk** Move the black knight 1 space right and 2 spaces up. Then return the knight to its original location and move it 2 spaces up and 1 space right. What do you notice? Is this always true? Explain.

Module 8 • Lesson 2   259

Build Understanding

The figure that results from a transformation, such as a translation, is called the **image**. The original figure is called the **preimage**.

> **Connect to Vocabulary**
> A **translation** is the movement of a figure along a straight line.

 → translation →

preimage   image

1 Aran says that if the pawn shown below is translated 2 inches right, the preimage and the image will have the same parallel line segments and will be the same height and width. Hiro says the parallel line segments will remain parallel but the height and width will not be the same. Who is correct?

A. Fill in the dimensions and angle measures. Are the dashed segments parallel? _____

B. Trace the pawn. Translate your tracing 2 inches right. What is the relationship between the dimensions, angle measures, and parallel segments of the preimage and image?

_____

_____

_____

C. Which student is correct? _____

D. What translation must Aran perform on the image so that it returns to the exact location of the preimage?

_____

Turn and Talk Does the direction or distance a figure is translated affect the side lengths, relationships between sides, or angle measures of the figure? Explain.

Step It Out

2 Hiro draws a sketch of a game piece on a **coordinate plane**. Then he translates it 3 units right and 3 units up.

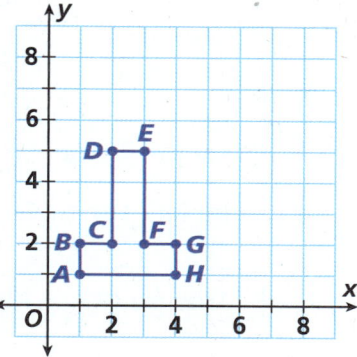

A. Draw the image of Figure *ABCDEFGH* on the coordinate plane after it is translated 3 units right and 3 units up.

B. **Prime notation**, adding apostrophes to each letter label, is used to label images. For instance, Point *A* in the preimage is labeled *A'* in the image and read as "A prime." Label the image you drew using prime notation.

C. Complete the table of ordered pairs.

Preimage	A(1, 1)	B(1, 2)	C(2, 2)				
Image	A'(4, 4)						

D. What do you notice about the relationship between the *x*- and *y*-values of each **vertex** of the preimage compared to the *x*- and *y*-values of each vertex of the image?

_____

_____

_____

_____

E. Translations in the coordinate plane can be described in mapping notation as $(x, y) \rightarrow (x \pm a, y \pm b)$ where *a* is the number of units the figure is translated horizontally and *b* is the number of units the figure is translated vertically. You read this notation as, "The ordered pair *x, y* is mapped to the ordered pair *x* plus or minus *a*, *y* plus or minus *b*."

Describe the translation of Figure *ABCDEFGH* using mapping notation.

$(x, y) \rightarrow (x + \underline{}, y + \underline{})$

F. What do you notice about the size, shape, angle measures, and relationship between the sides in the preimage and image?

_____

_____

_____

 **Turn and Talk** If Figure *ABCDEFGH* is translated using the rule $(x, y) \rightarrow (x - 2, y - 4)$, how does the image of this translation compare to the image of the translation described in Task 2?

Module 8 • Lesson 2   261

3 Triangle *DEF* is translated using the rule $(x, y) \rightarrow (x + 3, y - 4)$.

A. Use words to describe the distance and direction Triangle *DEF* is translated.

_____

B. Draw the image. Label it using prime notation.

C. Complete the table.

Triangle DEF	Triangle D'E'F'
D(2, 5)	

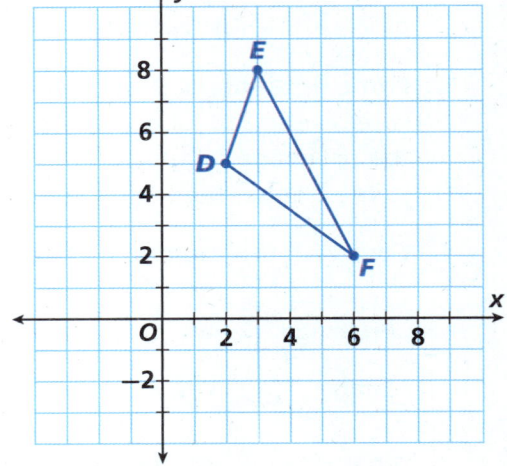

Check Understanding

1. The coordinates of a triangle's vertices are (2, 2), (4, 5), and (6, 1).

   A. If the triangle is translated using the rule $(x, y) \rightarrow (x + 3, y - 5)$, by how many units and in what direction was the preimage translated?

   _____

   B. What are the coordinates of the image's vertices?

   _____

   C. Write a true statement about the relationship of the line segments and angle measures when a translation is applied to a preimage.

   _____
   _____

   D. Will the line segment between (2, 2) and (4, 5) be parallel to its image?

   _____

2. The coordinates of the vertices of the preimage of a parallelogram are (1, 5), (3, 3), (3, 7), and (5, 5). The coordinates of the vertices of the image are (−5, 3), (−3, 1), (−3, 5), and (−1, 3). How far and in what direction was the parallelogram translated? Write your answer using mapping notation and practice reading your answer aloud.

   _____

Name _____

On Your Own

Solve Problems 3–5 using the graph of Buildings A, B, C, D, and E.

3. Shana translates Building B three units right and three units up. Draw the image of Building B in the new location.

4. **MP Model with Mathematics** Shana translates Building C to the location of Building E. Use mapping notation to describe the translation of Building C.

   _____

5. **MP Construct Arguments** The coordinates of the vertices of the image of Building D are (−7, 3), (−1, 3), (−1, −5), and (−7, −5). The coordinates of the vertices of the image of Building A are (1, 1), (3, 1), (3, 3), and (1, 3). Which of these is not a translation of the preimage? Explain by using the definition of a translation.

   _____
   _____
   _____

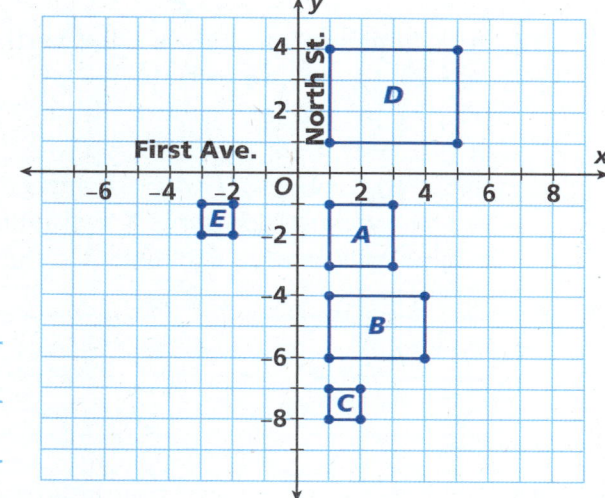

Use the triangles shown to answer Problems 6–7.

Triangle 2 is a translation of Triangle 1.

6. All the sides of Triangle 1 have a length of 3 inches. What is the length of each side of Triangle 2? _____

7. All the angles of Triangle 1 have a measure of 60°. What is the measure of each angle of Triangle 2? _____

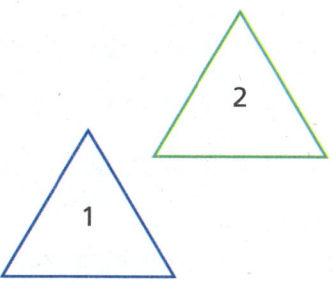

Use the description shown to answer Problems 8–9.

Square P'Q'R'S' is a translation of Square PQRS.

8. What is true about the angles of Square PQRS and Square P'Q'R'S'?

   _____

9. Opposite sides of Square PQRS are parallel and the same length. What is true about opposite sides of Square P'Q'R'S'?

   _____

Module 8 • Lesson 2

Solve Problems 10–13 using the graph of Houses B, C, D, and E.

10. **(MP) Attend to Precision** House B is translated using the rule $(x, y) \rightarrow (x - 3, y + 2)$. Draw House B in its new location.

11. **(MP) Model with Mathematics** The builder adds House A to her plan first with vertices at $(-1, 1)$, $(-5, 1)$, $(-5, 7)$, and $(-1, 7)$. Then she moves it so it has vertices at $(6, 2)$, $(2, 2)$, $(2, 8)$, and $(6, 8)$. Use mapping notation to describe how far and in what direction she translated the house.

_____

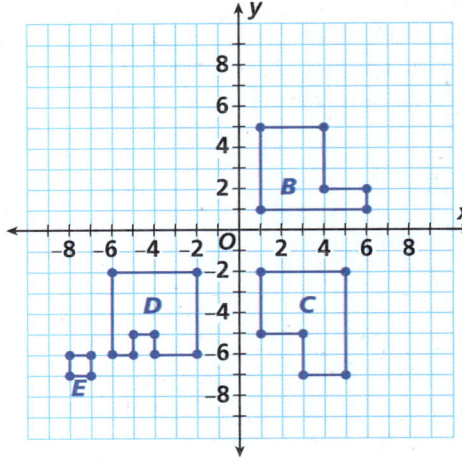

12. In its final location, House C has vertices at $(4, -2)$, $(4, -5)$, $(6, -5)$, $(6, -7)$, $(8, -7)$, and $(8, -2)$. In its final location, House D has vertices at $(-2, -2)$, $(-6, -2)$, $(-6, -6)$, $(-5, -6)$, $(-5, -5)$, $(-4, -4)$, $(-4, -6)$, and $(-2, -6)$. Which building represents a translation from its original placement? Explain.

_____

_____

_____

13. Building E is a shed. It is translated 1 unit left and 2 units up. Draw Building E in its new location.

14. Explain whether Figure B is a translation of Figure A below.

_____

_____

_____

_____

_____

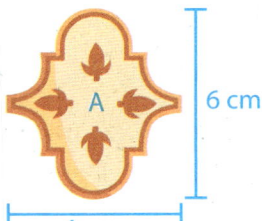

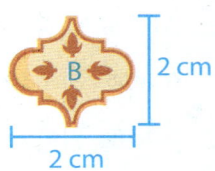

I'm in a Learning Mindset!

How does my mindset affect my ability to successfully translate figures?

_____

_____

Explore Translations

Use the graph to answer Problems 1–4.

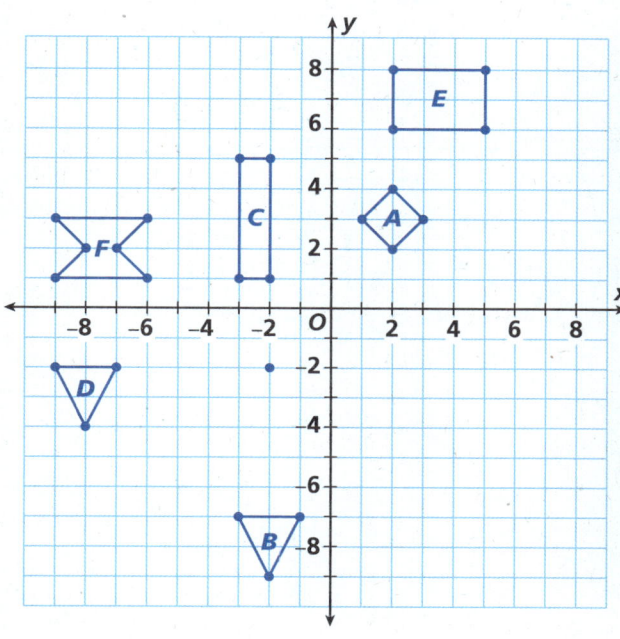

Elements in the pattern are translated.

1. Translate Figure A using the rule $(x, y) \rightarrow (x + 1, y - 4)$. Draw the image of Figure A. Practice reading the rule aloud.

2. **Model with Mathematics** How was Figure B translated to get Figure D? Write your answer using mapping notation.

3. **Construct Arguments** Why is Figure E not a translation of Figure C?

4. Figure F has vertices with coordinates at $(-6, 1)$, $(-9, 1)$, $(-8, 2)$, $(-9, 3)$, $(-6, 3)$, and $(-7, 2)$. If the figure is translated using the rule $(x, y) \rightarrow (x + 2, y + 5)$, what are the coordinates of the new vertices?

5. **Math on the Spot** Graph the translation of △XYZ 4 units right and 2 units down.

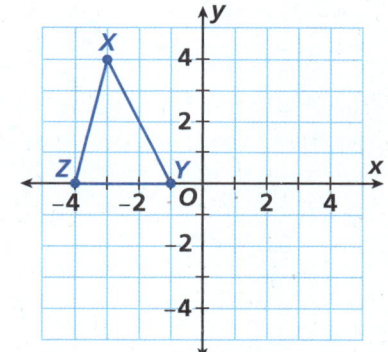

Test Prep

6. Which figure is a translation of Figure A?
   - Ⓐ Figure 1
   - Ⓑ Figure 2
   - Ⓒ Figure 3
   - Ⓓ Figure 4

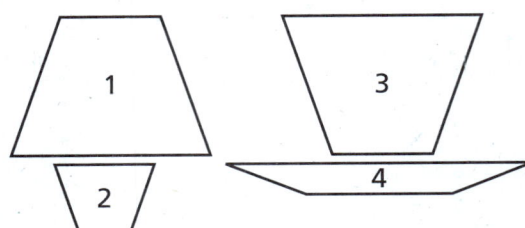

7. The coordinates of a triangle are given in the table. The triangle is translated using the rule $(x, y) \rightarrow (x - 3, y + 2)$. What are the coordinates of the image of the triangle?

Preimage coordinates	Image coordinates
(0, 1)	
(2, 3)	
(4, 2)	

8. A quadrilateral is translated 5 units right and 3 units down on a coordinate plane. Which expressions could be used to find one of the coordinates of the vertices of the image? Select all that are correct.
   - Ⓐ $x - 3$
   - Ⓑ $x - 5$
   - Ⓒ $x + 5$
   - Ⓓ $y - 3$
   - Ⓔ $y + 3$
   - Ⓕ $y + 5$

Spiral Review

9. What are the common factors of 6, 9, and 18?

10. Jovan is 15 years old. His sister is 6 years older than one-third his age. How old is Jovan's sister?

11. DeMarcus multiplies all the integers from −10 to −1 including −10 and −1. Should his answer be positive or negative? Explain your reasoning.

Connect Concepts and Skills

Lesson 3

Name _____

Explore Reflections

I Can reflect a figure over either axis in the coordinate plane and describe the reflection algebraically.

Spark Your Learning

The word "AMBULANCE" is often written backwards on the front of ambulances, so that it will appear forwards in the rear-view mirrors of cars.

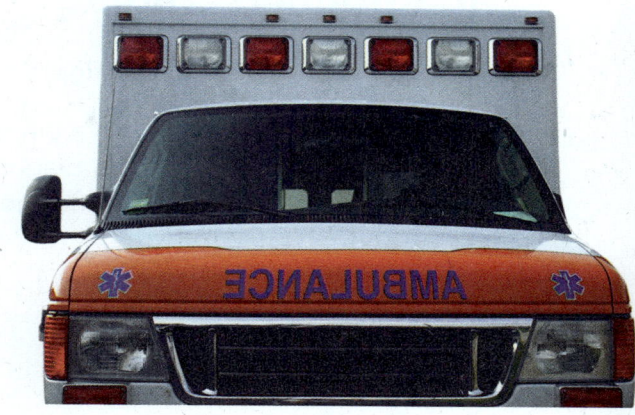

ƎƆNALUBMA

Use tracing paper to trace the word as it is shown above. What can you do with your result to make the word readable?

What effect do your actions have on the order of the letters, and what effect do your actions have on the individual letters themselves?

 **Turn and Talk** As you change the word "AMBULANCE" so that it is readable, which letters change their appearance and which do not? What is different about the letters that remain the same after the transition, as opposed to the letters that change?

Module 8 • Lesson 3   267

Build Understanding

1 How can you reflect a figure using tracing paper?

Draw the letter "N" on a piece of tracing paper, then fold the paper over the diagonal and trace the "N". Unfold the paper, and you should see the original "N" and its reflection:

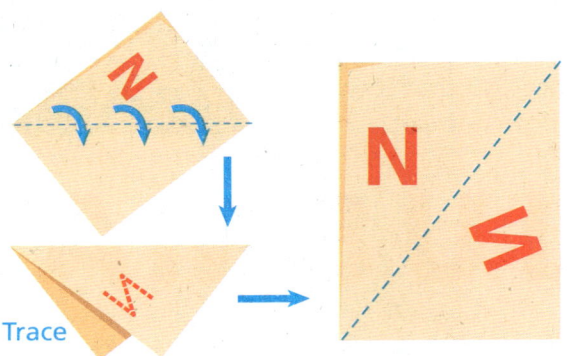

Trace

> **Connect to Vocabulary**
>
> A **reflection** is a transformation of a figure that flips the figure across a line, called the **line of reflection** so that each point on the preimage is the same distance from the line of reflection as the corresponding point on the image.

A. Find two line segments for the letter "N" that are parallel in the preimage. Are the corresponding segments in the image also parallel?

_____

B. Use a ruler to measure the length of a line segment in the preimage. Then measure the length of the corresponding line segment in the image. What do you notice about the lengths of the two segments?

_____

C. Use a protractor to measure an angle in the preimage and the **corresponding angle** in the image. What do you notice?

_____

D. What can you conclude about the way reflecting a figure affects side length, angle measure, and parallel line segments?

_____

_____

E. Look again at the "N" and its image on the paper. Why do you think the word *reflection* is used to describe such an image?

_____

_____

Turn and Talk Two students perform a reflection of the same shape. One reflects over a vertical line. The other reflects over a horizontal line. How are their reflections the same? How are they different?

Name _____

Step It Out

2 How can you reflect a figure over the *x*-axis or *y*-axis?

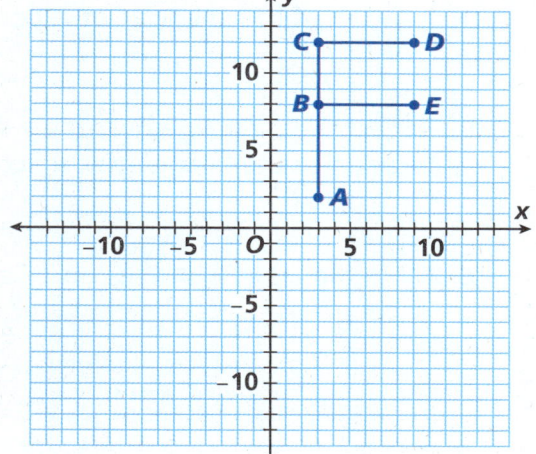

A. Reflect the image shown over the *x*-axis. Remember to keep each point of the image the same distance from the *x*-axis as the corresponding preimage point. For instance, Point C is 12 units from the *x*-axis, so Point C' in the image must also be 12 units from the *x*-axis. Label the points using prime notation.

B. The preimage is upright. Is the image also upright, or has it changed?

_____

C. Find the length of $\overline{AC}$ in the preimage (in units). What do you expect the length of $\overline{A'C'}$ to be? Find this length.

_____

D. The original letter "F" faces to the right. Reflect the original image over the *y*-axis. Does the new image face the same direction? If not, how is it different? Label the points using double-prime notation (").

_____

E. What are the coordinates of the points on the images corresponding to the labeled points on the preimage? Complete the table.

Point	Preimage	Image after reflection over *x*-axis	Image after reflection over *y*-axis
A	(3, 2)	(3, −2)	
B	(3, 8)		
C	(3, 12)		(−3, 12)
D	(9, 12)	(9, −12)	
E	(9, 8)		

F. Look at your table. In general:

A point (*a*, *b*) reflected over the *x*-axis has the coordinates (☐, ☐).

A point (*a*, *b*) reflected over the *y*-axis has the coordinates (☐, ☐).

 **Turn and Talk** On the grid, draw $\overline{DE}$ and $\overline{D'E'}$. Find the areas of Rectangle BCDE and Rectangle B'C'D'E'. What do you notice about these areas?

Module 8 • Lesson 3   269

3 On a piece of graph paper, draw a **parallelogram** in the third **quadrant** of the coordinate **plane** with vertices at the points shown.

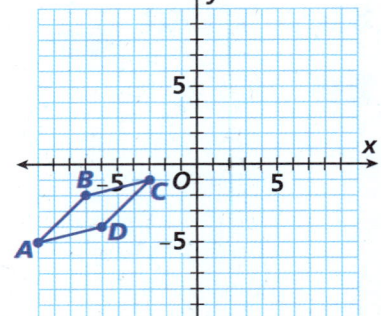

A. Reflect this preimage over the *x*-axis and describe the location of the image after reflection.

_____

B. Reflect the preimage over the *y*-axis and describe the location of the image after reflection.

_____

C. Fill in the table with the coordinates of the vertices of the images.

Point	Preimage	Image after reflection over *x*-axis	Image after reflection over *y*-axis
A	(−10, −5)		
B	(−7, −2)		
C	(−3, −1)		
D	(−6, −4)		
Any point	(a, b)		

Check Understanding

1. The coordinates of the vertices of a triangle are (2, 3), (5, 1), and (6, 4). After one reflection, the coordinates of the vertices of the triangle's image are (2, −3), (5, −1), and (6, −4). Over what line has the triangle been reflected?

_____

2. The coordinates of the vertices of a square are (−10, −2), (−5, −2), (−5, −7), and (−10, −7). The square is reflected over the *y*-axis.

   A. What are the coordinates of the vertices of the image?

   _____

   B. Show that the image still has parallel sides and the same angles as the preimage: the image's sides are segments of the lines $y =$ _____, $y =$ _____, $x =$ _____, and $x =$ _____, which meet at _____ angles.

   C. Does the image have the same side lengths as the preimage? Explain.

   _____
   _____

3. In your own words, describe the meaning of a reflection.

   _____

Name _____

On Your Own

Use the figures to answer Problems 4–7.

Figure Y is a reflection of Figure X.

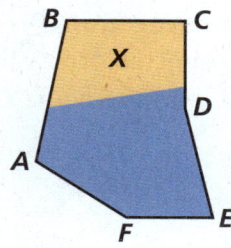

4. $\overline{AB}$ is 3 centimeters long. What is the length of the corresponding side of Figure Y? How do you know?

   _____

   _____

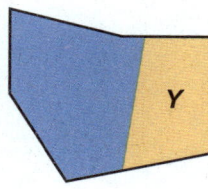

5. Angle A measures 115°. What is the measure of the corresponding angle in Figure Y?

   _____

6. $\overline{FE}$ is parallel to $\overline{BC}$. Are the corresponding sides in Figure Y also parallel?

   _____

7. Draw the line of reflection between Figures X and Y.

8. Draw a reflection of the preimage over the line shown.

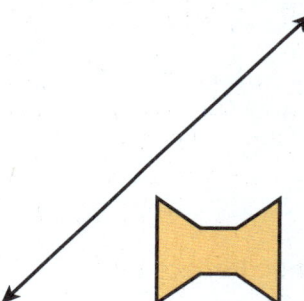

9. Marie is practicing her reflections on graph paper.

   A. Is Figure P a reflection of Figure N over the y-axis?

   _____

   B. Is Figure P a reflection of Figure M over the y-axis and then over the x-axis?

   _____

   C. Is Figure P a reflection of Figure M over the x-axis and then over the y-axis?

   _____

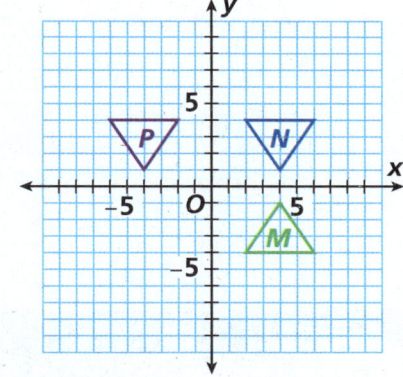

Module 8 • Lesson 3

10. Figure ABCD is a trapezoid in the second quadrant.

   A. **Attend to Precision** On the given graph, draw the image of Figure ABCD reflected across the y-axis. What are the coordinates of the vertices of ABCD and A'B'C'D'?

   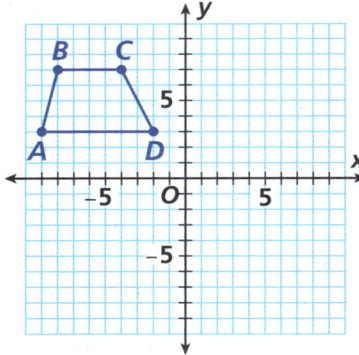

ABCD	A'B'C'D'

   B. **Model with Mathematics** Given any point (x, y) on ABCD, what are the coordinates of the corresponding point on A'B'C'D'?

   $(x, y) \rightarrow (\ \square\ ,\ \square\ )$

   C. Is A'B'C'D' facing the same direction as ABCD? Explain.

   _____

11. Draw a square with sides that are horizontal and vertical on a piece of paper.

   A. If you reflect the square over a vertical line, does it look any different? If you reflect the square over a horizontal line, does it look any different?

   _____

   B. In your original square, draw a right-angle mark in one corner. Reflect this square over a horizontal line. Does it look any different? If so, what is different?

   _____

   C. If you reflect the square from Part B over a vertical line, does it look any different? If so, what is different?

   _____

 I'm in a Learning Mindset!

How does my mindset affect my confidence with performing reflections?

_____

Explore Reflections

LESSON 8.3 More Practice/ Homework

ONLINE Video Tutorials and Interactive Examples

Construct Arguments Use the tiger images to answer Problems 1–3.

Tiger 1   Tiger 2

1. Could Tiger 2 be an image of Tiger 1 after one reflection? Explain.

   _____
   _____
   _____

Tiger 3   Tiger 4

2. Could Tiger 3 be an image of Tiger 1 after one reflection? Explain.

   _____
   _____
   _____

3. Could Tiger 4 be an image of Tiger 1 after one reflection? Explain.

   _____
   _____

4. The grid shows Figure R, a pair of arrows forming a right angle. On the grid, draw a reflection of R so that any point (a, b) on the preimage becomes (−a, b) on the image, R′.

   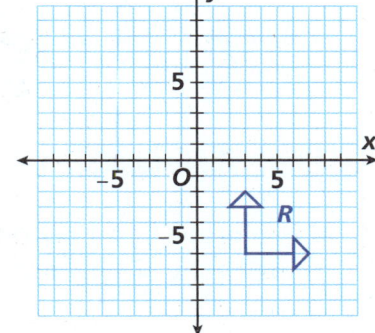

   A. Over what line did you reflect R?

   _____

   B. Both arrows in Figure R are 4 units long. How long are the arrows in Figure R′?

   _____

   C. What are the coordinates of the tips of the arrows on R′?

   _____

   D. On the same grid, reflect R′ over the x-axis to arrive at Figure R″. In which quadrant is R″?

   _____

   E. What are the coordinates of the point at which the arrows intersect in R″?

   _____

   F. In which directions do the arrows point in Figure R″?

   _____

Module 8 • Lesson 3

Test Prep

5. Select all the figures that could represent an image of the given figure after one reflection over a horizontal or vertical line through its center.

Ⓐ Ⓑ

Ⓒ  Ⓓ Ⓔ

6. A triangle with vertices at (−6, 5), (−5, 1), and (−8, 2) is reflected over the y-axis. What are the coordinates of the vertices of the image?

Preimage coordinates	Image coordinates
(−6, 5)	
(−5, 1)	
(−8, 2)	

7. Which of the following is a rule that represents what happens to the coordinates of any point on a figure after it is reflected over the x-axis and then the y-axis?

Ⓐ $(x, y) \rightarrow (x, -y)$
Ⓑ $(x, y) \rightarrow (-x, y)$
Ⓒ $(x, y) \rightarrow (y, x)$
Ⓓ $(x, y) \rightarrow (-x, -y)$

Spiral Review

8. Can a graph of a horizontal line represent a proportional relationship? Explain why or why not.

_____

_____

_____

9. A recipe calls for $2\frac{3}{4}$ cups of flour. Thomas is making $2\frac{1}{2}$ batches of the recipe. How many cups of flour does he need?

_____

10. A diamond figure has vertices with coordinates at (−5, −4), (−3, −2), (−1, −4), and (−3, −6). If the figure is translated 3 units right and 8 units up, what are the coordinates of the vertices of the image?

_____

Connect Concepts and Skills

Lesson 4

Name _____

Explore Rotations

I Can identify and perform rotations, and describe a rotation on a coordinate plane algebraically.

Spark Your Learning

Use tracing paper to trace a copy of this recycling symbol.

Place the tip of your pencil in the center of the symbol and turn the paper about that point. You'll see that the original design reappears three times in every full turn.

In the space provided, sketch a design that reappears every quarter of a full turn. Trace the shape on tracing paper, then turn it to check your work.

 **Turn and Talk** If the preimage and image of a figure look identical after being turned one-fourth turn clockwise or one-fourth turn counterclockwise, what must be true about the figure?

Module 8 • Lesson 4   **275**

Build Understanding

1 Trace the hexagon and Points P, Q, and R on tracing paper.

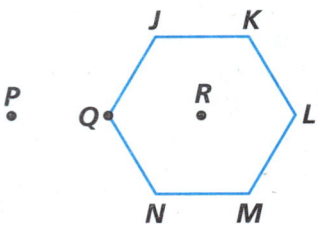

> **Connect to Vocabulary**
>
> A **rotation** is a transformation in which a figure is turned around a point. That point is called the **center of rotation**.

A. Use a ruler and protractor to complete the table.

Length of $\overline{JK}$	_____ cm
Measure of $\angle JQN$	_____ °

B. Place the tip of a pencil on Point R and rotate the hexagon 90° (one-fourth turn) clockwise about that point.

- What happens to the measure of $\angle JQN$?

  _____

- What happens to the length of $\overline{JK}$?

  _____

- Name a pair of parallel sides in the shape. What happens to the pair when the shape is rotated?

  _____
  _____

C. Move the center of rotation by placing the tip of your pencil on Point P. Rotate the shape about Point P. Describe the rotation. How is it different from the rotation in Part B?

  _____
  _____
  _____

D. Draw an arrow inside your hexagon that points to the top of the shape. When you rotate the shape 180° (one-half turn), what happens to the direction of the arrow in the image, and why?

  _____
  _____

Turn and Talk Can you make your hexagon change its shape using a rotation? Why or why not?

Step It Out

2 You can rotate the letter "N" and get the letter "Z." Figure 2 was formed by rotating Figure 1 90° clockwise about the **origin**.

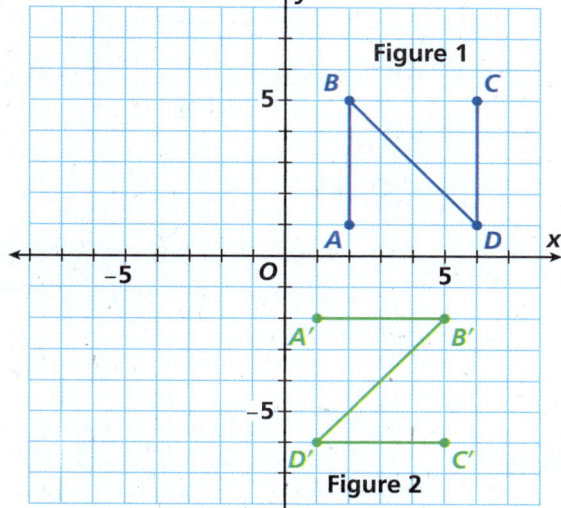

A. Use a ruler and protractor to measure the line segments and angles of both figures. What is the relationship between the side lengths and angle measures of the image and preimage?

_____

B. In Figure 1, $\overline{AB}$ is parallel to $\overline{DC}$. What is the relationship between $\overline{A'B'}$ and $\overline{D'C'}$ in Figure 2?

_____

C. Fill in the coordinates for each point.

Figure 1	A(2, 1)			
Figure 2	A'(1, −2)			

D. Look at the relationship between the coordinates of the vertices of Figure 1 and Figure 2. Write a rule to find the coordinates of the vertices of any figure rotated 90° clockwise about the origin.

(x, y) → (☐ , ☐)

E. Rotate Figure 2 180° counterclockwise about the origin. Label the result as Figure 3. Then fill in the table.

Figure 2	A'(1, −2)	B'(5, −2)	C'(5, −6)	D'(1, −6)
Figure 3	A"(−1, 2)			

F. Write a rule that represents the change in coordinates of any figure rotated 180° counterclockwise about the origin.

(x, y) → (☐ , ☐)

G. If you rotate the letter "W" 180° clockwise, what letter does it resemble?

_____

Turn and Talk Identify which uppercase letters look the same after a 180° rotation.

Module 8 • Lesson 4   277

3 Figure 1 is rotated to form Figure 2.

A. Describe the rotation.

_____

B. Fill in the table of vertex coordinates.

Q(1, 4)			
Q'(−1, −4)			

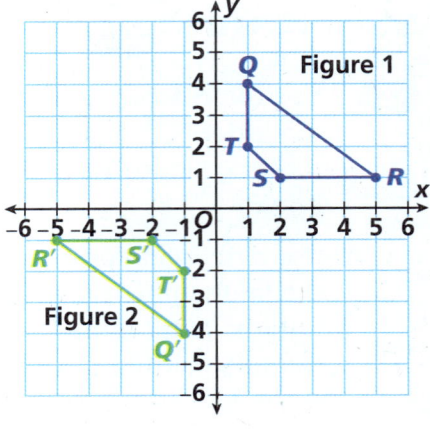

C. Write a rule that represents the change in coordinates of any figure rotated 180° about the origin.

$(x, y) \to (\boxed{}, \boxed{})$

4 A. △EFG has vertices (2, 4), (5, 1), and (1, 2). Graph the triangle and label it Figure 1.

B. Rotate △EFG by the rule $(x, y) \to (y, -x)$ and label the image Figure 2. Complete the sentence about the rotation:

To form Figure 2, Figure 1 underwent a rotation of 90° _____ about the origin.

C. Rotate △EFG by the rule $(x, y) \to (-y, x)$ and label the image Figure 3. Complete the sentence about the rotation:

To form Figure 3, Figure 1 underwent a rotation of _____ counterclockwise about the origin.

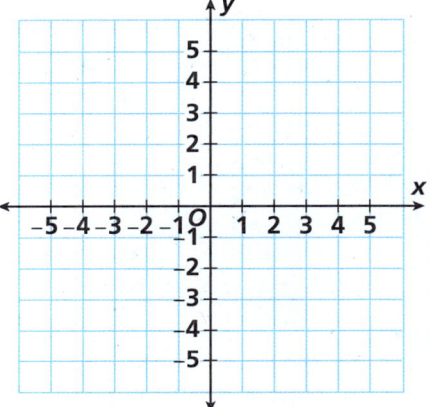

Check Understanding

1. Antoine and Bobby each rotated a pentagon about Point P, but they each got a different image. Which rotation is correct? Why?

_____

_____

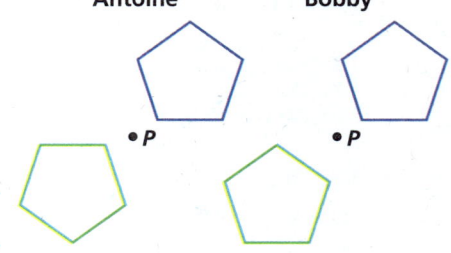

Antoine   Bobby

2. A. Draw rotations of Rectangle STUV 90°, 180°, and 270° clockwise about the origin.

B. What do all four figures have in common? They all have _____ side lengths and _____ angle measures, and their _____ sides are parallel.

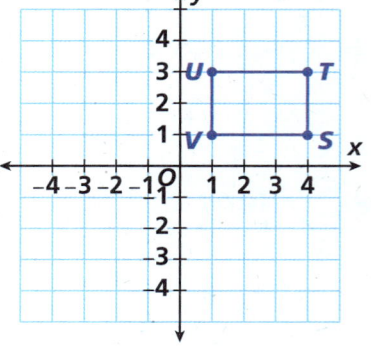

On Your Own

3. Victor rotated his initial, V, about Point P. What stayed the same between the preimage and image? What changed?

_____

_____

4. Sketch a rotation of the Figure WXYZ. Use Point W as the center of rotation.

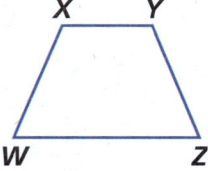

   A. What is the same about the two images?

   _____

   _____

   B. What is different about the two images?

   _____

5. Elias graphed the movement of one quarter-turn of a ceiling fan.

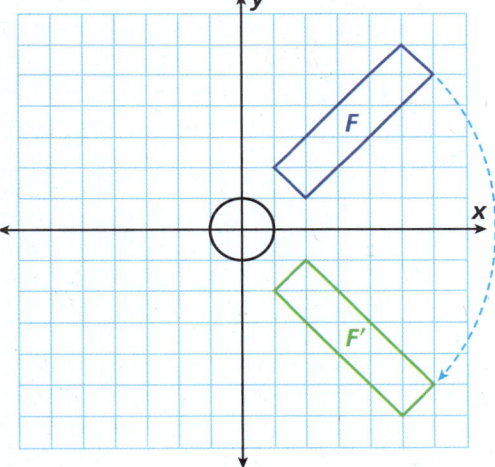

   A. Continue the rotation and draw the fan blade in the third and second quadrants after two more rotations of 90° each.

   B. Describe the rotation of the fan blade from F to F'.

   _____

   _____

   C. (MP) **Model with Mathematics** Describe the rotation from F to F' in mapping notation.

   _____

6. (MP) **Attend to Precision** Rotate each figure 180° about the origin.

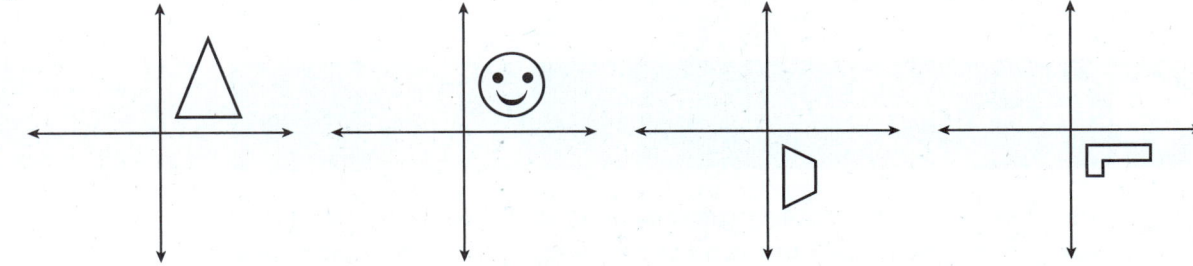

7. Describe the transformation of Figure 1 to Figure 2 using mapping notation.

   _____

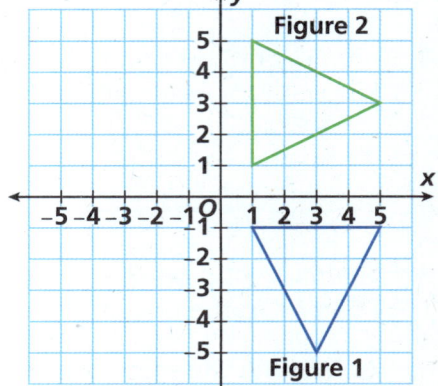

8. △JKL has an area of 3.25 square units. What happens to its area when it is rotated 180° about Point J?

   _____
   _____
   _____

9. The vertices of the preimage of a triangle are (−2, 1), (−5, 2), and (−3, 6). The triangle is rotated and its image has vertices at (1, 2), (2, 5), and (6, 3).

   A. Describe the rotation that resulted in the image.

   _____

   B. If the image is then rotated 90° clockwise, what are the coordinates of the new image?

   _____

10. **Attend to Precision** Rotate the shape by the rule $(x, y) \rightarrow (y, -x)$. Then rotate the new image according to the rule $(x, y) \rightarrow (-x, -y)$.

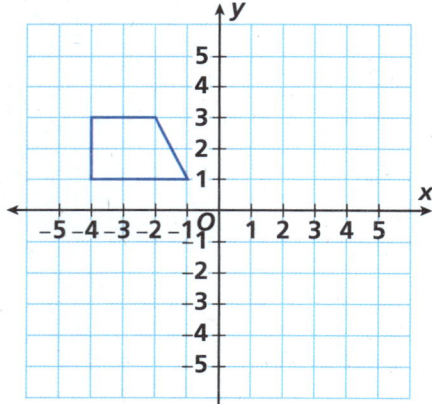

I'm in a Learning Mindset!

Do I have a fixed-mindset voice or growth-mindset voice in my head when I'm working with rotations? How can I tap into my growth-mindset voice?

_____
_____

Explore Rotations

LESSON 8.4
More Practice/ Homework

1. Which shape shows a rotation of the shaded figure following the rule $(x, y) \to (-x, -y)$?

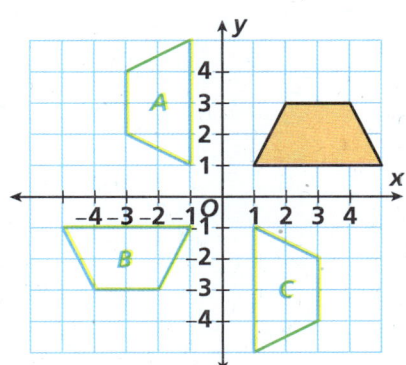

Windmill blades are a good example of rotation.

2. Sarika uses rotations to make designs. What characteristics of the design indicate it is a rotation?

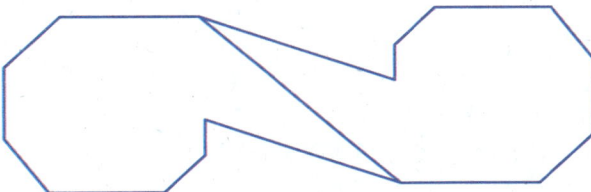

3. A triangle has vertices at $(-3, 4)$, $(-1, 0)$, and $(-4, 0)$. What are the coordinates of the vertices after it is rotated 180° about the origin?

4. **A.** Graph Rectangle *ABCD* with vertices at $A(1, 5)$, $B(3, 6)$, $C(5, 2)$, and $D(3, 1)$. Then draw a rotation of the rectangle 90° counterclockwise about the origin and list the coordinates of the vertices of the result.

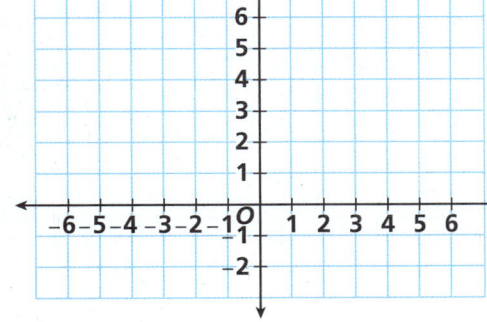

B. **Model with Mathematics** Describe the rotation in mapping notation.

Module 8 • Lesson 4   281

Test Prep

5. Draw a rotation of the parallelogram 90° counterclockwise about the origin.

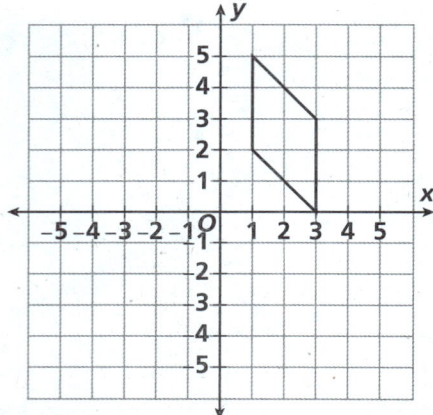

6. What rotation of △MNP about Point P could have produced △PQR?

   Ⓐ 90° clockwise
   Ⓑ 180° clockwise
   Ⓒ 270° counterclockwise
   Ⓓ 360° counterclockwise

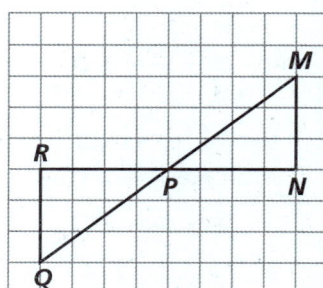

7. A pentagon has vertices at (−1, −1), (−5, −2), (−6, −4), (−4, −7), and (−2, −3). If the pentagon is rotated 180° clockwise about the origin, what are the coordinates of the vertices of the image?

Spiral Review

8. A figure has two pairs of parallel sides and four right angles. The figure is translated 4 units down. How many parallel sides does the image have?

9. Which figure is a reflection of Figure A?

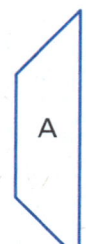 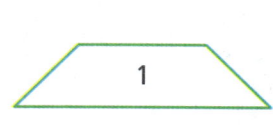  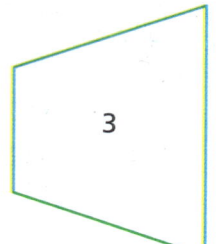 

Connect Concepts and Skills
Lesson 5

Name _____

Understand and Recognize Congruent Figures

I Can determine congruence by performing or describing a sequence of transformations that maps one figure onto another.

Spark Your Learning

Maribel wants to make a quilt like this one. She has quilt pieces that are triangles and quilt pieces that are parallelograms. Describe ways she can transform the shapes to match the pattern in the quilt.

Turn and Talk Design a second quilt using parallelograms and triangles. Exchange your design with a partner and have him or her describe the transformations you used to design your quilt.

Module 8 • Lesson 5   283

Build Understanding

1. Maribel needs to cut shapes out of fabric to prepare for a different quilt. Trace Figure 1 on a piece of paper and cut it out. Lay your cut-out on top of Figure 1 to make sure it is the same size and shape.

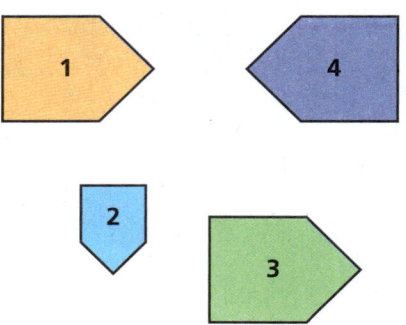

A. Experiment with transformations to move the cut-out shape on top of Figure 2. What transformations did you use? Explain how the figures are the same and how they are different.

_____

_____

_____

B. Experiment with transformations to move the cut-out shape over Figures 3 and 4. What transformations did you use?

_____

_____

C. What do you notice when you compare Figure 1 to Figures 3 and 4?

_____

_____

D. A figure is congruent to another if and only if a series of rotations, reflections, and translations can map one onto the other. Which figures are congruent?

_____

Connect to Vocabulary

Congruent figures are the same size and shape.

 Turn and Talk Is there a series of rotations, reflections, or translations you can perform on Figure 2 to produce Figure 1, 3, or 4? Explain.

284

Name _____

Step It Out

2 ▶ While preparing fabric for quilting, Maribel lays a grid over her fabric. She wants to cut out five congruent triangles. She draws the triangles on the coordinate grid below.

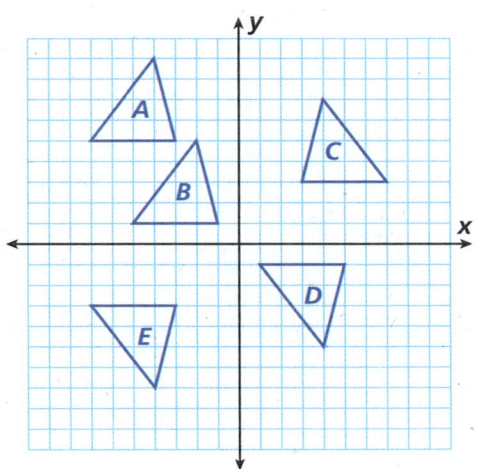

A. Triangle A is translated 2 units down and then reflected across the y-axis. Which triangle is the image of this sequence of transformations?

_____

B. Are the two triangles congruent? Explain how you know.

_____
_____
_____

C. Which two transformations can you perform on Triangle B to show that it is congruent to Triangle D?

_____
_____

D. Record the vertices of Triangle A and Triangle B. Use mapping notation to show how the vertices of Triangle A changed, and read the mapping notation aloud to another student. Explain how you know the shapes are congruent.

Triangle A → Triangle B

$(x, y) \rightarrow (x + \underline{}, y - \underline{})$

_____
_____
_____

Module 8 • Lesson 5

3 Maribel wants to cut a new shape. She will reflect Figure A across the x-axis and translate the image 5 units left. She claims that the order in which she performs the transformations matters. Is she correct?

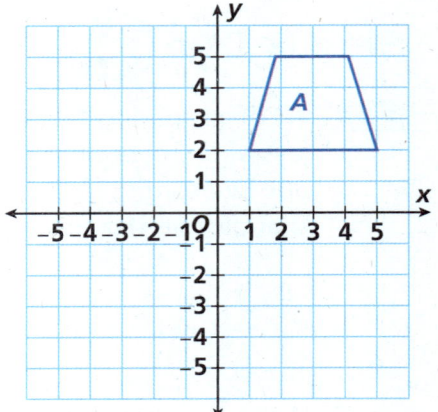

A. Reflect Figure A across the x-axis and then translate the figure 5 units left. Draw the final image.

Reverse the order of the transformations and draw the image again. How did the order you performed the transformations change the final image?

_____

_____

B. The vertices of Figure B have coordinates shown in the table. Figure B is rotated 90° clockwise about the origin, then reflected across the x-axis to form Figure C. Figure B is also reflected across the x-axis, and then rotated 90° clockwise about the origin to form Figure D. Complete the table.

Figure B	(0, 0)	(0, −3)	(2, −3)	(1, −1)	(2, 0)
Figure C		(−3, 0)			
Figure D		(3, 0)			

C. How did the order you performed the transformations on the figure change the final images, Figures C and D?

_____

_____

Check Understanding

Use the figures to answer Problems 1–2.

1. Which of these figures are not congruent to Figure 1? Why?

_____

_____

_____

2. A. What sequence of transformations can you perform on Figure 1 to produce Figure 3?

_____

_____

B. Use mapping notation to describe this sequence of transformations.

_____

On Your Own

3. Can a square ever be congruent to a pentagon? Explain.

_____

_____

Use the graph to answer Problems 4–10.

4. Open Ended What sequence of transformations can you perform on Figure C to produce Figure A?

_____

_____

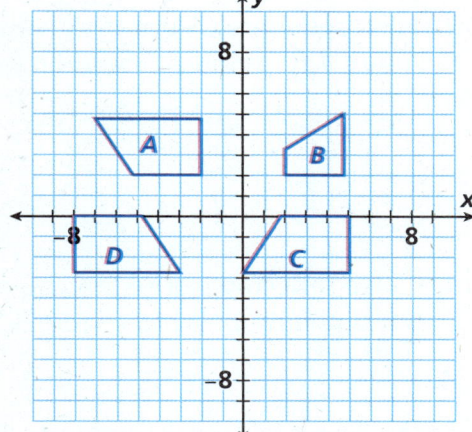

5. Figure D is translated 3 units right and reflected across the y-axis. Which figure will this sequence of transformations produce?

_____

6. Which figures are congruent to Figure A? How do you know?

_____

_____

_____

_____

7. Figure B is translated 3 units up and then reflected across the y-axis to form Figure E. Draw Figure E on the coordinate grid.

8. **Critique Reasoning** Nathan claims Figure B is congruent to Figure A. Is he correct? Explain.

_____

_____

9. Without performing a transformation on Figure A, how can you use tools to be sure it is congruent to Figure D?

_____

_____

_____

10. Without performing a transformation on Figure A, how can you use tools to be sure that it is not congruent to Figure B?

_____

_____

Use the figures to answer Problems 11–13.

11. Which figures are congruent to Figure 1? Which are not congruent to Figure 1?

    _____

    _____

12. What sequence of transformations can be performed on Figure 4 to produce Figure 1?

    _____

    _____

    _____

13. Kailee reflected Figure 5 across a vertical line and then translated it up. Which figure is the result?

    _____

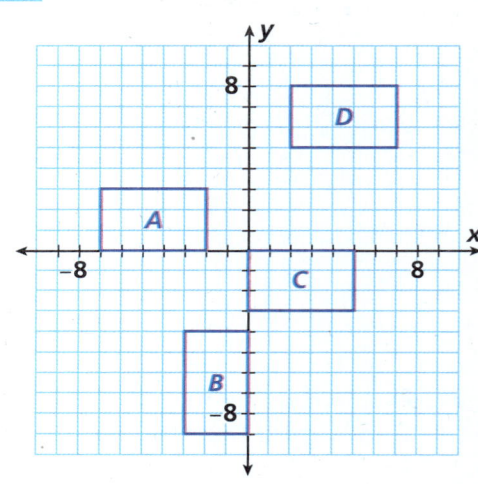

Use the graph to answer Problems 14–17.

14. Henrietta claims that Figure B can be transformed into Figure A by translating it 2 units right and rotating it 90° clockwise about the origin. Is she correct? If not, find and correct her error.

    _____

    _____

15. Figure C is rotated 90° clockwise about the origin and translated 4 units down. Which figure will this sequence of transformations produce?

    _____

16. How can you prove that Figure A is congruent to Figure C?

    _____

    _____

17. Figure B is translated 5 units left and then reflected across the x-axis to form Figure E. Draw Figure E on the coordinate grid.

I'm in a Learning Mindset!

How did I support the strategy I used to identify congruent figures?

_____

_____

Understand and Recognize Congruent Figures

Use the kites shown to answer Problems 1–3.

1. Draw a figure that is congruent to Figure 3. How can you prove that your figure is congruent using tracing paper?

   _____
   _____
   _____

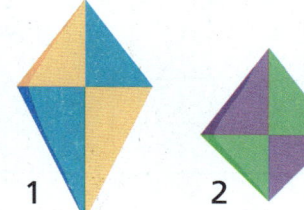
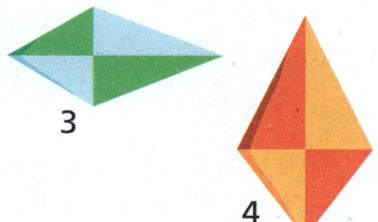

2. Mirai transforms Figure 1 into Figure 4. What sequence of transformations did Mirai perform?

   _____
   _____

3. **(MP) Reason** Can you perform a series of transformations on Figure 1 to form Figure 2? Explain.

   _____
   _____
   _____

Use the graph to answer Problems 4–7.

4. A. Figure B is reflected across the x-axis and translated 2 units left to form Figure E. Draw Figure E.
   B. Ricardo translates Figure B 2 units left and then reflects it across the x-axis. What is the same about Ricardo's drawing and your Figure E, and what is different?

   _____
   _____

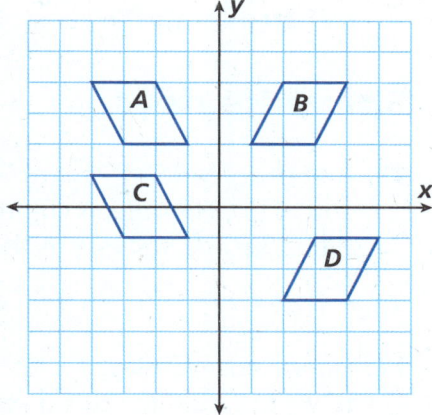

5. What transformation can be performed on Figure A to produce Figure C?

   _____

6. **Open Ended** What sequence of transformations can be performed on Figure B to produce Figure C?

   _____
   _____

7. Is Figure A congruent to Figure D? Explain.

   _____
   _____

Module 8 • Lesson 5

Test Prep

8. Select all figures that are congruent.

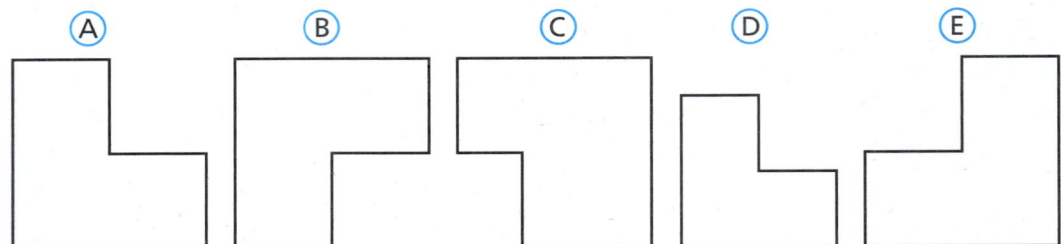

9. Figure A and its transformation Figure B are shown.

What transformations can be performed on Figure A to produce Figure B?

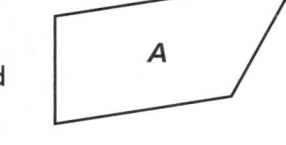

Ⓐ reflection across a vertical line followed by a translation to the right

Ⓑ reflection across a vertical line followed by a translation to the left

Ⓒ translation to the right followed by a reflection across a horizontal line

Ⓓ translation down followed by a reflection across a horizontal line

10. Triangle ABC is translated 2 units right and then reflected across the y-axis. Draw the image.

Spiral Review

11. Jose draws a triangle with vertices (4, 7), (4, 3), and (9, 3). He reflects the triangle across the x-axis. What are the vertices of the new image?

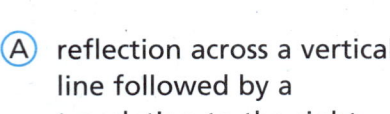

12. Figure A is translated 2 units right and 4 units up. Use mapping notation to write a rule for this translation.

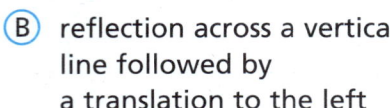

13. The average cost of a gallon of gas in January 2014 was $3.42 and was $2.36 in December 2014. What was the percent change in the average cost of a gallon of gas in 2014? Round to the nearest percent.

Module 8 Review

Vocabulary

For Problems 1–5, choose the correct term from the vocabulary box.

Vocabulary
image
reflection
rotation
translation
preimage

1. A(n) _____ is a transformation that slides a figure.

2. A(n) _____ is a transformation that flips a figure across a line.

3. A(n) _____ is a transformation that turns a figure about a point.

4. A(n) _____ is the original figure in a transformation.

5. A(n) _____ is the resulting figure in a transformation.

Concepts and Skills

6. Figure ABCD and its transformation, Figure FGHJ, are shown. Which transformation of Figure ABCD produced Figure FGHJ?

   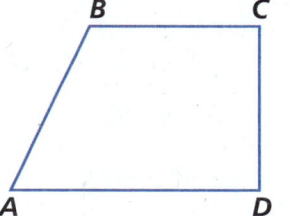

   A. vertical translation
   B. horizontal translation
   C. reflection across a vertical line
   D. reflection across a horizontal line

7. **MP Use Tools** Describe a sequence of transformations you could use to show that Triangle DEF is congruent to Triangle JKL. State what strategy and tool you will use to answer the question, explain your choice, and then find the answer.

   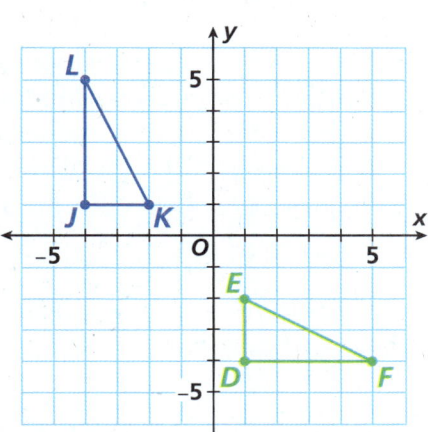

   _____
   _____
   _____
   _____

8. Triangle PQR has vertices P(2, −4), Q(4, −5), and R(7, −2). Triangle PQR is translated 6 units left and 3 units up to produce Triangle P'Q'R'. Complete the table with the coordinates of the vertices of Triangle P'Q'R'.

Vertex	x-coordinate	y-coordinate
P'		
Q'		
R'		

Module 8   291

For Problems 9–10, draw the image of each transformation.

9. Rotate Triangle RST 180° about the origin.

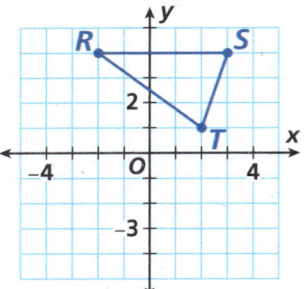

10. Translate Quadrilateral WXYZ 5 units right and 2 units down.

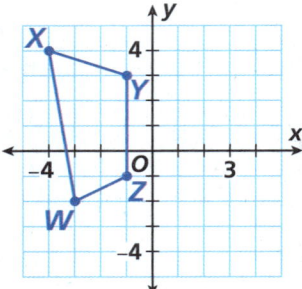

11. Side KN of Figure KLMN is parallel to Side LM. Figure KLMN is rotated 90° clockwise about Point P to produce Figure RSTU. Based on this information, select all statements that are true.

Ⓐ $\overline{ST}$ is parallel to $\overline{RU}$.

Ⓑ ∠R has the same measure as ∠N.

Ⓒ $\overline{RS}$ is the same length as $\overline{MN}$.

Ⓓ Figure RSTU is congruent to Figure KLMN.

Ⓔ ∠T has the same measure as ∠M.

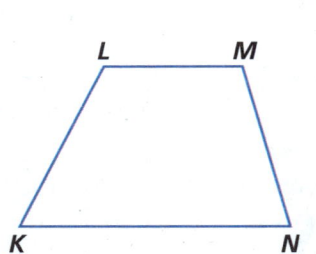

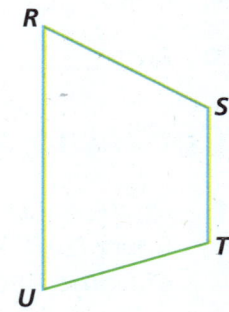

12. An artist is designing a logo for a new company by reflecting Triangle ABC across a vertical line and then translating it up and to the right to produce Triangle DEF. Find each measure.

measure of ∠D: _____ °

length of $\overline{EF}$: _____ in.

length of $\overline{DF}$: _____ in.

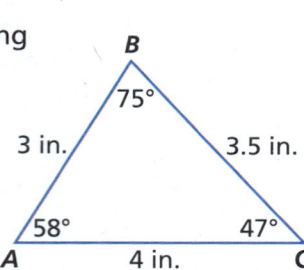

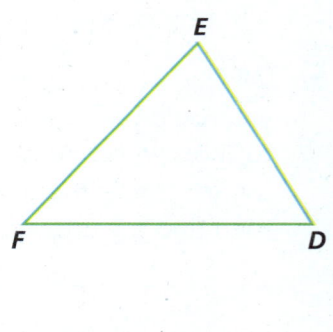

13. The point (a, b) is reflected across the x-axis and then translated 4 units to the right. What are the coordinates of the image of the point?

Ⓐ (−a, b + 4)

Ⓑ (−a + 4, b)

Ⓒ (a, −b + 4)

Ⓓ (a + 4, −b)

14. How many types of transformations did you study in this module? Name and define each of them.

_____

_____

Module 9

Draw and Analyze Two-Dimensional Figures

MOUSETRAP ON THE COORDINATE PLANE!

There is a mouse on the coordinate plane shown here. The mouse is at a location that has integer coordinates.

To find the mouse, first graph the following polygons.

A. Triangle *ABC* with vertices $A(-7, 7)$, $B(3, 7)$, and $C(-2, 2)$.

B. Parallelogram *EFGH* with vertices $E(-3, 5)$, $F(6, 5)$, and $G(3, 1)$. Where is vertex *H* located? _____

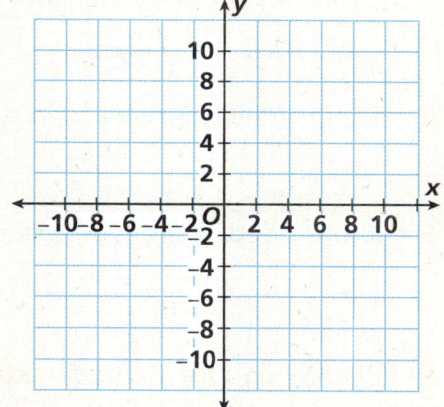

C. Square *KLMN* with vertices $K(-1, 4)$, $L(6, 4)$, and $M(6, -3)$. Where is vertex *N* located?
_____

D. Trapezoid *PQRS* with vertices $P(-3, 4)$, $Q(2, -1)$, $R(2, -6)$, and $S(-3, -9)$.

E. Now use these clues.

The mouse is located inside Triangle *ABC*.

The mouse is located inside Parallelogram *EFGH*.

The mouse is located outside Square *KLMN*.

The mouse is located outside Trapezoid *PQRS*.

 **Turn and Talk**

What are the coordinates of the location of the mouse? Explain how you know.

Module 9   293

Are You Ready?

Complete these problems to review prior concepts and skills you will need for this module.

Quadrilaterals

Classify each quadrilateral in as many ways as possible. Write *parallelogram*, *rectangle*, *square*, or *trapezoid*. If the figure is a quadrilateral only, write *quadrilateral*.

1.

2.

3. a four-sided figure with four right angles and four sides of equal length

4. a four-sided figure with no parallel sides

5. a four-sided figure with one pair of parallel sides

Polygons in the Coordinate Plane

Determine the length of each side of Quadrilateral *ABCD*.

6. Side *AB* _____   7. Side *CD* _____   8. Side *AD* _____

9. Draw triangle *FGH* with vertices *F*(−4, −4), *G*(−5, 2), and *H*(−1, −4) in the coordinate plane.

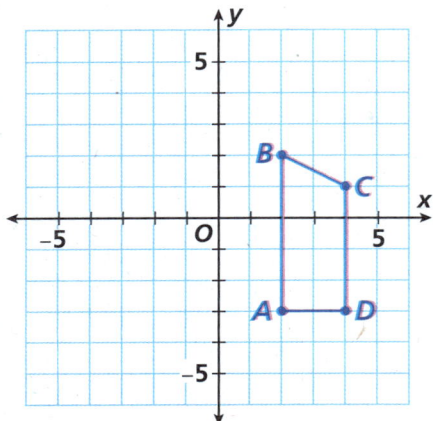

Build Conceptual Understanding

Lesson 1

Name _____

Draw Shapes with Given Conditions

I Can inscribe triangles in circles and draw geometric figures meeting given conditions.

Spark Your Learning

Parker plans to build a circular fire pit in a square area. He is drawing a model on paper to confirm his plans before he starts to build. How can Parker use paper folding and a compass to draw the largest possible circular fire pit in the space he has staked off? Trace Parker's square to a piece of paper and draw the circle for the fire pit.

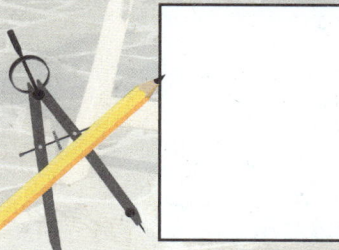

 **Turn and Talk** Brainstorm a list of characteristics specific to squares and circles.

Module 9 • Lesson 1   295

Build Understanding

1. A polygon is inscribed in a circle if every vertex of the polygon is on the circle. To investigate the kinds of triangles that can be inscribed in a circle, begin Parts A and B by using a compass to draw a circle with a radius of 0.5 inch. The **radius** of a circle is the distance from the circle's center to any point on the circle.

    A. Draw a circle and inscribe a triangle in it. Inscribe more than one if you can.

    B. A **diameter** is a segment that passes through the circle's center and has endpoints on the circle. Draw a circle and a diameter. Use the endpoints of the diameter and a third point on the circle to inscribe a triangle in the circle.

    C. Draw three circles, each with a diameter of 1 inch. Can you inscribe each triangle in one of the circles? If so, draw it. If not, justify your answer.

    a triangle with a 50° angle
    a triangle with a side of length 1.25 inches
    a triangle with a 30° angle and a 60° angle

Turn and Talk How many triangles can you draw in each of Parts A–C: none, only one, or more than one? Explain.

Name _____

2 ▸ Draw a hexagon with side lengths 2, 3, 4, 5, 6, and 7 units. The two longest sides are perpendicular. The longest side and the third-longest side are parallel.

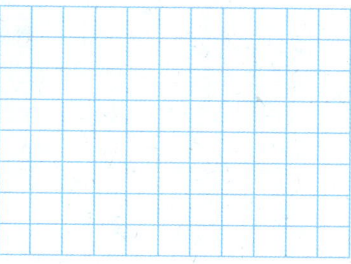

A. Begin by drawing the two longest sides perpendicular to each other. How can you draw two perpendicular segments?

_____

_____

B. Draw the third-longest side parallel to the longest side and connected to the second-longest side. How can you draw two parallel segments?

_____

C. Use a ruler or compass to draw the last three segments, or cut thin strips of paper. Use the segments to complete the hexagon.

D. Does the figure have any lines of symmetry? _____

3 ▸ Kaylee has a square piece of wood with a side length of 48 inches. She wants to use it to build the largest circular tabletop that she can.

A. Draw a square to model the piece of wood and label the square's side length. Then draw the diagonals to find the center of the square, which will also be the center of the circle, and draw the circle.

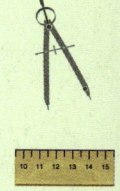

B. What is the diameter of the tabletop? How do you know?

_____

_____

_____

Check Understanding

1. Draw a circle. Can you inscribe an obtuse triangle? If so, inscribe an obtuse triangle and tell how many you can draw. If not, explain why not.

2. A square has a side length of 2.5 meters. What is the radius of the largest circle that fits inside the square?

_____

Module 9 • Lesson 1

On Your Own

3. **Use Tools** Draw a quadrilateral with two pairs of opposite sides that are parallel and equal in length, no right angles, and no lines of symmetry. What is the quadrilateral?

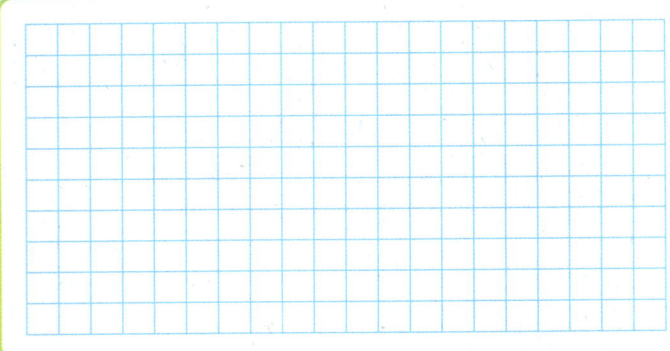

4. **Use Tools** Draw a circle and one of its diameters. Can you inscribe a triangle that has the diameter as a side and includes an obtuse angle? If so, draw the triangle. If not, justify your answer.

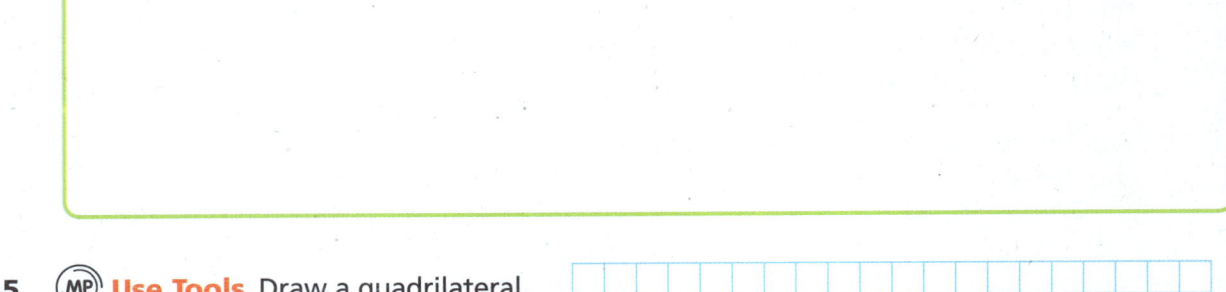

5. **Use Tools** Draw a quadrilateral with exactly one pair of parallel sides. What is the quadrilateral?

 I'm in a Learning Mindset!

Am I confident in my answer for Problem 4? What evidence do I have that I solved it correctly?

Name _____

Draw Shapes with Given Conditions

LESSON 9.1
More Practice/ Homework

ONLINE Video Tutorials and Interactive Examples

1. (MP) **Use Tools** Draw a decagon with eight sides of length 2 units and two sides of length 4 units. Any two sides that meet should be perpendicular, and the figure should contain parallel segments.

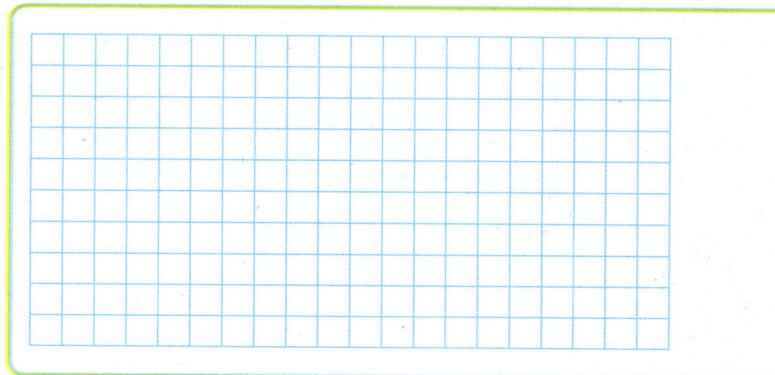

2. (MP) **Use Tools** Draw a quadrilateral with two pairs of congruent sides, no parallel sides, and one line of symmetry. What is the quadrilateral?

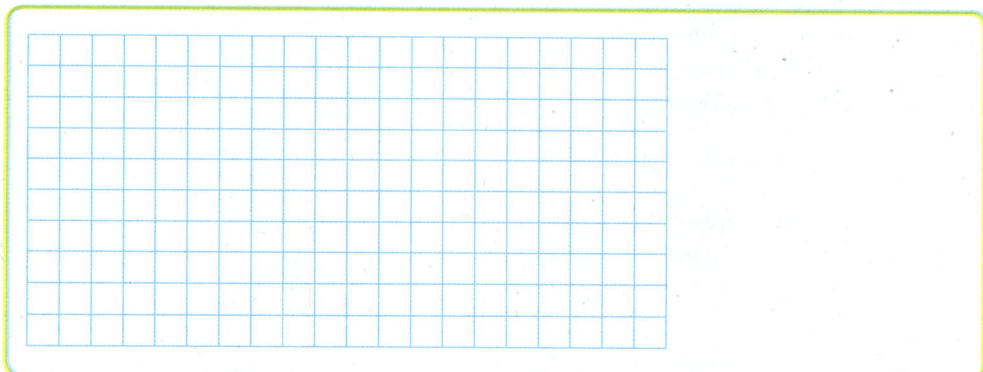

3. (MP) **Use Tools** Draw a circle with a radius of $\frac{3}{4}$ inch and a horizontal diameter. Inscribe a triangle that has the diameter as a side and a vertical line of symmetry.

Module 9 • Lesson 1   299

Test Prep

4. Match each figure with its description.

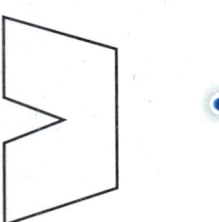

• hexagon with no symmetry

• hexagon with opposite sides parallel

• heptagon with one line of symmetry

5. A. Use tools to draw a quadrilateral with four sides of length 3 units, two pairs of parallel sides, and four lines of symmetry. What is the quadrilateral?

_____

B. What is the radius of the largest circle that fits inside your quadrilateral from Part A?

_____

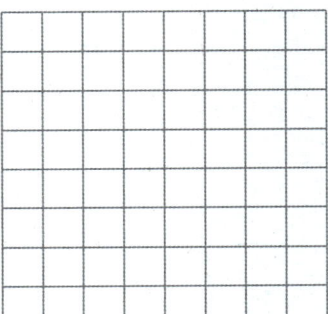

Spiral Review

6. This week, a department store is having a sale where everything is discounted 20%. A ski jacket originally sells for $185. How much will the ski jacket cost during the sale?

_____

7. What sequence of transformations can be performed on Figure 1 to produce Figure 2?

_____

_____

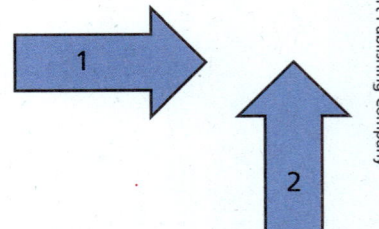

Lesson 2

Connect Concepts and Skills

Name _____

Draw and Construct Triangles Given Side Lengths

I Can determine whether three lengths could be side lengths of a triangle, and, given two side lengths, I can find the range of possible lengths for the third side.

Spark Your Learning

Martina is building a wind chime. She has pieces of metal pipe 2, 3, 4, and 5 inches long that she will use to make a triangular top for the wind chime. Which combinations of three lengths will **not** work for the top?

 **Turn and Talk** What do you notice about the set of lengths that did not make a triangle?

Module 9 • Lesson 2

Build Understanding

1 Can you draw a triangle with side lengths of 3, 4, and 8 units? There are different ways to model the situation and investigate. You can use thin strips of paper cut to the correct lengths, or you can use tools such as a ruler and compass or geometry software.

A. Use the longest side of your model as the possible base. Use your model to view the shorter sides in different positions. Can you draw a triangle? If so, draw one. If not, explain why you cannot.

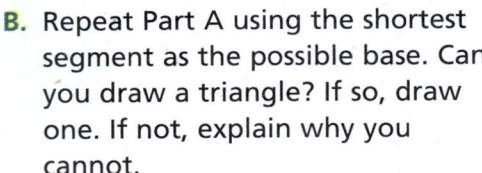

B. Repeat Part A using the shortest segment as the possible base. Can you draw a triangle? If so, draw one. If not, explain why you cannot.

C. Complete the statements describing the relationships among the three side lengths that do **not** form a triangle. Use *less than, equal to,* or *greater than*.

The sum of the lengths of the two shorter sides is _____ or equal to the length of the longer one.

2 Can you draw a triangle with side lengths of 3, 4, and 6 units?

A. Use the 6-unit segment as the possible base. Can you make a triangle? If so, draw it. If not, explain why you cannot.

_____

B. Use the 3-unit segment as the possible base. Can you make a triangle? If so, draw it. If not, explain why you cannot.

_____

C. Use the 4-unit segment as the possible base. Can you make a triangle? If so, draw it. If not, explain why you cannot.

_____

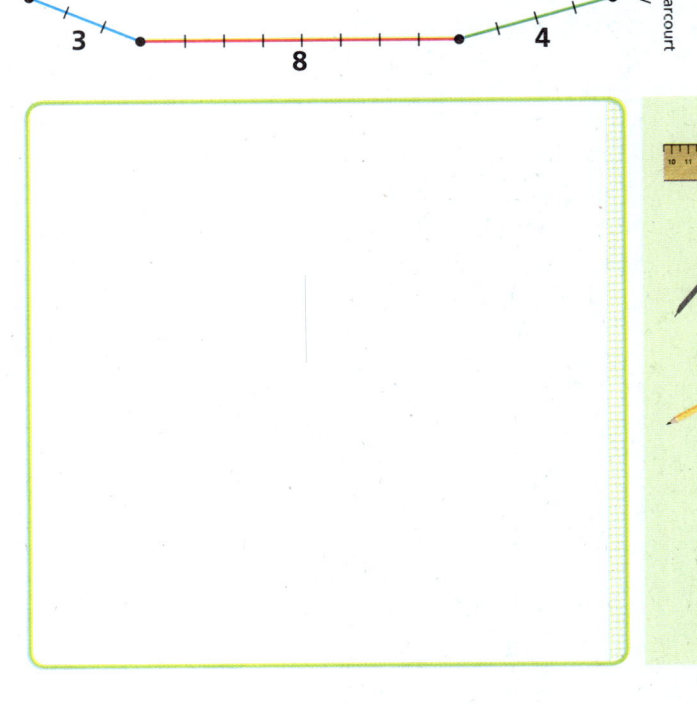

Name _____

D. How are the triangles you made in Parts A–C alike?

_____

E. Complete the statements describing the relationships between the three side lengths that form a triangle. Use *less than*, *equal to*, or *greater than*.

The sum of the lengths of the two shorter sides is _____ the length of the longest side.

F. Complete the summary of what you have discovered so far for three segments with lengths *a*, *b*, and *c*, where *c* is the greatest length.

If *a* + *b* is _____ than *c*, the segments cannot form a triangle.
If *a* + *b* is _____ than *c*, the segments form one triangle.

3 Can you draw a quadrilateral with side lengths of 2, 3, 4, and 5 units?

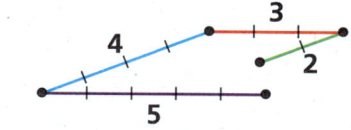

A. Make and use a model. Can you connect the endpoints to form a quadrilateral? If so, draw a quadrilateral. If not, explain why you cannot.

B. Using the same side lengths, can you make a quadrilateral that is different than the one you drew in Part A? If so, draw it. If not, explain why you cannot.

C. Make a conjecture about the number of quadrilaterals that can be made using four different segment lengths. Support your conclusion.

_____
_____
_____
_____
_____

Turn and Talk Is it possible that four segments cannot form a quadrilateral?

Module 9 • Lesson 2

Step It Out

4 In Parts A–C, let *a* and *b* be the shorter lengths and *c* be the longest length. Compare $a + b$ to c to determine if a triangle can be made. Write <, =, or >.

A. Nia wants to make a triangular picture frame from strips of wood that are 9 centimeters, 11 centimeters, and 15 centimeters long.

9 + 11 ☐ 15

Since the sum of the lengths of two shorter strips is _____ the length of the longest strip, Nia [can / cannot] make a triangle.

B. Gerard has pieces of string 6 inches, 5 inches, and 11 inches in length that he plans to use as a border for a collage.

6 + 5 ☐ 11

Since the sum of the lengths of two shorter pieces is _____ the length of the longest piece, Gerard [can / cannot] make a triangle.

C. Olivia gives her niece leftover pieces of ribbon from her art supplies. They are 12 inches, 10 inches, and 24 inches long.

12 + 10 ☐ 24

Since the sum of the lengths of two shorter pieces of ribbon is _____ the length of the longest, Olivia's niece [can / cannot] make a triangle.

D. Amil is making a bamboo frame. Given the side lengths shown for the first two sides, what is one possible side length that will form a triangular frame?

5 + 8 = _____, so one side length that will make a triangle is _____ inches.

8 in.   5 in.

Check Understanding

1. Max has three pieces of oak trim that are 7 inches, 11 inches, and 18 inches long. He wants to use them to make a triangular base for a candleholder. Will the pieces make a triangle? Explain.

_____
_____

2. Bella is making a sculpture for her garden. She has pieces of copper pipe that are 4 centimeters long and 13 centimeters long. What is a possible third length of copper pipe that will make a triangle? Justify your answer.

_____

304

On Your Own

3. Horace is making a shadow box in the shape of a triangle to hold his homerun baseballs. He has pieces of wood 12 inches, 12 inches, and 26 inches long. Show whether these pieces will make a triangle.

_____

4. Art An artist is going to make triangle earrings from glass rods with the lengths shown. Show whether these rods will make a triangle.

_____

_____

5. Alan makes triangular potholders and sews edging around the outside. He has pieces of edging 5 inches, 5 inches, and 10 inches long. Show whether these pieces will make a triangle.

_____

_____

Pieces to use:
1 cm
2 cm
2.5 cm

6. Open Ended The volleyball team is making a triangular banner for their last home game. They want two of the sides to be 4 feet long each. Determine one possible length for the third side. Justify your answer.

_____

_____

7. **(MP) Reason** Dante is constructing a quadrilateral with four sides, each 2 inches long. How many different quadrilaterals can he make? Explain.

_____

_____

_____

_____

Determine whether each set of numbers could be lengths of the sides of a triangle.

8. 17, 13, 11 _____   **9.** 11, 19, 35 _____   **10.** 6, 7, 13 _____

Two side lengths of a triangle are given. Find a possible third length.

11. 5 meters, 12 meters   **12.** 3 feet, 9 feet   **13.** 23 miles, 31 miles

Module 9 • Lesson 2   305

14. A craftsman makes stained glass crafts. He has metal strips of lengths 5 inches, 8 inches, and 11 inches. Show whether these strips will make a triangle.

_____

_____

15. Karissa is building a triangular landscape border around her mailbox. She has logs 4 feet, 5 feet, and 10 feet long. Show whether these logs will make a triangle.

_____

_____

16. Pierce is developing his own board game. The border of the board is going to be 3 pieces of cardboard, each 17 inches long. Show whether these lengths will make a triangle.

_____

17. **(MP) Construct Arguments** Risa has four sticks measuring 2 inches, 2.5 inches, 3 inches, and 8 inches. She wants to connect the sticks end to end to make a quadrilateral. Can she do it? Explain why or why not.

_____

_____

_____

Determine whether each set of numbers could be lengths of the sides of a triangle.

18. 8.5, 6, 10 _____   19. 2.5, 2.5, 4 _____   20. 5, 12, 18 _____

Two side lengths of a triangle are given. Find a possible third length.

21. 5 inches, 10 inches   22. 6 yards, 18 yards   23. 9 meters, 21 meters

_____   _____   _____

 I'm in a Learning Mindset!

How does my mindset affect my confidence in determining whether a set of side lengths could form a triangle?

_____

_____

Name _____

Draw and Construct Triangles Given Side Lengths

LESSON 9.2
More Practice/ Homework

ONLINE Video Tutorials and Interactive Examples

1. Haley is making a triangle-shaped box garden. She has wooden pieces of lengths 6 feet, 8 feet, and 13 feet. Show whether these pieces will make a triangle.

   _____

   _____

2. Students are making shapes with string in an art class. Ben has pieces of string measuring 4 inches, 2 inches, and 1.5 inches long. Show whether these lengths will make a triangle.

   _____

   _____

3. (MP) **Construct Arguments** The Culinary Club is making a triangle-shaped sign showing a piece of pie for their pie-eating competition. Two of the sides measure as shown. Determine a possible length for the third side. Justify your answer.

   _____

   _____

   _____

   _____

4. Seth wants to make a quadrilateral charm for a necklace. He has wire pieces with lengths 1 centimeter, 2 centimeters, 4 centimeters, and 5 centimeters. How many possible quadrilaterals are there with those side lengths?

   _____

   _____

Determine whether each set of numbers could be lengths of the sides of a triangle.

5. 2, 4, 6 _____   6. 16, 21, 33 _____   7. 1, 3, 3 _____

Two side lengths of a triangle are given. Find a possible third length.

8. 6 meters, 8 meters   9. 4 feet, 5 feet   10. 4.5 yards, 7 yards

Module 9 • Lesson 2   307

Test Prep

11. Lorelei is making decorative boxes in the shape of triangles. Which of the following could be the lengths of the sides of the boxes?

    Ⓐ 12 cm, 13 cm, 24 cm

    Ⓑ 12 cm, 13 cm, 25 cm

    Ⓒ 10 cm, 10 cm, 24 cm

    Ⓓ 10 cm, 10 cm, 22 cm

12. Lhu builds dollhouses with triangle-shaped roofs. Which of the following could be lengths of the edges of the roof of a dollhouse?

    Ⓐ 10 in., 10 in., 20 in.

    Ⓑ 10 in., 12 in., 24 in.

    Ⓒ 11 in., 12 in., 24 in.

    Ⓓ 11 in., 11 in., 20 in.

13. Select all the sets of numbers that could be lengths of the sides of a triangle.

    Ⓐ 2, 7, 9

    Ⓑ 4, 11, 13

    Ⓒ 6, 9, 12

    Ⓓ 6, 6, 14

    Ⓔ 8, 15, 21

    Ⓕ 9, 17, 27

14. An artist gets strips of metal from a salvage yard to make decorative wall art. The artist finds strips that are 2.5 feet and 3.5 feet long. Determine one possible length for the third strip if the artist wants to make a triangle.

_____

Spiral Review

15. Use geometry software to draw a quadrilateral with two pairs of parallel sides and four right angles. What is the most specific name that applies to the quadrilateral?

_____

16. Complete the inequality with the correct comparison symbol.

    -4 ☐ $|-4|$

Draw and Construct Triangles Given Angle Measures

I Can use tools to construct triangles when given angle measures and determine if no triangle or many triangles can be formed.

Spark Your Learning

A town is designing triangular flower beds for a park. Is it possible to choose three angle measures that will **not** form a triangle? If so, draw several examples.

 Turn and Talk Pick one of your examples above and describe how you could revise your drawing to form a triangle.

Build Understanding

1 You can use tools to determine whether you can construct a triangle with three given angle measures.

A. Is it possible to construct a triangle with angle measures of 25°, 75°, and 80°? If so, draw the triangle.

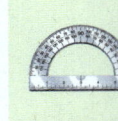

B. Is it possible to construct a larger or smaller triangle with those same angle measures? If so, draw an example. If not, explain why not.

C. Is it possible to construct a triangle with angle measures of 45°, 60°, and 55°? With angle measures of 45°, 60°, and 95°? If so, draw the triangles.

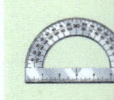

D. You have examined the number of unique triangles that can be formed using three given angle measures and the number of unique triangles that can be formed using three given side lengths. How do the numbers compare?

_____

_____

_____

 Turn and Talk What appears to be true about the sum of the measures of the angles of a triangle?

Name _____

Step It Out

2 Jenny draws a triangle that includes one angle that has a measure of 30°, one angle that has a measure of 90°, and one side that has a length of 1 inch. Without seeing her triangle, can you draw it?

    A. Can the given side of Jenny's triangle be a side of both given angles of the triangle? Can it be a side of only one of the angles? _____

    B. Think about how the given side and the given angles might be positioned. Draw all the triangles you can using the information given for Jenny's triangle. Label the known measures on your drawings.

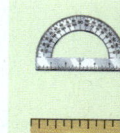

    C. Can Jenny's triangle be found among your drawings? Explain.

_____
_____

    D. Can you draw a triangle with one 90° angle and one 100° angle so that the side between the angles is 2 inches long? Why or why not?

_____
_____
_____

Check Understanding

1. Cliff wants to draw a triangle with a 30° angle and a 60° angle so that the side between them is 2 inches long. How many triangles can he draw?

_____

2.   **A.** If possible, construct a triangle with angle measures of 45°, 65°, and 70°.

    B. How many triangles are possible: none, one, or many?

_____

Module 9 • Lesson 3

On Your Own

3. Kara is making a picture out of tiles. One tile will be triangular with angle measures of 25°, 25°, and 130°.

   A. **Use Tools** Sketch a triangle with those angle measures.

   B. Do you have enough information to make Kara's triangle? Explain.

Use Tools For Problems 4–5, determine whether it is possible to draw a triangle with the given angle measures. If it is possible, use tools to draw a triangle.

4. 55°, 60°, 70°

5. 30°, 40°, 110°

6. **Use Tools** Kate is drawing a house. For the top of the house, she wants to make a triangle with angle measures of 30°, 30°, and 120°. Can Kate make a triangle with these angle measures? If so, use tools to draw the triangle. If not, explain why not.

7. Eduardo is building a triangular sandbox for a playground. He wants the triangle to include a 65° angle, a 50° angle, and at least one side that is 12 feet long. Draw at least one possible triangle on a separate piece of paper and estimate possible lengths of the other two sides of the triangle.

I'm in a Learning Mindset!

How does my mindset affect my confidence in determining whether it is possible to draw a triangle with given angle measures? How did I use tools to support my conclusion?

Name _____

Draw and Construct Triangles Given Angle Measures

LESSON 9.3
More Practice/Homework

1. **Use Tools** Vanessa wants to build a triangular table. Can she build a table with angle measures of 15°, 55°, and 110°? If so, draw the triangle.

2. Carlos wants to draw a triangle with angle measures of 55°, 60°, and 65°. How many different triangles can Carlos draw: one or more than one?

_____

For Problems 3–6, determine whether it is possible to draw a triangle with the given angle measures. If it is possible, use tools to draw a triangle.

3. 25°, 40°, 115°

4. 15°, 15°, 120°

5. 60°, 70°, 70°

6. 30°, 55°, 95°

7. **Construct Arguments** James sees a floor made of triangular tiles of different sizes. He notices that two triangles each have one angle with a measure of 35°, another with a measure of 45°, and one side with a length of 6 inches. Are the two triangles the same? Explain.

_____
_____
_____

Module 9 • Lesson 3

313

Test Prep

8. How many different triangles can be made with the angle measures 30°, 60°, and 90°?

- Ⓐ none
- Ⓑ one
- Ⓒ exactly two
- Ⓓ more than two

9. Each set of angle measures and/or side lengths can be used to form a triangle. Which conditions produce only one triangle? Choose all that apply.

- Ⓐ 35° angle, 55° angle, 90° angle
- Ⓑ 3-inch side, 4-inch side, 5-inch side
- Ⓒ 30° angle, 60° angle, 2-inch side joining the angles
- Ⓓ 28° angle, 80° angle, 1-meter side
- Ⓔ three 60° angles, three $\frac{3}{4}$-inch sides

10. Seamus draws a triangle with angles of measures 40°, 60°, and 80°. Edwina draws a triangle with these same angle measures. Which statement **cannot** be true?

- Ⓐ Edwina's triangle is not the same size as Seamus's triangle.
- Ⓑ Edwina's triangle is not the same shape as Seamus's triangle.
- Ⓒ The perimeter of Seamus's triangle is greater than the perimeter of Edwina's triangle.
- Ⓓ The area of Edwina's triangle is less than the area of Seamus's triangle.

Spiral Review

11. The vertices of a triangle are (5, 3), (−2, −5), and (0, −6). The triangle is rotated 180° about the origin. What are the coordinates of the vertices of the image?

12. Draw an octagon with six sides of length 3 units, one side of length 4 units, and one side of length 10 units. Every pair of sides that meet are perpendicular. The figure should have symmetry.

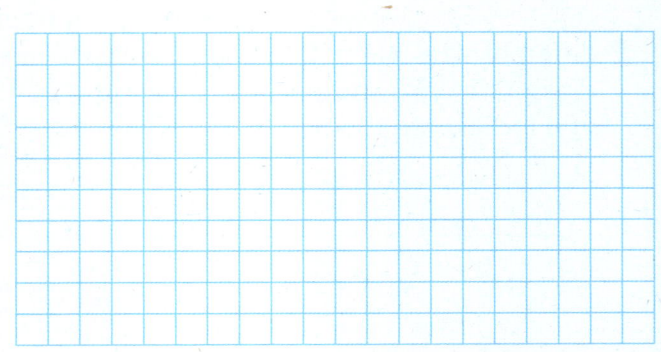

Apply and Practice
Lesson 4

Name _____

Draw and Analyze Shapes to Solve Problems

I Can draw and analyze shapes, including circles and triangles, to solve real-world problems.

Step It Out

1 Lucas is using strips of wood to construct a triangle. The first two strips are 4 feet long and 7 feet long. When Lucas nails them together, the two pieces of wood form a 50° angle.

A. Draw a model of the two strips after Lucas nailed them together.

B. Can he use a third strip to construct a triangle? If so, complete the model.

_____

C. How many triangles can be formed?

_____

Turn and Talk What if the third strip were 12 feet long? Would Lucas still be able to construct a triangle? Explain.

2 In this task, you will draw triangles given the lengths of two sides and the measure of an angle that is **not** between them.

A. Side AB: 8 units; Side BC: 6 units; Angle A: 40°

To construct Triangle ABC, you need to draw Side BC. Because Side BC is 6 units long, put the point of the compass at Point B, and draw part of a circle with radius 6 units. You can use this segment to help you open your compass to the correct radius.

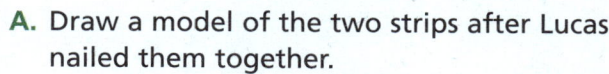
6 units

The circle intersects the other side of $\angle A$ in _____ point(s). You can draw _____ triangle(s). Draw the triangle(s).

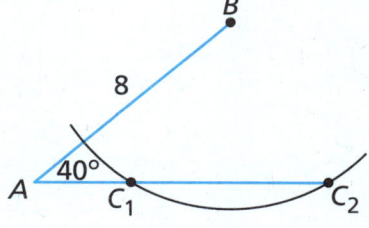

Module 9 • Lesson 4   315

B. Side *AB*: 5 units; Side *BC*: 7 units; Angle *A*: 90°

To draw Side *BC*, put the point of the compass on Point *B*, and draw part of a circle with radius 7 units. Use this 7-unit segment to open your compass to the correct radius.

|—————— 7 units ——————|

The circle intersects the other side of ∠*A* at _____ point(s).

You can draw _____ triangle(s). Draw the triangle(s).

C. Side *AB*: 6 units; Side *BC*: 9 units; Angle *A*: 120°

Use this segment to help you draw Side *BC*.

9 units

The circle intersects the other side of ∠*A* at _____ point(s).

You can draw _____ triangle(s). Draw the triangle(s).

D. How many triangles did you draw in Parts A–C given two sides and the measure of an angle that is not between them?

_____

_____

Turn and Talk How are the situations in Step It Out 1 and Step It Out 2 different? How are they the same?

Check Understanding

1. Draw a right triangle with two sides of lengths of 4 units and 5 units and the 90° angle between them.

2. Draw a right triangle with two sides of lengths 4 units and 5 units with the 90° angle not between them.

Name _____

On Your Own

3. A triangle with the largest possible base is drawn inside a circle. What part of the circle must coincide with the base of the triangle?

_____

4. **MP Use Tools** Use the diagram shown. Construct two different triangles that each have Side *AB* with a length of 8 units, Side *BC* with a length of 5 units, and a 35° angle that is not between them. Use the segment below to help you draw Side *BC*.

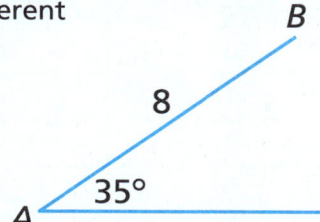

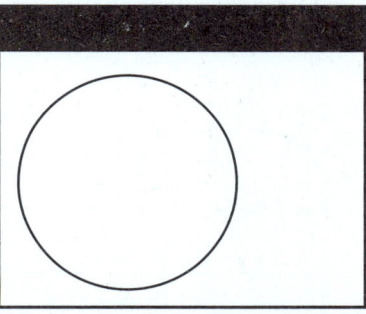

5. **STEM** An ethologist is a scientist who studies animal behavior. One ethologist studied the play behavior of a group of infant lowland gorillas and measured the portion of play time given to three types of play. Draw a circle graph to show the portion of the day for each type. The measure of the angle between the sides of the section for each behavior is given.

Solitary play: 150°
Social play: 195°
Mother-infant play: 15°

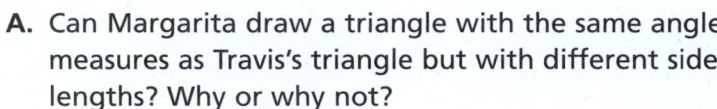

6. Travis draws a triangle with three 60° angles and three sides of length 5 inches.

A. Can Margarita draw a triangle with the same angle measures as Travis's triangle but with different side lengths? Why or why not?

_____
_____

B. Can she draw a triangle with the same side lengths as Travis's triangle but with different angle measures? Explain.

_____
_____

Module 9 • Lesson 4   **317**

7. **Use Tools** Students were surveyed about the number of siblings they have. Draw a circle graph to show the part of the group surveyed that each has a given number of siblings. The table shows the measure of the angle between the sides of the section for each number of siblings.

Siblings	Angle measure
0	40°
1	85°
2	95°
3	50°
4	50°
5 or more	40°

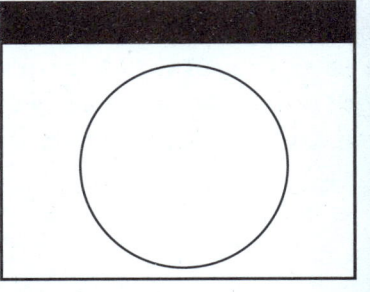

8. **Use Tools** Draw a triangle that has sides of length 7 units and 5 units with a 42° angle between them. Can you draw more than one triangle?

9. **Open Ended** Draw a figure that has at least one pair of parallel sides and at least one side that is 6 units long. The figure should also have at least one line of symmetry.

Name _____

Draw and Analyze Shapes to Solve Problems

LESSON 9.4
More Practice/ Homework

ONLINE Video Tutorials and Interactive Examples

1. **Open Ended** Draw a figure that has at least one pair of perpendicular sides, at least one side that is 4 units long, and at least one line of symmetry.

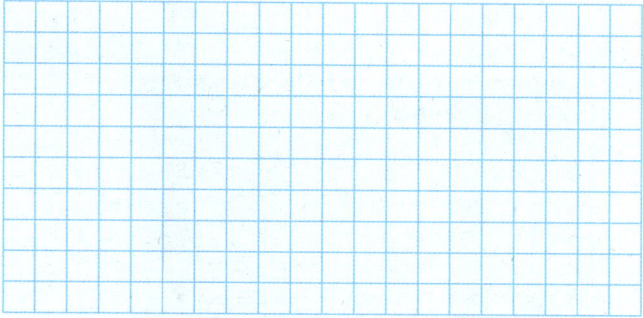

2. **Use Tools** How many triangles can you draw that have two sides of lengths 5 units and 2 units and a 68° angle between them? Draw the triangle(s).

3. A. **Use Tools** Complete the drawing to make Triangle(s) ABC with Side AB of length 9 units, Side BC of length 7 units, and Angle A with measure 45°. Use this segment to help you draw side BC.

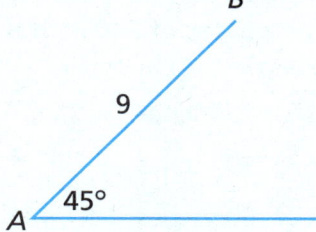
7 units

B. How many triangles with these measurements can you draw?

_____

4. **Reason** The two longest sides of a triangle are 7 inches and 10 inches long. Describe a possible length for the shortest side. Explain your reasoning.

_____
_____
_____

Module 9 • Lesson 4   319

Test Prep

5. Indicate whether one, none, or many triangles can be drawn with the given side lengths and/or angle measures.

	None	One	Many
6 feet, 6 feet, 8 feet	☐	☐	☐
40°, 40°, 112°	☐	☐	☐
68°, 22°, 90°	☐	☐	☐
7 meters, 6 meters, 12 meters	☐	☐	☐
6 inches, 10 inches, 45° angle between	☐	☐	☐
3 feet, 5 feet, 10 feet	☐	☐	☐

6. A triangle has two sides of lengths 20 centimeters and 8 centimeters. Which can be the length of the third side of the triangle? Select all that apply.

  (A) 30 centimeters

  (B) 22 centimeters

  (C) 14 centimeters

  (D) 8 centimeters

  (E) 6 centimeters

7. A road worker wants to place a circular map on a square sign that has a perimeter of 240 inches. What is the greatest possible radius of the circular map?

  (A) 15 inches

  (B) 30 inches

  (C) 60 inches

  (D) 120 inches

Spiral Review

8. Write an inequality to compare the integers −5 and −6.

_____

9. How many unique triangles can be made with sides of lengths 4 cm, 7 cm, and 12 cm: none, one, or many?

_____

Module 9 Review

Name _____

Vocabulary

Choose the correct term from the Vocabulary box.

Vocabulary
- diameter
- hexagon
- perpendicular
- quadrilateral
- radius

1. The distance from the center of a circle to any point on the circle is the _____ of the circle.

2. Two lines that intersect at a right angle are _____.

3. A _____ is a six-sided polygon.

4. A _____ of a circle is a line segment that passes through the center of the circle and has its endpoints on the circle.

Concepts and Skills

For Problems 5–6, draw a figure on the grid that matches each description.

5. A polygon with at least one pair of perpendicular sides, a side with a length of 8 units, and a side with a length of 6 units

6. An acute triangle with exactly one line of symmetry and one side with a length of 4 units

7. **MP Use Tools** Alisa drew the triangle shown. She claims it is the only distinct triangle that can be drawn with a 90° angle and two sides that measure 5 inches and 7 inches. Is Alisa correct? Why or why not? State what strategy and tool you will use to answer the question, explain your choice, and then find the answer.

_____
_____
_____

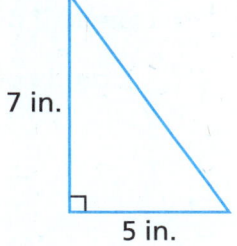

Module 9   **321**

8. Iris has three pieces of PVC piping that are 3 feet, 8 feet, and 14 feet long. She wants to use them to make a triangular base for a garden project. Can the pieces form a triangle? Explain.

   _____

9. Ernesto drew a quadrilateral that has exactly one pair of parallel sides and exactly one line of symmetry. Which shape could he have drawn?

   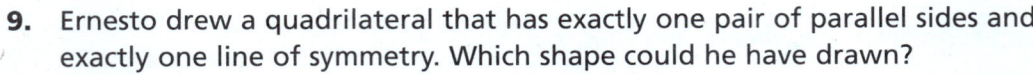

   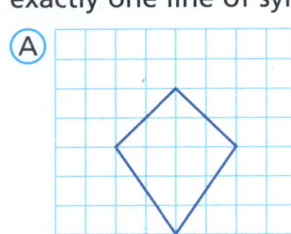 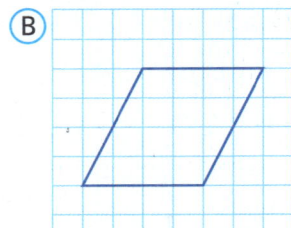 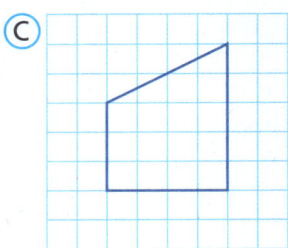 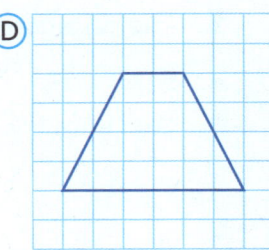

10. Two of the sides of a triangle measure 6 inches and 10 inches. Select all measurements that could be the length of the third side of the triangle.

    (A) 4 inches (D) 10 inches

    (B) 5 inches (E) 12 inches

    (C) 8 inches (F) 18 inches

11. For each set of measurements, tell whether exactly one triangle, more than one triangle, or no triangle can be constructed.

	Exactly one triangle	More than one triangle	No triangles
Angles that measure 60°, 60°, and 60°	☐	☐	☐
Sides that measure 4 cm, 8 cm, and 9 cm	☐	☐	☐
Sides that measure 15 mm, 20 mm, and 35 mm	☐	☐	☐

12. An artist is designing a logo for a new business. She starts by drawing a rectangle with a length of 10 centimeters and a width of 6 centimeters. What is the radius of the largest circle the artist can draw inside the rectangle if points on the circle can touch the sides of the rectangle?

    _____ centimeters

Module 10

Transformations and Similarity

DO YOU HAUL BONES?

A museum received a crate containing a set of dinosaur bones. You need to move the crate from its current location to the location marked on the grid. Each unit on the grid represents 1 meter.

How could you use a sequence of transformations to haul the crate to its new location?

_____
_____
_____
_____

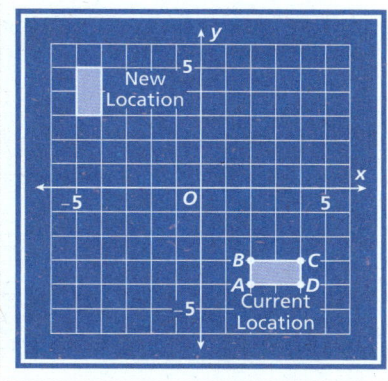

 Turn and Talk

Why might the museum not want you to use a reflection to move the crate?

323

Are You Ready?

Complete these problems to review prior concepts and skills you will need for this module.

Polygons in the Coordinate Plane

Determine the length, in units, of each side of the figure on the coordinate plane.

1. $\overline{LM}$ _____
2. $\overline{MN}$ _____
3. $\overline{NP}$ _____
4. $\overline{PQ}$ _____
5. $\overline{QR}$ _____
6. $\overline{LR}$ _____

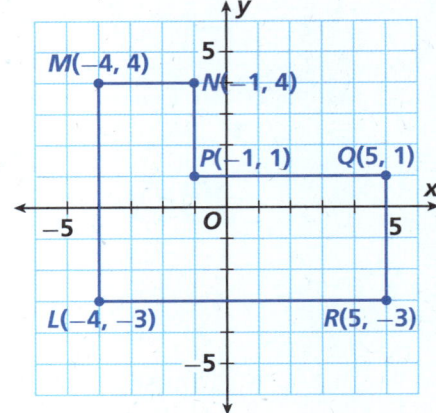

Scale Drawings

A scale drawing of a school cafeteria has a scale of 1 inch : 4 feet. Use this information to answer each question.

7. In the drawing, the cafeteria dining room has a length of 18 inches. What is the actual length of the dining room?

   _____

8. The actual width of the cafeteria kitchen is 42 feet. What is the width of the kitchen in the scale drawing?

   _____

Translations, Reflections, and Rotations

Draw the image of each transformation on the coordinate plane.

9. Rotate Triangle ABC 180° about the origin.

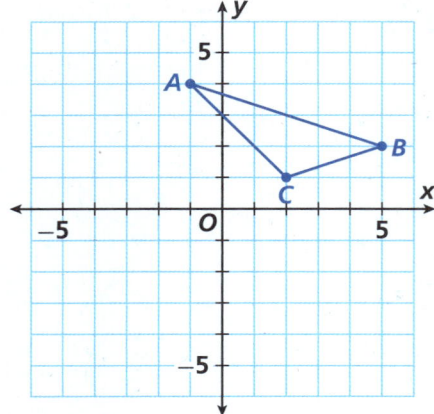

10. Reflect Triangle DEF across the y-axis, and then translate it 4 units down.

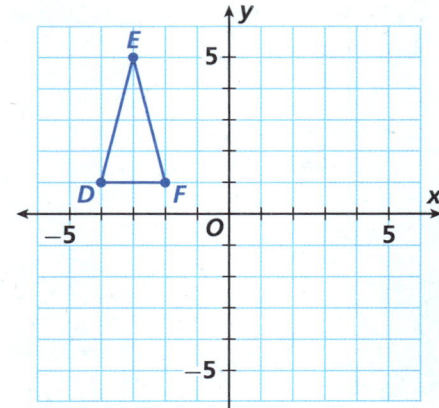

Investigate Reductions and Enlargements

I Can identify and perform enlargements and reductions.

Spark Your Learning

Rachel wants to enlarge her company logo for a sign. Sketch an **enlargement** of the **Roofs by Rachel** logo. Use your protractor to make sure the angle measurements of your enlargement stay the same as the original.

How are the two images alike? How are they different? Describe your findings.

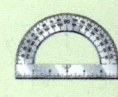

 **Turn and Talk** Write ratios comparing the lengths of the short and long sides of the original parallelogram and also of your enlarged parallelograms. What do you find?

Module 10 • Lesson 1

325

Build Understanding

Many computers and phones use reductions, called *thumbnails*, to represent images. **Reductions** are transformations that keep the proportions of the original image but are smaller in size.

1 **A.** Triangle *ABC* is a drawing of the side of a roof. Use a ruler and a protractor to measure △*ABC*.

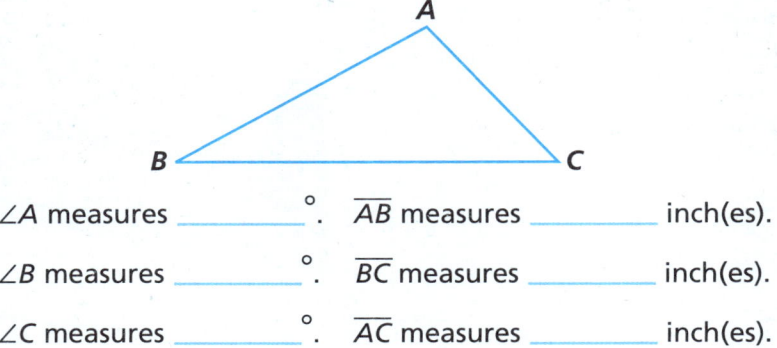

∠A measures _____°. $\overline{AB}$ measures _____ inch(es).

∠B measures _____°. $\overline{BC}$ measures _____ inch(es).

∠C measures _____°. $\overline{AC}$ measures _____ inch(es).

B. If △*A'B'C'* is a reduction of △*ABC* that results in △*A'B'C'* having a perimeter exactly half that of △*ABC*, what are the measurements of △*A'B'C'*?

∠A' measures _____°. $\overline{A'B'}$ measures _____ inch(es).

∠B' measures _____°. $\overline{B'C'}$ measures _____ inch(es).

∠C' measures _____°. $\overline{A'C'}$ measures _____ inch(es).

C. Draw △*A'B'C'* as a reduction.

D. Explain how you know it is a reduction.

_____

_____

_____

 Turn and Talk What would happen if you enlarged △*A'B'C'*? Could you make a new image that is congruent to the original figure △*ABC*? If so, how?

Name _____

Look at this photo. As the train tracks get closer to the front, they appear larger. A coordinate grid can help show how the tracks' apparent size changes.

2 ▶ Samuel wants to draw a railroad tunnel on a grid. First he draws the far end of the tunnel in blue as shown, then he decides to use rays to help him accurately enlarge the image.

A. Samuel draws two rays. Each starts at the origin and passes through a vertex of the blue preimage. He uses the rays to help sketch the floor of the tunnel closest to the viewer.

How do the rays help him draw the floor of the tunnel closest to the viewer?

_____
_____
_____
_____

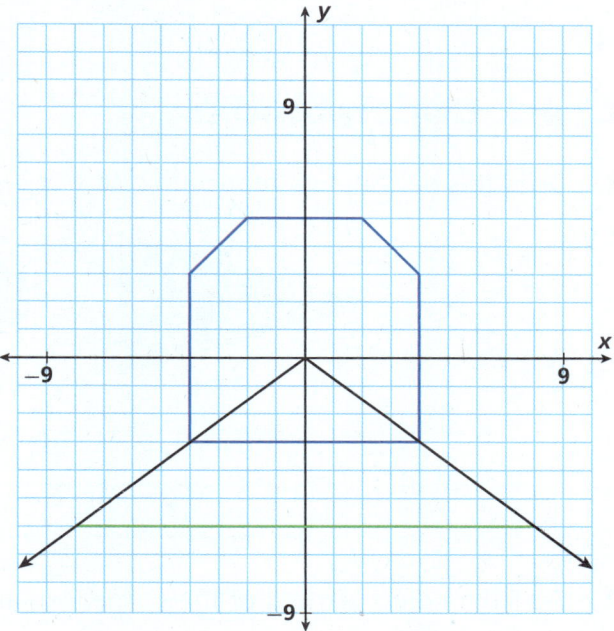

B. Draw additional rays from the origin through the vertices of Samuel's preimage. Use those rays to complete the enlarged image.

C. Look at your new image. Is it the same shape as the preimage? Explain how you know.

_____
_____
_____

Module 10 • Lesson 1

3 You can make reductions on a coordinate grid.

A. Draw rays from the origin through the vertices of the given shape. How can these rays help you reduce the shape?

_____
_____
_____

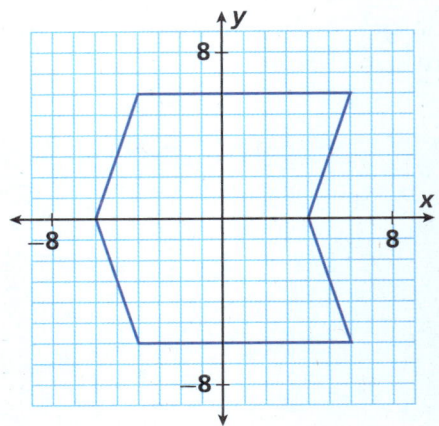

B. Reduce the shape so the sides are half the original length. Use the grid to sketch your new image.

C. How can you be sure your image shows an accurate reduction?

_____
_____

Check Understanding

1. Does this pair show a reduction? Why or why not?

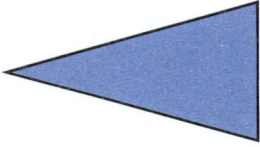

_____
_____
_____

2. Sketch an enlargement of the shape. Explain how you know it's an enlargement.

_____
_____

328

Name _____

On Your Own

3. Identify whether the transformation from each blue Figure A to green Figure B is an enlargement or a reduction.

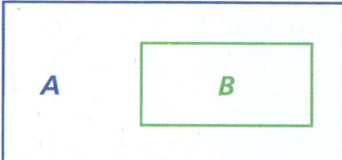 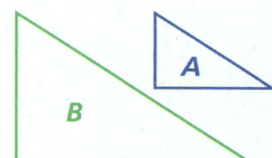 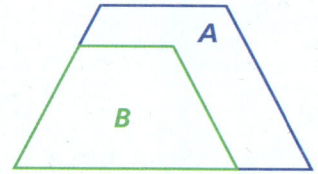

_____   _____   _____

4. Use the coordinate plane to sketch an enlargement with side lengths twice those in the figure shown.

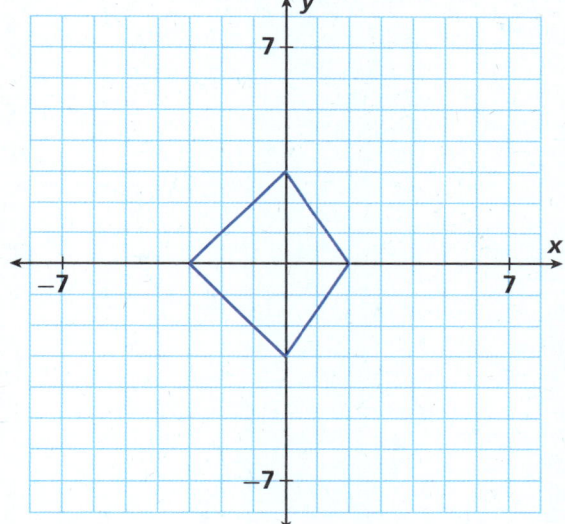

5. **Reason** Fredrick drew a reduction of a phone. Is the reduction accurate? Why or why not?

_____
_____
_____
_____
_____
_____

Module 10 • Lesson 1

6. **Use Tools** Draw a reduction of the figure with dimensions half those of the original figure.

 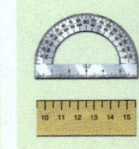

7. **Use Tools** Use the coordinate plane to reduce the side lengths of the figure by a factor of 2.

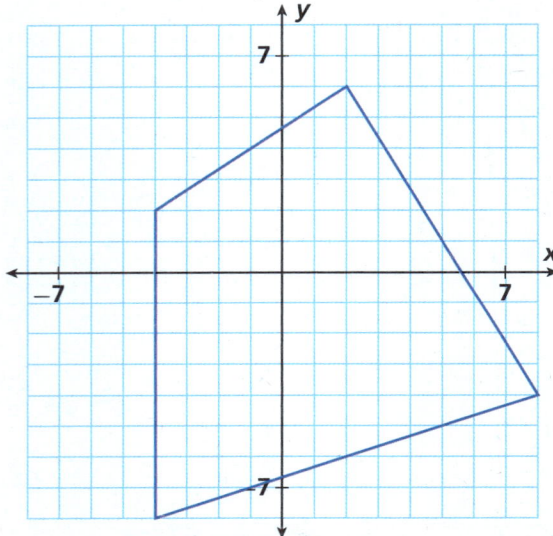

8. For each figure, determine if it is a reduction of Figure S.

  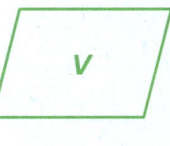

 **I'm in a Learning Mindset!**

How does my mindset affect my confidence with reducing and enlarging figures?

_____

_____

330

Investigate Reductions and Enlargements

**LESSON 10.1
More Practice/
Homework**

1. **(MP) Use Tools** In the space provided, sketch an enlargement that has sides $\frac{3}{2}$ the length of each given figure.

2. **A.** Use the coordinate plane to sketch a reduction of the irregular pentagon on the grid by any amount.

   _____

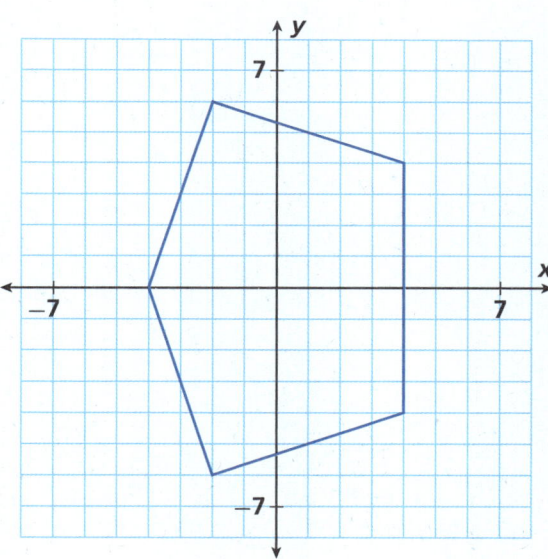

The Pentagon, in Washington, DC, is a regular pentagon.

B. Measure the angles of both figures with a protractor. Explain your findings.

_____

_____

3. A certain Figure Q is enlarged to form Figure P. Are Figures Q and P congruent? Why or why not?

_____

_____

Module 10 • Lesson 1

Test Prep

4. In which of the following has Figure 1 been enlarged to form Figure 2?

Ⓐ

Ⓒ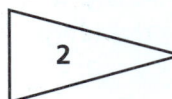

Ⓑ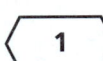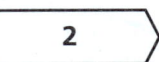

Ⓓ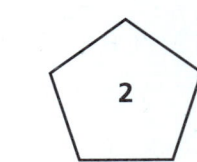

5. One of the shapes on the coordinate grid was transformed into the other shape. Which term could describe the transformation?

Ⓐ reflection Ⓑ enlargement Ⓒ translation Ⓓ rotation

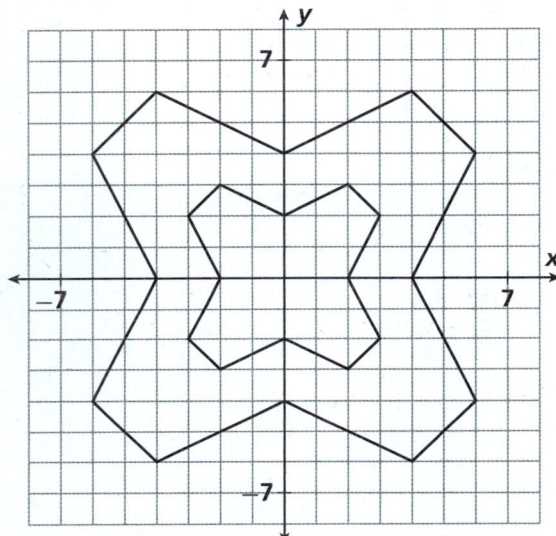

Spiral Review

6. Rotate △ABC 90° counterclockwise about the origin.

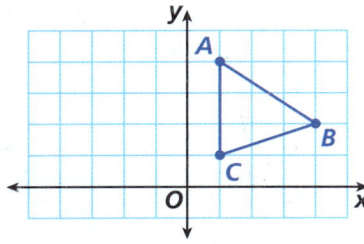

7. This design is made using only one type of transformation multiple times. Which one type of transformation is this?

_____

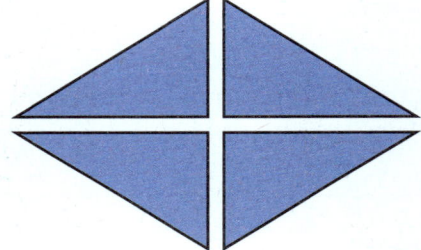

332

Connect Concepts and Skills

Lesson 2

Name _____

Explore Dilations

I Can identify and perform dilations given a scale factor and center of dilation, perform a dilation on a coordinate plane, and identify an algebraic rule for the dilation.

Spark Your Learning

On a computer, Raquel uses polygons and a circle to make a model of the top of London's Big Ben clock tower. Then she reduces it.

Compare Raquel's image and reduction. What do you find?

 **Turn and Talk** What is the relationship between the perimeter of Raquel's original image and her reduction? How does this relate to the relationship between the side lengths?

Module 10 • Lesson 2   333

Build Understanding

1 Rectangle R'S'T'U' is a dilation of Rectangle RSTU.

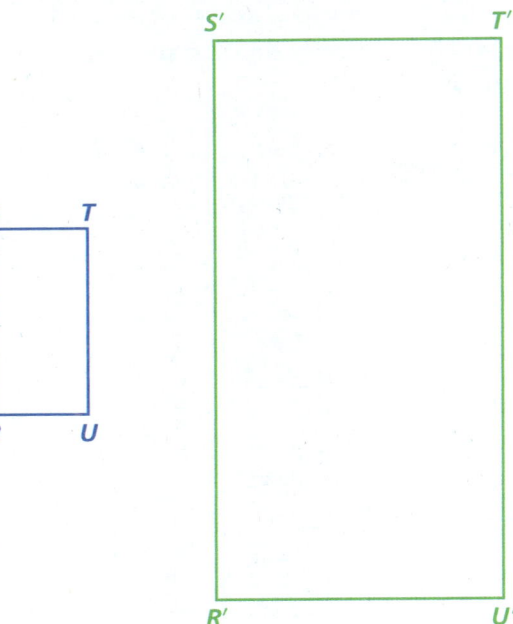

> **Connect to Vocabulary**
>
> A **dilation** is a transformation that produces an image that is proportional to its preimage.

A. Measure the sides of the figures, then fill in the table.

	RSTU	R'S'T'U'
Height (in.)		
Width (in.)		

What is the relationship between the measurements of the two rectangles?

_____

_____

B. What is the scale factor of this dilation?

_____

C. Points R and R' are an example of corresponding vertices. Use a ruler or straight edge to draw four rays, each extending from a vertex of the image to the corresponding vertex of the preimage, and continuing through to the left. What do you notice?

_____

D. Label the center of dilation for Rectangles RSTU and R'S'T'U' as Point P.

> **Connect to Vocabulary**
>
> The **scale factor** of a dilation is the ratio of the side lengths of the image to the preimage. The point of intersection of lines through each pair of corresponding vertices in a dilation is called the **center of dilation**.

Step It Out

2

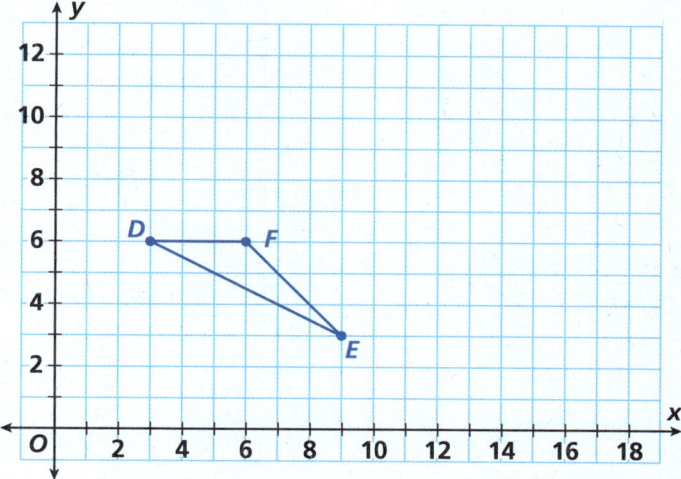

A. In order to dilate △DEF to form △D'E'F' with a scale factor of 2 and center of dilation (0, 0), first draw a ray from the center of dilation through Vertex D.

B. Find a point on the ray that is twice the distance from the center of dilation as Vertex D. Label it D'.

C. Give the ordered pairs for Vertices D and D'. How are these values related to the scale factor?

_____
_____

D. Predict the ordered pairs for Vertices E' and F'. Explain your reasoning.

_____
_____
_____

E. Draw △D'E'F' on the graph. Use rays from the center of dilation to draw your dilation.

F. Using the ordered pairs of △DEF, how would you make a dilation △D"E"F" with a scale factor of $\frac{1}{3}$ and center (0, 0)?

_____

G. Draw △D"E"F" on the graph. Use rays from the center of dilation to check your dilation. What are the coordinates of the vertices of △D"E"F"?

_____

H. What happens when you dilate △DEF with a scale factor of 1? Describe the resulting image.

_____

Module 10 • Lesson 2

3 △G'H'J' is a dilation of △GHJ. Find the scale factor and center of dilation. Represent the dilation algebraically.

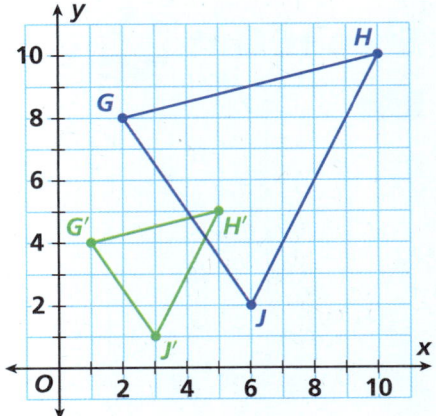

A. Complete the table.

G (2, 8)	→	G' (1, 4)
H	→	H'
J	→	J'

B. How are the corresponding coordinates for the image and the preimage related?

_____

_____

C. What is the scale factor of the dilation? _____

D. Circle the algebraic representation that best describes this dilation. Explain your reasoning.

$(x, y) \rightarrow (x + \frac{1}{2}, y + \frac{1}{2})$ $(x, y) \rightarrow (x - \frac{1}{2}, y - \frac{1}{2})$

$(x, y) \rightarrow (\frac{1}{2}x, \frac{1}{2}y)$ $(x, y) \rightarrow (2x, 2y)$

_____

_____

E. Draw rays through corresponding vertices of both figures to find the center of dilation. What is the center of dilation?

_____

Check Understanding

1. Does the pair of figures show a dilation with scale factor 4?

   A.

   B.

2. Polygon BCDE has vertices B(5, 1), C(5, 6), D(10, 6), and E(10, 1). If B'C'D'E' is a dilation of BCDE with scale factor 4 and center (0, 0), give the coordinates of B'C'D'E'.

_____

On Your Own

3. **Reason** Figure S' is a dilation of Figure S.

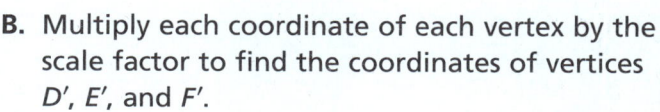

   A. Is the scale factor greater than 1 or less than 1? _____

   B. Is Figure S congruent to Figure S'? _____

   C. Is the dilation a reduction? _____

4. **Use Tools** Dilate △DEF with scale factor $\frac{3}{2}$ and center (0, 0).

   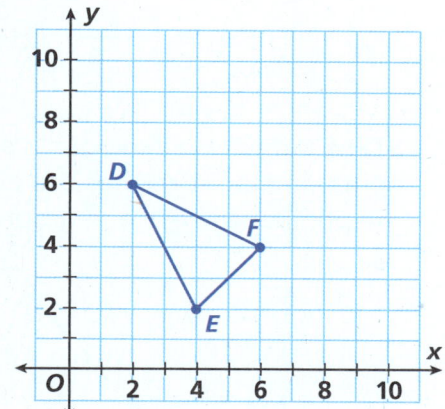

   A. Find the coordinates of vertices D, E, and F.

   _____

   B. Multiply each coordinate of each vertex by the scale factor to find the coordinates of vertices D', E', and F'.

   _____

   C. Graph and label the vertices D', E', and F'. Draw rays to connect each corresponding vertex with the center of dilation.

   D. Represent the dilation algebraically.

   _____

5. Figure J'K'L'M' is a dilation of Figure JKLM. The center of dilation is the origin, (0, 0).

J(3, 2)	→	J'(9, 6)
K(7, 4)	→	K'(21, 12)
L(7, 9)	→	L'
M(2, 5)	→	M'

   A. Given the coordinates of J, J', K, and K', what is the scale factor of the dilation?

   _____

   B. Use the scale factor to complete the table for points L' and M'.

   C. Represent the dilation algebraically.

   _____

Module 10 • Lesson 2

6. Graph △TUV with vertices T(4, 2), U(2, 0), and V(2, 4). Dilate the figure by a scale factor of $\frac{5}{2}$ with a center of dilation of (0, 0). Graph △T'U'V'.

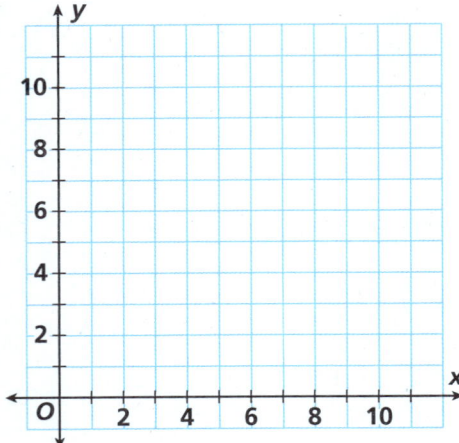

7. **STEM** An ophthalmologist is a doctor who studies the eye. The ophthalmologist records the effect of changes in lighting on the size of the pupil of the eye and graphs the results on a coordinate plane.

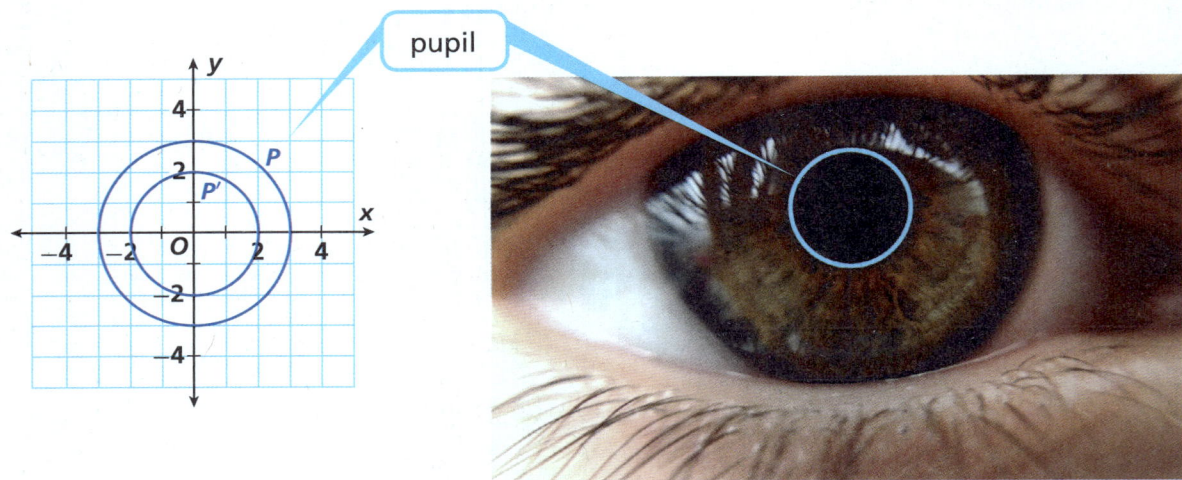

A. What is the scale factor of the dilation from P to P'? _____

B. Graph a dilation of P using scale factor $\frac{1}{3}$.

I'm in a Learning Mindset!

Did I have confidence in my answer? What specific evidence do I have that I found a scale factor of a dilation correctly?

_____

_____

Name _____

Explore Dilations

1. **MP Reason** Which shape shows a dilation of Figure V? Justify your reasoning.

    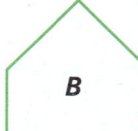 

   _____
   _____

2. **MP Use Tools** What is the scale factor of the dilation from the smaller square to the larger?

   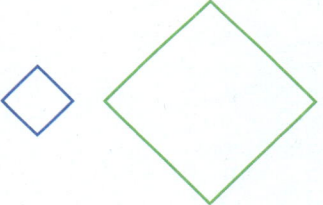

   _____

3. Identify the center of dilation for the given figures.

   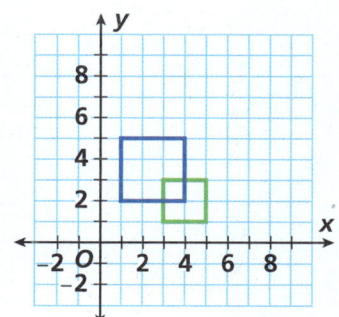

   _____

4. Polygon WXYZ has vertices W(4, 2), X(6, 4), Y(2, 3), and Z(4, 5). If W'X'Y'Z' is a dilation of WXYZ with center of dilation (0, 0) and vertex coordinates W'(2, 1), X'(3, 2), Y'(1, 1.5), and Z'(2, 2.5), find the scale factor.

   _____

Module 10 • Lesson 2

Test Prep

5. Dilate ABCD with a scale factor of 2 and center (0, 0).

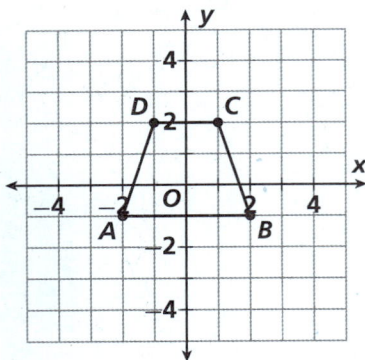

6. △MNP has vertices M(4, 8), N(12, 6), and P(2, 4). △M′N′P′ is a dilation of △MNP with a scale factor of $\frac{1}{2}$ and center (0, 0). Select the coordinates of the vertices of △M′N′P′.

- Ⓐ M′(1, 2), N′(2, 1), and P′(1, 2)
- Ⓑ M′(2, 4), N′(6, 3), and P′(1, 2)
- Ⓒ M′(4, 8), N′(12, 6), and P′(2, 4)
- Ⓓ M′(8, 16), N′(24, 12), and P′(4, 8)

7. A triangle has angles of 30°, 60°, and 90°. It is dilated by a scale factor of 3. Give the angle measures of the dilation of the triangle.

Spiral Review

8. Translate the shape three units up and two units left.

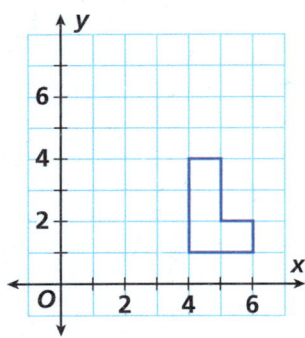

9. What single transformation is represented by the expression P(x, y) → P′(−x, −y)?

340

Connect Concepts and Skills
Lesson 3

Name

Understand and Recognize Similar Figures

I Can describe a sequence of transformations that exhibits the similarity between two figures.

Spark Your Learning

Jamar is using a website to make a customized phone case. To make a design for the case, he starts by drawing Parallelogram *ABCD*. Then he dilates the parallelogram using a vertex as the center of dilation. Finally, he translates the dilated parallelogram. Draw a possible final image for the figure and label it *A'B'C'D'*. Show your work.

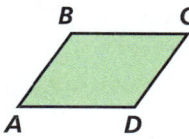

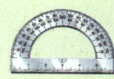

How are the sides and angles of *ABCD* and *A'B'C'D'* the same? How are they different?

_____

_____

 Turn and Talk Suppose Jamar uses the same translation first, followed by the same dilation. Would the answers to the above questions be different? Explain.

Module 10 • Lesson 3 341

Build Understanding

1 Bailey is going to use the shapes shown to make a customized phone case.

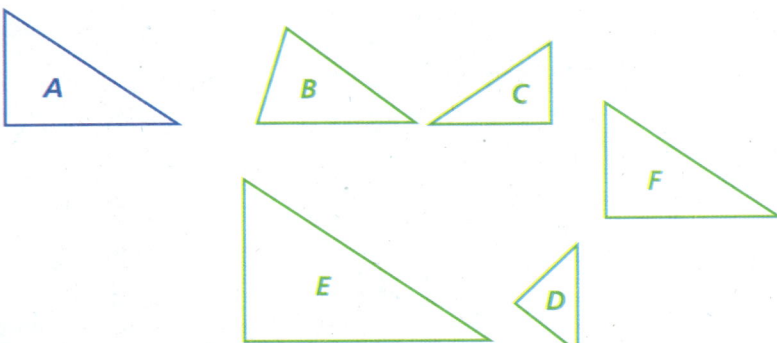

A. Which triangles are similar to Triangle A? You can use tracing paper, a protractor, and/or a ruler to help you decide which triangles are similar.

_____

> **Connect to Vocabulary**
>
> Two figures are **similar** if one can be obtained from the other by a transformation or sequence of transformations that may include dilation.

B. For each of the similar triangles you identified, describe a transformation or sequence of transformations that takes Triangle A to the other triangle.

_____
_____
_____
_____

C. Is Triangle A similar to Triangle B? Why or why not?

_____
_____

D. Bailey decides to add another triangle to her design. She dilates Triangle B using a scale factor of 1 and then rotates the image to form Triangle G. How are Triangle B and Triangle G related? Explain.

_____
_____
_____
_____

Turn and Talk If two figures are congruent can you always conclude that they are similar? Why or why not?

Name _____

Step It Out

2 Brendan uses a coordinate plane to draw figures for his custom phone case. He includes several similar figures in the design, as shown on the graph.

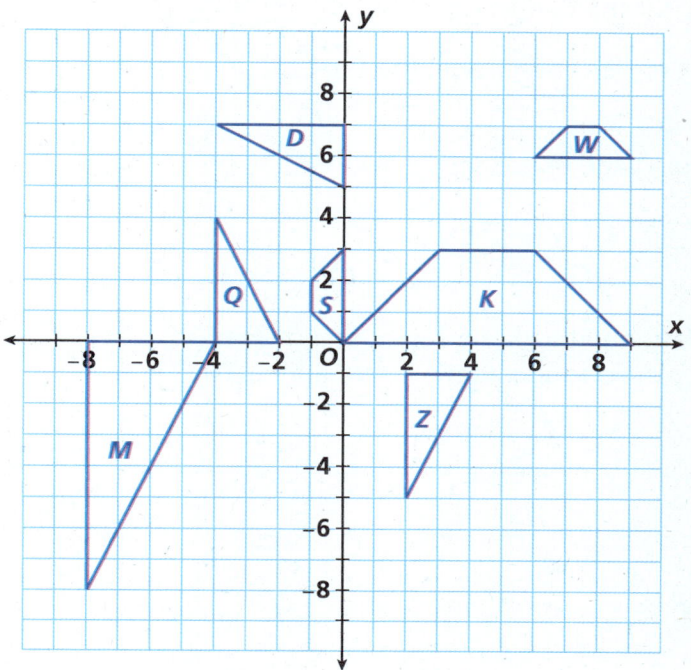

A. For each pair of similar figures, describe a sequence of transformations that can be used to map the first figure to the second figure.

Figure K to Figure W

_____

_____

Figure S to Figure K

_____

_____

B. Which pair of similar figures can be mapped from one to the other by the given sequence of transformations?

a dilation with scale factor $\frac{1}{2}$ and center of dilation (0, 0), followed by a reflection across the x-axis

_____

the dilation $(x, y) \rightarrow (2x, 2y)$ with a center of dilation (0, 0), followed by a translation 12 units left and 2 units up

_____

Module 10 • Lesson 3

3 For his phone case, Brendan makes an additional shape △ABC. He dilates the triangle using a dilation with a scale factor of $\frac{1}{2}$ and center of dilation (0, 0). Then he reflects the image across the y-axis.

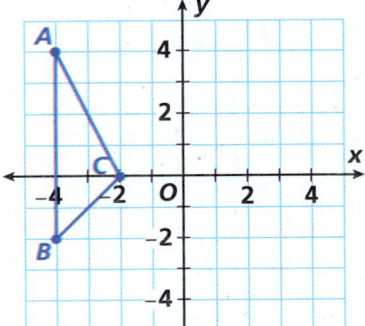

A. Draw the image of △ABC after the dilation.

B. Draw the final image after the reflection. Label the final image △A'B'C'.

C. What can you conclude about △ABC and △A'B'C'? Why?

_____

_____

D. Suppose Brendan uses a dilation with a scale factor of 1 instead of a scale factor of $\frac{1}{2}$. What can you conclude about △ABC and △A'B'C' in this case? Explain.

_____

_____

Check Understanding

1. Doretta is choosing tiles for a mosaic. She wants to choose two tiles that are similar but not congruent. Which pair of tiles could she use? Explain why she can only choose those tiles.

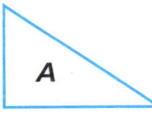  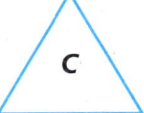 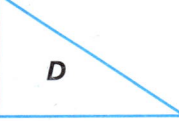 

_____

_____

2. Identify all pairs of similar figures on the coordinate plane. For each pair, describe the sequence of transformations that maps one figure to the other.

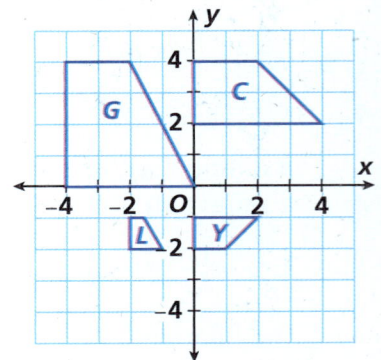

_____

_____

_____

344

Name _____

On Your Own

3. Ryan is a landscape architect. He uses the coordinate plane shown to design flower beds at a mall.

   A. To draw flower bed B, Ryan reflects flower bed A across the x-axis. Then he applies the dilation $(x, y) \rightarrow (2x, 2y)$. Draw and label flower bed B.

   B. To draw flower bed C, Ryan rotates flower bed A by 180° about the origin. Then he applies the dilation $(x, y) \rightarrow (2.5x, 2.5y)$. Draw and label flower bed C.

   C. What can you conclude about the three flower beds?
   _____

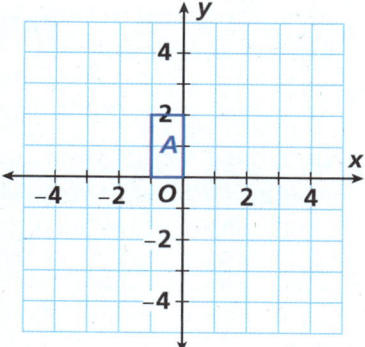

4. **Art** A car show has advertising posters in different shapes and sizes. They are shown as they appear next to each other on a wall at the car show.

   A. Circle all of the posters that are similar.

   B. For the posters you identified, describe a sequence of transformations that takes one poster to the other.
   _____

Use the graph to solve Problems 5–7.

5. Which pair of similar triangles can be mapped from one to the other by a dilation with scale factor $\frac{1}{3}$ and center of dilation (0, 0), followed by a rotation of 180° clockwise around the origin?
   _____

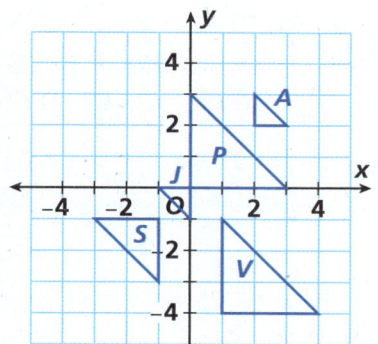

6. Which pair of similar triangles can be mapped from one to the other by a dilation with scale factor 3 and center of dilation (0, 0), followed by the translation $(x, y) \rightarrow (x - 6, y - 6)$?
   _____

7. Describe a sequence of transformations that can be used to map Triangle J to Triangle S.
   _____
   _____
   _____

8. Glass laboratory flasks come in a variety of shapes and sizes. Different flasks have different purposes, such as heating, measuring, and mixing. Are any of the flasks shown similar? Explain why or why not.

9. Describe a sequence of transformations that can be used to map △RST with vertices R(−1, 0), S(0, 1), and T(1, 0) to △JKL with vertices J(−4, 0), K(0, −4), and L(4, 0).

10. **Open Ended** The coordinates of the vertices of △ABC are A(0, 0), B(0, 4), and C(−2, 0). Give the coordinates of the vertices of a triangle, △DEF, that is similar to △ABC but not congruent to △ABC. Then describe a sequence of transformations that maps △ABC to △DEF.

11. (MP) **Use Repeated Reasoning** Jaycee draws a sequence of squares on the coordinate plane. First she draws the square shown and dilates it using (x, y) → (3x, 3y). Then she uses this same transformation to dilate the image. She continues dilating each image in this way to draw a total of six squares. What dilation could she use to map the first square she draws directly to the last square she draws?

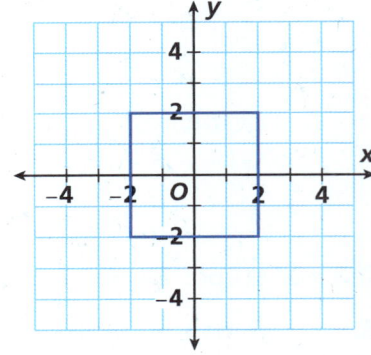

12. If Figure X is similar to Figure Y, and Figure Y is similar to Figure Z, can you conclude that Figure X is similar to Figure Z? Explain.

 **I'm in a Learning Mindset!**

Do I have a fixed-mindset voice or a growth-mindset voice in my head when I'm finding similar figures? How can I tap into my growth-mindset voice?

Name _____

LESSON 10.3
More Practice/ Homework

Understand and Recognize Similar Figures

Video Tutorials and Interactive Examples

1. **Use Tools** Keisha is using a coordinate plane to design the background image for a video game. She starts with △ABC.

   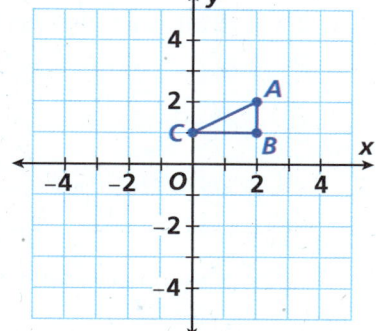

   A. To draw △DEF, Keisha translates △ABC using $(x, y) \rightarrow (x - 2, y)$. Then she applies the dilation with scale factor 2 and center of dilation (0, 0). Draw and label △DEF.

   B. To draw △GHJ, Keisha reflects △ABC using $(x, y) \rightarrow (x, -y)$. Then she applies the dilation with scale factor 2 and center of dilation (0, 0). Draw and label △GHJ.

   C. **Critique Reasoning** Keisha claims that all three triangles are similar. Do you agree or disagree? Explain.

   _____

   _____

2. Marco is trying different designs for a business logo. Several of the logos are shown.

   A. Circle all of the logos that are similar to each other.

   B. For the logos you identified, describe a sequence of transformations that takes one logo to the other.

   _____

3. **Math on the Spot** Consider the pairs of figures on the coordinate planes.

   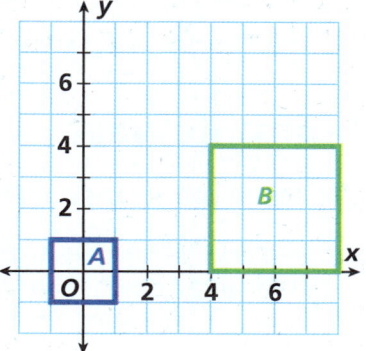

   A. Identify a sequence of transformations that will transform Figure A onto Figure B. Tell whether the figures are congruent. Tell whether they are similar.

   _____

   _____

   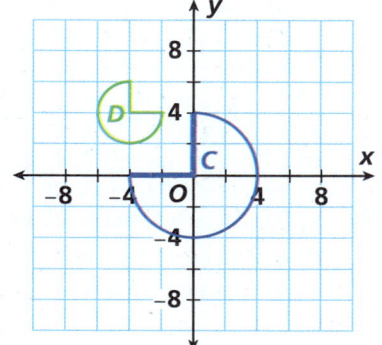

   B. Identify a sequence of transformations that will transform Figure C onto Figure D. Tell whether the figures are congruent. Tell whether they are similar.

   _____

   _____

Module 10 • Lesson 3   347

Test Prep

4. Figure *M* and Figure *N* are similar triangles. Which sequence of transformations can be used to map Figure *M* to Figure *N*?

   Ⓐ a dilation followed by a reflection

   Ⓑ a rotation followed by a dilation

   Ⓒ a translation followed by a rotation

   Ⓓ a dilation followed by a translation

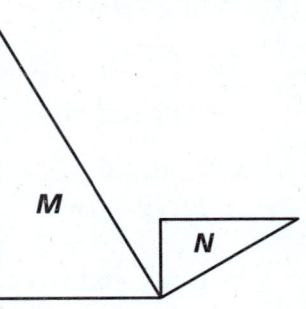

5. Select all of the figures that are similar to Trapezoid *RSTU*.

   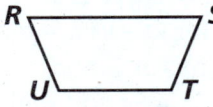

   Ⓐ

   Ⓓ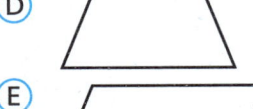

   Ⓑ

   Ⓔ

   Ⓒ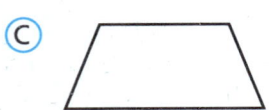

   Ⓕ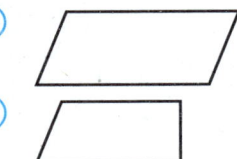

6. Maria draws △*PQR*. Then she applies a dilation with scale factor $\frac{1}{3}$ and center of dilation *P* to the triangle. Next, she translates the image 2 centimeters up and 3 centimeters right. She labels the final image as △*XYZ*. Which of the following must be true about △*PQR* and △*XYZ*?

   Ⓐ △*PQR* and △*XYZ* are congruent and similar.

   Ⓑ △*PQR* and △*XYZ* are congruent but not similar.

   Ⓒ △*PQR* and △*XYZ* are similar but not congruent.

   Ⓓ △*PQR* and △*XYZ* are neither similar nor congruent.

Spiral Review

Use the graph to answer Problems 7–8.

7. Justin makes a figure that is congruent to Figure *V* by reflecting Figure *V* across the *x*-axis and then translating the image 1 unit right. Draw this figure and label it Figure *F*.

8. Are Figure *V* and Figure *L* congruent? Explain why or why not.

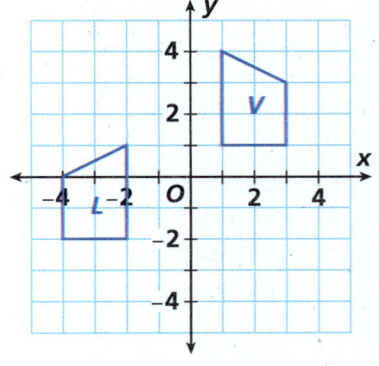

9. △*ABC* has vertices *A*(−2, −1), *B*(1, 2), and *C*(2, −4). If △*A'B'C'* is a dilation of △*ABC* with a scale factor of 2.5 and center of dilation (0, 0), give the coordinates of the vertices of △*A'B'C'*.

Module 10 Review

Vocabulary

Tell whether each statement is true or false. If it is false, correct the underlined word to make the statement true.

Vocabulary
- center of dilation
- congruent
- enlargement
- reduction
- similar
- transformation
- translation

1. The image of a dilation is always <u>congruent</u> to the preimage.
   _____

2. The preimage of a <u>reduction</u> is larger than the image.
   _____

3. Lines through each pair of corresponding vertices in a dilation intersect at the <u>center</u> of dilation. _____

4. A dilation is a type of <u>translation</u> that enlarges or reduces a figure.
   _____

Concepts and Skills

5. Triangle R'S'T' is a dilation of Triangle RST.

   A. What is the scale factor of the dilation? _____

   B. What are the coordinates of the center of the dilation? (____, ____)

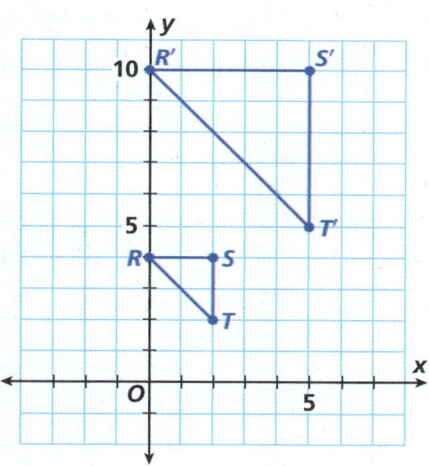

6. **Use Tools** Triangle JKL has vertices J(−1, −3), K(−2, 3), and L(4, 1). It is dilated by a scale factor of 5, with the origin as the center of dilation, to produce Triangle J'K'L'. What are the coordinates of the vertices of J'K'L'? State what strategy and tool you will use to answer the question, explain your choice, and then find the answer.

   _____

   _____

7. Triangle DEF has vertices D(−4, 0), E(1, 3), and F(3, −4). It is dilated by a scale factor of $\frac{3}{4}$, with the center of dilation at the origin. Use words from the box to complete the sentences about the dilation.

   - larger
   - negative
   - positive
   - smaller
   - x-axis
   - y-axis

   The image of the dilation is _____ than the preimage. The image of Vertex D is on the _____. The image of Vertex F has a _____ x-coordinate.

Module 10 349

Draw the image of each dilation in the coordinate plane. The center of each dilation is the origin.

8. Triangle ABC is dilated by a scale factor of 3 to form Triangle A'B'C'.

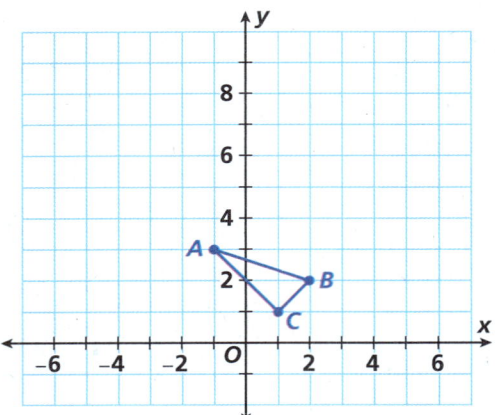

9. Quadrilateral FGHJ is dilated by a scale factor of $\frac{1}{2}$ to form Quadrilateral F'G'H'J'.

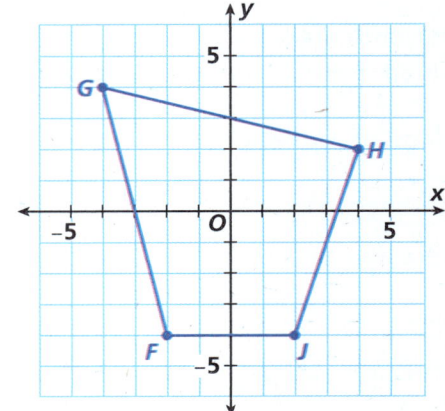

10. Quadrilaterals LMNP and WXYZ are similar. Which sequence of transformations could be used to obtain Quadrilateral WXYZ from Quadrilateral LMNP?

    Ⓐ 180° rotation, dilation

    Ⓑ vertical translation, dilation

    Ⓒ dilation, reflection across a horizontal line

    Ⓓ reflection across a horizontal line, vertical translation

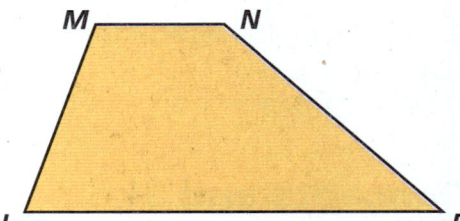

11. Which of these sequences of transformations result in figures that are similar but not congruent? Select all that apply.

    Ⓐ 180° rotation, dilation with a factor of $\frac{1}{4}$

    Ⓑ translation 3 units up, 90° clockwise rotation

    Ⓒ dilation with a factor of 4, translation 1 unit down

    Ⓓ reflection across the x-axis, translation 6 units right

    Ⓔ 90° counterclockwise rotation, reflection across the y-axis

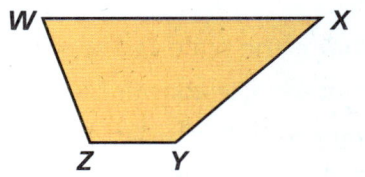

12. Are Triangles GHJ and LMN similar? Explain your reasoning.

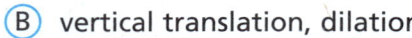

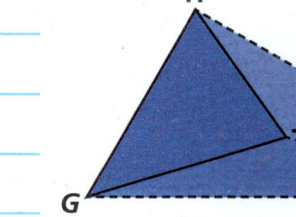

350

Unit 5
Similarity, Slope, and Linear Relationships

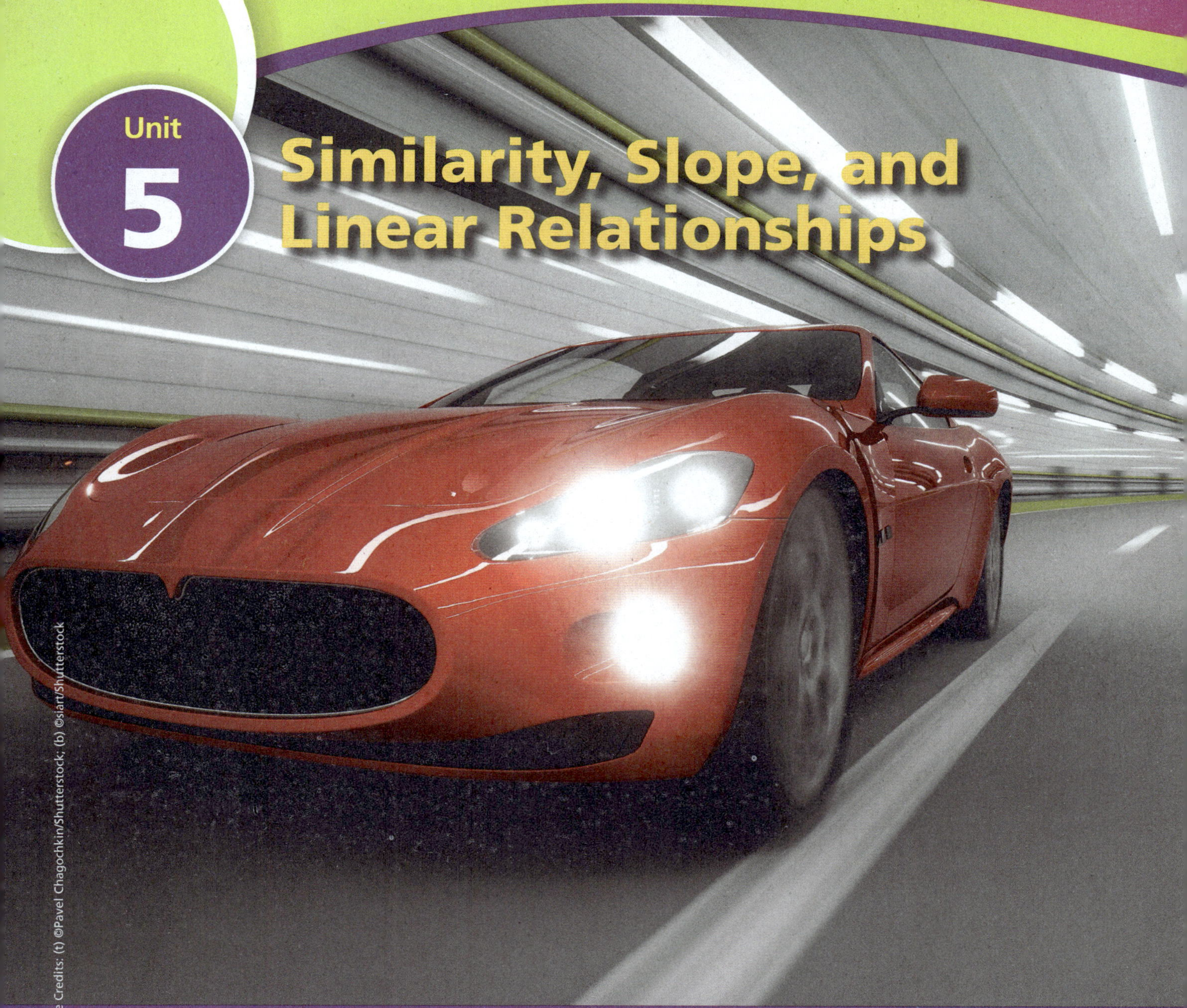

Auto Engineer

Auto engineers design new vehicles and improve existing vehicles. Some auto engineers work on improving a car's performance, fuel efficiency, or safety. Others specialize in certain components, such as brakes or electrical systems. Auto engineers must understand how some quantities, such as a car's braking distance, depend on other quantities, such as the car's speed.

STEM Task:

Three quantities related to a car engine's performance are torque, horsepower, and revolutions per minute (RPM). These quantities are related by the equation

$$\text{torque} = \frac{\text{horsepower}}{\text{RPM}} \cdot 5{,}252,$$

where torque is measured in pound-feet. How much torque is required to produce 300 horsepower at 2,500 RPM? At 5,000 RPM? How are the two related?

Unit 5   351

Learning Mindset
Challenge-Seeking Defines Own Challenges

As you grow, you discover the pleasure of setting your own goals and challenges, and designing ways to meet them. Maybe you want to learn a new language, write a book, or become more successful academically. Here are some things to keep in mind as you seek and define new challenges.

- Believe in your ability to improve skills that are a challenge for you now. Use positive self-talk to address any fixed-mindset voices telling you that you can't reach your goal. Believe in the power of "yet."

- Think about how you will handle unexpected difficulties. Don't become discouraged. Every failure can help you get closer the next time.

- Be flexible. You may find it necessary to adjust your plan or even redefine the end goal.

- Don't be afraid to ask for advice and assistance from content resources or people with more experience than you have currently.

Reflect

Q How do you know whether a task is the right level of challenge for you?

Q Was the STEM Task an appropriate challenge for you? If not, what reasonable challenge would you set for yourself?

Module 11

Angle Relationships

A Fox From Any Angle

The diagram shows the design for a fox made from folded paper.

Give an example of each type of angle pair in the design.

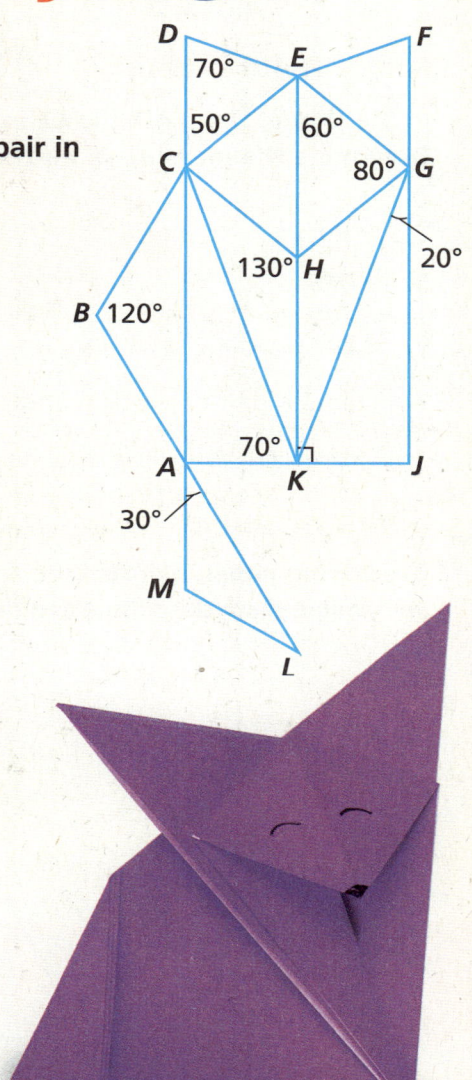

A. Vertical angles

_____

B. Adjacent supplementary angles

_____

C. Non-adjacent supplementary angles

_____

D. Adjacent complementary angles

_____

E. Non-adjacent complementary angles

_____

 **Turn and Talk**

How did you identify a pair of non-adjacent supplementary angles?

Module 11 353

Are You Ready?

Complete these problems to review prior concepts and skills you will need for this module.

Operations with Linear Expressions

Simplify each expression.

1. $x + 2x + 48$

2. $(n + 7) + 3(n + 1) + 90$

3. $180 - (68 + a)$

Angle Relationships

In the figure, Lines *AD* and *CE* intersect at Point *F*. Determine the measure of each angle.

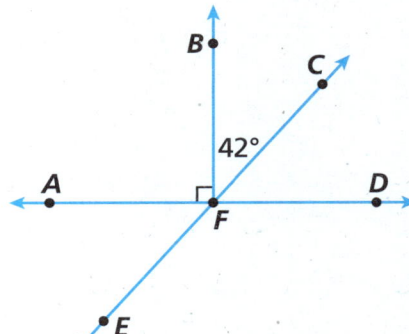

4. $\angle CFD$ _____

5. $\angle DFE$ _____

6. $\angle AFE$ _____

7. Name a pair of vertical angles in the figure.

   _____

Similar Figures

Use tracing paper, a protractor, and a ruler to determine whether the triangles in each pair are similar. If so, describe a sequence of transformations that demonstrates the similarity.

8.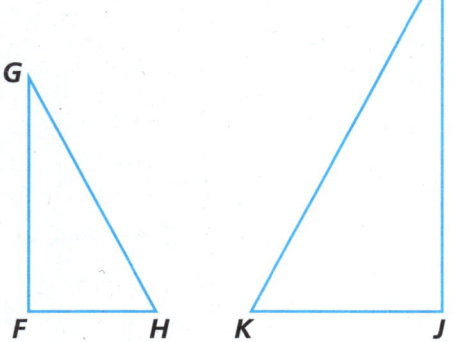

9.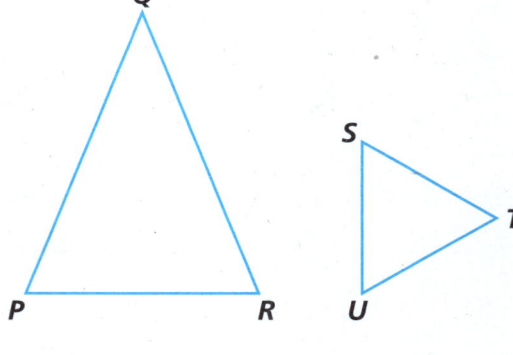

Connect Concepts and Skills

Lesson 1

Name _____

Develop Angle Relationships for Triangles

I Can find an unknown angle measure in a triangle.

Spark Your Learning

The angles of a triangle have a relationship with each other. Draw three unique triangles. What do you notice about the measures of the interior angles of the triangles?

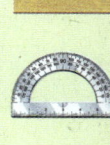

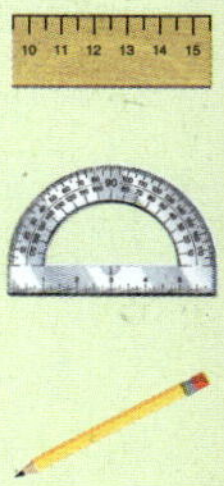

Turn and Talk What conjecture can you make about the sum of the measures of the angles of a triangle?

Module 11 • Lesson 1

355

Build Understanding

1 What is the sum of the measures of the three interior angles of a triangle?

A. Find the sum of the measures of the angles in each of the three triangles.

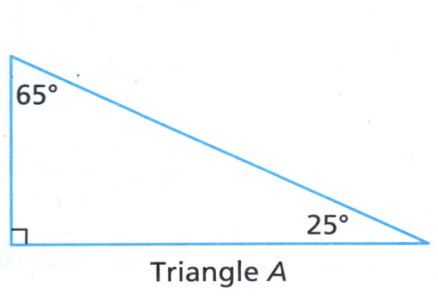
Triangle A

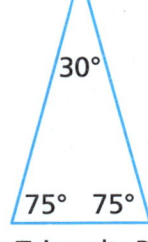
Triangle B

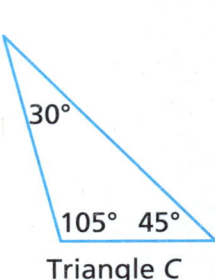
Triangle C

B. What do you notice about the sum of the measures of the three triangles?
_____

C. Do you think this is true for all triangles? Explain.
_____
_____

The **Triangle Sum Theorem** states that the measures of the three interior angles of a triangle sum to 180°.

D. The angles in a triangle measure $2x$, $3x$, and $4x$ degrees. Write and solve an equation to determine the angle measures.
_____
_____

Turn and Talk Discuss how to find an unknown measure of an angle in a triangle when the other two angle measures are given.

Name _____

Step It Out

The Triangle Sum Theorem can be used to draw conclusions about a triangle's interior angles.

  The dashed line segment represents an extension of one side of the triangle. Together with the right side of the triangle, the segment forms an angle, ∠4.

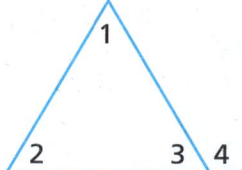

A. What is the sum of the measures of ∠3 and ∠4?

_____

B. An **exterior angle** of a polygon is an angle formed by one side of the polygon and the extension of an adjacent side. Which angle in the diagram is an exterior angle?

_____

C. If the measure of ∠3 is 60°, what is the measure of ∠4?

_____

D. If the measure of ∠3 is 60°, what is the sum of the measures of ∠1 and ∠2?

_____

E. Which angle has a measure equal to the sum of the measures of ∠1 and ∠2?

_____

F. A **remote interior angle** of an exterior angle of a polygon is an angle that is inside the polygon and is not adjacent to the exterior angle. Which two angles in the diagram are remote interior angles in relation to Angle 4?

_____

G. If the sum of the measures of ∠1 and ∠2 is 115°, what is the measure of ∠4?

_____

>  **Turn and Talk** A triangle has exterior Angle P with remote interior Angles Q and R. Can you determine which angle has the greatest measure? Why or why not?

Module 11 • Lesson 1   **357**

3 ▸ A machinist is drawing a triangular piece of an industrial machine.

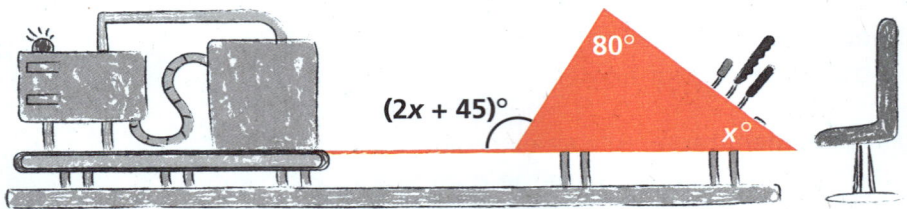

A. Write an equation and solve to find the value of x. Show your work.

☐x + ☐ = x + ☐

☐x − x = 80 − ☐

x = ☐

B. What is the measure of the unknown remote interior angle?

_____

C. Use the value of x from Part A to find the measure of the exterior angle.

2x + 45 = 2(☐) + 45 = ☐ + 45 = ☐

D. What is the measure of the exterior angle?

_____

Connect to Vocabulary

The measure of an exterior angle of a triangle is greater than either of the measures of the remote interior angles. This is the **Exterior Angle Theorem**.

Check Understanding

1. Two angles of a triangle have measures of 30° and 45°. What is the measure of the remaining angle?

_____

2. Dana draws a triangle with one angle that has a measure of 40°.

   A. What is the measure of the angle's adjacent exterior angle?

   _____

   B. What is the sum of the measures of the remote interior angles for the exterior angle adjacent to the 40° angle?

   _____

3. An exterior angle of a triangle has a measure of 80°, and one of the remote interior angles has a measure of 20°. Write and solve an equation to find the measure of the other remote interior angle.

_____

Name _____

On Your Own

4. A puppeteer is making a triangular hat for a puppet. If two of the three angles of the hat both measure 30°, what is the measure of the third angle?

_____

5. (MP) **Construct Arguments** Can a triangle have two obtuse angles? Explain your answer.

_____

_____

_____

_____

6. **STEM** In engineering, equilateral triangles can support the most weight and so are commonly found in the design of bridges and buildings. Equilateral triangles are triangles with three congruent sides and three congruent angles. What are the measures of the angles of an equilateral triangle?

_____

7. A triangle has one 30° angle, an unknown angle, and an angle with a measure that is twice the measure of the unknown angle. Find the measures of the triangle's unknown angles and explain how you found the answer.

_____

_____

_____

_____

For Problems 8–10, find the measures of the unknown third angles.

8.

9.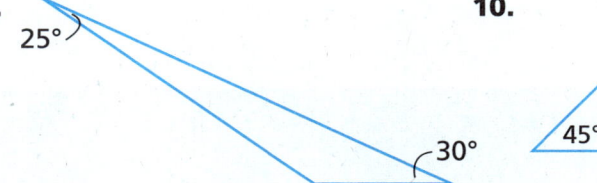

Module 11 • Lesson 1

359

11. **Open Ended** The measure of an exterior angle of a triangle is $x°$. The measure of the adjacent interior angle is at least twice $x°$. List three possible solutions for x.

   _____

12. The measure of an exterior angle of a triangle is 40°. What is the sum of the measures of the corresponding remote interior angles?

   _____

13. Steven is building a fin for a surfboard. In order to make the fin, he needs to know the value of x in the following diagram. Use your knowledge of triangle angle relationships to find the value of x.

   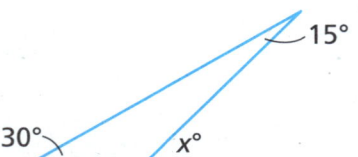

   _____

14. Find the value of x in the diagram. Explain how you found the answer.

   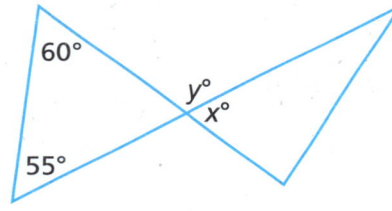

   _____
   _____
   _____
   _____
   _____

I'm in a Learning Mindset!

Was problem 13 an appropriate challenge for me? Why or why not?

_____
_____

Name _____

Develop Angle Relationships for Triangles

LESSON 11.1
More Practice/ Homework

ONLINE Video Tutorials and Interactive Examples

1. Find the value of x using your knowledge of the relationship between interior and exterior angles.

   _____

2. **Math on the Spot** Find the unknown measure in the triangle.

   _____

3. **Construct Arguments** Can the measure of an exterior angle of a triangle ever exceed 180°? Explain your reasoning.

   _____
   _____
   _____
   _____

4. **STEM** The measure of the angle formed at the center of an oxygen atom in a water molecule is about 105°. The angles formed at each hydrogen atom are congruent. What is the measure of the angle at each hydrogen atom?

   _____

   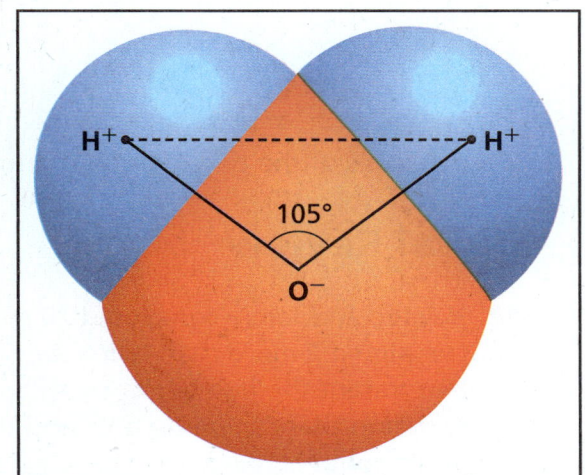

5. **Open Ended** One of the angles in a triangle measures 90°. Name three possibilities for the measures of the remaining two angles.

   _____
   _____

6. Find the value of x in the following diagram.

   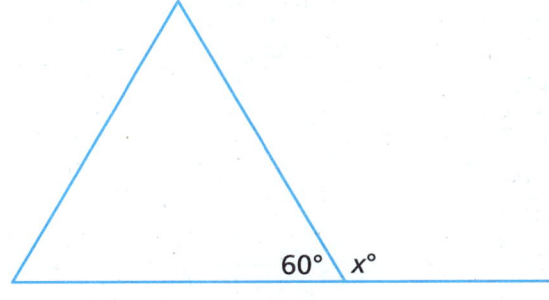

   _____

Module 11 • Lesson 1   361

Test Prep

7. Complete the table by entering the measures of the unknown angles for the following two triangles.

Triangle	Angle 1	Angle 2	Unknown angle
1	30°	60°	
2	45°	20°	

8. If an exterior angle of a triangle has a measure of 35°, what is the measure of the adjacent interior angle?

_____

9. Find the value of x.

$x = $ ☐

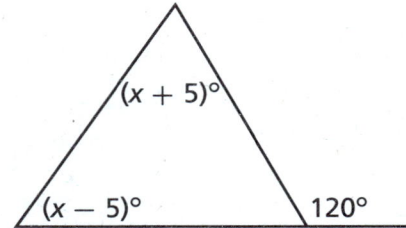

10. The measures of an exterior angle of a triangle and its adjacent interior angle add to what value?

- (A) 90°
- (B) 100°
- (C) 180°
- (D) 360°

11. The measure of an exterior angle of a triangle and the sum of the measures of the two remote interior angles are _____.

Spiral Review

12. Hayden and Jamie completed 20 math problems together. Jamie completed 2 more than twice the number that Hayden completed. Let p represent the number of math problems Hayden completed. Write an equation that can be used to find the number of math problems that Jamie completed.

_____

13. Does the equation $5(x - 3) = 10x - 15$ have one solution, infinitely many solutions, or no solution?

_____

14. Find the value of x, given that $4(3x + 2) = 44$.

_____

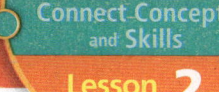

Investigate Angle-Angle Similarity

I Can use angle-angle similarity to test triangles for similarity and find unknown angle measures.

Spark Your Learning

Asa is comparing the architect's model of a barn with the finished building. He looks at the triangle that forms the front of the roof in the model and in the completed barn. Are the triangles similar? Why or why not?

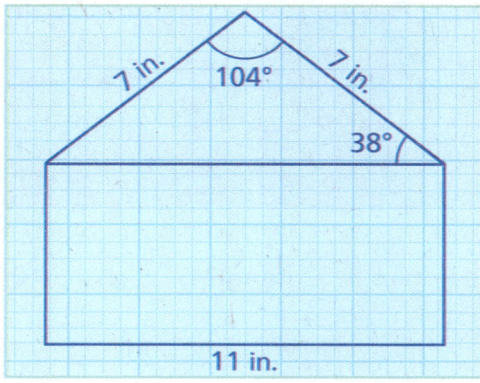
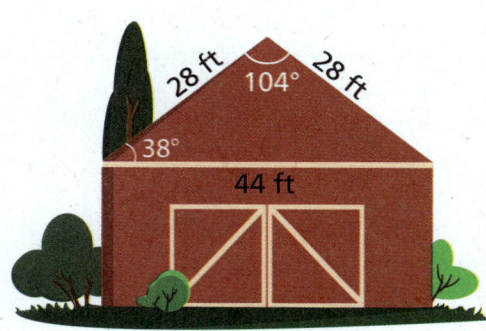

Turn and Talk Which is the easier way of deciding if the triangles are similar, comparing the angles or comparing the side lengths? Why?

Module 11 • Lesson 2

Build Understanding

Two triangles are similar if all three pairs of corresponding angles are congruent. What if only two out of three pairs of corresponding angles are congruent?

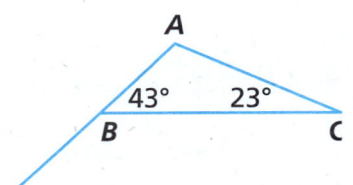

1 Using the given drawing by the set designer, Shawna is making a flag for a play. She has measured Angles *ABC* and *ACB* with a protractor, and they match Angles *E* and *F*, respectively, on the set designer's notes. Can she be sure that her flag is similar to the drawing without measuring the third angle?

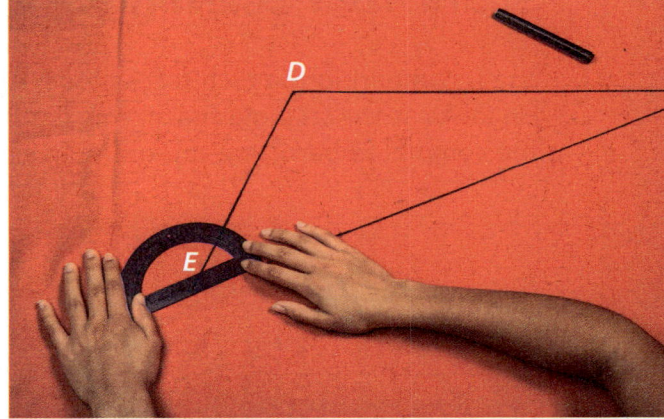

A. What do you know about the sum of the measures of the angles in a triangle?

_____
_____

B. How does knowing the sum of the measures of the angles in a triangle help you solve this problem?

_____
_____

C. Write and evaluate an expression to find the measure of the third angle of Triangle *ABC*, using the angle measures given.

_____

D. Write and evaluate an expression to find the measure of the third angle of Triangle *DEF* using the angle measures given.

_____

E. Based on your calculation of the measure of the third angle, can you now state with confidence whether Shawna's flag is similar to the drawing without measuring the third angle? Explain.

_____
_____
_____

The <mark>Angle-Angle Similarity Postulate</mark> states that two triangles are similar if they have two pairs of corresponding angles that are congruent.

 Turn and Talk When two triangles have two angle measures in common, will the third angle measure always be the same for both triangles? Explain.

Step It Out

2 In the two triangles shown, m∠A = m∠D and m∠C = m∠F.

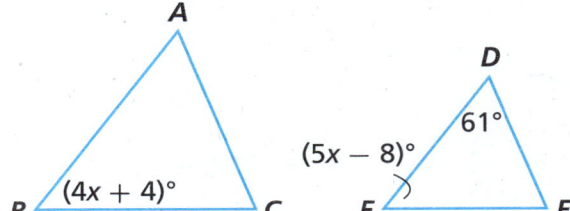

A. Do you know enough to say whether the two triangles are similar? Explain.

_____

_____

B. What does your answer to Part A imply about Angles B and E? Explain how you know.

_____

_____

C. What equation can you write relating the measures of Angles B and E? _____

D. Solve your equation from Part C for x. What is the measure of both Angles B and E? _____

E. How can you find the measure of Angle F?

_____

_____

_____

F. How can you find the measure of Angle C?

_____

G. Fill in the measures of the six angles:

m∠A = _____   m∠B = _____   m∠C = _____

m∠D = _____   m∠E = _____   m∠F = _____

Turn and Talk If you were given the measures of Angles A, C, D, and E from Part G, how could you determine whether the triangles are similar?

Module 11 • Lesson 2

3 The illustration shows a wheelchair ramp from the side. The support at $\overline{BC}$ binds the ramp to the floor. Are Triangles ABC and ADE similar?

A. What do the little squares at Points C and E mean?

_____

B. Do Triangles ABC and ADE both contain the same angle? If so, name it.

_____

C. Does that mean both triangles have two pairs of corresponding congruent angles? If so, name the corresponding congruent angles.

_____

D. Are Triangles ABC and ADE similar? Explain.

_____

Check Understanding

1. Which two triangles are similar?

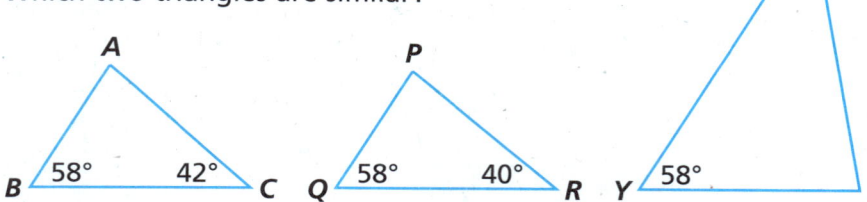

_____

2. Explain why △XYZ is similar to △LMZ.

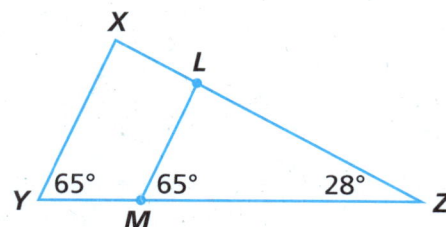

_____
_____

366

Name _____

On Your Own

3. **Reason** A graphic designer wants to reproduce the logo of a mountain-climbing club for some club stationery. The logo is a triangle with the angles shown.

   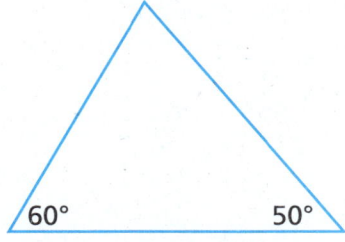

   A. The designer wants the base to be 2 inches long. How should the triangle be drawn?

   _____
   _____
   _____
   _____

   B. How can the Angle-Angle Similarity Postulate help the designer make sure the triangle is reproduced correctly?

   _____
   _____
   _____

4. Angles A, D, and G are congruent, and Angles C, F, and J are congruent.

   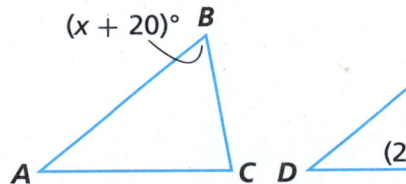

   A. Write an equation to find the measures of Angles B, F, and G.

   _____

   B. What is the measure of Angle E?

   _____

Use Triangles QRS and TUV to solve Problems 5 and 6.

5. Are Triangles QRS and TUV similar? How do you know?

   _____
   _____

   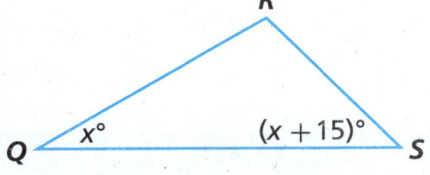

6. What is the measure of Angle R in terms of x?

   _____

   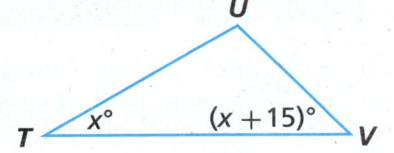

Module 11 • Lesson 2   367

7. **Reason** Are the triangles shown similar? Why or why not?

   _____
   _____
   _____
   _____

   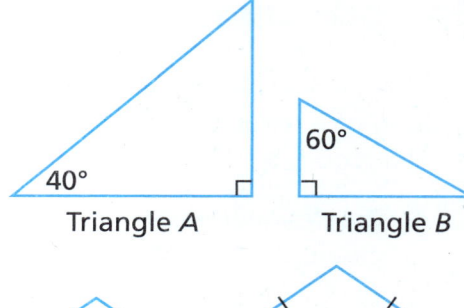

8. **Reason** Are the triangles shown similar? How do you know?

   _____
   _____

9. **Reason** Are the triangles similar? Explain.

   _____
   _____
   _____
   _____

10. Angle C is congruent to Angle F. What is the measure of Angle E?

    _____

    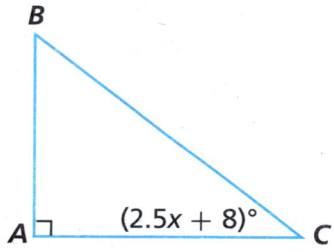
    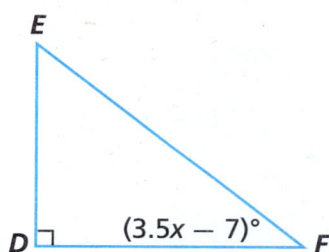

11. Does the diagram show similar triangles? Explain.

    _____
    _____
    _____
    _____
    _____

    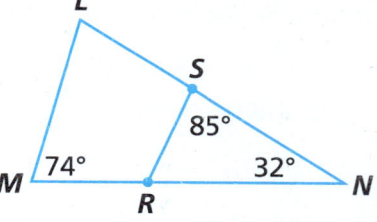

What challenges do I face trying to understand how to use angle relationships to determine whether two triangles are similar?

_____
_____

Name _____

Investigate Angle-Angle Similarity

LESSON 11.2
More Practice/ Homework

ONLINE Video Tutorials and Interactive Examples

1. One triangle shown is formed by the tree, its shadow, and a line of sight from the ground to the top of the tree. The other is formed by Manny, his shadow, and a line of sight from the ground to the top of his head.

   A. Are the two triangles similar? How do you know?

   _____
   _____
   _____

   B. Manny is $5\frac{1}{2}$ feet tall, and his shadow is $4\frac{1}{4}$ feet long. The shadow of the tree is 17 feet long. Can you determine the height of the tree? If so, how?

   _____
   _____

   C. What is the height of the tree?

   _____

2. **Reason** Explain whether the triangles are similar.

   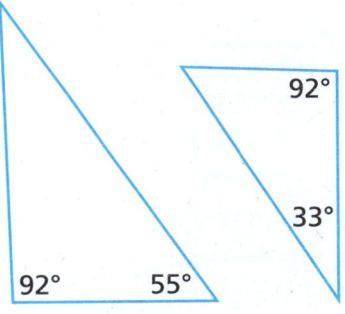

   _____
   _____
   _____

3. Consider the diagram for Parts A and B.

   A. The value of x is _____.

   B. The measure of Angle A is _____.

   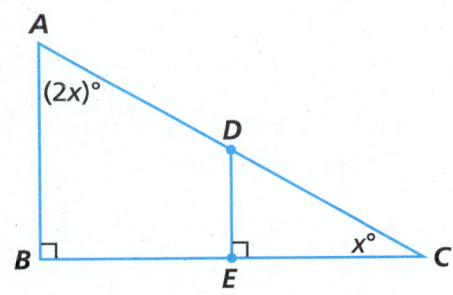

Module 11 • Lesson 2

369

Test Prep

4. Angle L is congruent to Angle P, and Angle N is congruent to Angle R. What is the measure of Angle Q?

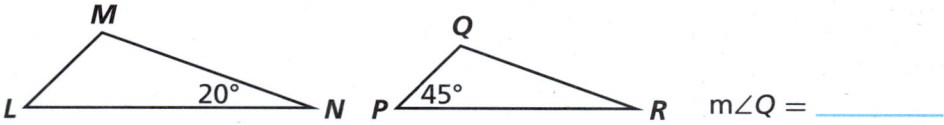

m∠Q = _____

5. Which triangles are similar?

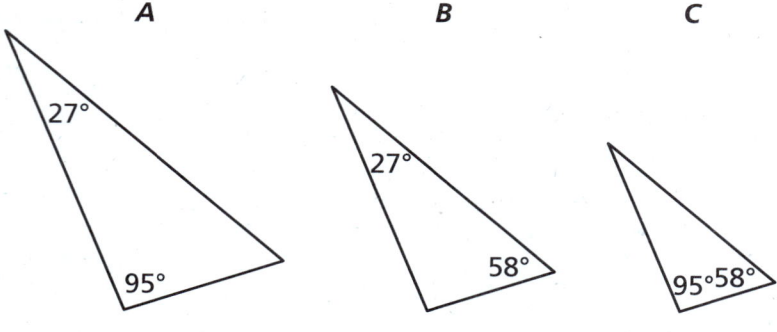

_____

6. The measures of two pairs of corresponding angles of two triangles are 24° and 55°. Explain why the two triangles are similar.

_____
_____

Spiral Review

7. Mrs. Kato has 6 bags of dried beans and a 2-pound bag of rice in one shopping bag. In another shopping bag she has a 5-pound bag of flour. The two shopping bags weigh the same amount. What is the weight of each bag of dried beans?

_____

8. A triangle is dilated with scale factor 4. Write a true statement about the image and preimage of the triangle.

_____
_____

9. Name a sequence of transformations that would map Figure A to Figure B.

_____
_____

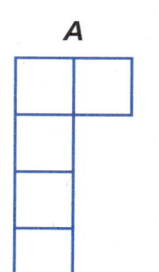

Connect Concepts and Skills

Lesson 3

Name _____

Explore Parallel Lines Cut by a Transversal

I Can identify the relationship between angle pairs as either supplementary or congruent.

Spark Your Learning

A walker sees these logs on a hike and notices that they make several angles.

Draw a representation of the logs and compare the lines and the angles in your drawing. How are the angles the same and how are they different?

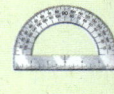

 **Turn and Talk** What pattern do you notice after measuring all the angles?

Module 11 • Lesson 3

Build Understanding

Like the logs, the diagram shows two parallel lines with a third line that cuts across the two parallel lines. This third line is called a **transversal**. The intersections of the lines form eight angles, including five special types of angle pairs. The angles in any of the special pairs will be either congruent or supplementary.

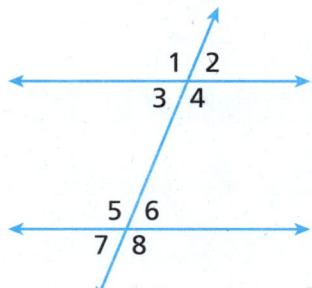

1 The term *alternate* means that two angles are on opposite sides of the transversal.

A. Alternate interior angles are angles on opposite sides of the transversal inside the parallel lines. Measure a pair of alternate interior angles with a protractor. Name the angles you found. Are they congruent or supplementary?

_____

_____

B. Alternate exterior angles are angles on the outer side of two lines cut by a transversal, on opposite sides of the transversal. Measure a pair of alternate exterior angles with a protractor. Name the angles you found. Are they congruent or supplementary?

_____

_____

The term *same-side* means that two angles are on the same side of the transversal.

C. Same-side interior angles are on the same side of the transversal and between the parallel lines. Measure a pair of same-side interior angles. Name the angles you found. Are they congruent or supplementary?

_____

_____

D. Same-side exterior angles are on the same side of the transversal but outside the parallel lines. Measure a pair of same-side exterior angles. Name the angles you found. Are they congruent or supplementary?

_____

_____

E. Corresponding angles are angles in the same position formed when a third line intersects two parallel lines. Measure two pairs of corresponding angles. Name the angles you found. Are they congruent or supplementary?

_____

_____

Step It Out

2 The diagram shows two parallel lines cut by a transversal. Find the value of x.

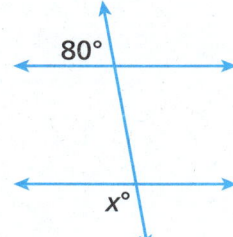

A. What kind of angle pair is formed by the two labeled angles?
_____

B. How are the two angles related to each other?
_____

C. Complete the equation to find the value of x.

x + 80 = ☐

x = ☐

3 The diagram shows two parallel lines cut by a transversal.

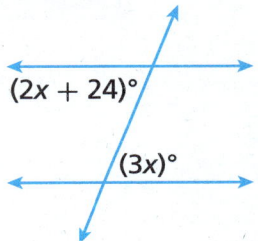

A. What kind of angle pair is formed by the two labeled angles?
_____

B. What is true about the measures of the angles?
_____

C. Complete and solve the equation to find the value of x.

3x = ☐

x = ☐

D. Find the measures of the angles.

3x = 3(☐) = 72

2x + 24 = 2(☐) + 24 = ☐ + 24 = 72

The angles both measure _____.

Turn and Talk Consider the diagram in Task 3. What happens if it is rotated so the parallel lines are vertical? Explain how this affects the relationships of the angle pairs.

Module 11 • Lesson 3

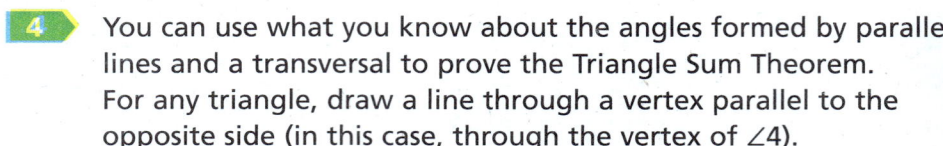

4 You can use what you know about the angles formed by parallel lines and a transversal to prove the Triangle Sum Theorem. For any triangle, draw a line through a vertex parallel to the opposite side (in this case, through the vertex of ∠4).

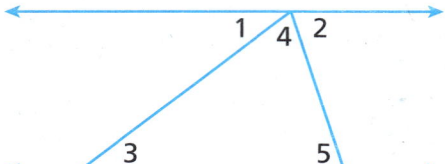

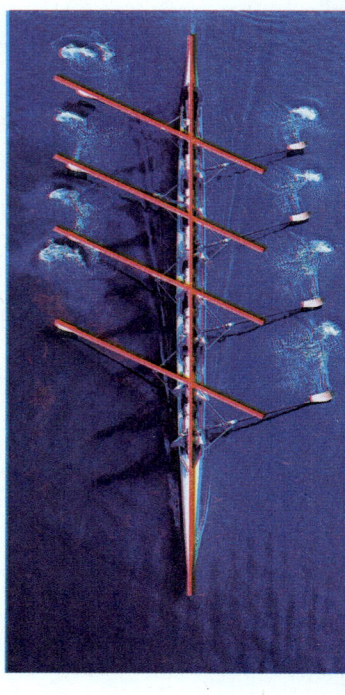

A. What is the sum of the measures of Angle 1, Angle 2, and Angle 4? How do you know?

_____

B. How would you classify the angle pairs ∠1 and ∠3, and ∠2 and ∠5?

_____

C. What does that tell you about their respective angle measures?

_____

D. Complete this statement: If m∠1 = m∠3 and m∠2 = m∠5, then

m∠3 + m∠4 + m∠5 = m∠☐ + m∠4 + m∠☐ = ☐ .

E. Make three copies of the triangle and arrange them so the three angles form a line. Use parallel lines and transversals to explain how your figure proves the Triangle Sum Theorem.

Check Understanding

Problems 1–2 show two parallel lines and a transversal. Find the values of *x*.

1.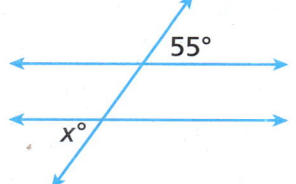

2.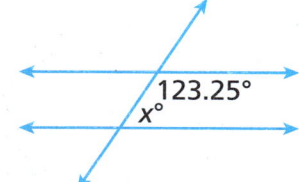

374

Name _____

On Your Own

3. The picture shows a bridge between two parallel river banks. What angle does the driver's right turn make with the river after crossing the bridge to continue on Northbridge Road?

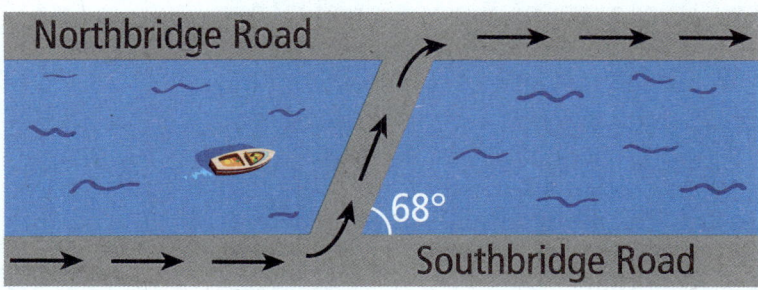

_____

Use the diagram showing two parallel lines and a transversal to answer Problems 4–6.

4. Which angle forms a pair of alternate interior angles with ∠ACB?

   _____

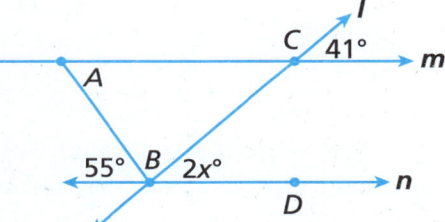

5. Which angle forms a pair of corresponding angles with the 41° angle?

   _____

6. Solve for x.

   _____

7. **(MP) Reason** The diagram shows two parallel lines cut by a transversal. Clarissa measured ∠1 and ∠2 with her protractor. She says the angles measure 43° and 142°, respectively. Is she correct? Explain.

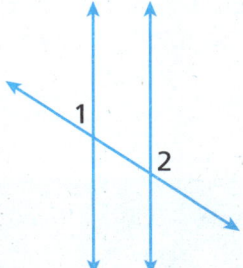

_____
_____
_____

Module 11 • Lesson 3

8. In the diagram, two parallel lines are cut by a transversal. Which of the numbered angles measures 152°?

_____

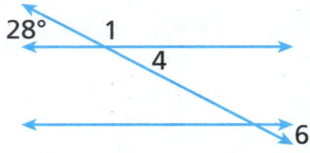

9. (MP) **Reason** You're not sure whether a pair of angles formed by two parallel lines and a transversal are same-side exterior angles or alternate exterior angles. Both angles measure 53°. Which of the two types must they be? Explain.

_____

_____

10. Which two angles have the same measure?

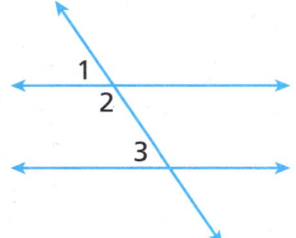

_____

11. Lines *m* and *n* are parallel. Find the following angle pairs in the diagram. If you can't find any, write *none*.

    alternate exterior _____

    corresponding angles _____

    same-side exterior _____

    alternate interior _____

    same-side interior _____

12. Two angles are same-side interior angles. The measures of the angles are represented by the expressions $10x + 9$ and $7x + 18$. What are the two angle measures?

_____

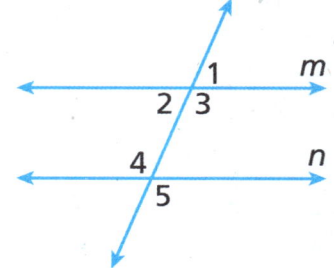

I'm in a Learning Mindset!

What can I do to increase my understanding of how to find unknown angle measures when parallel lines are cut by a transversal?

_____

_____

Name _____

Explore Parallel Lines Cut by a Transversal

LESSON 11.3
More Practice/ Homework

ONLINE Video Tutorials and Interactive Examples

1. A room in an attic has a sloping wall that makes an angle of 55° with the floor, which is parallel to the ceiling. What is the measure of an angle that forms a pair of same-side interior angles with that angle?

   _____

2. **Math on the Spot** Line *n* is parallel to Line *p*. Find the measure of each angle.

   _____
   _____

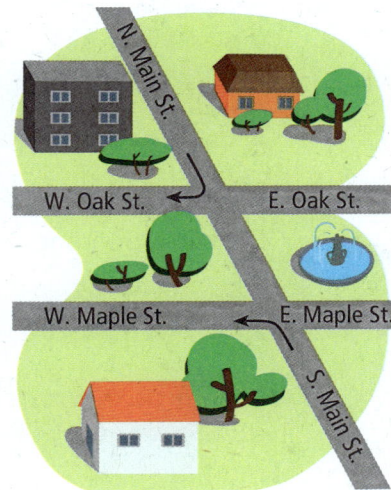

3. Oak Street runs parallel with Maple Street. The turn shown from North Main Street onto West Oak Street measures 65°. What is the measure of the turn shown from South Main Street onto West Maple Street? Explain.

   _____
   _____
   _____

4. Two parallel lines are cut by a transversal and two of the same-side interior angles formed have measures of $(4x + 3)°$ and $(x + 2)°$.

   A. How are the angles related?
   _____

   B. Write and solve an equation to find the value of *x*.
   _____

   C. What are the two angle measures?
   _____

5. **(MP) Reason** In the diagram, two parallel lines are cut by a transversal, and ∠1 and ∠6 do not form any of the kinds of angle pairs that you have learned. What is a way you can find the measure of ∠6 if you know that the measure of ∠1 is 132°? Explain.

   _____
   _____
   _____

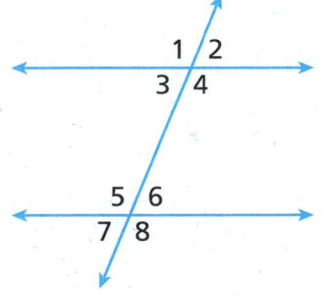

Module 11 • Lesson 3   377

Test Prep

6. Two parallel lines are cut by a transversal. A pair of same-side interior angles formed have measures of $(2x - 11)°$ and $(9x + 6.75)°$. What is the measure of the smaller angle?

   _____

7. What are the values of x and y?

   Ⓐ $x = 30; y = 76$
   Ⓑ $x = 76; y = 48$
   Ⓒ $x = 80; y = 54$
   Ⓓ $x = 132; y = 48$

   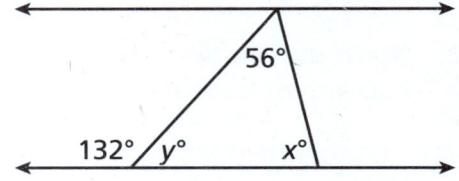

8. Two parallel lines are cut by a transversal. What kind of angle pair are Angles 1 and 2?

   Ⓐ alternate interior angles
   Ⓑ alternate exterior angles
   Ⓒ same-side exterior angles
   Ⓓ corresponding angles

   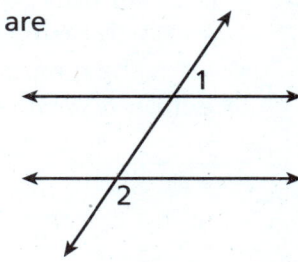

Spiral Review

9. If a unit circle with a center at (−3, 4) is reflected across the x-axis, where will the center of the reflected image lie?

   _____

10. One triangle has angles that measure 45° and 83°. Another triangle has angles that measure 45° and 52°. Are the triangles similar? How do you know?

    _____
    _____
    _____

11. An office manager is planning to set up three computer workstations and a printer in a space that is 22 feet wide. The printer takes up 4 feet.

    A. Write an equation that you could use to find the width w (in feet) of the space available for each computer workstation.

    _____

    B. What is the width of the space available for each computer workstation?

    _____

Module 11 Review

Vocabulary

In the diagram, Line *AF* is parallel to Line *BE*. Give one example of each type of figure in the diagram.

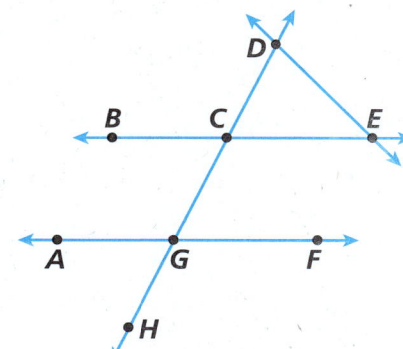

1. an exterior angle of a triangle _____

2. a remote interior angle of the exterior angle you named in Problem 1 _____

3. a transversal of a pair of parallel lines _____

4. a pair of alternate interior angles formed by a pair of parallel lines and a transversal _____

Concepts and Skills

5. If Triangle *ABC* is similar to Triangle *EDC*, which statements about the figures must be true?

    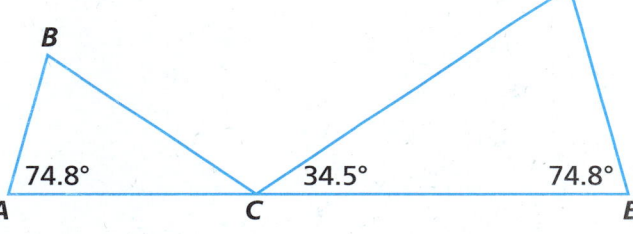

    Ⓐ Angle *B* measures 70.7°.

    Ⓑ Angle *ACB* measures 40.3°.

    Ⓒ Angle *A* is the largest interior angle of Triangle *ABC*.

    Ⓓ Triangle *EDC* can be produced from Triangle *ABC* by a dilation and a reflection.

    Ⓔ Triangle *EDC* can be produced from Triangle *ABC* by a rotation and a dilation.

6. In Triangle *JKL*, ∠*J* is congruent to ∠*L*. What is the measure of ∠*L*? _____

    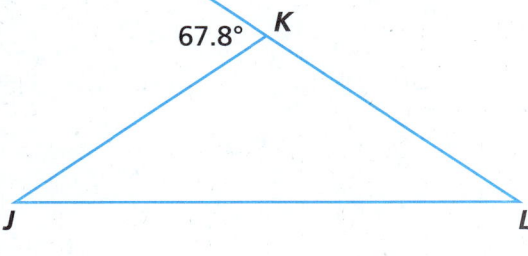

7. **Use Tools** A figure with parallel Lines *m* and *n* is shown. Find the measures of angles *A*, *B*, and *C*. State what strategy and tool you will use to answer the question, explain your choice, and then find the answer.

    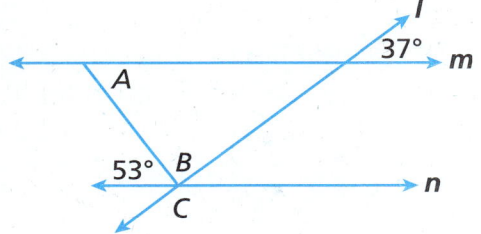

    _____
    _____
    _____

Module 11 379

8. In the figure, Segments SV and RU intersect at Point T. Anna claims that Triangle RST is similar to Triangle UVT. Is Anna's claim correct? Explain your reasoning.

_____

_____

_____

_____

_____

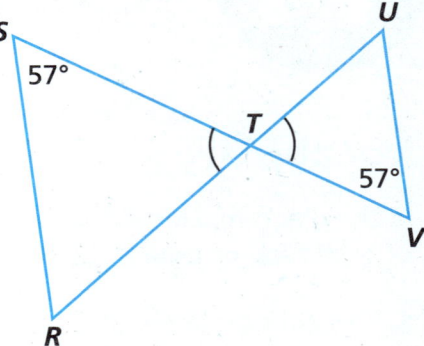

9. What is the value of x in the figure shown? _____

10. What is the value of z in the figure shown? _____

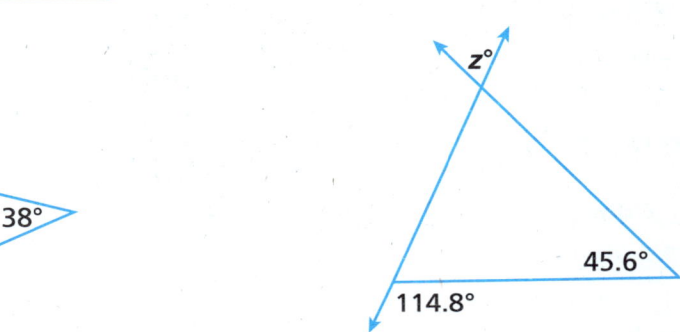

11. In the figure, Line a is parallel to Line b.

   A. Which equation can be used to determine the value of x?

   Ⓐ $3x = 2x + 20$

   Ⓑ $90 - 3x = 2x + 20$

   Ⓒ $3x = 180 - 2x + 20$

   Ⓓ $3x + 2x + 20 = 180$

   B. What are the values of x and y?

   x = _____

   y = _____

12. In the figure, Line ℓ is parallel to Line m. Select all true statements about the figure.

   Ⓐ $g = 54$

   Ⓑ $h = 126$

   Ⓒ $f = g$

   Ⓓ $g + h = 180$

   Ⓔ $f = h$

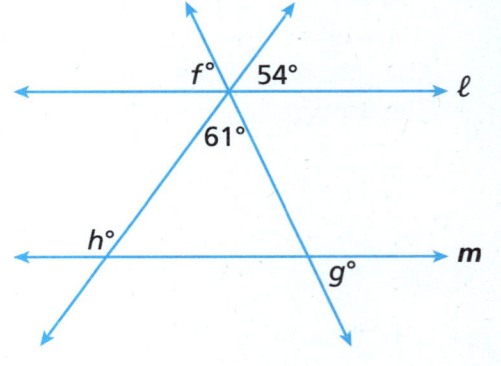

Module 12: Linear Relationships

Proportional Smoothies

The owners of a smoothie shop want the price of each size of smoothie to be proportional to the amount of liquid it contains. A small smoothie will be 16 fluid ounces and sell for $3.52.

Complete the shop's price chart by deciding how many fluid ounces the other smoothie sizes will have and then determine the price of each smoothie.

Smoothies		
Size	Fluid ounces	Price ($)
Kid-size		
Small	16	3.52
Medium		
Large		

 **Turn and Talk**

- Explain how you know that the prices of the smoothies are proportional to their volumes.

- The shop owners decide to charge $0.99 for each smoothie add-in. For smoothies with a single add-in, is the total price proportional to the fluid ounces? Explain.

Are You Ready?

Complete these problems to review prior concepts and skills you will need for this module.

Tables and Graphs of Equivalent Ratios

Complete each table to represent the relationship.

1. Collette runs 6.5 kilometers each week. Let d represent the total distance, in kilometers, she runs in w weeks.

w	2		5
d		19.5	

2. A theater charges a service fee of $0.95 per ticket bought online. Let t represent the total fee paid for ordering n tickets.

n	1	3	
t			$5.70

Identify Proportional Relationships

Tell whether each relationship is proportional. Explain your reasoning.

3.
x	6	8	12	15
y	48	64	96	120

4.
x	9	15	18	36
y	18	24	27	45

Similar Triangles

Tell whether each pair of triangles is similar. Explain your reasoning.

5.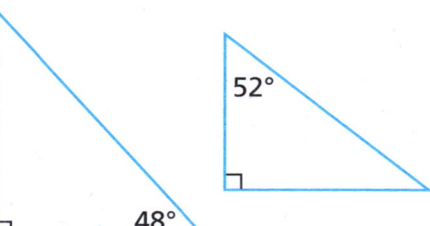

6.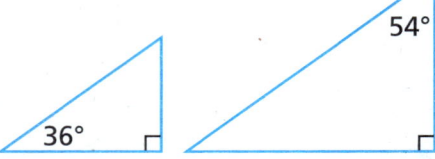

Build Conceptual Understanding

Lesson 1

Name _____

Explain Slope with Similar Triangles

 I Can determine the slope of a line and use it to find additional points on the line.

Spark Your Learning

A line passes through the origin. Two right triangles each have one side along the line and another side on the x-axis. How is △OAC related to △OBD?

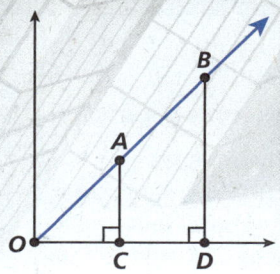

Turn and Talk Amie drew a different line through the origin and drew two new right triangles that have one side along the x-axis. How are her triangles different from the ones shown above? How are they the same?

Module 12 • Lesson 1

Build Understanding

1 Points on the line represent the vertical and horizontal distances a person would travel while climbing the path before steps were built to make the climb easier.

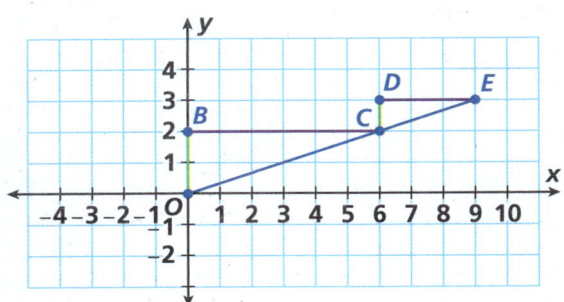

A. Write a sequence of transformations that maps one triangle onto the other to show that △OBC is similar to △CDE.

_____

_____

_____

> **Connect to Vocabulary**
>
> The **hypotenuse** of a right triangle is the side opposite the right angle. The **legs** of a right triangle are the sides adjacent to the right angle.

B. Complete the following based on △OBC and △CDE.

$\dfrac{\text{length of } \overline{OB}}{\text{length of } \overline{CD}} = \dfrac{\text{length of } \overline{BC}}{\text{length of } \overline{DE}}$ Corresponding sides of similar triangles are proportional.

$\dfrac{\square}{1} = \dfrac{\square}{3}$ Substitute.

$\dfrac{\square}{1} \times \dfrac{1}{6} = \dfrac{\square}{3} \times \dfrac{1}{6}$ _____

$\dfrac{\square}{6} = \dfrac{\square}{3}$ ← rise
               ← run   Multiply.

C. When moving from one point to another along a line, the change in the y-coordinates is the **rise** and the change in the x-coordinates is the **run**. The legs of △OBC and △CDE can help you visualize the rise and run. What does Part B show you about the rise-to-run ratios in △OBC and △CDE?

_____

384

Name _____

D. Explain how Parts A–C use similar triangles to show the slope of a line is constant in this situation. Why does this work in general?

> **Connect to Vocabulary**
>
> **Slope** is a measure of the steepness of a line and is described by the ratio of the line's rise to its run. A horizontal line has slope 0, and a vertical line's slope is undefined.

_____
_____
_____
_____
_____

2 A skateboard ramp is shown on a coordinate plane.

A. Does this line represent a proportional relationship? Explain.

_____
_____

B. Since the run between the origin and Point P is 1, the unit rate is equal to the rise-over-run ratio. Find the unit rate of the relationship modeled by the line. Complete the equation using the coordinates of Point P and the origin.

$$\text{unit rate} = \frac{\text{rise}}{\text{run}} = \frac{\Box - \Box}{\Box - \Box} = \frac{\Box}{\Box} = \Box \text{ in./ft}$$

> **Connect to Vocabulary**
>
> A rate is a comparison of two quantities that have different units. A **unit rate** is a rate with a denominator of one unit.

Turn and Talk Explain the relationship between the unit rate and the slope.

Check Understanding

1. Explain how you can use similar triangles from the diagram to show that slope is constant.

_____
_____
_____
_____

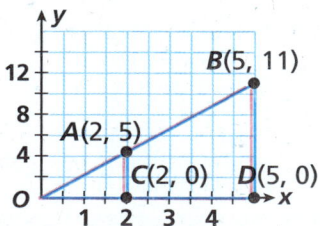

2. For the proportional relationship in Item 1, what is another way to describe the slope. Explain.

_____

Module 12 • Lesson 1   385

On Your Own

3. A mountain road has a grade, meaning it has an incline. A person drives their car from the bottom of the road, represented by (0, 0) to the peak's overlook. The overlook is a vertical distance of 750 feet and a horizontal distance of 150 feet from the bottom. What is the slope of the line that models this situation? _____

4. **(MP) Attend to Precision** Line ℓ passes through the origin and the point (4, 5). Suppose point (x, y) also lies on Line ℓ.

   A. The slope of Line ℓ from the origin to (4, 5) is _____.

   B. Show how to use similar triangles and the ratio of sides to confirm the slope of Line ℓ from the origin to (x, y) is the same as the slope from the origin to (4, 5).

   _____

   _____

   _____

5. Are Triangles OPQ and ORS similar? If so, give a sequence of transformations that maps △OPQ onto △ORS. What is the slope of line PR?

   _____

   _____

   _____

   _____

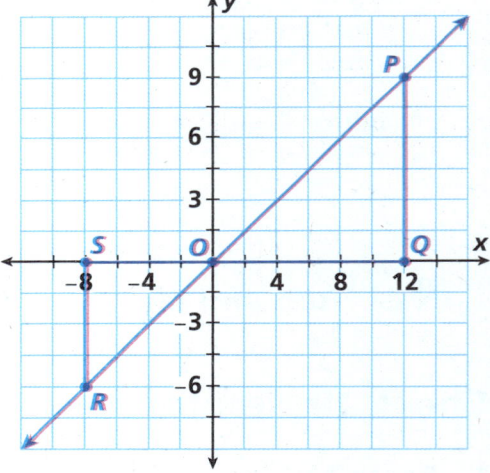

For problems 6-7, the line with its given points represents a proportional relationship. Find the slope expressed as a unit rate.

6. (5, 10) and (−3, −6)

7. (12, −2) and (20, 6)

   _____   _____

I'm in a Learning Mindset!

How was finding the slope of a line an appropriate challenge for me?

_____

_____

386

Explain Slope with Similar Triangles

LESSON 12.1 More Practice/Homework

Use the graph to answer Problems 1–4.

1. Use parallel lines cut by a transversal to Identify one pair of corresponding angles and describe what you know about them.

2. How is △PQR related to △STU? Explain.

3. What is the ratio of the length of the vertical side to the length of the horizontal side of each triangle?

4. Find the slope of the line using the origin and point U. How does the slope of the line relate to the similar triangle ratios found in Problem 3? Explain.

5. **Model with Mathematics** A person casts a shadow that aligns with the shadow of a tree. The person is 5.5 feet tall, and casts a shadow 8.25 feet long. The tree's shadow measures 22.5 feet long.

   A. Write an equation you can use to find the tree's height.

   B. How tall is the tree? How far is the person standing from the tree?

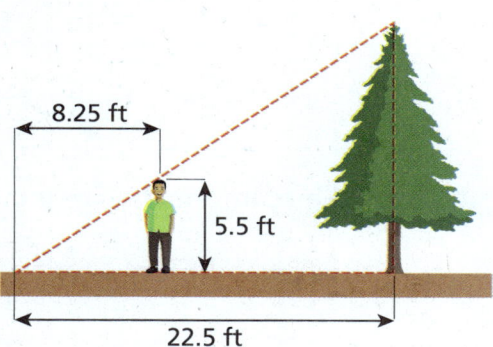

6. **Open Ended** Explain how it is possible to find the slope of a line given any two points on the line.

Module 12 • Lesson 1   387

Test Prep

7. A line passes through the origin, (3, 6), and (10, 20). Which of the following statements is not true?

- Ⓐ The points make two congruent triangles.
- Ⓑ The slope is 2.
- Ⓒ The points represent a proportional relationship.
- Ⓓ The slope is a unit rate.

Use the diagram at the right for questions 8–9.

8. Which of the following steps could be part of a sequence of transformations that would map Triangle *OAC* to Triangle *ABD*?

- Ⓐ dilation of 2
- Ⓑ dilation of $\frac{1}{2}$
- Ⓒ translation 2 right
- Ⓓ translation 2 left
- Ⓔ translation up 1
- Ⓕ translation down 1

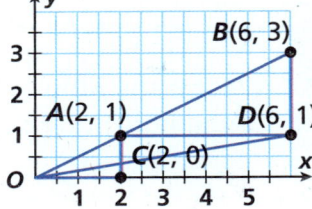

9. What is the slope of line *AB*? _____

Spiral Review

10. Find the value of *x*. Then find the measure of each angle.

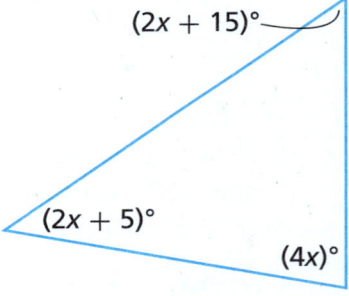

11. Jean-Paul wants to make a triangular figure. He has side lengths of 2, 5, 8, and 18 centimeters. Could he make a triangular figure out of any combination of these pieces? Explain.

12. Describe a transformation that maps *ABCD* onto *A'B'C'D'*.

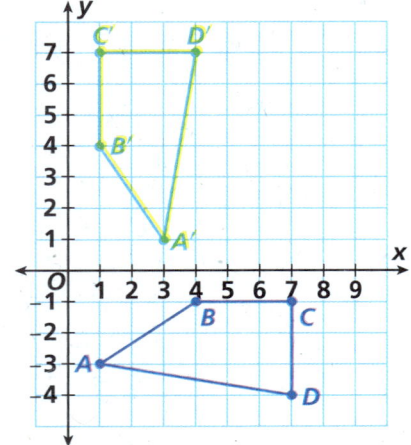

388

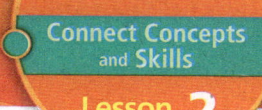

Lesson 2

Name _____

Derive $y = mx$

I Can write the equation of a line given a graph or a table of values.

Spark Your Learning

Asiah's literature class is studying a new book. To complete the assigned reading on time, she has made a schedule. Asiah records her progress in a graph. What can you interpret from the graph?

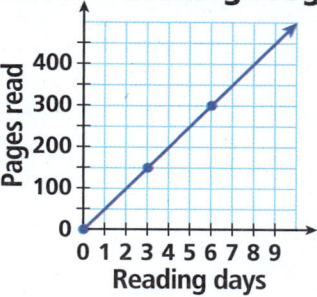

Turn and Talk How would the graph look different if Asiah read more pages per day?

Module 12 • Lesson 2

Build Understanding

1 Use the graph of Asiah's reading to answer the following questions.

A. The number of pages that Asiah has cumulatively read increases by $\frac{\boxed{} \text{ pages}}{1 \text{ day}}$.

B. The graph shows the number of pages that Asiah has read at the end of each day. Complete the table, including a general expression for the number of pages Asiah will read in x days.

Asiah's Reading Progress	
Reading days	**Pages read**
1	
2	
4	
7	
x	

C. Use the variable y to stand for the number of pages that Asiah has read. Write an equation to model the number of pages read after x days.

D. From the point at 1 day to the point at 2 days, how much does the graph rise?

E. What is the slope, or rise over run, for Asiah's graph? Explain your reasoning.

F. How is the slope related to the unit rate of this proportional relationship?

G. Look at the equation from Part C. What do you notice about the equation when you compare it to the slope from Part E?

H. Asiah decides she wants to adjust her schedule so she will finish the book earlier than the due date. How will this change the slope? Explain your reasoning.

Name _____

Step It Out

2 Don is a gifted wood carver, and he has started selling his wood carvings online. He tracks the total number of carvings sold.

Months in business	Carvings sold
2	5
6	15
8	20

A. Sketch a graph of the relationship between the number of months in business and the number of carvings sold.

B. Explain why the relationship is proportional.

_____

C. Write the slope m of the graph. Slope = $\frac{\text{rise}}{\text{run}}$ = _____.

D. Recall that the equation of a proportional relationship has the form $y = kx$ and that the slope m and the unit rate k are the same in a proportional relationship. Write an equation of the line in the form $y = mx$. _____

E. Use the linear equation to predict the number of carvings sold after being in business for 12 months. _____

Don's Carving Business

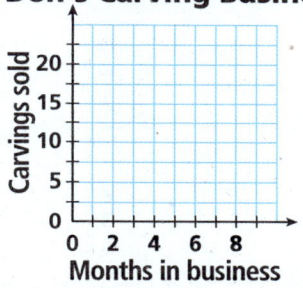

Connect to Vocabulary

A **linear equation** is an equation whose solutions form a straight line on a coordinate plane.

 **Turn and Talk** A line is modeled by the equation $y = mx$. Explain how the value of m affects the graph of the line.

Check Understanding

1. The Nguyen family is traveling cross-country, driving 300 miles each day. Let x represent the number of days in the trip and let y represent the total number of miles driven. Write an equation to model their trip.

_____

2. Write an equation for the line passing through points (0, 0), (4, 5), and (8, 10).

_____

Module 12 • Lesson 2

On Your Own

3. **Reason** A clothing store is going out of business. To sell their remaining inventory, the managers drop the price of each item $5 each week until the item sells.

A. A line is drawn to model the relationship between the number of weeks and the change in price. Is the slope of this line positive or negative? Explain.

_____

B. Write the equation of the line. _____

For Problems 4–5, sketch the graph of the line represented by the equation. Plot and label three points on each line.

4. $y = \frac{5}{3}x$

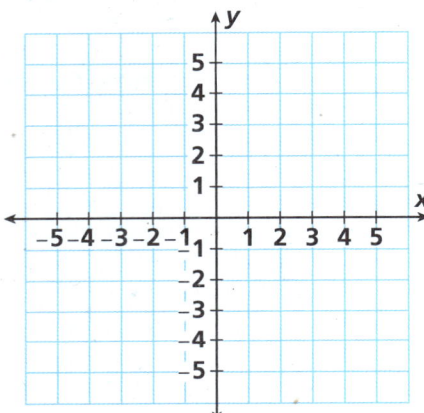

5. $y = -\frac{1}{4}x$

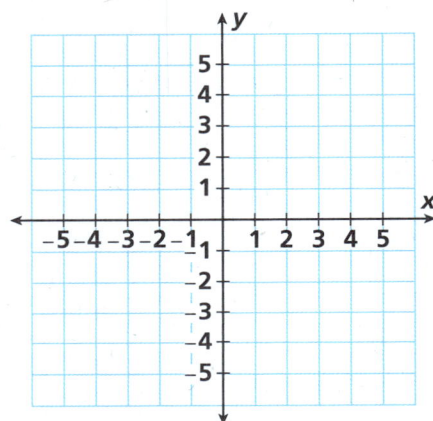

Model with Mathematics For Problems 6–7, write an equation that models the relationship shown in the table.

6.

x	y
−6	14
−3	7
3	−7
6	−14

7.

x	y
−8	−4
−4	−2
6	3
10	5

_____

 I'm in a **Learning Mindset!**

What challenges did I face writing an equation that modeled the relationship in the table for Problem 7?

_____

_____

Name _____

Derive y = mx

LESSON 12.2
More Practice/ Homework

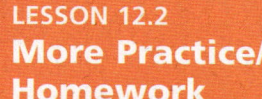
 Video Tutorials and Interactive Examples

1. Sean tutors math students to earn extra money.

   A. How much would Sean earn from 4 hours of tutoring?

   _____

   B. Write an equation to model Sean's earnings, y, after x hours.

   _____

Sean charges $20 per hour.

2. (MP) **Attend to Precision** An inch is exactly 2.54 centimeters. Write an equation to convert the number of inches x to the corresponding length in centimeters.

   _____

3. Write an equation of the line passing through the points $(-5, -25)$, $(0, 0)$, and $(3, 15)$.

   _____

4. **Math on the Spot** The graph shows the distance Caleb runs over time.

   A. Identify four points on the line.

   _____

   _____

   B. Determine the slope of the line.

   _____

   C. Write an equation of the line.

   _____

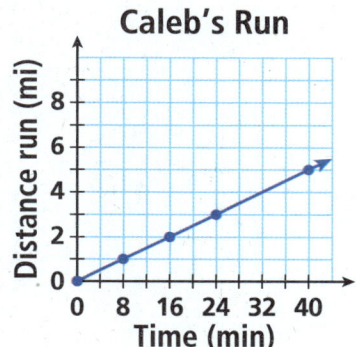

Caleb's Run

5. Sketch the graph of the line $y = 4x$.

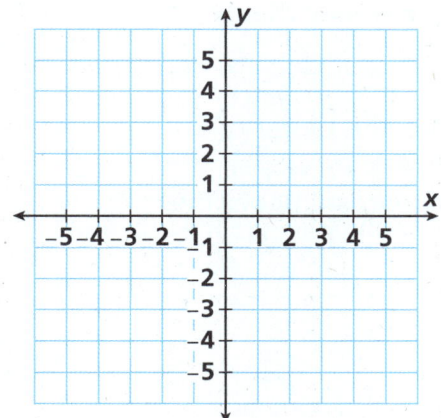

6. (MP) **Model with Mathematics** Write an equation that models the relationship shown in the table.

x	y
12	−9
8	−6
20	−15
32	−24

_____

Module 12 • Lesson 2

Test Prep

7. Which is an equation of the line passing through the points (−2, 5), (0, 0), and (4, −10)?

Ⓐ $y = -\frac{5}{2}x$
Ⓑ $y = -\frac{2}{5}x$
Ⓒ $y = \frac{2}{5}x$
Ⓓ $y = \frac{5}{2}x$

8. Complete the equation of the line passing through the points (−4, −2), (2, 1), and (−2, −1).

$y = \boxed{} x$

9. The value of a house has been increasing by $5,000 each year. Write an equation to show how the value will have changed x years from now.

$y = \boxed{} x$

10. Graph $y = \frac{2}{3}x$. Plot and label three points on the line.

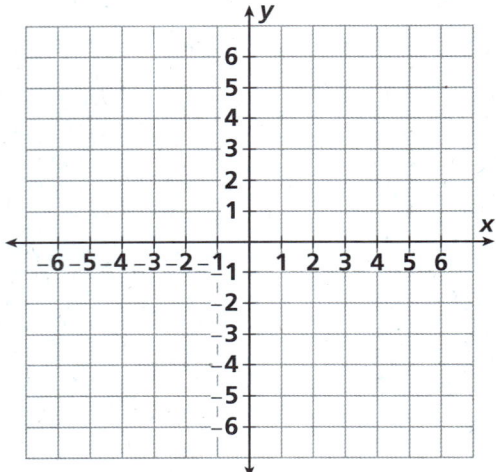

Spiral Review

11. Triangle *ABC* has vertices (1, 4), (5, 6), and (3, 10). It is reflected across the *y*-axis, making Triangle *A'B'C'*. What are the vertices of the new triangle?

_____

12. Quadrilateral *ABCD* is dilated by a scale factor of 2, with the center of dilation at the origin. The vertices of *ABCD* are *A*(0, 0), *B*(5, 0), *C*(5, 3), and *D*(0, 3). What are the coordinates of the image of Vertex *C* under the dilation?

_____

13. Solve the equation $3x - 2(x + 1) = 2x - 7$.

_____

Connect Concepts and Skills

Lesson 3

Derive and Interpret $y = mx + b$

I Can derive the equation for a line in the form $y = mx + b$ given the slope of the line and a point.

Spark Your Learning

Based on data from a science experiment, Sierra graphs Lines A, B, and C. Compare the lines. How are they the same? How are they different?

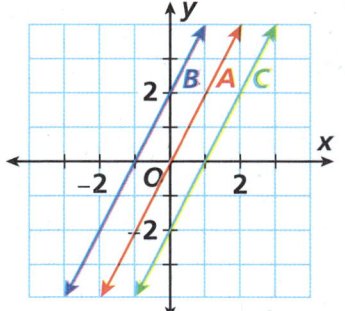

Turn and Talk What would be the equation of a line that passes through the origin and the point (1, −2)? Explain.

Module 12 • Lesson 3

Build Understanding

1 The **y-intercept** of a graph is the point where the graph crosses the y-axis, or the value of y when x equals 0. A line that passes through the origin can be represented by an equation of the form $y = mx$.

A. Consider a line with slope m and y-intercept b. Write the ordered pair that represents the y-intercept.

_____

B. Recall that slope is rise over run, or the ratio of change in y to change in x. Complete the equation for the slope m of the line using the point from Part A and another point on the line (x, y).

$m = \dfrac{y - \Box}{\Box - 0}$

C. Solve the equation from Part B for y.

The $y = mx + b$ form of the equation of a line is called **slope-intercept form**.

D. Identify the slope and y-intercept of each graph.

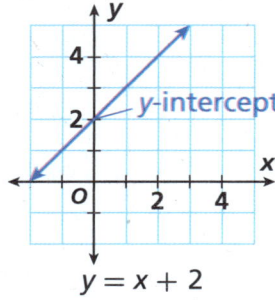

$y = x + 2$

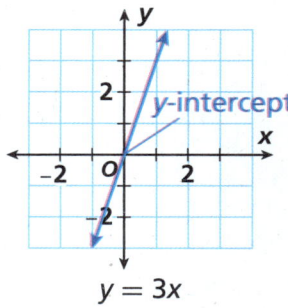

$y = -2x + 1$

$y = 3x$

slope: _____   slope: _____   slope: _____

y-intercept: _____   y-intercept: _____   y-intercept: _____

E. How do the coefficient m of x and the constant b in each equation relate to the slope and y-intercept?

_____

_____

Name _____

Step It Out

2 A. Is the slope of Line A positive or negative? _____

B. Find the slope of Line A. _____

C. What is the y-intercept of Line A? _____

D. Write the equation of Line A in slope-intercept form.

y = ☐ x + ☐

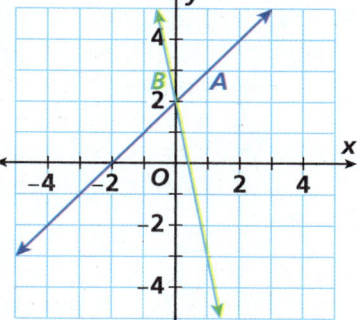

3 A line has a slope $m = -1$. One point on the line is (2, 4). Substitute the x, y, and m values into the slope-intercept form of an equation to find the y-intercept. Then write the equation of the line in slope-intercept form.

y = ☐ , m = ☐ , and x = ☐

$y = mx + b$

☐ = −1 (☐) + b

☐ = ☐ + b

☐ = b

The y-intercept is _____.

The equation of the line is y = ☐ x + ☐ .

> **Turn and Talk** Does the graph of $y = 3x - 3$ pass through the origin? If so, how do you know? If not, what is the y-intercept?

Check Understanding

1. Use the diagram from Task 2 to find the slope and y-intercept of Line B. Then write the equation of Line B in slope-intercept form.

   _____

2. The slope of a line is −3, and a point on the line is (4, −1). Can the equation of the line be expressed in slope-intercept form? If so, what is the equation? Does the line pass through the origin? How do you know?

   _____

   _____

Module 12 • Lesson 3

On Your Own

3. **A.** On the coordinate plane provided, plot the points $(-2, -2)$, $(-1, 1)$, and $(1, 7)$. Connect the points with a straight line.

   B. **Model with Mathematics** What is the equation of the line in slope-intercept form?

   _____

   C. Is $y = 3x + 1$ parallel to the line from Part A? Explain. (Hint: Graph this line too.)

   _____

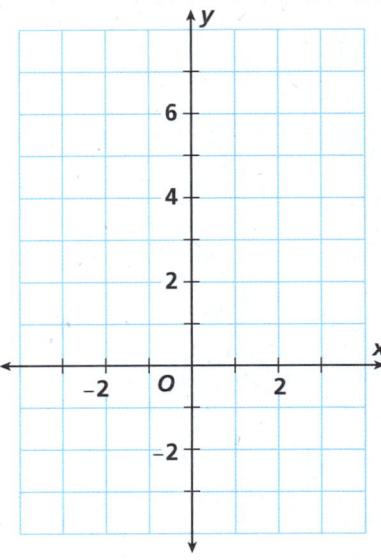

4. **Open Ended** Write an equation for a proportional relationship and an equation for a nonproportional one.

   _____

   _____

For Problems 5 and 6, write the equation in slope-intercept form, identify the slope, and identify the *y*-intercept.

5. $2y - 3x = 4$ _____

   _____

6. $-5 = -y - 3x$ _____

   _____

Model with Mathematics For Problems 7 and 8, write the slope-intercept form of the line with the given slope and point.

7. $m = 4$; $(2, 3)$

   _____

8. $m = -2$; $(5, 1)$

   _____

I'm in a Learning Mindset!

How does my understanding of equations in slope-intercept form impact my ability to find parallel lines?

_____

_____

Name _____

Derive and Interpret $y = mx + b$

LESSON 12.3
More Practice/ Homework

1. **MP Attend to Precision** Tasha wants to draw a line on a graph that is parallel to $y = 3x$. Give two examples of lines she could draw, one that is above the original line and one that is below the original line.

   _____

2. Shyann is trying to figure out whether her equation, $y = 5{,}683x + 976$, will pass through the origin. Will the line pass through the origin? How do you know?

   _____

3. Paulo identifies one point on a line as (6, 3), and he knows that the slope is 2. How can he derive the equation of the line?

   _____
   _____
   _____

4. **Math on the Spot** An arcade deducts 3.5 points from a 50-point game card for each game played. The linear equation $y = -3.5x + 50$ represents the number of points y on a card after x games played. Graph the equation using the slope and y-intercept.

   Points on Game Card
   (graph with y-axis "Points" 0 to 50, x-axis "Number of games played" 0 to 60)

Write each equation in slope-intercept form and identify the y-intercept.

5. $5 = 10x - 5y$

6. $12x = -4y - 8$

Identify the slope and state whether the line rises or falls from left to right.

7. $y = 3x - 11$

8. $y = -\frac{1}{2}x + 2$

Identify whether each relationship is proportional or nonproportional.

9. $y = \frac{3}{2}x$

10. $y = \frac{3}{2x} + 9$

Module 12 • Lesson 3   399

Test Prep

11. Find the equation of a line with slope −2 that contains the point (−3, 3).

$y = \boxed{} x - \boxed{}$

For Problems 12–14, complete each statement for the equation $y = \frac{1}{2}x - \frac{1}{2}$.

12. What is the slope of the line? _____

13. Does the line rise or fall from left to right? _____

14. The graph crosses the y-axis at $\left(0, \underline{}\right)$.

15. Roscoe has a pie baking business. His profit is given by the equation $y = 15x - 5$. Sheena has a cake baking business. Her profit is given by an equation with a graph that is parallel to the graph of the equation for Roscoe's profit. Which equation could represent Sheena's profit?

Ⓐ $y = 15x + 10$
Ⓑ $y = 3x - 1$
Ⓒ $y = 5x - 5$
Ⓓ $y = -15x - 3$

16. Identify whether each relationship is proportional or nonproportional.

	Proportional	Nonproportional
$y = x + 1$	☐	☐
$0 = 2x + y$	☐	☐
$y = \frac{5}{4}x$	☐	☐
$4 = x - y$	☐	☐

Spiral Review

17. Mr. Chin asked his class to solve the equation $8(3y - 5) = 9(y - 5) - 1$ for y. Explain how to solve for y. Then solve.

_____

_____

18. Claire wants to start a stamp collection. She spends $15 on an album to hold her stamps and $1.25 for each stamp. If she has $40, what is the maximum number of stamps she can buy?

_____

19. How many triangles can you construct with side lengths 5 inches, 8 inches, and 20 inches?

_____

Describe and Sketch Nonlinear Relationships

I Can convert between a verbal description of a relationship and its graph, and between a graph and a verbal description of a relationship.

Step It Out

A **linear relationship** is a relationship that can be written in the form $y = mx + b$ and whose graph is a line. The slope of a line is constant except in the case of a vertical line whose slope is undefined. A **nonlinear relationship** is a relationship whose graph is not a line.

1 Emanuel walks the North Trail at his local park. The graph shows his distance from the fountain at the center of the park as he walks along the trail. Use the graph to answer the questions.

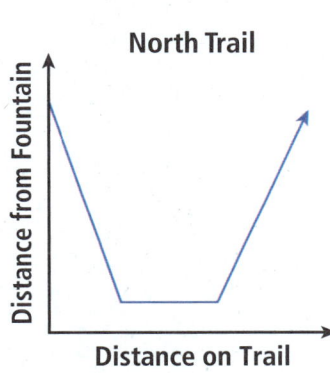

North Trail

A. Each section of the graph is linear / nonlinear .

B. The slope for the first part of his walk is positive / negative , which means his distance from the fountain is increasing / decreasing at a constant rate.

C. The slope for the second part of his walk is _____.

What does that mean about his distance from the fountain?

_____

D. The slope for the third part of his walk is positive / negative , which means his distance from the fountain is increasing / decreasing at a constant rate.

E. Emanuel returns to the park the next day and walks the South Trail.

The South Trail graph is linear / nonlinear .

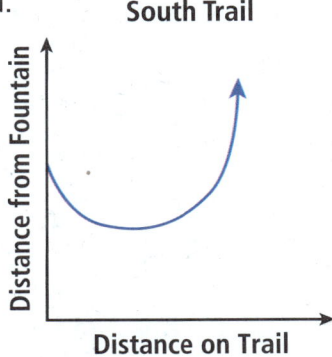

South Trail

F. Early on, does his distance from the fountain decrease at a constant rate? _____

Near the end, does his distance from the fountain increase at a constant rate? _____

How do you know? _____

Turn and Talk Describe potential scenarios for each path in relation to the fountain location.

Module 12 • Lesson 4   401

2 When a state fair opened, the number of people attending the fair gradually increased at a constant rate in the morning. Then the number of people remained constant through the afternoon. In the evening, the attendance gradually decreased at a constant rate until near the end of the night, when the number of people decreased swiftly at a constant rate as they all left.

A. Where should the graph of the situation begin and why?

It starts at _____ because there were

_____ people there until the fair opened.

B. Describe what happens to the graph as the number of people gradually increased at a constant rate in the morning. Will the slope of this part of the graph be positive or negative? Will it be steep or gradual?

It will be | positive / negative | and | steep / gradual |.

C. Describe what the graph looks like as the number of people remained constant through the afternoon.

This part of the graph will be _____.

D. Describe what happens to the graph as the number of people gradually decreased at a constant rate. Will the slope of this part of the graph be positive or negative? Will it be steep or gradual?

It will be | positive / negative | and | steep / gradual |.

E. Describe what happens to the graph near the end of the night, when the number of people decreased swiftly as they all left. Will the slope of this part of the graph be positive or negative? Will it be steep or gradual?

It will be | positive / negative | and | steep / gradual |.

F. Use what you described to sketch the situation.

G. Suppose the number of people attending the fair continued to gradually increase at a constant rate throughout the afternoon instead of remaining constant. Sketch a graph that represents this situation.

Name _____

3 Kevin says that this graph describes an airplane that takes off, climbs to cruising altitude, stays at the cruising altitude for the flight, and then descends for landing. Kate says that the graph better describes a model rocket that launches, rises to a maximum altitude, and then falls faster and faster until it reaches the ground.

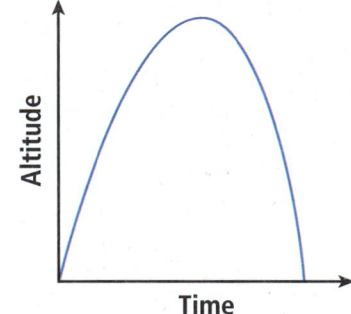

A. Is the graph linear, nonlinear, or a combination?

_____

B. Is the graph increasing at a constant rate? Is the graph decreasing at a constant rate?

_____

C. Is there a portion of the graph where the altitude is constant?

_____

D. Whose description does the graph better represent, Kevin's or Kate's? Why?

_____
_____
_____
_____

Turn and Talk Sketch a graph to represent the airplane flight that Kevin suggested.

Check Understanding

1. Describe the temperature changes shown in the graph.

_____
_____
_____
_____

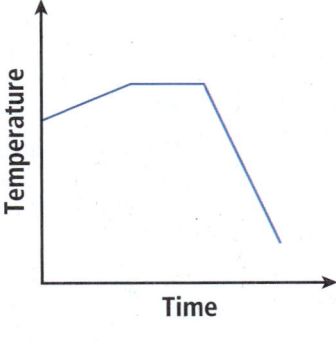

2. Selena hikes a trail. Her elevation decreases at a constant rate until she reaches a stream. Her elevation stays the same walking by the stream until she climbs a hill at a constant rate to reach the campground. She sits to rest once she gets back to the campground. Sketch a graph to represent the situation.

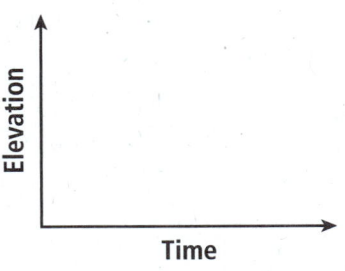

Module 12 • Lesson 4

On Your Own

3. The graph represents the speed of a swimmer during a race. Describe the swimmer's speed during the course of the race.

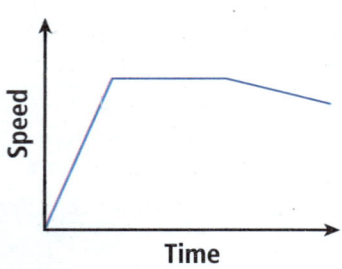

_____

_____

_____

_____

4. The value of a stock increases gradually at a constant rate at the beginning of the day. The value quickly decreases at a constant rate to below the original value during the middle of the day, and then stays the same for the rest of the day.

A. Sketch a graph that represents the situation.

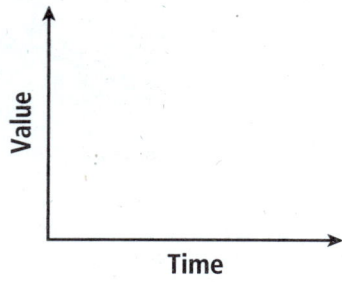

B. **(MP) Reason** How would the graph change if the value of the stock gradually decreased during the middle of the day?

_____

_____

5. Sketch a graph that shows a value that starts increasing rapidly, then continues increasing but more gradually, then increases rapidly again.

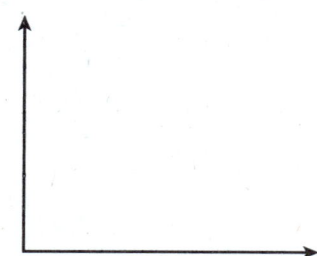

Name _____

For Problems 6–9, write a situation that the graph could represent.

6.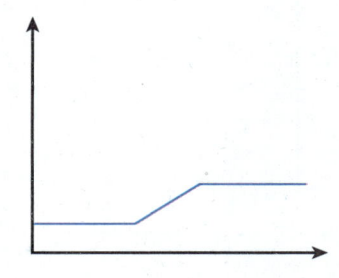

7.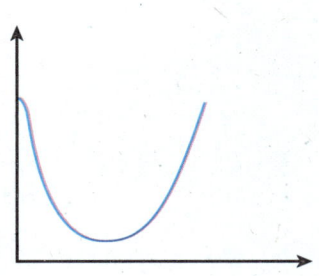

8.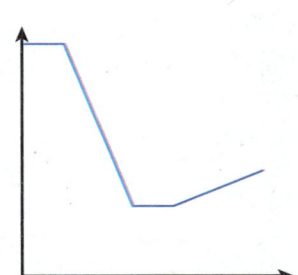

9.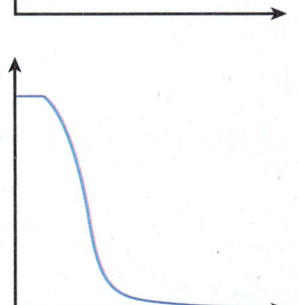

10. Manny completes a video game level. The elevation of his character is constant, then increases rapidly at a constant rate to a new constant elevation. The elevation then decreases rapidly at a constant rate to a new constant elevation to complete the level. Sketch a graph that represents the situation.

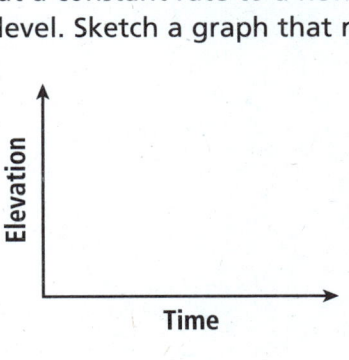

Module 12 • Lesson 4

405

The graph represents the height of a ball over time as the ball rolls across a ledge, then falls off. Use the graph to answer Problems 11–14.

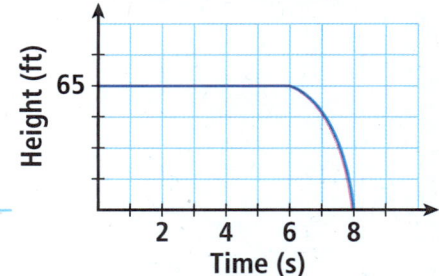

Height of Rolling Ball

11. Starting at what time and ending at what time, when is the graph linear?

_____

12. Starting at what time and ending at what time, when is the graph nonlinear?

_____

13. What does the linear part of the graph describe?

_____
_____

14. STEM What does the nonlinear part of the graph describe? Why is it nonlinear?

_____
_____
_____
_____
_____

Use the graph to answer Problems 15–16.

Fish Population at a Lake

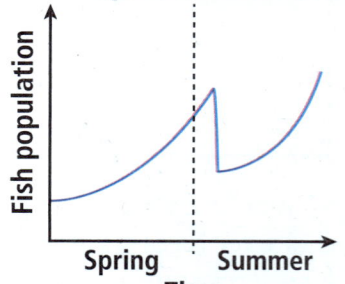

15. Social Studies What happens to the fish population in the spring? Use either the term *linear* or *nonlinear* in your response.

_____
_____

16. A fishing competition is held on the lake once a year.

  A. Which part of the graph shows the result of the competition? In what season is the competition held?

  _____

  B. Describe what happens to the fish population after the competition. Use either the term *linear* or *nonlinear* in your response.

  _____

Name _____

Describe and Sketch Nonlinear Relationships

LESSON 12.4
More Practice/ Homework

ONLINE Video Tutorials and Interactive Examples

1. **Open Ended** Write a situation that this graph could represent.

   _____
   _____
   _____
   _____
   _____

   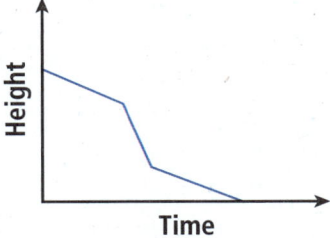

2. Darnell competes in an obstacle course. He climbs a ladder, runs across a bridge, then slides down a slide. Sketch a graph that represents his position above the ground as he completes the obstacle course.

   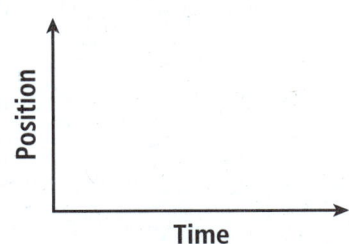

3. (MP) **Reason** The two graphs show the speeds of bicycles as they are coming to a stop. Describe how each of the bicycles comes to a stop.

   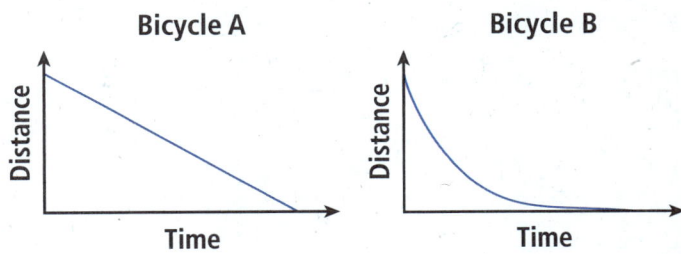

   _____
   _____

For Problems 4–5, sketch a graph that represents the given situation.

4. The temperature increased at a constant rate, then stayed the same for a while. Then it began increasing at a greater constant rate.

5. Rebecca drove at a constant speed on a street. She slowed at a constant rate to turn onto the highway, then sped up at a constant rate to drive at the speed limit.

Module 12 • Lesson 4

407

Test Prep

6. Which graph is a linear relationship decreasing at a constant rate?

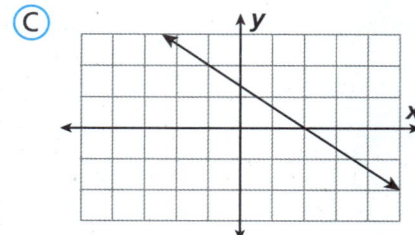

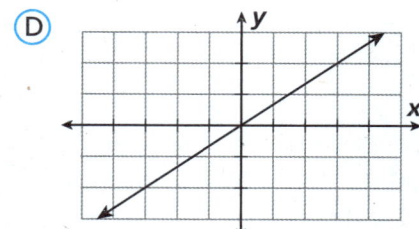

7. Select all statements that are true of the graph shown.

   Ⓐ The rate of the increase is greater than the rate of the decrease.

   Ⓑ The first segment of the graph is constant.

   Ⓒ The second segment of the graph increases at a constant rate.

   Ⓓ The rate of the decrease is greater than the rate of the increase.

   Ⓔ The third segment of the graph is decreasing.

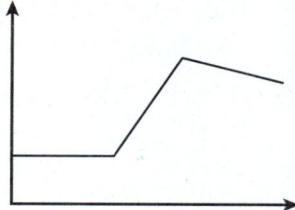

Spiral Review

8. Triangle *ABC* is dilated by a scale factor of 1.5 to form Triangle *DEF*. Are Triangles *ABC* and *DEF* congruent? Why or why not?

   _____
   _____
   _____

9. A triangle has angles measuring 45°, 55°, and 80°. It is dilated by a scale factor of 2. What are the angle measures of the dilated image?

   _____

Module 12 Review

Vocabulary

Choose the correct term from the box to complete each sentence.

Vocabulary
hypotenuse
leg
linear
nonlinear
rise
run
slope-intercept form

1. In a right triangle, the _____ is the side opposite the right angle, and a _____ is one of the sides that forms the right angle.

2. The slope of a non-vertical line is the ratio of the _____ to the _____ between any two points on the line.

3. A relationship between two variables whose graph is not a straight line is _____.

4. A relationship between two variables whose graph is a straight line is _____.

5. What is $y = mx + b$, and what do m and b represent?
   _____
   _____

Concepts and Skills

6. **MP Use Tools** The table and the equation each show a proportional relationship between time x, in seconds, and distance y, in meters. Who would finish a 100-meter race faster? How much faster? State what strategy and tool you will use to answer the question, explain your choice, and then find the answer.
   _____
   _____

Lauren's Run: $y = 8x$

Amani's Run	
Time (s)	Distance (m)
3	18
5	30
8	48

7. The graph shows right triangles *ABC* and *ADE*. The hypotenuse of each triangle lies on the same line.

   A. Explain how you know that the triangles are similar.

   _____

   _____

   _____

   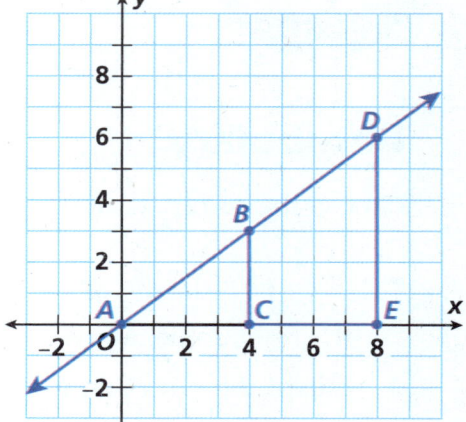

   B. How does knowing the triangles are similar help you show that the slope of the line through the hypotenuses is constant?

   _____

   _____

   _____

   _____

8. The graph shows how the temperature in a refrigerator changed over time, where *x* is the time in hours and *y* is the temperature in degrees Celsius. Use numbers from the box to complete the equation of the line shown in the graph.

   | (−4) | (−2) | (−0.5) | 0 | 0.5 | 2 | 4 |

   $y = \boxed{} x + \boxed{}$

   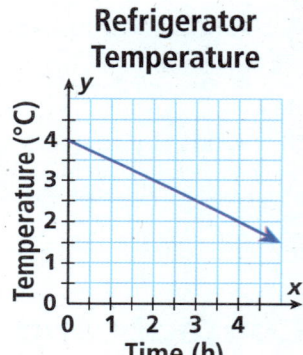

   Refrigerator Temperature

9. Write the slope-intercept form of the line with slope = −3, that passes through the point (−2, 11). _____

10. On the coordinate plane, draw the graph of a linear relationship that increases at a constant rate.

    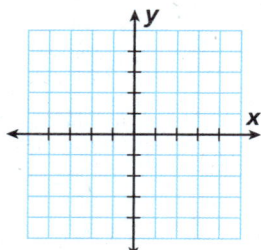

11. Can you describe a real-world linear relationship that can be modeled by the graph shown? Explain.

    _____

    _____

    _____

Unit 6
Applications of Real Numbers and Exponents

Historian

We know that the pyramids of Egypt were built about 5,000 years ago and that the people who built them used math to do so. But *how* do we know? Our knowledge is largely due to historians, who study the people, events, and ideas of the past and their influence on today's world. Historians use the information they gather to develop theories and draw conclusions about their subjects.

STEM Task:

An ancient Egyptian multiplication method based on doubling is used below to find 11×24. Use the method to find 13×24.

$11 \times 19 = 209$

①	19	19
②	38	38
4	76	
⑧	152	+152
16	304	
		209

Learning Mindset
Resilience Adjusts to Change

Resilience is the ability to "bounce back" after experiencing a disappointment or a defeat. When you encounter difficulty or setbacks, watch out for a fixed-mindset voice in your head telling you to give up. Here are some statements you can tell yourself to activate your growth-mindset voice and strengthen your resilience. Can you think of others?

- Mistakes and challenges are opportunities to learn.
- If this were easy, I would not learn anything from it.
- I have overcome challenges in the past, so I know I can do it again.
- When I solve this problem, I can be proud because it is not easy.
- I may be struggling, but I am still making progress.

Reflect

Q As you worked on the STEM Task, did anything trigger a fixed-mindset voice in your head? If so, what?

Q In the past, what situations have caused a fixed-mindset response in your head? What is your plan for activating your growth mindset when you encounter similar situations in the future?

Module 13

Real Numbers

Track the Distance

A group of five friends went running at the school track. They ran the distances shown.

Use the clues to determine which friend ran each distance.

- Ara and Tyrone ran the same distance.
- Morgan's distance written as a decimal has 3 nonzero digits.
- Shane's distance in miles is equal to a repeating decimal.
- Julius ran the greatest distance.
- Tyrone's distance in miles is given as a fraction in simplest form.

Ara ran _____ mile.   Morgan ran _____ mile.

Shane ran _____ mile.   Julius ran _____ mile.

Tyrone ran _____ mile.

 **Turn and Talk**

Another friend, Knox, ran farther than Shane but not as far as Tyrone. What possible distance could Knox have run? Explain.

Are You Ready?

Complete these problems to review prior concepts and skills you will need for this module.

Solve One-Step Equations

Solve each equation.

1. $x + 5 = 25$ _____
2. $x + 4 = 7$ _____
3. $x - 3 = 7$ _____
4. $x - 2 = 6$ _____
5. $19x = 76$ _____
6. $5x = 70$ _____
7. $\frac{x}{4} = 12$ _____
8. $\frac{x}{3} = 8$ _____

Rational Numbers on a Number Line

Plot each rational number on the number line.

9. 0.75
10. $-\frac{5}{8}$
11. -1.5
12. $1\frac{1}{8}$

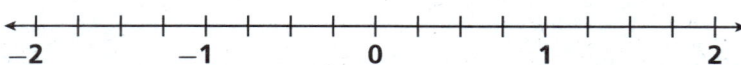

Convert Fractions to Decimals

13. How can you convert a fraction to a decimal?

   _____

   _____

Write each fraction as a decimal.

14. $\frac{4}{5}$
15. $\frac{3}{8}$
16. $\frac{11}{20}$
17. $\frac{3}{4}$
18. $\frac{1}{16}$
19. $\frac{13}{25}$

Connect Concepts and Skills

Lesson 1

Name _____

Understand Rational and Irrational Numbers

I Can determine whether a number is rational and write a given rational number as a fraction.

Spark Your Learning

In softball, a player's batting average is the number of hits divided by the number of at-bats. Write each player's batting average as a decimal.

What do you notice?

Player	Hits	At-bats
Jamilla	2	5
Callie	1	8
Mayumi	4	9
Elena	37	99
Kaycee	7	36

 Turn and Talk Do you think all fractions have decimal representations that either end or have digits that repeat? Try some additional fractions and discuss your conjecture.

Module 13 • Lesson 1   415

Build Understanding

A **rational number** is any number that can be written as a ratio in the form $\frac{a}{b}$, where a and b are integers and b is not 0. Every rational number can be written as a **terminating decimal** or a **repeating decimal**. Examples of rational numbers are shown:

$$\frac{3}{8} = 0.375 \qquad\qquad 7 = \frac{7}{1}$$

$$0.2 = \frac{1}{5} \qquad\qquad 0.11111\ldots = \frac{1}{9}$$

> **Connect to Vocabulary**
>
> An **irrational number** is a number that cannot be written in the form $\frac{a}{b}$, where a and b are integers and b is not 0.

 Is every number rational?

A. Consider the decimal 1.345345634567… .

Does the decimal appear to have a repeating pattern? Explain.

_____

Do you think 1.345345634567… is a rational number? Why or why not?

_____

B. You have learned that pi (π) is the ratio of the circumference of any circle to its diameter. The decimal value of pi is shown.

$\pi = 3.1415926535897932\ldots$

Pi is an irrational number, but it can be written as a ratio. How can this be?

_____
_____
_____
_____

There are two ways to write a repeating decimal. You can use an ellipsis (three dots) to show that the repeating pattern continues:

0.111… , 0.235235235… , and 0.244444444…

Or, you can write an overbar over the part of the decimal that repeats:

$0.\overline{1}$, $0.\overline{235}$, and $0.2\overline{4}$

 **Turn and Talk** Convert $\frac{1}{36}$ to a decimal. Write the decimal using an ellipsis and using an overbar. Explain the process you used.

Step It Out

2 ▶ A basketball player's free throw percentage is 82.5%, or 0.825. Write this as a fraction.

A. Identify the place value of the last digit in the terminating decimal. Use this to determine the denominator of the fraction. The digits to the right of the decimal point are the numerator of the fraction.

$$0.825 = \frac{825}{\Box}$$

B. Write the fraction in lowest terms. Identify the greatest common factor (GCF) of the numerator and denominator. Divide the numerator and denominator by the GCF.

$$0.825 = \frac{825}{\Box} = \frac{825 \div \Box}{\Box \div \Box} = \frac{\Box}{\Box}$$

3 ▶ You can also convert a repeating decimal to a fraction.

Write $0.\overline{18}$ as a fraction. Let x be the given decimal.

A. Write the first few repeating digits. $\quad x = 0.1818...$

B. Multiply both sides of the equation by 100 so that the two repeating digits appear just to the *left* of the decimal point. $\quad 100x = $ _____

C. Subtract an expression equal to x from both sides.

$$100x = \underline{}$$
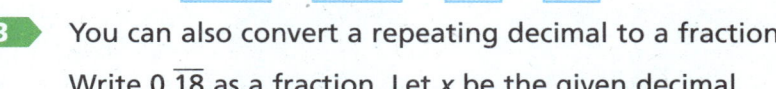
$$99x = \underline{}$$

D. Solve for x. Then simplify the fraction. $\quad x = \dfrac{\Box}{\Box} = \dfrac{\Box}{\Box}$

Check Understanding

1. Convert $\frac{1}{18}$ to a decimal.

   A. Write the decimal form. _____

   B. Is this number rational? Explain.

   _____

For Problems 2–4, write the rational number as a simplified fraction or as a mixed number in simplest form.

2. 1.905

3. 0.828282...

4. $0.4\overline{3}$

Module 13 • Lesson 1

On Your Own

5. **STEM** The atomic weight of an element is the total mass of the protons, neutrons, and electrons. The ratio of the mass of the protons in radon to the atomic mass of radon is 0.387387387... . Write the decimal as a fraction.

   _____

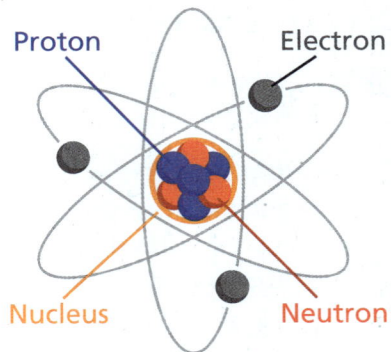

6. Convert $\frac{1}{15}$ to a decimal. Write the decimal using an ellipsis, then write the decimal using an overbar.

   _____

7. **Critique Reasoning** Mitchell was asked to write 0.616161... as a fraction. His work is shown. Do you agree with his answer? If not, explain the error and correct it.

   Let $x = 0.616161...$
   Then $10x = 6.16161...$
   Subtract: $10x = 6.16161...$
   $-x -0.616161...$
   $9x = 6$
   $x = \frac{6}{9} = \frac{2}{3}$

   _____
   _____
   _____
   _____
   _____
   _____

For Problems 8–13, write the number as a fraction or mixed number in simplest form.

8. 4.024

9. −1.111...

10. $-0.\overline{39}$

11. $0.61\overline{4}$

12. 2.484848...

13. 0.7222...

 I'm in a Learning Mindset!

How am I using feedback to solve problems about rational numbers?

_____
_____

Name _____

Understand Rational and Irrational Numbers

LESSON 13.1
More Practice/ Homework

ONLINE Video Tutorials and Interactive Examples

1. Kara and Nathan participated in a 60-minute maze race.

   A. Use ratio notation and decimal notation to describe the relationship between Kara's time and the total time of the race.

   _____

   B. Is the relationship in Part A rational or irrational? Justify your answer.

   _____
   _____

Kara: 32 minutes

Nathan: 40 minutes

2. **Math on the Spot** Write the decimal $0.\overline{63}$ as a fraction in simplest form.

   _____

3. The average number of hourly visitors to an art exhibit is $45.1\overline{3}$. Write the average number of hourly visitors as a mixed number in simplest form.

   _____

4. **(MP) Critique Reasoning** Katrina said the number 0.101100111000... is a rational number because it consists only of the digits 0 and 1, and these digits repeat. Do you agree or disagree? Explain.

   _____
   _____
   _____

5. Convert $\frac{1}{27}$ to a decimal. Write the decimal using an ellipsis, then write the decimal using an overbar.

Write the rational number as a fraction or mixed number in simplest form.

6. 0.606060...

7. −8.725

8. 0.424242...

9. 1.52888...

10. $-10.\overline{7}$

11. $0.\overline{57}$

Module 13 • Lesson 1

419

Test Prep

12. Midori wrote a ratio of two integers. Which of the following must be true about the number Midori wrote?

- Ⓐ The decimal form of the number is a terminating decimal.
- Ⓑ The decimal form of the number is a repeating decimal.
- Ⓒ The number is rational.
- Ⓓ The number is irrational.

13. Which of the following is $0.\overline{15}$ written as a fraction in simplest form?

- Ⓐ $\frac{1}{15}$
- Ⓑ $\frac{1}{9}$
- Ⓒ $\frac{3}{20}$
- Ⓓ $\frac{5}{33}$

14. Paolo keeps track of his favorite baseball player's batting average, and notices the average is 0.4727272... . If his player has 55 at bats, what is the number of hits?

_____ hits

Spiral Review

15. Maria is saving for a scooter that costs $170. She has $54 already. She gets an allowance of $8 each week. How many weeks will it take for Maria to save at least enough money to buy the scooter? Write an inequality to represent the situation.

_____

16. In the figure, line p is parallel to line q. Write an equation you can use to find the value of y, and explain why you can use it. Then solve the equation and use your result to help you find the measure of ∠1.

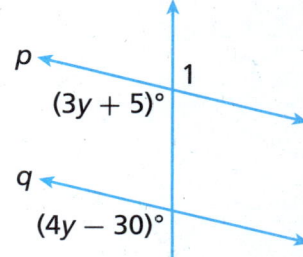

_____
_____
_____

420

Connect Concepts and Skills

Lesson 2

Name _____

Investigate Roots

 evaluate square roots and cube roots.

Spark Your Learning

Aaron plans to make origami cranes, which can be folded from a square piece of paper. He starts by drawing small squares with side lengths 1 inch, 2 inches, 3 inches, and 4 inches.

Find the area of each square. What do you notice about the relationship between the side lengths and the area of each square?

4 in.
2 in.
1 in.
3 in.

 **Turn and Talk** Consider a square with an area of 23 square inches. Explain how you would determine the length of each side for such a square.

Module 13 • Lesson 2   421

Build Understanding

1 ▶ Aaron is also planning to make origami cubes of different sizes. The edge lengths of the cubes are 1 inch, 2 inches, 3 inches, and 4 inches.

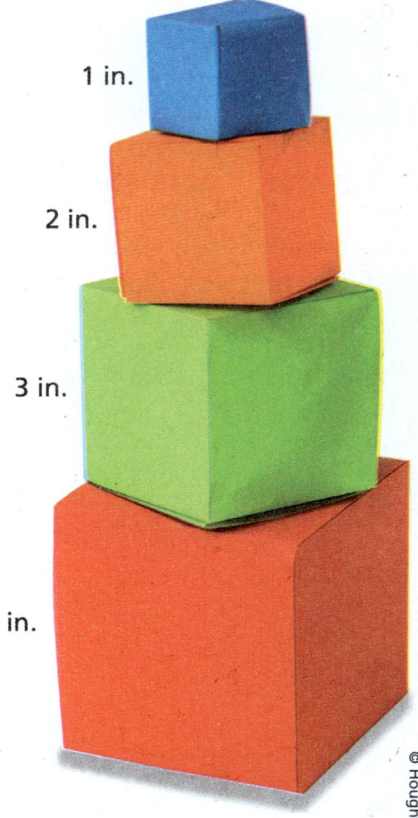

A. Talk to a partner, then write down a formula to determine the volume of a cube.

_____

_____

B. Find the volume of each of the cubes. Complete the table and look for patterns.

Edge length (in.)	Volume (in³)
1	
2	
3	
4	

C. What do you notice about how the volumes change as the edge length increases?

_____

_____

D. If you are given the volume of a cube, how can you find the edge length?

_____

_____

E. What is the edge length of a cube with a volume of 125 cubic inches? Why is it difficult to express the edge length of a cube with a volume of 10 cubic inches?

_____

_____

_____

Turn and Talk A student completed the table in Part B and claimed it is impossible for a cube to have a volume of exactly 50 cubic centimeters since this number will not appear in the "Volume" column. Do you agree? Why or why not?

Step It Out

The **square root** of a positive number p is x when $x^2 = p$. Note that every positive number has two square roots. For example, $3^2 = 9$ and $(-3)^2 = 9$, so the two square roots of 9 are 3 and -3. These are sometimes written together as ± 3, and read as "plus or minus three."

A **perfect square** is a whole number whose square roots are integers. For example, 16 is a perfect square since its square roots are the integers 4 and -4. The square root of any number that isn't a perfect square is another example of an irrational number.

The symbol $\sqrt{}$ (**radical symbol**) is used to indicate the positive square root, or **principal square root**, of a number. So, $\sqrt{16} = 4$.

2 Use the information about roots to evaluate each expression.

A. Find the square roots of 81.

$\boxed{}^2 = 81$ and $\boxed{}^2 = 81$.

So, the square roots of 81 are _____ and _____ .

B. Find $\sqrt{\frac{4}{9}}$.

Both $\left(\boxed{\frac{}{}}\right)^2 = \frac{4}{9}$ and $\left(-\boxed{\frac{}{}}\right)^2 = \frac{4}{9}$.

The square root symbol indicates the principal square root.

So, $\sqrt{\frac{4}{9}} = \boxed{\frac{}{}}$.

Suppose Aaron wants a square piece of origami paper with an area of 2 square centimeters.

C. What is the length of one side of the piece of paper? Use a square root symbol in your answer.

_____ centimeters

D. Is 2 a perfect square? Why or why not?

yes / no ; There is / is not an integer whose square is 2.

E. Is the square root of 2 rational or irrational?

rational / irrational ; $\sqrt{2}$ can / cannot be written as a ratio of two integers.

Module 13 • Lesson 2

The **cube root** of a positive number p is x when $x^3 = p$. Every positive number has one cube root. For example, $4^3 = 64$, so the cube root of 64 is 4. The symbol for a cube root is similar to the symbol for square root and written as $\sqrt[3]{\ }$. $\sqrt[3]{64} = 4$ is read out loud as, "The cube root of 64 equals 4."

A **perfect cube** is a whole number whose cube root is an integer. For example, 64 is a perfect cube, since its cube root is an integer, 4.

3 Find the cube root of $\frac{8}{27}$.

$\boxed{}^3 = 8$ and $\boxed{}^3 = 27$, so $\left(\frac{\boxed{}}{\boxed{}}\right)^3 = \frac{8}{27}$.

So, the cube root of $\frac{8}{27}$ is $\frac{\boxed{}}{\boxed{}}$. You also can write $\sqrt[3]{\frac{8}{27}} = \frac{\boxed{}}{\boxed{}}$.

4 Solve each problem.

A. What is the side length of the square picture frame shown?

$x^2 = 100$ Write the equation.

$x = \pm\sqrt{100}$ Apply the definition of square root.

$x = \pm \underline{}$ Find integers that equal 100 when squared.

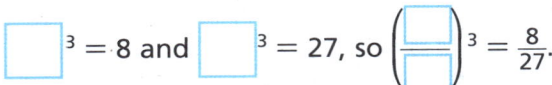

100 in²

The side length of the picture frame is _____ inches.

Note that the square root −10 is not used since it is not a possible length for a real-world object.

B. Solve for y: $y^3 = \frac{1}{14}$.

$y = \sqrt[3]{\frac{1}{14}}$ Apply the definition of cube root.

Since no rational number when cubed equals $\frac{1}{14}$, _____ represents the solution to $y^3 = \frac{1}{14}$.

Check Understanding

1. Solve each equation.

A. $x^2 = 7$ $x =$ _____

B. $x^3 = \frac{1}{64}$ $x =$ _____

For Problems 2–4, find the indicated root.

2. $\sqrt{121}$ **3.** $\sqrt{\frac{16}{25}}$ **4.** $\sqrt[3]{125}$

On Your Own

5. A band stores their equipment in a large cube. The cube has sound-dampening foam designed to allow the drummer to play inside the cube when the band is practicing.

125 cubic feet

A. Is 125 a perfect cube? Why or why not?

_____

_____

B. What is the edge length of the band's cube? Explain.

_____

6. Find the square roots of 400.

_____

7. Find the cube root of $\frac{8}{125}$. Show how you can check that you found the cube root correctly.

_____

8. **Reason** A student claimed 7 and −7 are the two cube roots of 343. Do you agree or disagree? Explain.

_____

_____

9. Solve the equation $x^2 = 196$. Show your work and explain your steps.

10. Solve the equation $z^3 = \frac{125}{216}$. Show your work and explain your steps.

Module 13 • Lesson 2   425

11. **Open Ended** A square tile has an area of less than 1 square foot. The area and length are rational numbers. What is a possible area for the tile in square feet? What is the corresponding edge length?

_____

12. **Use Repeated Reasoning** What do perfect squares have in common?

    A. Complete the table of squares.

x	1	2	3	4	5	6	7	8	9	10	11	12
x^2												

    B. What do you notice about the ones digit in each of the perfect squares in your table?

    _____

    C. Suppose you extend the table and continue to find perfect squares. Do you think the number 10,402 will eventually appear in the x^2 row? Explain.

    _____
    _____
    _____

13. Does the square root of 0 exist? What about the cube root of 0? Explain your answers.

    _____

For Problems 14–16, find each root.

14. $\sqrt{225}$ 15. $\sqrt[3]{729}$ 16. $\sqrt[3]{\frac{64}{343}}$

For Problems 17–19, solve each equation.

17. $x^2 = \frac{1}{49}$ 18. $n^3 = 19$ 19. $y^3 = \frac{27}{125}$

I'm in a Learning Mindset!

How did I model constructive feedback when solving Problem 12B?

_____
_____

Name _____

LESSON 13.2 More Practice/ Homework

Investigate Roots

1. A puzzle maker built the cube puzzle shown.

   A. What is the edge length of the cube puzzle? Explain.
   _____

   216 cubic inches

   B. Suppose the puzzle maker wants to build a larger cube puzzle and wants the volume to be a perfect cube when measured in cubic inches. If the volume must be less than 1000 cubic inches, what are some volumes the puzzle maker could use? Explain.
   _____
   _____
   _____

2. Find the square roots of 169. Then find $\sqrt{169}$. Explain why the answers are not exactly the same.
   _____

3. Solve the equation $y^3 = \frac{64}{729}$. Show your work and explain your steps.

4. **Math on the Spot** Solve each equation for x.

   A. $x^2 = 81$

   B. $x^2 = \frac{25}{144}$

   _____   _____

For Problems 5–7, find each root.

5. $\sqrt{289}$
6. $\sqrt[3]{512}$
7. $\sqrt[3]{\frac{1}{1,000}}$

For Problems 8–10, solve each equation.

8. $z^2 = \frac{81}{121}$
9. $x^3 = 343$
10. $y^3 = \frac{8}{729}$

Module 13 • Lesson 2

Test Prep

11. Which of the following is NOT a perfect cube?
- Ⓐ 1
- Ⓑ 8
- Ⓒ 9
- Ⓓ 27

12. Iris wrote a square root of 144 on a piece of paper. Which one of the following must be true about the number she wrote?
- Ⓐ The number is 12.
- Ⓑ The number is −12.
- Ⓒ The number multiplied by itself equals 144.
- Ⓓ None of the above is true.

13. Which of the following is an irrational number?
- Ⓐ $\sqrt[3]{1}$
- Ⓑ $\sqrt{2}$
- Ⓒ $\sqrt[3]{27}$
- Ⓓ $\sqrt{25}$

14. Which number when squared makes 26?
- Ⓐ 52
- Ⓑ 13
- Ⓒ 5.5
- Ⓓ $\sqrt{26}$

15. A square flower bed has an area of $\frac{169}{36}$ square yards. What is the perimeter of the flower bed?

 yards

Spiral Review

16. The segment with endpoints (0, 8) and (−6, 0) is dilated with the center of dilation at the origin to become a segment with endpoints (0, 6) and (−4.5, 0). What is the scale factor of the dilation?

_____

17. For what value of m does $5 - 3x = m + mx$ have no solution?

_____

18. Frankie and Marcel are picking apples. Frankie has 18 apples, which is 2 more than 4 times the number of apples Marcel has. How many apples does Marcel have?

_____

Order Real Numbers

I Can accurately order a list of real numbers containing fractions, decimals, and irrational numbers.

Step It Out

All **real numbers** correspond to a position on a number line. Real numbers include rational and irrational numbers.

1 Estimate $\sqrt{50}$ to the nearest tenth.

A. Find the two perfect squares closest to 50, one greater than 50 and one less than 50.

_____ and _____

B. What are the square roots of the two perfect squares?

_____ and _____

C. The whole number that most closely estimates $\sqrt{50}$ is _____.

D. Refine your estimate of $\sqrt{50}$. Circle the true statement. Then underline the value closer to 50.

$7.0^2 < 50 < 7.1^2$ $\quad$ $7.2^2 < 50 < 7.3^2$ $\quad$ $7.4^2 < 50 < 7.5^2$

$7.1^2 < 50 < 7.2^2$ $\quad$ $7.3^2 < 50 < 7.4^2$ $\quad$ $7.5^2 < 50 < 7.6^2$

2 Estimate $\sqrt[3]{100}$ to the nearest hundredth.

A. Find the two perfect cubes closest to 100, one greater than 100 and one less than 100.

_____ and _____

B. What are the cube roots of the two perfect cubes?

_____ and _____

C. Circle the pair of cubes $\sqrt[3]{100}$ lies between.

4.5^3 $\quad$ 4.6^3 $\quad$ 4.7^3 $\quad$ 4.8^3 $\quad$ 4.9^3 $\quad$ 5.0^3

D. Within your interval, test cubes of values expressed in hundredths. Which cube is closest to 100? "Approximately equal to" is represented by the ≈ symbol.

_____ is closest to 100, so $\sqrt[3]{100} \approx$ _____.

 Turn and Talk What is your strategy for estimating a square root or a cube root to the nearest hundredth?

Module 13 • Lesson 3

3 You can use estimates of square roots to help you estimate and compare numerical expressions involving square roots.

A. Compare the values below. Use < or > to complete each statement.

2 ◯ 6, so $\sqrt{3}+2$ ◯ $\sqrt{3}+6$. $\sqrt{7}$ ◯ $\sqrt{3}$, so $2\sqrt{7}$ ◯ $2\sqrt{3}$.

−1 ◯ −3, so $\sqrt{7}-1$ ◯ $\sqrt{7}-3$. $\sqrt{11}$ ◯ $\sqrt{21}$, so $5\sqrt{11}$ ◯ $5\sqrt{21}$.

6 ◯ 7, so $2\sqrt{6}$ ◯ $2\sqrt{7}$. $\sqrt{3}$ ◯ $\sqrt{5}$, so $8\sqrt{3}$ ◯ $8\sqrt{5}$.

B. Complete each statement with consecutive integers.

_____ < $\sqrt{8}+3$ < _____   _____ < $\sqrt[3]{25}+2$ < _____

_____ < $\sqrt{13}-1$ < _____   _____ < $\sqrt{111}-4$ < _____

4 A. Identify the consecutive integers between which each number is located.

_____ < $\frac{3}{2}$ < _____   _____ < $-\sqrt{12}$ < _____

_____ < π < _____   _____ < −4.75 < _____

_____ < $\sqrt{5}$ < _____   _____ < $\sqrt{3}-8$ < _____

_____ < $0.\overline{3}$ < _____   _____ < $-\frac{17}{3}$ < _____

B. Use the comparisons to plot and label the points on the number line.

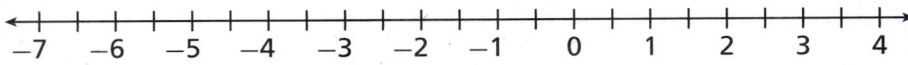

Check Understanding

For Problems 1–3, use < or > to compare the expressions.

1. $\sqrt{6}$ ◯ $\sqrt{7}$ 2. $\sqrt{10}$ ◯ $\sqrt[3]{25}$ 3. $\sqrt{5}+4$ ◯ $\sqrt{50}+1$

Use the information to solve Problems 4–5.

Amber is designing a side table with a length of $\sqrt{7}$ feet and a width of $\sqrt{3}$ feet. Estimate the dimensions to the nearest tenth, then label the points on the number line.

4. $\sqrt{3}$ feet

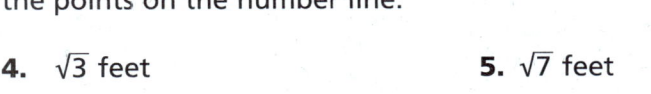

5. $\sqrt{7}$ feet

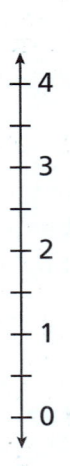

On Your Own

6. Answer the questions and complete the statements in Parts A–C. Then complete the statement in Part D.

A. Is $\sqrt{14}$ between 3.0 and 3.5 or 3.5 and 4.0? _____

To the nearest integer, $\sqrt{14} \approx$ _____.

B. Is $\sqrt{35}$ between 5.75 and 5.85 or 5.85 and 5.95? _____

To the nearest tenth, $\sqrt{35} \approx$ _____.

C. Is $\sqrt{75}$ between 8.655 and 8.665 or 8.665 and 8.675? _____

To the nearest hundredth, $\sqrt{75} \approx$ _____.

D. (MP) **Reason** How do the intervals selected in Part B help you estimate the value of the square root?

_____

_____

_____

7. Estimate $\sqrt{84}$

A. to the nearest integer.
$\sqrt{84} \approx$ _____

B. to the nearest tenth.
$\sqrt{84} \approx$ _____

8. Estimate $\sqrt[3]{60}$

A. to the nearest integer.
$\sqrt[3]{60} \approx$ _____

B. to the nearest tenth.
$\sqrt[3]{60} \approx$ _____

9. History The Spiral of Theodorus was used to prove the irrationality of several square roots. Estimate $\sqrt{2}$ to the nearest hundredth. Show your work.

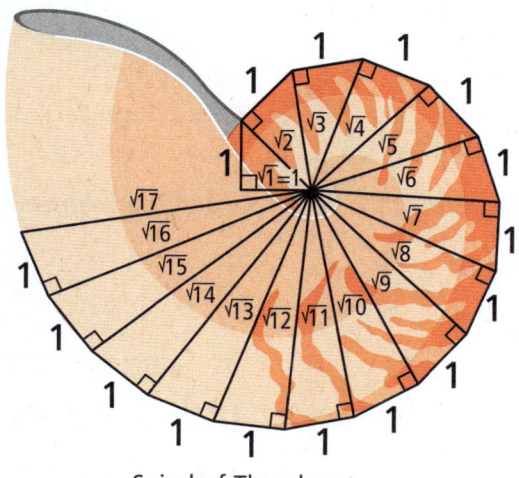
Spiral of Theodorus

Module 13 • Lesson 3

For Problems 10–13, use < or > to complete each statement.

10. $\sqrt{15} - 4$ ◯ $\sqrt{15} - 7$ **11.** $2\sqrt{18}$ ◯ $2\sqrt{21}$

12. $-\sqrt[3]{30}$ ◯ -3 **13.** $\sqrt{8} + 1$ ◯ $\sqrt{17} - 2$

For Problems 14–17, complete each inequality using the greatest possible integer for comparison.

14. $\sqrt{42} > $ _____ **15.** $\sqrt{150} > $ _____

16. $\sqrt{245} > $ _____ **17.** $\sqrt{398} > $ _____

For Problems 18–21, circle the lesser of the two numbers.

18. $\sqrt{30} + 4$ 8   **19.** $\sqrt{11}$ $\sqrt{20} - 2$

20. $\sqrt{7}$ $\sqrt[3]{40}$ **21.** $15 - \sqrt{2}$ $\sqrt{125}$

For Problems 22–25, complete each inequality using a pair of consecutive integers.

22. _____ $< \sqrt{10} + 4 <$ _____   **23.** _____ $< \sqrt{92} - 11 <$ _____

24. _____ $< \sqrt[3]{50} - 1 <$ _____   **25.** _____ $< \sqrt[3]{100} + 2 <$ _____

26. Which number is the best approximation for $\frac{\pi}{3}$: 1, 1.03, 1.05, or 1.07?

_____

27. (MP) **Reason** Is there a limit to the number of decimal places to which you can approximate an irrational number? Explain.

_____

_____

_____

For Problems 28–29, plot the values of the expressions on the number line.

28. $\sqrt{10}, \frac{7}{4}, 2.\overline{2}, (\sqrt{13} - 1)$

29. $-\sqrt{15}, -\frac{5}{3}, -\sqrt[3]{27}, (\sqrt{12} - 6)$

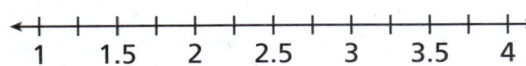
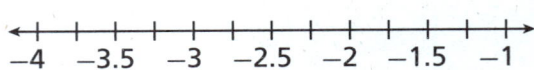

For Problems 30–31, order the expressions from greatest to least.

30. $\frac{2}{3}, \sqrt{2}, \frac{2}{9}, (\sqrt{3} - 1), \frac{10}{9}$

_____

31. $0.\overline{7}, 2\sqrt{3}, (\sqrt{32} - 8), (-2 + \sqrt{19}), \left(4 - \frac{21}{4}\right)$

_____

Name _____

Order Real Numbers

LESSON 13.3
More Practice/ Homework

ONLINE
Video Tutorials and Interactive Examples

1. **MP Attend to Precision** Through calculations, Jack and Kelsey estimated the diameter of the fountain in the park. If the actual length is 15 feet, which student's estimate is more accurate? Explain your reasoning.

   _____
   _____

2. Complete the inequality with consecutive integers.

   _____ < $\sqrt{357}$ < _____

3. **Math on the Spot** Compare the expressions. Write <, >, or =.

   $\sqrt{6} + 3$ ◯ $6 + \sqrt{3}$

4. Estimate $\sqrt{74}$ and $\sqrt[3]{74}$ to the nearest tenth.

   _____

5. **Open Ended** Identify two rational numbers and one irrational number between $\sqrt{2}$ and $\sqrt{3}$. Show how you know they are in this range.

   _____
   _____

For Problems 6–7, plot the expressions on the number line.

6. $\sqrt{17}$, $\frac{\pi}{2}$, π, $\frac{11}{4}$

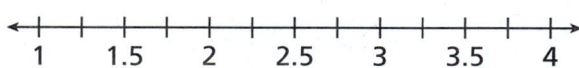

7. $\sqrt{15}$, $(\sqrt{22} - 6)$, $\frac{16}{5}$, $(-5 + \sqrt{25})$

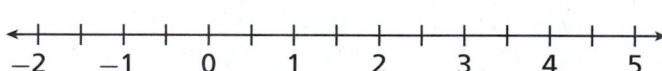

8. Order the expressions from least to greatest.

   $\sqrt{31}$, $\frac{29}{9}$, $(\sqrt{24} + 2)$, $\sqrt[3]{90}$

   _____

9. Order the expressions from greatest to least.

   $(\sqrt[3]{99} - 5)$, $(-\sqrt{45} + 9)$, $(\sqrt{71} - 8)$, $\frac{12}{7}$, $-\frac{8}{5}$

   _____

Module 13 • Lesson 3

Test Prep

10. Which numbers make the inequality true? Select all that apply.

$7 < \boxed{} < 8$

- Ⓐ $\sqrt{56}$
- Ⓑ $\sqrt{99} - 1$
- Ⓒ $\sqrt{38} + 1$
- Ⓓ $3\sqrt{3} + 2$
- Ⓔ $2\sqrt{2} + 3$

11. Which is the best estimate of $\sqrt{200}$?

- Ⓐ 14.0
- Ⓑ 14.1
- Ⓒ 14.2
- Ⓓ 14.3

12. Which is the best estimate of $\sqrt[3]{84}$?

- Ⓐ 4.38
- Ⓑ 4.39
- Ⓒ 4.40
- Ⓓ 4.41

13. Order the numerical expressions from least to greatest.

$-\dfrac{52}{5} \qquad -\sqrt{130} \qquad -3 - \sqrt{47}$

___

Spiral Review

14. What is the measure of ∠PQS in the figure shown?

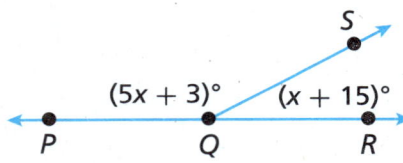

15. The vertices of △ABC are A(−9, 12), B(6, −18), and C(15, 3), while those of △DEF are D(6, 8), E(−4, −12), and F(−10, 2). Given that the two triangles are similar, describe a sequence of transformations that exhibits their similarity.

16. A chef used some bouillon cubes when making chicken noodle soup. The volume of each of the bouillon cubes was $\dfrac{1}{27}$ cubic inch. How long was an edge of one of the bouillon cubes that the chef used?

Review

Name _____

Vocabulary

For Problems 1–4, give two examples of each type of number.

1. rational number

   _____

2. irrational number

   _____

3. terminating decimal

   _____

4. repeating decimal

   _____

5. Explain how the terms *perfect square* and *square root* are related.

   _____
   _____
   _____

Concepts and Skills

6. Select all numbers that are irrational.

   Ⓐ $-\frac{5}{12}$ Ⓒ $0.\overline{15}$ Ⓔ $\frac{1}{6}$

   Ⓑ $\frac{\pi}{2}$ Ⓓ $\sqrt{5}$ Ⓕ $\sqrt{25}$

7. Determine whether each number is rational or irrational.

	Rational	Irrational
$\sqrt{49}$	☐	☐
$\sqrt{90}$	☐	☐
$\sqrt{125}$	☐	☐
$\sqrt{169}$	☐	☐

8. **ⓂⓅ Use Tools** Write a fraction equivalent to $0.\overline{24}$. State what strategy and tool you will use to answer the question, explain your choice, and then find the answer.

   _____
   _____
   _____

Module 13

For Problems 9–10, write each repeating decimal as a fraction.

9. $0.\overline{18}$ _____

10. $0.3\overline{6}$ _____

11. Do you see a pattern in the number 0.31311311131111…? Is it rational or irrational? Explain your reasoning.

_____

_____

_____

_____

For Problems 12–13, find all solutions of the equation.

12. $x^3 = 11$

$x = $ _____

13. $n^2 = 0.16$

$n = $ _____

14. A cube has a volume of 216 cubic inches. What is the edge length of the cube?
- Ⓐ 6 inches
- Ⓑ 15 inches
- Ⓒ 18 inches
- Ⓓ 36 inches

15. Explain why the equation $x^2 = 64$ has two solutions, but the equation $x^3 = 64$ has only one solution.

_____

_____

_____

_____

For Problems 16–17, estimate the value of the root to the nearest whole number.

16. $\sqrt{53}$ _____

17. $\sqrt[3]{118}$ _____

18. Select all values that are greater than 4.
- Ⓐ $\sqrt[3]{8}$
- Ⓑ $\sqrt{9}$
- Ⓒ $\sqrt{10}$
- Ⓓ $\sqrt[3]{12} + 2$
- Ⓔ $\sqrt{27}$
- Ⓕ 2π

For Problems 19–20, plot the set of numbers at their approximate locations on the number line.

19. $\sqrt[3]{6}$, $\sqrt[3]{39}$, and $\sqrt[3]{150}$

20. $\sqrt{2}$ and $\sqrt{8}$

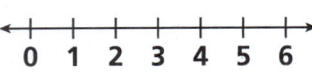

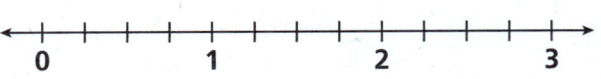

Module 14

The Pythagorean Theorem

Try Your Angle

A worker is making wooden triangles to use as obstacles for minigolf. The sides of the triangles can have any of the lengths shown. A triangle can be isosceles, but none of the triangles can be equilateral.

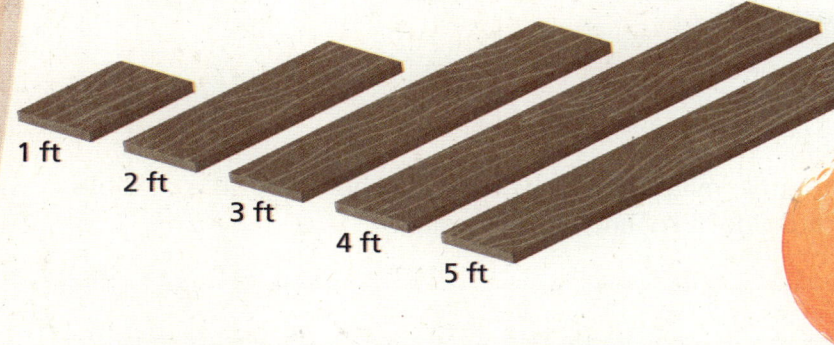

1 ft   2 ft   3 ft   4 ft   5 ft

Name the side lengths of four different triangles to be used as obstacles. No two triangles should have the same set of lengths.

Triangle 1: _____, _____, and _____

Triangle 2: _____, _____, and _____

Triangle 3: _____, _____, and _____

Triangle 4: _____, _____, and _____

 **Turn and Talk**

How do you know that each set of lengths can form a triangle?

Are You Ready?

Complete these problems to review prior concepts and skills you will need for this module.

Order of Operations

Determine the value of each expression.

1. $18 + 7^2 - 24$ _____
2. $2(10 - 4)^2 + 8$ _____
3. $8^2 + 5^2$ _____
4. $20^2 - 12^2$ _____

Draw Shapes with Given Conditions

For Problems 5–6, state whether a triangle can be formed from the set of side lengths. Write *yes* or *no*.

5. 1 centimeter, 2 centimeters, and 4 centimeters _____

6. 2 centimeters, 2 centimeters, and 3 centimeters _____

7. Two sides of a triangle measure 6 inches and 8 inches. What is a possible length of the third side? Explain your reasoning.

   _____
   _____
   _____

Use Roots to Solve Equations

For Problems 8–11, solve the equation.

8. $a^2 = 100$
9. $c^2 = 35$

10. $b^2 = 144$
11. $x^2 = 225$

12. A square park has an area of 8100 square meters.

    A. Write an equation that can be used to determine the side length *s*, in meters, of the park.

       _____

    B. Solve your equation, and interpret the solution.

       _____
       _____

Lesson 1

Name _____

Prove the Pythagorean Theorem and Its Converse

I Can prove the Pythagorean Theorem and its converse.

Spark Your Learning

The given squares form a right triangle. Find the side length and area of each. What patterns do you notice about the squares and side lengths?

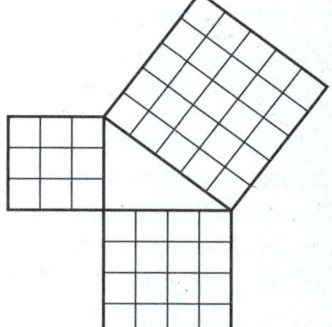

Turn and Talk What types of objects in the real world are in the shape of a right triangle? Can you find some right triangles in the classroom?

Module 14 • Lesson 1   439

Build Understanding

The **Pythagorean Theorem** states that in a right triangle, the square of the length of the hypotenuse is equal to the sum of the squares of the lengths of the legs.

If a and b are the lengths of the legs and c is the length of the hypotenuse, then $a^2 + b^2 = c^2$. If a, b, and c are all integers, they are called a **Pythagorean triple**.

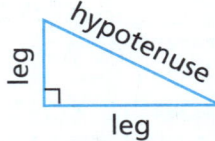

1 Pythagoras was a Greek philosopher and mathematician who is credited with being the first to prove the Pythagorean Theorem. You can use what you know about similar triangles to prove the Pythagorean Theorem.

A. Using △ABC, draw a line from Point C perpendicular to the hypotenuse. Label the point where this line intersects the hypotenuse as Point D. This breaks the length c into two parts and forms two smaller triangles. Label $\overline{AD}$ as length e, and label $\overline{DB}$ as length f. Repeat the labels in the two smaller triangles.

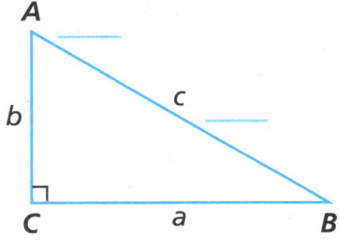 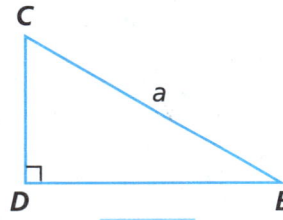 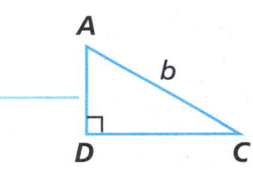

B. Because of Angle-Angle Similarity, △ABC is similar to △CBD and △ACD.

What do you know about the corresponding sides of similar triangles?

_____

C. Use similar triangles to compare corresponding hypotenuses and corresponding longer legs in △CBD and △ABC. $\dfrac{a}{c} = \dfrac{f}{\boxed{}}$

Use similar triangles to compare corresponding hypotenuses and corresponding shorter legs in △ABC and △ACD. $\dfrac{c}{b} = \dfrac{b}{\boxed{}}$

D. Multiply to rewrite the equations. $cf = $ _____ and $b^2 = $ _____

E. Use addition to write $a^2 + b^2$ in terms of c, e, and f. Then simplify to complete the proof.

Consider this statement: *If I am in this class, then I am in the 7th grade*. The converse of this statement is: *If I am in the 7th grade, then I am in this class*. The converse of a theorem reverses the hypothesis and the conclusion.

The Pythagorean Theorem states:
If a triangle is a right triangle, then the sum of the squares of the shorter sides is equal to the square of the longest side.

The converse of that statement is:
If the sum of the squares of the two shorter sides of a triangle is equal to the square of the longest side, then the triangle is a right triangle.

2 Show that, given a triangle *ABC* with side lengths *a*, *b*, and *c*, if $a^2 + b^2 = c^2$, then the triangle is a right triangle with a right angle at *C*.

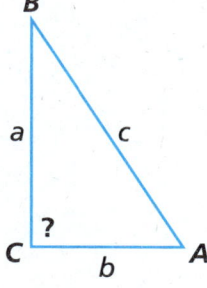

A. Let Triangle *DEF* be a triangle such that $EF = a$, $DF = b$, $DE = x$, and *F* is a right angle. We need to show that Triangles *ABC* and *DEF* are congruent.

B. Can we apply the Pythagorean Theorem to Triangle *DEF*? Why or why not? If so, what can we conclude?

_____
_____

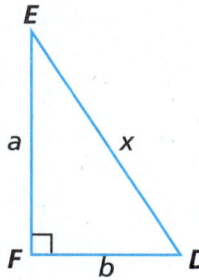

C. How can we relate *x* to *c*?

_____
_____

D. What can you conclude about the measure of Angle *C*? Explain, and include the classification for Triangle *ABC*.

_____
_____
_____
_____

Check Understanding

1. Explain how the equations in Part C of Task 1 can be rewritten as in Part D.

_____
_____

2. In a triangle, side *a* measures $\sqrt{100}$ inches, side *b* measures 24 inches, and side *c* measures 26 inches. Can these measures be the side lengths of a right triangle? Do these measures form a Pythagorean Triple?

_____

Module 14 • Lesson 1

On Your Own

3. In your own words, summarize the Pythagorean Theorem.

_____

_____

Determine whether each set of three side lengths forms a right triangle.

4. 8, 11, and 13

5. 12, 35, and 37

_____

_____

6. **(MP) Reason** Show how to justify the reasoning in Part E of Task 1.

$a^2 + b^2 = cf + ce$

$a^2 + b^2 = c\ (\underline{})$ _____ Property

$a^2 + b^2 = c\ \underline{}$ Substitute _____ for _____.

$a^2 + b^2 = c\ (\underline{})$ Multiply.

7. **STEM** A high school is converting an entry staircase into a ramp to increase accessibility. The entrance door is 7 feet off the ground. By law, a ramp this high needs to start 24 feet away from the building. If the length of the ramp is 25 feet, will the ramp form a right triangle with the building?

A. Fill in the measurements on the illustration shown.

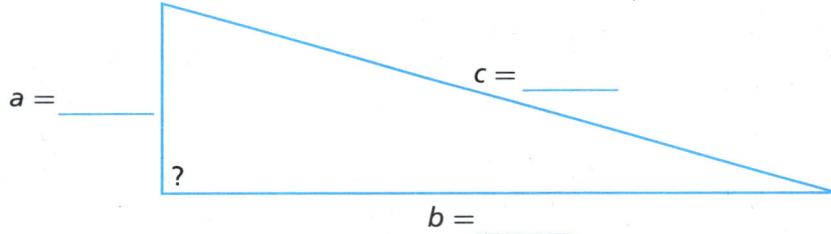

B. Determine whether the ramp forms a right triangle.

Does $\boxed{}^2 + \boxed{}^2 = \boxed{}^2$?

Does $\boxed{} + \boxed{} = \boxed{}$?

Does the 25-foot ramp form a right triangle? _____

 I'm in a Learning Mindset!

How did I apply the feedback I was given about the Pythagorean Theorem to my understanding of the converse of the Pythagorean Theorem?

_____

Prove the Pythagorean Theorem and Its Converse

LESSON 14.1 More Practice/ Homework

1. **Open Ended** Draw a right triangle on graph paper. Measure the length of each leg and the hypotenuse. Write an equation using your triangle's side lengths to show the Pythagorean Theorem holds true for your triangle.

   _____

   _____

2. Show whether the measures 8 feet, 15 feet, and 17 feet make a right triangle. If each side were multiplied by a factor a, would the new triangle also be a right triangle?

   _____

   _____

   _____

   _____

3. **Math on the Spot** Lynnette is buying a triangular parcel of land. If the lengths of the three sides are 300 yards, 400 yards, and 500 yards, will the parcel of land have a right angle? Explain.

   _____

   _____

4. **Use Structure** Right Triangle ABC is shown. Segment CD is perpendicular to the hypotenuse, Segment AB.

   A. Label the missing sides of the similar triangles created by Segment CD.

   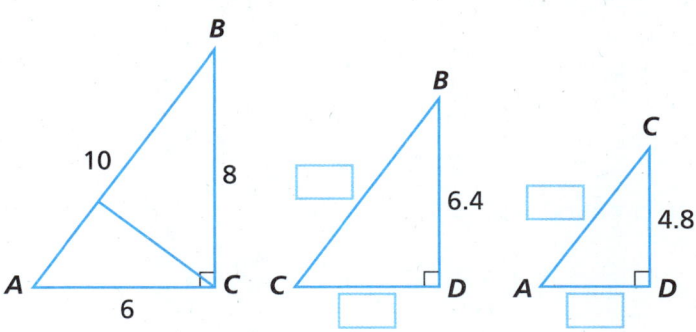 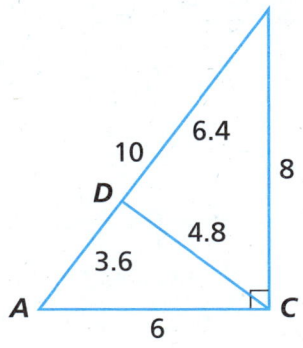

   B. Write equations that show that the two smaller triangles are right triangles.

   _____

Module 14 • Lesson 1

Test Prep

5. Which are examples of Pythagorean triples? Select all that apply.
   - (A) 6, 8, 10
   - (B) 8, 10, 12
   - (C) 10, 16, 15
   - (D) 12, 16, 20
   - (E) 14, 18, 20

6. Identify in the table whether the measurements could be the side lengths of a right triangle.

	Right triangle	Not a right triangle
6, 8, and 14	☐	☐
3, 4, and 5	☐	☐
9, 12, and 15	☐	☐
5, 6, and 7	☐	☐
6, 8, and 10	☐	☐
5, 7, and 12	☐	☐

7. Amber claims that a triangle with sides measuring 3 inches, 6 inches, and 9 inches is a right triangle because 3 + 6 = 9. Explain her error.

   _____

   _____

   _____

Spiral Review

8. Solve the equation $5x - 7 = 2(x + 8)$

   _____

9. Order the numbers from least to greatest.

   $\frac{10}{4}$, -3, $\sqrt{8}$, 2.7

   _____

Connect Concepts and Skills

Lesson **2**

Name _____

Apply the Pythagorean Theorem

I Can apply the Pythagorean Theorem to solve real-life problems involving the legs and hypotenuse of a right triangle, including problems in three dimensions.

Spark Your Learning

A builder is replacing the stairway shown at the right. They must get a building permit from the county which indicates the specific dimensions of the new stairway. How can the builder determine the distance, c?

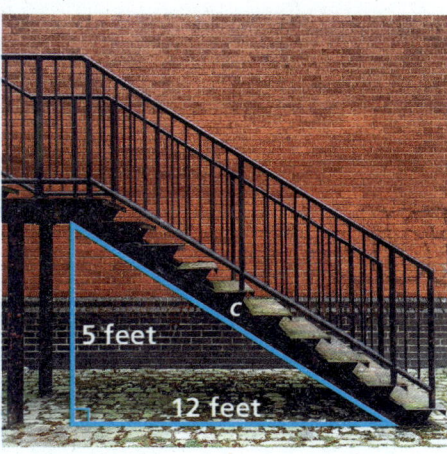

 **Turn and Talk** Why can we use the Pythagorean Theorem to model this real-life situation?

Module 14 • Lesson 2

445

Build Understanding

1 ▶ The red team and blue team are playing Capture the Flag. The teams place their flags at opposite corners of the field. The red team sends two players, Alfredo and Angelina, from the red flag to capture the blue flag.

A. Alfredo must follow the white arrows to the flag. How far does he run? Explain.

_____

_____

_____

B. Angelina must follow the black arrow to the flag. Use grid paper to find the side length of a square that matches the hypotenuse and estimate how far she runs.

_____

_____

C. Write the equation that models using the Pythagorean Theorem to determine how far she runs. Then solve the equation. Round to the nearest tenth.

_____

_____

D. How much farther does Alfredo run than Angelina?

Alfredo runs _____ meters farther than Angelina.

 **Turn and Talk** Will the direct route between two points always be shorter than a route with a right angle? Why or why not?

Step It Out

The Pythagorean Theorem can be used to find lengths inside a three-dimensional object by finding right triangle relationships inside the object.

2 Jada wants to ship a 3-foot curtain rod to a customer. The **biggest** box at the post office is shown. Jada wants to know if the box is large enough to ship the curtain rod.

A. The longest distance in the box is the diagonal AD between opposite corners.

It forms the hypotenuse of $\triangle ACD$.

What is the length of $\overline{DC}$? _____ inches

B. To find the length of $\overline{AD}$ we must know the length of $\overline{AC}$. Look at the bottom of the box. $\overline{AC}$ is the hypotenuse of another right triangle, $\triangle ABC$. Use the Pythagorean Theorem to find the length of $\overline{AC}$. Round to the nearest tenth if necessary.

$$a^2 + b^2 = c^2$$

$$\boxed{}^2 + \boxed{}^2 = c^2$$

$$\boxed{} = c^2$$

$$c = \sqrt{\boxed{}} \approx \boxed{}$$

The length of $\overline{AC}$ is about _____ inches.

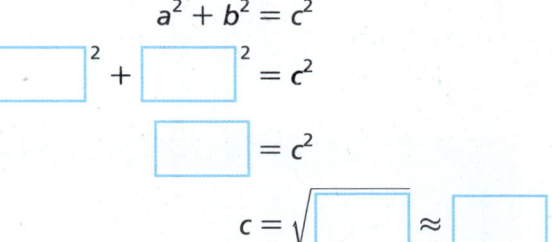

C. Use the length of $\overline{AC}$ to find the length of $\overline{AD}$. Round to the nearest tenth of an inch.

$$AC^2 + CD^2 = AD^2$$

$$\boxed{}^2 + \boxed{}^2 = c^2$$

$$\boxed{} = c^2$$

$$c = \sqrt{\boxed{}} \approx \boxed{}$$

The length of $\overline{AD}$ is about _____ inches.

D. About how long is the longest rod that could fit in the box?

_____ inches

E. Can the curtain rod fit in the box? _____

Module 14 • Lesson 2

3 Cara measured the radius and outside length of an ice cream cone. Identify the right triangle in the cone, then use Cara's measurements to find the height of the cone. Round your final answer to the nearest hundredth.

$$\boxed{}^2 + b^2 = \boxed{}^2$$

$$\boxed{} + b^2 = \boxed{}$$

$$b^2 = \boxed{} - \boxed{}$$

$$b = \sqrt{\boxed{}}$$

$$b \approx \boxed{}$$

The height of the cone is about _____ centimeters.

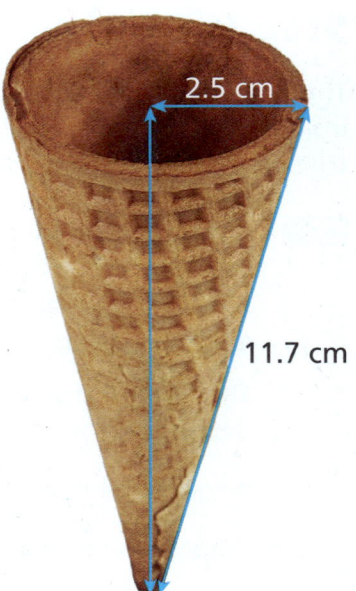

2.5 cm

11.7 cm

 **Turn and Talk** Cara has another ice cream cone. The radius and the height of the second cone are known. Explain how to use these dimensions to find the outside length of the cone.

Check Understanding

1. Computer monitors are measured diagonally, from corner to corner. If the rectangular screen of a 40-inch monitor is 35 inches wide, what is the height of the monitor? Round to the nearest tenth.

   _____

2. A 20-inch rod fits perfectly in a box 15 inches tall. What is the measurement of x in the diagram? Round to the nearest tenth.

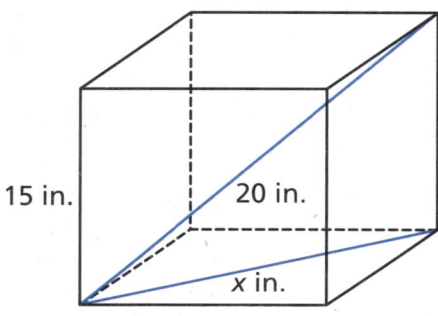

15 in.   20 in.

x in.

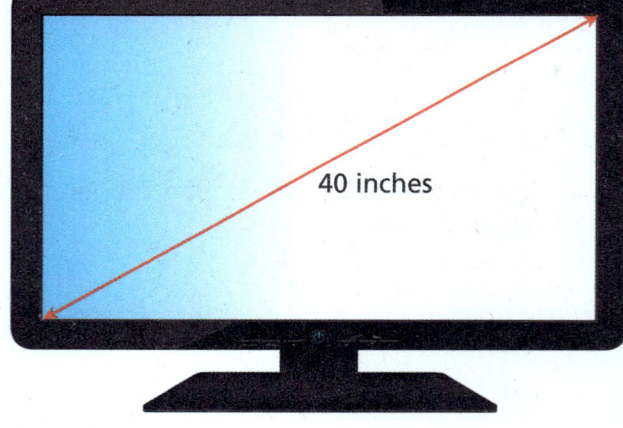

40 inches

Name _____

On Your Own

3. Alexa can follow the sidewalk from the library to the school or she can travel across the grass directly.

   A. Which route is longer?

   _____

   B. What is the difference between the lengths of the two routes?

   _____

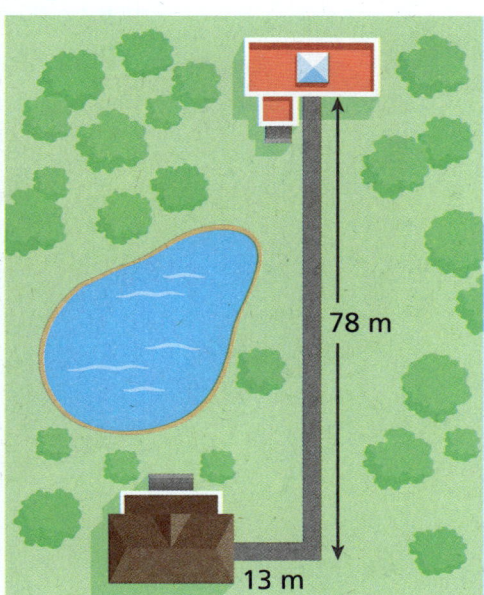

4. **Open Ended** Brianne purchased a box with a base diagonal length of 45 inches. What are two possible pairs of dimensions for the length and width of the box? Round to the nearest tenth.

   _____
   _____

5. A cone 10 meters tall with a radius of 4 meters at the base. What is the measurement of x in the diagram? Round to the nearest hundredth.

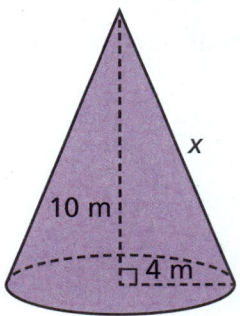

   _____

6. A. Which is taller, Cone A or Cone B?

	x	y
Cone A	10 cm	17 cm
Cone B	12 cm	18 cm

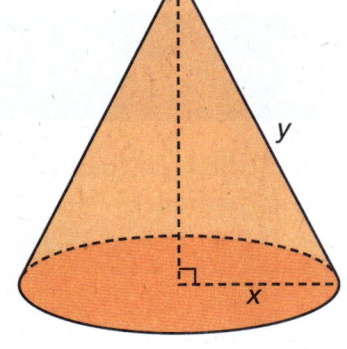

   _____

   B. By how much? Round to the nearest hundredth.

   _____

Module 14 • Lesson 2   449

For Problems 7–10, find the value for the unknown measurement. Round to the nearest tenth.

7.

8.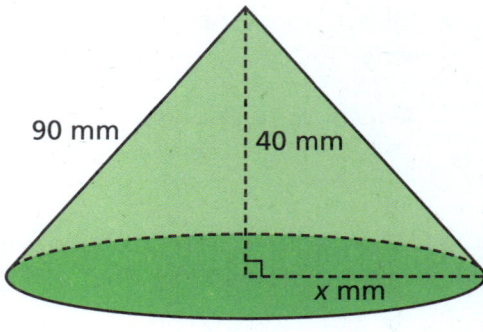

9.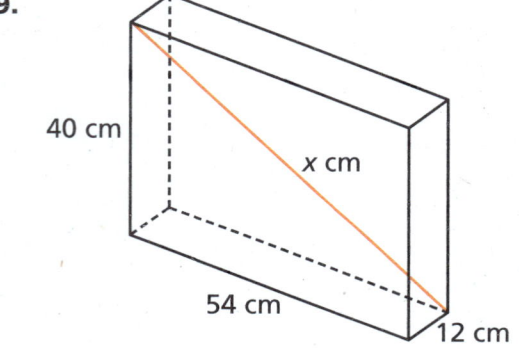

10.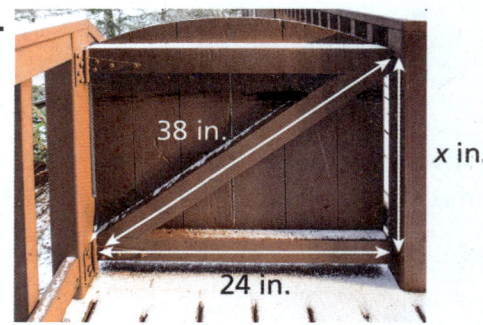

11. **Use Structure** The Maron Luggage Company has a suitcase large enough to fit a 34-inch baseball bat inside. The suitcase has a width of 11 inches and a depth of 17 inches. Its length is a whole number. What is its minimum length? Assume its minimum length must be a whole number of inches.

I'm in a Learning Mindset!

What strategy did I use to overcome barriers to solving problems that apply the Pythagorean Theorem?

Apply the Pythagorean Theorem

1. The distances between Centerville, Springfield, and Capital City form a right triangle. The distance between Centerville and Springfield is 913 kilometers and the distance between Springfield and Capital City is 976 kilometers.

    A. What is the direct distance between Centerville and Capital City? Round to the nearest kilometer.

    _____

    B. Anwell travels from Centerville to Springfield, then on to Capital City. Yue travels directly from Centerville to Capital City. How much farther does Anwell travel than Yue? Round to the nearest kilometer.

    _____

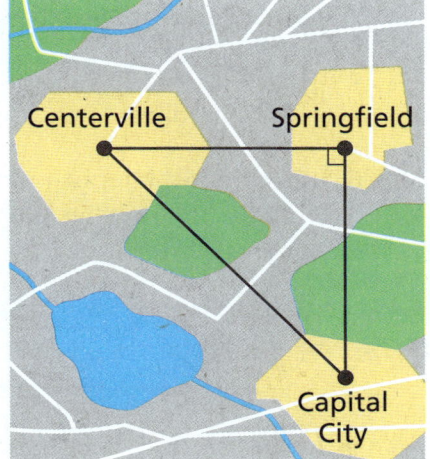

2. **Attend to Precision** Find the radius of the ice cup shown. Round to the nearest tenth.

    _____

3. **Math on the Spot** A child has an empty box that measures 4 inches by 6 inches by 3 inches. What is the length of the longest pencil that will fit into the box, given that the length of the pencil must be a whole number of inches? Do not round until your final answer.

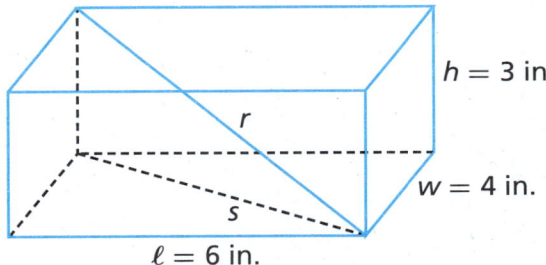

_____

4. Mr. Johnston supports a young tree by using a stake and a rope forming a right angle with the ground. What is the length of the rope? Round to the nearest tenth.

    _____

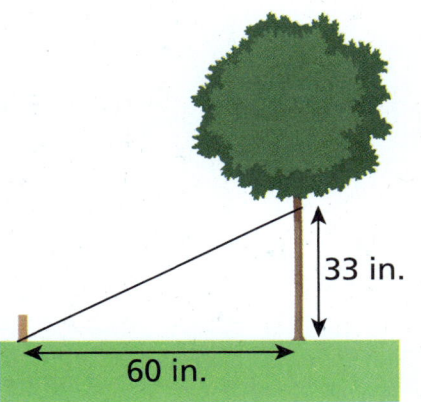

Test Prep

5. The state of Wyoming is almost rectangular, with an approximate width of 365 miles and an approximate height of 276 miles. If you fly across the state from opposite corners, what is the best approximation of the distance you travel?

  Ⓐ 448 miles
  Ⓑ 450 miles
  Ⓒ 458 miles
  Ⓓ 462 miles

6. Calculate the length of the longest rod that can fit in a box measuring 100 centimeters by 130 centimeters by 400 centimeters. Round to the nearest tenth.

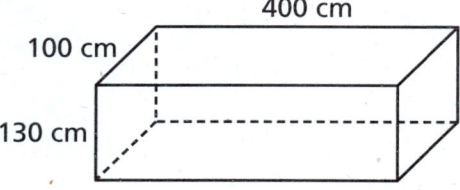

_____ centimeters

7. Which set of measurements could possibly fit the given cone diagram?

  Ⓐ $x = 3, y = 4, z = 5$
  Ⓑ $x = 9, y = 6, z = 10$
  Ⓒ $x = 3, y = 8, z = 5$
  Ⓓ $x = 6, y = 10, z = 8$

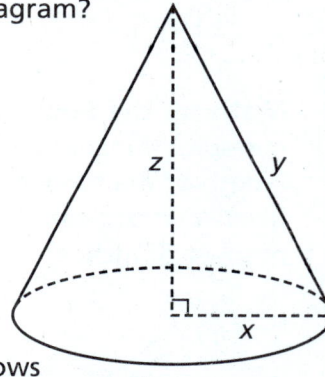

Spiral Review

8. Luna knows that a line crosses the y-axis at (0, −1). She also knows that the point (3, 2) is on the line. What is the slope of this line?

_____

9. Reflect the triangle across the y-axis and draw the image.

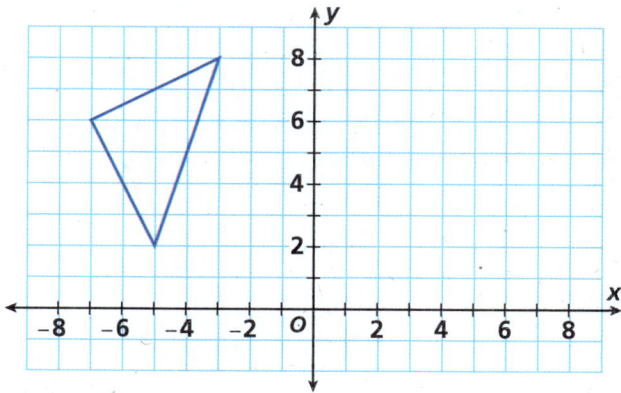

Apply the Pythagorean Theorem in the Coordinate Plane

I Can apply the Pythagorean Theorem to find the lengths of line segments on the coordinate plane, including line segments that are part of a composite figure.

Step It Out

1 To find the distance between two points in a coordinate system (on a coordinate plane), draw a right triangle using the horizontal and vertical lines of the grid, with the given points as endpoints of the hypotenuse. Use the Pythagorean Theorem to find the distance between the points.

A. Plot the Points $P(9, 8)$ and $Q(2, 4)$, then use a straightedge to draw a line segment between the points.

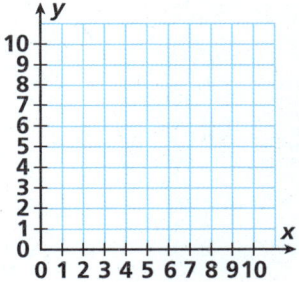 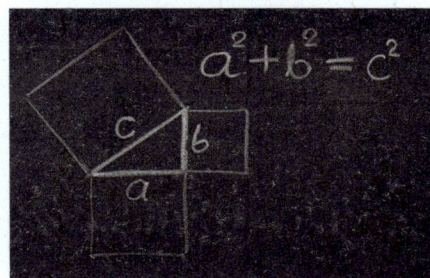

B. Use the horizontal and vertical lines of the coordinate system to draw the legs of a right triangle with Point P and Point Q as vertices.

C. Determine the lengths of the horizontal and vertical legs, then use the Pythagorean Theorem to determine the length of $\overline{PQ}$. Round to the nearest tenth.

$$a^2 + b^2 = c^2$$

$$\boxed{}^2 + \boxed{}^2 = c^2$$

$$\boxed{} + \boxed{} = c^2$$

$$\boxed{} = c^2$$

$$c = \sqrt{\boxed{}} \approx \boxed{}$$

The distance between Points P and Q is approximately _____ units.

Turn and Talk How many right triangles can you draw using a given pair of points as endpoints of the hypotenuse? Justify your reasoning.

Module 14 • Lesson 3   453

2 The Purple Moving Company drew their logo on graph paper. They want to know the perimeter of the design.

A. Complete the table with the coordinates.

Point	Coordinates
V	(1, 10)
W	
X	
Y	
Z	

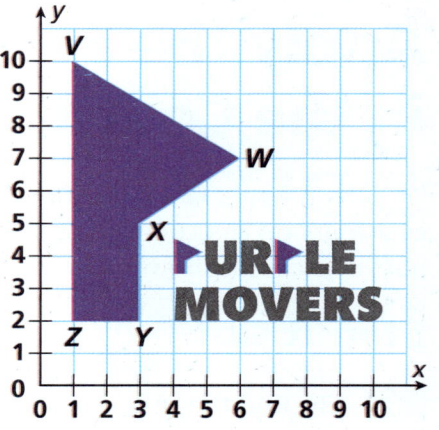

B. Draw horizontal and vertical grid lines to draw the legs of a right triangle with $\overline{VW}$ as the hypotenuse. Use the Pythagorean Theorem to calculate the length of $\overline{VW}$. Round to the nearest tenth.

_____ units

C. Use the same method to determine the length of $\overline{WX}$. Round to the nearest tenth.

_____ units

D. What is the perimeter of the Purple Moving Company logo? Round to the nearest tenth.

_____ units

Check Understanding

1. On the graph provided, draw a right triangle with Points G and H as endpoints of the hypotenuse. Find the distance between Points G and H. Round to the nearest tenth.

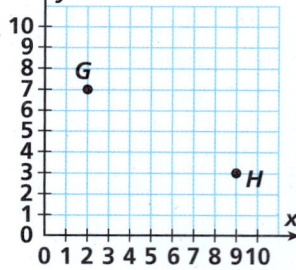

2. A. On your own paper, plot the points (−2, 6) and (5, −5). Find the distance between these two points. Round to the nearest tenth.

   B. What is the perimeter of a triangle that has (−2, 6) and (5, −5) as the end points of its hypotenuse? Round to the nearest tenth.

3. On your own paper, plot the points (3, 60) and (−5, 45). Find the distance between these two points. Round to the nearest tenth if necessary.

Name _____

On Your Own

4. **Use Structure** The town halls of Havertville and Northtown are shown on the map. If the distance between grid lines represents 1 mile, what is the distance between the two town halls? Round your answer to the nearest tenth.

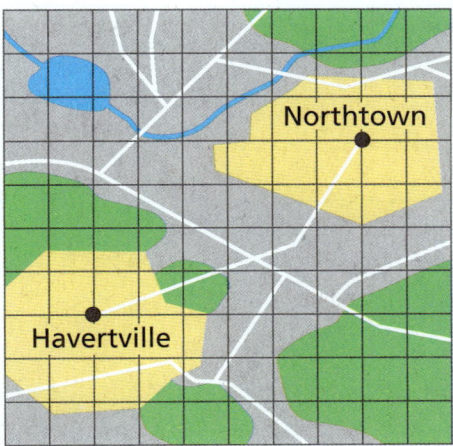

Use the graph to answer Problems 5–6.

5. **Attend to Precision** Which point is exactly 10 units from (0, 0)?

   _____

6. What is the distance between Points E and H? Round to the nearest tenth.

   _____ units

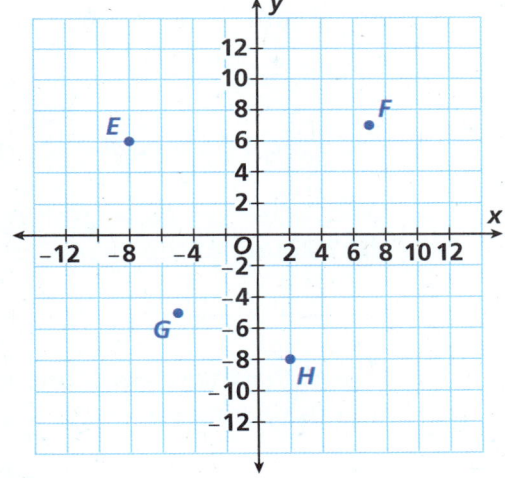

7. On your own paper, graph the points (−5, 4) and (4, 2). Use the grid lines to draw a right triangle with the given points as endpoints of the hypotenuse.

   A. Give two possible coordinate pairs for the third vertex.

   _____

   B. Find the distance between the given points. Round to the nearest tenth of a unit.

   _____

   C. Find the perimeter of the triangle to the nearest tenth of a unit.

   _____

Module 14 • Lesson 3   455

8. **Critique Reasoning** Elena plots the points (1, −1), (1, 2), and (5, 2). She says that the length of the hypotenuse of the right triangle formed by these points, rounded to the nearest tenth, is equal to 2.6 units, and the perimeter of the triangle is 9.6 units. Is Elena correct? How do you know?

_____

_____

_____

_____

_____

9. Georgia placed a grid over the map of the post office and the local library. The distance between grid lines is 0.5 mile.

   A. Give the coordinates of the post office and the library.

   _____

   B. Find the distance between the two buildings. Round to the nearest hundredth.

   _____

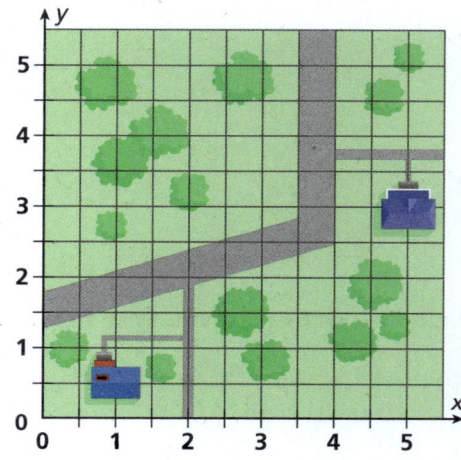

10. Ali drew the 3-pointed star shown on the graph.

    A. What is the perimeter of this 3-pointed star? Round to the nearest tenth.

    _____

    B. Explain how you used right triangles to find the perimeter.

    _____

    _____

    _____

    _____

    _____

    _____

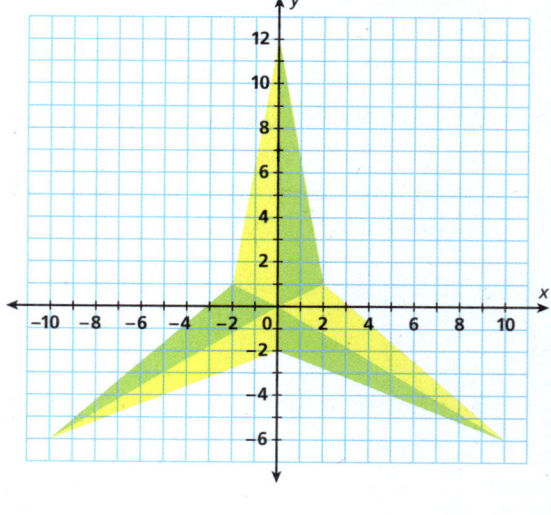

Name _____

Apply the Pythagorean Theorem in the Coordinate Plane

LESSON 14.3
More Practice/ Homework

ONLINE Video Tutorials and Interactive Examples

1. Renee takes a boat directly from the lodge to the campsite. If the distance between grid lines represents 500 feet, how far does Renee travel? Round to the nearest 10 feet.

   _____

   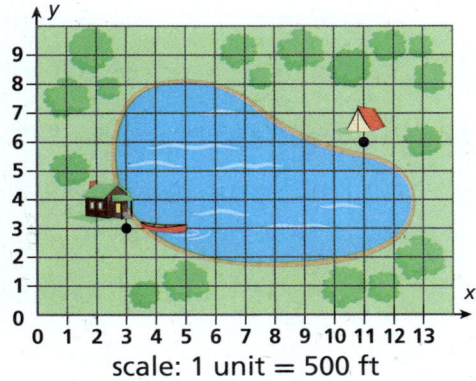
   scale: 1 unit = 500 ft

2. **(MP) Use Tools** On your own paper, plot the Points $E(-2, 2)$ and $F(8, 10)$. Use the vertical and horizontal grid lines to draw a right triangle with these two points as endpoints of the hypotenuse.

   A. Label the third vertex of your right triangle Point G. Identify two possible coordinate pairs for Point G.

   _____

   B. What is the distance between Points E and F? Round to the nearest tenth of a unit.

   _____

   C. What is the perimeter of △EFG? Round to the nearest tenth of a unit.

   _____

3. **(MP) Use Tools** On your own paper, graph the points $(-2, -4)$ and $(4, -1)$. Use the grid lines to draw a right triangle with the given points as endpoints of the hypotenuse.

   A. Give a possible coordinate pair for the third vertex.

   _____

   B. What is the vertical distance between the points? What is the horizontal distance between the points?

   _____

   C. Find the distance between the given points. Round to the nearest tenth of a unit.

   _____

   D. What is the perimeter of the triangle you drew? Round to the nearest tenth of a unit.

   _____

Module 14 • Lesson 3

Test Prep

4. Which set of is the distance between Point A and Point C on Parallelogram ABCD?

   Ⓐ 4.8 units   Ⓒ 5.2 units

   Ⓑ 5 units   Ⓓ 5.4 units

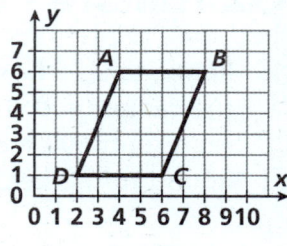

Use the graph for Problems 5–7.

5. Which two points are exactly 5 units apart?

   Ⓐ J and K   Ⓒ N and P

   Ⓑ L and M   Ⓓ Q and R

6. How far apart are L and M?

   Ⓐ 6 units   Ⓒ $\sqrt{12}$ units

   Ⓑ $\sqrt{9}$ units   Ⓓ $\sqrt{18}$ units

7. Which two points are $\sqrt{29}$ units apart?

   Ⓐ J and L   Ⓒ N and P

   Ⓑ P and M   Ⓓ Q and R

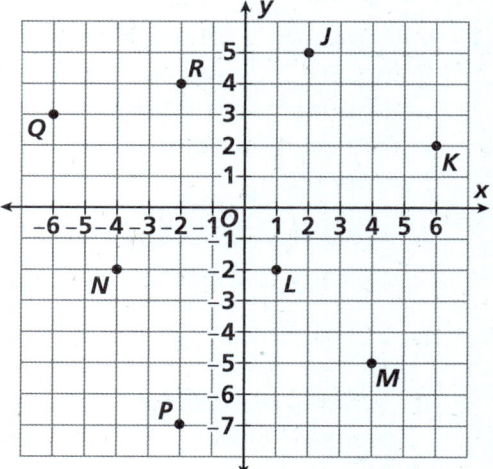

8. What is the perimeter of Trapezoid EFGH?

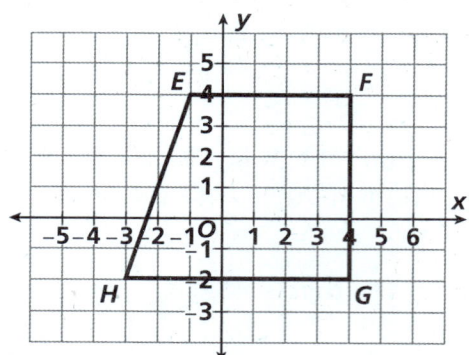

   Ⓐ 24 units   Ⓒ 25 units

   Ⓑ 24.3 units   Ⓓ 25.3 units

Spiral Review

9. Find the value of x that makes the equation true.
   $12x = 4(x + 2) + 20$

10. A line has a slope of 8 and crosses the y-axis at (0, 12). Write an equation of the line in slope-intercept form.

Module 14 Review

Name _____

Vocabulary

For Problems 1–3, choose the correct term from the Vocabulary box to complete each sentence.

Vocabulary
hypotenuse
leg
Pythagorean Theorem
Pythagorean triple

1. The _____ describes the relationship among the lengths of the sides of any right triangle.

2. A _____ of a right triangle is one of the sides that forms the right angle.

3. A _____ is a set of three whole numbers that could be the side lengths of a right triangle.

4. Write the converse of this statement: *If a triangle has a right angle, then it is a right triangle*.

   _____

Concepts and Skills

5. Which set of side lengths could form a right triangle?

   Ⓐ 5 cm, 5 cm, and 10 cm
   Ⓑ 6 cm, 7 cm, and 8 cm
   Ⓒ 8 cm, 15 cm, and 17 cm
   Ⓓ 9 cm, 12 cm, and 16 cm

6. **Use Tools** The diagram represents a set of beams that form part of a bridge support. Label $\overline{AB}$ and $\overline{BD}$ with their lengths, rounded to the nearest foot. State what strategy and tool you will use to answer the question, explain your choice, and then find the answer.

   _____
   _____

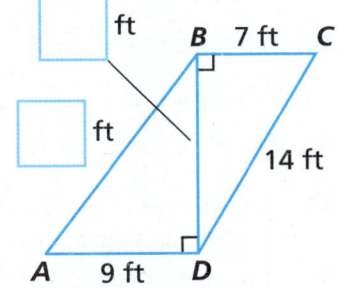

For Problems 7 and 8, determine the unknown side length of each right triangle to the nearest hundredth.

7. What is the length of $\overline{JL}$?

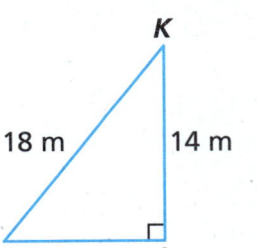

_____ meters

8. What is the length of $\overline{ST}$?

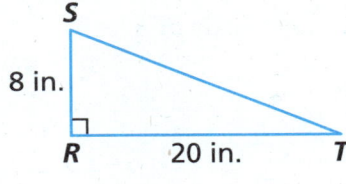

_____ inches

9. The steps shown can be used to prove the Pythagorean Theorem.

Step 1: Draw a figure using two squares. 	**Step 2:** Draw two congruent right triangles inside the figure. 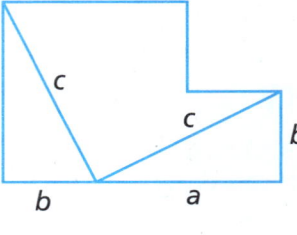
Step 3: Rotate the two triangles. 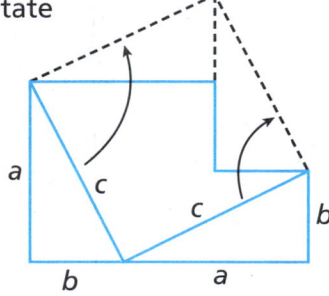	**Step 4:** The resulting figure is a square of side length c. 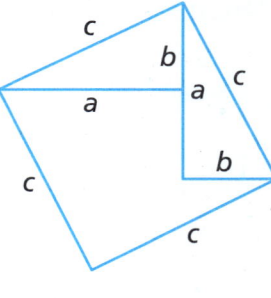

Explain how the steps prove the Pythagorean Theorem. *Hint:* Write expressions for the total area of the figures in Step 1 and in Step 4.

_____

_____

_____

_____

10. Which set of three side lengths form a right triangle?

    Ⓐ 3 ft, 5 ft, 12 ft   Ⓒ 12 ft, 13 ft, 16 ft

    Ⓑ 5 ft, 12 ft, 13 ft   Ⓓ 13 ft, 16 ft, 24 ft

11. Meg is making a scale model of an Egyptian pyramid. The model is a right square pyramid as shown. To the nearest centimeter, what is the base length b of the model?

    Ⓐ 12 cm   Ⓒ 23 cm

    Ⓑ 16 cm   Ⓓ 48 cm

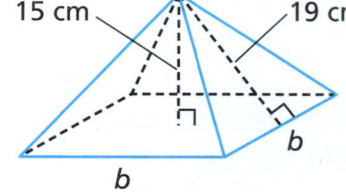

For Problems 12–14, determine the distance between the pair of points to the nearest hundredth of a unit.

12. $A(-2, 1)$ and $B(3, 5)$ _____ units

13. $C(-5, -2)$ and $D(0, -4)$ _____ units

14. $E(7, 3)$ and $F(-2, 6)$ _____ units

Module 15

Exponents and Scientific Notation

A-Mazing Expressions

Find a path through the maze by evaluating each of the expressions shown. You can move from one space to the next only if the value of the expression in the space you are in is less than the value of the expression in the space you are moving to. You can move left, right, up, or down, but not diagonally.

START

$(4 + 2) \div 5^2$	$(8 \div 10^2) + 2.3$	$1.5 \times 6 - 4 \times 2$
$1.8 \div 10^2$	$12 - 3.8 + 4.7$	$15 + (7 - 5)^3$
$5 \times 71 - 340$	$0.8^2 + 4^3$	$(1.4 \times 10^2) \div 5$
$(10 + 2)^2 - 1$	2.46×10^2	6.74×10^3

FINISH

 Turn and Talk

Explain how to determine whether you can move from 2.46×10^2 to 6.74×10^3 without performing any operations.

Are You Ready?

Complete these problems to review prior concepts and skills you will need for this module.

Order of Operations

For Problems 1–8, determine the value of each expression.

1. 36×10^5 _____

2. 1.24×10^4 _____

3. $179 \div 10^3$ _____

4. $1.5 \div 10^2$ _____

5. $(3.5 \times 10^3) + (4.27 \times 10^3)$ _____

6. $(6.7 \times 10^4) - (5.82 \times 10^2)$ _____

7. $(8.3 \times 10^3) \times (9.71 \times 10^2)$ _____

8. $(5.52 \times 10^2) \div (4.6 \times 10^3)$ _____

Solve Multi-Step Problems

9. At a grocery store, sliced turkey from the deli counter costs $7.92 per pound. A customer purchases 0.625 pound of sliced turkey. Excluding tax, how much change will she receive if she pays with a $20 bill?

    $ _____

10. It takes Steven 12.25 minutes to run 1.4 miles. At this rate, how long will it take him to run 2.6 miles?

    _____ minutes

11. An account with $600 earns 4% simple interest per year. The next year all the money is put into a new account that earns 4.5% simple interest per year. How much money does the account have at the end of the second year? Explain.

    _____

    _____

    _____

12. Anthony has two cube-shaped pots with an interior edge length of 8 inches and two cube-shaped pots with an interior edge length of 6.5 inches. He wants to fill each pot full of potting soil. His bag of potting soil is one cubic foot. How much soil will he have left after he fills each pot full of soil?

    _____

Lesson 1

Know and Apply Properties of Exponents

I Can use properties of integer exponents to simplify expressions.

Spark Your Learning

Alex has a rope that is 2^4, or 16 feet long. He folds the rope in half and cuts it, so he now has two pieces of rope that are each 2^3, or 8 feet long. Alex then folds each of the new pieces in half and cuts them, so he now has four pieces of rope that are each 2^2, or 4 feet long. Alex repeats this process until his pieces of rope are each 1 foot long. What would happen if Alex took each 1-foot section of rope and continued this process? What pattern do you notice?

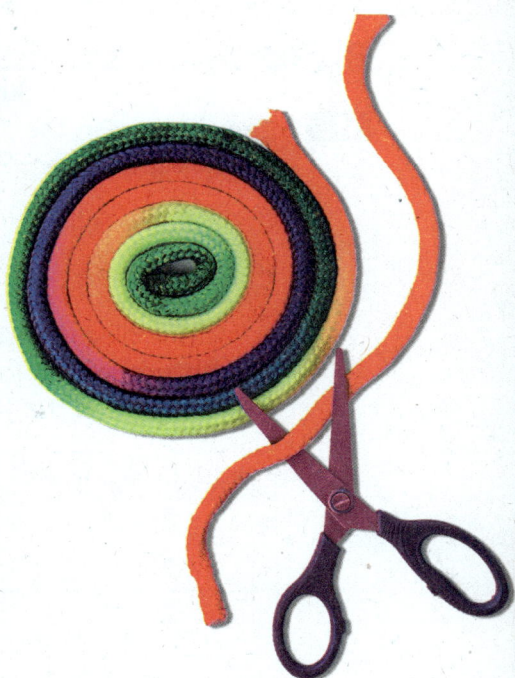

Turn and Talk Look for patterns in how these pairs are related: 2^{-3} and 2^3, 2^{-2} and 2^2, 2^{-1} and 2^1. What generalization can you make about a^{-b}, where a and b are natural numbers (1, 2, 3,...)?

Module 15 • Lesson 1 463

Build Understanding

1 The patterns in the Spark Your Learning lead to the following two properties of exponents.

If $a \neq 0$ and b is an integer, then $a^{-b} = \dfrac{1}{a^b}$.

If $a \neq 0$, then $a^0 = 1$.

> **Connect to Vocabulary**
>
> In the **power** 2^4, 2 is the **base** and 4 is the **exponent**.
> The **properties of exponents** are rules for operations with exponents.

A. You can look for patterns to develop the product of powers property for multiplying powers with the same base. Complete the table.

Product of powers	Factors	Single power
$3^2 \cdot 3^4$	$(3 \cdot 3) \cdot (3 \cdot 3 \cdot 3 \cdot 3)$	3^6
$7^3 \cdot 7^2$		
$2^4 \cdot 2^3$		

 $2^1 = 2$

 $2^2 = 4$

 $2^3 = 8$

B. How are the exponents in the left column and the exponent in the right column related?

_____

_____

C. You can also look for patterns to develop the quotient of powers property for dividing powers with the same base. Complete the table.

 $2^4 = 16$

Quotient of powers	Factors	Single power
$\dfrac{2^7}{2^4}$	$\dfrac{2 \cdot 2 \cdot 2 \cdot 2 \cdot 2 \cdot 2 \cdot 2}{2 \cdot 2 \cdot 2 \cdot 2}$	2^3
$\dfrac{6^5}{6^3}$		
$\dfrac{5^8}{5^2}$		

D. How are the exponents in the left column and the exponent in the right column related?

_____

_____

E. Make a conjecture about two additional properties of exponents based on your findings.

_____

_____

> **Turn and Talk** Can you use the properties of exponents you discovered to simplify $5^2 \cdot 2^5$? If so, how? If not, why not?

Name _____

Step It Out

2 ▶ In 2002, a high school student broke the record for folding a sheet of paper in half multiple times. When the paper was opened, the number of regions formed was $(2^4)^3$. How many times did the student fold the paper? To answer, you can develop the power of a power property.

A. First look for patterns using specific examples of a power of a power. Complete the table.

Power of powers	Expanded form	Factors	Single power
$(5^2)^3$	$5^2 \cdot 5^2 \cdot 5^2$	$(5 \cdot 5) \cdot (5 \cdot 5) \cdot (5 \cdot 5)$	5^6
$(7^4)^2$			
$(8^3)^2$			
$(4^3)^3$			

B. How are the exponents in the far-left column and the exponent in the far-right column related?

The _____ of the exponents in the far-left column equals the _____ in the far-right column.

C. Complete the conjecture about a property of exponents based on your findings:

If $a \neq 0$, and m and n are integers, then $\left(a^{\square}\right)^{\square} = a^{\square}$.

D. The number of regions formed by the high school student's folded paper was $(2^4)^3$. Use a single exponent to write this expression.

$(2^4)^3 = 2^{\square}$

E. How many times did the student fold the paper in half?

The student folded the paper ____ times. This is because 1 fold results in $2^{\square}$ regions, 2 folds results in $2^{\square}$ regions, and so on.

Continuing the pattern shows that ____ folds results in $\boxed{}^{12}$ regions.

Turn and Talk Does the property of exponents you discovered apply to negative powers? For example, can you use it to simplify $(7^{-2})^2$? Explain.

Module 15 • Lesson 1

3 Simplify each expression.

A. $2^4 \cdot 2^9$

$= 2^{\square + \square}$ Apply the product of powers property.

$= 2^{\square}$ Add the exponents.

$= \underline{\qquad}$ Simplify.

B. $3^3 \cdot 3^{-5}$

$= 3^{\square + \square}$ Apply the product of powers property.

$= 3^{\square}$ Add the exponents.

$= \dfrac{\square}{\square}$ Write the power without a negative exponent.

$= \underline{\qquad}$ Simplify.

$3^0 = 1,\ 3^1 = 3,\ 3^2 = 9$

C. $(4 + 8)^0$

$= \square^0$ Simplify within parentheses.

$= \underline{\qquad}$ Simplify.

D. $\dfrac{(5^2)^5}{5^6}$

$= \dfrac{\square}{\square}$ Apply the power of powers property in the numerator.

$= \square^{\square}$ Apply the quotient of powers property.

$= \underline{\qquad}$ Simplify.

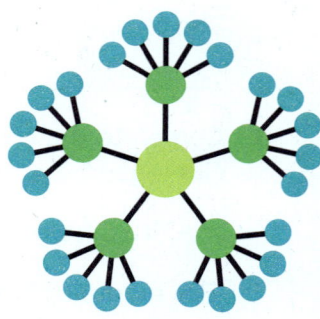

Powers of 5

Check Understanding

1. If $a \neq 0$ and m is an integer, what is the value of $a^m \cdot a^{-m}$? How do you know?

_____

2. Simplify $3^0 - 3^4 \cdot 3^{-5}$. Show your work and write the result as a fraction.

_____

466

Name _____

On Your Own

3. **STEM** According to one estimate, the number of stars in the Milky Way Galaxy is about $10^2 \cdot 10^3 \cdot 10^6$.

   A. Write the number of stars in the Milky Way Galaxy as a single power. Which property of exponents did you use?

   _____

   B. Write the estimated number of stars in the Milky Way Galaxy without using exponents.

   _____

4. The formula for the volume V of a cube with edge length s is $V = s^3$. The formula for the surface area A of the cube is $A = 6s^2$.

   A. A cube has edges of length 2 centimeters. Write expressions using exponents for the volume of the cube (in cubic centimeters) and for the surface area of the cube (in square centimeters).

   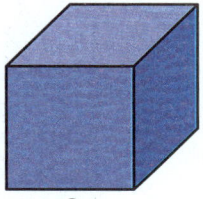

   _____

   B. **(MP) Reason** What is the ratio of the cube's volume to its surface area? Use the expressions you wrote in Part A and show how to simplify the ratio. Show your work and name any properties of exponents you use.

For Problems 5–7, use the table shown.

Description	Distance (m)
Distance from the Sun to Saturn	$(10^2)^6$
Diameter of the Solar System	$10^5 \cdot 10^8$
Diameter of Saturn	$((10^2)^2)^2$
Diameter of the disc of the Milky Way	$\dfrac{10^{23}}{10^2}$

5. What is the greatest distance shown? Write it as a power of 10 with a single exponent.

   _____

6. What is the least distance shown? Write it as a power of 10 with a single exponent.

   _____

7. The distance from Earth to the star Vega is approximately 10^{17} meters. Which of the distances in the table, if any, are less than this?

   _____

   _____

Module 15 • Lesson 1

8. **Open Ended** Write an expression involving two or more operations and three or more powers of 5 that can be simplified to $\frac{1}{5}$.

___

9. **Use Repeated Reasoning** You can look for patterns to develop the power of a product property.

   A. Complete the table.

Power of product	Factors	Product of powers
$(4 \cdot 3)^2$	$(4 \cdot 3) \cdot (4 \cdot 3) = (4 \cdot 4) \cdot (3 \cdot 3)$	$4^2 \cdot 3^2$
$(2 \cdot 9)^2$		
$(5 \cdot 8)^3$		

   B. Look for patterns in the table. State a property of exponents based on what you observe.

   ___

   C. Show two different ways to simplify the expression $(3 \cdot 2)^5$.

   ___
   ___

For Problems 10–13, simplify each expression. Write your answer without using exponents.

10. $3^2 \cdot 3^0 \cdot 3^4$

11. $\dfrac{4^6 \cdot 4^{-2}}{4^5}$

12. $\dfrac{2^5}{(2^2)^5}$

13. $8^0 + 8^6 \cdot 8^{-4}$

I'm in a Learning Mindset!

What is challenging about solving a problem involving exponents? Can I work through it on my own, or do I need help?

___
___

Know and Apply Properties of Exponents

LESSON 15.1 More Practice/ Homework

Problems 1–2 involve crayon production.

1. According to one crayon manufacturer, the average number of crayons produced in its factories each day is greater than $\frac{10^4 \cdot 10^6}{10^3}$.

   A. Write the number of crayons as a single power of 10. Which property or properties of exponents did you use?

   _____
   _____

   B. Write the number of crayons without using exponents.

   _____

2. One of the boxes produced by the crayon manufacturer contains $2^2 \cdot 2^0 \cdot 2^4$ crayons. How many crayons are in the box?

   _____

3. Katie and Lawrence collect guitar picks. Katie has $(2^2)^4$ guitar picks in her collection. Lawrence has $(3^2)^2$ guitar picks in his collection. Who has more guitar picks? How many more?

   _____

4. **Reason** Simplify $3^0 + 3^4 \cdot 3^{-6}$. Show your work and explain your steps.

For Problems 5–8, simplify each expression.

5. $8^{-1} \cdot 8^{-5} \cdot 8^3$

6. $4^3 \cdot 4^{-4} \cdot 4^2$

7. $\frac{9^{-2} \cdot 9^7}{9^3}$

8. $\frac{[6^3]^5}{6^{18}}$

Module 15 • Lesson 1

Test Prep

9. Which expression is equivalent to $3^2 \cdot 3^{-8} \cdot 3^0$?

  Ⓐ $\frac{1}{3^6}$
  Ⓒ 3^6
  Ⓑ $\frac{1}{3^{-6}}$
  Ⓓ 3^0

10. Draw a line to match each expression to its value.

$\frac{4^2 \cdot 4^{-4}}{4^3}$ • • $\frac{1}{1{,}024}$

$4^2 \cdot 4^8 \cdot 4^{-7}$ • • $\frac{1}{256}$

$\frac{4^6}{4 \cdot 4^3}$ • • 1

$4^{-2} \cdot 4^2 \cdot 4^{-4}$ • • 16

$\frac{4^3 \cdot 4^0}{4^2 \cdot 4}$ • • 64

11. What is the value of the expression $(-2 + 9)^5 \cdot (4 + 3)^{-3} + 7^0$?

  Ⓐ $\frac{1}{343}$
  Ⓒ 49
  Ⓑ $1\frac{1}{49}$
  Ⓓ 50

Spiral Review

12. Complete each figure so it is congruent to the figure shown.

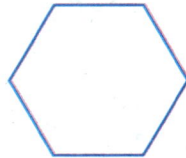 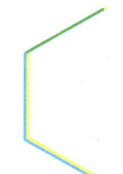 

13. The coordinates of the vertices of the preimage of a triangle are (2, 1), (3, 4), and (4, 1). The coordinates of the vertices of the image are (3, 3), (4, 6), and (5, 3). How far and in what direction was the triangle translated?

_____

Apply and Practice
Lesson 2

Name _____

Understand Scientific Notation

I Can use scientific notation to describe very large or very small quantities and to compare quantities.

Step It Out

1 What does one trillion dollars look like? If you could stack one trillion one-dollar bills, the stack would be about 68,000 miles tall. This is more than one-fourth the distance to the moon!

The **standard,** or **decimal, form** of a number is one way to write numbers. It uses the base-ten system to show all of a number's digits. For example, the way to write one trillion in standard form is 1,000,000,000,000.

There is a shorthand way, called **scientific notation**, to write large numbers without so many zeros. 1,000,000,000,000 in scientific notation is 1×10^{12}.

A. To write 68,000 miles in scientific notation, first move the decimal point to the left to get a number that is greater than or equal to 1 but less than 10.

$$68{,}000.$$
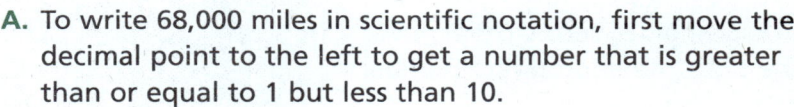

The decimal point moves _____ places to the left.

Remove the extra zeros to get the first factor for scientific notation: _____.

> **Connect to Vocabulary**
>
> **Scientific notation** is a method of writing very large or very small numbers by using powers of 10. In scientific notation, a number is written as the product of two factors. The first factor is greater than or equal to 1 but less than 10, and the second factor is a power of 10.

B. Use this factor and a power of 10 to write the number in scientific notation.

$68{,}000 = $ _____ $\times\ 10^{\square}$

When you write a number in scientific notation, its value does not change.

C. Write one billion, 1,000,000,000, in scientific notation.

$1{,}000{,}000{,}000 = $ _____ $\times\ 10^{\square}$

 **Turn and Talk** Is the number 16×10^7 written in scientific notation? Why or why not?

Module 15 • Lesson 2   471

2 You also can use scientific notation for very small numbers. The thickness of a dollar bill is about 0.0043 inches. Write this quantity in scientific notation.

A. First move the decimal point to the right to get a number that is greater than or equal to 1 but less than 10.

0.0043   The decimal point moves _____ places to the right.

Remove the extra zeros to get the first factor: _____.

B. Since 0.0043 is less than 1, you moved the decimal point to the right, so the exponent in the power of 10 will be negative.

0.0043 = _____ × 10^☐

3 In 2016, the United States Mint produced about 9.1×10^9 pennies. Write this quantity in standard form.

A. Use the power of 10 to determine how many places you will need to move the decimal point.

Move the decimal point _____ places.

B. Write the number with placeholder zeros. Then move the decimal point to the right the appropriate number of places.

9.100000000   So, 9.1×10^9 = _____.

4 Scientific notation makes it easy to compare quantities.

A. The table shows the number of half-dollar coins produced in 2016. Use a ratio to compare these quantities.

2016 Half-Dollar Production	
Denver Mint	2.1×10^6
All U.S. mints	4.2×10^6

$$\frac{4.2 \times 10^6}{2.1 \times 10^6}$$

The powers of 10 are the same: $\frac{10^6}{10^6} = 10^0$ or _____.

Compare the first factors: $\frac{\boxed{}}{2.1}$ = _____.

So, the total number of half-dollar coins minted is about $\boxed{} \cdot \boxed{}$ = _____ times the number of half-dollar coins minted in Denver.

 **Turn and Talk** Why is scientific notation a good way to express very large or very small numbers that you are estimating?

472

B. Use the ratio $\frac{3.45 \times 10^{-8}}{3.45 \times 10^{-11}}$ to compare 3.45×10^{-8} and 3.45×10^{-11}.

First compare the powers of 10. Compare the greater power to the lesser power.

$\frac{\Box}{10^{-11}} = 10^{\Box} = $ _____

Compare the first factors: $\frac{\Box}{3.45} = $ _____.

So, 3.45×10^{-8} is $\Box \cdot \Box = $ _____ times greater than 3.45×10^{-11}.

C. Use a ratio to compare 4.8×10^9 and 12,000,000.

Write 12,000,000 in scientific notation. 12,000,000 = _____

Compare the powers of 10. Compare the greater power to the lesser power.

$\frac{10^9}{\Box} = 10^{\Box} = $ _____

Compare the first factors: $\frac{4.8}{\Box} = $ _____.

So, 4.8×10^9 is _____ × _____ = _____ times greater than 12,000,000.

D. Use a ratio to compare 0.00222 and 66,600.

In scientific notation, 0.00222 = _____.

In scientific notation, 66,600 = _____.

66,600 is _____ × _____ = _____ times greater than 0.00222.

Check Understanding

1. Which number is greater: 8.9×10^5 or 2.1×10^7? How can you tell without writing the numbers in standard notation?

_____

2. Write 0.000501 in scientific notation.

_____

3. Write 5.31×10^3 in standard form.

_____

Module 15 • Lesson 2

On Your Own

4. The photo shows a road sign in western Australia.

   A. Write the distance to Rome in scientific notation.

   _____

   B. Write the distance to Sydney in scientific notation.

   _____

   C. **(MP) Reason** Explain how you can use the scientific notation version of the distances to determine whether it is farther to Rome or to Sydney.

   _____
   _____

5. **STEM** The diameter of a carbon atom is approximately 0.000000017 centimeter.

   A. When the diameter is expressed in scientific notation, will the exponent be positive or negative? How do you know?

   _____

   B. Write the diameter in scientific notation. Show your work and explain your steps.

For Problems 6–7, use the table which shows the number of miles on the odometers of several cars.

Car	Miles
A	7.51×10^4
B	6.03×10^3
C	1.1×10^5
D	4×10^4
E	8.9×10^3

6. Write the number of miles on Car A's odometer in standard form.

   _____

7. **(MP) Attend to Precision** Nicole wants to buy a used car with fewer than 50,000 miles on the odometer. Which of the cars shown should Nicole consider? Explain.

   _____
   _____

Name _____

For Problems 8–9, use the table of bridge lengths shown.

Bridge	Length (ft)
Atchafalaya Basin	9.6×10^4
General W.K. Wilson Jr.	3.2×10^4
Manchac Swamp	1.2×10^5
Frank Davins Memorial	2.9×10^4

8. Which of the bridges shown is the longest? How do you know?

   _____

   _____

9. How many times longer is the Atchafalaya Basin Bridge than the General W.K. Wilson Jr. Bridge? Explain.

   _____

   _____

   _____

10. **STEM** A geologist is comparing two rock samples. Sample A has a mass of 0.0015 gram. Sample B has the mass shown on the scale.

    A. Write the masses in scientific notation.

    _____

    B. How many times greater is the mass of Sample B than the mass of Sample A? Show your work.

11. **Use Tools** Most calculators display scientific notation when a result is longer than the number of digits the screen can display.

    A. To find out how your calculator displays scientific notation, enter 2^{40} and press the ENTER key. What does the calculator display? What number in scientific notation does it represent?

    _____

    B. Write the value of 2^{40} rounded to the nearest trillion.

    _____

Module 15 • Lesson 2

475

12. **(MP) Reason** What must be true about the exponent when you write a whole number between 1 and 10 in scientific notation? Why? Give an example.

For Problems 13–16, write each number in scientific notation.

13. 47,100,000

14. 6,004

15. 0.0000000009

16. 0.00053

For Problems 17–20, write each number in standard form.

17. 3.2×10^8

18. 5.111×10^2

19. 1.06×10^{-3}

20. 7.7×10^{-9}

For Problems 21–24, determine which number is greater and tell how many times greater.

21. 2×10^5 and 8×10^9

22. 3.9×10^4 and 1.3×10^{-1}

23. 24,000,000 and 2.4×10^{10}

24. 1.5×10^{-6} and 0.0063

25. **Social Studies** The Smithsonian Institution in Washington, D.C., is the world's largest museum, with approximately 15.4×10^7 artifacts. Explain why this number is not written in scientific notation and show how to write it correctly.

Name _____

Understand Scientific Notation

LESSON 15.2
More Practice/ Homework

ONLINE Video Tutorials and Interactive Examples

1. A group of researchers in Hawaii estimated that the number of grains of sand on Earth is 7,500,000,000,000,000,000. Write this number using scientific notation.

   _____

2. A snail moves across a table at a rate of 0.00093 mile per hour. Write this rate in scientific notation.

   _____

3. **Math on the Spot** The approximate population of Brazil in 2008 is shown. Write this number in standard form.

   _____

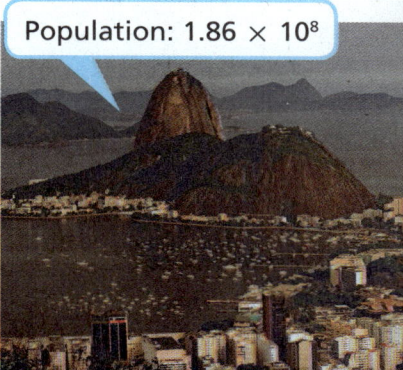

Population: 1.86×10^8

For Problems 4–7, write each number in scientific notation.

4. 239,000,000,000

5. 405

6. 0.0000101

7. 0.00000000000006

For Problems 8–11, write each number in standard form.

8. 5.5×10^5

9. 6.07×10^7

10. 2.04×10^{-4}

11. 4×10^{-6}

For Problems 12–14, determine which number is greater and tell how many times greater.

12. 7×10^{12} and 3.5×10^9

13. 1.4×10^{-5} and 2.8×10^{-4}

14. 16,000 and 1.6×10^8

15. **Open Ended** Write two numbers in scientific notation so that the second number is 10 times greater than the first number.

Module 15 • Lesson 2

Test Prep

16. Kendrick wants to write the number 0.000065 in scientific notation. What exponent should he use for the power of 10?
- Ⓐ −5
- Ⓑ −4
- Ⓒ 4
- Ⓓ 5

17. Jenna collected data about the number of annual visitors to two sports blogs. The table shows the data. The number of visitors to Sports Space is _____ times the number of visitors to Team Zone.

Blog	Annual visitors
Sports Space	4.8×10^5
Team Zone	12,000

- Ⓐ 4
- Ⓑ 40
- Ⓒ 400
- Ⓓ 4,000

18. What is 5.003×10^3 written in standard form?
- Ⓐ 0.0005003
- Ⓑ 0.005003
- Ⓒ 5,003
- Ⓓ 5,003,000

19. Which of the following numbers is greatest?
- Ⓐ 6.1×10^7
- Ⓑ 8.9×10^6
- Ⓒ 55,000,000
- Ⓓ 9,070,000

Spiral Review

20. The figure shows the dimensions of a rectangular city park. A member of the parks commission is considering a new diagonal path that would cut through the park from A to C. If the path is built, how much shorter would it be to walk along the path from A to C rather than walking along the edge of the park from A to C? Explain.

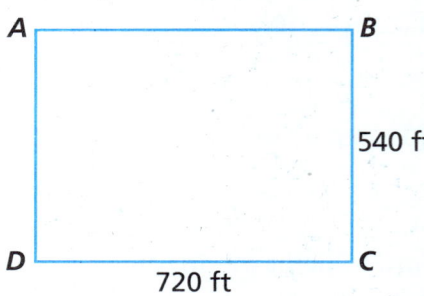

_____

_____

_____

21. What is the height of the cone shown? Round to the nearest tenth of a centimeter.

_____

22. Simplify the expression $7^0 + \dfrac{7^2}{(7^3)^2}$.

_____

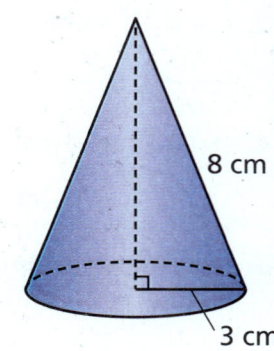

Compute with Scientific Notation

I Can compute with numbers in scientific notation and choose appropriate units for very large or small quantities.

Step It Out

1 You can add and subtract with scientific notation to analyze the data in the table.

National Park Visitors, 2016	
Park	Visitors
Great Smoky Mountains	1.13×10^7
Grand Canyon	5.97×10^6
Yellowstone	4.26×10^6

A. How many more people visited Grand Canyon National Park than Yellowstone National Park?

To add or subtract with scientific notation, first express the quantities with the same power of 10. These data have the same power of 10.

Use the Distributive Property:
$5.97 \times 10^6 - 4.26 \times 10^6 = (5.97 - 4.26) \times 10^6$

Subtract the first factors: $5.97 -$ _____ $=$ _____.

Express the difference with the same power of 10.

_____ $\times 10^6$ more people, or _____ more people, visited Grand Canyon National Park than Yellowstone National Park.

B. What was the total number of visitors to Great Smoky Mountains National Park and Grand Canyon National Park?

Since the numbers are written with different powers of 10, we need to rewrite one so they have the same power of 10. To do this, multiply the first factor by 10 and divide the power of 10 by 10.

$1.13 \times 10^7 = (1.13 \times 10) \times (10^7 \div 10) =$ _____ $\times$ _____

Now add the first factors: _____ $+$ _____ $=$ _____.

Express the sum with the same power of 10: _____ $\times 10^6$.

To write your answer in scientific notation, determine how to write the first factor as a number between 1 and 10. In this case, divide 17.27 by 10. To keep the value the same, multiply 10^6 by 10 to get 10^7.

_____ $\times 10^6 =$ _____ $\times 10^7$

 **Turn and Talk** How could you solve the problem in Part B by rewriting the quantity for the Grand Canyon rather than the Great Smoky Mountains?

Module 15 • Lesson 3

2 You can multiply or divide numbers in scientific notation by multiplying or dividing the first factors and multiplying or dividing the powers of 10.

A. Find $(3.3 \times 10^{-4}) \times 500$. Write your answer in scientific notation.

$$(3.3 \times 10^{-4}) \times 500 = (3.3 \times 10^{-4}) \times \left(5 \times 10^{\boxed{}}\right)$$
$$= (3.3 \times 5) \times \left(10^{-4} \times 10^{\boxed{}}\right)$$
$$= \underline{} \times 10^{\boxed{}}$$

Rewrite the product in scientific notation.

$16.5 \times 10^{-2} = \underline{} \times 10^{\boxed{}}$

B. Find $(8.864 \times 10^{15}) \div (1.6 \times 10^{4})$. Write your answer in scientific notation.

$$(8.864 \times 10^{15}) \div (1.6 \times 10^{4}) =$$
$$(8.864 \div \underline{}) \times \left(10^{15} \div 10^{\boxed{}}\right)$$
$$= \underline{} \times 10^{\boxed{}}$$

C. Many calculators have a key labeled EE that allows you to enter values in scientific notation. The display may look like scientific notation with the "×" replaced by "E." For example, 4.1×10^9 may appear as 4.1E9.

Use a calculator to check your answer to Part B. Write the quotient as it appears on your calculator. Then write it in scientific notation.

_____

 Turn and Talk How could you find the product in Part A of Task 2 without first writing 500 in scientific notation?

Check Understanding

Add or subtract. Express your answer in scientific notation.

1. $(5.7 \times 10^8) + (3.2 \times 10^6)$ 2. $(1.3 \times 10^{-4}) - (7.5 \times 10^{-5})$

Multiply or divide. Express your answer in scientific notation.

3. $(2.8 \times 10^7) \times (3.5 \times 10^{-3})$ 4. $(7.2 \times 10^{12}) \div (3 \times 10^5)$

Name _____

On Your Own

For Problems 5–7, use the data shown about the average number of vehicles per day crossing each bridge. Express your answers in scientific notation.

112,000 vehicles per day

Golden Gate Bridge

5. Find the total average number of vehicles per day crossing the bridges.

6. How many more vehicles cross the San Francisco-Oakland Bay Bridge each day than the Golden Gate Bridge, on average?

7. **(MP) Use Structure** What is the average number of vehicles that cross each bridge in one year?

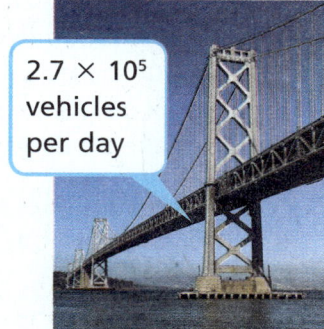
2.7×10^5 vehicles per day

San Francisco-Oakland Bay Bridge

8. **STEM** A typical *Escherichia coli* (or *E. coli*) bacterial cell is about 7.9×10^{-5} inch long. Suppose you could line up *E. coli* cells, end to end, across a Petri dish with a diameter of 2 inches. About how many cells would fit across the dish? Explain your method.

For Problems 9–10, a ream of paper contains 500 sheets. A case of paper contains 10 reams.

9. An office supply store gets a delivery of 400 cases. How many sheets of paper are in the delivery? Express your answer in scientific notation.

10. A ream of paper is 4.5×10^{-2} meter thick.

    A. **(MP) Use Tools** Use a calculator to find the thickness of a single sheet of paper. Write your answer in scientific notation.

    B. Express the answer to Part A using a more appropriate unit of length.

Module 15 • Lesson 3   481

11. About how many sesame seeds are in one gram of sesame seeds?

_____

A single sesame seed weighs approximately 4×10^{-6} kg.

12. Open Ended Write two numbers in scientific notation so that all of the following are true.
- Both numbers are greater than 1×10^2.
- Both numbers are less than 1×10^6.
- The product of the two numbers is 5×10^6.

_____

13. **(MP) Reason** New Zealand consists of hundreds of islands. Most of the population lives on the North Island, which has an area of 1.14×10^5 square kilometers, and the South Island, which has an area of 151,000 square kilometers. The North Island and South Island make up almost all of New Zealand's area.

A. Which island has a greater area? How many square kilometers greater is it? Express your answer in scientific notation.

_____

B. The combined population of the North and South islands is about 4.8×10^6. Find the approximate combined population density of people per square kilometer, rounded to the nearest unit. Explain your steps.

_____
_____
_____

14. **(MP) Critique Reasoning** Tim was asked to find the difference of 5.9×10^7 and 2.4×10^7. His work is shown here. Did he find the difference correctly? If so, name the mathematical properties he used. If not, explain his error and find the correct difference.

$(5.9 \times 10^7) - (2.4 \times 10^7)$
$= (5.9 - 2.4) + (10^7 - 10^7)$
$= 3.5 + 0$
$= 3.5$

_____
_____
_____

15. The top speed at which a Galapagos tortoise can travel is 3×10^{-1} km/h. At its top speed, how far does the tortoise travel in one minute? Use an appropriate unit of length for your answer.

_____

Compute with Scientific Notation

LESSON 15.3 More Practice/Homework

1. School District A has 5.6×10^5 students. School District B has 2.5×10^5 students. What is the total number of students in the two school districts?

   _____

The mass of a typical aphid is shown in the photo. The mass of a typical worker ant is 3×10^{-6} kilogram. Use this information to answer Problems 2–3. Use a calculator to verify your answers.

2. What is the combined mass of an aphid and a worker ant?

   _____

3. How much greater is the mass of a worker ant than the mass of an aphid?

   _____

Aphid mass: 2×10^{-7} kg

4. **(MP) Attend to Precision** A factory produces boxes of paper clips that each contain 2.5×10^2 paper clips. Every hour, the factory produces 8,000 boxes. Assuming the factory operates 24 hours per day, how many paper clips are produced in one week? Express your answer in scientific notation.

   _____

5. **Math on the Spot** The table shows the approximate areas of the surfaces of three oceans given in square meters. What is the total area? Write the answer in scientific notation using more appropriate units.

Ocean	Atlantic	Indian	Arctic
Area (m²)	7.68×10^{13}	6.86×10^{13}	1.41×10^{13}

   _____

Add or subtract. Express your answer in scientific notation.

6. $(7.7 \times 10^6) - (2.5 \times 10^6)$

7. $(3.9 \times 10^4) + (7.5 \times 10^5)$

8. $(5.22 \times 10^{-2}) + (3.85 \times 10^{-3})$

9. $(1.4 \times 10^{-7}) - (4.4 \times 10^{-8})$

Multiply or divide. Express your answer in scientific notation.

10. $(7.2 \times 10^4) \times (1.8 \times 10^3)$

11. $(8.4 \times 10^{-5}) \div (4.2 \times 10^{-6})$

12. $(4.1 \times 10^{12}) \times (3.5 \times 10^{-7})$

13. $(5.2 \times 10^{-3}) \div (4 \times 10^6)$

Test Prep

14. Draw a line to match each expression with its correct value.

$(2 \times 10^4) + (2 \times 10^3)$ •   • 1×10^1

$(2 \times 10^4) - (2 \times 10^3)$ •   • 2.2×10^4

$(2 \times 10^4) \times (2 \times 10^3)$ •   • 4×10^7

$(2 \times 10^4) \div (2 \times 10^3)$ •   • 1.8×10^4

The table shows the total seasonal attendance for four soccer teams. Use the table to answer Problems 15–17.

Team	Seasonal attendance
Aviators	2.3×10^4
Wranglers	16,000
Barracudas	8.9×10^3
Manatees	20,200

15. What was the combined seasonal attendance for the Aviators and the Wranglers?

Ⓐ 2.46×10^4 attendees

Ⓑ 3.9×10^4 attendees

Ⓒ 3.68×10^8 attendees

Ⓓ 3.9×10^8 attendees

16. How much greater was the Wranglers' seasonal attendance than the Barracudas' seasonal attendance? Write your answer in scientific notation.

_____

17. The Aviators' season consisted of 8 games. What was the average attendance per game? Express your answer in scientific notation and in standard form.

_____

Spiral Review

18. Ava wants to use $\triangle PQR$ to prove the Pythagorean Theorem. She draws $\overline{QT}$ as shown. She starts her proof by identifying three similar triangles in the figure and writing proportions based on their side lengths. Complete the proportions.

$\dfrac{QR}{TR} = \dfrac{PR}{\boxed{}}$ $\dfrac{QP}{TP} = \dfrac{PR}{\boxed{}}$

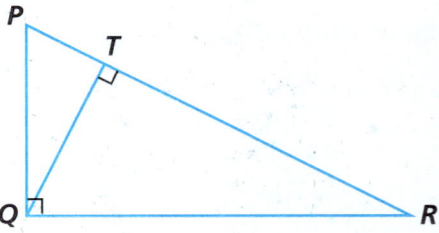

19. Use the Pythagorean Theorem to find the distance between the points $(2, 3)$ and $(-1, -2)$. Round to the nearest tenth.

_____

20. Order the numbers from least to greatest: $3 + \sqrt{5}$, π, $\dfrac{5}{2}$, $6 + \sqrt{2}$, $-\sqrt{16}$.

Module 15 Review

Vocabulary

In Problems 1–3, complete each sentence with the correct operation to explain the properties of exponents.

1. To raise a power to a power, keep the base the same and _____ the exponents.

2. To divide two powers with the same base, keep the base the same and _____ the exponents.

3. To multiply two powers with the same base, keep the base the same and _____ the exponents.

4. What is the difference between the standard form of a number and the number written in scientific notation?

   _____
   _____
   _____
   _____

Concepts and Skills

5. **Use Tools** Write an expression with a single exponent that is equivalent to $8^{-4} \cdot (8^2)^4$. State what strategy and tool you will use to answer the equation, explain your choice, and then find the answer.

   _____
   _____

6. Compare each expression to 6^6.

	Less than 6^6	Greater than 6^6	Equal to 6^6
$(6^{-1} \cdot 6^4)^2$	☐	☐	☐
$\dfrac{6^8}{(6^2)^2}$	☐	☐	☐
$\left(\dfrac{6^2}{6^0}\right)^4$	☐	☐	☐

7. Select all the expressions equivalent to $\dfrac{9^3 \cdot 9^5}{9^2}$.

   Ⓐ 3^8 Ⓒ 9^6 Ⓔ 27^2

   Ⓑ 3^{12} Ⓓ 9^4 Ⓕ 27^4

8. What are possible values for a and b in the equation $\frac{4^a}{4^b} = 4^{-1}$? What must be true about the values of a and b?

   $a =$ _____ $b =$ _____

   _____

9. The diameter of Earth is about 1×10^4 kilometers, and the diameter of a basketball is about 2×10^{-4} kilometer. About how many times as great is the diameter of Earth as the diameter of a basketball?

   Ⓐ 5,000 times as great as
   Ⓑ 50,000 times as great as
   Ⓒ 50,000,000 times as great as
   Ⓓ 500,000,000 times as great as

10. A bee hummingbird has a mass of 0.0023 kilogram. What is the mass of a bee hummingbird written in scientific notation?

    _____ kilogram

11. Naomi says that 9.8×10^5 is greater than 3.2×10^6. Is Naomi correct? Explain your reasoning.

    _____
    _____
    _____
    _____

12. Which expression is equivalent to $\frac{(8 \times 10^3) + (4 \times 10^3)}{(3 \times 10^{-2})}$?

    Ⓐ 4×10^1
    Ⓑ 4×10^4
    Ⓒ 4×10^5
    Ⓓ 4×10^8

13. What is the difference between 8.5×10^{-4} and 2.8×10^{-4}, written in standard form?

    _____

14. Mount Everest is growing at a rate of about 1.1×10^{-5} meter per day. Express this rate using units of a more appropriate size, and explain why the units you chose are more appropriate.

    _____
    _____
    _____
    _____

15. An elephant has a mass of 4,500 kilograms. How many mice, with a mass of 2×10^{-2} kilogram each, would it take to equal the mass of the elephant?

    Write your answer in standard form. _____ mice

Unit 7

Area and Volume

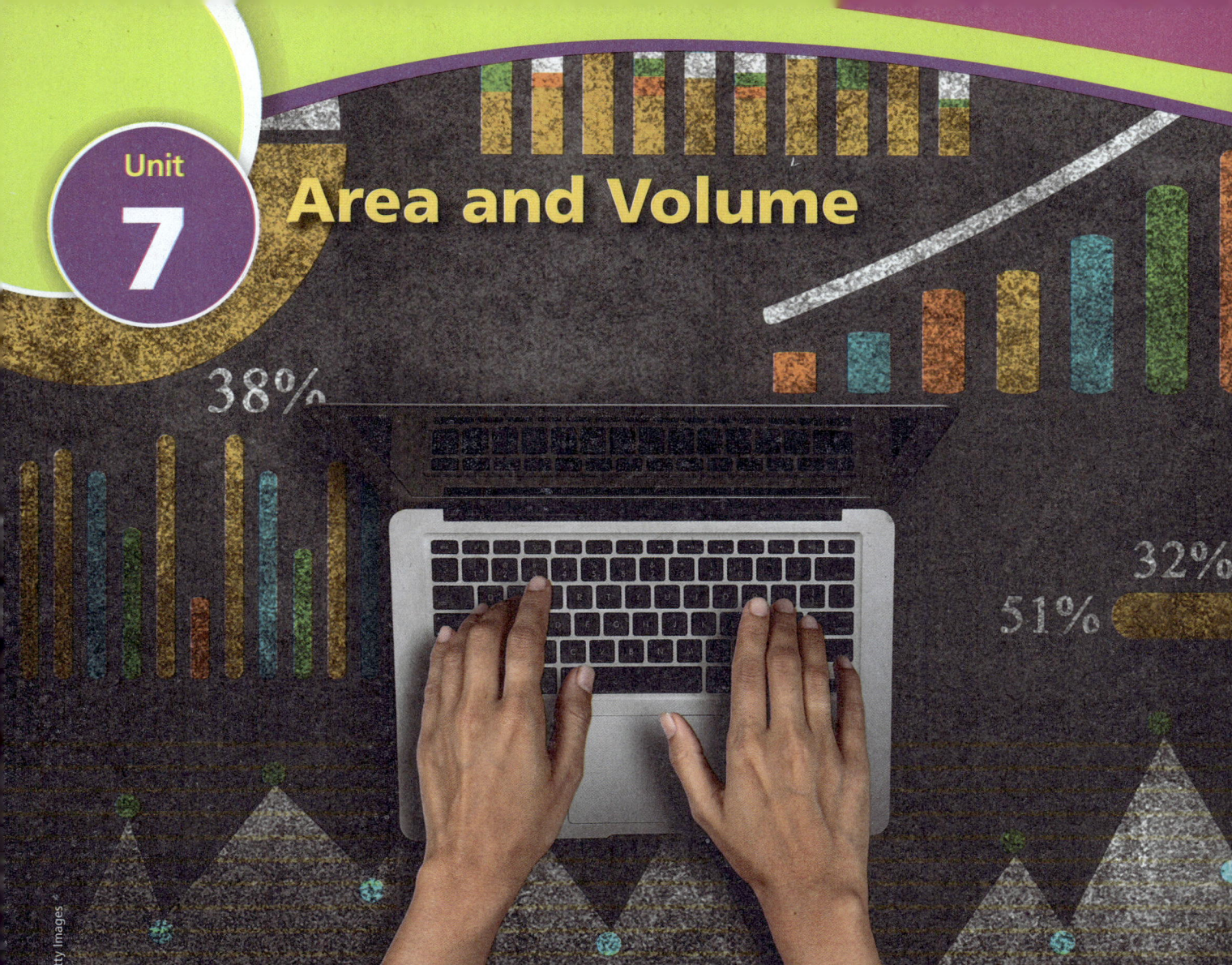

Data Analyst

A data analyst helps companies make good business decisions by collecting, analyzing, and storing data. The data may be related to sales, market research, costs, errors, or just about anything. A data analyst looks for patterns and trends in the data and then presents the results in a meaningful way.

STEM Task:

A rectangular electronic game board is 16.5 inches by 12 inches. It includes a grid with 8 rows of 8 squares, each 0.5 inch on a side. When you aim a laser at any of the red squares, data are collected on the accuracy of the hits. What are the ratios of (a) the area of one square to the area of the board, and (b) the combined area of the squares to the area of the board? Explain.

Learning Mindset
Perseverance Learns Effectively

Perseverance is the ability to stick with a task until it is complete. But it can be difficult to persevere when a task seems too big or complicated. If you feel overwhelmed by a task, try dividing it into smaller, easier steps. Here's how:

- Identify the end goal of the task. Then work backward. What do you need to do before you can reach the end goal? What do you need to do before that? And before that?

- Alternatively, start by identifying just the first step. Sometimes completing the first step will help you see the second step.

- Each step should be specific and small enough to feel achievable. If a step feels overwhelming, break it down into even smaller steps.

Reflect

Q What steps were involved in completing the STEM Task?

Q Can you compute a ratio from the STEM Task more efficiently by refining how you used an area formula? Explain.

Module 16

Analyze Figures to Find Circumference and Area

What Comes Next in the Pattern?

The figures shown are squares, non-square rectangles, and triangles.

Find the area of each figure in square centimeters. Look for patterns.

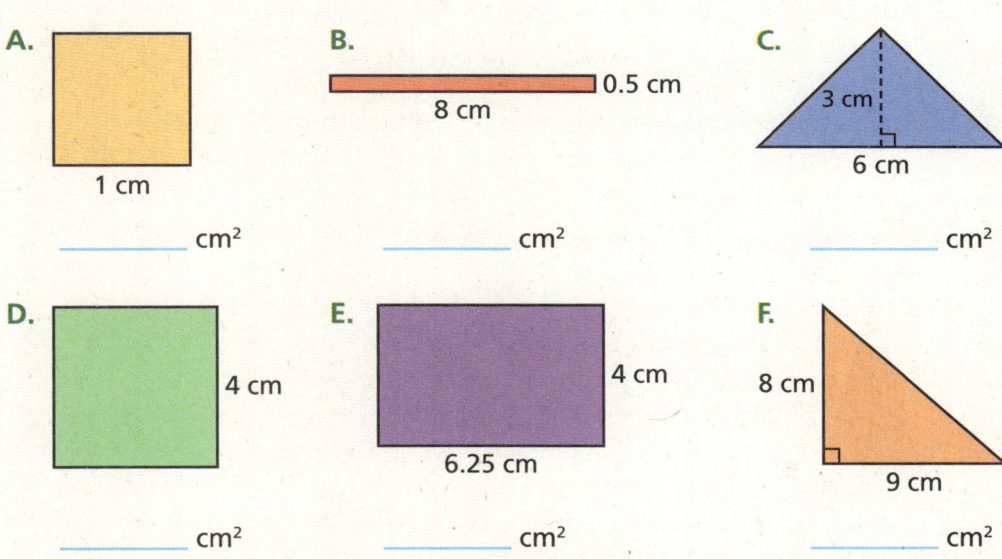

A. 1 cm square

_____ cm²

B. 8 cm × 0.5 cm

_____ cm²

C. triangle, 6 cm base, 3 cm height

_____ cm²

D. 4 cm square

_____ cm²

E. 6.25 cm × 4 cm

_____ cm²

F. right triangle, 9 cm × 8 cm

_____ cm²

 **Turn and Talk**

If the pattern continues, what three figures will appear in the next row? What will the areas of the figures be? Explain.

Module 16 — 489

Are You Ready?

Complete these problems to review prior concepts and skills you will need for this module.

Solve One-Step Equations

Solve the equation.

1. $\frac{x}{2} = 5$ for x _____
2. $2w = \frac{10}{3}$ for w _____
3. $\frac{h}{20} = \frac{5}{4}$ for h _____

Evaluate Algebraic Expressions

Evaluate each given expression for $n = -3$.

4. $4n + n$ _____
5. $-n + n^2$ _____
6. $3 - n^2$ _____

Area of Quadrilaterals and Triangles

7. What is the area of a rectangle that has a base of 5 centimeters and a height of 2 centimeters?

   _____

8. What is the area of a square with a side length of 2.5 feet?

   _____

9. What is the area of the triangle shown?

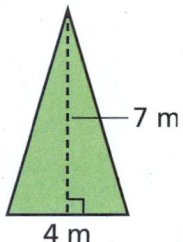

   _____

10. What is the area of the parallelogram shown?

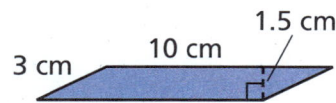

   _____

Lesson 1

Name _____

Derive and Apply Formulas for Circumference

 I Can find the circumference of a circle when I know either the radius or the diameter.

Spark Your Learning

A woodworker has twelve spokes. To make the wheel's rim, there are two pieces of wood that can be curved using steam. They are 6 feet and 8 feet long.

The measure along the spokes from the center to the inside of the rim is shown. Is the 6-foot piece of wood long enough to curve around for the wheel's rim? Is the 8-foot piece of wood long enough? Use measuring tools, large paper, and string to help solve.

1 ft

 **Turn and Talk** Did this experiment give you an idea of how much longer a string that makes up the rim of a wheel must be than one of the spokes? Explain.

Module 16 • Lesson 1   491

Build Understanding

1 ▶ Find circular objects or objects that have a circular face. For each object, follow the steps to complete the table.

A. List the name of the object in the table.

B. Measure and record the circumference of the circular face.

C. Measure and record the diameter of the circular face.

D. Calculate the ratio of the circumference to the diameter. Write the ratio as a decimal in the table.

Object	Circumference, C	Diameter, d	Ratio, $\frac{C}{d}$
small bowl	about 16 in.	5 in.	

5 in.

Connect to Vocabulary

The **circumference** of a circle is like the perimeter of a rectangle; it is the distance around the figure.

 **Turn and Talk** Describe what you notice about the ratio $\frac{C}{d}$ in your table. Does the relationship between the circumference and diameter of a circle appear to be proportional? Explain.

2 ▶ Pi, represented by the symbol π, is the ratio of a circle's circumference to its diameter. You can use this relationship to find a formula for circumference.

A. Write an equation for π using C for circumference and d for diameter.

$\pi = \dfrac{\boxed{}}{\boxed{}}$

Connect to Vocabulary

The ratio of circumference to diameter, $\frac{C}{d}$, is the same for all circles and is called π or **pi**. The value of π can be approximated by 3.14 or by $\frac{22}{7}$.

B. How can you rewrite the equation as a formula for circumference C?

C = $\boxed{}$ · $\boxed{}$

C. How are diameter and radius related?

The diameter is equal to _____ times the radius.

D. Rewrite your equation for C in terms of the radius r.

C = $\boxed{}$ · 2 $\boxed{}$

Step It Out

3. Juanita wants to put a circular fence around the edge of the circular garden shown. How much fencing will she need to the nearest foot? Use 3.14 for π.

14 ft

$C = \pi d$

$C \approx 3.14 \cdot \square$

$C \approx \square$

Juanita will need about _____ feet of fencing.

4. The circumference of a men's adult basketball hoop is about 56.52 inches. The diameter of a basketball is about 9.55 inches. Show that the ball can fit through the hoop. Use 3.14 for π.

Find the diameter of the hoop using $C = \pi d$.

$C = \pi d$

$\square \approx \square \cdot d$

$\square \approx d$

$\square \approx d$

The diameter of the hoop is about _____ inches, which is / is not greater than the diameter of the basketball.

Check Understanding

1. At a park, the jogging trail is a circle with a radius of 200 meters. How far is it around the trail? Use 3.14 for π. Show your work.

   _____

2. A contractor is installing a semicircular window with a radius of 3.5 feet. Find the distance around the window. Use $\frac{22}{7}$ for π. Explain your answer.

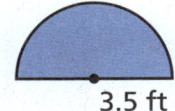

3.5 ft

Module 16 • Lesson 1   493

On Your Own

3. Toni rides the Ferris wheel shown for 15 revolutions.

   56 ft

   A. How far does Toni travel in one revolution? Use $\frac{22}{7}$ for π.

   _____

   B. How far does Toni travel for the entire ride?

   _____

4. **(MP) Reason** Paul is making a ball toss game for his club booth at the fair. He wants to make the circumference of the holes at least 3 inches greater but not more than 4 inches greater than the circumference of the ball. One person suggests that Paul make the diameter of the hole 1 inch greater than that of the ball. Another suggests the diameter should be 2 inches greater. Which suggestion should Paul choose? Explain.

   _____
   _____
   _____
   _____

5. **Health and Fitness** Juan runs a total of 11,775 feet around a circular track, burning 12 calories each lap. The track's diameter is 150 feet. How many calories does Juan burn? Round your answer to the nearest whole number. Use 3.14 for π.

   _____

For Problems 6–7, find the circumference. Round your answer to the nearest hundredth. Use 3.14 for π.

6.
   10 m

7.
   21 cm

I'm in a Learning Mindset!

Did my strategy for deriving and applying circumferences work? How did I adjust my strategy when I got stuck?

_____
_____

Name _____

LESSON 16.1
More Practice/ Homework

Derive and Apply Formulas for Circumference

ONLINE
Video Tutorials and Interactive Examples

1. **Math on the Spot** A counter recorded 254 revolutions of the bicycle wheel shown. How far did the bicycle travel? Use $\frac{22}{7}$ for π.

   A. How far does the wheel roll for one tire revolution?

   _____

   B. What is the total distance recorded?

   _____

diameter $\frac{5}{4}$ ft

2. **Use Structure** Hans opens a circular window that is 3.5 feet across at its widest point. What is the circumference of the window to the nearest whole number? Use 3.14 for π.

   _____

3. **STEM** Forest rangers estimate the age of trees by dividing a tree's radius by its average ring width, which represents a year's worth of growth. If an oak tree has a circumference of 151 inches and an average ring width of $\frac{1}{2}$ inch, approximately how old is the tree to the nearest whole year? Use 3.14 for π.

   _____

For Problems 4–9, find the circumference. Round your answer to the nearest hundredth. Use 3.14 for π.

4.  25 m

5. 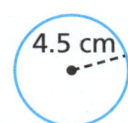 4.5 cm

6.  28 in.

7.  19 ft

8.  3 mm

9.  35 in.

Module 16 • Lesson 1   495

Test Prep

10. What is the circumference of the circle to the nearest hundredth? Use 3.14 for π.

   Ⓐ 26.69 in.
   Ⓑ 53.38 in.
   Ⓒ 106.76 in.
   Ⓓ 907.46 in.

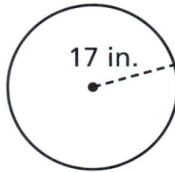

11. Randy is designing a circular garden that is 18 feet in diameter. He is buying plastic edging that costs $1.50 per foot. He can only buy edging in whole-foot amounts. How much does it cost Randy to buy edging for his garden? Use 3.14 for π.

_____

For Problems 12 and 13, find the circumference of each circle to the nearest hundredth. Use 3.14 for π.

12.

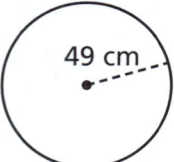

_____

13.

_____

Spiral Review

14. Nada is making square coasters with sides of 3 inches. On each coaster is a circular design. What is the radius of the largest circle that fits on one of the coasters?

_____

15. In the circle in the diagram, $\overline{AC}$ is the diameter and $\overline{BD}$ is the radius that splits the upper semicircle in half. What is the measure of ∠ABD?

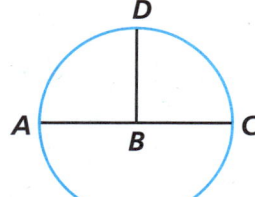

_____

Connect Concepts and Skills

Lesson 2

Name _____

Derive and Apply a Formula for the Area of a Circle

I Can use formulas for the area and circumference of a circle to solve problems and informally derive the relationship between the circumference and the area.

Spark Your Learning

A designer plans for a circular rug in a 9-foot by 9-foot square bedroom. What is the largest area of a rug that can fit in the bedroom?

Turn and Talk How close do you think your estimate of the rug's area was? Explain.

Module 16 • Lesson 2

497

Build Understanding

1 Use a parallelogram to find the area of a circle.

A. Use a compass to draw a circle on a piece of paper. Cut out the circle. Fold the circle in half three times as shown to get wedges of equal size.

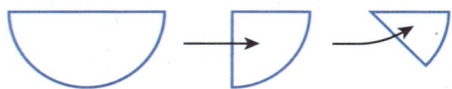

B. Cut the circle along the fold lines to separate the circle into eight equal wedges.

C. Arrange the wedges to form a figure resembling a parallelogram. Label the base of the parallelogram in terms of the circumference C. Label the height of the parallelogram in terms of the radius r.

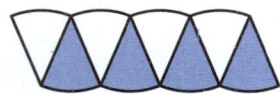

D. Use the labels on your parallelogram of wedges to substitute for b and h in the formula for area of a parallelogram.

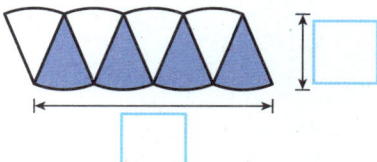

$A = b \cdot h$

$A = \boxed{} \cdot \boxed{}$

E. The formula for the circumference of a circle is $C = \pi \boxed{}$.

So half of the circumference can be written in terms of the radius as:

$\frac{1}{2}C = \pi \boxed{}$

F. Finally, complete the formula for the area of your parallelogram of wedges.

$A = \frac{1}{2}C \cdot r$

$A = \boxed{} \cdot r$ Substitute for $\frac{1}{2}C$.

$A = \boxed{}$ Write using an exponent.

G. The parallelogram of wedges is made from a circle, so the formula for the area of a circle is:

$A = \boxed{}$

Turn and Talk How could you make your parallelogram of wedges look more like a parallelogram with straight edges?

Name _____

Step It Out

2 The formula for the area of a circle is $A = \pi r^2$. This formula allows you to find the area of a circle if you know the radius or diameter. How can you find the area if you know only the circumference?

A. Write the formula for circumference using r. Then solve for r.

$$C = \pi d$$

$$C = \boxed{}$$

$$\frac{C}{\boxed{}} = r$$

B. Substitute the expression for r into the formula for area of a circle and simplify.

$$A = \pi r^2$$

$$A = \pi \left(\frac{\boxed{}}{\boxed{}} \right)^2 \quad \text{Substitute for } r.$$

$$A = \frac{\boxed{}}{\boxed{} \cdot \boxed{}} \quad \text{Simplify.}$$

C. Use your formula to find the area, to the nearest square meter, of the pen shown. Use 3.14 for π.

$$A = \frac{\boxed{}}{\boxed{}}$$

$$A = \frac{\boxed{}^2}{4\pi} \approx \boxed{} \text{ square meters}$$

65 m of fencing

Check Understanding

1. The new circular community swimming pool has a diameter of 64 feet.

A. What is the radius of the community pool?

_____

B. What is the area of the surface of the pool? Use 3.14 for π.

_____

2. To the nearest square centimeter, what is the area of a circle with a circumference of 75.36 centimeters? Use 3.14 for π.

_____

Module 16 • Lesson 2

On Your Own

3. A circular mirror has the radius shown.

   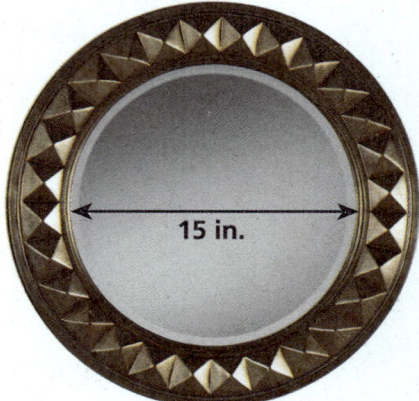

   A. To the nearest hundredth, what is the area of the mirror? Use 3.14 for π.

   _____

   B. The mirror has a frame. The radius of the mirror with the frame is 11 inches. To the nearest hundredth, what is the area of the mirror with the frame?

   _____

   C. (MP) **Reason** To the nearest hundredth, what is the area of the frame?

   _____

4. A disk is shaped like a flat circular plate. Its circumference is 26.69 inches. To the nearest hundredth, what is the area of the disk? Use 3.14 for π.

   _____

5. (MP) **Critique Reasoning** A classmate states that if the radius of a circle is doubled, then its area is doubled. Do you agree or disagree? If you disagree, how much larger do you think the area will be? Explain.

   _____
   _____
   _____

For Problems 6–7, find the area to the nearest hundredth. Use 3.14 for π.

6.

7.

_____

 I'm in a **Learning Mindset!**

How effective were the strategies I used to find the area of a circle using the circumference of the circle?

_____
_____

Name

Derive and Apply a Formula for the Area of a Circle

LESSON 16.2
More Practice/ Homework

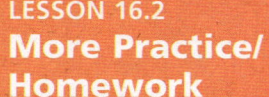

ONLINE Video Tutorials and Interactive Examples

1. To make grape juice, water is added to a large cylindrical vat of grapes. If the diameter of the vat is 16 feet, what is the area of the base of the vat? Use 3.14 for π. Round to the nearest hundredth.

   _____

2. **Math on the Spot** A group of historians are building a tepee to display at a local multicultural fair. The tepee has a height of 7 feet 4 inches at its center, and it has a circular floor of radius 14 feet. What is the area of the floor of the tepee to the nearest square foot? Use $\frac{22}{7}$ for π.

   _____

3. The face of a clock has a circumference of 14π inches. What is its area to the nearest hundredth? Use 3.14 for π.

   _____

4. A carpenter cuts a circle out of a piece of wood. The radius of the circle is about 23 inches. The carpenter cuts the circle into two semicircles. What is the area of one semicircle to the nearest hundredth? Use 3.14 for π.

   _____

5. **(MP) Use Structure** Four identical circles are lined up in a row with no gaps between them. A line segment from the beginning to the end of the row that passes through the centers of all the circles measures 68 cm. What is the combined area of all the circles to the nearest hundredth? Use 3.14 for π.

   _____

6. Ms. Flynn's class is painting a circular canvas. Its diameter is 5 feet. What is the area of the canvas to the nearest whole number? Use 3.14 for π.

   _____

For Problems 7–12, find the area of each circle described. Use 3.14 for π. Round to the nearest hundredth.

7. Radius of 10 centimeters

8. Diameter of 2 feet

9. Circumference of 62.8 inches

10. Diameter of 8 inches

11. Circumference of 18.84 miles

12. Radius of 99 millimeters

Module 16 • Lesson 2   501

Test Prep

13. Larry drew a circle with a circumference of 40.82 centimeters. What is the approximate area of the circle to the nearest thousandth? Use 3.14 for π.

_____

14. Safeta put a circular placemat on a table. The radius of the placemat is 7.5 inches. What is the area of the placemat to the nearest hundredth? Use 3.14 for π.

_____

15. The length of the curved part of a semicircle is 25.12 inches. What is the approximate area of the semicircle? Use 3.14 for π.

- Ⓐ 25.12 in²
- Ⓑ 50.24 in²
- Ⓒ 100.48 in²
- Ⓓ 200.96 in²

16. On a middle school basketball court, there is a large circle painted on the floor. The diameter of the circle is 12 feet. What is the area of the circle to the nearest hundredth? Use 3.14 for π.

- Ⓐ 18.84 ft²
- Ⓑ 113.04 ft²
- Ⓒ 452.16 ft²
- Ⓓ 1,808.64 ft²

17. Find the area of a circle with a radius of 33 millimeters to the nearest hundredth. Use 3.14 for π.

_____

Spiral Review

18. Carlos drew a figure on the smartboard and said it was a triangle with angles of 100°, 35°, and 55°. Nate said that was impossible. Who is correct? Explain.

_____

_____

19. The diameter of a wheel is 3 feet. What is the circumference to the nearest hundredth? Use 3.14 for π.

_____

Apply and Practice
Lesson 3

Name _____

Areas of Composite Figures

I Can break a composite figure into simple shapes and use area formulas to find its area.

Step It Out

1 Rahim drew an outline of the front of a house on grid paper. He wants to find the area of his model.

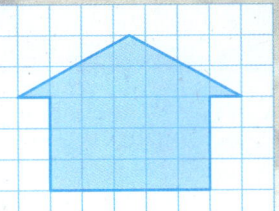

A. Separate the **composite figure** into simple geometric figures. What simple geometric figures are used to form the outline?

_____

B. Determine the dimensions and then find the area of each of the simple geometric figures.

_____
_____

C. Find the area of the composite figure.

_____
_____

Turn and Talk Can you separate the composite figure into different simple geometric figures? Explain.

Module 16 • Lesson 3

2 A section of a basketball court is shown.

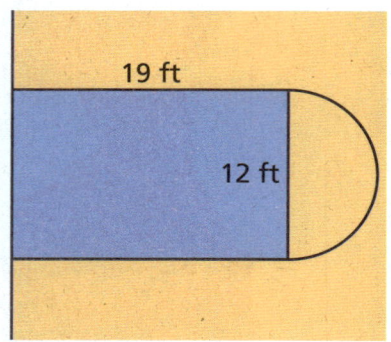

A. Determine the simple geometric figures that are used in the composite figure.

___

B. Find the dimensions of the simple geometric figures.

___

C. How is the area of a semicircle related to the area of a circle with the same radius?

___

D. Find the area of the simple geometric figures to the nearest square foot. Use 3.14 for π.

___

E. Find the area of the composite figure.

___

Turn and Talk Describe the method you would use to determine the simple geometric figures of a composite figure.

Name _____

3 The manager of a hotel wants to put new carpet in the lobby. The dimensions of the lobby are shown. There is a statue with a circular base in the lobby that does not need to have carpet under it.

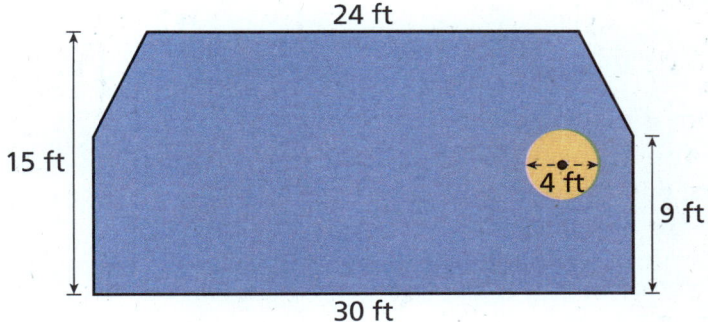

A. Determine the simple geometric figures that are in the composite figure. Find the dimensions of the simple geometric figures.

_____

_____

_____

B. Find the areas of the simple geometric figures. Use 3.14 for π.

_____

_____

_____

C. Find the area of the lobby that needs carpet. Explain how you found the area.

_____

_____

_____

Check Understanding

1. Find the area of the composite figure.

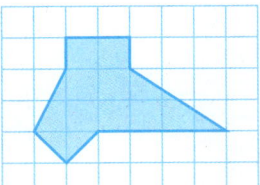

_____

2. Farrah has a piece of paper that is 11 inches long and 8 inches wide. She cuts a semicircle with a radius of 4 inches out of the piece of paper. What is the area of the piece of paper she has left after the cut to the nearest hundredth? Use 3.14 for π.

_____

Module 16 • Lesson 3

On Your Own

3. Greg designed a trophy using grid paper. What is the area of the drawing of the trophy shown?

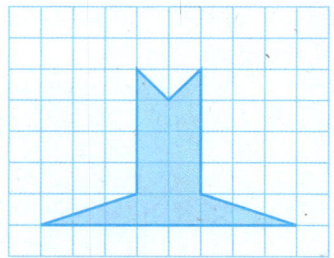

_____

4. **(MP) Attend to Precision** Clara is making a pennant. She attaches a rectangle that is 1 inch wide and 6 inches long to a triangle that has a base of 6 inches and a height of 28 inches. What is the area of the pennant?

_____

5. **Financial Literacy** Mary is installing carpet in a closet for a customer. A floor plan of the closet is shown. Mary charges $5.60 per square foot of carpet, plus a $150 installation fee.

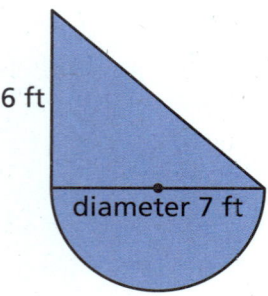

How much should Mary charge the customer to the nearest cent? Use 3.14 for π.

_____

For Problems 6–9, find the area of the composite figure shown to the nearest half unit. Use 3.14 for π.

6.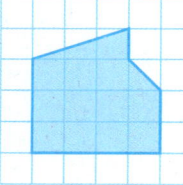

7.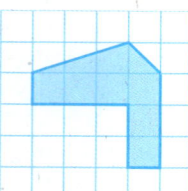

8.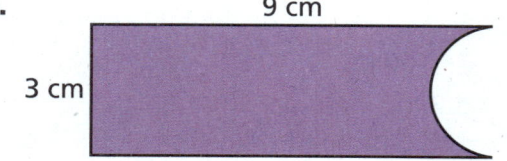

9.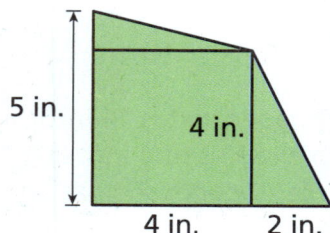

506

Name _____

Areas of Composite Figures

LESSON 16.3
More Practice/Homework

ONLINE Video Tutorials and Interactive Examples

1. A driveway consists of two rectangles. One rectangle is 80 feet long and 15 feet wide. The other is 30 feet long and 30 feet wide. What is the area of the driveway?

   _____

2. **MP Use Tools** A patio is made of two sections. One is shaped like a trapezoid, and the other like a semicircle. The bases of the trapezoid are 12 feet and 8 feet. The height of the trapezoid is 4 feet. The diameter of the semicircle is the same as the trapezoid's shorter base. Use geometry software or another tool to draw a model of the patio. Find the patio's area. Use 3.14 for π.

   _____

3. **Open Ended** Juanita is making a ribbon as shown.

   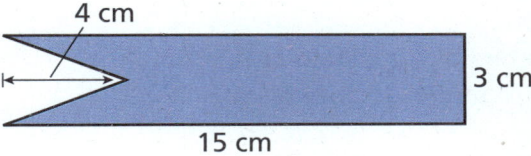

   Explain two different ways you can find the area of the ribbon. Then find the area of the ribbon.

   _____
   _____
   _____
   _____

For Problems 4–5, find the area of the composite figure. Use 3.14 for π.

4.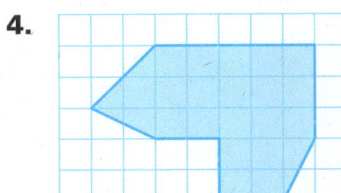

5.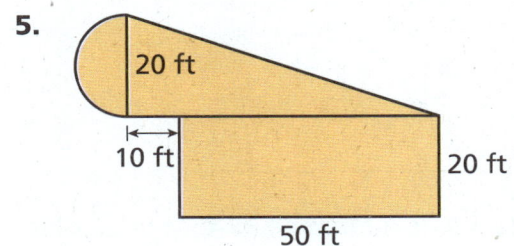

Module 16 • Lesson 3

507

Test Prep

6. A model of a plot of grass behind a building is shown. What is the area of the plot of grass?

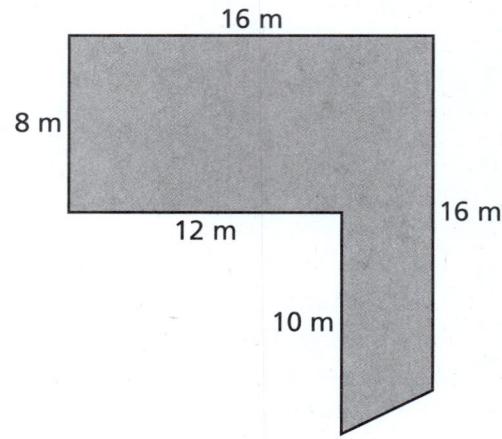

7. Eric is designing a logo for a company. The logo consists of two identical parallelograms joined at their longest sides. One of the parallelograms has a base of 2.5 centimeters and a height of 1.25 centimeters. What is the area of the logo?

8. Find the approximate area of the composite figure. Use 3.14 for π.

   Ⓐ 159.48 cm²   Ⓒ 288 cm²

   Ⓑ 231.48 cm²   Ⓓ 344.52 cm²

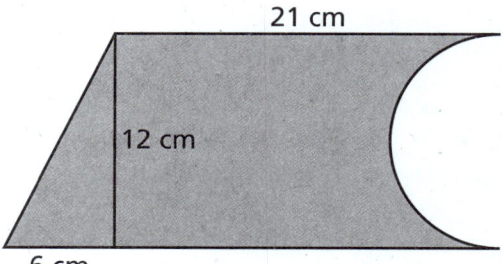

Spiral Review

9. As a sprinkler rotates in a circle, it waters all the grass within 7.5 meters. How many square meters of grass does the sprinkler water? Use 3.14 for π and round your answer to the nearest hundredth of a square meter.

10. What is the perimeter of △FGH shown?

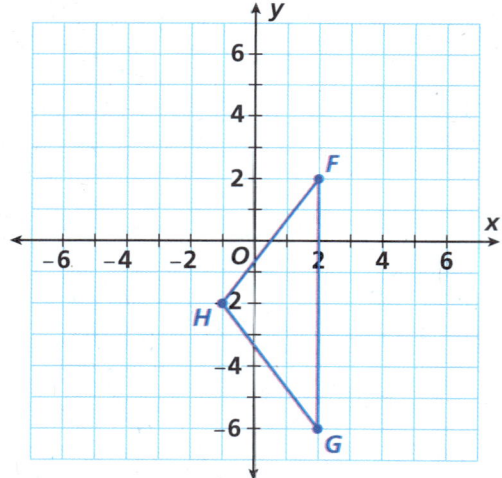

11. A window-washer is climbing a 37-foot ladder leaning against a building. The ladder touches the building 35 feet above the ground. What is the distance from the bottom of the ladder to the base of the building?

Module 16 Review

Vocabulary

Choose the correct term from the Vocabulary box.

Vocabulary
- circumference
- composite figure
- pi

1. The distance around a circle
   _____

2. A figure made up of simple geometric figures
   _____

3. The ratio of the distance around a circle to the distance across the circle
   _____

Concepts and Skills

Use the circle for Problems 4–5.

4. Calculate the circumference of the circle in terms of π.
   _____

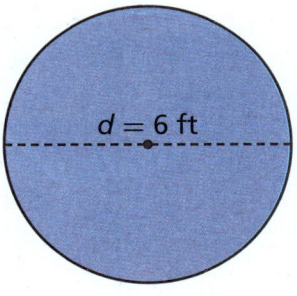
$d = 6$ ft

5. What is the area of the circle in terms of π?
   _____

6. Given that $\pi \approx 3.14$, which values are reasonable for the area of a circle with radius 5 inches? Select all that apply.
   - Ⓐ 10π in²
   - Ⓑ 15.7 in²
   - Ⓒ 25π in²
   - Ⓓ 31.4 in²
   - Ⓔ 78.5 in²

7. **Use Tools** Given that the circumference of a circle is 8π centimeters, calculate the area of the circle in terms of π. State what strategy and tool you will use to answer the question, explain your choice, and then find the answer.
   _____
   _____

Module 16

8. To the nearest square inch, what is the area of a circle with a circumference of 15.8 inches? Use 3.14 for π.

9. A circular garden has a diameter of 24 feet. What is the area of the garden to the nearest hundredth? Use 3.14 for π.

10. A parking lot is a composite figure consisting of two rectangles. One part of the parking lot is 160 feet long and 80 feet wide. The other part is 70 feet long and 45 feet wide. What is the area of the parking lot?

For Problems 11–12, calculate the area of the given figure.

11.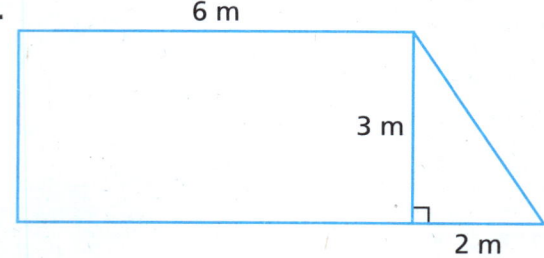

Ⓐ 48 m²

Ⓑ 34 m²

Ⓒ 21 m²

Ⓓ 24 m²

12.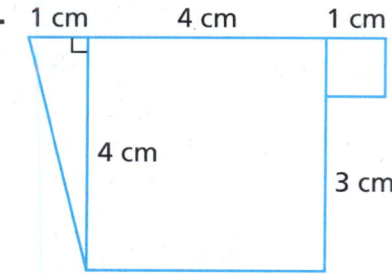

13. The new circular community water fountain has a diameter of 192 feet. What is the area of the surface of the circular community water fountain? Use 3.14 for π. Round to the nearest square foot.

Module 17

Cross Sections, Surface Area, and Volume

The Prism Family

Each of the rectangular prisms shown is made from cubes with an edge length of 1 centimeter. All of the prisms in this family have something in common.

Investigate by finding the dimensions, surface area, and volume of each prism. How are they all related?

A.

Dimensions:

_____, _____, _____

Surface area: _____

Volume: _____

B.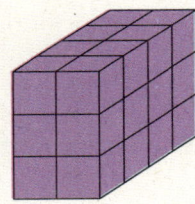

Dimensions:

_____, _____, _____

Surface area: _____

Volume: _____

C.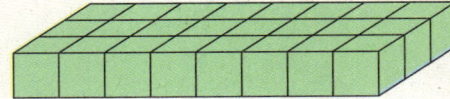

Dimensions:

_____, _____, _____

Surface area: _____

Volume: _____

 Turn and Talk

Describe the family of rectangular prisms.

Are You Ready?

Complete these problems to review prior concepts and skills you will need for this module.

Explore Volume

Each rectangular prism is composed of cubes with an edge length of 1 inch. Determine the volume of each prism.

1. 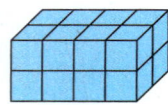 _____ in³

2.  _____ in³

Nets and Surface Area

For Problems 3–4, draw a net of each prism. Then use the net to determine the surface area of the prism.

3.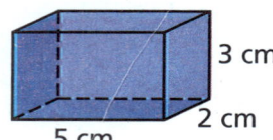

   _____ cm²

4.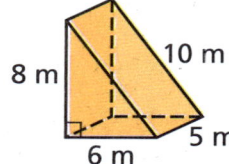

   _____ m²

Area of Circles

For Problems 5–6, determine the area of each circle. Use 3.14 for π. Round each answer to the nearest hundredth.

5.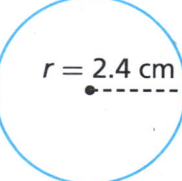

   _____ cm²

6.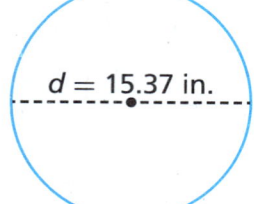

   _____ in²

7. On the ice of a hockey rink, there is one circle with a 12-inch diameter, and one with a 24-inch diameter. How much more area does the larger circle have than the smaller? Explain how you know. Use 3.14 for π.

   _____

   _____

Build Conceptual Understanding

Lesson 1

Name _____

Describe and Analyze Cross Sections of Solids

I Can identify the shapes of cross sections of solids and solve problems involving the areas of cross sections.

Spark Your Learning

Cassie and Amanda are making a cylindrical layer cake with four different-flavored layers. Amanda wants a circular piece of cake with only one flavor. Cassie wants a piece of cake with a rectangular face and all four flavors. Show how each girl could make a single cut to the cake to get the piece she wants. Can both girls get the piece of cake they want from the same cake? Explain.

 **Turn and Talk** For each type of cut, does the location where the cake is cut change the shape of the piece of cake? Explain.

Module 17 • Lesson 1

513

Build Understanding

A **cross section** is an inside view made by making a cut or slice. In this lesson, only cuts made parallel or perpendicular to the base will be shown.

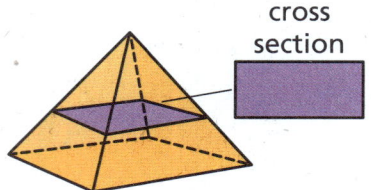

1 Analyze the shipping box shown, which is in the shape of a **rectangular prism** with two square faces. What are the figures formed when slicing the box from different directions?

A. The box is a prism. What polygon describes the two-dimensional bases of this prism? What polygon describes the other faces?

_____
_____

B. Suppose you slice the prism parallel to its base as shown. What two-dimensional figure is the cross section?

_____

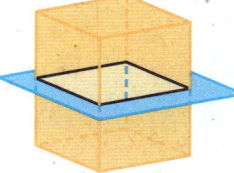

C. Suppose you slice the prism perpendicular to its base as shown. What two-dimensional figure is the cross section?

_____

D. Consider the **pyramid** shown. Identify the two-dimensional base and faces. What is the name of this pyramid?

_____
_____

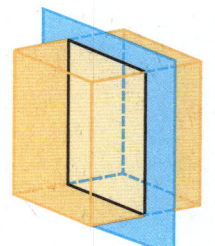

E. Suppose you slice the pyramid parallel to its base. What two-dimensional figure is the cross section?

_____

F. Suppose you slice the pyramid perpendicular to its base, through the vertex. What two-dimensional figure is the cross section?

_____

Name _____

2 Rajesh is doing a research project on the Pentagon, which is located near Washington, D.C. Rajesh sketched a pentagonal prism to help him model the Pentagon.

A. When Rajesh slices the pentagonal prism parallel to the bases, the result is a plane figure that has the same shape as the _____. So the figure is a _____.

B. When you slice the pentagonal prism perpendicular to the bases, the result is a figure of the same type as _____. So the figure of this cross section is a _____.

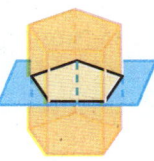 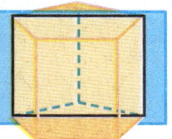

C. Now consider a hexagonal pyramid. The two-dimensional figure that results from slicing the hexagonal pyramid parallel to the base is a _____.

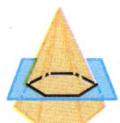 

D. The two-dimensional figure that results from slicing the hexagonal pyramid perpendicular to the base, but not through the vertex, is a _____.

Turn and Talk How are the following related: the shape of a base and the cross section of a slice parallel to the base of a prism or pyramid? The shape of the faces and the cross section of a slice perpendicular to the base?

Check Understanding

1. A triangular prism is sliced parallel to its base. What two-dimensional figure is the cross section? Use a sketch to support your answer.

2. What cross section is made when a hexagonal pyramid like the one in Task 2 is sliced perpendicular to its base through its vertex?

   _____

3. Suppose the box of cereal shown is sliced parallel to its base. What is the resulting cross section?

   _____

4. Compare the cross sections made from slicing the cereal box parallel to its base and slicing it perpendicular to its base.

   _____
   _____

Module 17 • Lesson 1

On Your Own

For Problems 5 and 6, use the picture of the hotel with a roof in the shape of a regular pentagonal pyramid.

5. **Use Structure** Describe how the roof can be sliced to make a cross section in the shape of a pentagon.

6. **Use Structure** Describe how the roof can be sliced to make a cross section in the shape of a triangle.

7. **Reason** The diameter of a sphere is 8 inches. What are the circumference and area of the cross section formed by a plane slicing through the sphere's center? Round to the nearest hundredth. Use 3.14 for π.

For Problems 8–13, identify the shape of the two-dimensional cross section shown.

8. perpendicular to base of a rectangular prism

9. perpendicular to base, not through vertex of a rectangular pyramid

10. perpendicular to base and through vertex of a square pyramid

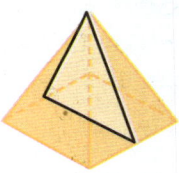

11. parallel to base of a pentagonal prism

12. parallel to base of a hexagonal prism

13. parallel to base of a square pyramid

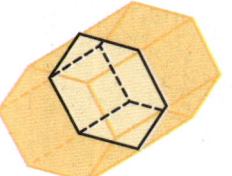
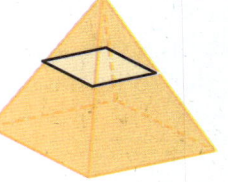

I'm in a Learning Mindset!

What methods are most effective for analyzing cross sections of solids?

Describe and Analyze Cross Sections of Solids

LESSON 17.1 More Practice/ Homework

For Problems 1 and 2, describe the two-dimensional figure that results from slicing the given three-dimensional figure.

1. Slice parallel to the base

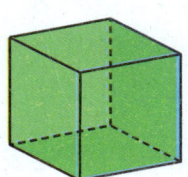

2. Slice perpendicular to the base, not through the vertex

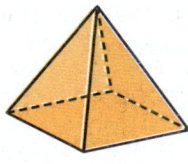

For Problems 3–5, tell whether the slice must be parallel or perpendicular to the base to make the given cross section.

3. A slice of a pentagonal pyramid results in a pentagon.

4. A slice of a triangular prism results in a triangle.

5. A slice of a hexagonal pyramid results in a triangle.

6. **Use Repeated Reasoning** A sphere has a radius of 12 inches.

   A. Describe the cross section formed by slicing through the sphere's center.

   B. Describe the cross sections formed by slicing the sphere many times, each time farther from the center of the sphere.

7. **Use Structure** What cross sections might you see when slicing a cone that you would not see when slicing a pyramid or a prism?

Module 17 • Lesson 1

Test Prep

8. Two chefs are working on cylindrical cakes. David wants to make a stripe of frosting in his cake, and he makes a cut that shows a rectangle. Terri wants to put a layer of frosting in the middle of her cake, so she makes a cut that shows a circle. How was Terri's cut different from David's?

   _____

9. Select all of the following three-dimensional figures that could have a cross section of a triangle when sliced parallel to the base, perpendicular to the base through the vertex, or perpendicular to the base *not* through the vertex.

   Ⓐ cone   Ⓓ triangular pyramid
   Ⓑ triangular prism   Ⓔ sphere
   Ⓒ rectangular prism

10. Match each description of slicing a three-dimensional figure with the resulting two-dimensional figure shown.

    Slice a square pyramid parallel to base

    Slice a non-square rectangular prism parallel to base

    Slice a square pyramid perpendicular to base through the vertex

    Slice a pentagonal prism parallel to base

    A (rectangle)
    B (pentagon)
    C (square)
    D (triangle)

Spiral Review

11. Find the area of the composite figure.

    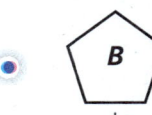

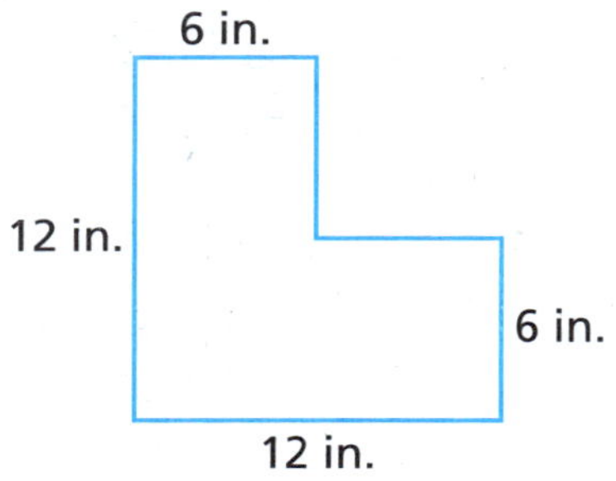

    6 in.
    12 in.
    6 in.
    12 in.

    _____

12. How many unique triangles can be made with the angle measures 48°, 64°, and 68°: none, one, or infinitely many?

    _____

Connect Concepts and Skills
Lesson 2

Name _____

Derive and Apply Formulas for Surface Areas of Cubes and Right Prisms

I Can derive and apply the formulas for surface area of any right prism.

Spark Your Learning *SMALL GROUPS*

Sara is wrapping a gift box with dimensions 10 inches by 14 inches by 5 inches with wrapping paper. What is the least amount of wrapping paper she will need to cover the gift box without any overlap?

Turn and Talk What is the difference between area and surface area?

Module 17 • Lesson 2   519

Build Understanding

1 A wooden toy box is represented by the net shown with it.

A. How many faces make up the toy box? How does the net show these faces?

_____

_____

B. Are any of the faces congruent? If so, which ones?

_____

_____

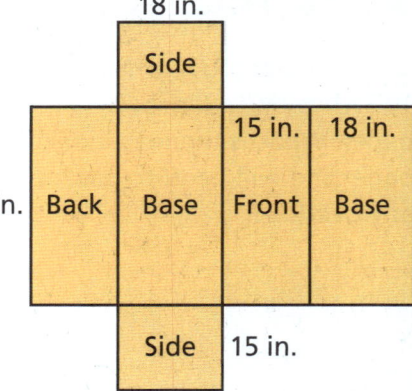

C. What is the shape of the two bases? What is their combined area?

_____

D. What is the combined area of the front and back faces?

_____

E. What is the combined area of the left and right faces?

_____

F. How can you find the total **surface area** of the box? What is this value?

_____

G. Use the net to derive a formula for surface area of a box with length ℓ, width w, and height h:

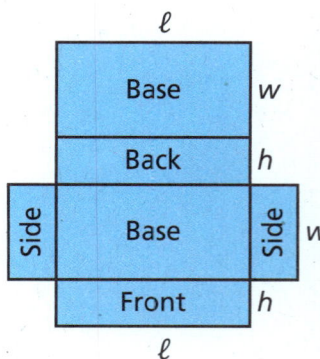

Surface area = $2\ell w +$ ☐ + ☐

Since ℓw is the area of a | base / front or back / side |, replace ℓw with B: $2B + 2\ell h + 2wh$.

Both parts of the expression $2\ell h + 2wh$ contain an h, so factor it out: $2B + h($ ☐ + ☐ $)$.

Since $2\ell + 2w$ represents the | area / perimeter | of the base, replace $2\ell + 2w$ with P:

Surface Area = $2B +$ ☐ h

Turn and Talk How could you change the surface area formula for a cube to make it simpler?

Step It Out

The surface area of a right prism is $S = 2B + Ph$, where B is the base area, P is the base perimeter, and h is the height of the prism.

2 A foundation has the water bottle shown as giveaways for its annual fundraiser. What is the approximate surface area of the water bottle, treating the top surface as flat and ignoring the spout?

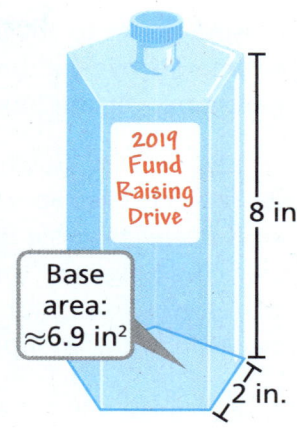

A. From the picture, the area of the base is approximately ☐ square inches and the height is ☐ inches.

The perimeter of the base is ☐ × ☐ = ☐ inches.

B. Find the approximate surface area. Treat the top surface as flat. Ignore the spout.

$S = 2B + Ph$

$S \approx 2\boxed{} + \boxed{}(\boxed{})$

$S \approx \boxed{} + \boxed{}$

$S \approx \boxed{}$

The surface area of the water bottle is approximately ☐ square inches.

Check Understanding

1. A couch cushion needs to be covered with fabric. The dimensions of the cushion are 1.5 feet long by 1.5 feet wide by 0.5 foot high. What is the least amount of fabric needed to cover the couch cushion?

2. Bobby is sanding a five-sided storage chest with the dimensions shown. The base is a regular pentagon. If he sands only the outside of the chest, how much area must he sand?

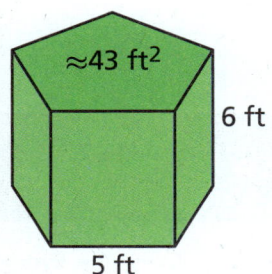

3. A photographer's darkroom needs a new coat of black paint on all surfaces of the room, including the ceiling and the floor. The room is a cube with edge length 11 feet. How much surface area must be painted?

Module 17 • Lesson 2

On Your Own

4. Lily is using paper to cover a box with dimensions 7 centimeters by 10 centimeters by 5 centimeters. What is the least amount of paper Lily will need to cover the box? _____

5. **(MP) Use Structure** Gavin is making a scale replica of a tent for his social studies project. The replica is in the shape of a triangular prism. It has an isosceles triangle base with side lengths 6 inches, 5 inches, and 5 inches. The height of the triangle is 4 inches, and the depth of the tent is 7 inches. How much fabric will Gavin need to make the outside of the replica, including the "floor"? _____

6. Blake made a storage bin out of poles in the shape of a regular hexagonal prism, as shown. He wants to cover the surface area of the prism, including the floor, with a tarp to protect his things from the weather. What is the approximate surface area that the tarp will cover? Explain.

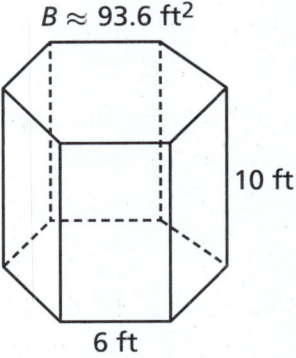

_____

_____

Find the surface area of each prism.

7.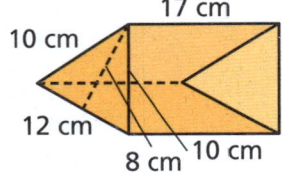

8.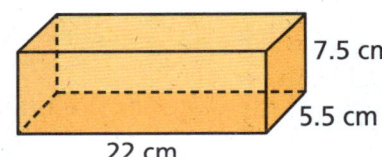

_____

9.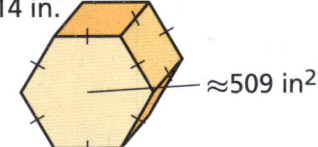

10.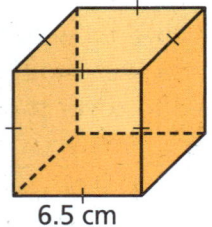

_____

I'm in a Learning Mindset!

How does using the formulas for surface area of right prisms help me find surface area more efficiently?

_____

_____

Name _____

Derive and Apply Formulas for Surface Areas of Cubes and Right Prisms

LESSON 17.2
More Practice/ Homework

ONLINE Video Tutorials and Interactive Examples

1. **(MP) Use Structure** Melissa baked a cake. The box for the cake is in the shape of a cube with edges 9 inches in length. Draw a supporting picture and find how many square inches of cardboard are needed to make the box.

2. Sue is upholstering a rectangular ottoman that measures 21 centimeters by 18 centimeters by 15 centimeters. What will be the total square centimeters of fabric that Sue must use to cover all faces of the ottoman?

   _____

3. A drawing of the attic in a house is shown. It needs insulation on all sides. How many square feet of insulation are needed?

   _____

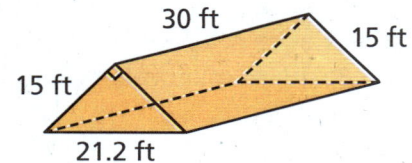

Find the surface area of each prism.

4. **Math on the Spot**

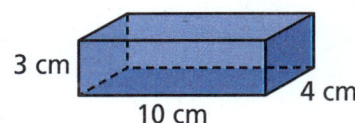

5.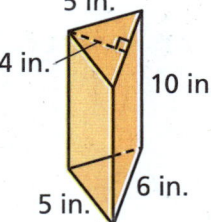

   _____   _____

Find the surface area. Round to the nearest tenth if necessary.

6. Regular pentagon base

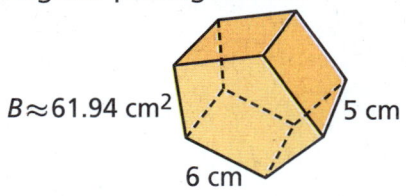

7.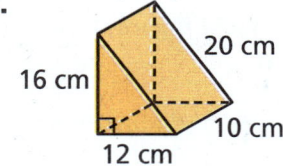

Module 17 • Lesson 2

523

Test Prep

8. Find the surface area of the figure.

    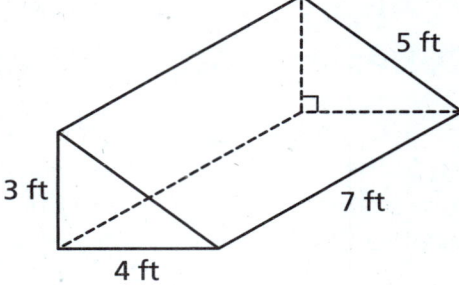

    A) 41 ft²
    B) 69 ft²
    C) 75 ft²
    D) 96 ft²

9. Mark bought a jewelry box in the shape of a cube. The jewelry box has edge lengths of 6 inches. What is the total surface area of the jewelry box?

    A) 36 in²
    B) 108 in²
    C) 216 in²
    D) 1,296 in²

10. Find the surface area of a rectangular prism with length of 4.7 inches, width of 6.4 inches, and height of 8.2 inches. Round to the nearest tenth.

    _____

11. The height of a regular hexagonal prism is 3.9 millimeters, and each side of its base is 4.2 millimeters long. The area of the base is approximately 45.8 square millimeters. Find the surface area of the prism. Round to the nearest tenth.

    _____

Spiral Review

12. Identify the two-dimensional figure that results from slicing a cylinder parallel to its base.

    _____

13. Find the area of the composite figure.

    _____

    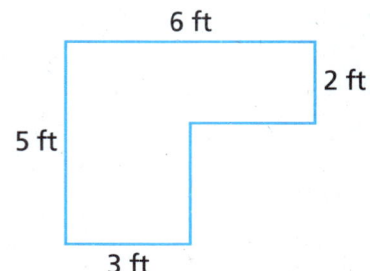

Connect Concepts and Skills

Lesson 3

Name _____

Derive and Apply a Formula for the Volume of a Right Prism

I Can accurately apply the formula to find the volume of right prisms.

Spark Your Learning

Use unit cubes or graph paper to find how many 1-inch cubes could fit into a rectangular prism with edge lengths shown. Describe how you found your answer.

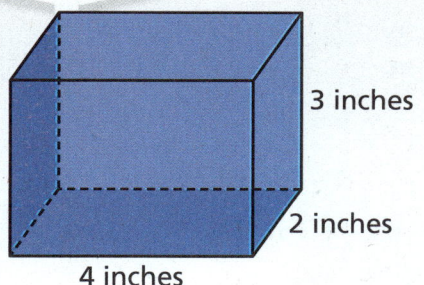

3 inches
2 inches
4 inches

Turn and Talk How are the dimensions of the box related to the number of unit cubes required to fill it?

Module 17 • Lesson 3   525

Build Understanding

1 To derive the formula for volume of any right prism, imagine filling a right rectangular prism with 1-inch cubes.

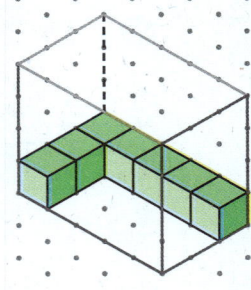

A. How many 1-inch cubes can be placed along the length of the prism shown here? The width of the prism?

_____

B. How many cubes are needed to make one horizontal layer in the prism? Explain how you found your answer.

_____
_____

C. How is completing the first layer like finding the area of the base or a cross section of the prism? How is it different?

_____
_____
_____

D. How will the number of cubes needed to make the first layer compare to the number of cubes needed to complete any other layer?

_____

E. How many layers will it take to fill the prism shown? How did you find your answer?

_____
_____

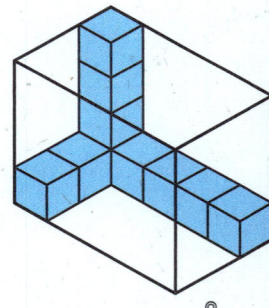

F. Using the concept of "layers," how can you determine the number of cubes it will take to fill up the entire volume of the prism? What is the volume of the prism?

_____
_____

G. Using Parts A through F, complete the statements to derive the formula for the volume V of a right prism.

V = (length × _____) × _____

V = area of the _____ × _____

Turn and Talk Using what you know about the formulas for area of triangles and trapezoids, will this same formula work for other types of prisms?

Step It Out

The formula for volume, $V = Bh$, is the area of the base (B) of a prism multiplied by its height (h).

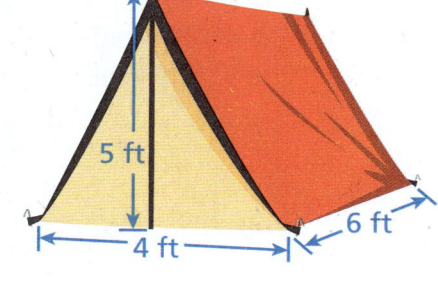

2 Find the volume of the tent shown.

A. Since the tent is shaped like a prism, the base of the prism is a triangle / rectangle.

B. Write an expression for the area of the base of the prism.

$B = (\square)(\square)(\square)$

C. The length of the tent is $\square$ feet. This represents the base / height of the prism.

D. Use the formula.

$V = Bh$

$V = (\square \cdot \square \cdot \square)\square = \square$ ft³

3 A hexagonal prism has a volume of 60 cubic centimeters. The hexagonal base has an area of 12 square centimeters. Find the height of the prism.

A. The base of this prism is a hexagon / rectangle.

B. Use the formula.

$V = Bh$

$\square = \square h$

$\square = h$; So, the height of the hexagonal prism is $\square$ centimeters.

Check Understanding

1. A rectangular sandbox measures 4 feet by 7 feet by 2 feet. How many cubic feet of sand can the sandbox hold? _____

2. A triangular prism has a base length of 1.5 centimeters, a base height of 3 centimeters, and a height of 12 centimeters.

   A. Find the volume of the prism. _____

   B. A pentagonal prism has the same volume as the triangular prism in Part A. Its base has an area of $4\frac{1}{2}$ square centimeters. Find its height.

Module 17 • Lesson 3

On Your Own

3. Leah is filling a cube-shaped box with packing material and gift items. Each edge length of the box is 20 inches. What is the largest possible volume of all the presents inside the box?

4. **(MP) Use Structure** A lantern is represented by the pentagonal prism shown. What is the area of the base of the lantern? Explain your reasoning. Round to the nearest tenth.

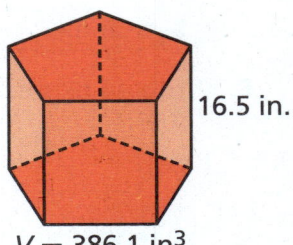

16.5 in.

$V = 386.1$ in^3

5. A rectangular fish tank can hold 142.5 cubic meters of water. Its base is 9.5 meters by 5 meters. What is the height?

6. A triangular prism has the dimensions shown. What is the length x if its volume is 72 cubic feet?

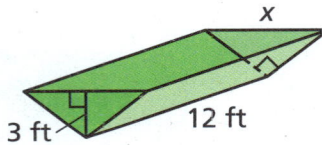

For Problems 7–8, find the volume of the figure.

7.
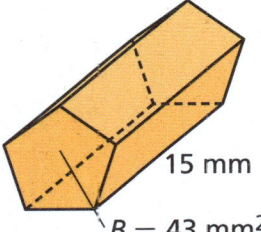

8.
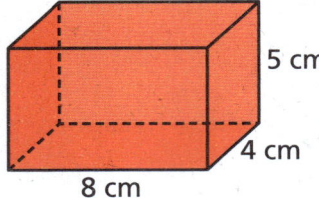

I'm in a Learning Mindset!

Did I manage my time well when I applied the formulas for volumes of right prisms? What can I do to manage my time better?

Name _____

Derive and Apply a Formula for the Volume of a Right Prism

LESSON 17.3
More Practice/Homework

ONLINE
Video Tutorials and Interactive Examples

1. The Truit family rented a cabin in the shape of a triangular prism. The cabin is 30 feet deep. What is the volume of the cabin?
   _____

2. A piece of copper tubing is in the shape of a hexagonal prism. The area of the base of the prism is 3 square centimeters. The volume of the prism is 51 cubic centimeters. What is the length of the tubing?
   _____

3. **Open Ended** A restaurant's walk-in commercial refrigerator has a capacity of 120 cubic feet. It is a rectangular prism 6 feet tall. Using graph paper, model the possible dimensions of the length and width of the refrigerator's footprint. (Hint: Have each square on the graph paper represent one square foot.) Are your answers reasonable? Explain.
   _____
   _____
   _____
   _____
   _____

4. **Math on the Spot** Find the volume of the triangular prism.

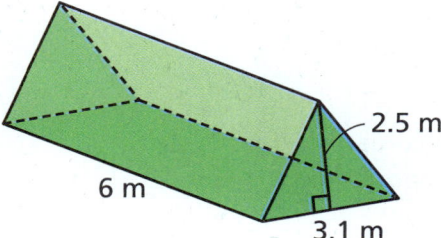

_____

For Problems 5–6, find the volume of each figure.

5.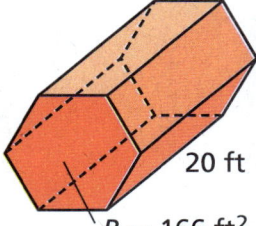

   20 ft
   $B = 166$ ft²

6.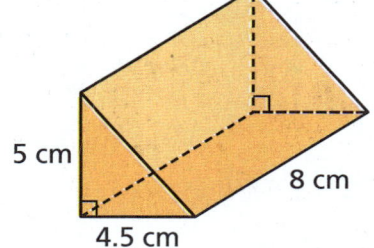

   5 cm
   8 cm
   4.5 cm

Module 17 • Lesson 3   529

Test Prep

7. Jerome bought an aquarium that measured 12 inches by 18 inches by 24 inches. Lim bought an aquarium that was 12 inches by 30 inches by 12 inches. Both aquariums are rectangular prisms. How much more volume does Jerome's aquarium have than Lim's?

   _____

8. An attic for a dollhouse is represented by a triangular prism with the dimensions shown. What is the volume of the attic?

   Ⓐ 11.5 in³   Ⓒ 44 in³

   Ⓑ 22 in³   Ⓓ 88 in³

   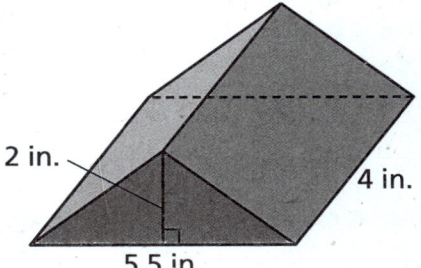

9. The volume of an octagonal prism is 1,260 cubic meters. The base has an area of 28 square meters. Write and solve an equation to find the height of the prism.

   _____

10. A rectangular prism has a volume of 98 cubic feet, a width of 2 feet, and a length of 7 feet. Find the height of the rectangular prism.

    _____

Spiral Review

11. Use geometry software to draw a quadrilateral with two pairs of parallel sides and four right angles. What is the quadrilateral?

    _____

12. Find the surface area of the right triangular prism.

    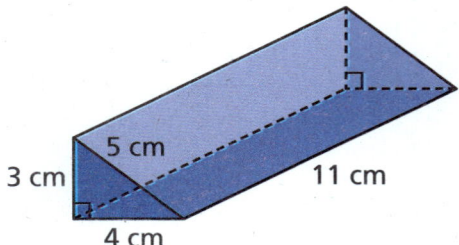

13. Find the approximate surface area of the regular pentagonal prism.

    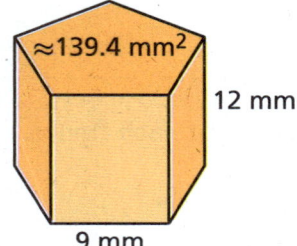

530

Lesson 4

Find Volume of Cylinders

I Can find the volume of a cylinder or the dimensions of a cylinder given the volume.

Spark Your Learning

You have seen that the volume of a rectangular prism is the area of the base times the height. This may be written as $V = Bh$. Since the area of the rectangular base is the length times the width, the formula can also be written as $V = \ell wh$.

Rectangular Prism

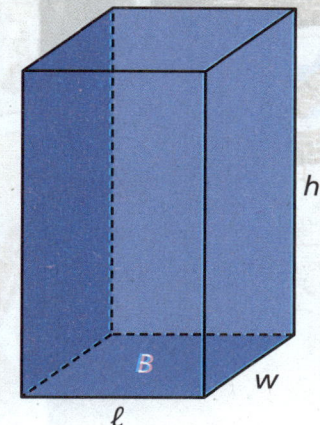

Cylinder

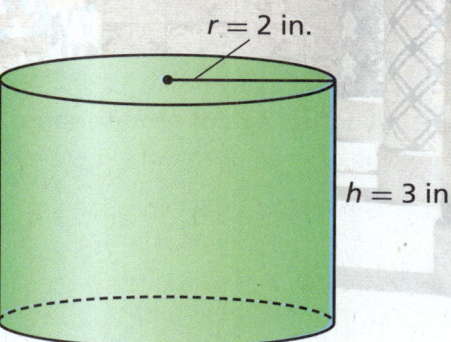

The base of a cylinder is a circle. What is the volume of the cylinder shown? (*Hint*: Recall that the formula for the area A of a circle is $A = \pi r^2$.) Show your steps.

Turn and Talk How is finding the volume of a cylinder similar to finding the volume of a rectangular prism? How is it different?

Module 17 • Lesson 4

Build Understanding

The formula for the volume of a cylinder is similar to the formula for the volume of a rectangular prism. The formula states that the volume V is the product of the area of the base B and the height h. The only difference is in how to calculate B. You can use the fact that the base of a cylinder is a circle to write the formula in terms of the radius r.

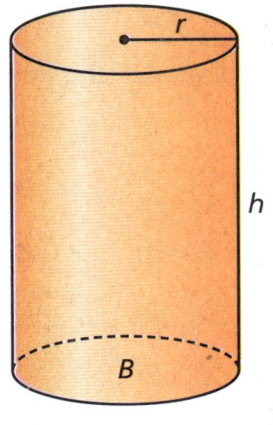

Connect to Vocabulary

A cylinder is a three-dimensional figure with two parallel, congruent circular bases connected by a curved lateral surface.

$V = Bh$

or

$V = \pi r^2 h$

1. Find the volume of the cylindrical can of tomato soup shown. Leave your answer in terms of π.

   A. What information do you need to know in order to use the formula $V = \pi r^2 h$?

   _____

   _____

   B. What are the radius and the height of the cylinder?

   _____

   _____

   C. Show how to substitute for r and h in the formula. Then simplify and leave your answer in terms of π. Be sure to include an appropriate unit for the volume.

   _____

   _____

   _____

   D. Now show how to use 3.14 as an approximation for π. Round the volume to the nearest tenth.

   _____

   _____

   _____

 **Turn and Talk** How can you use estimation to show that the volume you found is reasonable?

Step It Out

2 Find the volume of the cylinder shown. First write the volume in terms of π. Then substitute 3.14 for π, and express the volume in scientific notation with the first factor rounded to the nearest tenth.

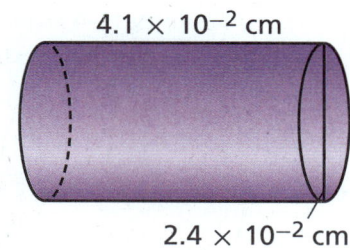

4.1 × 10⁻² cm

2.4 × 10⁻² cm

The diameter is 2.4×10^{-2} centimeter, so the radius is

_____ × 10 [ ] centimeter.

Now use the formula for the volume of a cylinder.

$V = \pi r^2 h$

$= \pi(\underline{\hspace{1cm}} \times 10^{-2})^2 (\underline{\hspace{1cm}} \times 10^{-2})$

$= \pi(\underline{\hspace{1cm}} \times 10^{-4})(\underline{\hspace{1cm}} \times 10^{-2})$

$\approx (3.14)(\underline{\hspace{1cm}} \times 10^{\boxed{}})$

$\approx \underline{\hspace{1cm}} \times 10^{-6}$

$\approx \underline{\hspace{1cm}} \times 10^{-5}$ cubic centimeter

3 The volume of the cylinder shown is 602.88 cubic feet. Find the height of the cylinder. Use 3.14 for π.

4 ft

Use the formula for the volume of a cylinder to solve for h.

$V = \pi r^2 h$

_____ $\approx (3.14)(\underline{\hspace{1cm}})^2 h$

_____ $\approx (3.14)(\underline{\hspace{1cm}}) h$

_____ $\approx (\underline{\hspace{1cm}}) h$

$h \approx \dfrac{\boxed{}}{\boxed{}} = \underline{\hspace{1cm}}$ feet

Check Understanding

1. The volume of this cylinder is 32π yd³. Find the height.

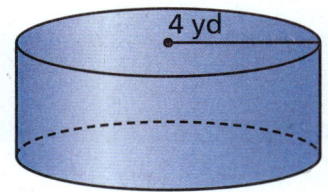

4 yd

2. Find the volume to the nearest tenth. Use 3.14 for π.

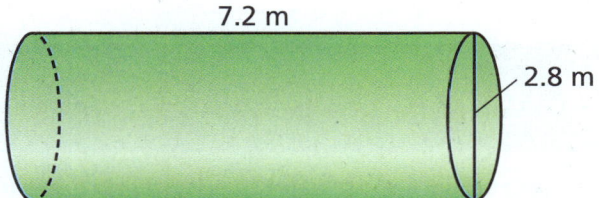

7.2 m

2.8 m

Module 17 • Lesson 4 533

On Your Own

For Problems 3–4, find the volume of each cylinder. Use 3.14 for π. Round the volume to the nearest tenth.

3.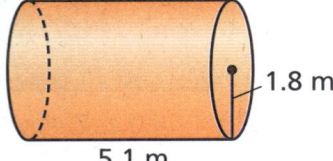

4.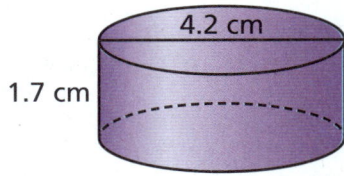

_____   _____

For Problems 5–6, find the approximate height of each cylinder. Use 3.14 for π.

5. Volume = 37.68 in³

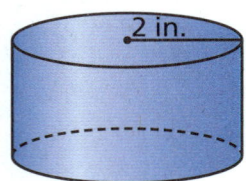

6. Volume = 146.952 cm³

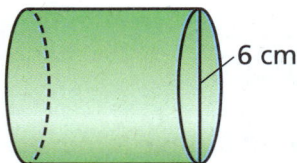

_____   _____

7. Find the approximate volume of the cylinder shown. Use 3.14 for π. Express the volume in scientific notation and round the first factor to the nearest tenth. _____

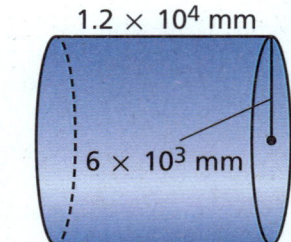

8. **Open Ended** Give the radius and height of a cylinder whose volume is greater than 1,000 cubic feet but less than 2,000 cubic feet. _____

9. **(MP) Attend to Precision** Consider a cylinder with the radius and height shown in the image.

   A. Find the approximate volume of the cylinder using the π key on your calculator. Round your answer in a way that seems most appropriate.

   _____

   B. Explain how you decided how many digits to include in your answer.

   _____
   _____

I'm in a Learning Mindset!

What methods are most effective in helping me use the formula for the volume of a cylinder?

_____

Name _____

Find Volume of Cylinders

LESSON 17.4
More Practice/ Homework

ONLINE Video Tutorials and Interactive Examples

1. The radius of a cylinder is 49 feet, and the height is 180 feet. Find the volume of the cylinder. Leave your answer in terms of π.

   _____

2. **Math on the Spot** Find the approximate volume of each cylinder. Use 3.14 for π. Round the volume to the nearest cubic unit.

   A. 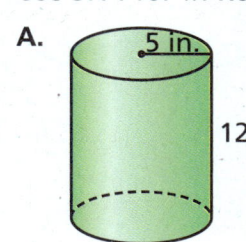   B. 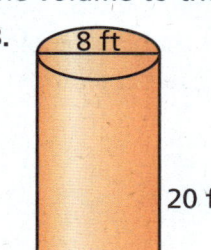   C.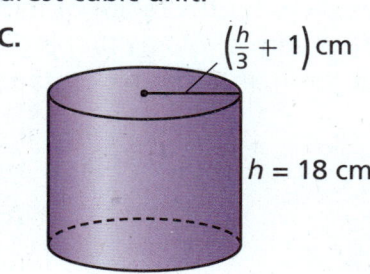

For Problems 3–4, approximate the volume of each cylinder. Use 3.14 for π. Round the volume to the nearest cubic unit.

3. 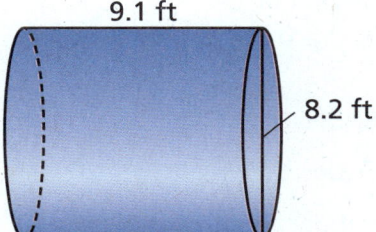   4.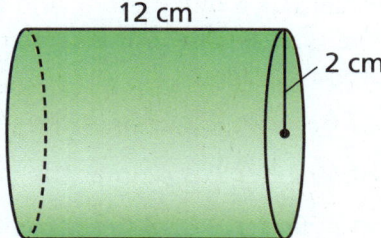

5. A cylinder has diameter d and height h. Write a formula for the volume V of the cylinder in terms of d and h.

   _____

For Problems 6–7, find the approximate height of each cylinder. Use 3.14 for π.

6. Volume = 7.85 ft³   7. Volume = 668.6944 m³

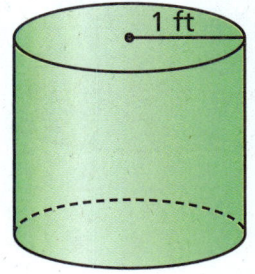   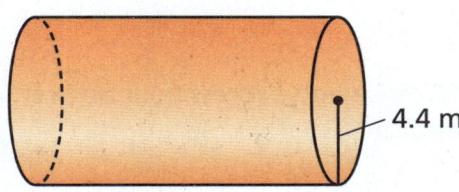

Module 17 • Lesson 4   535

Test Prep

8. Which of the following values for the radius and height of a cylinder result in a cylinder with the greatest volume?

   Ⓐ radius = 1 ft; height = 4 ft
   Ⓒ radius = 3 ft; height = 2 ft
   Ⓑ radius = 2 ft; height = 3 ft
   Ⓓ radius = 4 ft; height = 1 ft

9. Which value or values for the radius of the cylinder shown result in a cylinder with a volume that is greater than 100 cubic centimeters but less than 600 cubic centimeters? Select all that apply.

   Ⓐ 1 cm
   Ⓓ 6 cm
   Ⓑ 3 cm
   Ⓔ 8 cm
   Ⓒ 5 cm
   Ⓕ 10 cm

10. The cylinder shown has a volume of 62.8 cubic inches. Which of the following is closest to the height of the cylinder?

   Ⓐ 5 in.
   Ⓒ 20 in.
   Ⓑ 10 in.
   Ⓓ 30 in.

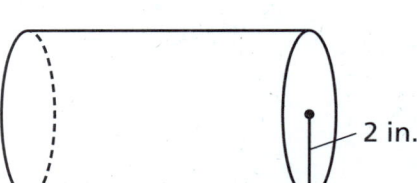

11. The radius of Cylinder P is 6 millimeters, and the radius of Cylinder Q is 3 millimeters. The cylinders have the same height. Which is a true statement about the cylinders?

   Ⓐ The volume of Cylinder P is 2 times the volume of Cylinder Q.
   Ⓑ The volume of Cylinder P is 4 times the volume of Cylinder Q.
   Ⓒ The volume of Cylinder P is 18 times the volume of Cylinder Q.
   Ⓓ The volume of Cylinder P is 36 times the volume of Cylinder Q.

Spiral Review

12. Find the height of the cone. Round your answer to the nearest tenth of a centimeter.

   _____

13. Write the number 0.0000000058 in scientific notation.

   _____

14. Find the difference and express your answer in scientific notation.

   $(3.4 \times 10^6) - (4.9 \times 10^5)$

   _____

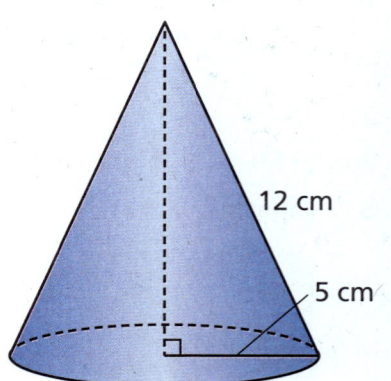

Apply and Practice
Lesson 5

Name _____

Find Volume of Cones and Spheres

I Can find the volume of a cone and a sphere, and find the dimensions of a cone and a sphere, given their volumes.

Step It Out

1 In a **right cone**, a line drawn from the vertex perpendicular to the base passes through the center of the base. The distance from the vertex to the center of the base is the height of the right cone.

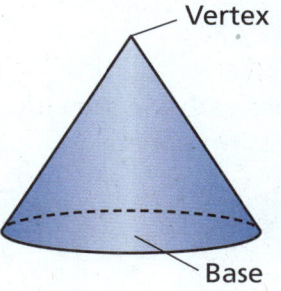

You can use the following reasoning to develop a formula for the volume of a cone.

A. Consider a cone with radius r and height h. Imagine that the cone is made of cardboard and has an open top, as shown. Also, consider a cylinder with the same radius and the same height.

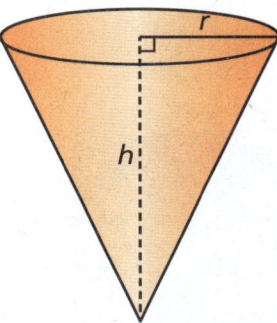
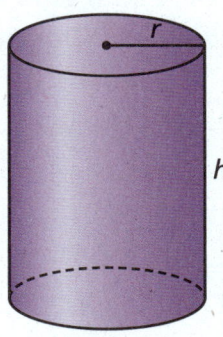

You can fill the cone with sand and pour the sand into the cylinder. It takes 3 cones full of sand to fill the cylinder completely.

This means the volume of the cone is ____ the volume of the cylinder.

B. Complete the following to write a formula for the volume of a cone.

volume of cone = $\dfrac{\Box}{\Box}$ volume of cylinder

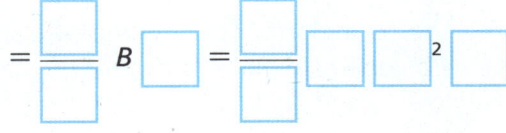

Turn and Talk How is the formula for the volume of a cone similar to the formula for the volume of a cylinder? How is it different?

Module 17 • Lesson 5

537

2 A **sphere** is a three-dimensional figure with all points the same distance from the center. The radius of a sphere is the distance from the center to any point on the sphere.

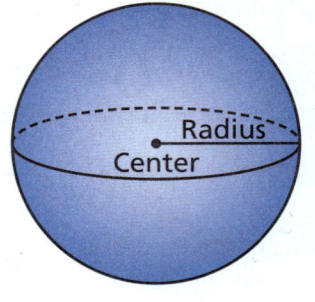

You can use the following reasoning to develop a formula for the volume of a sphere.

A. Start with a sphere of radius r. How is the height of the sphere related to the radius?

$h = $ _____ r

B. Consider a cylinder with the same radius and the same height as the sphere.

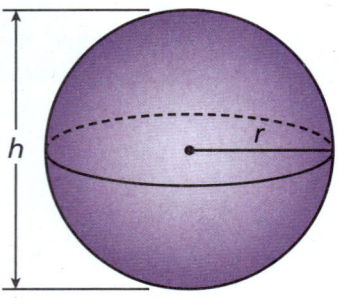 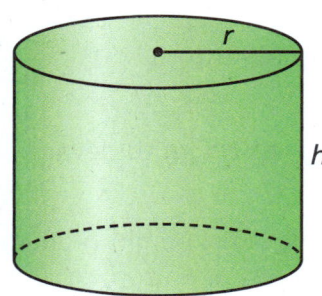

Imagine filling the sphere with sand and pouring the sand into the cylinder. The sand will fill $\frac{2}{3}$ of the cylinder.

volume of sphere = $\dfrac{\square}{\square}$ volume of cylinder

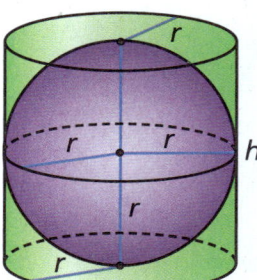

$= \dfrac{\square}{\square} \pi r^2 h$

$= \dfrac{\square}{\square} \pi r^2 (\underline{})$

$= \dfrac{\square}{\square} \pi r^3$

 Turn and Talk How is the formula for the volume of a sphere similar to the formula for the volume of a cone? How is it different?

Name _____

3 ▶ You can use a formula to find the volume of a cone when you know, or can calculate, its radius and height.

The cone-shaped party hat shown here has a radius of 3 inches. Find the volume of the cone. Use $\frac{22}{7}$ for π.

$V = \frac{1}{3}\pi r^2 h$

$\approx \frac{1}{3}\left(\frac{22}{7}\right)(\underline{\hspace{1cm}})^2(\underline{\hspace{1cm}})$

$= \frac{1}{3}\left(\frac{22}{7}\right)(\underline{\hspace{1cm}})(\underline{\hspace{1cm}})$

$= \underline{\hspace{1cm}}$

The volume of the cone is approximately _____ cubic inches.

7 in.

4 ▶ You can use a formula to find the volume of a sphere when you are given or can calculate its radius.

Approximate the volume of the sphere. Use $\frac{22}{7}$ for π and leave your answer as an improper fraction.

To find the volume, use the volume formula with

$r = \underline{\hspace{1cm}}$.

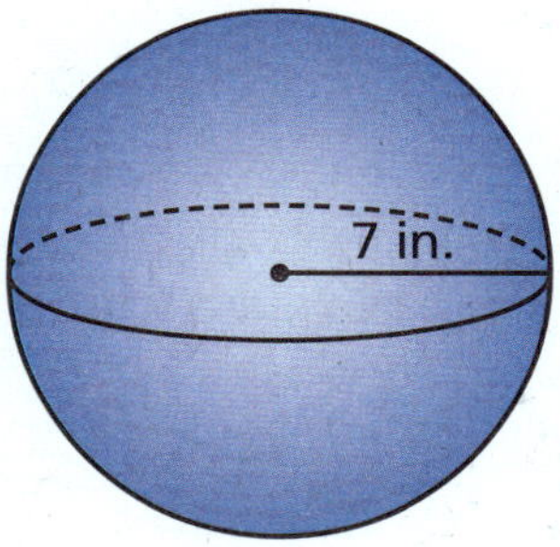

$V = \frac{4}{3}\pi r^3$

$\approx \frac{4}{3}\left(\frac{22}{7}\right)(\underline{\hspace{1cm}})^3$

$= \frac{4}{3}\left(\frac{22}{7}\right)(\underline{\hspace{1cm}})$

$= \underline{\hspace{1cm}}$

7 in.

The volume of the sphere is approximately _____ cubic inches.

Check Understanding

1. **A.** A cone has a radius of 6 inches and a slant height of 10 inches. What is the height of the cone? _____

   B. What is the volume of the cone in Part A? Leave your answer in terms of π. _____

2. Approximate the volume of a sphere with a diameter of 20 meters. Leave your answer in terms of π. Then use 3.14 for π and round the volume to the nearest tenth.

_____

Module 17 • Lesson 5

539

On Your Own

3. The cone-shaped candle shown has a radius of 6 centimeters.

   A. Find the volume of the cone. Leave your answer in terms of π.

   B. **Construct Arguments** A cylinder has the same radius and height as the cone. What is the volume of the cylinder in terms of π? Explain how you know.

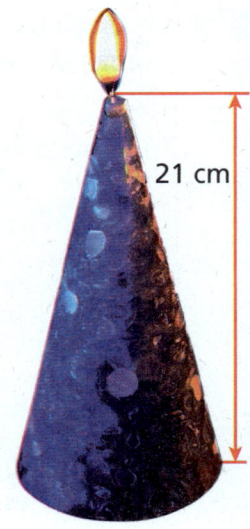

21 cm

4. Consider the spherical marble shown in the photo.

   A. **Attend to Precision** What is the volume? Leave your answer in terms of π. Round the first factor in scientific notation to the nearest tenth.

   B. Find the volume of the marble to the nearest cubic millimeter using $\frac{22}{7}$ for π. Explain your method.

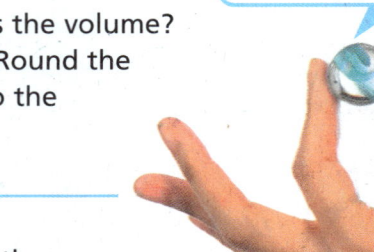

Radius 5×10^{-3} m

For Problems 5–6, find the approximate volume of the cone. Use 3.14 for π and round the volume to the nearest tenth.

5.
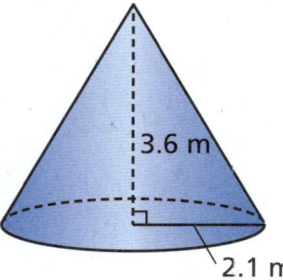
3.6 m, 2.1 m

6.
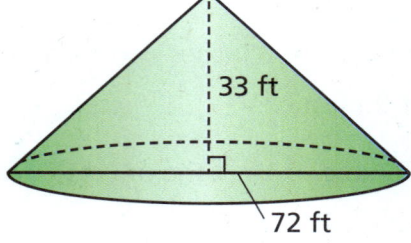
33 ft, 72 ft

Use the cone-shaped hedge shown to answer Problems 7–8.

7. What is the volume of the cone? Leave your answer in terms of π.

_____

8. Find the approximate volume of the cone using $\frac{22}{7}$ for π. Round the volume to the nearest tenth.

_____

9. The radius of a basketball is 12 centimeters. Approximate the volume of the basketball. Use $\frac{22}{7}$ for π and round the volume to the nearest tenth.

_____

For Problems 10–12, find the approximate volume of each sphere. Use 3.14 for π and round the volume to the nearest tenth.

10.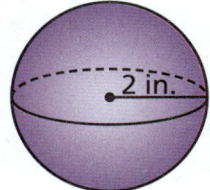

11.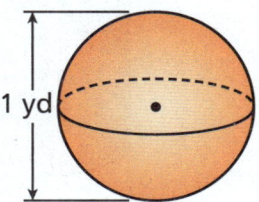

_____

12.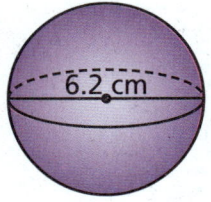

_____

For Problems 13–14, find the approximate volume of each cone. Use 3.14 for π.

13.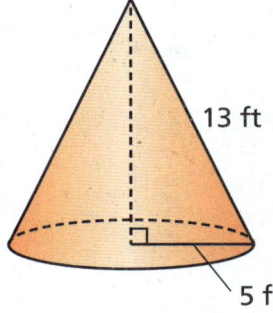

14.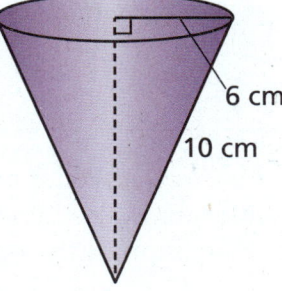

_____

Module 17 • Lesson 5

541

15. **Open Ended** In the photo, V represents the volume of the spherical plant shown. Determine a possible radius for the sphere. Justify your answer.

_____

_____

_____

16. **Critique Reasoning** The cone and cylinder shown have the same radius. The height of the cylinder is 3 times the height of the cone. Jared looked at the solids and concluded that the volume of the cylinder must be 3 times the volume of the cone. Therefore, he said the volume of the cylinder is 3 × 40, or 120 cubic centimeters.

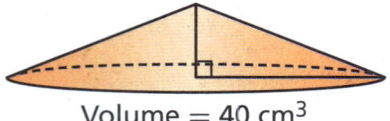

Volume = 40 cm³

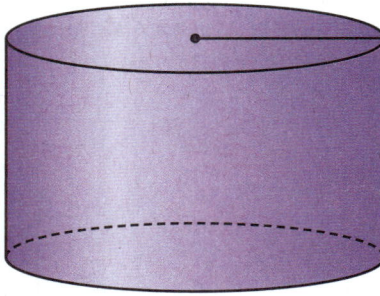

Do you agree with Jared's reasoning? Explain.

_____

_____

_____

17. Consider a set of cones that all have a radius of 1 centimeter. The heights of the cones are 1 centimeter, 2 centimeters, 3 centimeters, 4 centimeters, and 5 centimeters.

   A. Complete the table. Leave the volumes in terms of π.

Height (cm)	1	2	3	4	5
Volume (cm³)					

   B. **Model with Mathematics** Write an equation that gives the volume y of a cone with radius 1 centimeter if you know the height x of the cone. Describe the graph of the equation.

_____

_____

542

Name _____

Find Volume of Cones and Spheres

**LESSON 17.5
More Practice/ Homework**

ONLINE Video Tutorials and Interactive Examples

1. **Math on the Spot** Approximate the volume of a sphere with a radius of 7 feet, both in terms of π and to the nearest tenth. Use 3.14 for π.

   _____

2. A cone has a height of 6×10^3 millimeters and a radius of 2×10^3 millimeters. Find the volume of the cone. Leave your answer in scientific notation and in terms of π.

   _____

Approximate the volume of each cone. Use 3.14 for π and round the volume to the nearest tenth.

3. 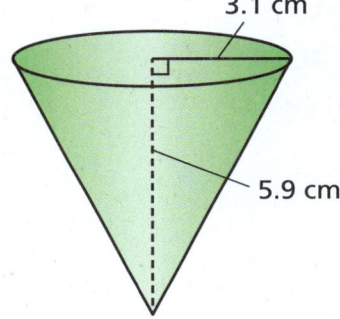 3.1 cm, 5.9 cm

4. 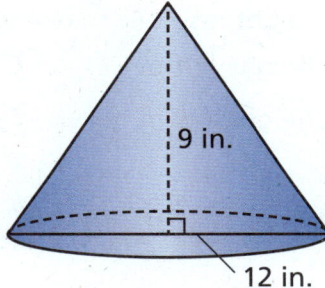 9 in., 12 in.

For Problems 5–6, approximate the volume of the sphere. Use 3.14 for π and round the volume to the nearest tenth.

5. 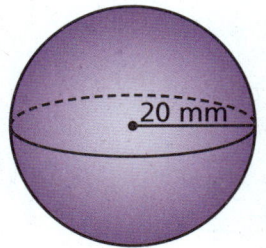 20 mm

6. 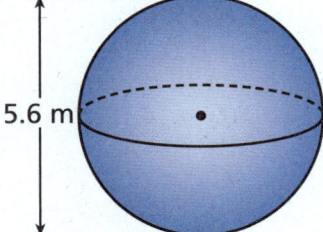 5.6 m

7. **MP Critique Reasoning** A student was asked to find the exact volume of the sphere shown, leaving the answer in terms of π. The student's work is shown. Explain the student's error.

   $V = \frac{4}{3}\pi r^3 = \frac{4}{3}\pi(6)^3 = \frac{4}{3}\pi(216) = 288\pi \text{ ft}^3$

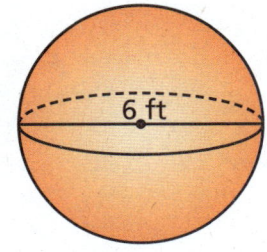 6 ft

Module 17 • Lesson 5

Test Prep

8. Fill in the formula for the volume of the cone shown here by writing a numerical value in each box.

   $V = \dfrac{\Box}{\Box} \pi \left(\Box\right)^2 \left(\Box\right)$

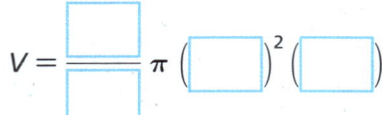

12.9 cm

16.4 cm

9. A student has a set of six spheres with radii 1, 2, 3, 4, 5, and 6 centimeters. Which of the following is the volume of a sphere in the set? Select all that apply.
   - (A) $\frac{4}{3}\pi$ cm³
   - (B) $\frac{8}{3}\pi$ cm³
   - (C) $\frac{32}{3}\pi$ cm³
   - (D) 36π cm³
   - (E) 125π cm³
   - (F) 288π cm³

10. Which radius and height result in a cone with the least volume?
    - (A) radius = 7 m; height = 1 m
    - (B) radius = 5 m; height = 5 m
    - (C) radius = 3 m; height = 10 m
    - (D) radius = 1 m; height = 15 m

Spiral Review

11. Solve $3x - 1 = 5$.

12. A triangle has sides of length 3 inches, 5 inches, and 6 inches. Is the triangle a right triangle? Explain how you know.

13. Approximate the volume of a cylinder with a radius of 3.4 meters and a height of 1.2 meters. Use 3.14 for π and round the volume to the nearest tenth.

Apply and Practice
Lesson 6

Name _____

Solve Multi-Step Problems with Surface Area and Volume

I Can solve multi-step surface area and volume problems.

Step It Out

1 Products come in various shapes and sizes. Knowing the surface area and volume of these products helps with shipping costs.

A. The regular pentagonal prism shown has a surface area of approximately 191 square centimeters. Find the approximate volume of the prism.

Use the surface area to find the approximate height.

Surface Area = $2B + Ph$ ☐ ≈ 2(☐) + ☐ h

$B ≈ 43$ cm², 5 cm

191 ≈ ☐ + 25h

Subtract 86 from both sides: ☐ ≈ 25h

Divide both sides by 25: ☐ ≈ h

The approximate height h is _____ centimeters. Use the approximate height to find the volume.

Volume = Bh ≈ ☐ × ☐ = ☐ cm³

The volume is approximately _____ cubic centimeters.

B. Find the surface area of the rectangular prism with a square base. First use the volume to find the height.

Volume = Bh = ☐ = (☐)h

Divide both sides by ☐ : ☐ = h

Use the height you found to determine the surface area.

Surface Area = $2B + Ph$ = 2(☐) + (☐)(☐) = ☐

The surface area is _____ square inches.

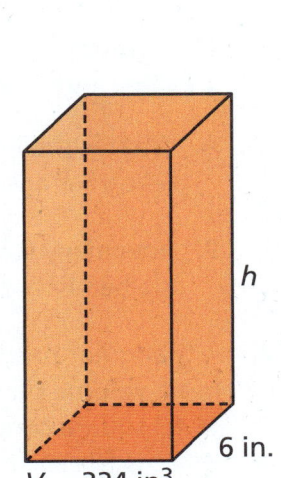

$V = 324$ in³, 6 in.

Module 17 • Lesson 6   545

2. Holly has an empty cylindrical container. She places four tennis balls, each with a diameter of 2.6 inches, inside the container. What is the approximate volume of air remaining inside the container?

1.5 in.

10.5 in.

A. Find the volume of the cylindrical container to the nearest hundredth. Use 3.14 for π.

$V = \pi r^2 h$

$= \pi(\underline{\hspace{1cm}})^2 (\underline{\hspace{1cm}})$

$\approx (\underline{\hspace{1cm}})(\underline{\hspace{1cm}})(\underline{\hspace{1cm}})$

$\approx \underline{\hspace{1cm}}$ in³

B. Find the volume taken up by the four tennis balls to the nearest hundredth. Use 3.14 for π.

$V = \frac{4}{3}\pi r^3 \cdot 4$

$= \frac{4}{3}\pi(\underline{\hspace{1cm}})^3 \cdot 4$

$\approx \frac{4}{3}(\underline{\hspace{1cm}})(\underline{\hspace{1cm}}) 4$

$\approx (\underline{\hspace{1cm}}) 4$

$= \underline{\hspace{1cm}}$ in³

C. Subtract to find the difference.

_____

Turn and Talk Find the volumes in Parts A and B in terms of π. In Part C, use 3.14 to complete the calculations. Why are the answers slightly different?

Check Understanding

1. The interior of a barrel used to store rice has a radius of 4 inches and a height of 7 inches.

   A. What is the interior volume of the barrel in cubic inches? Give your answer in terms of π. _____

   B. How many scoops of rice can the barrel hold if each scoop is a hemisphere with radius 1 inch? _____

2. A triangular prism with an equilateral triangle as its base has a volume of 64.98 cubic centimeters, a base area of 10.83 square centimeters, and a triangle edge length of 5 centimeters. What is the surface area of the prism in square centimeters?

_____

On Your Own

3. **Use Structure** Lonnie makes a regular hexagonal prism as shown with a surface area of approximately 244.8 square inches to collect his change. What is the approximate volume of change the prism will hold in cubic inches?

   A. What is the approximate height of the prism? _____

   B. What is the approximate volume of the prism? _____

3 in.

$B \approx 23.4$ in^2

4. **Social Studies** The USDA estimates that 15 million households in the United States were food-insecure in 2017. To help people in their community who might be food-insecure, a school has a fundraiser to fill a truck with canned goods for the local food bank. If the cube-shaped boxes used to store the canned goods have a surface area of 24 square feet and the truck will hold 128 boxes, what is the maximum volume of canned goods the students can collect?

   A. What is the edge length of 1 box? _____

   B. What is the volume of canned goods that the truck can carry?

   _____

5. A trapezoidal prism has a volume of 585 cubic centimeters. The area of the base is 39 square centimeters. If the base has sides measuring 4, 6.5, 6.5, and 9 centimeters, what is the surface area of the prism?

   _____

6. **Attend to Precision** Maribelle decorates candleholders in the shape of open-topped regular pentagonal prisms. Each candleholder holds an approximate volume of 275 cubic centimeters of wax. The area of the base of the holder is approximately 27.5 square centimeters and the edge length of the base is 4 centimeters. What is the approximate surface area of the candleholder (not including a top)?

   A. What is the approximate height of the candleholder? _____

   B. What is the approximate surface area of the candleholder? _____

7. **Reason** A rectangular prism has a 10-inch by 2-inch base and a surface area of 424 square inches. What is the volume of a column of 8 rectangular prisms with these dimensions stacked base to base?

   _____

8. **Attend to Precision** A conical container can hold up to 654 cubic centimeters of sand. If the radius of the cone is 5 centimeters, what is the height of the cone? Round your answer to the nearest whole centimeter. Use 3.14 for π.

   _____

Module 17 • Lesson 6

9. **Use Structure** The tent shown is a triangular prism. What is the amount of space inside the tent?

   A. About how long is the tent from the front to the back?

   _____

   B. What formula will find the space inside the tent? What is the space inside the tent?

   _____

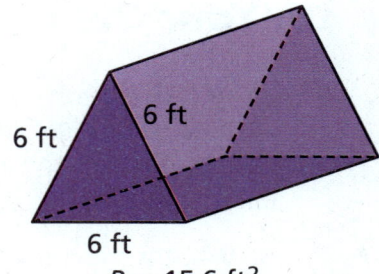

$B \approx 15.6 \text{ ft}^2$
Surface area $\approx 157.2 \text{ ft}^2$

10. **Reason** The conical cup, cylindrical cup, and hemispherical bowl shown have the same unknown radius r. If the height of each container is the same as that radius, which of the containers holds the most liquid? Explain.

    _____

    _____

    _____

11. **Attend to Precision** A cylindrical water tank is 7 feet tall and has a diameter of 12 feet. If the tank is currently half full, how much more water can be poured into the tank? Use $\frac{22}{7}$ for π and round your answer to the nearest cubic foot.

    _____

12. **Attend to Precision** Brittany makes dough and packages it in cylindrical containers that each have a height of 4 inches. What is the radius of each container if a pack of 6 containers contains 169.56 cubic inches of dough? Use 3.14 for π and round the radius to the nearest tenth of an inch.

    _____

13. **STEM** Cinder cone volcanoes are roughly cone-shaped, with heights ranging between 300 feet and 1,200 feet. Approximate the volume of a cinder cone volcano with a height of 350 feet and a diameter of 1,100 feet. Use 3.14 for π, and round your answer to the nearest cubic foot.

    _____

14. **Attend to Precision** Sonia fills half of the spherical bowl shown with sand using the cylindrical scoop shown. How many scoops of sand will it take to fill half of the bowl?

    _____

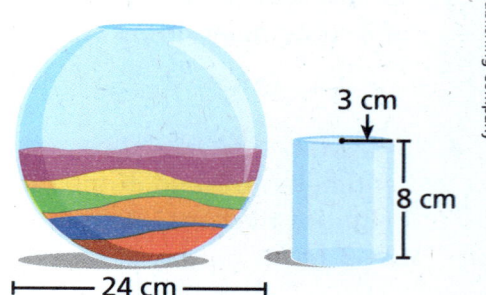

548

Name _____

LESSON 17.6
More Practice/ Homework

Solve Multi-Step Problems with Surface Area and Volume

ONLINE Video Tutorials and Interactive Examples

1. **MP Use Structure** The cargo area of the moving truck shown will be completely filled by 45 identical cube-shaped boxes with no empty space in the truck remaining. What will be the surface area of one layer of boxes on the floor of the truck bed?

   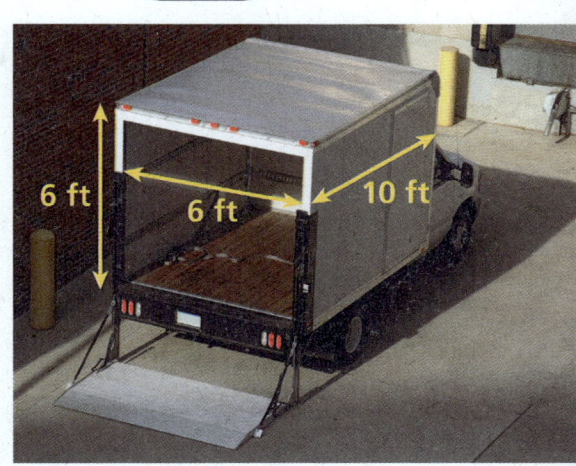

   A. What is the edge length of one box? _____

   B. What is the surface area of one layer of boxes on the floor of the truck bed?

   _____

   C. How many boxes make up this one layer?

   _____

2. **Math on the Spot** Find the volume of milk, in cubic inches, that the carton shown can hold when it is filled up to the top of the rectangular part of the carton.

   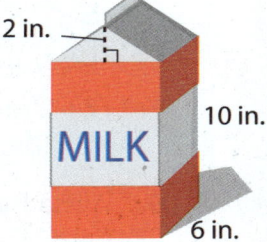

   _____

3. **MP Critique Reasoning** Eddie measures and finds the volume of the baseball shown. Does he approximate the volume correctly? Explain.

   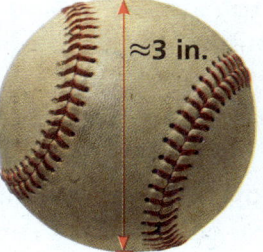

   $V = \frac{4}{3}\pi r^3$

   $\approx \frac{4}{3}(3.14)(3^3)$

   $\approx 113 \text{ in}^3$

   _____
   _____

4. A grain silo is in the shape of a cylinder. The area of the circular roof is 803.84 square feet. If 13,665.28 cubic feet of grain fits in the silo, what is the height of the silo?

   _____

5. A funnel in the shape of a cone has a diameter of 4 centimeters and a height of 9 centimeters. What is the volume of the funnel, to the nearest cubic centimeter? Use 3.14 for π.

   _____

Module 17 • Lesson 6   **549**

Test Prep

6. A cube has a surface area of 1,176 square inches. What is the volume of the cube?

- Ⓐ 14 in³
- Ⓑ 196 in³
- Ⓒ 1,728 in³
- Ⓓ 2,744 in³

7. Ina makes cakes in a pan shaped like a rectangular prism. The base is an 8-inch by 12-inch rectangle, and the volume is 288 cubic inches. Find the surface area of a cake baked in this pan.

_____

8. Suppose you are given the base area, the perimeter of the base, and the surface area of a triangular prism. Select all the steps needed to find the volume of the prism.

- Ⓐ Find the height of the prism using the surface area formula.
- Ⓑ Find the height of the prism using the volume formula.
- Ⓒ Find the height of the triangle.
- Ⓓ Use the area of the base and the height to find the volume.
- Ⓔ Use the area of the base and the height of the prism to find the volume.

9. Alissa has an 8.2-inch-tall water bottle with a radius of 1.5 inches. Find the volume of the water bottle, rounded to the nearest hundredth of a cubic inch. Use 3.14 for π.

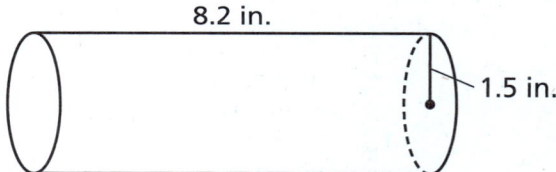

_____

10. A waffle cone has a volume of 31.25π cubic centimeters and a radius of 2.5 centimeters. What is the height of the cone?

- Ⓐ 5 cm
- Ⓑ 6.25 cm
- Ⓒ 15 cm
- Ⓓ 30 cm

Spiral Review

11. Simplify.

$\dfrac{7^4 \cdot 7^3}{7^5} =$ _____

12. A bike wheel has a 16-inch diameter. Approximately how far will the wheel travel in three rotations? Use 3.14 for π.

_____

Module 17 Review

Vocabulary

1. Select all three-dimensional figures that have each characteristic.

For Problems 2–4, tell whether each statement is true or false. If it is false, tell what word could replace the underlined word to make the statement true.

	Cylinder	Cone	Sphere
A vertex	☐	☐	☐
A curved surface	☐	☐	☐
Exactly one circular base	☐	☐	☐
Two parallel circular bases	☐	☐	☐

2. A cross section is a <u>two</u>-dimensional figure formed when a three-dimensional figure is cut.
   _____

3. A <u>pentagon</u> is a polygon with six sides. _____

4. A triangular prism has three faces that are <u>triangles</u>.
   _____

Concepts and Skills

5. (MP) **Use Tools** The cylinder shown has a radius of 8 centimeters and a height of 14 centimeters. What is the approximate volume of the cylinder? (Use $\frac{22}{7}$ for π.) State what strategy and tool you will use to answer the question, explain your choice, and then find the answer.

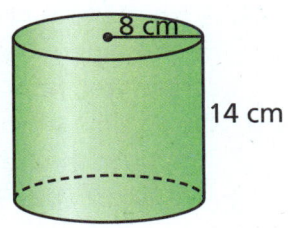

6. A school garden club is making the garden bed shown. It needs to hold 24 cubic feet of soil when full. Draw a rectangle on the grid that represents a possible length and width of the bed.

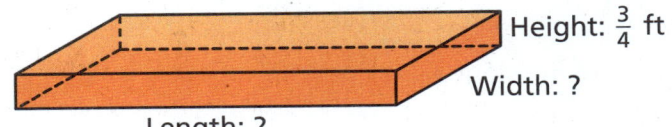

Height: $\frac{3}{4}$ ft
Width: ?
Length: ?

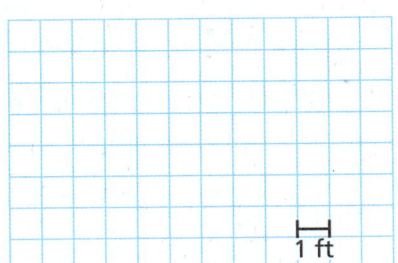

7. A cone-shaped pile of sand has a base diameter of 7 feet and a height of 2.4 feet, as shown. To the nearest tenth of a cubic foot, what is the volume of the pile of sand? (Use $\frac{22}{7}$ for π.)

   _____ cubic feet

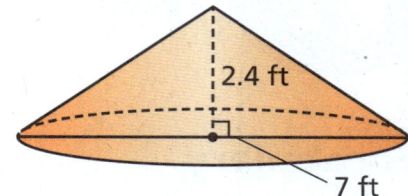

8. The bases of the triangular prism are isosceles triangles. Darren and Riya each cut the prism to make a cross section. The cross section from Darren's cut is a triangle. The cross section from Riya's cut is a rectangle. How did each of them cut the prism?

   _____
   _____

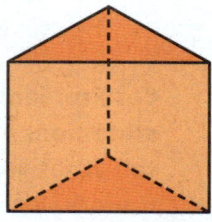

9. A sphere has a diameter of 12 inches, as shown. To the nearest cubic inch, what is the volume of the sphere? (Use 3.14 for π.)

   _____ cubic inches

10. The surface area of a cube is 150 square meters. What is the volume of the cube?

    Ⓐ 25 m³
    Ⓑ 125 m³
    Ⓒ 15,625 m³
    Ⓓ 625 m³

11. A frozen yogurt stand has two types of containers. To the nearest cubic centimeter, how much greater is the volume of the cylinder-shaped container than the cone-shaped container? (Use 3.14 for π.)

    _____ cubic centimeters

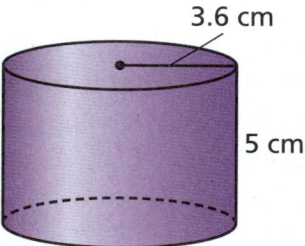

12. The cylinder is sliced horizontally by a plane as shown. Select all reasonable statements for the figure.

    Ⓐ The cross section is parallel to the base of the cylinder.
    Ⓑ The cross section is a rectangle.
    Ⓒ The cross section is a circle.
    Ⓓ The cross section will have the same dimensions as the base of the cylinder.
    Ⓔ The cross section in the figure would be the same if the cylinder were sliced vertically instead of horizontally.

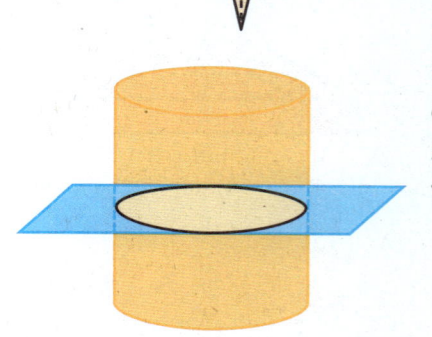

Unit 8

Data Analysis and Sampling

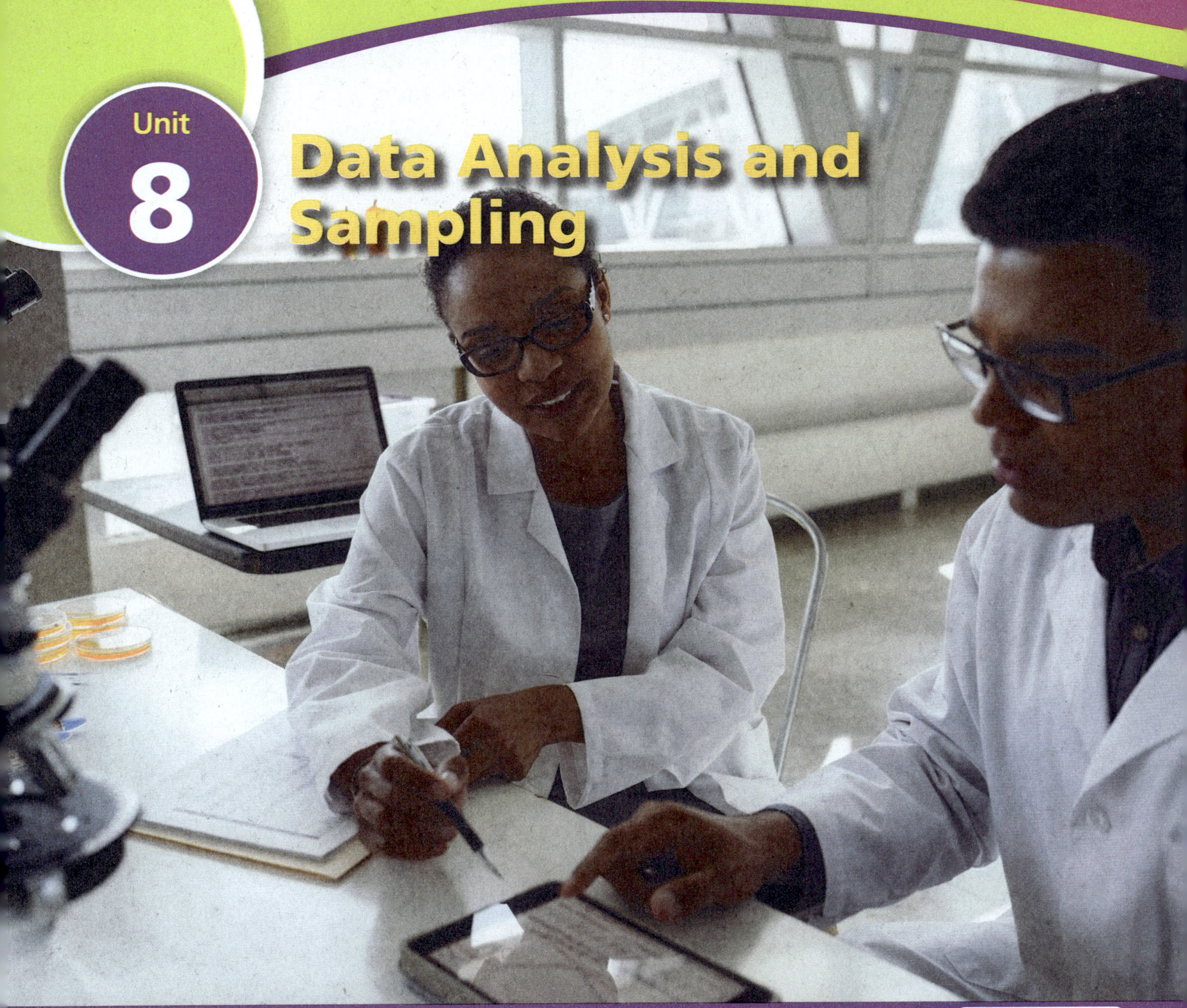

Research Assistant

STEM POWERING INGENUITY

A research assistant collects or verifies information in a laboratory setting, or even in an office for a field such as law or media. Responsibilities of a research assistant may include conducting surveys, analyzing data, providing quality control, managing information storage, and preparing results for presentation or publication. Research assistants often use computers to help them perform these tasks.

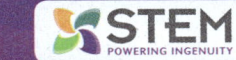

STEM Task:

Work as a class to record the birth month of each class member. Assign the number 1 to represent January, the number 2 to represent February, and so on. Use the class data to make a dot plot. What observations and conclusions can you make by looking at the dot plot? What questions do the data raise? Explain your thinking.

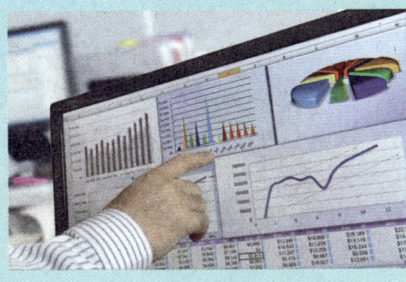

Learning Mindset
Resilience Manages the Learning Process

Resilience is the ability to move forward when obstacles arise. Developing resilience allows you to identify a barrier, learn from it, and overcome the challenges it presents. Here are some ways you can increase your resilience.

- Consider where you are within the learning process. Do you think you may encounter barriers to completing a task? If so, try to identify them.

- Review the steps you are taking to direct your learning. Monitor your feelings, motivation, and interest level to keep yourself on task.

- If necessary, modify learning situations and activities so that they lead to successful conclusions.

Reflect

Q What strategies did you use to overcome barriers you encountered during the STEM Task?

Q What steps can you take to direct your learning and better understand how to collect and analyze data?

Module 18
Proportional Reasoning with Samples

WHICH FRACTION DOES NOT BELONG?

Each diagram represents a fraction. All but one of the fractions can be matched with a partner, but not based on the shapes of the models.

Write the fraction that each model represents.

A.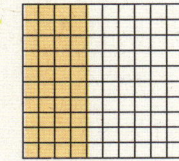

B.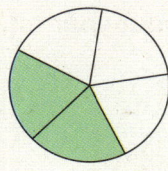

C.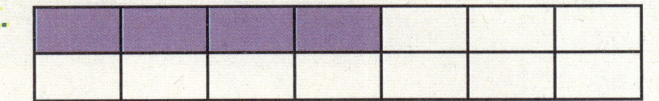

D.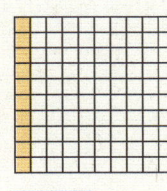

E.

🔄 **Turn and Talk**

How can you pair up the fractions? Which is the fraction that does not belong? Explain your answers.

Are You Ready?

Complete these problems to review prior concepts and skills you will need for this module.

Statistical Data Collection

For Problems 1–2, tell whether the question is a statistical question. Explain your reasoning.

1. How many days are in the month of March?

2. How tall are the giraffes at the zoo?

3. Write a statistical question about your school.

Representing Equivalent Ratios

Complete the table of equivalent ratios.

4.

Size (oz)	Price ($)
4	1.00
	2.00
10	
12	

5.

Time (h)	Distance (mi)
	84
3	126
5	
	336

Use Ratio and Rate Reasoning

Write an equation to model each proportional relationship. Then solve the problem.

6. The ratio of tables, x, to chairs, y, in a restaurant is 2 to 7. The restaurant has a total of 12 tables. How many chairs does it have?

    Equation: _____ Solution: _____ chairs

7. Let x represent the number of batteries and y represent the cost of the batteries. A package of 8 rechargeable batteries costs $12. At this rate, how much would a package of 20 rechargeable batteries cost?

    Equation: _____ Solution: $_____

Build Conceptual Understanding
Lesson 1

Name _____

Understand Representative Samples

I Can identify the population and sample for a given survey scenario and say whether a sample is random. I can determine whether a sample is likely to be representative of the population.

Spark Your Learning

In the fall, the residents of a large city will be voting on whether to use state funding to build a new football stadium. A research analyst wants to know the opinion of all the registered voters of the city in order to predict the outcome of the upcoming vote. Without polling all the residents, how can the research analyst be sure that the poll represents the opinion of the registered voters?

 **Turn and Talk** Is it reasonable for the research analyst to poll every eligible resident of the city about using state funding to build a new stadium? Explain.

Module 18 • Lesson 1   557

Build Understanding

1 ▶ A chain restaurant is thinking of entering a city for the first time. The owners want to determine if the teenagers in the city like the kind of food served by the restaurant.

A. In this case, what is the population the restaurant needs to survey? Is it reasonable for them to survey the entire population? Why or why not?

_____

_____

> **Connect to Vocabulary**
>
> When information is being gathered about a group, the entire group of objects or individuals considered for a survey is the **population**.

When a population is too large to survey, a subset of the population, or a sample, is used to represent the population. If the sample is representative, it can be used to infer data about the population. The restaurant owners made a list of possible samples.

> **Connect to Vocabulary**
>
> A **sample** is part of the population that is chosen to represent the entire group.
> A **representative sample** is a sample that has the same characteristics as the population.
> When a sample does not accurately represent the population, it has **bias**.

List of potential samples of the population:
1. Survey every 10th person coming out of a competitor's restaurant.
2. Call every 100th person in the local phonebook.
3. Survey 10% of the students at the city's middle schools and high schools.
4. Survey teenagers leaving a fast-food restaurant.

B. Which of the potential samples are more likely to be representative of the population? Why?

_____

C. Of the representative samples of the population, which is most representative of the entire population? Explain.

_____

_____

D. Which of the potential samples are biased? Explain.

_____

_____

_____

A sample in which every member of the population has an equal chance of being selected is a **random sample**.

2 Aiden asks the survey question shown to determine what genre of music to play at an employee event.

A. He asks every tenth employee on a list of all employees. Is this sample random? Explain.

_____

B. Is the sample in Part A representative of the population? Explain.

_____
_____

C. On Thursday, he asks every third employee that gets off the elevator on the fifth floor the survey question. Is this sample biased? Explain.

_____
_____

D. Is the sample in Part C a random sample? Explain.

_____

 **Turn and Talk** Does a random sample always generate a representative sample? Explain.

Check Understanding

1. Isabella wants to know the favorite sport of the students in her school. She randomly asks every fifth person entering the football game Friday night. Is this sample biased? Explain.

_____
_____

2. Noah assigned a number to each of the 200 students in seventh grade. He put the numbers in a bag. Noah randomly chose 30 numbers and surveyed those students. Identify the population and sample.

_____
_____

3. Wyatt wants to poll the opinion of a neighborhood about safety. Give an example of a biased sample. Justify your answer.

_____
_____

Module 18 • Lesson 1

On Your Own

For Problems 4–5, use this survey information: Every hundredth resident of voting age listed on the county census was surveyed about building a library.

4. Identify the population and sample.

   A. Population: _____

   B. Sample: _____

5. **(MP) Reason** Is the sample random? Is the sample representative of the population? Explain.

   _____

   _____

For Problems 6–7, identify the population and sample. Determine whether each sample is random and whether it is biased. Explain your reasoning.

6. Juanita surveys 50 adults at a local swimming pool during the summer to determine the favorite month of adults in her city.

   A. Population: _____

   B. Sample: _____

   C. Random? _____

   D. Representative? _____

7. Cameron surveys every tenth student who walks into school to determine the favorite type of movie of students in his school.

   A. Population: _____

   B. Sample: _____

   C. Random? _____

   D. Representative? _____

8. **(MP) Construct Arguments** Addison surveys every 25th customer who leaves a grocery store to determine whether students at her school prefer to pack a lunch or purchase a lunch. Is her sample biased? Explain.

   _____

   _____

 I'm in a **Learning Mindset!**

What barriers are there to my understanding of representative samples?

_____

_____

Name _____

LESSON 18.1
More Practice/ Homework

Understand Representative Samples

1. The president of a national soccer fan club, Abdul, wants to determine if the club's 10,000 members are in favor of using club dues to make a new online video to support their team in the upcoming championship. He assigns a number to each member and uses a random number generator to choose 250 members to survey.

   A. Identify the population and sample.

   _____
   _____

   B. Is the sample representative of the entire population? Explain.

   _____
   _____

   C. Suppose 212 of the 250 members in a random sample are in favor of using club dues to make a new video for their team. What can Abdul conclude about the results of the survey? Explain.

   _____
   _____
   _____
   _____

2. **Math on the Spot** Determine whether the sample is representative or biased. Explain.

   A. A teacher chooses the grades of 50 students at random from his classes to calculate the average grade earned in his class.

   _____

   B. Seventy-five people exiting a bookstore are surveyed to find out the average amount of time spent reading each day by people in the area.

   _____
   _____

3. **Open Ended** A random sample of 10 students and a random sample of 200 students are chosen from a student population of 1,200 students. Which sample do you think is more likely to be representative of the population? Explain.

   _____
   _____

Test Prep

4. Jayla wants to know the favorite sports team of the adults in her city. Which survey method is representative of the population?

   Ⓐ Randomly survey 1,000 adults as they leave a professional basketball game.

   Ⓑ Randomly survey 2,000 adults in one neighborhood.

   Ⓒ Survey every 100th adult customer who enters the local grocery store.

   Ⓓ Survey every 20th student who enters the high school.

For Problems 5–6, determine whether each situation *does* or *does not* show bias.

5. Haley wants to know if people use the store's bags or bring their own reusable bags. She surveys every tenth person who leaves a grocery store.

   This situation does / does not show bias.

6. Josiah wants to know the favorite pet of adults in his city. Josiah assigned a number to each of the 200 people on the list to adopt a dog from a dog shelter. He puts the numbers in a hat. Josiah randomly chose 40 numbers and surveyed those people.

   This situation does / does not show bias.

7. Fayard wants to know the favorite instrument of students in his school. He puts the names of all the students in a jar, draws 5 names, and surveys those students. Suppose Julia conducts the same survey in the same way, but she draws 15 names. Which method is more representative? Explain.

   _____

   _____

Spiral Review

8. A fully-inflated beach ball floating in the ocean is spherical and has a diameter of 0.6 meter. What is the beach ball's volume? Give your answer in terms of π and also to the nearest tenth of a cubic meter by using 3.14 for π.

   _____

9. The radius of a cylinder is 14 inches. A plane perpendicular to the base passes through its center. Given that the cylinder's height is equal to the radius, describe the cross-section formed. Is it the same cross-section that would result if the plane passed through the base, but not its center? Explain.

   _____

   _____

   _____

Connect Concepts and Skills

Lesson 2

Name _____

Make Inferences from a Random Sample

I Can use proportional reasoning to make inferences about populations based on the results of a random sample.

Spark Your Learning

At a grocery store, a bin is filled with trail mix made by mixing raisins with a large 30-pound bag of nuts. Zane buys a small bag of a trail mix that contains $1\frac{1}{2}$ pounds of nuts and $\frac{1}{2}$ pound of raisins. If the nuts and raisins in Zane's bag are proportional to the nuts and raisins in the bin of trail mix, how many pounds of raisins do you think the store used to make the entire bin of trail mix?

 **Turn and Talk** How is the connection between the sample (small bag) and population (large bin) of trail mix similar to the sample and population of a survey?

Module 18 • Lesson 2

563

Build Understanding

1 To estimate the number of pets that students in your school have, conduct a survey of ten randomly selected students in your class.

A. Plot the results of your survey on the grid provided.

B. According to my survey, most students in my school have _____ pets.

C. According to my survey, about _____ % of the students in my school have more than two pets.

D. According to my survey, about _____ % of the students in my school have zero pets.

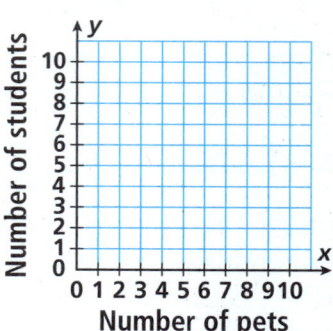

Conduct the same survey again using a second set of ten randomly selected students in your class.

E. Plot the results of your survey on the grid provided.

F. According to my survey, most students in my school have _____ pets.

G. According to my survey, about _____ % of the students in my school have more than two pets.

H. According to my survey, about _____ % of the students in my school have zero pets.

I. Compare the results from both of your samples.

- Are the results from the two samples exactly the same?

  _____

- Will a different sample give a different estimate?

  _____

A sample ratio can be used to estimate a population ratio. However, because different samples will likely vary, a sample ratio must be considered as only an estimate of the population ratio.

Turn and Talk Discuss how samples from random surveys can be improved to obtain better estimates about a population.

Name _____

Step It Out

To make inferences about a population based on a random representative sample, you can use proportional reasoning.

2 Javier randomly selects 12 cartons of eggs from the grocery store. He finds that 2 cartons have at least one broken egg.

Suppose there are 144 cartons of eggs at the grocery store. What is an estimate of the total number of those 144 cartons that have at least one broken egg?

A. Identify the sample.

_____

B. Identify the population.

_____

C. Write the ratio of cartons with at least one broken egg to the total number of cartons in the sample.

$\frac{\Box}{\Box}$

D. Use the sample ratio to write an equation for the proportional relationship, where x is the population size and y is the number of cartons in the population with at least one broken egg.

$y = \frac{\Box}{\Box} \cdot 144$

E. Use your equation in Part D to estimate the number of cartons in the population that have at least one broken egg.

_____
_____

Turn and Talk Discuss how to write an equation for the proportional relationship using a decimal or a percent for the sample ratio.

Module 18 • Lesson 2

3 A worker randomly selects one out of every 7 sets from the 3,500 sets of headphones produced. The results are shown.

4 of 500 defective

A. The ☐ population / sample ☐ is the total of 3,500 sets of headphones produced. The 500 selected for testing is the ☐ population / sample ☐.

B. Write the ratio of defective headphones to total headphones in the sample. Then write the ratio as a decimal and as a percent.

$$\frac{\Box}{\Box} = \Box = \Box\%$$

C. Write and solve an equation to find the number of headphones in the population that can be estimated to be defective.

$$y = \frac{\Box}{\Box} \cdot 3{,}500$$

There would be about ☐ defective headphones.

Check Understanding

1. William conducted a random survey of the students in his school regarding the number of hours of sleep they got last night. The box plot shows the results of his survey. Make an inference about the entire population.

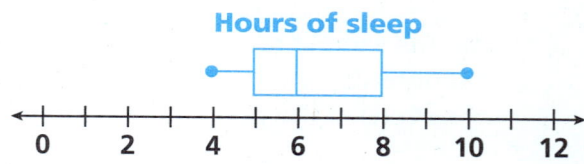

Hours of sleep

_____

_____

2. Hazel assigned a number to each of the 100 students in the band and put the numbers in a bag. She randomly chose 20 numbers and found that 3 students did not complete their homework for today. Make an inference about the number of students in the band that did not do their homework. If Hazel randomly chose 20 more numbers, what results would you expect? Explain.

_____

_____

_____

On Your Own

For Problems 3–5, make an inference about the ages of all drama club students at a theater conference using the dot plot showing the ages of students in a random sample of conference attendees.

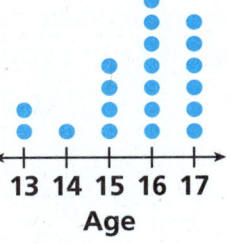

3. Most drama club students at the conference are _____ 15 years old.

4. About _____% of the students at the conference are 16 years old or older.

5. **(MP) Construct Arguments** Would you think that it is likely for the number of 16-year-old students and the number of 17-year-old students to be almost equal in another random sample of conference attendees? Explain.

   _____

   _____

6. A manager randomly selects 1,500 ink pens produced today and finds 12 of them defective. There were 12,000 ink pens produced today. Make an inference about the number of ink pens produced today that are defective.

   The sample ratio of defective pens is $\dfrac{\boxed{}}{\boxed{}}$ or $\boxed{}$%.

   Inference: In the 12,000 population, the number of defective pens is estimated to be $\boxed{} \cdot 12{,}000 = \boxed{}$.

7. Gabby assigned a number to each of the 120 athletes at her school and put the numbers in a box. She randomly chose 25 numbers and found that 10 athletes were female. Use this sample to make an inference about how many athletes at Gabby's school are female.

   _____

8. A random sample of dry-erase board markers at Juan's school shows that 9 of the 60 dry-erase board markers do not work. There are 200 dry-erase board markers at Juan's school. Make an inference about the number of dry-erase board markers at Juan's school that do not work.

   _____

9. A mail carrier randomly inspects every 20th letter being mailed. Out of 600 letters in the sample, 3 were open. There were 18,000 letters being mailed. Make an inference about the number of all the letters being mailed that were open.

   _____

Module 18 • Lesson 2

For Problems 10–13, use the box plot, which shows the results of a survey of the number of minutes that people at a variety of randomly selected gyms exercise. Make an inference about the number of minutes that people at gyms exercise according to this survey.

Minutes of exercise

10. According to the survey, 75% of people at gyms exercise for _____ minutes or longer.

11. According to the survey, 25% of people at gyms exercise for more than _____ minutes.

12. According to the survey, _____ % of people at gyms exercise from 15 to 50 minutes.

13. According to the survey, _____ % of people at gyms exercise from 15 to 30 minutes.

14. **Health and Fitness** Would the owners of another gym be able to use data from a survey like the one in Problems 10–13 to make inferences about the number of minutes people exercise at their gym? Explain your reasoning.

_____
_____
_____
_____

15. A wildlife park manager is working on a request to expand the park. In a random selection during one week, 3 of every 5 cars have more than 3 people inside. If about 5,000 cars come to the park in a month, estimate how many cars that month would have more than 3 people inside. Show your work.

_____
_____
_____

 I'm in a Learning Mindset!

How is making inferences from random samples similar to the way I make decisions when I am learning something new?

_____

Name _____

Make Inferences from a Random Sample

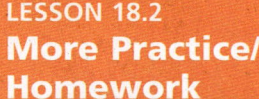

LESSON 18.2
More Practice/ Homework

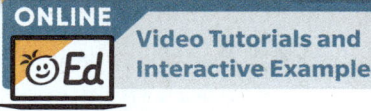

1. Xavier surveyed a random sample of the grade levels of the Spanish Club members in the county. The bar graph shows the results of his survey.

   A. The largest number of students in the Spanish Club are in _____ grade.

   B. The same number of students in the Spanish Club are in the _____ grade as are in the 11th and 12th grades combined.

   C. If there are 300 students in the Spanish Club in the county, predict how many are 10th graders.

   _____

   D. Of the 300 students, predict about how many are 9th graders.

   _____

   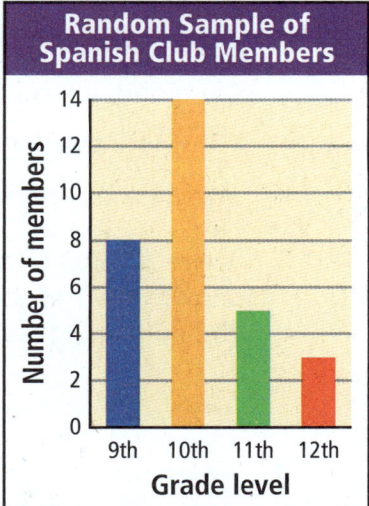

   E. Xavier conducted another random survey of the grade levels of the Spanish Club members in the county. In what grade would you expect to find the most students in Spanish Club? Explain.

   _____
   _____
   _____

2. A manager at a factory finds that in a random sample of 200 clocks, 15 are defective.

   A. What percent of the clocks are defective?

   _____

   B. Of the 10,000 clocks from which the sample was chosen, about how many clocks are probably not defective?

   _____

   C. The next day the manager finds only 8 of the 200 randomly selected clocks are defective. About how many clocks out of the 10,000 produced that day are probably defective?

   _____

3. **(MP) Use Structure** Based on a sample survey, a tutoring company claims that 90% of their students pass their classes. Out of 300 students, how many would you predict will pass?

   _____

Module 18 • Lesson 2   569

Test Prep

4. Ronnie surveyed a random selection of real-estate agents in his town about the numbers of bedrooms in the houses for sale that week. The dot plot shows the results. Which inference is correct?

   Ⓐ Most of the houses have fewer than 3 bedrooms.

   Ⓑ Some houses have 0 bedrooms.

   Ⓒ More than 50% of the houses have exactly 3 bedrooms.

   Ⓓ 80% of the houses have 3 or 4 bedrooms.

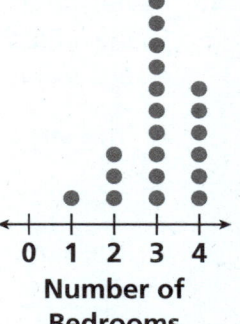

5. There are 300 computers at an electronics store. A random sample shows that 1 of 25 sampled computers has a malfunction. Estimate the number of computers that have malfunctions.

   _____

6. Jaylen used the seat number for each of 6,500 fans' seats at a football game. He randomly chose 200 numbers and found that 36 of those people had also bought a parking voucher. Estimate how many of the 6,500 fans at the game bought a parking voucher. Explain.

   _____

   _____

   _____

Spiral Review

7. Two right triangles on a coordinate plane have hypotenuses on the same line, which passes through the origin. An endpoint of one of the hypotenuses is (−2, 5). An endpoint of the other hypotenuse is (6, k). What is the value of k?

   _____

8. What is the center of dilation for the given figures?

   _____

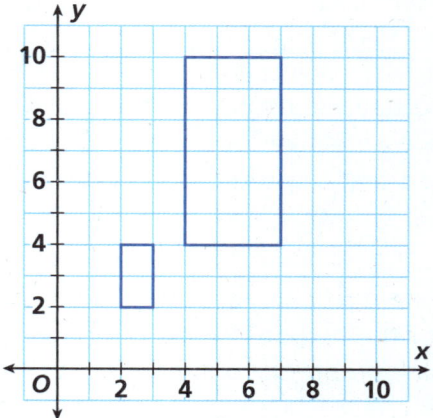

Make Inferences from Repeated Random Samples

I Can use multiple random samples of the same size from a population to make inferences about a survey result.

Step It Out

1 The results of a school-wide survey of all students at a middle school about renaming the school mascot from Grizzlies to Bears are shown at the right. Since all students in the school were surveyed, these ratios are the population ratios. The students in a math class had an assignment to collect random samples of 20 students in the school and compare the sample ratio to the population ratio. The results are shown below. Find each sample ratio for those who prefer "Bears," and write it as a percent.

BEARS Mascot **70%**

GRIZZLIES Mascot **30%**

A. Sample 1: 13 students prefer "Bears"

Sample ratio of those who prefer "Bears": $\frac{\square}{20} = \square\%$

B. Sample 2: 16 students prefer "Bears"

Sample ratio of those who prefer "Bears": $\frac{\square}{20} = \square\%$

C. Sample 3: 15 students prefer "Bears"

Sample ratio of those who prefer "Bears": $\frac{\square}{20} = \square\%$

D. Do these sample ratios support the finding that 70% of the entire school population prefer the mascot name "Bears"? Explain.

_____

_____

Turn and Talk Why are the sample ratios different from the population ratio?

Module 18 • Lesson 3

2 A bagel shop offering regular or toasted bagels makes the claim shown. Use each method to explore how much variation can be expected from a sample.

60% prefer toasted bagels

A. Construct a mock population by placing 60 red slips of paper (for toasted) and 40 blue slips of paper (for not toasted) in a bag.

B. Randomly select 10 slips of paper from the bag and record the results in the column for Sample 1. Be sure to return each slip of paper to the bag before you draw another.

C. Repeat Step B nine more times, recording your results in the table.

	Samples									
	1	2	3	4	5	6	7	8	9	10
Toasted bagels (red)										
Untoasted bagels (blue)										
Sample ratio of toasted bagels										

D. Plot the results in the dot plot.

E. How do the sample ratios compare with the population ratio?

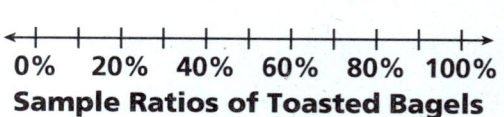

Sample Ratios of Toasted Bagels

_____

_____

_____

 Turn and Talk How can repeated random samples of the same size from a population help you to understand the variation in the sample ratios?

Check Understanding

A company claims that 75% of employees prefer day shifts to night shifts.

1. The manager took a random sample of 20 employees and found that 16 employees prefer the day shift. Does the sample ratio support the company's claim about the population ratio? Explain.

_____

2. With repeated samples, is the average of sample ratios more likely to approximate the population ratio than a single sample?

_____

572

On Your Own

3. **Health and Fitness** The results of a survey about whether students at a middle school prefer to participate in basketball or football are shown.

65%

35%

Bella used a random number generator to generate 10 samples of the population.

Numbers 1–65: basketball
Numbers 66–100: football

Sample 1	62	1	73	53	85	31	79	68	8	14	13	29	30	25	61	28	26	67	24	80
Sample 2	48	66	65	59	58	21	85	92	34	56	67	76	82	26	28	18	93	39	73	97
Sample 3	99	12	92	45	13	2	62	40	96	64	100	69	35	70	93	14	78	48	67	15
Sample 4	85	32	25	37	8	49	28	24	60	31	43	61	94	16	58	63	59	12	52	1
Sample 5	28	36	3	78	46	6	54	52	99	59	39	65	84	80	81	98	75	14	53	79
Sample 6	60	66	53	40	18	55	72	38	44	69	49	51	93	17	34	67	64	89	91	13
Sample 7	28	56	93	7	84	29	57	11	35	74	87	65	78	80	27	85	99	41	91	40
Sample 8	58	46	82	56	24	26	12	67	73	61	6	52	68	29	48	21	43	85	49	2
Sample 9:	3	43	98	76	17	88	44	13	65	23	87	2	18	93	49	60	58	57	86	29
Sample 10	57	11	8	3	68	98	1	67	97	29	23	99	59	56	65	72	60	79	89	30

A. Use the random numbers from each sample to complete the table.

	Samples									
	1	2	3	4	5	6	7	8	9	10
Numbers 1–65										
Numbers 66–100										
Sample ratio of numbers 1–65										

B. Plot the results from the table in the dot plot.

C. How does the Sample 9 ratio compare to the population ratio?

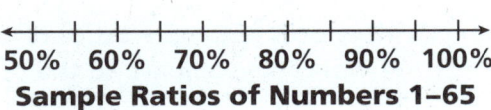

Sample Ratios of Numbers 1–65

_____

D. **Use Structure** How do the sample ratios compare to the population ratio?

_____

Module 18 • Lesson 3

4. A factory owner surveyed employees about whether they prefer working 5 regular workdays or 4 longer workdays. The results are shown.

   A. Construct a mock population using blue and green slips of paper.

   Blue: prefer 5 regular workdays
   Green: prefer 4 longer workdays

   - Place 10 blue slips and 40 green slips in a hat.
   - Randomly select a sample of 10 slips of paper from the hat, and record the ratio.
   - Replace the slips, and repeat for 10 samples.

	Samples									
	1	2	3	4	5	6	7	8	9	10
5 workdays (blue)										
4 workdays (green)										
Sample ratio of 5 workdays										
Sample ratio of 4 workdays										

B. Plot the ratios of those who prefer 5 workdays in the dot plot.

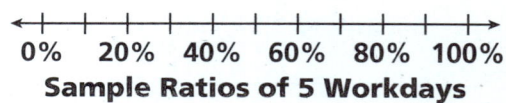

Sample Ratios of 5 Workdays

C. How do the sample ratios of those who prefer 5 workdays compare to the population ratio?

_____

_____

D. **(MP) Attend to Precision** Plot the ratios of those who prefer 4 workdays in the dot plot.

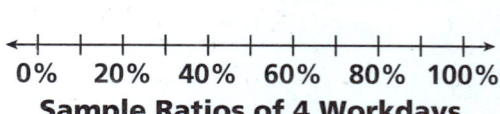

Sample Ratios of 4 Workdays

E. How do the sample ratios of those who prefer 4 workdays compare to the population ratio?

_____

_____

Make Inferences from Repeated Random Samples

LESSON 18.3 More Practice/Homework

1. A poll was conducted among all students at a middle school about whether they prefer blue or red. The resulting population ratios are shown.

   55%
   45%

   A. Glen used a random number generator to generate the sample ratios shown in the chart.

   Numbers 1–55: students who prefer blue
   Numbers 56–100: students who prefer red

	Samples									
	1	2	3	4	5	6	7	8	9	10
Blue preference	12	11	13	8	11	12	10	9	10	9
Red preference	8	9	7	12	9	8	10	11	10	11
Sample ratio of blue preference	60%	55%	65%	40%	55%	60%	50%	45%	50%	45%

   The sample ratio for blue preference in Sample 1 is [above / below] the population ratio.

   The sample ratio for blue preference in Sample 8 is [above / below] the population ratio.

   B. Plot the results for blue preference from the table on the dot plot.

   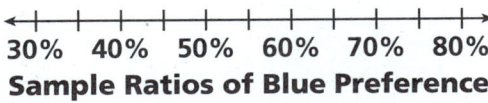

   Sample Ratios of Blue Preference

   C. **Open Ended** How do the sample ratios Glen generated compare to the population ratio?

   D. **Reason** Predict what would happen to the sample ratios in the dot plot as more samples are taken.

Module 18 • Lesson 3

575

Test Prep

2. Abner researched and found that 60% of students in his school ride the bus to school. Abner took a random sample of 50 students and found that 38 ride the bus to school. Which statement correctly describes the sample ratio?

   Ⓐ The sample ratio is 38%, which is below the population ratio.

   Ⓑ The sample ratio is 38%, which is above the population ratio.

   Ⓒ The sample ratio is 76%, which is below the population ratio.

   Ⓓ The sample ratio is 76%, which is above the population ratio.

3. The population ratio of male employees in a large office is 55%. Random samples of 20 employees are taken. Select how the sample ratio varies in relation to the actual ratio of the population.

	5% Above	10% Above	5% Below	10% Below
45% of employees are male.	☐	☐	☐	☐
10 out of 20 employees are male.	☐	☐	☐	☐
60% of employees are male.	☐	☐	☐	☐
13 out of 20 employees are male.	☐	☐	☐	☐

4. Research claims that 30% of dental customers have had braces. Julie used a random number generator to generate samples, where numbers 1–3 represent having braces and numbers 4–10 represent not having braces. One sample is shown. How does the sample compare to the population?

   Sample 5: 2, 1, 7, 5, 8, 3, 9, 6, 8, 4, 3, 2, 3, 5, 6, 8, 6, 7, 2, 8

   _____
   _____
   _____

Spiral Review

5. The results of a random survey about the number of siblings of students are shown in the box plot. Make an inference about the larger student population.

   _____
   _____

6. Libby bought 224 ounces of flour. If each bag contains 32 ounces of flour, how many bags of flour did Libby buy?

   _____

Module 18 Review

Vocabulary

Dana wants to know how many students at her school watch sports on television. She selects 40 students from her school to survey. Use this information to answer each question.

1. What is the population in this situation?

2. What is the sample?

3. What is the difference between a representative sample and a biased sample in this situation?

Concepts and Skills

4. A theater owner wants to survey the audience about the types of plays they want to see. At a sold-out show, there are 100 people in VIP seats, 700 on the main floor, and 400 in the balcony. Which sample can best help the owner see the preferences of all the audience members?

    A) 5 people in VIP seats, 20 on the main floor, and 35 in the balcony

    B) 5 people in VIP seats, 35 on the main floor, and 20 in the balcony

    C) 20 people in VIP seats, 20 on the main floor, and 20 in the balcony

    D) 10 people in VIP seats, 7 on the main floor, and 4 in the balcony

5. **Use Tools** There are 580 students at Alejandro's school. He surveys a random sample of 60 students and finds that 21 of them regularly bring their lunch. Based on these results, estimate how many students at Alejandro's school regularly bring their lunch. State what strategy and tool you will use to answer the question, explain your choice, and then find the answer.

6. A city librarian wants to see if visitors want to add a cafe to the library. On a Monday morning, the librarian surveys every fourth visitor to the library. Is this sample likely to be representative of all library visitors? Explain.

_____

_____

_____

7. A factory produces a batch of 4,800 pens. The company dictates that if a random sample of the batch shows that more than 2% of the pens are defective, the batch needs additional testing. A worker checks a random sample of 60 pens from the batch and finds that 2 are defective. Based on this information, which statement(s) about the sample are true? Select all that apply.

   Ⓐ It indicates the batch needs additional testing.

   Ⓑ It indicates probably about 96 pens in the batch are defective.

   Ⓒ It indicates there are probably about 160 defective pens in the batch.

   Ⓓ It indicates probably about 4,580 pens in the batch have no defects.

   Ⓔ It indicates that about 1.25% of the pens in the batch are defective.

8. A company makes short-sleeved and long-sleeved T-shirts. The company checks a random sample of 60 T-shirts of each type. It finds that 4 short-sleeved shirts have problems and 1 long-sleeved shirt has problems. How many T-shirts should the company predict have problems in a shipment of 3,000 shirts of each type?

   _____ total T-shirts

9. An inspector takes 20 different random samples of 25 apples each from a shipment of 2,000 apples. Based on the data, which is the most reasonable prediction of the number of apples in the shipment that weigh more than 7 ounces?

   Ⓐ about 200 apples   Ⓒ about 520 apples

   Ⓑ about 320 apples   Ⓓ about 560 apples

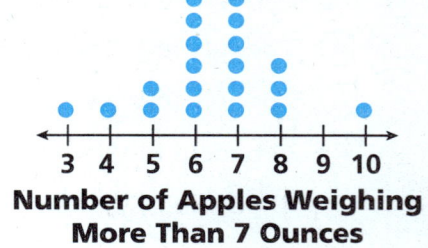

Number of Apples Weighing More Than 7 Ounces

10. Karen and Zeb each use a computer program to randomly select 50 students from the school directory. They ask the students about the school rules. They find that 68% from Karen's sample and 72% from Zeb's sample say the rules are fair. Explain why Karen and Zeb got different results, even though they used the same sampling method.

_____

_____

_____

Module 19

Use Statistics and Graphs to Compare Data

And the Best Player Is...

Three friends have a tournament to see who is best at playing a popular game on their phones. They each play the game 9 times. Their scores are shown.

Find the mean, median, range, and interquartile range for each player. Who is the best player?

A.

Arianna's Scores		
68	88	89
90	77	75
67	41	98

Mean: _____
Median: _____
Range: _____
Interquartile range: _____

B.

Deshauna's Scores		
98	79	41
93	24	93
91	31	35

Mean: _____
Median: _____
Range: _____
Interquartile range: _____

C.

Mayumi's Scores		
90	65	78
10	67	71
97	81	80

Mean: _____
Median: _____
Range: _____
Interquartile range: _____

 **Turn and Talk**

Which player do you think is the best player? Justify your answer.

Are You Ready?

Complete these problems to review prior concepts and skills you will need for this module.

Mean

Find the mean of each set of data.

1. The table lists the weights of a random sample of 11 tents from an outdoor store. What is the mean weight? _____

Tent Weights (ounces)		
79	73	77
81	76	50
64	56	47
59	75	

2. 17, 25, 22, 18, 18, 20 _____

3. 48, 12, 35, 57, 42, 15, 74, 29 _____

4. 24, 27, 29, 31, 8, 16, 24, 19, 11 _____

Dot Plots

Rosa is growing pea plants for a science experiment. The dot plot shows the heights of her 11 plants. Use the dot plot to determine each measure of center or variability.

5. Mean _____

6. Median _____

7. Range _____

Height of Pea Plants (cm)

Box Plots

A karate studio offers 10 classes per week for middle school students. The numbers of students in the classes are listed.

13, 15, 14, 10, 12, 10, 13, 16, 15, 13

8. Use the number line to make a box plot of the data set. Be sure to give the box plot a title.

9. Median _____

10. Range _____

11. Interquartile range _____

580

Apply and Practice
Lesson 1

Name _____

Compare Center and Spread of Data Displayed in Dot Plots

I Can compare two data sets displayed in dot plots and make inferences about two populations.

Step It Out

1 At the end of the first week of school, Mr. Parrish asked 15 freshman students how much time they spent studying that week. He also surveyed 15 sophomore students to investigate whether their habits were different.

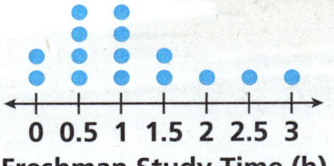
Freshman Study Time (h)

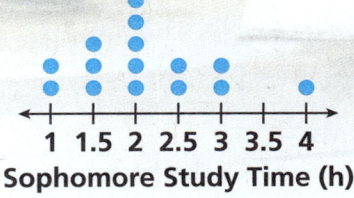
Sophomore Study Time (h)

A. Compare the shapes of the dot plots by describing where the values are clustered in each plot.

_____
_____
_____

B. Find the **median** and **mean** of each data set.

Freshman: median = _____   Sophomore: median = _____

Freshman: mean = _____   Sophomore: mean = _____

C. Find the **range** for each data set.

Freshman range: 3 − _____ = _____ hours

Sophomore range: 4 − _____ = _____ hours

Both data sets have a range of _____ hours.

D. What do the data tell you about study habits?

_____
_____

Turn and Talk How does a dot plot help you look at trends in data?

Module 19 • Lesson 1

581

2 Bill grows oranges and Carla grows apples. Each selected 13 trees at random and counted the pieces of fruit they produced to the nearest hundred.

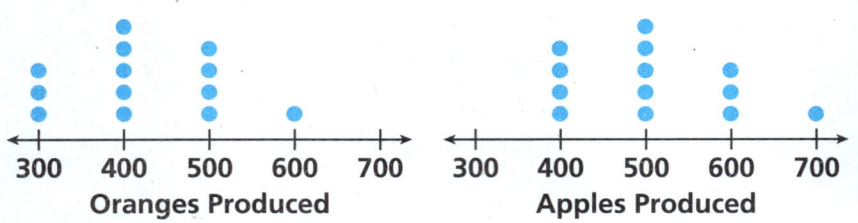

A. How are the shapes of the dot plots alike in terms of their peaks?

B. What is the median of each data set? Compare the medians of the plots.

C. Use the dot plots to compare the ranges of the data.

Check Understanding

The members of two book clubs kept track of how many hours they spent reading over one weekend. Use the dot plots for Problems 1–3.

1. Compare the means of the data sets and draw one conclusion.

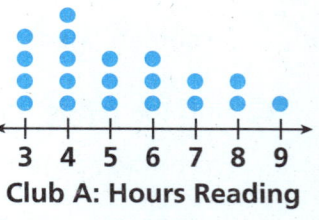

2. Compare the ranges of the data sets and draw one conclusion.

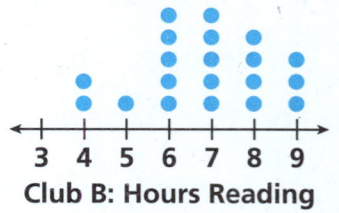

3. Draw one conclusion from the shape of the data distribution.

582

On Your Own

4. The dot plots show recorded wait times for two food trucks.

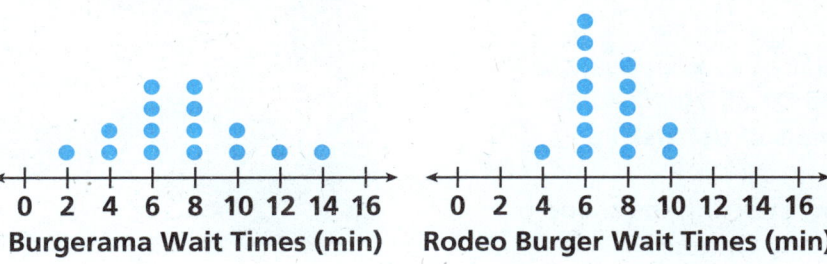 

A. **Use Structure** Visually compare the spreads of the data sets.

_____

_____

B. **Use Structure** Visually compare the centers of the data sets.

_____

C. Complete the table to verify your visual assessments.

	Burgerama	Rodeo Burger
Number of observations		
Median		
Range		

D. Do you expect the means to be about the same or to be different for each data set? Explain your visual assessment.

_____

_____

_____

_____

E. Find the mean to the nearest tenth to check your visual assessment.

Burgerama mean: _____   Rodeo Burger mean: _____

F. **Construct Arguments** Based on the data, which restaurant would have more predictable wait times? Explain.

_____

_____

_____

Module 19 • Lesson 1

5. Fabulous Fashions selected employees at random to review salary distribution for the company.

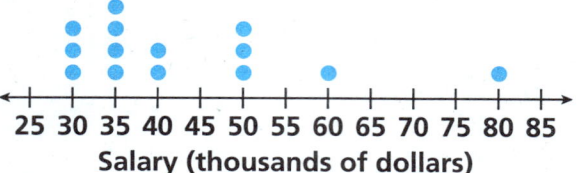

A. What is the median? Describe the shape of the data, including any clusters.

_____

_____

B. What is the range of the data? _____

C. **Use Structure** What do the data in the dot plot tell you about what most employees earn?

_____

_____

6. The dot plots show the ages in years of the players for both the Wolves and the Jets basketball teams.

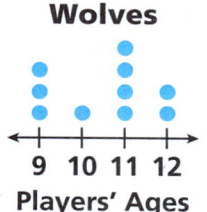
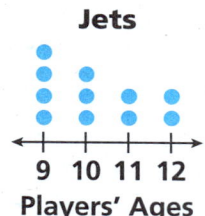

A. Compare the shapes of the dot plots.

_____

_____

B. Compare the modes and medians of the data sets.

_____

_____

C. What is the range of each data set?

_____

D. **Use Structure** What do the dot plots tell you about the ages of the players on the two teams?

_____

_____

Name _____

Compare Center and Spread of Data Displayed in Dot Plots

LESSON 19.1
More Practice/ Homework

ONLINE Video Tutorials and Interactive Examples

Tallahassee and Key West are at opposite ends of the state of Florida. The dot plots show high temperatures recorded in each city in May of one year. Use this information for Problems 1–7.

Tallahassee High Temperatures–May

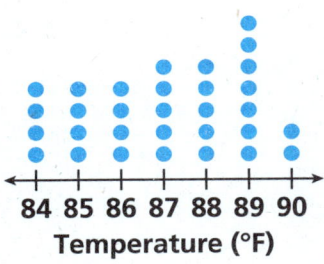

84 85 86 87 88 89 90
Temperature (°F)

Key West High Temperatures–May

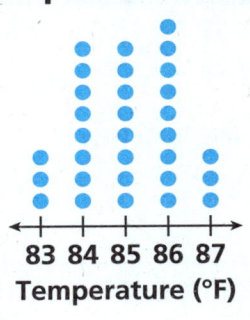

83 84 85 86 87
Temperature (°F)

1. Calculate the ranges of the data sets.

2. Which city's temperatures have the greater spread?

3. Calculate the medians of the data sets.

4. Which city's temperatures have the greater median?

5. What was the mean high temperature in May for each city, rounded to the nearest degree?

6. What was the difference between the median and the mean for each city?

7. **Geography** What do you learn about the temperatures for May in these cities by comparing their dot plots?

Module 19 • Lesson 1

585

Test Prep

Use the dot plots for Problems 8–11.

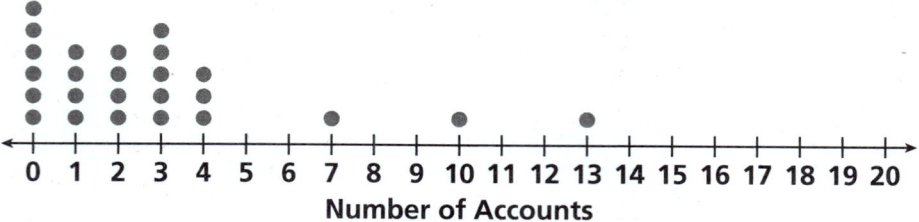

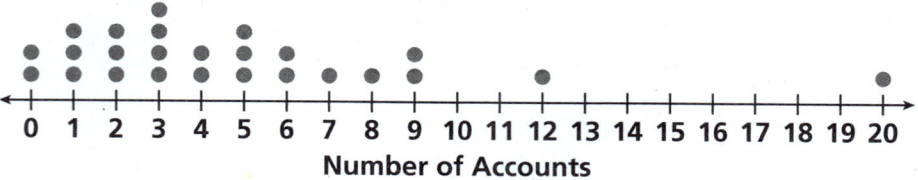

8. What is the median for the middle school data?

   (A) 0   (B) 1   (C) 2   (D) 3

9. What is the median for the high school data?

   (A) 3   (B) 4   (C) 5   (D) 6

10. Which of the following best describes the shape of the data in the middle school dot plot?

    (A) Most of the data points are less than 2.

    (B) Most of the data points are 5 or more.

    (C) Most of the data points are 4 or less.

    (D) There are no outliers.

11. What can you conclude about the variations among populations represented in this survey?

    _____
    _____

Spiral Review

12. What is the solution of the equation $2w - 3 = 11$? _____

13. If the slope of a line is 3 and the y-intercept is 0, what is an equation that represents the line?

    _____

Apply and Practice
Lesson 2

Name _____

Compare Center and Spread of Data Displayed in Box Plots

I Can compare two data sets displayed in box plots and make inferences about two populations.

Step It Out

1 The sixth- and seventh-grade students are having a reading contest. Their progress is shown in the **box plots**.

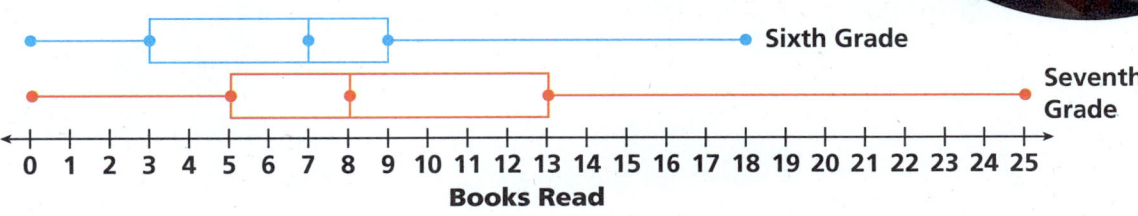

A. Describe the shapes of the box plots.

_____
_____
_____

B. Compare the medians of the data sets.

_____

C. Find the ranges and the **interquartile ranges**. Complete the table.

	Sixth grade	Seventh grade
Range		
Interquartile range		

D. Why would the data sets appear to have similar spreads using interquartile range and very different spreads using the range?

_____
_____

E. Explain what the left whiskers of the box plots tell you about the data sets.

_____
_____

 **Turn and Talk** Can you project the winner of the contest based on this data? Explain.

Module 19 • Lesson 2   **587**

2 The times in minutes for students to complete a test on paper and the same test on a computer are shown.

Paper: 42, 48, 52, 54, 59, 61, 61, 64, 65, 67, 68, 70, 72, 75, 80

Computer: 46, 47, 48, 50, 52, 55, 58, 60, 62, 64, 64, 64, 69, 73, 74

A. Find the five key values that describe the test scores collected from pencil-and-paper exams.

The least value, the minimum, is _____ minutes.

The greatest value, the maximum, is _____ minutes.

The median, or middle value, is _____ minutes.

The **lower quartile** is the median of only the values less than the median, so $Q_1 =$ _____ minutes.

The **upper quartile** is the median of the top half of the data, so $Q_3 =$ _____ minutes.

B. Identify the five key values for the sample of computer exam scores.

Minimum: _____ Median: _____ Maximum: _____

Q_1: _____ Q_3: _____

C. Sketch box plots to represent each sample.

D. Compare the medians and spreads of the box plots. Which testing format takes students longer to complete?

Paper

Computer

42 44 46 48 50 52 54 56 58 60 62 64 66 68 70 72 74 76 78 80
Time to Complete Exam (min)

_____
_____

Check Understanding

1. Two groups of 8 violin students kept track of the hours they practiced in a week.

   The results are:
   A: 0, 1, 3, 5, 5, 6, 6, 8   B: 2, 3, 3, 3, 5, 6, 9, 10

   Group A

   Group B

   0 1 2 3 4 5 6 7 8 9 10
   Hours Practicing Per Week

   Sketch box plots representing each data set. Draw one conclusion based on the plots.

   _____

2. About how many data points fall below the median of a data set?

   _____

Name _____

On Your Own

3. The box plots show the distribution of ages for players on two football teams.

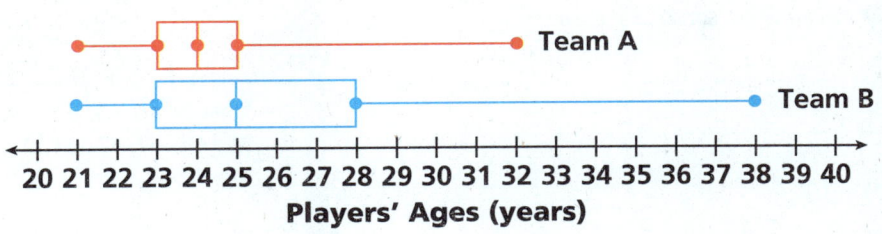

A. **Use Structure** How are the distributions alike?

_____
_____

B. Which measure of spread would you choose to describe these data sets? Use it to compare the spread of the data in these sets.

_____
_____
_____
_____

C. Use the box plots to complete the table.

D. Compare the medians of the box plots.

_____
_____
_____

	Team A	Team B
Minimum		
Lower quartile		
Median		
Upper quartile		
Maximum		

E. Explain the significance of the age 25 years in each box plot.

_____
_____
_____

F. **Reason** Where is the greatest difference in the box plots? Justify your choice.

_____
_____
_____

Module 19 • Lesson 2

4. Each year the Academy Awards honor excellence in film, including awards for Best Actor and Best Actress. The data sets shown are random samples of the ages in years at which these awards have been won.

Best actor: 29, 53, 40, 62, 36, 49, 53, 37, 44, 31, 41, 49, 51, 48, 32

Best actress: 22, 41, 27, 22, 38, 60, 62, 30, 36, 49, 21, 33, 26, 38, 28

A. Find the five key values for each data set.

B. Sketch box plots to represent each sample.

Best Actor

Best Actress

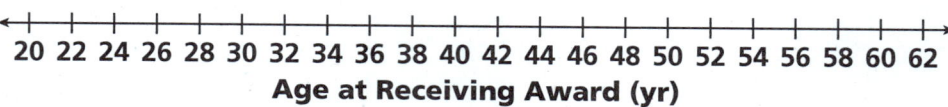

Age at Receiving Award (yr)

C. Compare the medians and spreads of the box plots.

D. **Critique Reasoning** After looking at the box plots, Tomás expresses surprise that most award-winning actresses are under the age of 41. Martha disagrees, pointing out that the right whisker is the longest part of the Best Actress box plot. Therefore, she argues, there are more winners between the ages of 41 and 62 than in the other intervals. Determine which friend is correct, and explain why.

E. What do the box plots for the samples tell you about the populations?

F. **Open Ended** Add two more possible ages to the data set for Best Actress winners so that the median of the data set does not change. Do not use the median age of 33 years.

Name _____

Compare Center and Spread of Data Displayed in Box Plots

LESSON 19.2
More Practice/ Homework

ONLINE Video Tutorials and Interactive Examples

Ms. Horvat is investigating prices of laptop computers at her local stores. She visits two different stores and selects a random sample of computers, recording their prices.

1. The box plot representing the data from Store A is shown.

   The five key values for the data from Store B are:

   minimum = $300, Q_1 = $500, median = $800, Q_3 = $1,000, maximum = $1,500

   A. Use the key values to sketch the box plot for Store B.

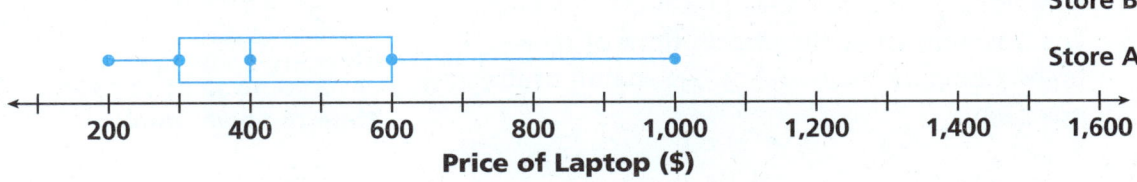

Store B

Store A

Price of Laptop ($)

   B. Compare the medians and shapes of the box plots.

   _____
   _____

   C. Compare the spreads of the box plots.

   _____
   _____
   _____
   _____

   D. **(MP) Use Structure** The price $1,000 is a key value for each box plot. Explain the significance of this price for each store's data.

   _____
   _____
   _____

   E. For each store, compare the spread of the lower half of the data with the spread of the upper half of the data.

   _____
   _____
   _____
   _____

Module 19 • Lesson 2

Test Prep

2. Which measures are used to make a box plot? Select all that apply.
   - Ⓐ maximum
   - Ⓑ mean
   - Ⓒ median
   - Ⓓ minimum
   - Ⓔ mode

3. When comparing two sets of data represented by box plots, compare the shape, _____, and _____.

4. Which is the preferred measure of spread for a data set with outliers?
   - Ⓐ interquartile range
   - Ⓑ mean
   - Ⓒ median
   - Ⓓ range

5. Moesha and Justin are competing in an online game to see who can solve puzzles in less time. The box plots show the distributions of their times. Compare the medians and shapes of the box plots.

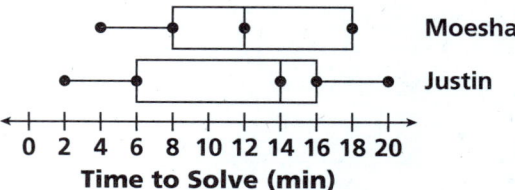

Spiral Review

6. The two dot plots show the points students in a driver's education class received on a quiz before and after their instructor awarded extra credit. How do the means, medians, and ranges of the two data sets compare? Explain.

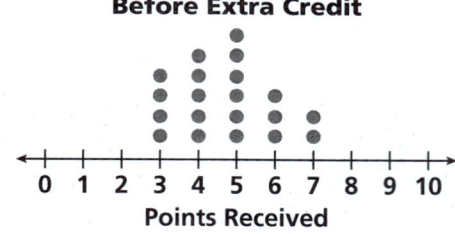 

7. What is $(9.5 \times 10^{-6}) \div (5 \times 10^4)$? Express your answer in scientific notation.

8. Simplify the expression $(2^{-3})^x \cdot (2^x)^7$ by rewriting it with a single exponent.

Apply and Practice
Lesson 3

Name _____

Compare Means Using Mean Absolute Deviation and Repeated Sampling

I Can use the means and MADs to assess the amount of visual overlap of two numerical data distributions.

Step It Out

1 The numbers of minutes students spent completing a math puzzle in January and in June of the same year are shown.

A. Recall that to find a **mean absolute deviation (MAD)**, find the average distance the data points are from the mean of the data set. Complete the table.

B. The MADs for these data sets happen to be the same. Find the ratio of the difference of the means to the MAD to the nearest tenth. The difference of the means is about _____ times the MAD.

C. When two data sets are displayed in dot plots, the points might overlap a lot, a little, or not at all. The centers might be close or far apart. The ratios of the difference of the means to the MADs can help you describe the separation between the two distributions. The greater the ratio, the greater the separation. When the MADs of the data sets are similar, these ratios will be similar.

These plots show the puzzle-solving data. The yellow shading shows values within the MAD, that is values that have an absolute deviation that is less than or equal to the MAD. Looking at the plots, you can see that the means are about 3.5 MADs apart.

January				
12	18	20	16	11
14	16	22	17	14

June				
12	6	3	4	9
4	5	8	9	10

	January	June
Mean		
MAD		

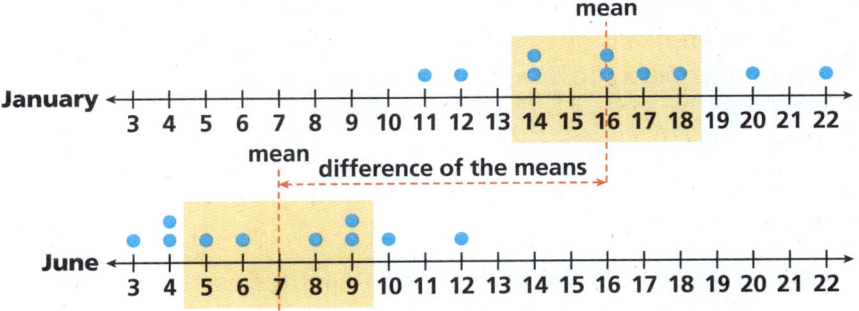

The distance between the means is _____, which is about _____ times the MAD, which indicates that there is a large / small separation between the centers of the data and a lot of / not much overlap in the two distributions.

Module 19 • Lesson 3

593

2 The first plot shows the heights in inches of sixth-grade students in the orchestra. The second shows the heights in inches of eighth-grade students in orchestra.

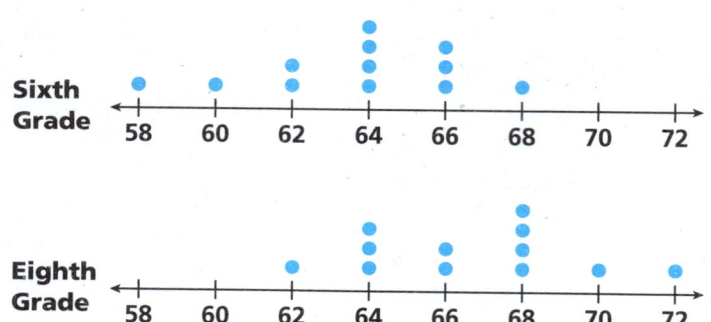

A. Complete the table. Round to the nearest tenth.

B. For each plot, draw a dashed vertical segment to show the mean. Then, shade the region that shows the values that are within the MAD.

	Sixth Grade	Eighth Grade
Mean		
MAD		

C. Find the ratio of the difference of the means to the MAD for each data set.

Grade 6: $\frac{\text{difference of the means}}{\text{MAD}} = $ _____   Grade 8: $\frac{\text{difference of the means}}{\text{MAD}} = $ _____

D. What do the ratios you calculated in Part C tell you about the separation between the two distributions? Do the dot plots support this?

_____
_____
_____
_____

Check Understanding

1. The difference of the means of two data sets is 0.5. Both data sets have a MAD of 1. How does the difference in the means compare to the MADs? If the data were displayed in dot plots, how much overlap would you expect to see? Explain.

_____
_____

2. A survey of adults and teens recorded the daily time in minutes each person spent messaging on a cell phone. The results are shown.

   Adults: 5, 10, 20, 15, 10   Teens: 50, 60, 40, 10, 80

   Complete the statement: The MAD for _____ is more than _____ times the MAD for _____, so the variation for _____ is much greater than for _____.

594

Name _____

On Your Own

3. A video game company is developing two games. One group is writing computer code for "Find the Gem." The other group is writing code for "Cross the Ocean." The plots show how long each programmer spent writing code for that game.

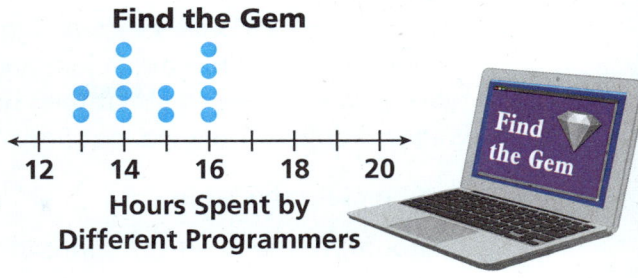

A. To the nearest tenth, what is the mean of each sample data set?

   Find the Gem: _____

   Cross the Ocean: _____

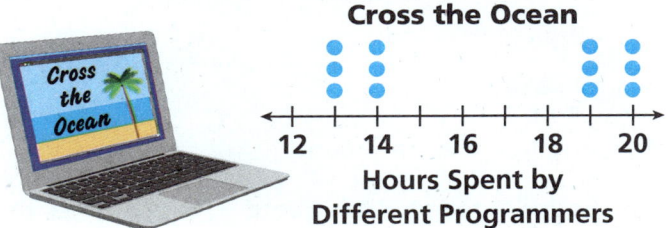

B. Which distribution do you predict will have the greater MAD? Why?

   _____

   _____

C. (MP) **Attend to Precision** What is the MAD of each data set?

   MAD of "Find the Gem" _____   MAD of "Cross the Ocean" _____

D. Complete the statement. Does your answer support your prediction in Part B?

   The MAD for "Cross the Ocean" is _____ times the MAD for "Find the Gem."

   _____

For Problems 4–7, write the approximate ratio of the difference of the means to the MADs for the given data sets. Then tell how much overlap you would expect to see in dot plots of the same sample data.

4.

	Sample A	Sample B
Mean	45	48
MAD	1.5	1.5

5.

	Sample A	Sample B
Mean	112	107
MAD	4.8	5.2

6.

	Sample A	Sample B
Mean	36	43
MAD	14	14

7.

	Sample A	Sample B
Mean	27.5	27.2
MAD	0.09	0.09

Module 19 • Lesson 3

8. **Reason** Randomly selected high school students with summer jobs and adult workers were surveyed about their hourly wages in dollars. The data are shown.

   Hourly Wage of Students ($)

15.00	15.00	15.00	15.00	15.00
15.25	15.25	15.50	15.50	15.50
15.75	16.00	18.00	19.00	20.00

   Hourly Wage of Adults ($)

15.00	15.00	16.00	17.50	18.00
19.00	21.00	22.00	24.00	25.00
27.00	28.00	28.00	31.50	32.00

   A. Complete the table.

   Round to the nearest hundredth.

	Students	Adults
Mean		
MAD		

   B. Complete the statement.

   The MAD for adults is about _____ times the MAD for students. This means the variation in the wages for adults is much _____ than the variation in the wages for students.

   C. **Open Ended** Suggest a change to one hourly wage in the student table so that the MAD will be less than before.

   _____

9. Randomly selected seventh-graders in two classes are each asked to measure the entire length of their pointer finger and its length from the tip to the middle joint. The ratio of the lengths is recorded. The data are then organized for each class.

   Class 1 Length Ratios

   Class 2 Length Ratios

   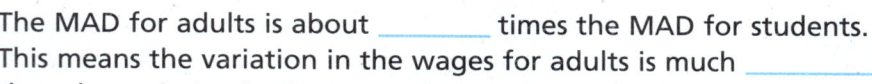

   A. Do the two data sets overlap a lot, a little, or not at all?

   _____

   B. Find the means, the MADs, and the ratio of the difference of the means to the MADs for each data set. Round your answers to the nearest hundredth.

   Class 1: mean _____ MAD _____ ratio _____

   Class 2: mean _____ MAD _____ ratio _____

   C. Do your answers to Part B support your answer to Part A? Explain.

   _____
   _____

Compare Means Using Mean Absolute Deviation and Repeated Sampling

LESSON 19.3
More Practice/ Homework

ONLINE Video Tutorials and Interactive Examples

1. **STEM** Akuchi is experimenting with the effect of using plant food on the growth of sunflowers. The dot plots show the heights in inches of randomly selected sunflowers.

A. What are the means of each sample data set?

The mean height of sunflowers that grew with no food is _____ inches.

The mean height of sunflowers that grew with food is _____ inches.

B. What are the mean absolute deviations of the sample data?

The MAD for the sunflowers that grew with no food is _____ inches.

The MAD for the sunflowers that grew with food is _____ inches.

Are the data differences visually separate? Explain why you would expect them to be.

_____

_____

2. **Math on the Spot** The tables show the number of minutes per day students spend outside of school reading and doing their math homework.

Minutes spent outside of school reading	Minutes spent outside of school doing math homework
15, 15, 15, 20, 30, 30, 30, 30, 45, 60	25, 30, 30, 30, 30, 40, 45, 45, 55, 60

What is the difference of the means as a multiple of the approximate mean absolute deviations? _____

Module 19 • Lesson 3

597

Test Prep

Use this information for Problems 3 and 4.

Two lab groups are each given a bag of identically shaped beads with letters. The groups are instructed to select 20 beads randomly and then record the number of vowels in the sample. They each perform the process 8 times, and their data are shown.

Group A	3	1	0	2	3	4	1	2
Group B	3	0	4	4	2	1	4	2

3. What is the difference of the means for Group A and Group B?
   - Ⓐ 0.5 vowel
   - Ⓑ 1 vowel
   - Ⓒ 2 vowels
   - Ⓓ 4.5 vowels

4. What is the ratio of the difference of the means to the MAD for Group B?
   - Ⓐ 0.4
   - Ⓑ 0.5
   - Ⓒ 1
   - Ⓓ 1.25

Spiral Review

5. The box plots represent data for the daily temperatures in one month for two cities in Colorado at different altitudes.

   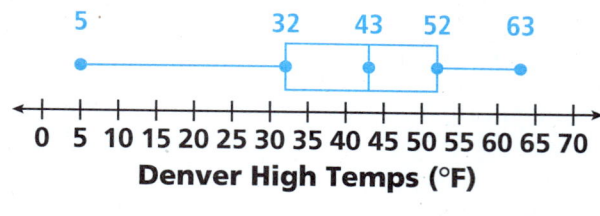
   Denver High Temps (°F)

   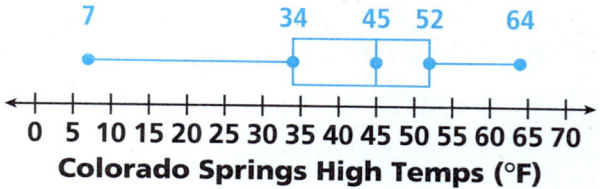
   Colorado Springs High Temps (°F)

   How do the medians compare?

   _____
   _____

6. A tourist traced a semicircle while walking half-way around a circular fountain at an arboretum. The tourist walked a total of 15π feet. What is the straight-line distance between the tourist's starting and ending points?

   _____

7. Write $0.4\overline{09}$ as a fraction in simplest form. Is $0.4\overline{09}$ rational or irrational?

   _____

Module 19 Review

Vocabulary

1. How is a dot plot similar to a box plot? How are they different?
   _____
   _____

2. How are the median and upper quartile of a data set related?
   _____
   _____

Concepts and Skills

3. Cheri skated 10 laps on a skating rink, and Kristen skated 9 laps. The dot plots show the time it took them to skate each lap. Plot a dot on Kristen's dot plot to show a time she must get on her tenth lap so that her median time is equal to Cheri's median time.

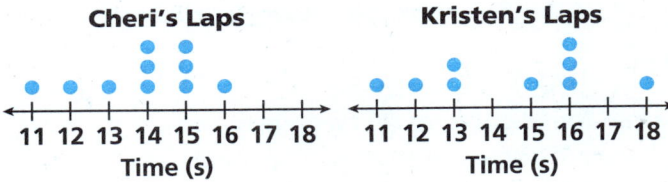

4. **Use Tools** A shipment includes 500 boxes of wheat cereal and 500 boxes of corn cereal. The dot plots show the masses of a random sample of 20 boxes of each type. Which cereal has a greater median mass? How much greater? State what strategy and tool you will use to answer the question, explain your choice, and then find the answer.

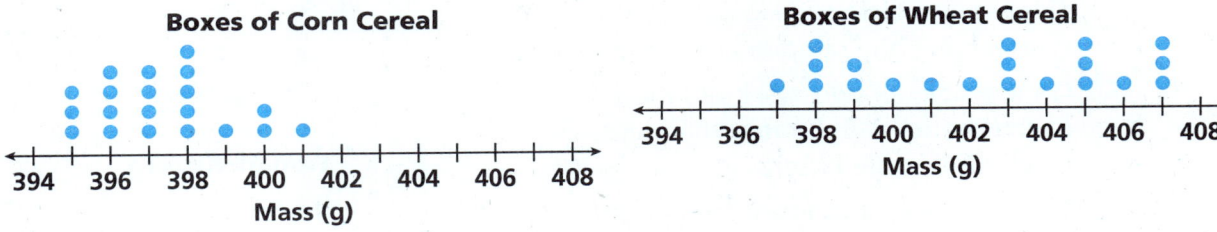

_____
_____
_____

5. The box plot shows the numbers of students in a random sample of 30 classes at Lincoln Middle School and a random sample of 30 classes at Fairview Middle School. Which statements about the classes at the two schools are supported by the random samples? Select all that apply.

   Ⓐ There is little overlap in the distributions of the samples.

   Ⓑ The number of students per class is more variable at Lincoln than at Fairview.

   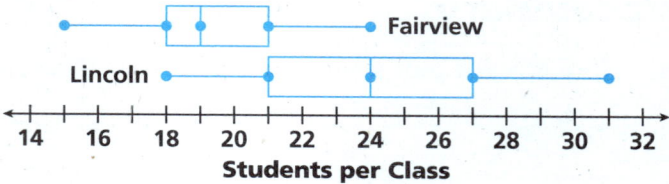

   Ⓒ A typical class at Lincoln has about 10 more students than a typical class at Fairview.

   Ⓓ About half the sampled classes at Lincoln have more students than the largest sampled class at Fairview.

   Ⓔ The interquartile range for the number of students per class at Fairview is about 3 times the interquartile range at Lincoln.

6. Ignacio surveyed a random sample of students at his school about the number of math problems they had for homework on Monday and on Friday. The box plot shows his results. What is the difference in the ranges of the two data sets? _____ problems

   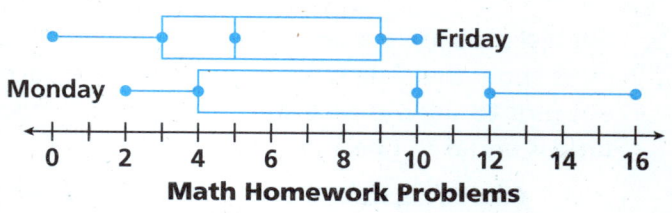

7. The dot plots show the weights of a random sample of 20 two-week-old male kittens and 20 two-week-old female kittens at a shelter. The mean weight of the males is 11.75 ounces, and the mean weight of the females is 11 ounces. The difference in the mean weights is about 0.6 times the mean average deviation of either sample. Which statement is best supported by the random samples?

   Ⓐ There is a lot of overlap between the two samples; the samples are similar.

   Ⓑ There is very little overlap between the two samples; the samples are very different.

   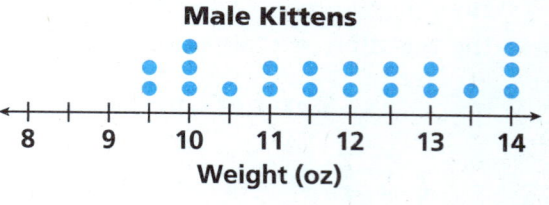

   Ⓒ On average, all two-week-old male kittens at the shelter weigh more than all two-week-old female kittens.

   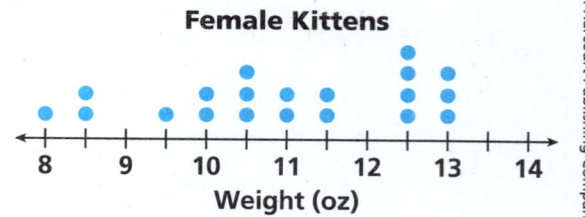

   Ⓔ There is more variation in the weights of all two-week-old male kittens at the shelter than in the weights of all two-week-old female kittens.

600

Unit 9: Probability

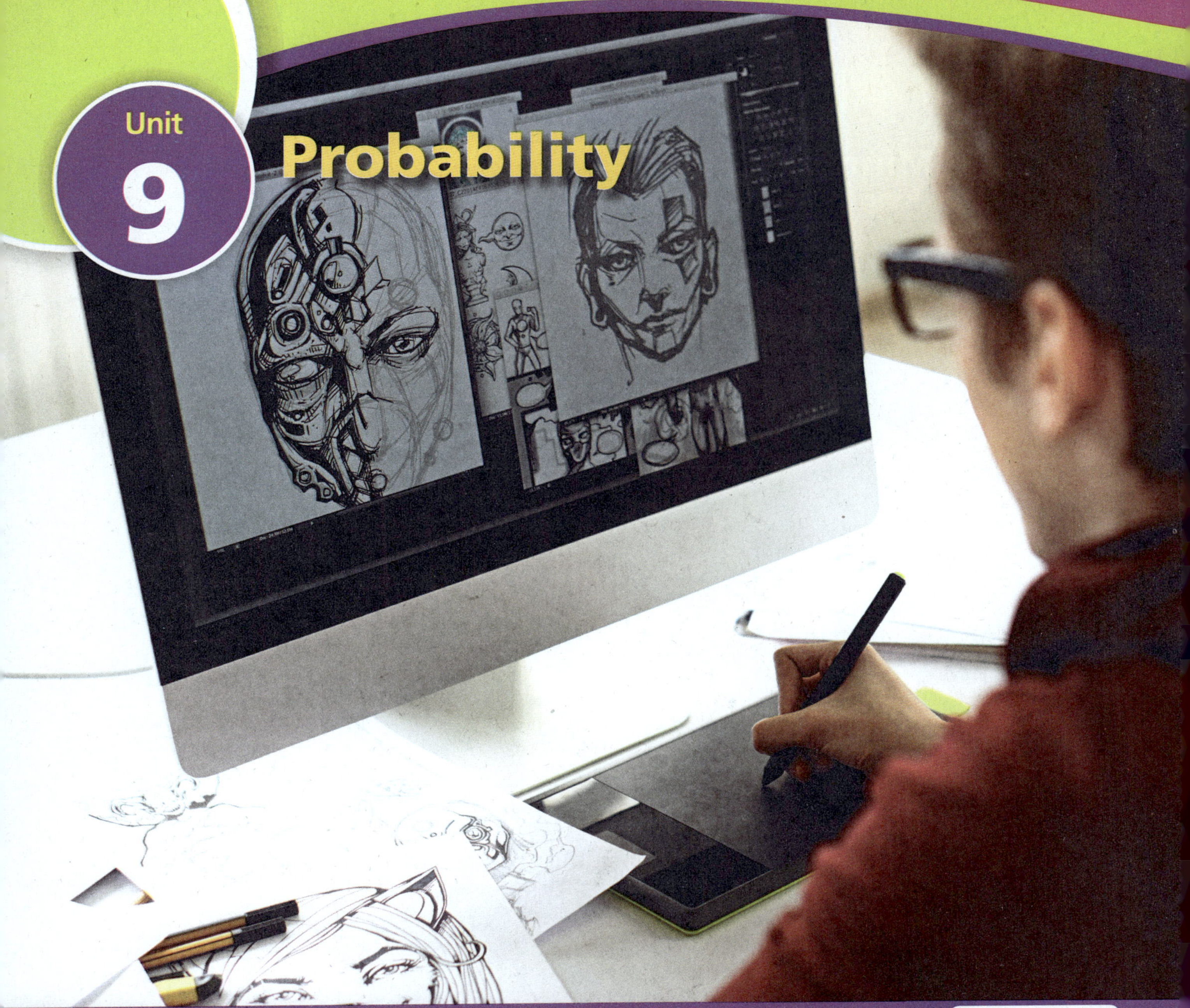

Game Designer

A game designer usually works as part of a team that designs games. Video game designers help develop computer games for a variety of platforms, from large consoles to mobile phones. Shigeru Miyamoto, sometimes called the father of modern video games, is a Japanese game designer who has invented some of the world's most famous and successful video games.

STEM Task:

Work with a partner to invent a simple board game for two players. Your game should use up to ten cards and/or one or two number cubes. Choose the goal of the game and decide how players move on the board. Then play the game with your partner several times. Do you think you designed a fair game? Explain why or why not.

Learning Mindset
Challenge-Seeking Makes Plans to Meet Goals

A challenge is a problem that requires work and determination to solve. A challenging project may include both short- and long-term tasks. By definition, a challenge is not easy—that is why mastering a challenge is such a rewarding experience. You can feel a sense of pride because you know you accomplished something difficult. Here are some tips for tackling a challenge.

- Divide the challenge into smaller steps. Think about how each step leads to completion of the entire project or task.

- Decide how and where to find the information and knowledge you need to complete each step.

- Work with others to brainstorm, check work, share knowledge, and give and receive support.

Reflect

Q What steps did you take to complete the STEM Task?

Q What challenges did you and your partner identify while working on the STEM Task? How did you address them?

Module 20
Understand and Apply Experimental Probability

Go for the Gold!

In the first four levels of a video game, players roam through a castle collecting gold coins and bars. To reach Level D, a player must have a total of at least 10 more gold bars than coins. The table shows the number of coins or gold bars that Miguel collected in each of the first three levels.

Complete the table by sketching the missing gold coins and gold bars.

Level	Ratio of Coins to Gold Bars	Number of Coins Collected	Number of Gold Bars Collected
A	2:3	○○○○	
B	6:8	○○○○○○○○○○	
C	4:10		▭▭▭▭▭ ▭▭▭▭▭ ▭▭▭▭▭

 **Turn and Talk**

Does Miguel advance to Level D? Justify your answer.

Are You Ready?

Complete these problems to review prior concepts and skills you will need for this module.

Statistical Data Collection

The dot plot shows the heights of students in one class. Use this information for Problems 1–2.

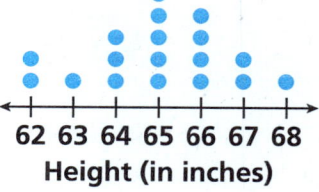

1. What unit of measure was used? How was it measured?
   _____

2. How many students are in the class? Explain.
   _____
   _____

Fractions, Decimals, and Percents

Write each fraction as a decimal and a percent.

3. $\frac{3}{5}$ 4. $\frac{12}{16}$ 5. $\frac{5}{8}$

   _____   _____   _____

Write each decimal as a percent and a fraction in simplest form.

6. 0.35   7. 0.7   8. 0.125

   _____   _____   _____

Use Ratio and Rate Reasoning

9. One out of every 3 players on a soccer team is new this season. There are 15 players on the team in all. How many of the players are new?

   _____ new players

10. There are 515 students who attend Central Middle School. Three out of every 5 students live within 1 mile of the school. How many students at Central Middle School live within 1 mile of the school?

    _____ students

11. How can you use proportional reasoning to write a ratio that is equivalent to another ratio?

    _____
    _____

604

Build Conceptual Understanding

Lesson 1

Name _____

Understand Probability of an Event

I Can describe the likelihood of an event.

Spark Your Learning

A gumball machine contains 50 gumballs. There are 25 blue, 10 red, 12 green, and 3 yellow gumballs in the machine. Bart puts a coin in and turns the wheel to receive a gumball. What is an outcome that is likely to occur? Not likely? As likely as not? Certain? Impossible?

 Turn and Talk How would you describe the likelihood of receiving a red gumball, using the given phrases?

Module 20 • Lesson 1

Build Understanding

Probability describes how likely an event is to occur. It is a measure between 0 and 1 as shown on the number line, and can be written as a fraction, a decimal, or a percent. The probability of an event is written as *P*(event).

> **Connect to Vocabulary**
>
> The **probability of an event** measures the likelihood that the event will occur.

The closer the probability of the event is to 0, the less likely the event is to occur. The closer the probability of the event is to 1, the more likely the event is to occur. An event with probability 0 is impossible. An event with probability 1 is certain.

Impossible	Unlikely	As likely as not	Likely	Certain
0		$\frac{1}{2}$		1
0		0.5		1.0
0%		50%		100%

1 Tell whether each event is impossible, unlikely, as likely as not, likely, or certain. Then tell whether the probability is 0, close to 0, $\frac{1}{2}$, close to 1, or 1.

A. A bag contains pieces of paper labeled with the numbers 1 through 100. A piece of paper with the number 13 is selected at random.

_____

B. Two number cubes are rolled. The sum of the numbers is 1.

_____

C. A number cube is rolled, and the result is an even number.

_____

_____

D. A bowl contains 26 disks. Each disk is labeled with a different letter of the alphabet. A consonant is selected at random.

_____

E. Twelve middle-school students are selected to complete a survey. None of the students are in tenth grade.

_____

> **Turn and Talk** What do you know about the value of the probability of an event that is likely?

Name _____

Often the same experiment is repeated many times. Each repetition of an experiment is called a **trial**, and each result of a trial is an **outcome**. A set of one or more possible outcomes for a trial is an **event**. A **sample space** is the set of all possible outcomes for an experiment.

> **Connect to Vocabulary**
>
> An **experiment** is an activity involving chance in which results are observed.

2 Roll a number cube 10 times. How likely is each event in the table?

A. What is the sample space of all possible outcomes when you roll the number cube once?

_____

B. Roll a number cube 10 times and record the results in the table.

Event	Frequency
Roll a 2	
Roll a 1, 3, 4, 5 or 6	
Roll an odd number	
Roll a number less than 7	

C. How many trials did you perform? How many events did you record?

_____

D. Judging from the results of your trials, which events are certain when rolling a number cube?

_____

E. Judging from the results of your trials, which events are likely? Which events are unlikely? Which events are as likely as not?

_____
_____

 **Turn and Talk** Based on your results from the table, what number or number range might you use to describe the probability of rolling a 2? Explain.

Check Understanding

1. Tell whether choosing a blue marble from a jar containing 4 blue marbles and 12 red marbles is unlikely, as likely as not, or likely. Is the probability closer to 0 or 1?

_____

2. What number and what percent describe the probability of a certain event? What number and what percent describe the probability of an impossible event?

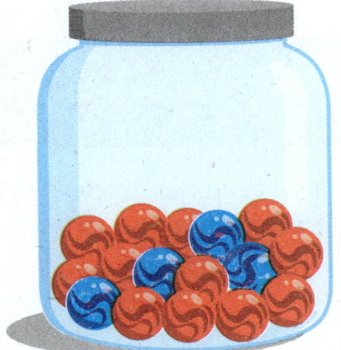

Module 20 • Lesson 1

On Your Own

3. Mina opens a book 15 times and records whether the page number is even or odd. How many trials did she conduct? Name two events that she recorded.

   _____

4. Orlando has a bowl with 12 green disks and 8 yellow disks. Is the probability of randomly selecting a green disk unlikely, as likely as not, or likely?

   _____

5. (MP) **Reason** A container holds 20 red, 20 blue, and 10 green marbles. Is the probability of choosing a blue marble greater than or less than the probability of choosing a marble that is not blue? Explain.

   _____

   _____

   _____

   For Problems 6–7, describe the probability of each event in words. Then describe each probability with a number or a number range.

6. Roll a number greater than 5 on a standard number cube.

   _____

7. Pick a number less than or equal to 30 from a bag with 40 pieces of paper numbered 1 through 40.

   _____

8. **Open Ended** Ask 6 students their age and record the results. Pick one age from the results. How many students stated this age? Describe in words the probability that a student in your class is this age, judging from the results.

   _____

 I'm in a **Learning Mindset!**

Did I select appropriate challenges as part of learning how to describe the probability of an event?

_____

_____

Name _____

Understand Probability of an Event

LESSON 20.1
More Practice/ Homework

ONLINE Video Tutorials and Interactive Examples

1. Mia rolls two standard number cubes. Is a sum greater than 12 impossible, unlikely, as likely as not, likely, or certain?

   _____

2. A machine makes 50 parts. Out of the 50 parts, 3 are defective. Describe the probability that a randomly selected part is not defective, using a number or a number range.

   _____

3 out of 50 parts are defective.

3. **Open Ended** Write a situation where the probability of an event occurring is unlikely.

   _____
   _____
   _____

4. Rocky has a box of pens. He has 11 black pens, 8 blue pens, and 6 red pens. He randomly selects a pen from the box. Use a number or number range to describe the probability that the pen he selects is blue.

   _____

Flip a coin eight times and record the results of *heads* or *tails*. Use the results for Problems 5–9.

5. List the sample space of all possible outcomes when you flip a coin once.

   _____

6. What experiment did you perform? How many trials of the experiment did you conduct? What events did you record?

   _____

7. How many times did the coin land heads up? Based only on these results, does getting *heads* seem to be impossible, unlikely, as likely as not, likely, or certain?

   _____

8. How many times did the coin land tails up? Based only on these results, does getting *tails* seem to be impossible, unlikely, as likely as not, likely, or certain?

   _____

9. **(MP) Reason** Are the results of your experiment what you would expect? Explain.

   _____

Module 20 • Lesson 1

Test Prep

10. Adam has 10 blocks numbered 1 through 10. Which describes the probability of randomly choosing a block that has an even number?

　Ⓐ impossible

　Ⓑ unlikely

　Ⓒ as likely as not

　Ⓓ likely

　Ⓔ certain

11. Bella finds some beach glass. She finds 14 pieces of brown beach glass, 12 pieces of white beach glass, 12 pieces of green beach glass, and 2 pieces of blue beach glass. She lets her sister pick one piece at random to keep. Describe the probability that her sister picks a piece of blue beach glass, using a number or a number range.

_____

12. A bowl contains 4 blue marbles and 12 red marbles. Soo-jin picks a marble from the bowl. Describe a likely event.

_____

13. A community service club has 12 seventh-graders and 12 eighth-graders. The name of each student is put in a hat, and a name is drawn at random. Which number or number range describes the probability that the student selected is a seventh-grader?

　Ⓐ a number greater than 0 and less than $\frac{1}{2}$

　Ⓑ a number greater than $\frac{1}{2}$ and less than 1

　Ⓒ 1

　Ⓓ $\frac{1}{2}$

Spiral Review

14. A patio is shaped as a composite figure consisting of two rectangles. One part of the patio is 20 feet long and 15 feet wide. The other part is 15 feet long and 10 feet wide. What is the area of the patio?

_____

15. An aquarium is a rectangular prism. The volume of the aquarium is 6,480 cubic inches. The length of the aquarium is 30 inches, and the height is 18 inches. What is the width of the aquarium?

_____

Connect Concepts and Skills

Lesson 2

Name _____

Find Experimental Probability of Simple Events

I Can find an experimental probability and its complement.

Spark Your Learning

Toss a paper cup a number of times and record the different ways that the cup lands on a table. Describe each way that the cup lands as likely or unlikely. Organize your results in a table.

Outcome	Frequency
Open end up	
Open end down	
On its side	

Turn and Talk How do you think increasing the number of times you toss the cup would change your results?

Module 20 • Lesson 2

611

Build Understanding

1 Conduct an experiment by flipping a coin. Record your results in the table. Repeat until you have conducted the experiment 20 times.

Outcome	Frequency
Heads	
Tails	

A. How many trials did you conduct?

___

B. Do the outcomes appear to be equally likely? Explain.

___

___

C. Use the number of times each event occurs compared to the number of trials to approximate the probability of each event.

Outcome	Probability
Heads	$\dfrac{heads}{20} = \dfrac{\square}{20}$
Tails	$\dfrac{tails}{20} = \dfrac{\square}{20}$

D. If you flip the coin only four times, do you think it is possible that you might record only *tails* and no *heads*? What if you flip a coin 100 times? Compare the chances of the two possibilities.

___

___

E. What happens to the number of times each outcome occurs as you perform more trials?

___

___

___

F. What is the sum of the probabilities in Part C?

___

Turn and Talk Are there any outcomes that did not occur in your set of trials? Explain why or why not.

Name _____

Step It Out

The **experimental probability** of an event is found by comparing the number of times an event occurs to the total number of trials.

experimental probability = $\frac{\text{number of times the event occurs}}{\text{total number of trials}}$

2 Muriel has a spinner with red, blue, and green sections. She spins the spinner 50 times and records the results in a table.

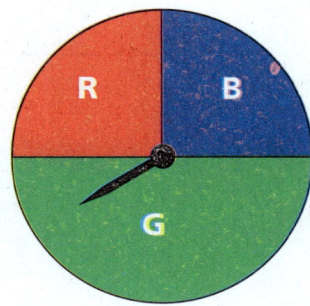

Event	Frequency
Red	14
Blue	12
Green	24

A. Find the experimental probability of each outcome.

_____

B. What conclusions can you make about the spinner using the experimental probabilities?

_____
_____
_____

C. How would you find the experimental probability of the spinner landing on a color that is not red, and what is that experimental probability in this example?

_____
_____

Connect to Vocabulary

The **complement** of an event is the set of all outcomes in the sample space that are *not* included in the event. The sum of the probability of an event and the probability of its complement is 1.

D. How is the experimental probability of the spinner landing on a color that is not red related to the experimental probability of the spinner landing on red?

_____

Module 20 • Lesson 2

A **simulation** is a model of an experiment that would be difficult to actually perform. A simulation can be used to find an experimental probability and make a prediction.

3 A softball player hits the ball and reaches base safely about 30% of the time. The player hits the ball but is called "out" about 50% of the time. The player strikes out about 20% of the time.

A. How could you use a random number generator to simulate what might happen the next 25 times the player comes up to hit the ball?

_____

_____

B. Perform the simulation. Record your results.

Event	Frequency
Hit - Safe	
Hit - Out	
Strikeout	

C. Make a prediction based on your simulation.

_____

D. Combine the results of your simulation with the results of all the simulations. How do the total results of the class compare to your simulation?

_____

_____

Check Understanding

1. Allison rolls a standard number cube 30 times and records her results. The number of times she rolled a 4 is 6. What is the experimental probability of rolling a 4? What is the experimental probability of not rolling a 4?

_____

2. Kelly averages 90% correct on her math assignments. She wants to perform a simulation to predict the number of questions she will answer correctly out of her next 70 questions. What is a simulation she could use to make this prediction?

_____

_____

Name _____

On Your Own

3. Andreas is performing an experiment involving rolling a number cube. He rolls the number cube 60 times and records the results in the table.

    A. **Reason** Are the outcomes equally likely? Explain.

    _____

    _____

    B. Find the experimental probabilities to complete the table.

Outcome	Frequency	Experimental Probability
1	8	
2	11	
3	10	
4	7	
5	11	
6	13	

4. **Open Ended** Ask 8 students how many letters are in their first name. Record the number of letters for each answer. Describe one event from your experiment and find the experimental probability of this event.

    _____

    _____

5. **Use Tools** A football quarterback completes 60% of attempted passes. Describe a simulation that you can perform in order to predict how many passes out of 40 this quarterback will complete.

    _____

    _____

6. Jean estimates that her friend completes a new level of a video game on the first try 20% of the time. She conducts a simulation to predict how many times out of 80 her friend would complete a new level on the first try. Jean uses a random number generator. Every digit that is 8 or 9 represents completing the level. What is the probability that her friend completes a new level on the first try, written as a percent?

Digit	0	1	2	3	4	5	6	7	8	9
Frequency	10	9	6	7	8	12	4	6	7	11

Module 20 • Lesson 2

7. Diego has a spinner that is divided into four sections labeled A, B, C, and D as shown. He spins the spinner many times and records the results. The results are shown in the table.

Letter	A	B	C	D
Frequency	14	24	14	12

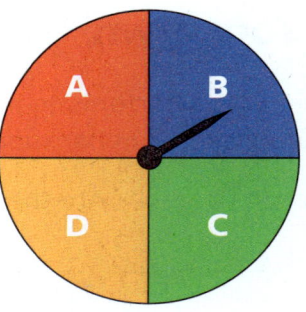

A. Add the frequency of each event to find the total number of times that he spun the spinner. Then find the experimental probability of spinning each letter.

_____

B. What is the probability of the complement of spinning D?

_____

C. **Construct Arguments** What conclusion can Diego make about the bias of the spinner he used, based on the experimental probabilities? Explain your reasoning.

_____
_____
_____
_____
_____

8. Dustin buys packs of trading cards. He reads that half of the packs contain a bonus card. Dustin uses a coin to perform a simulation to estimate how many packs will contain a bonus card if he buys 20 packs. He uses heads to represent a pack with a bonus card. The results of his simulation are shown.

H, H, T, H, T, T, T, H, T, H, H, T, T, H, T, H, H, T, H, H

How many packs in this simulation did not contain a bonus card?

_____

 I'm in a Learning Mindset!

Am I willing to accept new challenges while learning about probability?

_____

Name _____

Find Experimental Probability of Simple Events

LESSON 20.2
More Practice/ Homework

ONLINE Video Tutorials and Interactive Examples

1. Luther is performing an experiment involving a triangular pyramid with sides labeled 1–4. He shakes it in a jar and empties the jar without looking 80 times. Using a table, he records the number of the face it lands on. Find the experimental probabilities to complete the table.

Outcome	Frequency	Experimental Probability
1	19	$\frac{\Box}{80}$
2	17	$\frac{\Box}{80}$
3	23	$\frac{\Box}{80}$
4	21	$\frac{\Box}{80}$

2. **(MP) Use Tools** Marcela gets to school later than her friend Kim about half the time. Describe a way to simulate this event for 10 school days. Then perform the simulation. How many times does it show Marcela arriving later than Kim? What is the experimental probability of this event?

_____
_____

3. **Math on the Spot** For one month, Terry recorded the time at which her school bus arrived. She organized her results in a frequency table. Find the experimental probability that the bus will arrive between 8:20 and 8:24. Find the experimental probability that the bus will arrive after 8:19.

Time	8:15–8:19	8:20–8:24	8:25–8:30
Frequency	10	11	3

_____

4. **(MP) Use Tools** Wei has two different routes he takes to a park. He labels the routes A and B. He takes route B about 33% of the time. Describe a simulation Wei could perform using a number cube to estimate the number of times he will take route B to get to the park if he goes to the park 60 times.

_____
_____
_____
_____

Module 20 • Lesson 2   **617**

Test Prep

5. Asia has a jar of marbles. She randomly selects a marble from the jar, records its color, and returns it to the jar. She repeats this 74 times. Her results are shown in the table.

Outcome	Frequency
Red	13
Blue	20
Green	22
Yellow	19

What is the experimental probability of Asia choosing a green marble?

_____

6. Jordan performed an experiment using a number cube. He rolled a number cube 50 times. He found that he rolled a 6 a total of 8 times. What is the experimental probability that he did *not* roll a 6?

- Ⓐ $\frac{3}{25}$
- Ⓑ $\frac{4}{25}$
- Ⓒ $\frac{21}{25}$
- Ⓓ $\frac{22}{25}$

7. Juan rolls a number cube 40 times. He rolls a 3 on the number cube 6 times. What is the experimental probability that he rolls a 3?

_____

Spiral Review

8. Emma selects coins at random from a jar, putting the coin back each time after selecting it. She conducts 28 trials and selects 7 pennies, 12 nickels, and 9 dimes. Based on the results, describe in words the likelihood that she selects a penny.

_____

9. Juana and Andy completed 10 math problems total. Juana completed 6 of the problems. Write an equation to determine the number of math problems that Andy completed, then solve the equation. How many of the math problems did Andy complete?

_____

Connect Concepts and Skills

Lesson 3

Name _____

Find Experimental Probability of Compound Events

I Can determine the experimental probability of compound events.

Spark Your Learning

Felix was attending an awards dinner and the menu had the choices shown for appetizer and entrée. What is the sample space for his dinner selection?

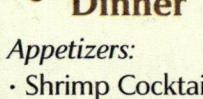

Appetizers:
· Shrimp Cocktail
· Garden Salad

Entrees:
· Roast Beef
· Chicken Marsala
· Vegetarian Lasagna

 Turn and Talk The menu also had a choice of two drinks. When considering that choice, how does that affect the total number of combinations that are available to order?

Module 20 • Lesson 3

619

Build Understanding

At Felix's awards dinner, T-shirts were being handed out to the award winners. The choices for the shirts are shown. The selection of a shirt is a compound event due to the available choices in different categories.

> **Connect to Vocabulary**
> A coin landing heads up when flipped or rolling a 6 on a number cube are simple events. A **compound event** is an event that includes two or more simple events.

1 Define the sample space of the shirt choices.

A. How many colors are there? What are the choices?

_____

B. How many sizes are there? What are the choices?

_____

C. Write all the possible combinations of sizes and colors.

_____

_____

_____

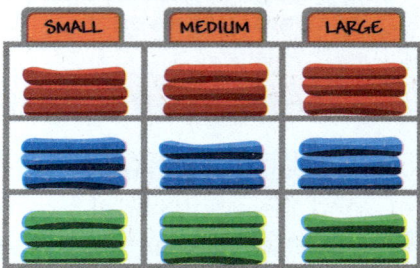

D. There are _____ possible outcomes for this compound event.

E. In the table, fill out the shaded boxes with headings for the sizes and colors of the shirts. Then fill in the table to show the sample space, all the possible outcomes when a shirt is selected.

F. Suppose a compound event includes two simple events. Explain how many rows and columns are needed in a table of the sample space.

_____

_____

_____

_____

 **Turn and Talk** Does it matter whether sizes or colors are listed in rows or columns? Explain.

Name _____

Step It Out

Conducting a survey is a type of experiment. Each time a question is asked of one person counts as one trial. Each answer is an outcome. Compare the number of times one answer is given to the total number of times a question is asked to find the experimental probability that a new, randomly chosen person, if asked, will give this answer.

2 Guests at the awards were asked for their dinner order. The number of people who gave each answer is shown. Find the experimental probability that a dinner guest orders roast beef and salad.

	Roast beef	Chicken Marsala	Vegetarian lasagna
Shrimp cocktail	15	32	12
Garden salad	24	22	15

Awards Dinner

Appetizers:
· Shrimp Cocktail
· Garden Salad

Entrees:
· Roast Beef
· Chicken Marsala
· Vegetarian Lasagna

A. Find the total number of dinner orders.

15 + 32 + ☐ + 24 + 22 + 15 = ☐

B. Find the experimental probability.

$P(\text{roast beef, salad}) = \dfrac{\text{number of orders for roast beef with salad}}{\text{total number of orders (total trials)}}$

$= \dfrac{\Box}{\Box}$, or $\dfrac{\Box}{\Box}$

3 The T-shirt choices of some award winners are shown in the table. What is the experimental probability that an award winner does NOT select a medium green T-shirt?

	Small	Medium	Large
Red	4	8	8
Green	2	5	7
Blue	3	4	9

A. Find the experimental probability of choosing a medium green T-shirt.

$P(\text{medium, green}) = \dfrac{\text{number of medium green T-shirts selected}}{\text{total number of T-shirts selected (total number of trials)}}$

$= \dfrac{\Box}{\Box} = \dfrac{\Box}{\Box}$, or ☐ %

B. Find the complement of the event in Part A, the experimental probability of NOT choosing a medium green T-shirt.

$P(\text{NOT medium, green}) = 1 - P(\text{medium, green})$

$= 1 - \dfrac{\Box}{\Box} = \dfrac{\Box}{\Box}$, or ☐ %

Module 20 • Lesson 3

4. A party bundle sold by an event planning company contains party favors and table decorations. The party favors are key chains, pens, and wristbands. The table decorations are flowers and candles. The company packs party bundles and stores them in a warehouse, choosing the party favor and decorations for each bundle at random. Tatiana simulates choosing a bundle from the warehouse and checking its contents.

A. List the compound events that occur when checking the bundles.

_____

_____

_____

B. Describe the two choices that together make up each compound event.

_____

C. How can you use a number cube and a coin to simulate the experiment?

_____

_____

D. Tatiana simulates 100 trials of the experiment and records the results shown in the table. What is the experimental probability that the next choice of a bundle includes pens and candles?

	Key chain	Pen	Wristband
Flowers	21	19	18
Candles	18	14	10

$P(\text{pens, candles}) = \dfrac{\text{number of pens/candles bundles selected}}{\text{total number of party bundles selected (total trials)}}$

$= \dfrac{\boxed{}}{\boxed{}} = \dfrac{\boxed{}}{\boxed{}}$, or $\boxed{}$ %

Check Understanding

The table shows the average daily breakfast orders for toast at a diner.

	Wheat	White	Rye
Butter	20	32	8
Dry	7	10	3

1. How many possible outcomes are in the sample space of toast choices?

_____

2. What is the experimental probability that a customer orders buttered white toast? Write your answer as a fraction and a percent.

_____

On Your Own

3. A tea bar offers tea in the varieties shown.

   A. How many rows and columns represent the sample space?
   _____

   B. How many possible outcomes are in the sample space?
   _____

Teas
• Hibiscus tea
• Macha tea
• Black tea

Sizes
• Small
• Large

4. **(MP) Model with Mathematics** Sabah works at a movie theater. One evening, she tracks the popcorn orders at the concessions stand.

   A. Sabah sold 125 orders of popcorn. Complete the table to show the number of times a large popcorn without butter was sold.

	Small	Medium	Large
With butter	18	15	36
Without butter	19	22	

   B. Find the experimental probability of a new customer ordering a large popcorn without butter. _____

5. **(MP) Construct Arguments** When simulating a compound event by rolling a number cube and flipping a coin, does it matter which one is done first? Explain your answer.
   _____
   _____

The table shows activities chosen. For Problems 6–9, use the table to determine the experimental probability of the choice and its complement.

	Swimming	Boating	Arts & Crafts	Field Sports
Morning	48	36	16	25
Afternoon	45	30	40	35

6. swimming in the afternoon _____

7. field sports in the morning _____

8. boating in the morning _____

9. arts & crafts in the afternoon _____

Module 20 • Lesson 3

Use Tools For Problems 10–12, tell how you could use the tools shown to simulate each compound event.

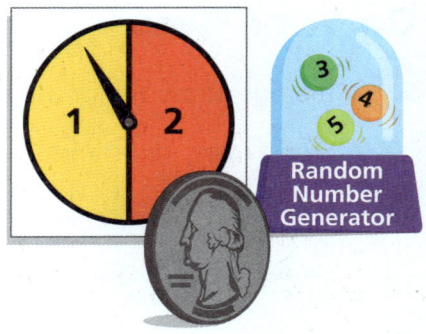

10. Choosing a pet at the animal shelter: a male or female; a cat, a dog, or a rabbit

    _____
    _____
    _____

11. Choosing colors for a shed: a red, blue, or yellow shed with white, gray, or black trim

    _____
    _____
    _____

12. Choosing an activity: going hiking or going swimming, traveling by bus or traveling by bicycle

    _____
    _____
    _____

13. **Open Ended** Write a word problem that includes finding the possible outcomes and the size of the sample space for a compound event. Then find the size of the sample space described in your problem.

    _____
    _____
    _____
    _____
    _____
    _____
    _____

 I'm in a Learning Mindset!

If you want to adjust the level of challenge in a simulation, would changing the order of simple events work? Why or why not?

_____
_____

Find Experimental Probability of Compound Events

LESSON 20.3 More Practice/Homework

1. **Math on the Spot** A compound event is simulated by flipping a coin (H or T) and rolling a number cube (1–6).

   A. List all the different possible outcomes.

   _____

   B. Represent the sample space using the table.

	1	2	3	4	5	6
H						
T						

Nico rolled two number cubes 250 times. The table shows his results. Use the table for Problems 2–4.

NC2 \ NC1	1	2	3	4	5	6
1	6	7	3	8	9	7
2	4	8	6	5	10	2
3	7	6	11	9	8	7
4	6	7	6	8	9	5
5	3	5	9	7	6	4
6	6	8	5	3	4	26

2. Find the experimental probability of rolling a 5 on the first number cube and a 2 on the second number cube.

   _____

3. A. Find the experimental probability of rolling a 1 on the second number cube.

   _____

   B. Use the complement to find the experimental probability of NOT rolling a 1 on the second number cube.

   _____

4. **Reason** Find the experimental probability of rolling double sixes. Is this experimental probability close to what you would expect? Explain.

   _____
   _____

Module 20 • Lesson 3

Test Prep

5. Carlotta is doing an experiment by flipping a coin and rolling a number cube. Select all that apply to the sample space of the experiment.

    Ⓐ The possible outcomes for the simulation can be represented in a table with 2 rows and 6 columns.

    Ⓑ The possible outcomes for the simulation can be represented in a table with 6 rows and 2 columns.

    Ⓒ The sample space of the simulation can only be represented by a table.

    Ⓓ The sample space has 36 total possible outcomes.

    Ⓔ The sample space has 8 total possible outcomes.

6. Ali runs a simulation using a coin and random number generator with output from 1 to 5. The table shows the results of the simulation.

	1	2	3	4	5
Heads (H)	12	8	11	14	8
Tails (T)	9	10	9	7	12

    A. Find the experimental probability of the outcome H-4.

    B. Use the complement to find the experimental probability of *not* H-4.

Spiral Review

7. Octavia found that in a population, 35% of customers bought socks. She took a random sample of 150 customers and found that 42 bought socks. Describe the sample ratio. Is it above or below the population ratio?

8. Using a number or number range, describe the probability of rolling a 3 on a number cube.

9. A graph of the equation $D = 2.25t$ shows the distance Han walks over time, where t is time in hours on the horizontal axis and D is distance in miles on the vertical axis. Another line is drawn on the graph to represent the distance Marcus walks over time. If Marcus walks at a steady speed of 2 miles per hour, how will the two lines compare?

Apply and Practice
Lesson 4

Name _____

Use Experimental Probability and Proportional Reasoning to Make Predictions

I Can use proportional reasoning or percent expressions to make a prediction based on an experimental probability.

Step It Out

1 Jessica bowls in several leagues, and she is very good at closing out frames. Over the past few years, she has closed out 8 of every 10 frames she has bowled. This season Jessica will bowl 35 games, or 350 frames. How many frames can Jessica expect to close out this season?

A. **Method 1: Use a proportion.**

Write a proportion. 8 out of 10 is how many out of 350?

$$\frac{8}{10} = \frac{x}{\boxed{}}$$

Multiply $\frac{8}{10}$ by a form of 1 to keep the equation true and to find the value of x.

$$\frac{8}{10} \cdot \frac{\boxed{}}{\boxed{}} = \frac{x}{\boxed{}}$$

The value of x is $8 \cdot \boxed{} = \boxed{}$.

B. **Method 2: Use a percent.**

Write $\frac{8}{10}$ as a percent and a decimal: $\boxed{}$% and $\boxed{}$.

Find $\boxed{}$% of 350: $\boxed{} \cdot 350 = \boxed{}$.

So Jessica can expect to close out about _____ frames.

C. If Jessica closes out 288 frames this season, was her average over the past few years a good predictor of her performance?

_____

Turn and Talk Which method do you prefer for making a prediction, using a proportion or a percent?

Module 20 • Lesson 4

627

2 The middle school that Carmen and Richard attend has 925 students. The schedule options for first period include only math and English. In order to find out whether students prefer first period math or first period English, Carmen and Richard took a poll of 100 randomly selected students. The results are shown.

1st period Math 79, 1st period English 21

A. Method 1
Use proportional reasoning to predict the number of students in the whole school who will state that they prefer first period math.

_____ out of 100 is how many out of 925?

$$\frac{\boxed{}}{100} = \frac{x}{\boxed{}}$$

Multiply by a form of 1: $\frac{79}{100} \cdot \frac{\boxed{}}{\boxed{}} = \frac{x}{925}$.

The value of x is $79 \cdot \boxed{} = \boxed{}$.

About _____ students will state that they prefer first period math.

B. Method 2
Use a percent to predict the number of students in the whole school who will state that they prefer first period math.

79 out of 100 is _____ %, so find _____ % of _____, the number of students in the whole school.

$\boxed{} \cdot 925 = \boxed{}$

About _____ students will state that they prefer first period math.

Check Understanding

1. A doctor takes a random sample of her patients and finds that 40% are between the ages of 13 and 21. She has 1,100 patients in total. Use the experimental probability from the survey to predict how many of her patients are between the ages of 13 and 21.

   _____

2. A company sold 660 watches. A consumer advocate group found that 5% of this type of watch were defective, when the group conducted a random survey of 100 watches. Estimate the number of watches sold that were defective.

   _____

Name _____

On Your Own

3. **Model with Mathematics** In a sample of 100 randomly selected concert attendees, the concert organizers find that 11 of them left the show early. The concert originally had 2,040 attendees.

   A. Use proportional reasoning to estimate how many of the total number of attendees left the concert early.

   B. **Attend to Precision** Explain why the answer in Part A cannot be a decimal.

   _____

4. **Model with Mathematics** In D'Andre's class, 5 of the 25 students are 5 feet tall or shorter. There are 400 students in D'Andre's grade at his school.

   A. Set up a proportional relationship to estimate the total number of students who are 5 feet tall or shorter in D'Andre's grade.

   _____

   B. Estimate how many students in D'Andre's grade are *over* 5 feet tall.

   _____

5. **STEM** According to the US Forest Service, the most common tree type found in timberlands in the state of Florida is the longleaf pine tree. In a sample population, 35% of trees were of this type.

   A. Write a percent expression to estimate the number of acres of longleaf pine trees in Florida.

   There are approximately 17.4 million acres of forested land in Florida.

   _____

   B. Evaluate the percent expression to estimate how many acres of longleaf pine trees there are in Florida.

   _____

Module 20 • Lesson 4   **629**

For Problems 6–7, the following samples were taken to see how many people preferred Candidate A. Predict the number of people who prefer Candidate A based on the information given.

6. Sample size: 200
Number of favorable responses: 100
Population: 1,000

_____

7. Sample size: 100
Percent favorable: 35%
Population: 1,800

_____

8. Social Studies Jiang was concerned about a busy intersection because it did not have a stop sign. She asked 100 people near the intersection. Seventy-five of the people supported putting in a stop sign. The town's population is 4,480. Write a percent expression and also use proportional reasoning to estimate how many people in town support the stop sign. Then explain why the survey results might *not* represent opinions in town.

_____
_____
_____
_____

9. (MP) Attend to Precision Luis used proportional reasoning to predict that the number of people riding buses past his window each day would be 100.6 people. How should he express his answer? Explain.

_____

For Problems 10–11 use this information.

The birthstones of a sample of 100 students and teachers in Claire's school are provided. The school has a total of 510 teachers and students.

Garnet (January): 6
Amethyst (February): 15
Aquamarine (March): 8
Diamond (April): 9
Emerald (May): 9
Pearl (June): 7
Ruby (July): 11
Peridot (August): 6
Sapphire (September): 8
Opal (October): 4
Topaz (November): 10
Tanzanite (December): 7

10. Write and evaluate a percent expression to estimate the total number of teachers and students at the school who have the amethyst as their birthstone.

_____

11. Write and solve a proportion to estimate how many more teachers and students at the school have the garnet than the opal as their birthstone.

_____

Name _____

Use Experimental Probability and Proportional Reasoning to Make Predictions

LESSON 20.4
More Practice/ Homework

ONLINE Video Tutorials and Interactive Examples

1. Ms. Kalidova asked her class to use a percent expression to predict the result of the upcoming election for class president of the seventh grade. Results of a poll conducted of 50 students are provided in the graph. Assume the seventh grade has 350 students and everyone votes for one of the two candidates. Write a percent expression and evaluate it to find how many votes Andrew should expect to receive.

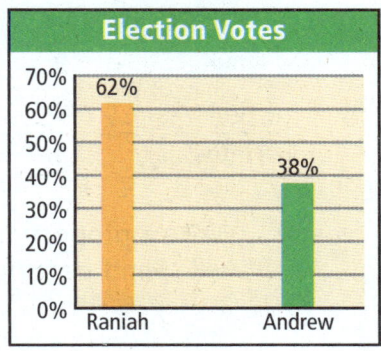

_____

2. **Open Ended** Write a real-world problem involving a sample and a population that can be modeled by this proportion: $\frac{66}{100} = \frac{x}{2,500}$.

_____

_____

_____

3. Shane plays baseball. The chart shows the results of his first 100 times at bat. Write a proportion and solve it to predict the number of home runs Shane will hit in his next 460 times at bat.

Out	63
Walk	8
Single	15
Double	8
Triple	1
Home run	5

_____

4. **Math on the Spot** Professor Burger found that the experimental probability of his making a strike in bowling is 20%. Out of 400 throws, about how many could he predict would be strikes?

_____

(MP) Model with Mathematics For Problems 5–6, use the following scenario.

In one weekend, 1,200 people attend a play at the theater downtown. A survey of 100 people who attended found that 45 gave the play at least 4 stars out of 5. Use the indicated method to estimate how many people in all would give the play at least 4 stars.

5. Solve using a proportion.

6. Solve using a percent.

Module 20 • Lesson 4   631

Test Prep

Use the chart for Problems 7–8. The chart shows the number of hours each student spends training for their favorite sport, per 100 hours.

Simone	12
Javier	9
Robert	15
Natasha	8

7. Write a proportion and make a prediction for the number of hours Simone will spend training over a 2,000-hour period.

   _____

8. Use a percent equation and make a prediction for the number of hours Javier will spend training over a 2,000-hour period.

   _____

9. Jabrin was tossing a ball up in the air and catching it. He found that in 50 tries, he could catch it 45 times. He is going to do this 600 more times. Predict how many times Jabrin will catch the ball out of these 600 tosses.

   _____

10. Considering the proportions/percent equations and the corresponding values of x given, which combination is correct?

    Ⓐ $\frac{40}{100} = \frac{x}{900}$; $x = 49$ Ⓒ $\frac{25}{100} = \frac{x}{750}$; $x = 175$

    Ⓑ $0.20(1,200) = x$; $x = 300$ Ⓓ $0.70(500) = x$; $x = 350$

Spiral Review

11. A vegetarian restaurant offers 52 vegetarian meals on its menu. Four of the meals include eggplant. Shan picks a dish at random from the menu with his eyes closed. What is the probability that he orders a meal that does not include eggplant? Write the probability as a fraction.

    _____

12. Jake is saving for a new tablet. It costs $250, and he has $100. He earns $5 per week for doing chores. Jake wants to figure out how many weeks it will take for him to have at least enough money to buy a new tablet. Write an inequality and solve it to determine the number of weeks it will take.

    _____

Review

Name _____

Vocabulary

Complete each sentence using terms from the Vocabulary box.

Vocabulary
- event
- experiment
- outcome
- probability
- sample space
- trial

1. The _____ of an experiment is the set of all possible outcomes of the experiment.

2. The _____ of an event is a number from 0 to 1, or from 0% to 100%, that describes its likelihood.

3. Each repetition of a probability _____ is called a _____.

4. Rolling a number less than 4 on a number cube is an _____ that consists of more than one _____.

Concepts and Skills

5. The chance that a baseball player will get a hit is estimated to be 23%. How would you describe this likelihood?

   Ⓐ certain   Ⓑ likely   Ⓒ unlikely   Ⓓ as likely as not

6. A news report states that a hurricane will reach land on Monday or Tuesday, but Tuesday is more likely. Give a number or number range to describe the probability that the hurricane will reach land on Tuesday.

   _____

7. Indira drew 3 animals: an eagle, a snake, and a shark. She drew each animal twice, once with green eyes and once with red eyes. Ten students chose their favorite drawing. Three of them chose the shark with red eyes. How many possible outcomes are in the sample space of the experiment? Based on the results, what is the experimental probability that a shark with red eyes is *not* picked, written as a percent?

   _____

8. **Ⓜ️ Use Tools** Sophia randomly selects a marble from a bag of marbles and then replaces it. The results of 300 trials are shown. Based on this data set, what is the experimental probability of selecting a red marble from the bag? State what strategy and tool you will use to answer the question, explain your choice, and then find the answer.

Red	57
White	105
Blue	138

_____

Module 20   633

9. In each cycle of a stoplight, the light is green for 30 seconds, yellow for 5 seconds, and red for 85 seconds. Liam conducts 500 trials of a simulation to estimate the likelihood that the stoplight will be a particular color when a car reaches it. Use the results to find the probability of each event.

Event	Experimental Probability
Getting a green light	
Getting a yellow light	
Not getting a red light	

Simulation Results	
Outcome	Frequency
Green light	115
Yellow light	15
Red light	370

10. A bag holds 6 plain bagels, 3 raisin bagels, 2 cheddar bagels, and 1 onion bagel. Grace chooses 4 bagels from the bag at random without replacing them. Select all possible compound events.

    A All of the bagels are raisin bagels.
    B There are exactly 2 plain bagels.
    C More than half the bagels are cheddar bagels.
    D There are more onion bagels selected than raisin bagels.
    E The number of cheddar bagels is equal to the number of plain bagels.

11. The experimental probability that Teresa will make a free-throw shot in basketball is 50%. Describe a simulation that can be used to estimate the probability that Teresa will make both of her next 2 free-throw shots.

    _____
    _____
    _____

12. The table shows the blood types of the last 300 people to donate blood at a blood bank. Use this information to answer each question.

    A. What is the experimental probability that the next person to donate blood will have type O blood?

    _____

    B. If 50 people donate blood on Friday, how many can be expected to have type O blood? _____ people

Blood Donations	
Blood type	Frequency
O	144
A	93
B	49
AB	14

13. The experimental probability of winning a prize when playing a carnival game is estimated to be 4%. Based on this information, approximately how many times would a player need to play the game to win 10 prizes?

    A 25 times   B 40 times   C 250 times   D 400 times

Module 21: Understand and Apply Theoretical Probability

ANALYZING ROCK-PAPER-SCISSORS

Destiny and Mateo are in the semi-finals of a Rock-Paper-Scissors tournament. Rock-Paper-Scissors is a game for two players, using the three hand signals shown. Players count, "1, 2, 3, go!" and then each player makes a hand signal for rock, paper, or scissors. Each player has an equal chance of winning.

Rock (R) beats scissors (S); Scissors (S) beat paper (P); Paper (P) beats rock (R)

A. The table shows the results of Destiny and Mateo's match. Complete the table by filling in the missing entries.

Destiny	R	P	S	S	S	P	P	P	P	R
Mateo	P	R	P	S	R	S	R	P	R	R
Winner	M	D	D	X						

The winner of this round of the semi-finals is _____ !

B. Complete the statements. Write each experimental probability as a fraction and as a decimal.

- Destiny (D) chose Rock _____ times. $P(DR) = \frac{\square}{10}$ or _____
- Mateo (M) chose Rock _____ times. $P(MR) = \frac{\square}{10}$ or _____
- Destiny chose Paper _____ times. $P(DP) = \frac{\square}{10}$ or _____
- Mateo chose Paper _____ times. $P(MP) = \frac{\square}{10}$ or _____

 **Turn and Talk**

Calculate each player's experimental probability of choosing scissors. Explain your method of calculation.

Are You Ready?

Complete these problems to review prior concepts and skills you will need for this module.

More Likely, Less Likely, Equally Likely

Use the spinner for Problems 1–3.

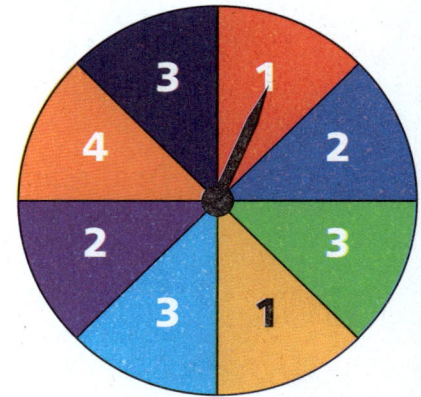

1. Which event is more likely than spinning a 1?

   _____

2. Which event is less likely than spinning a 1?

   _____

3. Which event is equally likely as spinning a 1?

   _____

Experimental Probability

The number of each type of bar in a variety pack of granola bars can vary. The table shows the number of peanut butter bars in a random sample of 300 variety packs. Use this information for Problems 4–6.

Number of Peanut Butter Bars per Pack	Frequency
0	11
1	29
2	60
3	75
4	71
5	39
6	15

4. What is the experimental probability that a variety pack will have exactly 3 peanut butter bars?

   _____
   _____

5. What is the experimental probability that a variety pack will have at most 4 peanut butter bars?

   _____
   _____

6. Esme buys 15 variety packs. How many packs can she expect will have more than 2 peanut butter bars? Explain your reasoning.

   _____
   _____
   _____
   _____

Connect Concepts and Skills

Lesson 1

Name _____

Find Theoretical Probability of Simple Events

I Can find the theoretical probability of a simple event.

Spark Your Learning (SMALL GROUPS)

Dominic wants to play a balloon dart game at the county fair. He can play Game 1 or Game 2. If he pops a blue balloon with a dart, he wins a prize. Which game should Dominic play if he wants a better chance of winning a prize? Assume that Dominic gets one throw, and it will hit a balloon in either game.

Turn and Talk Explain what changes could be made to Game 1 so that Dominic has the same chance of winning a prize when playing either game.

Module 21 • Lesson 1

637

Build Understanding

1 Clara is playing a game where she chooses to spin one of the spinners shown. If the spinner lands on a section labeled "A," she wins a pair of headphones. Which spinner will give her a better chance of winning?

Spinner 1

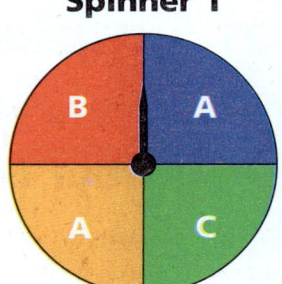

A. Total number of sections for each spinner:

Spinner 1 has a total of _____ sections of the same area.

Spinner 2 has a total of _____ sections of the same area.

B. Number of sections labeled "A" for each spinner:

Spinner 1 has _____ sections labeled "A."

Spinner 2 has _____ sections labeled "A."

Spinner 2

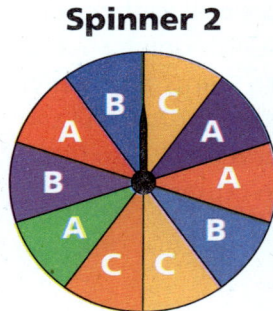

C. What is the ratio of sections labeled "A" to total number of sections for each spinner?

Spinner 1: $\frac{\square}{4}$ Spinner 2: $\frac{\square}{10}$

D. How can you make the ratios in Part C easier to compare?

_____

_____

E. What is the ratio of sections labeled "A" to total number of sections for each spinner, written as fractions with a common denominator?

Spinner 1: $\frac{\square}{20}$ Spinner 2: $\frac{\square}{20}$

F. Which spinner should Clara spin to give her a better chance of winning a pair of headphones? Explain.

_____

_____

_____

G. Which spinner should Clara spin to give her a better chance of landing on "C"? Explain.

_____

_____

Turn and Talk Describe another way to compare the ratios in Part C.

Name _____

Step It Out

If the outcomes of an experiment are equally likely, you can find the theoretical probability of an event without performing the experiment.

$$P(\text{event}) = \frac{\text{number of equally likely outcomes in the event}}{\text{total number of equally likely outcomes in the sample space}}$$

When a probability is given as a fraction, it is usually written in simplest form.

> **Connect to Vocabulary**
>
> If all possible outcomes are equally likely, the **theoretical probability** of an event is the ratio of the number of possible outcomes in the event to the total number of possible outcomes in the sample space.

2 Lindsay is going to draw one tile from the bag shown without looking. The tiles are the same size and cannot be told apart by touch, so each tile has an equal chance of being chosen. What is the theoretical probability that she selects a red tile?

A. Identify the sample space.

5 [red / blue / green] tiles

6 [red / blue / green] tiles

9 [red / blue / green] tiles

B. Find the total number of equally likely possible outcomes in the sample space by adding.

green tiles + red tiles + blue tiles = total number of tiles

☐ + ☐ + ☐ = ☐

There are _____ equally likely outcomes in the sample space.

C. Identify the total number of possible outcomes included in the event "selects a red tile." Is each possible outcome equally likely?

There are _____ red tiles in the bag, so there are _____ possible outcomes included in this event. Each of these possible outcomes [is / is not] equally likely.

D. Find the theoretical probability that Lindsay will select a red tile. Then, **write the ratio in simplest form**.

$$P(\text{red tile}) = \frac{\text{number of red tiles}}{\text{total number of tiles}} = \frac{\square}{\square} = \frac{\square}{\square}$$

E. Probability can be written as a fraction, decimal, or percent. Write the theoretical probability that Lindsay draws a red tile from the bag as a fraction, a decimal, and a percent.

_____

Module 21 • Lesson 1

3 Miguel is deciding if he should do his chores or homework first. To help him decide, he flips a coin.

A. Miguel flips the coin once. Find the theoretical probability of the coin landing on heads and the theoretical probability of the coin landing on tails. Write each as a decimal.

P(Heads) = ☐   P(Tails) = ☐

B. Predict the number of times the coin will land on heads and tails out of 20 flips using the theoretical probability.

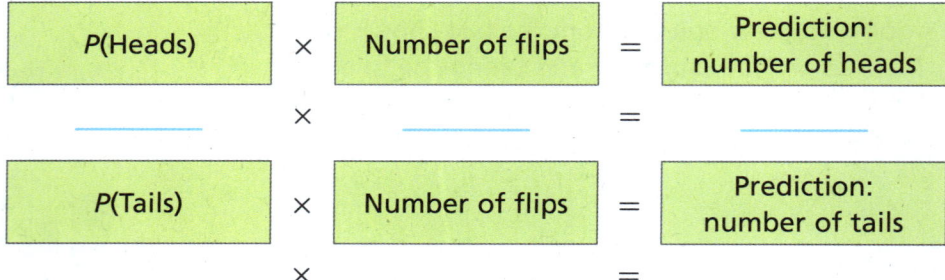

| P(Heads) | × | Number of flips | = | Prediction: number of heads |

____ × ____ = ____

| P(Tails) | × | Number of flips | = | Prediction: number of tails |

____ × ____ = ____

C. Flip a coin 20 times. Record the outcomes in the frequency column. Then give the experimental probability to the nearest percent.

Outcome	Heads	Tails
Frequency		
Experimental probability		

D. Compare the theoretical and experimental probabilities of the coin landing on heads and tails. Are the probabilities equal? Why isn't experimental probability always the same as theoretical probability?

_____
_____
_____

Check Understanding

1. Eric's coach said he could spin a spinner with 4 equal sections labeled 1–4, or roll a number cube labeled 1–6. If Eric gets a 1, he does not have to run a sprint. If Eric does not want to run a sprint, which should he pick? Explain.

_____
_____

2. Pam tossed a coin 50 times. She found the probability of getting heads was 45%. Was this a theoretical or experimental probability? Explain.

_____

Name _____

On Your Own

3. **Use Structure** Amara has the choice to select one card from Pile 1 or Pile 2 without looking. If she selects a yellow card, she wins a game. Which pile should Amara pick from to give her a better chance of winning? Explain your reasoning.

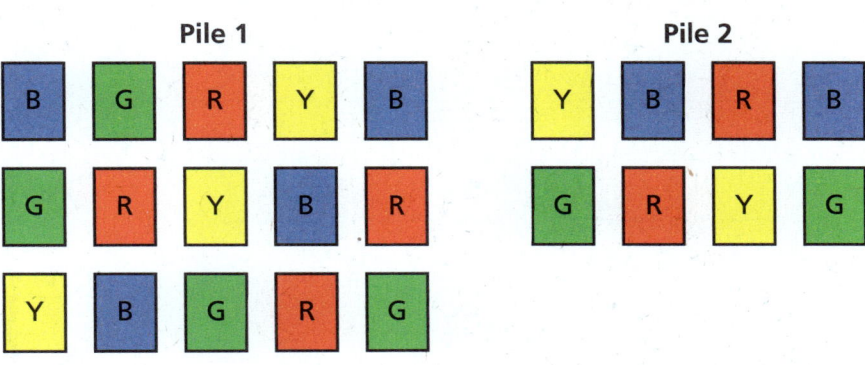

_____
_____
_____

4. **Reason** The table shows the results of rolling a number cube 50 times. Compare the experimental probability and theoretical probability of rolling a 5. Give a possible reason why the probabilities are different. Explain your reasoning.

Outcome	1	2	3	4	5	6
Frequency	10	9	5	6	7	13

_____
_____
_____

For Problems 5–8, use the gift boxes shown. Find the theoretical probability of randomly selecting each gift box. Write the probability as a fraction in simplest form.

5. yellow box: ☐   6. purple box: ☐

7. blue box: ☐   8. green box: ☐

green   blue   blue   purple

yellow   purple   green   blue

9. A bag contains 5 red balls, 8 white balls, and 7 black balls. What is the theoretical probability of randomly selecting a black ball from the bag?

_____

10. Chase can spin a spinner centered on Board 1 or Board 2. He wants the spinner to land on a section labeled "R." Which board should he choose? Explain.

_____
_____
_____
_____

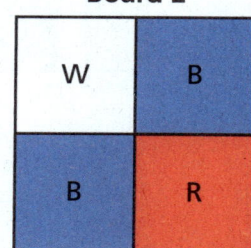

Board 1

Board 2

11. Edith spun a spinner with 5 equal sections labeled 1–5. The spinner landed on 1 five times, on 2 three times, on 3 four times, on 4 three times, and on 5 five times. For which number is the experimental probability the same as its theoretical probability? Explain.

_____
_____
_____
_____

Use Structure For Problems 12–13, use the flowers shown. Find the theoretical probability of selecting the color listed. Write the probability as a fraction in simplest form, a decimal, and a percent.

12. orange flower

_____

13. purple flower

_____

I'm in a Learning Mindset!

Was finding theoretical probabilities of simple events an appropriate challenge for me?

_____

Name _____

Find Theoretical Probability of Simple Events

LESSON 21.1
More Practice/ Homework

ONLINE Video Tutorials and Interactive Examples

Luke has a bag of 52 beads. Half the beads are rough. The other half are smooth. There are 13 red beads, 13 blue beads, 13 green beads, and 13 black beads. Use this information for Problems 1–5. Write each probability as a fraction in simplest form.

1. What is the theoretical probability of selecting a smooth bead?

   _____

2. What is the theoretical probability of selecting a blue bead?

   _____

3. What is the theoretical probability of selecting a rough bead?

   _____

4. What is the theoretical probability of not selecting a red bead?

   _____

5. **(MP) Reason** One hundred times, Luke picks one bead then puts it back into the bag. The results are shown. What are the experimental probability and theoretical probability of picking a black bead? Name a possible reason why the probabilities are not the same.

Outcome	Red	Blue	Green	Black
Frequency	21	26	33	20

   _____
   _____
   _____

6. **Math on the Spot** Find the probability of the event. Write your answer as a fraction, as a decimal, and as a percent.

   A. draw one of the 4 L's from a bag of 100 letter tiles

   _____

   B. roll a number less than 4 on a number cube

   _____

Module 21 • Lesson 1

643

Test Prep

7. Brice can win a game by selecting a letter tile with the letter B from a bag. He wants to choose a bag that will give him the best chance of winning. Which statement is correct?

- Ⓐ Brice has the best chance only with Bag 1.
- Ⓑ Brice has the best chance only with Bag 2.
- Ⓒ Brice has the best chance only with Bag 3.
- Ⓓ Brice has the best chance with either Bag 1 or Bag 3.

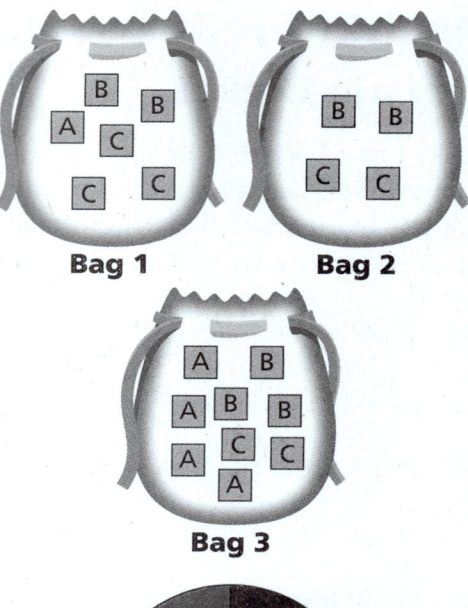

Bag 1   Bag 2

Bag 3

8. Use the spinner shown to match the theoretical probability to the correct event.

P(Y) •   • $\frac{1}{2}$

P(R) •   • 0.375

P(B) •   • 12.5%

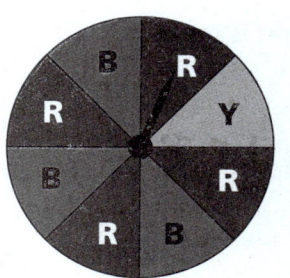

9. The table shows the results of flipping a coin 10 times. How do the theoretical and experimental probabilities of the coin landing on heads compare?

Outcome	Heads	Tails
Frequency	3	7

Spiral Review

10. A soccer team made 2 goals out of 32 attempts in a game. What is the experimental probability that the team made a goal on any given shot? Write the probability as a decimal.

11. The experimental probability that Jason makes a free throw is 72%. If Jason shoots 50 free throws, about how many can you expect him to make? Explain.

Find Theoretical Probability of Compound Events

I Can find the theoretical probability of a compound event.

Step It Out

1. Lucas spins the two spinners shown. Spinning each number on one spinner is equally likely. He wants to find the probability that the sum of the two numbers he spins is 3.

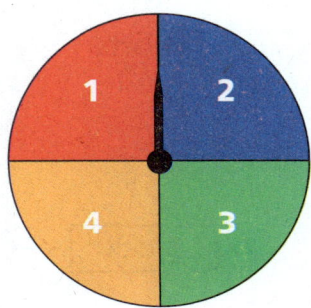

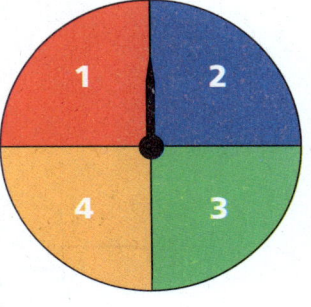

A. Lucas makes a table to represent the sample space of sums. Each entry in the table is the sum of the numbers in the corresponding row and column. Complete the remainder of the table.

+	1	2	3	4
1	2	3	4	
2	3	4		
3	4			
4				

B. The table in Part A shows:

- There are _____ possible outcomes with a sum of 3.

- There are _____ equally likely outcomes in the sample space.

C. Find the theoretical probability of spinning a sum of 3.

$$P(\text{sum of 3}) = \frac{\text{number of equally likely outcomes that add to 3}}{\text{total number of equally likely outcomes in the sample space}}$$

$$= \frac{\Box}{16}$$

$$= \frac{\Box}{\Box}$$

D. Determine another possible outcome in the sample space that has the same probability as that of spinning a sum of 3.

$P(\text{sum of 3}) = P(\underline{\qquad})$

 **Turn and Talk** Explain why spinning a sum of 3 is a compound event.

Module 21 • Lesson 2

2 Aria can choose one pair of shorts (black or white), one shirt (red, blue, or green), and one pair of shoes (brown or tan) as her outfit. Find the probability of choosing an outfit at random and getting white shorts, a blue shirt, and tan shoes.

A. Complete the **tree diagram** to represent the sample space.

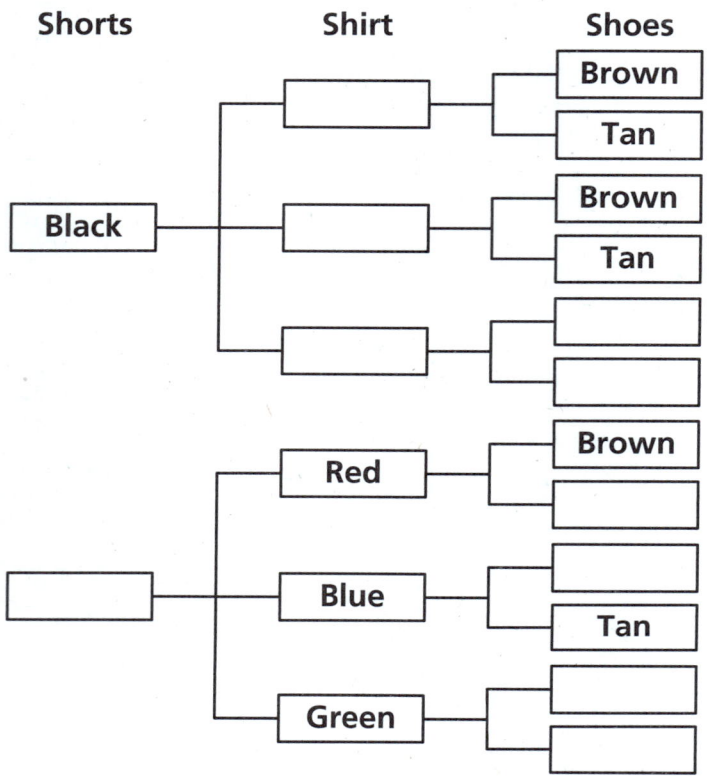

B. The tree diagram shows that there are _____ equally likely outcomes in the sample space.

C. Find the probability P(white, blue, tan).

P(white, blue, tan) = $\frac{\text{number of equally likely outcomes in the event (white, blue, tan)}}{\text{total number of equally likely outcomes in the sample space}}$

=

D. Find the probability of selecting white shorts and a blue shirt when selecting clothes at random.

P(white, blue) = $\frac{\text{number of equally likely outcomes in the event (white, blue)}}{\text{total number of equally likely outcomes in the sample space}}$

=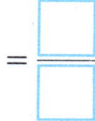

Name _____

3 Ethan draws cards from a hat that contains three cards labeled A, B, and C. He has an equal chance of drawing each card. He draws one card at a time, records the result, and replaces it before the next draw. What is the probability that Ethan draws the A-card 3 times in a row?

Winning Combination

| A | A | A |

A. Complete the organized lists to represent the sample space.

A on first draw		
A	A	A
A	A	B
A	A	C
A	B	A
A	B	B
A	B	C
A	C	
A	C	
A	C	

B on first draw		
B	A	A
B	A	B
B	A	C
B	B	
B	B	
B	B	
B	C	
B	C	
B	C	

C on first draw		
C	A	
C	A	
C	A	
	B	
C		A
C		B
C	C	C

B. The organized lists show that there are _____ equally likely outcomes in the sample space.

C. Find the probability P(A, A, A). Write the probability as a fraction, decimal, and percent. Round to the nearest hundredth and whole percent.

$P(A, A, A) = \dfrac{\text{number of equally likely outcomes in the event (A, A, A)}}{\text{total number of equally likely outcomes in the sample space}}$

= ☐/☐ or ☐ or ☐ %

The probability that Ethan draws the A-card 3 times in a row is about _____ %.

Turn and Talk How do you think you could use the organized lists to find the probability of drawing 2 or more A-cards in any order?

Check Understanding

1. What are some ways that you can represent the sample space of a compound event?

_____

2. Mila spins two spinners. One spinner has two equal sections labeled 1 and 2. The other spinner has three equal sections labeled 1, 2, and 3. What is the probability that the sum of the two spins is 4?

_____

Module 21 • Lesson 2   647

On Your Own

3. **Use Structure** Wyatt rolls two number prisms in the shape of triangular prisms, labeled 1 to 3 as shown.

    A. Complete the table to represent the sample space for the sum of these two number prisms.

+	1	2	3
1			
2			
3			

    B. What is the probability that Wyatt rolls a sum of 3?

    _____

    C. What event has the same probability as rolling a sum of 3? Explain.

    _____
    _____

    D. Name an event that is less likely than a sum of 3. Explain.

    _____
    _____
    _____

    E. Name an event that is more likely than a sum of 3. Explain.

    _____
    _____
    _____

Model with Mathematics Find each probability. Give your answer as a simplified fraction, a decimal to the nearest hundredth, and a percent to the nearest whole percent.

F. $P(\text{sum of 4})$

_____

G. $P(\text{sum of 6})$

_____

H. $P(\text{sum} < 10)$

_____

I. $P(\text{sum} > 10)$

_____

4. **Use Structure** Layla tosses three coins.

   A. Complete the tree diagram to show the sample space for how the coins can land. H represent heads and T represent tails.

   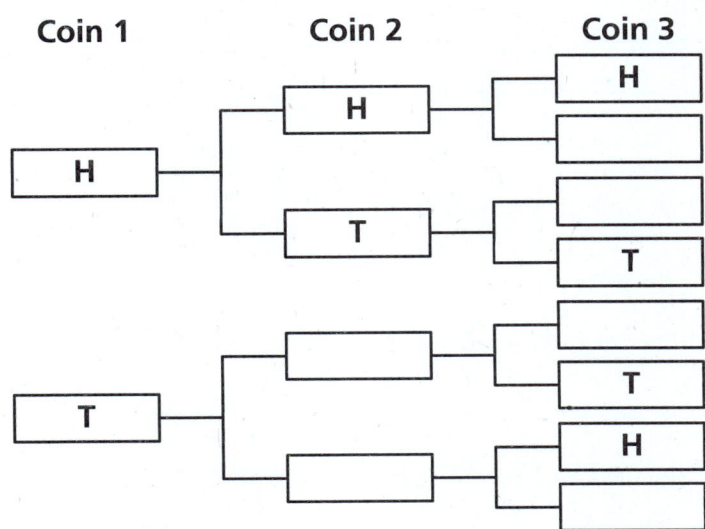

   B. What is the probability that exactly two coins land heads up? Write the probability as a fraction, decimal, and percent.

   _____

   C. What is the probability that exactly two coins land tails up? Compare this probability to the probability that exactly two coins land heads up.

   _____

   D. What is the probability that exactly three coins land tails up? Write the probability as a fraction, decimal, and percent.

   _____

   E. Name an event that has the same probability as that of three tails? Explain.

   _____
   _____

   F. Compare the theoretical probability of getting at least one head and the theoretical probability of getting at least two tails.

   _____
   _____
   _____
   _____

5. **Use Structure** Daniel is going to spin the spinner shown and roll a number cube.

A. Make an organized list to show the sample space for spinning the spinner and rolling the number cube.

_____
_____
_____

B. What is the probability that Daniel gets a sum of 5?

_____

C. What is the probability that Daniel gets a sum of 3?

_____

D. Compare the probability of getting a sum of 5 and the probability of getting a sum of 3.

_____
_____

E. **Open Ended** Give an example of an event that is more likely than getting a sum of 8. Explain your reasoning.

_____
_____
_____
_____

F. **Open Ended** Give an example of an event that is as likely as getting a sum of 6. Explain your reasoning.

_____
_____
_____
_____

6. **Reason** How is finding the theoretical probability of a compound event similar to finding the theoretical probability of a simple event?

_____
_____
_____

Name _____

Find Theoretical Probability of Compound Events

LESSON 21.2
More Practice/Homework

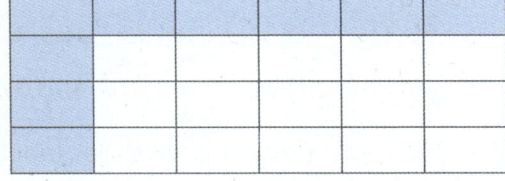
ONLINE Video Tutorials and Interactive Examples

1. **(MP) Use Structure** Christian has a red box with tiles numbered from 1 to 5 and a green box with tiles numbered from 1 to 3. He draws a tile from each box, and then finds the sum.

   A. Make a table to represent the sample space for drawing a particular sum from the numbers in the two boxes.

   B. What is the probability of drawing a sum of 7?
   _____

   C. Name an event that is more likely than drawing a sum of 7.
   _____

2. **(MP) Use Structure** Lucy can choose one sandwich (ham or turkey), one side (apples or grapes), and one drink (milk or water). Lucy has an equally likely chance of choosing any combination.

   A. Make a tree diagram to find the sample space.

   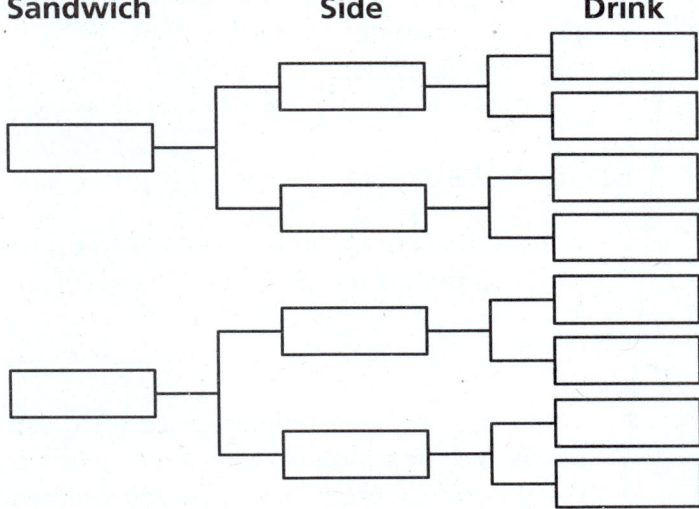

   B. What is the probability Lucy picks a ham sandwich and grapes?
   _____

   C. What is the probability Lucy chooses milk with a turkey sandwich and apples?
   _____

   D. **(MP) Reason** Name an event that is equally as likely as choosing ham and apples.
   _____

3. **(MP) Attend to Precision** How many different possible outcomes are there for the experiment described here?

   Step 1 Toss a number cube.
   Step 2 Toss a fair coin.
   Step 3 Spin the spinner.

   There are _____ different possible outcomes.

Module 21 • Lesson 2

Test Prep

4. Emma is going to flip a coin, resulting in H for heads or T for tails, and spin the spinner shown. Which list correctly represents the sample space?

   Ⓐ H, T, 1, 2, 3, 4, 5, 6

   Ⓑ H-1, H-2, H-3, H-4, H-5, H-6

   Ⓒ H-1, H-2, H-3, H-4, H-5, H-6, T-1, T-2, T-3, T-4, T-5, T-6

   Ⓓ H-T-1, H-T-2, H-T-3, H-T-4, H-T-5, H-T-6

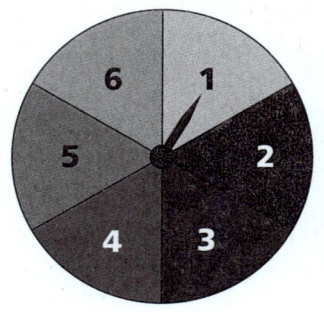

5. Luna rolls two number cubes labeled 1–6. Match the probability to the correct event.

   P(sum of 5)   •   • $\frac{1}{6}$

   P(sum less than 4)   •   • $\frac{1}{9}$

   P(sum of 7)   •   • $\frac{5}{18}$

   P(sum greater than 8)   •   • $\frac{1}{12}$

6. Carson can choose one type of vehicle (car or truck), one color (blue, red, or silver), and one type of transmission (standard or automatic). How many possible outcomes are there?

   _____

Spiral Review

7. Aaliyah spins the spinner shown. What is the theoretical probability that the spinner will land on an even number?

   _____

8. You and 19 other people are entered in a drawing. One person will be randomly selected to win a prize. What is the theoretical probability that you will win the prize? Explain.

   _____

   _____

   _____

   _____

Apply and Practice
Lesson 3

Name _____

Use Theoretical Probability and Proportional Reasoning to Make Predictions

I Can use theoretical probability to make predictions about real-world situations.

Step It Out

1 Sadie spins the spinner shown 80 times. Predict how many times she will spin a 2 or 3.

A. The theoretical probability of spinning a 2 or 3 is _____, or _____ %.

B. Solve by using proportional reasoning.

$\frac{1}{2} = \frac{x}{\square}$ $\begin{aligned} 1 \times \square &= x \\ 2 \times 40 &= 80 \end{aligned}$ So $x = \square$.

Sadie will spin a 2 or 3 about ____ times.

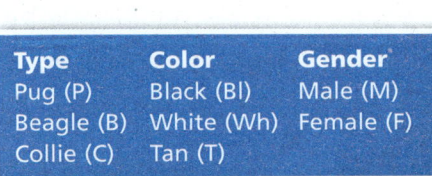

C. Solve by multiplying the probability by the number of trials.

P(spinning 2 or 3) × number of trials

$\square$ % × $\square$ = $\square$

Sadie will spin a 2 or 3 about ____ times.

2 Jamie volunteers at an animal shelter. The types, colors, and genders of dogs are shown. Predict how many times out of 90 Jamie will randomly select a tan, male pug to walk. Assume an equal chance for her to select each dog.

Type	Color	Gender
Pug (P)	Black (Bl)	Male (M)
Beagle (B)	White (Wh)	Female (F)
Collie (C)	Tan (T)	

A. Make an organized list for the sample space.

B. The theoretical probability of selecting a tan, male pug is ____.

C. Solve by multiplying the probability by the number of trials.

$\square$ × $\square$ = $\square$

Jamie will select a tan, male pug about ____ out of 90 times.

Module 21 • Lesson 3

3 Ezekiel randomly draws a card from the stack shown. Which is more likely: drawing a card that is NOT red or drawing a green card?

A. First find P(red). Then find the **complement**, P(NOT red).

$$P(red) = \frac{\text{number of outcomes in event "draw a red card"}}{\text{total number of equally likely outcomes in sample space}} = \frac{\square}{\square}$$

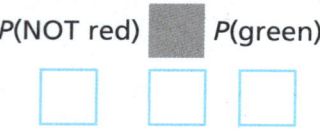

$$P(NOT\ red) = 1 - P(red) = 1 - \frac{\square}{\square} = \frac{\square}{15}$$

B. Complete the inequality statement to compare P(NOT red) and P(green).

P(NOT red) ▩ P(green)

□ □ □

So P(NOT red) / P(green) is more likely.

4 Isla is resetting her door code. The code is a 3-digit number made up of the digits 0 through 9. The digits can be repeated. Isla used a random number generator to select a code, so all possible codes are equally likely. Would you predict that the door code 567 will be generated more than 5 out of 8,000 times?

A. First find the number of equally likely outcomes in the sample space.

Imagine drawing a tree diagram. There are 10 possible outcomes for the first digit, and each of those has 10 possible outcomes for the second digit, and each of those 10 more for the third digit.

The sample space has 10 × 10 × 10 = _____ equally likely outcomes.

B. Find the probability of randomly generating the code 567, and use it to predict the number of times out of 8,000 you would expect code 567 to be generated.

$$P(567) = \frac{\square}{1{,}000}$$

P(567) × number of trials

□ × □ = □

I would / would not predict that the code 567 will be generated more than 5 out of 8,000 times.

Check Understanding

1. A bag of marbles contains 5 red, 3 blue, and 12 yellow marbles. Predict the number of times Hazel will select a blue marble out of 500 trials.

2. Kai flips a coin and spins a 3-sector spinner labeled 1–3. Predict the number of times Kai will get the outcome (heads, 2) in 300 trials.

Name _____

On Your Own

3. **(MP) Construct Arguments** Bryson selects a folder from a pile. The folder is blue. There are 8 blue folders, 9 yellow folders, and 3 orange folders left in the pile. He selects a second folder without looking. Is it likely that Bryson selects matching folders? Explain your reasoning.

   _____
   _____
   _____
   _____

(MP) Model with Mathematics An eight-sided game piece has 8 congruent triangular sides. The sides are labeled 1–8. Nevaeh rolls the game piece 400 times. Use this information for Problems 4–6.

4. Write and solve a proportion to predict how many times the game piece will land on 7.

   _____

5. Write and solve a proportion to predict how many times the game piece will land on 3 or 5.

   _____

6. Use multiplication to predict how many times the game piece will land on a number less than or equal to 3.

   _____

Liliana spins a spinner with equal-sized sections numbered 1 through 4 a total of 300 times. Use this information for Problems 7–8.

7. Write and solve a proportion to predict the number of times Liliana can expect to spin a 3.

   _____

8. Use multiplication to predict the number of times Liliana can expect to spin an even number.

   _____

9. A box has 12 red tiles, 15 blue tiles, and 23 purple tiles. LaTanisha randomly selects a tile without looking 2,000 times. Each time a tile is selected, it is replaced before the next selection. Predict the number of times LaTanisha selects a blue or red tile.

   _____

Module 21 • Lesson 3

10. Ezra is resetting the code on his safe. The code is a 3-digit number made up of the digits 0 through 5. The digits can be repeated. Ezra will randomly draw numbers from a hat to select a code, replacing the number after each draw. Is it likely that Ezra will randomly select the safe code 123 more than 10 times out of 4,320 random codes drawn from the hat? Solve using multiplication. Explain your reasoning.

Model with Mathematics Elliot rolls two number cubes 900 times. Their sides are labeled 1–6. Use this information for Problems 11–14.

11. Write and solve a proportion to predict the number of times Elliot can expect to roll a sum of 11.

12. Write and solve a proportion to predict the number of times Elliot can expect to roll two odd numbers.

13. Use multiplication to predict the number of times Elliot can expect to roll one even number and one odd number.

14. Use multiplication to predict the number of times Elliot can expect to roll the same number on both cubes.

15. **Construct Arguments** The security desk for an office building has visitor's badges with codes consisting of one letter (A–Z) and 1 digit (0 through 9). A visitor can select a badge at random, and badges are returned at the end of each day. Is it likely that the badge L7 is the first badge selected more than 5 times in 365 days? Explain your reasoning. (*Hint*: Imagine making a a rectangular array. There would be 26 × 10 different badge codes.)

Use Theoretical Probability and Proportional Reasoning to Make Predictions

LESSON 21.3 More Practice/Homework

1. Oliver selects a glove from his drawer. The glove is blue. There are 3 red gloves, 6 black gloves, and 11 blue gloves left in the drawer. He selects a second glove from the drawer without looking. Is it more likely than not that Oliver selects a glove of the same color? Explain your reasoning.

2. If you roll a number cube 20 times, about how many times do you expect to roll a number greater than 4?

Use Structure Victoria spins the two spinners shown 500 times. Use this information for Problems 3–5.

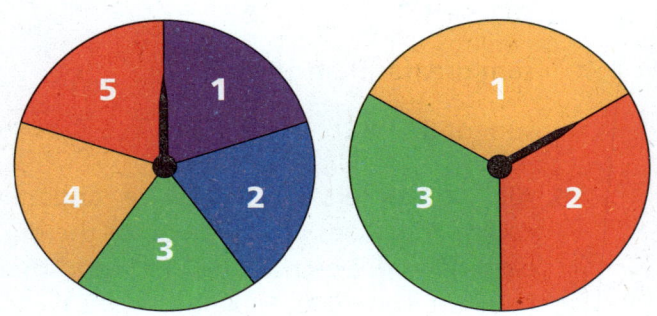

3. Solve a proportion to predict the number of times the sum is 4.

4. Solve a proportion to predict the number of times the sum is 4, 5, or 6.

5. Use a percent equation to predict the number of times the sum is less than or equal to 3.

Model with Mathematics There are 5 red, 18 green, and 17 blue pens in a bag. Leah selects a pen 800 times without looking. After each selection, she replaces the pen in the bag. Use this information for Problems 6–7.

6. Use multiplication to predict the number of times that Leah selects a pen that is red or green.

7. Use multiplication to predict the number of times that Leah selects a pen that is not red.

Module 21 • Lesson 3

Test Prep

8. Leo has 10 red cards, 20 black cards, 20 yellow cards, and 25 white cards in a bag. He randomly selects a card 300 times. He replaces the card after each selection. Predict how often Leo will select a white card.

- Ⓐ about 12 times
- Ⓑ about 75 times
- Ⓒ about 100 times
- Ⓓ about 150 times

9. Scarlet rolls a number cube labeled 1–6 and spins the spinner shown 2,100 times. Match the prediction to the correct event.

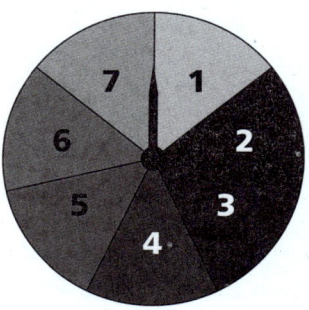

sum of 5	●	● about 300 times
sum less than 7	●	● about 50 times
sum of 13	●	● about 200 times
sum greater than 10	●	● about 550 times
sum of 8 or 9	●	● about 750 times

10. All 3,000 lockers at a school are randomly assigned 3-digit combination codes. The codes are made up of the digits 0 through 9. The digits can be repeated. Describe the likelihood that fewer than 5 of the lockers will have the code 000. Explain.

Spiral Review

11. Levi rolled a number cube. The number cube landed on 1 four times, 2 two times, 3 one time, 4 two times, 5 three times, and 6 six times. Which experimental probability is the same as the theoretical probability?

12. Brent rolls two number cubes labeled 1–6. What is the probability that Brent rolls a sum of 5?

Apply and Practice

Lesson 4

Name _____

Conduct Simulations

I Can use a simulation to test the probability of simple and compound events.

Step It Out

1 What is the experimental probability that you first find a winner on the second plate you check at the fundraiser dinner shown?

20% of the plates are winners!

A. $P(\text{winning sticker}) = \boxed{}\% = \dfrac{\boxed{}}{10}$

B. Carlos uses whole numbers from 1 to 10 to design a simulation. He generates one number at random to simulate checking one plate.

Winning: 1, 2
Non-winning: 3, 4, 5, 6, 7, 8, 9, 10

The table shows the results from Carlos's experiment: generating numbers for each trial until a winning number (1 or 2) appears. Complete the table.

Trial	Numbers generated	Plates checked
1	5, 8, 1	3
2	1	1
3	4, 8, 9, 2	4
4	5, 1	2
5	7, 8, 2	
6	8, 9, 10, 6, 2	
7	2	
8	3, 5, 7, 1	
9	9, 8, 2	
10	8, 6, 3, 4, 9, 2	

C. For Trial 1, a winning number appeared after _____ plate(s).

For Trial 2, a winning number appeared after _____ plate(s).

How many of the 10 trials showed a winner on the second plate?

_____

D. The experimental probability of first finding a winner on the second plate is $\dfrac{\boxed{}}{\boxed{}}$, or _____ %.

Module 21 • Lesson 4

659

2 The chance that Amir will make a free throw at any given time is shown. Find the experimental probability that Amir will make at least 3 of the next 5 free throws he attempts.

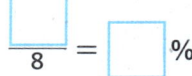
60% free-throw success

A. Design a simulation to model this compound event. Use whole numbers from 1 to 5. Amir makes free throws _____ % of the time. Let 1, 2, and 3 represent a successful free throw, and let _____ and _____ represent a missed free throw.

B. Amir conducted 8 trials generating five random numbers from 1 to 5. Complete the table.

Trial	Numbers Generated	Successful Free Throws
1	3, 1, 4, 4, 5	2
2	5, 2, 1, 3, 2	4
3	2, 5, 4, 2, 4	
4	4, 3, 5, 4, 5	
5	2, 1, 3, 3, 4	
6	3, 4, 2, 3, 2	
7	1, 1, 5, 4, 5	
8	4, 5, 1, 2, 1	

C. Find the experimental probability that Amir makes at least 3 of the next 5 free throws he attempts. $\frac{\square}{8} = \square$ %

 Turn and Talk Design another simulation to find the probability that Amir makes at least 3 of his next 5 free throws. Explain your reasoning.

Check Understanding

There is a 70% chance that Reagan will catch an early bus home from work. A computer generated 8 sets of random numbers from 1 to 10. The numbers 1–7 represent a success and 8–10 represent a missed bus. The table shows the results. Use it for Problems 1 and 2.

Trial	Numbers Generated
1	1, 9, 1, 2, 10, 6, 5, 2, 7, 2
2	8, 10, 4, 10, 2, 2, 3, 6, 7, 10
3	6, 9, 9, 10, 4, 10, 10, 2, 6, 6
4	8, 8, 2, 3, 4, 6, 5, 6, 5, 3
5	1, 10, 1, 2, 5, 6, 9, 4, 10, 3
6	7, 1, 9, 1, 6, 3, 3, 7, 5, 6
7	2, 5, 2, 7, 5, 5, 10, 5, 6, 3
8	9, 6, 10, 4, 9, 6, 8, 9, 9, 9

1. Find the experimental probability that Reagan will miss the early bus twice but catch it the third time.

2. Find the experimental probability that Reagan will catch the early bus at least 7 of the next 10 times.

On Your Own

Use the table and the information given for Problems 3 and 4.

Geography Over a 100-year period, the probability that a hurricane struck Reyna's city in any given year was 20%. Reyna performed a simulation to find the experimental probability that a hurricane would strike the city in at least 4 of the next 10 years. In Reyna's simulation, 1 represents a year with a hurricane.

Trial	Numbers Generated
1	2, 5, 3, 2, 5, 5, 1, 4, 5, 2
2	1, 1, 5, 2, 2, 1, 3, 1, 1, 5
3	4, 5, 4, 5, 5, 4, 3, 5, 1, 1
4	1, 5, 5, 5, 1, 2, 2, 3, 5, 3
5	5, 1, 5, 3, 5, 3, 4, 5, 3, 2
6	1, 1, 5, 5, 1, 4, 2, 2, 3, 4
7	2, 1, 5, 3, 1, 5, 1, 2, 1, 4
8	2, 4, 3, 2, 4, 4, 2, 1, 3, 1
9	3, 2, 1, 4, 5, 3, 5, 5, 1, 2
10	3, 4, 2, 4, 3, 5, 2, 3, 5, 1

3. According to Reyna's simulation, what was the experimental probability that a hurricane would strike the city in at least 4 of the next 10 years?

4. According to the simulation, what was the experimental probability that a hurricane strikes the city for the first time on the eighth year? Explain.

5. **Open Ended** Keith wants to use the spinner shown to simulate an event with a 75% chance of occurring. Describe a situation Keith could be simulating. Then describe how the spinner can be used.

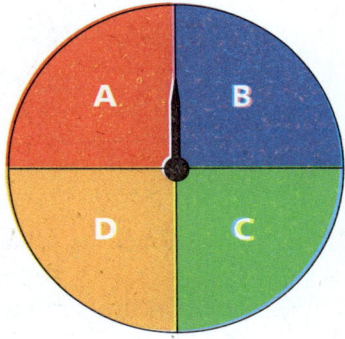

Module 21 • Lesson 4

6. **Use Tools** Dave wants to generate random numbers to simulate an event with a 25% chance of occurring. Describe a model he could use.

   _____
   _____
   _____

7. **Reason** Is it possible to perform a simulation several times and get different experimental probabilities for the same event? Explain.

   _____
   _____
   _____

8. **STEM** A quality control technician wants to determine how much variation can be expected in a random sample of light bulbs produced at a plant. The known rate of defective light bulbs is 5%. Describe a simulation the technician could use to find the experimental probability that a sample of 100 bulbs will include at least 5 defective bulbs.

   _____
   _____
   _____
   _____
   _____

9. **Use Tools** Allie is a softball player. She has a batting average of 0.600. This means that Allie gets a hit 60% of the time.

   A. Design a simulation using slips of paper and a box to find the experimental probability of Allie getting a hit at least 2 out of 5 times.

   _____
   _____
   _____
   _____

   B. Perform the simulation and use your results to predict the probability of Allie getting a hit at least 2 out of 5 times.

   _____
   _____
   _____

LESSON 21.4
More Practice/ Homework

Conduct Simulations

1. There is a card under 30% of the chairs at a booster meeting. Finn wants to find the probability that the first card he finds will be under the third chair that he checks. He generates 10 sets of random numbers from 1 to 10. The numbers 1–3 represent a chair with a card and 4–10 represent a chair without a card. Complete the table and find the experimental probability of the event.

Trial	1	2	3	4	5	6	7	8	9	10
Numbers Generated	6, 5, 1	8, 1	10, 1	7, 8, 4, 1	9, 3	5, 4, 2	3	9, 5, 8, 2	7, 3	9, 6, 8, 4, 7, 3
Chairs Checked										

2. **Math on the Spot** There is a 20% chance that a particular volcano will erupt during any given decade. A random number generator generated 10 sets of random numbers from 1 to 5 as shown. The number 1 represents the volcano erupting. Find the experimental probability that the volcano will erupt in 1 or 2 of the next 5 decades.

Trial	Numbers Generated
1	3, 1, 3, 4, 2
2	3, 2, 2, 4, 5
3	1, 3, 3, 2, 5
4	5, 3, 4, 5, 4
5	5, 5, 3, 2, 4
6	2, 3, 3, 4, 2
7	1, 2, 4, 1, 4
8	1, 3, 2, 1, 5
9	1, 2, 4, 2, 5
10	5, 5, 3, 2, 4

3. Sia makes 10% of the shots she attempts in soccer at any given time. A random number generator was used to generate 5 sets of random numbers from 1 to 10 as shown, where number 1 represents a successful shot and numbers 2–10 represent a missed shot. Find the experimental probability that Sia will make at least 2 of the next 10 shots.

Trial	Numbers Generated
1	5, 4, 8, 4, 8, 6, 7, 1, 7, 4
2	6, 9, 4, 6, 6, 4, 6, 8, 8, 6
3	10, 1, 8, 2, 3, 2, 9, 3, 5, 7
4	3, 6, 10, 5, 5, 4, 10, 6, 1, 5
5	8, 1, 9, 9, 3, 7, 4, 5, 1, 10

Module 21 • Lesson 4

Test Prep

4. There is a 25% chance that Jahil will hit an archery target on any given attempt. Which model can be used to find the experimental probability that Jahil will hit the target on at least 3 of the next 4 attempts?

Ⓐ Use a computer to generate whole numbers from 1 to 8 where numbers 1–2 represent hitting the target and numbers 3–8 represent not hitting the target.

Ⓑ Use a calculator to generate whole numbers from 1 to 8 where numbers 1–6 represent hitting the target and numbers 7–8 represent not hitting the target.

Ⓒ Use a computer to generate whole numbers from 1 to 4 where numbers 1–2 represent hitting the target and numbers 3–4 represent not hitting the target.

Ⓓ Use a calculator to generate whole numbers from 1 to 4 where numbers 1–3 represent hitting the target and number 4 represents not hitting the target.

5. At a gym, 50% of the customers get a free training session. Let the number 1 represent a customer receiving a free training session and the number 2 represent not receiving a free training session. A calculator generated random numbers, 1 and 2, until a number that represents a customer receiving a free training session appeared. The results are shown in the table. Find the experimental probability that you must ask exactly 2 customers before you find a customer that received a free training session.

Trial	Numbers Generated
1	1
2	2, 2, 1
3	2, 1
4	1
5	2, 2, 1

_____ %

6. Out of 12 trials, a simulation showed Ming getting a place in a summer art program 10 times. What is the experimental probability of the event, according to the simulation?

_____

Spiral Review

7. Vera is going to flip a coin 50 times. Use multiplication to predict the number of times the coin lands on heads.

_____

8. Juan spins two spinners each with 4 equal sections labeled 1–4 and adds the results. What is the probability that Juan spins a sum greater than 3?

_____

Module 21 Review

Vocabulary

1. How is theoretical probability different from experimental probability?

   _____
   _____
   _____
   _____
   _____

2. What is a *simulation* in probability? Write a definition in your own words.

   _____
   _____

Concepts and Skills

3. A box contains 4 red pencils, 6 yellow pencils, and 5 blue pencils. What is the probability of randomly selecting a yellow pencil from the box?

   _____

4. Select the situation with a $\frac{1}{3}$ probability of randomly selecting a blue marble from a bag.

   Ⓐ A bag containing 1 white, 4 red, 3 blue, 2 green, and 4 black marbles

   Ⓑ A bag containing 2 white, 6 red, 8 blue, 5 green, and 5 black marbles

   Ⓒ A bag containing 3 white, 2 red, 5 blue, 3 green, and 2 black marbles

   Ⓓ A bag containing 3 white, 3 red, 3 blue, 3 green, and 3 black marbles

5. **Use Tools** A stack of cards contains 25 red cards, 25 blue cards, 25 green cards, and 25 yellow cards. A card is drawn from the stack at random and then replaced 300 times. The results are shown. Which experimental probability from this experiment is closest to the expected theoretical probability based on the sample space? State what strategy and tool you will use to answer the question, explain your choice, and then find the answer.

Experimental Results	
Outcome	Frequency
Red	74
Blue	68
Green	78
Yellow	80

   _____
   _____

Module 21   665

6. Ginny rolls two number cubes numbered 1 to 6. Complete the table by determining the theroretical probability of each event.

Event	Probability
Rolling double 3s	
Rolling a sum of 7	
Rolling two even numbers	

7. Harry spins the spinner shown 60 times. How many times can he be expected to get a number less than 3?

   _____ times

8. A restaurant serves buttermilk, gingerbread, and pecan pancakes with strawberry, banana, or blueberry topping. Each week, the manager randomly selects one pancake type and one topping to be the breakfast special. There is an equal chance that each type and topping is picked. For about how many of the 52 weeks in a year can the restaurant be expected to have banana pecan pancakes as the breakfast special?

   (A) 6 weeks   (B) 9 weeks   (C) 12 weeks   (D) 17 weeks

9. Sula designs greeting cards for her friends. Each friend has a 30% chance to get a musical greeting card. Design a simulation that can be used to estimate the probability that a friend who receives 2 greeting cards will receive at least one musical greeting card.

   _____
   _____
   _____
   _____

10. A kitten has an equal chance of being male or female. In a litter of 3 kittens, the outcomes {MMM, MMF, MFM, MFF, FMM, FMF, FFM, FFF} are theoretically equally likely. Jaime used random numbers to simulate 400 litters of 3 kittens each. The table shows the result of the simulation. For which type of litter of 3 kittens is the frequency from the simulation less than the expected theoretical frequency?

Simulation Results	
Outcome	Frequency
3 males	63
2 males, 1 female	151
1 male, 2 females	130
3 females	56

   (A) 3 male kittens   (C) exactly 2 male kittens
   (B) 3 female kittens   (D) exactly 2 female kittens

Selected Answers

UNIT 1

MODULE 1, LESSON 1
On Your Own
3. Yes 5. Yes

More Practice/Homework
1. Yes 3. No 5. Yes 7. A
9. $94.20

MODULE 1, LESSON 2
On Your Own
5. yes; $k = 21$ 7. yes; $y = 7x$
9. No 11. $k = 42$; $y = 42x$
13. 100; 300; 2

More Practice/Homework
1. yes; $k = 9$ 3. The table represents a proportional relationship; $k = 24$; $y = 24x$
5. $k = 8$; $y = 8x$ 7. Table 2
9. It takes 24 h to build each chair. 11. A 13. Yes

MODULE 1, LESSON 3
On Your Own
5. 110 beats per min 7A. 12 min
B. 3 mi in 36 min C. Naomi
9. 4:1; No 11. $y = \frac{1}{60}x$; $\frac{5}{12}$ c
13. $8/h 15. $3\frac{1}{3}$ mi/h

More Practice/Homework
1. 3.8 g/cm³ 3. Maria's
5. $2.60 per lb 7. $3\frac{1}{2}$ ft²/h 9. $9/h
11. 17 mi/h 13. 20 min/lb 15. B
17. up to 14 bracelets

MODULE 1, LESSON 4
On Your Own
3A. It takes Yazmin 16 min to jog 1 mi. B. Yes; 16; $y = 16x$
5. Proportional

More Practice/Homework
1A. Yes B. $k = 15$ yd² per gal; $y = 15x$ 5. B 7. $3.50 per sandwich

MODULE 1, LESSON 5
On Your Own
3A. 30 ft³/min B. 1,800 ft³/h
C. $y = 1,800x$; 10,800 ft³ of water D. 15,300 ft³ of water
5A. 384,000 ft/h B. 72.7 mi/h
C. $y = 72.7x$; 218.1 mi

More Practice/Homework
1. 5.7 mi/h 3. 5.5 mi/h
5. 84.48 km 7. $15 9. B 11. >
13. −15, −5, −2, 1, 3, 8 15. 8

MODULE 1, LESSON 6
On Your Own
3B. $\frac{5 \text{ ft}}{1 \text{ in.}}$ C. $y = 5x$ D. 17.5 ft
E. 8 in. 5A. 7.5 feet per unit
B. $y = 7.5x$; about 47 ft

More Practice/Homework
1A. $y = 22.5x$ B. length: 18 m; width: 9 m 3. 14.7 in. 5. 10; 18
7.

Hours	Parts
2	40
3	60
5	100
8	160

MODULE 2, LESSON 1
On Your Own
5. 69 students 7. 2.5%
9A. 54 feet B. no
11. 56%; decrease 13. 75%; increase 15. 146.25 yd to 153.75 yd 17. 14.7 to 15.3
19A. |1,592 m − 1,600 m| = 8 m
B. 0.5% C. 1.25%

More Practice/Homework
1. 30% 3. 217 bacteria
5. 147 orders to 153 orders
7. increase of 87.5% 9. A, D
11. D 13A. 24 or $\frac{1}{24}$ B. $h = 24d$ or $d = \frac{1}{24}h$

MODULE 2, LESSON 2
On Your Own
3. $42 5. $133,860 7A. $y = 2.5x$
B. $30; $42 C. 75% D. $y = 0.75x$
9. $87.84 11. 150% 13. $30,000
15A. Possible answer: $p − 0.08p$ and $0.92p$ B. 0.92

More Practice/Homework
1. 25% 3. $120 5. $3.38
7. $352.00 9. $y = 3.4x$ 11. B
13. C 15. 237.5 g to 262.5 g

MODULE 2, LESSON 3
On Your Own
5. $290 7. $33.59 9. $900
11. $24.44 13. $250 15. $32.50
17. $676.18 19. $5.54
21. $y = 1.2x$ 23. $y = 1.2x$; $207.18

More Practice/Homework
1. $89.10 3. $16.32 5. 7%
7. $166.07 9. $126.36
11. $256.10 13. $600
15. D 17. 384 students

MODULE 2, LESSON 4
On Your Own
5. commission: $1,500; fees: $54
7. $141.60 9. $9,600 11. $1,637.50
13A. Irma also gets $11 for each delivery of pet supplies.
B. $4,044.80 C. Possible answer: In addition to a different base salary and a different commission rate for groceries, she will earn a commission rate for pet supplies instead of a fixed delivery fee. D. $3,597.26

More Practice/Homework
1. $6,500 3. $64,700 5. $1,925
7. $80,425 9. A, C, E 11. $1,215
13. 7.5% 15. $28.20

Selected Answers **SA1**

Selected Answers

MODULE 2, LESSON 5
On Your Own
3A. $57.60 **B.** $576.00
5A. $7,047 **B.** $21,547
7. $26,000 **9A.** $30 **B.** $2,150
C. 17 years

More Practice/Homework
1. $3,784.38 **3.** $15,225 **5.** B
7. 9 years **9.** −1

UNIT 2

MODULE 3, LESSON 1
On Your Own
3A. The ball ends up on the 31-yard marker; 6 yards to the right. **B.** The ball ends up on the 21-yard marker. **C.** They lost ground; They lost 4 yards because $6 + (-10) = -4$.
5. −10 **7.** 40

More Practice/Homework
1. 55°F **3.** 4°F **5.** yes **7.** C
9. negative **11.** $7.50

MODULE 3, LESSON 2
On Your Own
3. 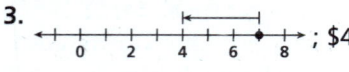 ; $4
5. 4 **7.** 30; (−40); (−20); −40; −40 m **9.** agree **11.** 40 °C
13. −50 **15.** 9 **17.** 0

More Practice/Homework
1. −4
3.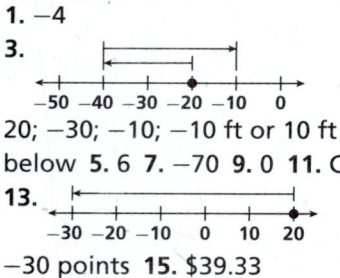
20; −30; −10; −10 ft or 10 ft below **5.** 6 **7.** −70 **9.** 0 **11.** C
13.
−30 points **15.** $39.33

MODULE 3, LESSON 3
On Your Own
5. $-5 + 13 + (-5) = 3$ **7.** 40 °F
9. 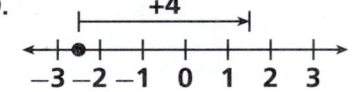 ;
Evan added $2\frac{1}{2} + 4$ instead of $\left(-2\frac{1}{2}\right) + 4$. The correct answer is $1\frac{1}{2}$. **11B.** $18.75 **13.** Possible answer: $-1\frac{1}{4}; \frac{1}{2}$ **15.** Possible answer: −5; 5 **17.** increase of 7 °F

More Practice/Homework
1.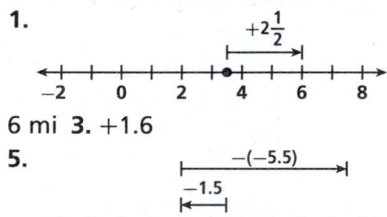
6 mi **3.** +1.6
5.
+4.5 **7.** B **9.** D **11.** 0.2 kg

MODULE 4, LESSON 1
On Your Own
3. $-10 + (-15) = -25$; She owes $25. **5.** $11.50 + 0.25 = \$11.75$
7. 3 **9.** $-\frac{13}{14}$ **11.** $3\frac{1}{2}$ **13.** $-11 + 5 = -6$; −6 floors **15.** $22\frac{1}{8} + \left(-16\frac{1}{5}\right) = 5\frac{37}{40}$; $5\frac{37}{40}$, or 5.925 miles **17.** −46 **19.** $-12\frac{1}{8}$ **21.** 9.26

More Practice/Homework
1A. $75\frac{1}{2} + \left(-92\frac{1}{4}\right)$ **B.** $-16\frac{3}{4}$ ft, or $16\frac{3}{4}$ ft below **3.** $28 + (-9) = 19$; $19 profit **5.** 15 **7.** 13.84 **9.** $-7\frac{17}{35}$
11. 0 **13.** $46.72 + (-24.61) = \$22.11$ **15.** C **17.** $-2\frac{1}{3}$ **19.** $9.49

MODULE 4, LESSON 2
On Your Own
5. $-15 - 2 = -17$; −17 °F
7A. $-56.2 - 27.7 = -83.9$ points
B. Yes **9.** $15.50 - 5.37 = 10.13$; $10.13 **11.** 26 units **13.** 0.67 unit
15. $65.02 - (-9.78) = 74.8$; $74.80
17. $41.7 + (-41.7) = 0$

19. $-13\frac{1}{4} + 10\frac{3}{4} = -2\frac{1}{2}$
21. $21.85 + (-6.03) = 15.82$
23. $0 + 5 = 5$

More Practice/Homework
1. $23 - (-12) = 35$; 35 °F
3. $3\frac{1}{3} - 1\frac{2}{3} = 1\frac{2}{3}$ mi **5.** $\frac{5}{12}$ **7.** −259
9. C **11.** $14,505 - (-282) = 14,787$; 14,787 ft **13.** 32
15. 8.9 miles

MODULE 4, LESSON 3
On Your Own
7. The balance in his checking account decreases by $500.
9. negative **11.** negative
13. negative **15.** −160 **17.** 90
19. 2 **21.** $\frac{1}{7}$ **23.** −6
25A.
−2 **B.** Negative

More Practice/Homework
1. Overall, missed landings on aerial cartwheels lowered the scores by 10 points. **3.** positive
5. negative **7.** Possible answer: Let $-10 \div (-5) = n$. Then $-10 = -5 \times n$. For $-5 \times n$ to be negative, n must be positive.
9. 43 **11.** $-4\frac{2}{3}$
13. A, C **15.** $43.52
17.
;1

MODULE 4, LESSON 4
On Your Own
5A. 0.45 h **B.** 23.4 mi
7A.

Fraction	Decimal
$\frac{1}{8}$	0.125
$\frac{2}{8}$	0.250
$\frac{3}{8}$	0.375

Possible answer: Each decimal is 0.125 more than the previous decimal. **B.** yes **9.** −8.5; Each charge decreased the value of

Selected Answers

the gift card by $8.50. **11.** 0.625
13. 0.777..., or $0.\overline{7}$
15. 10.3636..., or $10.\overline{36}$
17. Possible answer: $\frac{3}{-5}, -\left(\frac{3}{5}\right)$
19. Possible answer: $-7\frac{3}{5} = -\frac{38}{5} = \frac{-38}{5}$, -38 and 5 are integers. **21.** -7.5

More Practice/Homework
1A. 0.5625 pound **B.** $13.50
3. 4.875 **5.** -0.6 **7.** -5.4
9A.

Fraction	Decimal
$\frac{1}{9}$	0.111...
$\frac{2}{9}$	0.222...
$\frac{3}{9}$	0.333...

Possible answer: Each decimal is 0.111... more than the previous decimal. **B.** yes **11.** The values, in order, are -8, 8, 6, and -6.
13. $-11 + (-13) = -24$; the price decreased by $24 over the two years.

MODULE 4, LESSON 5
On Your Own
3A. -3.76 °F; when elevation increases by 0.2 mile, temperature drops about 3.76 °F.
B. 3.76 °F; when elevation decreases by 0.2 mile, temperature increases about 3.76 °F. **C.** The temperature changes are opposites. **5.** $-12\frac{1}{2}$ feet per second **7.** 5 containers; Possible answer: The quotient is $5\frac{1}{4}$ containers. So he can fill 5 whole containers and he'll have $\frac{1}{4} \times \frac{2}{3} = \frac{1}{6}$ cup of blueberries left over.
9. $\frac{\frac{-2}{4}}{\frac{-3}{4}}$, or $\frac{\frac{-1}{2}}{\frac{-3}{4}}$; $\frac{\frac{-1}{2}}{\frac{-3}{4}} = \frac{-1}{2} \div \frac{-3}{4} = \frac{-1}{2} \times \frac{4}{-3} = \frac{2}{3}$, and 2 and 3 are integers. **11.** $\frac{35}{36}$ **13.** -0.7
15. -0.8

More Practice/Homework
1. -20 ft **3A.** $4(3)(-12.50) = -150$; $-$150 **B.** 1 and 7, 2 and 6, 3 and 5, 4 and 4, 5 and 3, 6 and 2, 7 and 1 **C.** 9 **5.** $\frac{3}{2}$, or $1\frac{1}{2}$
7. -20 **9.** B
11.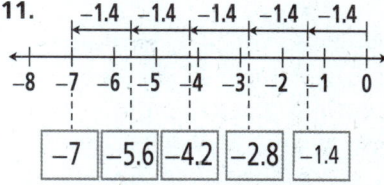

$(-1.4) + (-1.4) + (-1.4) + (-1.4) + (-1.4) = -7$

MODULE 5, LESSON 1
On Your Own
5A. LA = 543 ft; CA = 14,787 ft; IN = 937 ft; FL = 345 ft
B. not reasonable; elevations are both negative; difference must be < -282 **7.** 0.4 **9.** 5.075
11. -6.2 **13A.** $9 - 3$; 6
B. $4 \cdot 6 + 6$; 30
15A. $20 - \left[2\frac{1}{2}(5.50) + 2(0.45)\right]$
B. $5.35 **17.** $2\frac{1}{5}$ lb **19.** 0
21. $\frac{1}{2} \times \left(33 \times \frac{1}{11}\right) = \frac{1}{2} \times 3 = 1\frac{1}{2}$

More Practice/Homework
1. $11\frac{3}{4}$ ft, or 11.75 ft
3. Commutative Property of Addition; Associative Property of Addition; $\frac{1}{8}$ **5.** 10 loaves; about $0.88 per loaf **7.** $(7 + 2.6)9 \div (4 - 2.8)$ **9.** C **11.** C **13.** -21.1 °F

MODULE 5, LESSON 2
On Your Own
3A. 1.47 h **5.** 4 batches
7A. Possible answer: $900 **B.** no, too large **9A.** 5,760 m **B.** 5.76 km
C. Possible answer: about 1 h 45 min **11A.** 157 in. **B.** 48 min

More Practice/Homework
1. Possible answer: $3,300; underestimate **3A.** 23.9 min **5.** C
7. C **9.** Nicolas; 7 ft **11.** 39 doses

MODULE 5, LESSON 3
On Your Own
5. $7(2f + 3)$ **7.** $3(x - 10)$ **9.** $-1.3x - 15.2$ **11.** $4(7x) + (4)(3)$; $28x + 12$
13. Possible answer: $2L + (L - 1)$ and $3L - 1$ **15A.** Possible answer: $3x + 5(2x)$ and $13x$ **B.** Possible answer: The expression $3x + 5(2x)$ shows how many regular-sized quilts (3) and larger quilts (5) the customer ordered. The expression $13x$ shows that the total material used could also make 13 regular-sized quilts.
17. yes **19.** no
21. $2\left(5 - \frac{1}{4}x\right) + 2\left(5 - \frac{1}{4}x\right) + \left(5 - \frac{1}{4}x\right) + \left(5 - \frac{1}{4}x\right)$; $30 - \frac{3}{2}x$
23. $-12s - 1\frac{2}{5}$ **25.** $24x - 56$
27. $18p + 9 = 9(2p + 1)$
29. Possible answer: $2(7x) + 2(3x)$; it shows that the length is $7x$ and the width is $3x$.

More Practice/Homework
1. $9\frac{3}{4}t - 1$ **3.** $6y - 5$ **5.** $77c + 21$
7. $2.2s - 5$ **9.** D **11.** B, C
13. Positive

UNIT 3

MODULE 6, LESSON 1
On Your Own
3. Possible answer: $2x + 48 = 120$
5. Possible answer: $2(x + 2\frac{1}{2}) = 6\frac{1}{3}$
7. Possible answer: $0.70(x + 35) = 44.80

More Practice/Homework
1. Possible answer: $2x + 40.6 = 72.2$ **3.** $0.85x + 2.95 = 8.86$
5. Possible answer: $0.20(x + 25) = 13$ **7.** Possible answer: $19.50(x + 3) = 146.25$
9. $0.10x + 2 = 2.8$ **11.** A
13. $26.39

Selected Answers **SA3**

Selected Answers

MODULE 6, LESSON 2
On Your Own
3A. Possible answer: $\frac{637.50 - 200}{17.50} = 25$ h B. $17.50x + 200 = 637.50$; 25 h 5. $6(x + 5) = 72$; 12 in.
7. $h = -12$ 9. $y = -\frac{7}{15}$

More Practice/Homework
1. $0.50b + 4.50 = 22$; 35 bulbs
3. $2(x + 1\frac{1}{2}) = 4\frac{1}{2}$; $\frac{3}{4}$ c nuts
5. $m = 50$; $3 = 0.2(50) - 7$ (true)
7. $t = -6$; $-3(-6 + 6) = 0$ (true)
11. B 13. $16.50(h + 4) = 123.75$; 3.5 h 15. 5 apples for $2.50

MODULE 6, LESSON 3
On Your Own
3. Glenna 45, Val 80, Kim 55
5A. $x + (\frac{1}{2}x + 4) = 10$ B. $x = 4$
C. 4 home runs D. 6 home runs E. Possible answer: Add the answers in Parts C and D.
9. $p = 1$ 11. $t = 0.4$ 13. $n = -\frac{11}{7}$
15. $b = -4$

More Practice/Homework
1. 39 feet, 9 feet 5. $a = 3$ 7. $x = 30$
9. $x = 7.5$ 11. C 13. 3 hours
15. $39,500 17. $2\frac{3}{11}$ seconds

MODULE 6, LESSON 4
On Your Own
3. yes; one solution 5. Alex is not correct. 7. infinitely many solutions

More Practice/Homework
1. no 3. Blake is not correct.
7. 1 9. 3 11. one solution; $x = 4.2$ 13. C 15. $10.5x$
17. C 19A. 2.7 meters
B. 3.78 meters

MODULE 6, LESSON 5
On Your Own
3A. $t = 30$ B. They are at the same height after 30 seconds.
C. 45 feet 5. $\ell + (\ell + 3) = 49$;

Josh is 26 years old and Lynette is 23. 9. $(2x + 11)°$ 11. Ethan is incorrect. 13. $2,480
15. $x = 16$; 37° and 53°
17A. $3x + 7 + 5x + 3 = 90$
B. $x = 10$ C. 53°

More Practice/Homework
1. any number of games of bowling 3. 4.8 months
5A. $2x + 45 + 3x + 55 = 135$; $x = 7$ B. 59° 7. D 9. $\frac{1}{2}$ ounce of oil per hour

MODULE 7, LESSON 1
On Your Own
5. $4x \leq 24$; $x \leq 6$ ft
7. $x \geq 3$

9. $x > -10$

11. $4x \leq 24$; $x \leq 6$ 13. no
15. $x > 11.2$

17. $x < -3\frac{3}{5}$

More Practice/Homework
1A. $12x > 72$; $x > 6$ ft
B. $12x \leq 156$; $x \leq 13$ ft C. longer than 6 ft and no longer than 13 ft
3. $-3t > -24$; $t < 8$ min
5. B. 7. at least 8 9. $x = 65°$

MODULE 7, LESSON 2
On Your Own
3. $23d + 20 \geq 140$ 5. not a solution 7. $22 - 0.25w < 18$
9. $\frac{1}{4}x - 3 < 6$

More Practice/Homework
1. $5t + 40 \geq 500$ 3. Possible answer: $7x + 5 > 50$

5. 10 less than 2 times a number is greater than 22. 7. $75b + 800 \leq 1,200$ 11. $d - 31 \geq 15$; $d \geq 46$

MODULE 7, LESSON 3
On Your Own
3A. $2,100 - 25d < 1,500$; $d > 24$
B.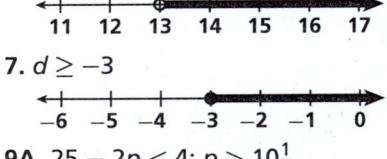

C. no, only whole numbers; The number of tables will be less than 1,500 after more than 24 days.
5. $x > 13$

7. $d \geq -3$

9A. $25 - 2p < 4$; $p > 10\frac{1}{2}$
B. at least 11 people
13. $z \leq -2$

15. $t \leq 1\frac{1}{2}$

17. $b \geq -3$

More Practice/Homework
1. $x \leq 7$
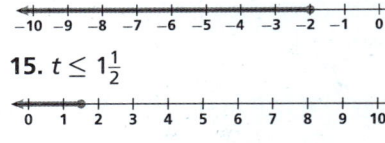
3. $r > \frac{1}{2}$
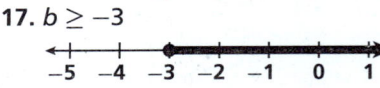

5. at least 50 tickets 7. at least 7 pieces 9. $36\frac{2}{3}$ mi 11. $3f + 6 = 18$

UNIT 4

MODULE 8, LESSON 1
On Your Own
5. yes 7. 1 pair of parallel lines; The parallel lines stay 4 centimeters apart

Selected Answers

More Practice/Homework
1. on the bottom 3A. yes; flip B. no
5.

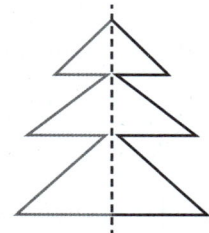

7. rhombus 9. the same size
11. $32.10

MODULE 8, LESSON 2
On Your Own
5. Building D 7. 60° 9. Opposite sides are parallel and the same length. 11. $(x, y) \rightarrow (x + 7, y + 1)$

More Practice/Homework
3. Figure E is not the same size or shape as Figure C.
5.

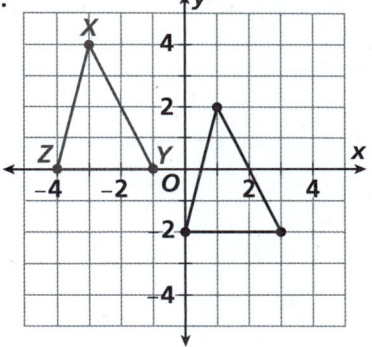

7. (−3, 3); (−1, 5); (1, 4)
9. 1 and 3 11. positive

MODULE 8, LESSON 3
On Your Own
5. 115°
7.

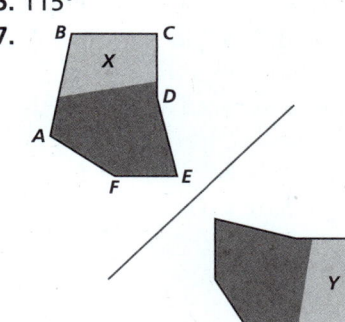

9A. yes B. yes C. yes 11A. no; no B. yes C. yes

More Practice/Homework
1. yes 3. no 5. A, C 7. D
9. $6\frac{7}{8}$ cups

MODULE 8, LESSON 4
On Your Own
3. The size and shape of the letter stayed the same. The V now opens down instead of up.
5A.

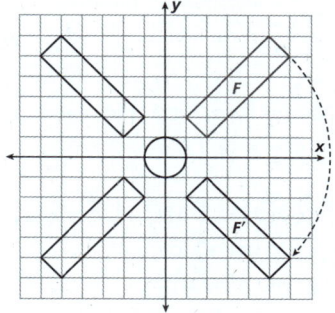

B. 90° clockwise about the origin C. $(x, y) \rightarrow (y, -x)$
7. $(x, y) \rightarrow (-y, x)$ 9A. 90° clockwise B. (2, −1), (5, −2), and (3, −6)

More Practice/Homework
1. Figure B
3. (3, −4), (1, 0), (4, 0)
5.

7. (1, 1), (5, 2), (6, 4), (2, 3), and (4, 7) 9. Figure 4

MODULE 8, LESSON 5
On Your Own
3. no 5. Figure C 9. Possible answer: I can use a ruler to measure and compare the side lengths. I can use a protractor to measure and compare the angles. 11. Figures 2, 4, and 5 are congruent; Figures 3 and 6 are not congruent. 13. Figure 1
15. Figure B

More Practice/Homework
1. Trace Fig. 3 and place it over my figure to show that they match exactly in size and shape. 3. no 5. a translation 3 units down 7. yes 9. C
11. (4, −7), (4, −3), (9, −3)
13. 31% decrease

MODULE 9, LESSON 1
On Your Own
3. The quadrilateral is a parallelogram. 5. The quadrilateral is a trapezoid that is not a parallelogram.

More Practice/Homework
3. Possible answer shown (reduced):

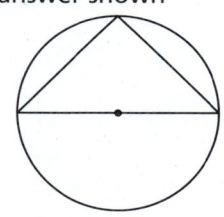

5A. The quadrilateral is a square. B. 1.5 units 7. Possible answer: a rotation followed by a translation

MODULE 9, LESSON 2
On Your Own
3. 12 + 12 < 26, so the pieces will not make a triangle.
5. 5 + 5 = 10, so these pieces will not make a triangle. 7. an infinite number of quadrilaterals
9. no 15. 4 + 5 < 10, so these logs will not make a triangle.
17. no 19. yes

More Practice/Homework
1. 6 + 8 > 13, so these pieces will make a triangle. 3. One possible side length is 5 ft; 3 + 3 = 6, so the length of the third side must

Selected Answers

be less than 6 ft. **5.** no **7.** yes
11. A **13.** B, C, E **15.** rectangle

MODULE 9, LESSON 3
On Your Own
3A.

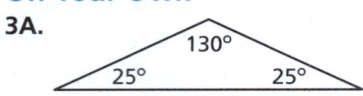

B. no **5.** possible **7.** Possible answers: 14 ft and 14 ft, or 10 ft and 12 ft

More Practice/Homework
1. yes **3.** possible **5.** not possible **7.** They may or may not be the same. **9.** B, C, E **11.** (−5, −3), (2, 5), (0, 6)

MODULE 9, LESSON 4
On Your Own
3. a diameter of the circle
5.

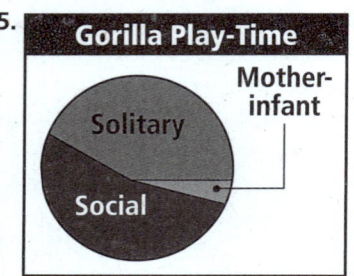

7.

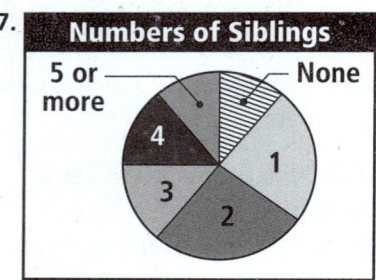

More Practice/Homework
3B. two triangles **5.** one; none; many; one; one; none **7.** B **9.** none

MODULE 10, LESSON 1
On Your Own
3. Left to right: reduction; enlargement; reduction **5.** no
7.

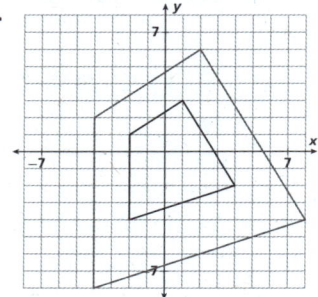

More Practice/Homework
3. no **5.** B **7.** reflection

MODULE 10, LESSON 2
On Your Own
3A. greater than 1 **B.** no **C.** no
5A. 3 **B.** $L'(21, 27)$; $M'(6, 15)$
C. $(x, y) \rightarrow (3x, 3y)$ **7A.** $\frac{2}{3}$
7B.

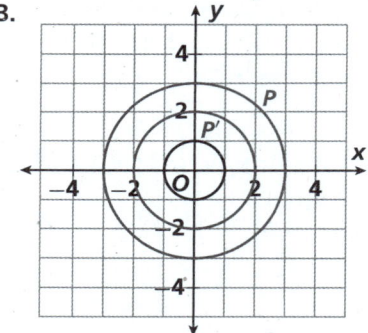

More Practice/Homework
1. Figure B is the correct shape. **3.** (7, −1)
5.

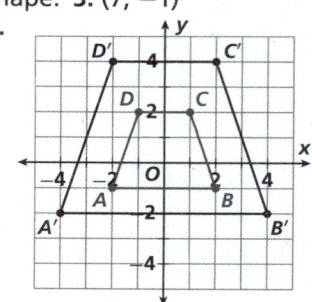

7. 30°, 60°, and 90°
9. rotation of 180° about the origin

MODULE 10, LESSON 3
On Your Own
3A, B.

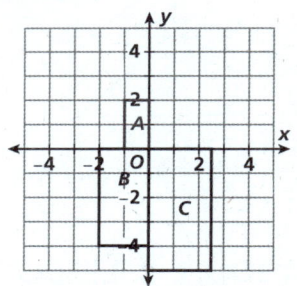

C. The flower beds are all similar.
5. Triangle P and Triangle J
7. Possible answer: dilation with scale factor 2 and center of dilation (0, 0), followed by a translation 1 unit left and 1 unit down **9.** Possible answer: dilation with scale factor 4 and center of dilation (0, 0), followed by a reflection across the x-axis **11.** $(x, y) \rightarrow (243x, 243y)$

More Practice/Homework
1A, B.

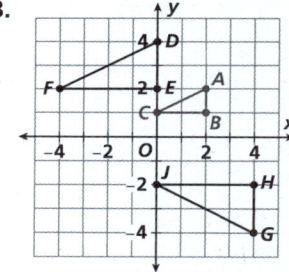

C. agree **3A.** Possible answer: dilation centered at (0, 0) with scale factor 2, translation $(x, y) \rightarrow (x + 6, y + 2)$; not congruent; similar **B.** Possible answer: reflection across the y-axis, dilation centered at (0, 0) with scale factor $\frac{1}{2}$, translation $(x, y) \rightarrow (x − 4, y + 4)$; not congruent; similar **5.** B, C, D

Selected Answers

7.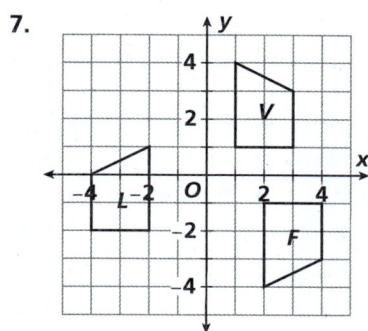

9. A'(−5, −2.5), B'(2.5, 5), C'(5, −10)

UNIT 5

MODULE 11, LESSON 1
On Your Own
5. no 7. 50°, 100° 9. 125°
13. x = 45

More Practice/Homework
1. x = 152.6 3. no

7.
Triangle	Unknown angle
1	90°
2	115°

9. 60 11. equal 13. one solution

MODULE 11, LESSON 2
On Your Own
5. yes 7. no 9. no 11. no

More Practice/Homework
1A. yes B. yes C. 22 ft 3A. 30
B. 60° 5. Triangles A, B, and C
7. 8 oz 9. Possible answer: a rotation and a reflection

MODULE 11, LESSON 3
On Your Own
3. 112° 5. ∠CBD 7. no
9. alternate exterior angles
11. none; ∠3 and ∠5; ∠1 and ∠5; ∠3 and ∠4; ∠2 and ∠4

More Practice/Homework
1. 125° 3. 115° 7. B 9. (−3, −4)
11A. 3w + 4 = 22 B. 6 ft

MODULE 12, LESSON 1
On Your Own
3. 5 5. yes 7. m = 1

More Practice/Homework
1. ∠RPQ and ∠UST; They are congruent. 5A. $\frac{5.5}{8.25} = \frac{x}{22.5}$
B. 15 feet tall; 14.25 feet away
7. A 9. $\frac{1}{2}$ 11. No

MODULE 12, LESSON 2
On Your Own
3A. The slope is negative because the price is decreasing. B. y = −5x
5. Possible points shown.

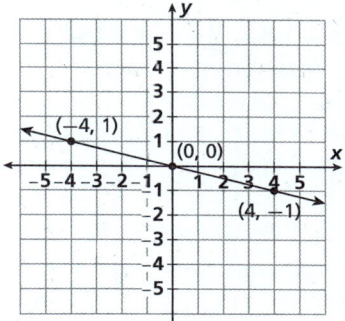

7. $y = \frac{1}{2}x$

More Practice/Homework
1A. $80 B. y = 20x 3. y = 5x
5.

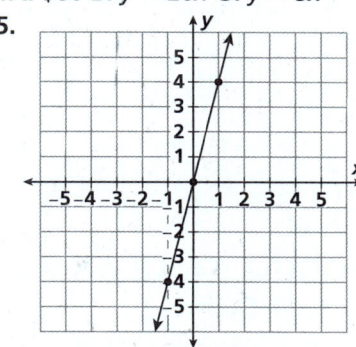

7. A 9. 5,000 11. A'(−1, 4), B'(−5, 6), C'(−3, 10) 13. x = 5

MODULE 12, LESSON 3
On Your Own
3B. y = 3x + 4 C. yes; The lines have the same slope 5. $y = \frac{3}{2}x + 2$; slope = $\frac{3}{2}$ y-intercept = 2
7. y = 4x − 5

More Practice/Homework
1. Possible answer: y = 3x + 2; and y = 3x − 2 3. Substitute the coordinates of the given point and the slope into the equation y = mx + b. 5. y = 2x − 1; y-intercept = −1 7. 3; rises
9. proportional 11. −2; 3
13. rise 15. A 17. Distribute values on both sides of the equal sign. Then combine like terms. $y = -\frac{2}{5}$ 19. 0 triangles

MODULE 12, LESSON 4
On Your Own
3. increases rapidly at the beginning; is constant speed during the middle; gradually decreases near the end 11. from 0 seconds to 6 seconds 13. the ball staying at the same height as it rolls across the ledge
15. It increases according to a nonlinear relationship.

More Practice/Homework
3. Bicycle A slows down at a constant rate. Bicycle B slows down rapidly at first, then gradually comes to a stop.
5. Possible answer shown.

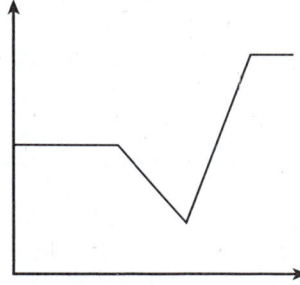

7. A, B, C, E 9. 45°, 55°, 80°

Selected Answers **SA7**

Selected Answers

UNIT 6

MODULE 13, LESSON 1
On Your Own
5. $\frac{43}{111}$ 7. no 9. $-1\frac{1}{9}$ 11. $\frac{553}{900}$ 13. $\frac{13}{18}$

More Practice/Homework
1A. $\frac{32}{60} = 0.533333\ldots$ B. rational
3. $45\frac{2}{15}$ hourly visitors
5. $0.037037037\ldots$; $0.\overline{037}$ 7. $-8\frac{29}{40}$
9. $1\frac{119}{225}$ 11. $\frac{19}{33}$ 13. D
15. $54 + 8w \geq 170$

MODULE 13, LESSON 2
On Your Own
5A. yes B. 5 ft; $5^3 = 125$
7. $\frac{2}{5}$; Possible answer:
$\left(\frac{2}{5}\right)^3 = \frac{8}{125}$ 9. $x = \pm 14$
13. yes; yes 15. 9 17. $x = \pm\frac{1}{7}$
19. $y = \frac{3}{5}$

More Practice/Homework
1A. 6 in.; $6^3 = 216$ B. 343 in³, 512 in³, or 729 in³ 3. $y = \frac{4}{9}$
5. 17 7. $\frac{1}{10}$ 9. $x = 7$ 11. C
13. B 15. $8\frac{2}{3}$ 17. $m = -3$

MODULE 13, LESSON 3
On Your Own
7A. 9; B. 9.2 9. $\sqrt{2} \approx 1.41$
11. < 13. > 15. 12 17. 19
19. $\sqrt{20} - 2$ 21. $\sqrt{125}$
23. -2; -1 25. 6; 7 27. no
29. $-\sqrt{15}$, $-\sqrt[3]{27}$, $(\sqrt{12} - 6)$, $-\frac{5}{3}$
    −4 −3.5 −3 −2.5 −2 −1.5 −1
31. $2\sqrt{3}$, $(-2 + \sqrt{19})$, $0.\overline{7}$, $\left(4 - \frac{21}{4}\right)$, $(\sqrt{32} - 8)$

More Practice/Homework
1. Kelsey's 3. <
7. $\sqrt{22} - 6$, $-5 + \sqrt{25}$, $\frac{16}{5}$, $\sqrt{15}$
   −2 −1 0 1 2 3 4
9. $-\sqrt{45} + 9$, $\frac{12}{5}$, $\sqrt{71} - 8$, $\sqrt[3]{99} - 5$, $-\frac{8}{5}$ 11. B 13. least: $-\sqrt{130}$; greatest: $-3 - \sqrt{47}$ 15. Possible answer: a dilation with a scale factor of $\frac{2}{3}$; center of dilation

at the origin; followed by a reflection across the y-axis

MODULE 14, LESSON 1
On Your Own
3. Possible answer: For a right triangle with legs a and b, and hypotenuse c, $a^2 + b^2 = c^2$.
5. yes

More Practice/Homework
3. yes; Possible answer: Since $300^2 + 400^2 = 500^2$, the parcel is a right triangle, which has a right angle. 5. A, D
7. Possible answer: She did not use the correct formula for the Pythagorean Theorem. $3^2 + 6^2 \neq 9^2$ 9. -3, $\frac{10}{4}$, 2.7, $\sqrt{8}$

MODULE 14, LESSON 2
On Your Own
3A. sidewalk route B. 11.9 m
5. 10.77 m 7. 28.8 in. 9. 68.3 cm
11. 28 inches

More Practice/Homework
1A. 1,336 km B. 553 km 3. 7 in.
5. C 7. D
9.

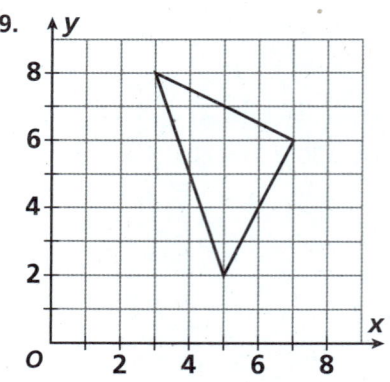

MODULE 14, LESSON 3
On Your Own
5. Point E 7A. $(-5, 2)$ or $(4, 4)$
B. 9.2 units C. 20.2 units
9A. $(1, 0.5)$, $(5, 3)$ B. 4.72 mi

More Practice/Homework
1. 4,270 ft 3A. $(-2, -1)$ or $(4, -4)$

B. 3 units; 6 units C. 6.7 units
D. 15.7 units 5. A 7. C 9. $x = 3.5$

MODULE 15, LESSON 1
On Your Own
3A. 10^{11}; product of powers property
B. 100,000,000,000 (one hundred billion) stars 5. diameter of Milky Way disc; 10^{21} m 7. distance from the Sun to Saturn, diameter of the Solar System, and diameter of Saturn 9B. If $a \neq 0$ and $b \neq 0$ and m is an integer, then $(ab)^m = a^m b^m$. C. $(3 \cdot 2)^5 = (6)^5 = 7,776$; $(3 \cdot 2)^5 = 3^5 \cdot 2^5 = 243 \cdot 32 = 7,776$
11. $\frac{1}{4}$ 13. 65

More Practice/Homework
1A. 10^7; product of powers property, quotient of powers property B. 10,000,000 (10 million) 3. Katie; 175 5. $\frac{1}{512}$
7. 81 9. A 11. D

MODULE 15, LESSON 2
On Your Own
5A. negative B. 1.7×10^{-8} cm
7. Car B, Car D, and Car E
9. 3 times longer 11A. Possible answer: 1.099511628E12; $1.099511628 \times 10^{12}$
B. 1,000,000,000,000
13. 4.71×10^7 15. 9×10^{-10}
17. 320,000,000 19. 0.00106
21. 8×10^9 is 40,000 times greater than 2×10^5.
23. 2.4×10^{10} is 1,000 times greater than 24,000,000.
25. The first factor is not greater than or equal to 1 but less than 10. 1.54×10^8

More Practice/Homework
1. 7.5×10^{18} 3. 186,000,000
5. 4.05×10^2 7. 6×10^{-14}
9. 60,700,000 11. 0.000004
13. 2.8×10^{-4} is 20 times greater than 1.4×10^{-5}. 17. B 19. A
21. 7.4 cm

Selected Answers

MODULE 15, LESSON 3
On Your Own
5. 3.82×10^5 vehicles **7.** Golden Gate Bridge: 4.088×10^7 vehicles; San Francisco-Oakland Bay Bridge: 9.855×10^7 vehicles
9. 2×10^6 sheets
11. approximately 250 seeds
13A. South Island; 3.7×10^4 km² greater **B.** approximately 18 people per square kilometer **15.** 5 meters

More Practice/Homework
1. 8.1×10^5 students **3.** 2.8×10^{-6} kg **5.** 1.595×10^8 km²
7. 7.89×10^5 **9.** 9.6×10^{-8}
11. 2×10^1 **13.** 1.3×10^{-9}
15. B **17.** 2.875×10^3 or 2,875 attendees **19.** 5.8 units

UNIT 7

MODULE 16, LESSON 1
On Your Own
3A. about 176 ft **B.** about 2,640 ft
5. 300 calories **7.** about 131.88 cm

More Practice/Homework
1A. about $\frac{55}{14}$ or 3.9 ft **B.** about $997\frac{6}{7}$ or 997.9 ft **3.** 48 years
5. about 28.26 cm **7.** about 59.66 ft **9.** about 28.26 in.
11. $85.50 **13.** 27.63 in. **15.** 90°

MODULE 16, LESSON 2
On Your Own
3A. 176.63 in² **B.** 379.94 in²
C. 203.31 in² or 203.32 in²
5. Disagree; 4 times as large
7. 254.34 m²

More Practice/Homework
1. 200.96 ft² **3.** 153.86 in²
5. 907.46 cm² **7.** 314 cm² **9.** 314 in²
11. 28.26 mi² **13.** 132.665 cm²
15. C **17.** 3,419.46 mm² **19.** 9.42 ft

MODULE 16, LESSON 3
On Your Own
3. 12 square units **5.** $375.29
7. 8 square units
9. 22 square inches

More Practice/Homework
1. 2,100 square feet **3.** 39 cm²
5. about 1,757 square feet
7. 6.25 square centimeters
9. 176.63 square meters
11. 12 feet

MODULE 17, LESSON 1
On Your Own
5. parallel to the base
7. circumference: 25.12 in.; area: 50.24 in² **9.** trapezoid
11. pentagon **13.** square

More Practice/Homework
1. square **3.** parallel
5. perpendicular **7.** Possible answer: circles **9.** A, B, D
11. 108 in²

MODULE 17, LESSON 2
On Your Own
5. 136 in² **7.** 640 cm²
9. $\approx$ 2,194 in²

More Practice/Homework
1. 486 cm² **3.** 1,761 ft²
5. 184 in² **7.** 672 cm²
9. C **11.** 189.9 mm² **13.** 21 ft²

MODULE 17, LESSON 3
On Your Own
3. 8,000 in³ **5.** 3 m **7.** 645 mm³

More Practice/Homework
1. 5,625 ft³ **5.** 3,320 ft³ **7.** 864 in³ more **9.** $V = Bh$; $1,260 = 28h$; $h = 45$ m **11.** rectangle
13. approximately 818.8 mm³

MODULE 17, LESSON 4
On Your Own
3. 51.9 m³ **5.** 3 in. **7.** 1.4×10^{12} mm³
9A. Possible answer: 140.55 cm³

More Practice/Homework
1. $432,180\pi$ ft³ **3.** 480 ft³
5. $V = \pi\left(\frac{d}{2}\right)^2 h$ or $V = \frac{\pi}{4}d^2h$
7. 11 m **9.** B, C, D **11.** B
13. 5.8×10^{-9}

MODULE 17, LESSON 5
On Your Own
3A. 252π cm³ **B.** 756π cm³
5. 16.6 m³ **7.** $\frac{3,887}{96}\pi$ ft³
9. 7,241.1 cm³ **11.** 0.5 yd³
13. 314 ft³
17A.

Height (cm)	1	2	3	4	5
Volume (cm³)	$\frac{1}{3}\pi$	$\frac{2}{3}\pi$	π	$\frac{4}{3}\pi$	$\frac{5}{3}\pi$

B. $y = \frac{1}{3}\pi x$

More Practice/Homework
1. $\frac{1,372}{3}\pi$ ft³; 1,436.0 ft³
3. 59.3 cm³ **5.** 33,493.3 mm³
7. The student forgot to find the radius by taking half the diameter. **9.** A, C, D, F **11.** $x = 2$
13. 43.6 m³

MODULE 17, LESSON 6
On Your Own
3A. 11 in. **B.** 257.4 in³ **5.** 468 cm³
7. 2,560 in³ **9A.** 7 ft **B.** volume; 109.2 ft³ **11.** 396 ft³ of water.
13. 110,815,833 ft³

More Practice/Homework
1A. 2 ft **B.** 184 ft² **C.** 15 **3.** no
5. 38 cm³ **7.** 312 in² **9.** 57.93 in³
11. 49

UNIT 8

MODULE 18, LESSON 1
On Your Own
5. yes; yes **7A.** all students in Cameron's school **B.** every tenth student that walks into school
C. yes **D.** yes

Selected Answers

More Practice/Homework
1A. Population: 10,000 members of the fan club; Sample: the 250 members chosen at random **B.** yes **C.** An overwhelming majority of club members are in favor. **3.** the sample of 200 students **5.** does not **7.** Julia's method **9.** a rectangle with a length of 28 inches and a width of 14 inches; no

MODULE 18, LESSON 2
On Your Own
3. at least **5.** yes **7.** 48 female athletes **9.** 90 letters **11.** 50 **13.** 25 **15.** Possible answer: 3,000 cars

More Practice/Homework
1A. 10th **B.** 9th **C.** 140 10th graders **D.** 80 9th graders **E.** Possible answer: 10th grade **3.** 270 students **5.** 12 laptop computers **7.** $k = -15$

MODULE 18, LESSON 3
On Your Own
3B.

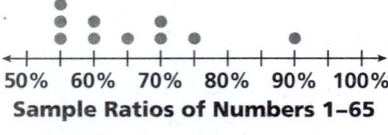

C. Slightly above the population ratio **D.** Possible answer: Most sample ratios are close to the population ratio.

More Practice/Homework
1A. above; below **B.**

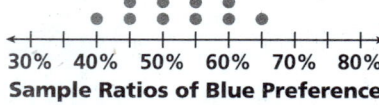

C. Possible answer: cluster around the population ratio of 55% or maybe slightly below it **D.** Possible answer: would cluster more tightly around 55% **3.** top down: 10% Below, 5% Below, 5% Above, 10% Above

MODULE 19, LESSON 1
On Your Own
5A. $37,500; clustered from $30,000 to $40,000 **B.** $50,000

More Practice/Homework
1. Tallahassee: 6°, Key West: 4°
3. Tallahassee: 87°, Key West: 85°
5. Tallahassee: 87°, Key West: 85°
7. Possible answer: The temperatures in Key West were more consistent and cooler than those in Tallahassee. Although Tallahassee is farther north, it got hotter in May than Key West. **9.** B **11.** Possible answer: HS students have more variation in the number of accounts than MS students. **13.** $y = 3x$

MODULE 19, LESSON 2
On Your Own
3A. Possible answer: On both teams, 25% of the players are ages 21–23, and 75% or more of the players are under 29.
B. Possible answer: I chose the interquartile range because it is less affected by outliers. The interquartile range for Team A is 2 yr, and the IQR for Team B is 5 yr. Team B has greater variability in players' ages.
C.

	Team A	Team B
Minimum	21	21
Lower quartile	23	23
Median	24	25
Upper quartile	25	28
Maximum	32	38

D. The medians are similar.
F. Possible answer: the data above the median

More Practice/Homework
1B. Possible answer: median A < median B; Store B prices vary more, but both stores have outlier high prices. **C.** Possible answer: The interquartile range for Store B is greater than the interquartile range for Store A. Both box plots have long right whiskers, so there may be high outliers at both stores.
D. Possible answer: 75% of the prices in the sample from Store B ≤ $1,000, while all prices in the sample from Store A ≤ $1,000. **E.** Possible answer: For Store A, the spread of the upper half of the data is 3 times the spread of the lower half. For Store B, the spread of the upper half of the data is a little less than $1\frac{1}{2}$ times the spread of the lower half. **3.** median; spread **5.** Possible answer: Medians are close, but median Moesha < median Justin; Justin's times tend to be more varied.
7. 1.9×10^{-10}

MODULE 19, LESSON 3
On Your Own
3A. 14.7 h; 16.5 h **B.** Cross the Ocean **C.** 1h; 3h **D.** 3; yes **5.** 1; some overlap **7.** 3; little or no overlap

More Practice/Homework
1A. 32; 39.4 **B.** 2 in.; 2.2 in.
3. A **5.** Colorado Springs was 2 °F higher. **7.** $\frac{9}{22}$; rational

UNIT 9

MODULE 20, LESSON 1
On Your Own
3. 15 trials; opening to an odd page, opening to an even page **5.** less **7.** likely; a number greater than $\frac{1}{2}$ and less than 1

Selected Answers

More Practice/Homework
1. impossible 5. Possible answer: {heads, tails} or {heads, tails, lands on side} 11. a number greater than 0 and less than $\frac{1}{2}$ 13. D 15. 12 inches

MODULE 20, LESSON 2
On Your Own
3A. yes B. The probabilities, in order, are $\frac{2}{15}, \frac{11}{60}, \frac{1}{6}, \frac{7}{60}, \frac{11}{60}$, and $\frac{13}{60}$. 5. Possible answer: Use random integers 1–10, where 1–6 represent completed passes. Perform 40 trials. 7A. $P(A) = \frac{7}{32}$; $P(B) = \frac{3}{8}$; $P(C) = \frac{7}{32}$; $P(D) = \frac{3}{16}$ B. $\frac{13}{16}$ C. The spinner is somehow biased in favor of the section labeled B.

More Practice/Homework
1. The probabilities, in order, are $\frac{19}{80}, \frac{17}{80}, \frac{23}{80}$, and $\frac{21}{80}$. 3. between: $\frac{7}{24}$; after: $\frac{7}{12}$ 5. $\frac{11}{37}$ 7. $\frac{3}{20}$ 9. $10 = 6 + x$; $x = 4$; four math problems

MODULE 20, LESSON 3
On Your Own
3A. 2 by 3 or 3 by 2 B. 6 possible outcomes 5. no 7. $\frac{1}{11}, \frac{10}{11}$ 9. $\frac{8}{55}, \frac{47}{55}$

More Practice/Homework
1A. 1H, 1T, 2H, 2T, 3H, 3T, 4H, 4T, 5H, 5T, 6H, 6T 1B. Row 1: 1H, 2H, 3H, 4H, 5H, 6H; Row 2: 1T, 2T, 3T, 4T, 5T, 6T 3A. $\frac{4}{25}$ 3B. $\frac{21}{25}$ 5. A, B 7. 28%; below 9. Both lines will pass through the origin, but the line for Han will be steeper than the line for Marcus.

MODULE 20, LESSON 4
On Your Own
3A. About 224 people B. because there cannot be partial people 5A. 0.35(17,400,000) B. about 6.09 million acres 7. 630 people 9. 101 people; Possible answer: no such thing as 0.6 of a person 11. about 10 more people

More Practice/Homework
1. 133 votes 3. 23 home runs 5. $\frac{45}{100} = \frac{x}{1,200}$; $x = 540$ 7. $\frac{12}{100} = \frac{x}{2,000}$; 240 h 9. 540 times 11. $\frac{12}{13}$

MODULE 21, LESSON 1
On Your Own
3. pile 2 5. $\frac{1}{8}$ 7. $\frac{3}{8}$ 9. 35% or $\frac{7}{20}$ 11. 3 13. $\frac{3}{5}$, 0.6, 60%

More Practice/Homework
1. $\frac{1}{2}$ 3. $\frac{1}{2}$ 5. theoretical probability: $\frac{13}{52}$ or $\frac{1}{4}$; experimental probability: $\frac{1}{5}$ 7. D 9. The theoretical probability is greater. 11. 36

MODULE 21, LESSON 2
On Your Own
3A. From left to right, top: 2, 3, 4; middle: 3, 4, 5; bottom: 4, 5, 6 B. $\frac{2}{9}$ C. rolling a sum of 5 D. Possible answer: Rolling a sum of 2 E. Possible answer: Rolling a sum of 4 F. $\frac{1}{3}$, 0.3, 33% G. $\frac{1}{9}$, 0.11, 11% H. 1, 1, 100% I. 0, 0, 0% 5A. 1, 1; 1, 2; 1, 3; 1, 4; 1, 5; 1, 6; 2, 1; 2, 2; 2, 3; 2, 4; 2, 5; 2, 6; 3, 1; 3, 2; 3, 3; 3, 4; 3, 5; 3, 6 B. $\frac{3}{18}$ or $\frac{1}{6}$ C. $\frac{2}{18}$ or $\frac{1}{9}$ D. Possible answer: The probability of getting a sum of 5 is greater than the probability of getting a sum of 3.

More Practice/Homework
1A.

+	1	2	3	4	5
1	2	3	4	5	6
2	3	4	5	6	7
3	4	5	6	7	8

B. $\frac{2}{15}$ C. Possible answer: drawing a sum of 6 3. 48 5. From top to bottom: $\frac{1}{9}, \frac{1}{12}, \frac{1}{6}, \frac{5}{18}$ 7. $\frac{4}{9}$

MODULE 21, LESSON 3
On Your Own
3. not likely 5. $\frac{2}{8} = \frac{x}{400}$; about 100 times 7. $\frac{1}{4} = \frac{x}{300}$; about 75 times 9. about 1,080 times 11. $\frac{1}{18} = \frac{x}{900}$; about 50 times 13. about 450 times 15. not likely; It would probably be chosen less than twice.

More Practice/Homework
1. yes 3. about 100 times 5. about 100 times 7. about 700 times 9. From top to bottom: about 200 times; about 750 times; about 50 times; about 300 times; about 550 times 11. landing on 5

MODULE 21, LESSON 4
On Your Own
3. 20% 7. yes 9A. Possible answer: Use whole numbers 1–5. Let 1–3 represent Allie getting a hit and 4–5 represent Allie not getting a hit. Draw 5 slips of paper from a box with numbers 1–5, replacing the slip of paper after each draw. Repeat 10 times.

More Practice/Homework
1. Chairs Checked: 3; 2; 2; 4; 2; 3; 1; 4; 2; 6; experimental probability: 20% 3. 20% 5. 20 7. about 25 times

Interactive Glossary

As you learn about each new term, add notes, drawings, or sentences in the space next to the definition. Doing so will help you remember what each term means.

Pronunciation Key

ă add, map	g go, log	n nice, tin	p pit, stop	û(r) burn, term
ā ace, rate	h hope, hate	ng ring, song	r run, poor	yōō fuse, few
â(r) care, air	hw which	ŏ odd, hot	s see, pass	v vain, eve
ä palm, father	ĭ it, give	ō open, so	sh sure, rush	w win, away
b bat, rub	ī ice, write	ô taught, jaw	t talk, sit	y yet, yearn
ch check, catch	îr tier	ôr order	th thin, both	z zest, muse
d dog, rod	j joy, ledge	oi oil, boy	th this, bathe	zh vision, pleasure
ĕ end, pet	k cool, take	ou pout, now	ŭ up, done	
ē equal, tree	l look, rule	ōō took, full	ōō pull, book	
f fit, half	m move, seem	ōō pool, food	ōōr cure	

ə the schwa, an unstressed vowel representing the sound spelled *a* in *above*, *e* in *sicken*, *i* in *possible*, *o* in *melon*, *u* in *circus*

Other symbols:
- separates words into syllables
' indicates stress on a syllable

A

My Vocabulary Summary

absolute value [ăb′sə-lōōt′ văl′ōō] The distance of a number from zero on a number line; shown by | |

valor absoluto Distancia a la que está un número de 0 en una recta numérica. El símbolo del valor absoluto es | |

Addition Property of Equality [ə-dĭsh′ən prŏp′ər-tē ŭv ĭ-kwŏl′ĭ-tē] The property that states that if you add the same number to both sides of an equation, the new equation will have the same solution

Propiedad de Igualdad de la Suma Propiedad que establece que puedes sumar el mismo número a ambos lados de una ecuación y la nueva ecuación tendrá la misma solución

Addition Property of Opposites [ə-dĭsh′ən prŏp′ər-tē ŭv ŏp′ə-zĭt] The property that states that the sum of a number and its opposite equals zero

Propiedad de la suma de los opuestos Propiedad que establece que la suma de un número y su opuesto es cero

Interactive Glossary

My Vocabulary Summary

additive inverse [ăd′ĭ-tĭv ĭn-vûrs′] The opposite of a number; the sum of the number and its additive inverse is 0

inverso aditivo El opuesto de un número; la suma del número y su inverso aditivo es 0

---

adjacent angles [ə-jā′sənt ăng′gəls] Angles in the same plane that have a common vertex and a common side

ángulos adyacentes Ángulos en el mismo plano que comparten un vértice y un lado

---

alternate exterior angles [ôl′tər-nĭt′ ĭk-stîr′ē-ər ăng′gəls] For two lines intersected by a transversal, a pair of angles that lie on opposite sides of the transversal and outside the other two lines

ángulos alternos externos Dadas dos rectas cortadas por una transversal, par de ángulos no adyacentes ubicados en los lados opuestos de la transversal y fuera de las otras dos rectas

---

alternate interior angles [ôl′tər-nĭt′ ĭn-tîr′ē-ər ăng′gəls] For two lines intersected by a transversal, a pair of nonadjacent angles that lie on opposite sides of the transversal and between the other two lines

ángulos alternos internos Dadas dos rectas cortadas por una transversal, par de ángulos no adyacentes ubicados en los lados opuestos de la transversal y entre de las otras dos rectas

---

Angle-Angle Similarity Postulate [ăng′gəl-ăng′gəl sĭm′ə-lăr′ĭ-tē pŏs′chə-lāt′] Two triangles are similar if they have pairs of corresponding angles that are congruent

Postulado de Semejanza Ángulo-Ángulo Dos triángulos son semejantes si tienen dos pares de ángulos correspondientes y congruentes

Interactive Glossary

My Vocabulary Summary

B

base [bās] The number that is used as a factor when a number is raised to a power

base Cuando un número es elevado a una potencia, el número que se usa como factor es la base

base (of a polygon or three-dimensional figure) [bās (ŭv ā pŏl′ē-gŏn′ ôr thrē′dĭ-mĕn′shə-nəl fĭg′yər)] A side of a polygon; a face of a three-dimensional figure by which the figure is measured or classified

base (de un polígono o figura tridimensional) Lado de un polígono; cara de una figura tridimensional según la cual se mide o se clasifica la figura

bias [bī′əs] When a sample does not accurately represent the population

sesgada Cuando una muestra no representa precisamente la población

box plot [bŏks plot] A graph that shows how data are distributed by using the median, quartiles, least value, and greatest value; also called a box-and-whisker plot

gráfica de mediana y rango Gráfica que muestra los valores máximo y mínimo, los cuartiles superior e inferior, así como la mediana de los datos

C

center of dilation [sĕn′tər ŭv dī-lā′shən] The point of intersection of lines through each pair of corresponding vertices in a dilation

centro de una dilatación Punto de intersección de las líneas que pasan a través de cada par de vértices correspondientes en una dilatación

Interactive Glossary

My Vocabulary Summary

center of rotation [sĕn′tər ŭv rō-tā′shən] The point about which a figure is rotated
centro de una rotación Punto alrededor del cual se hace girar una figura

circumference [sər-kŭm′fər-əns] The distance around a circle
circunferencia Distancia alrededor de un círculo

coefficient [kō′ə-fĭsh′ənt] The number that is multiplied by the variable in an algebraic expression
coeficiente Número que se multiplica por la variable en una expresión algebraica

commission [kə-mĭsh′ən] A fee paid to a person for making a sale
comisión Pago que recibe una persona por realizar una venta

common denominator [kŏm′ən dĭ-nŏm′ə-nā′tər] A denominator that is the same in two or more fractions
denominador común Denominador que es común a dos o más fracciones

complement of an event [kŏm′plə-mənt ŭv ən ĭ-vĕnt′] The set of all outcomes in the sample space that are *not* included in the event
complemento de un evento Conjunto de todos los resultados del espacio muestral que *no* están incluidos en el evento

complementary angles [kŏm′plə-mĕn′tə-rē ăng′gəls] Two angles whose measures add to 90°
ángulos complementarios Dos ángulos cuyas medidas suman 90°

Interactive Glossary **G5**

Interactive Glossary

My Vocabulary Summary

composite figure [kəm-pŏz′ĭt fĭg′yər] A figure made up of simple geometric shapes
figura compuesta Figura formada por figuras geométricas simples

compound event [kŏm-pound′ ĭ-věnt′] An event made up of two or more simple events
suceso compuesto Suceso que consista de dos o más sucesos simples

cone [kōn] A three-dimensional figure with one vertex and one circular base
cono Figura tridimensional con un vértice y una base circular

congruence transformation [kŏng′grōō-əns trăns′fər-mā′shən] A transformation that results in an image that is the same shape and the same size as the original figure
transformación de congruencia Una transformación que resulta en una imagen que tiene la misma forma y el mismo tamaño como la figura original

congruent [kŏng′grōō-ənt] Having the same size and shape; the symbol for congruent is ≅
congruentes Que tienen la misma forma y el mismo tamaño expresado por ≅

constant of proportionality [kŏn′stənt ŭv prə-pôr-shə-năl′ĭ-tē] A constant ratio of two variables related proportionally
constante de proporcionalidad Razón constante de dos variables que están relacionadas en forma proporcional

continuous graph [kən-tĭn′yōō-əs grăf] A graph made up of connected lines or curves
gráfica continua Gráfica compuesta por líneas rectas o curvas conectadas

Interactive Glossary

My Vocabulary Summary

coordinate [kō-ôr dn-ĭt, -āt] One of the numbers of an ordered pair that locate a point on a coordinate graph

coordenada Uno de los números de un par ordenado que ubica un punto en una gráfica de coordenadas

---

coordinate plane [kō-ôr′dn-ĭt plān] A plane formed by the intersection of a horizontal number line called the *x*-axis and a vertical number line called the *y*-axis

plano cartesiano Plano formado por la intersección de una recta numérica horizontal llamada eje *x* y otra vertical llamada eje *y*

---

corresponding angles (for lines) [kôr′ĭ-spŏn′dĭng ăng′gəls (fôr līns)] For two lines intersected by a transversal, a pair of angles that lie on the same side of the transversal and on the same sides of each of the other two lines

ángulos correspondientes (en líneas) Dadas dos rectas cortadas por una transversal, el par de ángulos ubicados en el mismo lado de la transversal y en los mismos lados de las otras dos rectas

---

corresponding angles (of polygons) [kôr′ĭ-spŏn′dĭng ăng′gəls (ŭv pŏl′ē-gŏn′s)] Angles in the same relative position in polygons with an equal number of sides

ángulos correspondientes (en polígonos) Ángulos en la misma posición formaron cuando una tercera línea interseca dos líneas

---

corresponding sides [kôr′ĭ-spŏn′dĭng sīds] Matching sides of two or more polygons

lados correspondientes Lados que se ubican en la misma posición relativa en dos o más polígonos

---

cross section [krôs sĕk′shən] The intersection of a three-dimensional figure and a plane

sección transversal Intersección de una figura tridimensional y un plano

Interactive Glossary

My Vocabulary Summary

cube (geometric figure) [kyoob (jē'ə-mĕt'rĭk fĭg'yər)] A rectangular prism with six congruent square faces

cubo (figura geométrica) Prisma rectangular con seis caras cuadradas congruentes

cube root [kyoob root] A number, written as $\sqrt[3]{x}$, whose cube is x

raíz cúbica Número, expresado como $\sqrt[3]{x}$, cuyo cubo es x

cylinder [sil'ən-dər] A three-dimensional figure with two parallel, congruent circular bases connected by a curved lateral surface

cilindro Figura tridimensional con dos bases circulares paralelas y congruentes, unidas por una superficie lateral curva

D

degree [dĭ-grē'] The unit of measure for angles or temperature

grado Unidad de medida para ángulos y temperaturas

dependent variable [dĭ-pĕn'dənt vâr'ē-ə-bəl] The output of a function; a variable whose value depends on the value of the input, or independent variable

variable dependiente Salida de una función; variable cuyo valor depende del valor de la entrada, o variable independiente

diameter [di-am'i-tər] A line segment that passes through the center of a circle and has endpoints on the circle; or the length of that segment

diámetro Segmento de recta que pasa por el centro de un círculo y tiene sus extremos en la circunferencia, o bien la longitud de ese segmento

Interactive Glossary

My Vocabulary Summary

dilation [dĭ-lā′shən] A transformation that enlarges or reduces a figure

dilatación Transformación que agranda o reduce una figura

dimension [dĭ-měn′shən] The length, width, or height of a figure

dimensión Longitud, ancho o altura de una figura

Distributive Property [dĭ-strĭb′yə-tĭv prŏp′ər-tē] For all real numbers a, b, and c, $a(b + c) = ab + ac$, and $a(b - c) = ab - ac$

Propiedad Distributiva Dados los números reales a, b, y c, $a(b + c) = ab + ac$, y $a(b - c) = ab - ac$

dividend [dĭv′ĭ-děnd′] The number to be divided in a division problem

dividendo Número que se divide en un problema de división

divisor [dĭ-vī′zər] The number you are dividing by in a division problem

divisor El número entre el que se divide en un problema de división

dot plot [dŏt plŏt] A visual display in which each piece of data is represented by a dot above a number line

diagrama de puntos Despliegue visual en que cada dato se representa con un punto sobre una recta numérica

E

enlargement [ĕn-lärj′mənt] An increase in size of all dimensions in the same proportions

agrandamiento Aumento de tamaño de todas las dimensiones en las mismas proporciones

Interactive Glossary

My Vocabulary Summary

equation [ĭ-kwā′zhən] A mathematical sentence that shows that two expressions are equivalent
ecuación Enunciado matemático que indica que dos expresiones son equivalentes

equilateral triangle [ē′kwə-lăt′ər-əl trī′ăng′gəl] A triangle with three congruent sides
triángulo equilátero Triángulo con tres lados congruentes

equivalent fractions [ĭ-kwĭv′ə-lənt frăk′shəns] Fractions that name the same amount or part
fracciones equivalentes Fracciones que representan la misma cantidad o parte

event [ĭ-vĕnt′] An outcome or set of outcomes of an experiment or situation
suceso Un resultado o una serie de resultados de un experimento o una situación

experiment [ĭk-spĕr′ə-mənt] In probability, any activity based on chance, such as tossing a coin
experimento En probabilidad, cualquier actividad basada en la posibilidad, como lanzar una moneda.

experimental probability [ĭk-spĕr′ə-mĕn′tl prŏb′ə-bĭl′ĭ-tē] The ratio of the number of times an event occurs to the total number of trials, or times that the activity is performed
probabilidad experimental Razón del número de veces que ocurre un suceso al número total de pruebas o al número de veces que se realiza el experimento

exponent [ĭk-spō′nənt] The number that indicates how many times the base is used as a factor
exponente Número que indica cuántas veces se usa la base como factor

expression [ĭk-sprĕsh ən] A mathematical phrase that contains operations, numbers, and/or variables
expresión Enunciado matemático que contiene operaciones, números y/o variables

G10 Interactive Glossary

Interactive Glossary

My Vocabulary Summary

exterior angle (of a polygon) [ĭk-stîr′ē-ər ăng′gəl (ŭv ā pŏl′ē-gŏn′)] An angle formed by one side of a polygon and the extension of an adjacent side

ángulo extreno de un polígono Ángulo formado por un lado de un polígono y la prolongación del lado adyacente

Exterior Angle Theorem [ĭk-stîr′ē-ər ăng′gəl thē′ər-əm] The measure of an exterior angle of a triangle is greater than either of the measures of the remote interior angles

Teorema del Ángulo Exterior La medida de un ángulo exterior de un triángulo es mayor que cualquiera de las medidas de los ángulos interiores no adyacentes

F

fee [fē] A fixed amount or a percent of an amount

tarifa Cantidad fija o porcentaje de una cantidad

frequency [frē′kwən-sē] The number of times the value appears in the data set

frecuencia Cantidad de veces que aparece el valor en un conjunto de datos

G

gratuity [grə-t′ī-tē] A tip, or monetary percent that is given or paid in addition to the price of a service

gratificación Una propina o porcentaje monetario, que se da o paga además del precio de un servicio

Interactive Glossary

My Vocabulary Summary

H

height [hīt] In a pyramid or cone, the perpendicular distance from the base to the opposite vertex

In a triangle or quadrilateral, the perpendicular distance from the base to the opposite vertex or side

In a prism or cylinder, the perpendicular distance between the bases

altura En una pirámide o cono, la distancia perpendicular desde la base al vértice opuesto

En un triángulo o cuadrilátero, la distancia perpendicular desde la base de la figura al vértice o lado opuesto

En un prisma o cilindro, la distancia perpendicular entre las bases

hypotenuse [hī-pŏt′n-ōōs′] In a right triangle, the side opposite the right angle

hipotenusa En un triángulo rectángulo, el lado opuesto al ángulo recto

I

image [ĭm′ĭj] A figure resulting from a transformation

imagen Figura que resulta de una transformación

independent variable [ĭn′dĭ-pĕn′dənt vâr′ē-ə-bəl] The input of a function; a variable whose value determines the value of the output, or dependent variable

variable independiente Entrada de una función; variable cuyo valor determina el valor de la salida, o variable dependiente

Interactive Glossary

My Vocabulary Summary

inequality [ĭn-ĭ-kwŏl'ĭ-tē] A mathematical sentence that shows the relationship between quantities that are not equivalent

desigualdad Enunciado matemático que muestra una relación entre cantidades que no son equivalentes

---

infinitely many solutions [ĭn'fə-nĭt-lē mĕn'ē sə-lōō'shəns] Occurs when every value of x creates a true mathematical statement, or if the graphs of two linear equations overlap and therefore intersect at infinitely many points

soluciones infinitas Ocurre cuando cada valor de x crea un enunciado matemático verdadero, o si las gráficas de dos ecuaciones lineales se superponen y por tanto se intersecan en puntos infinitos

---

interior angles [ĭn-tîr'ē-ər ăng'gəls] Angles on the inner sides of two lines cut by a transversal

ángulos internos Ángulos en los lados internos de dos líneas intersecadas por una transversal

---

interquartile range [ĭn'tər-kwôr'tĭl' rānj] The difference between the upper and lower quartiles in a box-and-whisker plot

rango entre cuartiles La diferencia entre los cuartiles superior e inferior en una gráfica de mediana y rango

---

inverse operations [ĭn-vûrs' ŏp'ə-rā'shəns] Operations that undo each other: addition and subtraction, or multiplication and division

operaciones inversas Operaciones que se cancelan mutuamente: suma y resta, o multiplicación y división

Interactive Glossary

My Vocabulary Summary

irrational number [ĭ-răsh′ə-nəl nŭm′bər] A number that cannot be expressed as a ratio of two integers or as a repeating or terminating decimal

número irracional Número que no se puede expresar como una razón de dos enteros ni como un decimal periódico o finito

isolate the variable [ī′sə-lāt′ thə vâr′ē-ə-bəl] To get a variable alone on one side of an equation or inequality in order to solve the equation or inequality

despejar la variable Dejar sola la variable en un lado de una ecuación o desigualdad para resolverla

L

legs [lĕgs] In a right triangle, the sides that form the right angle; in an isosceles triangle, the pair of congruent sides

catetos En un triángulo rectángulo, los lados adyacentes al ángulo recto. En un triángulo isósceles, el par de lados congruentes

like terms [līk tûrms] Terms that have the same variable(s) raised to the same exponent

términos semejantes Términos que contienen las mismas variables elevada a las mismas exponente

line of reflection [līn ŭv rĭ-flĕk′shən] A line that a figure is flipped across to create a mirror image of the original figure

línea de reflexión Línea sobre la cual se invierte una figura para crear una imagen reflejada de la figura original

Interactive Glossary

My Vocabulary Summary

linear equation [lĭn′ē-ər ĭ-kwā′zhən] An equation whose solutions form a straight line on a coordinate plane

ecuación lineal Ecuación cuyas soluciones forman una línea recta en un plano cartesiano

linear relationship [lĭn′ē-ər rĭ-lā′shən-shĭp′] A relationship whose graph is a straight line

relación lineal Relación cuya gráfica es una línea recta

lower quartile [lou′ər kwôr′tĭl′] The median of the lower half of a set of data

cuartil inferior La mediana de la mitad inferior de un conjunto de datos

M

markdown [märk′doun′] The amount of decrease in a price

margen de descuento Cantidad en la que disminuye un precio

markup [märk′ŭp′] The amount of increase in a price

margen de aumento Cantidad en la que aumenta un precio

Interactive Glossary

My Vocabulary Summary

mean [mēn] The sum of the items in a set of data divided by the number of items in the set; also called *average*

media La suma de todos loselementos de un conjunto de datos dividida entre el número de elementos del conjunto. También se llama *promedio*

mean absolute deviation (MAD) [mēn ăb′sə-lōōt′ dē′vē-ā′shən] The mean distance between each data value and the mean of the data set

desviación absoluta media (DAM) Distancia media entre cada dato y la media del conjunto de datos

median [mē′dē-ən] The middle number, or the mean (average) of the two middle numbers, in an ordered set of data

mediana El número intermedio, o la media (el promedio), de los dos números intermedios en un conjunto ordenado de datos

mode [mōd] The number or numbers that occur most frequently in a set of data; when all numbers occur with the same frequency, we say there is no mode

moda Número o números más frecuentes en un conjunto de datos; si todos los números aparecen con la misma frecuencia, no hay moda

multiple [mŭl′tə-pəl] The product of any number and any nonzero whole number is a multiple of that number

múltiplo El producto de un número y cualquier número cabal distinto de cero es un múltiplo de ese número

Multiplication Property of Equality [mŭl′tə-plĭ-kā′shən prŏp′ər-tē ŭv ĭ-kwŏl′ĭ-tē] The property that states that if you multiply both sides of an equation by the same number, the new equation will have the same solution

Propiedad de Igualdad de la Multiplicación Propiedad que establece que puedes multiplicar ambos lados de una ecuación por el mismo número y la nueva ecuación tendrá la misma solución

Interactive Glossary

My Vocabulary Summary

N

no solution [nō sə-lōō′shən] Occurs when no value of *x* makes an equation true, or when a system of two equations has graphs that never intersect because lines are parallel

sin solución Ocurre cuando ningún valor de x hace que una ecuación sea verdadera, o cuando un sistema de dos ecuaciones tiene gráficas que nunca se intersecan porque son rectas paralelas

nonlinear relationship [nŏn-lĭn′ē-ər rĭ-lā′shən-shĭp′] A relationship whose graph is not a straight line

relación no lineal Relación cuya gráfica no es una línea recta

number line [nŭm′bər līn] A line used to plot real numbers including integers, rational numbers, and irrational numbers

recta numérica Recta que se usa para marcar números reales que incluyen enteros, números racionales y números irracionales

O

opposites [ŏp′ə-zĭt] Two numbers are opposites if, on a number line, they are the same distance from 0 but on different sides

opuestos Dos números que están a la misma distancia de cero en una recta numérica

Interactive Glossary

My Vocabulary Summary

origin [ôr′ə-jĭn] The point where the *x*-axis and *y*-axis intersect on the coordinate plane; (0, 0)
origen Punto de intersección entre el eje *x* y el eje *y* en un plano cartesiano: (0, 0)

outcome [out′kŭm′] A possible result of a probability experiment
resultado Posible resultado de un experimento de probabilidad

outlier [out′lī′ər] A value much greater or much less than the others in a data set
valor atípico Un valor mucho mayor o menor que los demás valores de un conjunto de datos

P

parallel lines [păr′ə-lĕl′ līns] Lines in a plane that do not intersect
líneas paralelas Líneas que se encuentran en el mismo plano pero que nunca se intersecan

parallelogram [păr′ə-lĕl′ə-grăm′] A quadrilateral with two pairs of parallel sides
paralelogramo Cuadrilátero con dos pares de lados paralelos

percent change [pər-sĕnt′ chānj] The amount stated as a percent that a number increases or decreases
porcentaje de cambio Cantidad en que un número aumenta o disminuye, expresada como un porcentaje

Interactive Glossary

My Vocabulary Summary

percent decrease [pər-sĕnt′ dĭ-krēs′] A percent change describing a decrease in a quantity

porcentaje de disminución Porcentaje de cambio en que una cantidad disminuye

percent increase [pər-sĕnt′ ĭn-krēs′] A percent change describing an increase in a quantity

porcentaje de incremento Porcentaje de cambio en que una cantidad aumenta

perfect cube [pûr′fĭkt kyo͞ob] A cube of a whole number

cubo perfecto El cubo de un número cabal

perfect square [pûr′fĭkt skwâr] A square of a whole number

cuadrado perfecto El cuadrado de un número cabal

pi (π) [pī] The ratio of the circumference of a circle to the length of its diameter; $\pi \approx 3.14$ or $\frac{22}{7}$

pi (π) Razón de la circunferencia de un círculo a la longitud de su diámetro; $\pi \approx 3.14$ ó $\frac{22}{7}$

population [pŏp′yə-lā′shən] The entire group of objects or individuals considered for a survey

población Grupo completo de objetos o individuos que se desea estudiar

Interactive Glossary

My Vocabulary Summary

power [pou′ər] A number produced by raising a base to an exponent
potencia Número que resulta al elevar una base a un exponente

preimage [prē-ĭm′ĭj] The original figure in a transformation
imagen original Figura original en una transformación

prime notation [prīm nō-tā′shən] Used to label transformed images by adding apostrophes to each letter label
notación prima Se utiliza para marcar imágenes transformadas agregando apóstrofes a cada letra

principal [prĭn′sə-pəl] The initial amount of money borrowed or saved
capital Cantidad inicial de dinero depositada o recibida en préstamo

principal square root [prĭn′sə-pəl skwâr root] The nonnegative square root of a number
raíz cuadrada principal Raíz cuadrada no negativa de un número

prism [prĭz′əm] A polyhedron that has two congruent polygon-shaped bases and other faces that are all parallelograms
prisma Poliedro con dos bases congruentes con forma de polígono y caras con forma de paralelogramo

Interactive Glossary

My Vocabulary Summary

probability [prŏb′ə-bĭl′ĭ-tē] A number from 0 to 1 (or 0% to 100%) that describes how likely an event is to occur

probabilidad Un número entre 0 y 1 (ó 0% y 100%) que describe qué tan probable es un suceso

---

probability of an event [prŏb′ə-bĭl′ĭ-tē ŭv ən ĭ-vĕnt′] The probability of an event is the ratio of the number of outcomes in the event to the total number of outcomes in the sample space

probabilidad de un evento Razón del número de resultados del evento con respecto al número total de resultados del espacio muestral

---

properties of exponents [prŏp′ər-tēz ŭv ĭk-spō′nənts] Rules for operations with exponents

propiedades de exponentes Reglas de operaciones con exponentes

---

proportional relationship [prə-pôr′shə-nəl rĭ-lā′shən-shĭp′] A relationship between two quantities in which the ratio of one quantity to the other quantity is constant

relación proporcional Relación entre dos cantidades en que la razón de una cantidad a la otra es constante

---

pyramid [pĭr′ə-mĭd] A polyhedron with a polygon base and triangular sides that all meet at a common vertex

pirámide Poliedro cuya base es un polígono; tiene caras triangulares que se juntan en un vértice común

Interactive Glossary

My Vocabulary Summary

Pythagorean Theorem [pĭ-thăg′ə-rē′ən thē′ər-əm] In a right triangle, the square of the length of the hypotenuse is equal to the sum of the squares of the lengths of the legs

Teorema de Pitágoras En un triángulo rectángulo, la suma de los cuadrados de los catetos es igual al cuadrado de la hipotenusa

Pythagorean triple [pĭ-thăg′ə-rē′ən trĭp′əl] A set of three positive integers a, b, and c such that $a^2 + b^2 = c^2$

Tripleta de Pitágoras Conjunto de tres números enteros positivos de cero a, b y c tal que $a^2 + b^2 = c^2$

Q

quadrant [kwŏd′rənt] The x- and y-axes divide the coordinate plane into four regions. Each region is called a quadrant

cuadrante El eje x y el eje y dividen el plano cartesiano en cuatro regiones. Cada región recibe el nombre de cuadrante

quadrilateral [kwŏd′rə-lăt′ər-əl] A polygon with four sides and four angles

cuadrilátero Polígono que tiene cuatro lados y cuatro ángulos

quartile [kwôr′tĭl] Three values, one of which is the median, that divide a data set into fourths.

cuartiles Cada uno de tres valores, uno de los cuales es la mediana, que dividen en cuartos un conjunto de datos.

Interactive Glossary

My Vocabulary Summary

R

radical symbol [răd′ĭ-kəl sĭm′bəl] The symbol $\sqrt{}$ used to represent the nonnegative square root of a number

símbolo de radical El símbolo $\sqrt{}$ con que se representa la raíz cuadrada no negativa de un número

radius [rā′dē-əs] A line segment with one endpoint at the center of the circle and the other endpoint on the circle, or the length of that segment

radio Segmento de recta con un extremo en el centro de un círculo y el otro en la circunferencia, o bien se llama radio a la longitud de ese segmento

random sample [răn′dəm săm′pəl] A sample in which each individual or object in the entire population has an equal chance of being selected

muestra aleatoria Muestra en la que cada individuo u objeto de la población tiene la misma oportunidad de ser elegido

range [rānj] In statistics, the difference between the greatest and least values in a data set

rango (en estadística) Diferencia entre los valores máximo y mínimo de un conjunto de datos

rate of change [rāt ŭv chānj] A ratio that compares the amount of change in a dependent variable to the amount of change in an independent variable

tasa de cambio Razón que compara la cantidad de cambio de la variable dependiente con la cantidad de cambio de la variable independiente

ratio [rā′shō] A comparison of two quantities by division

razón Comparación de dos cantidades mediante una división

Interactive Glossary **G23**

Interactive Glossary

My Vocabulary Summary

rational number [răsh′ə-nəl nŭm′bər] Any number that can be expressed as a ratio of two integers
número racional Número que se puede escribir como una razón de dos enteros

real number [rē′əl nŭm′bər] A rational or irrational number
número real Número racional o irracional

reciprocal [rĭ-sĭp′rə-kəl] One of two numbers whose product is 1
recíproco Uno de dos números cuyo producto es igual a 1

rectangular prism [rĕk-tăng′gyə-lər prĭz′əm] A polyhedron whose bases are rectangles and whose other faces are parallelograms
prisma rectangular Poliedro cuyas bases son rectángulos y cuyas caras tienen forma de paralelogramo

reduction [rĭ-dŭk′shən] A decrease in the size of all dimensions of a figure
reducción Disminución de tamaño en todas las dimensiones de una figura

reflection [rĭ-flĕk′shən] A transformation of a figure that flips the figure across a line
reflexión Transformación que ocurre cuando se invierte una figura sobre una línea

remote interior angle [rĭ-mōt′ ĭn-tîr′ē-ər ăng′gəl] An interior angle of a polygon that is not adjacent to the exterior angle
ángulo interno remoto Ángulo interno de un polígono que no es adyacente al ángulo externo

Interactive Glossary

My Vocabulary Summary

repeating decimal [rĭ-pēt´ĭng dĕs´ə-məl] A decimal in which one or more digits repeat infinitely
decimal periódico Decimal en el que uno o más dígitos se repiten infinitamente

representative sample [rĕp´rĭ-zĕn´tə-tĭv săm´pəl] A sample that has the same characteristics of the population
muestra representativa Muestra que tiene las mismas características de la población

retail price [rē´tāl´ prīs] The amount an item is sold for after a company adds a markup
precio de venta al por menor Cantidad en la que se vende un artículo después que una compañía le agrega un aumento de precio

right cone [rīt kōn] A cone in which a perpendicular line drawn from the base to the tip (vertex) passes through the center of the base
cono recto Cono en el que una línea perpendicular trazada de la base a la punta (vértice) pasa por el centro de la base

rise [rīz] The vertical change when the slope of a line is expressed as the ratio $\frac{rise}{run}$, or "rise over run"
distancia vertical El cambio vertical cuando la pendiente de una línea se expresa como la razón $\frac{distancia\ vertical}{distancia\ horizontal}$, o "distancia vertical sobre distancia horizontal"

rotation [rō-tā´shən] A transformation in which a figure is turned around a point
rotación Transformación que ocurre cuando una figura gira alrededor de un punto

Interactive Glossary

My Vocabulary Summary

run [rŭn] The horizontal change when the slope of a line is expressed as the ratio $\frac{rise}{run}$, or "rise over run"

distancia horizontal El cambio horizontal cuando la pendiente de una línea se expresa como la razón $\frac{distancia\ vertical}{distancia\ horizontal}$, o "distancia vertical sobre distancia horizontal"

S

sales tax [sāl tăks] A percent of the cost of an item that is charged by governments to raise money

impuesto sobre la venta Porcentaje del costo de un artículo que los gobiernos cobran para recaudar fondos

same-side exterior angles [săm-sīd ĭk-stîr′ē-ər ăng′gəls] A pair of angles on the same side of a transversal but outside the parallel lines

ángulos externos del mismo lado Par de ángulos que se encuentran del mismo lado de una transversal, pero por la parte exterior de las rectas paralelas

same-side interior angles [săm-sīd ĭn-tîr′ē-ər ăng′gəls] A pair of angles on the same side of a transversal and between two lines intersected by the transversal

ángulo internos del mismo lado Dadas dos rectas cortadas por una transversal, par de ángulos ubicados en el mismo lado de la transversal y entre las dos rectas

sample [săm′pəl] A part of the population that is chosen to represent the entire group

muestra Una parte de la población que se elige para representar a todo el grupo

Interactive Glossary

My Vocabulary Summary

sample space [săm′pəl spās] All possible outcomes of an experiment
espacio muestral Conjunto de todos los resultados posibles de un experimento

scale [skāl] The ratio between two sets of measurements
escala La razón entre dos conjuntos de medidas

scale drawing [skāl drô′ĭng] A drawing that uses a scale to make an object smaller than or larger than the real object
dibujo a escala Dibujo en el que se usa una escala para que un objeto se vea mayor o menor que el objeto real al que representa

scale factor [skāl făk′tər] The ratio used to enlarge or reduce similar figures
factor de escala Razón empleada para agrandar o reducir figuras semejantes

scientific notation [sī′ən-tĭf′ĭk nō-tā′shən] A method of more conveniently writing very large or very small numbers by using powers of 10
notación científica Método que se usa para escribir números muy grandes o muy pequeños mediante potencias de 10

segment [sĕg′mənt] A part of a line between two endpoints
segmento Parte de una línea entre dos extremos

similar [sĭm′ə-lər] Figures with the same shape but not necessarily the same size
semejantes Figuras que tienen la misma forma, pero no necesariamente el mismo tamaño

Interactive Glossary **G27**

Interactive Glossary

My Vocabulary Summary

similarity transformation [sĭm′ə-lăr′ĭ-tē trăns′fər-mā′shən] A transformation that results in an image that is the same shape, but not necessarily the same size, as the original figure

transformación de semejanza Una transformación que resulta en una imagen que tiene la misma forma, pero no necesariamente el mismo tamaño como la figura original

---

simple interest [sĭm′pəl ĭn′trĭst] A fixed percent of the principal, found using the formula $I = Prt$, where P represents the principal, r the rate of interest, and t the time

interés simple Un porcentaje fijo del capital. Se calcula con la fórmula $I = Cit$, donde C representa el capital, i, la tasa de interés y t, el tiempo

---

simulation [sĭm′yə-lā′shən] A model of an experiment, often one that would be too difficult or too time-consuming to actually perform

simulación Representación de un experimento, por lo regular de uno cuya realización sería demasiado difícil o llevaría mucho tiempo

---

slant height (of a right cone) [slant hīt (ŭv ā rīt kōn)] The distance from the vertex of a right cone to a point on the edge of the base

altura inclinada (de un cono recto) Distancia desde el vértice de un cono recto hasta un punto en el borde de la base

---

slope [slōp] A measure of the steepness of a line on a graph; equal to the rise divided by the run

pendiente Medida de la inclinación de una línea en una gráfica. Razón de la distancia vertical a la distancia horizontal

Interactive Glossary

My Vocabulary Summary

slope-intercept form [slōp-ĭn′tər-sĕpt′ fôrm] A linear equation written in the form $y = mx + b$, where m represents slope and b represents the y-intercept

forma de pendiente-intersección Ecuación lineal escrita en la forma $y = mx + b$, donde m es la pendiente y b es la intersección con el eje y

---

solution of an equation [sə-lōō′shən ŭv ən ĭ-kwā′zhən] A value or values that make an equation true

solución de una ecuación Valor o valores que hacen verdadera una ecuación

---

solution of an inequality [sə-lōō′shən ŭv ən ĭn′ĭ-kwŏl′ĭ-tē] A value or values that make an inequality true

solución de una desigualdad Valor o valores que hacen verdadera una desigualdad

---

sphere [sfîr] A round three-dimensional figure with a central point and all points whose distance from the center is less than or equal to the radius

esfera Una figura redonda tridimensional con un punto central y todos los puntos cuya distancia desde el centro es menor o igual que el radio

---

square (numeration) [skwâr (nōō′mə-rā′shən)] A number raised to the second power

cuadrado (en numeración) Número elevado a la segunda potencia

---

square root [skwâr rōōt] A number that is multiplied by itself to form a product is called a square root of that product

raíz cuadrada El número que se multiplica por sí mismo para formar un producto se denomina la raíz cuadrada de ese producto

Interactive Glossary

My Vocabulary Summary

standard form of a number [stăn′dərd fôrm ŭv ā nŭm′bər] A way of writing a number by using digits

forma estándar de un número Manera de escribir un número usando dígitos

Subtraction Property of Equality [səb-trăk′shən prŏp′ər-tē ŭv ĭ-kwŏl′ĭ-tē] The property that states that if you subtract the same number from both sides of an equation, the new equation will have the same solution

Propiedad de igualdad de la resta Propiedad que establece que puedes restar el mismo número de ambos lados de una ecuación y la nueva ecuación tendrá la misma solución

supplementary angles [sŭp′lə-měn′tə-rē ăng′gəls] Two angles whose measures have a sum of 180°

ángulos suplementarios Dos ángulos cuyas medidas suman 180°

surface area [sûr′fəs âr′e-ə] The sum of the areas of the faces, or surfaces, of a three-dimensional figure

área total Suma de las áreas de las caras, o superficies, de una figura tridimensional

T

terminating decimal [tûr′mə-nāt′ĭng děs′ə-məl] A decimal number that ends, or terminates

decimal finito Decimal con un número determinado de posiciones decimales

Interactive Glossary

My Vocabulary Summary

theoretical probability [thē′ə-rĕt′ĭ-kəl prŏb′ə-bĭl′ĭ-tē] The ratio of the number of possible outcomes in the event to the total number of possible outcomes in the sample space

probabilidad teórica Razón del número de las maneras que puede ocurrir un suceso al número total de resultados igualmente probables

---

tip [tĭp] Another word for gratuity, a monetary percent that is given or paid in addition to the price of a service

propina Otra palabra para gratificación, que es un porcentaje de dinero que se da o se paga adicionalmente al precio de un servicio

---

transformation [trăns′fər-mā′shən] A change in the size or position of a figure

transformación Cambio en el tamaño o la posición de una figura

---

translation [trăns-lā′shən] A movement (slide) of a figure along a straight line

traslación Desplazamiento de una figura a lo largo de una línea recta

---

transversal [trans-vûr′səl] A line that intersects two or more other lines

transversal Línea que cruza dos o más líneas

---

trapezoid [trăp′ĭ-zoid′] A quadrilateral with at least one pair of parallel sides

trapecio Cuadrilátero con al menos un par de lados paralelos

Interactive Glossary

My Vocabulary Summary

tree diagram [trē dī′ə-grăm′] A branching diagram that shows all possible combinations or outcomes of an event

diagrama de árbol Diagrama ramificado que muestra todas las posibles combinaciones o resultados de un suceso

trial [trī′əl] Each repetition or observation of an experiment

prueba Una sola repetición u observación de un experimento

Triangle Sum Theorem [trī′ăng′gəl sŭm thē′ər-əm] The theorem that states that the measures of the angles in a triangle add up to 180°

Teorema de la suma del triángulo Teorema que establece que las medidas de los ángulos de un triángulo suman 180°

triangular prism [trī-ăng′gyə-lər prĭz′əm] A polyhedron whose bases are triangles and whose other faces are parallelograms

prisma triangular Poliedro cuyas bases son triángulos y cuyas demás caras tienen forma de paralelogramo

U

unit rate [yōō′nĭt rāt] A rate in which the second quantity in the comparison is one unit

tasa unitaria Una tasa en la que la segunda cantidad de la comparación es la unidad

upper quartile [ŭp′ər kwôr′tīl′] The median of the upper half of a set of data

cuartil superior La mediana de la mitad superior de un conjunto de datos

Interactive Glossary

My Vocabulary Summary

V

vertex [vûr′tĕks′] On an angle or polygon, the point where two sides intersect; on a polyhedron, the intersection of three or more faces; on a cone or pyramid, the top point

vértice En un ángulo o polígono, el punto de intersección de dos lados; en un poliedro, el punto de intersección de tres o más caras; en un cono o pirámide, la punta

vertical angles [vûr′tĭ-kəl ăng′gəls] A pair of opposite congruent angles formed by intersecting lines

ángulos opuestos por el vértice Par de ángulos opuestos congruentes formados por líneas secantes

volume [vŏl′yōōm] The amount of space enclosed within a three-dimensional region; or the number of cubic units needed to fill that space

volumen La cantidad de espacio dentro de una región tridimensional; o la cantidad de unidades cúbicas necesarias para llenar ese espacio

X

x-axis [ĕks′-ăk′sĭs] The horizontal axis on a coordinate plane

eje x El eje horizontal del plano cartesiano

Interactive Glossary

My Vocabulary Summary

x-intercept [ĕks-ĭn'tər-sĕpt'] The *x*-coordinate of the point where the graph of a line crosses the *x*-axis

intersección con el eje x Coordenada *x* del punto donde la gráfica de una línea cruza el eje *x*

Y

y = mx [wī ē'kwəls ĕm ĕks] The form for a linear equation that passes through the origin and has a *y*-intercept of 0

y = mx Ecuación que representa una ecuación lineal que pasa por el origen, la intersección con cada uno de los ejes es 0

y-axis [wī'-ăk sĭs] The vertical axis on a coordinate plane

eje y El eje vertical del plano cartesiano

y-intercept [wī-ĭn'tər-sĕpt'] The *y*-coordinate of the point where the graph of a line crosses the *y*-axis

intersección con el eje y Coordenada *y* del punto donde la gráfica de una línea cruza el eje *y*

Index

A

AA (Angle-Angle) Similarity Postulate, 364–370, 382, 383, 440
absolute value (||), 118, 155
   addition of, 118–120
   of numbers, 42, 90
   opposites and, 90
   showing on a number line, 42
   subtraction of, 119, 131
addition
   of absolute value (||), 118–120
   additive inverse, 107
   Associative Property of, 138, 157, 159–165, 175–177, 188
   Commutative Property of, 120, 157, 158, 160, 165, 175–177, 188
   in equations, 190–194
   of exponents, 464–470
   of fractions, 90
   of negative integers, 97–104
   properties of, applying to multi-step problems, 159–166
   Property of Equality, 138
   Property of Opposites, 107, 138
   of rational numbers, 89–114, 117–124
   with scientific notation, 479–486
   of temperature, 92–93, 95
additive inverse, 107
adjacent angles, 216, 223
   complementary, 353
   supplementary, 353
algebra
   The development of algebra skills and concepts is found throughout the book.
   algebraic representations of dilations, 333–340, 341–348
   coefficients, 202
   equations
      containing decimals, 479–486, 532–536, 539–541, 543–544, 546–552
      linear, 189–222
      modeling with, 15, 17
      multi-step, 201–208
      one-step, 4, 188, 373–374, 414, 490
      for proportional relationships, 12–18, 29, 35–42, 43, 44
      solving with Distributive Property, 479
      for taxes and gratuities, 67–72
      two-step, 189–194, 195–200
      using roots to solve, 421–428, 438, 445–452, 453–460
   expressions
      applying, 490
      operations with, 354
      properties of operations, 159–166, 167–174, 175–177, 180, 479
   for taxes and gratuities, 67–72
   translating figures on the coordinate plane, 259–266
   variables, 189–194, 195–200, 201–208
      isolating, 202
alternate exterior angles, 372–378
alternate interior angles, 372–378, 379
angle-angle similarity, 363–370, 440
Angle-Angle (AA) Similarity Postulate, 364–370, 382, 383, 440
angles, 353–380
   adjacent, 216, 223
      complementary, 353
      supplementary, 353
   alternate exterior, 372–378
   alternate interior, 372–378, 379
   complementary, 216, 218, 223, 353
   congruent, 359, 363–370, 371–380, 383
   corresponding, 268, 360, 363–378, 440
   exterior, 357–362, 379
   interior, 356–362, 379
   in linear equations, 216, 220
   non-adjacent complementary, 353
   non-adjacent supplementary, 353
   obtuse, 359
   parallel lines cut by transversal, 371–378
   relationships between, 354
   right, 220
   same-side exterior, 372
   same-side interior, 372
   supplementary, 216, 219, 221, 223, 360–361, 371–380
   in triangles, 355–362
   triangles, drawing and constructing given measures of, 309–314
   vertical, 216, 219, 223, 353
area
   of circles, 498, 531
   of composite figures, 503–508, 518
   of cross sections, 513–518
   of cylinder bases, 531–536
   of parallelograms, 490, 508
   of squares, 421
Are You Ready?, appears in every module. 4, 54, 90, 116, 158, 188, 226, 252, 294, 324, 354, 382, 414, 438, 462, 490, 512, 556, 580, 604, 636
art, 305
assessment
   Are You Ready?, appears in every module. 4, 54, 90, 116, 158, 188, 226, 252, 294, 324, 354, 382, 414, 438, 462, 490, 512, 556, 580, 604, 636
   Check Understanding, appears in every lesson. *See, for example,* 7, 14, 22, 30, 37, 45, 56, 62, 68, 74, 80, 93, 100, 108
   Module Review, appears in every module. 51–52, 85–86, 113–114, 155–156, 183–184, 223–224, 247–248, 291–292, 321–322, 349–350, 379–380, 409–410, 435–436, 459–460, 485–486, 509–510, 551–552, 577–578, 599–600, 633–634, 665–666
Associative Property
   of Addition, 138, 157, 159, 160, 165, 175–177, 188
   of Multiplication, 161, 164, 188

B

bar models, 3, 19, 35, 38, 40
base of exponents, 464
base ten system, 471–478
bias, 558
box plots, 566, 568, 576, 580, 598, 600
   shapes of, 587–592

C

calculators
   in generating trials of random numbers, 660, 664
   scientific notation on, 475, 480
careers
   archaeologist, 185
   astronomer, 1
   auto engineer, 351
   data analyst, 487
   film director, 87
   game designer, 601
   historian, 411
   puzzle designer, 249
   research assistant, 553
center
   comparing spread of data and, when displayed
      in box plots, 587–592
      in dot plots, 581–586
   of dilation, 333–340, 341–348
   of rotation, 276–282
challenge-seeking, 250, 256, 264, 272, 280, 288, 298, 306, 312, 330, 338, 346, 352, 360, 368, 376, 386, 392, 398, 602, 608, 616, 624, 642
Check Understanding, appears in every lesson. *See, for example,* 7, 14, 22, 30, 37, 45, 56, 62, 68, 74, 80, 93, 100, 108
circles
   area of, 498, 531
   base of cylinder as, 531, 532
   deriving and applying formula for area of, 497–502

Index

circles (continued)
  deriving and applying formula for circumference of, 491–496
  diameter of, 296–300, 321, 492–496, 499–502, 509
  inscribing polygons in, 296–299
  inscribing triangles in, 296–299
  pi (π) and, 416, 492
  radius of, 296–300, 321, 492, 493, 500, 509
circumference, 416, 509
  deriving and applying formula for, 491–496
cluster of data points, 582, 584, 586
coefficient, 202
coins, flipping of, 609, 612, 616, 617, 622–626, 640, 644, 649, 651, 652, 664
commissions, proportional reasoning in determining, 73–78, 85
common denominators, 202
Commutative Property
  of Addition, 120, 157, 158, 160, 165, 175–177, 188
  of Multiplication, 134, 161, 164
compare
  angle-angle similarity, 363–370
  irrational numbers, 430–432
  quantities, 5–10
  rates, 20
  rational numbers, 226
compasses, 295–297, 301–308, 315–320
complementary angles, 216, 218, 223, 353
complement of an event, 613, 654
complex fractions
  comparing scales, 45, 48
  computing unit rates involving, 19–26
composite figures, 509, 610
  area of, 503–508, 518
  volume of, 546
compound events
  experimental probability of, 619–626
  simulations in testing, 659–664
  theoretical probability of, 645–652
computers, in generating trials of random numbers, 660, 664
cones, 448–452
  diameter of, 537–544
  height of, 537–544
  radius of, 537–544
  right, 537
  slant height of, 539
  volume of, 537–544
    formula for, 537–544
congruence, transformations and, 251–292, 349
congruent angles, 359, 363–370, 371–380
conjectures, making, 303

constant of proportionality, 11–18, 22, 30–34, 51
  markup rate as, 63, 65
constant rates, 7–10, 12, 19, 20, 22, 32, 34, 38, 42
constant ratios, 30–34
converse of the Pythagorean Theorem, 439–444
  proving, 439–444
coordinate notation, 350
coordinate plane
  enlargements on the, 329
  linear equations on the, 391
  mapping notation, 261–265
  ordered pairs on the, 4, 324, 336
  polygons in the, 252, 293, 294, 325, 334–340, 343–348
  prime notation, 261–262
  Pythagorean Theorem in the, 453–460
  quadrants of the, 270
  reductions on the, 327–332
  reflections on the, 267–274
  shapes on the, 327–332, 335–340, 347–348, 349–350
  transformations on the, 324, 332, 343–348, 384, 386, 388
  translating figures on the, 259–266
  unit rates, 385
  vertex, 261
corresponding angles, 268, 360, 363–378, 440
cross sections, describing and analyzing, of solids, 513–518
cube roots, 424–428, 429–436, 467
  symbol for ($\sqrt[3]{}$), 424
  of zero, 426
cubes
  deriving and applying formula for surface areas of, 519–524
  edge length of, 422, 436, 467
  perfect, 424–428
  volume of, 422, 467
cylinders
  area of the base of, 531
  formula for the volume of, 531–535
  height of, 531–534, 536, 537
  radius of, 532–534, 536, 537
  volume of, 531–536
cylindrical containers
  volume of, 546

D

data
  collecting statistical, 556, 604
  comparing center and spread of, when displayed
    in box plots, 587–592
    in dot plots, 581–586

  comparing means of using mean absolute deviation and repeated sampling, 593–600
  mean of, 580
  median of, 580
  points, cluster of, 582, 584, 586
  range in, 580
  sample, 594
  using statistics and graphs to compare, 579–600
decagons, 178, 299
decimal notation, 419
decimals
  addition of, 116
  converting fractions to, 414
  multiplication of, 54, 116
  multi-step linear equations involving, 203
  repeating, 416–420, 435
  terminating, 416–419
  writing fractions as, 141–148, 414–419, 604
  writing probability as, 639, 643, 647
  writing rational numbers as, 141–148, 156
denominators
  in fractions, 152
  greatest common factor of, 417
density, as a unit rate, 25
diagrams. See under represent
diameter, 296–300, 321, 492–496, 499–502, 509
  of cylinders, 531–536
  of spheres, 467, 537–544
differences. See also subtraction
  absolute value and, 119, 131
dilations, 342–348, 349
  algebraic representation of, 336, 337
  centers of, 334–340, 337, 349
  exploring, 333–340
  images of, 349
  scale factor for, 334–340, 344–348, 349, 350, 370
dimensions, 45
discounts, 61–66
  equations for, 61–66
Distributive Property, 134, 138, 157, 164, 167, 177, 178, 188, 197, 204, 208, 223, 479
division
  in equations, 417
  in finding unit rate, 21
  of fractions, 116
  with fractions and mixed numbers, 4
  of integers, 141–148
  long, 414
  of mixed numbers, 116
  Property of Equality, 197
  of rational numbers, 133–140, 149–154

Index

with scientific notation, 480–486
in two-step equations, 196–200
dot plots, 580. *See also under* **represent**
  comparing center and spread of data displayed in, 581–586
  range of, 582
  shapes of, 582, 584
drawings
  of circles and other figures, 295–300
  scale, 43–50, 324

E

elevations, changes in, 121
enlargements
  on the coordinate plane, 329
  investigating, 325–332
  sketching, 328
equations. *See also under* **represent**
  absolute value (|||), 118–120
  for commissions and fees, 73–78
  cube roots, 424
  differences of rational numbers, 125–132
  division of rational numbers, 149–154
  linear, 187–224
    applying, 195–200, 215–222
    deriving, 389–394, 395–400
    multi-step, 201–208
    two-step, 189–194
  markups and discounts, 61–66
  modeling with, 15, 17
  multiplication of rational numbers, 149–154
  multi-step, 201–208, 532–536, 538–544, 546–552
  one-step, 4, 188, 414, 490
  percent change, 55–60
  products of rational numbers, 133–140
  for proportional relationships, 12–18, 29, 33, 35–42, 43, 44
  quotients of rational numbers, 133–140
  with rational numbers, 141–148
  rise/run, 384–385, 387
  simple interest, 79–84
  slope-intercept form, 395–400
  solutions of, 196–200
  with square roots, 423
  sums of rational numbers, 117–124
  for taxes and gratuities, 67–72
  two-step, 189–194
  using roots to solve, 438
  $y = mx$, 389–394
  $y = mx + b$, 395–400, 401
equilateral triangles, 176, 359
equivalent fractions, 142, 156
equivalent ratios, 3, 11–18, 23, 556
  proportional reasoning in writing, 604

estimates, in checking for reasonableness of answer, 169, 170, 172, 173, 429
events
  complement of, 613
  compound
    experimental probability of, 619–626
    simulations in testing, 659–664
    theoretical probability of, 645–652
  experimental probability of, 605–610
  simple
    finding experimental probability of, 611–618
    simulations in testing, 614–618, 659–664
    theoretical probability of, 637–644
experimental probability, 603–634, 635, 636, 665
  comparing to theoretical probability, 640–644, 665
  conducting simulations to test, 614–618, 659–664
  of events, 605–610
    compound, 619–626
    simple, 611–618
  proportional reasoning in making predictions, 627–632
  understanding, 605–610
experiments, 607
exponents
  laws or properties of, 463–470, 485
expressions
  adding, subtracting, and factoring with rational coefficients, 175–182
  algebraic, evaluating, 490
  simplifying, 463–470
exterior angles, 372–378, 357–362, 379
  alternate, 372–378, 379
  same-side, 372–378
Exterior Angle Theorem, 358

F

factors, of linear expressions with rational coefficients, 175–182
fees, proportional reasoning in determining, 73–78
figures. *See also* composite figures
  congruent, 283–290, 349
  similar, 341–348, 354
  three-dimensional, analyzing
    deriving and applying formula for surface areas of cubes and right prisms, 519–524
    solving multi-step problems with surface area and volume, 525–530, 545–550

translating on the coordinate plane, 259–266
two-dimensional, analyzing, 489–510
  areas of composite, 503–508, 518
  areas of cross sections, 513–518
  deriving and applying formula for area of circles, 497–502
  deriving and applying formula for circumference of circles, 491–496
  describing and analyzing cross sections of solids, 513–518
Financial Literacy, 59, 63, 75, 81–83, 110, 122, 129, 130, 153, 170, 506
flipping of coins, 609, 612, 616, 617, 622–626, 640, 644, 649, 651, 652, 664
formulas
  deriving and applying
    for area of circles, 497–502
    for circumference of circles, 491–496
    for surface area of cubes and right prisms, 519–524
  for perimeter, 195
  for Pythagorean Theorem, 440
  for the volume of a cone, 537–544
  for the volume of a cube, 422
  for the volume of a cylinder, 531–536
  for the volume of a sphere, 537–544, 548, 549
fractions
  addition of, 90, 116
  common denominator, 202
  complex, 19–26, 45, 48
  converting to decimals, 414, 415, 418, 419
  decimals and percents written as, 604
  denominator of, 152
  division of, 116
  division of mixed numbers and, 4
  equivalent, 142, 156
  expressing ratios as, 3, 12
  numerator of, 152
  rational numbers as, 415–420
  subtraction of, 90
  writing as decimals, 141–148, 414–420
  writing in lowest terms, 417, 418
  writing probability as, 613, 621, 639, 643, 645–652

G

geography, 49, 585, 661
geometry
  analyzing figures in finding
    areas of composite figures, 503–508, 518
    areas of cross sections, 513–518
    circumference and area, 489–510
    formula for area of circles, 497–502
    formula for circumference of circles, 491–496

Index **IN3**

Index

geometry (continued)
  analyzing surface area and volume
    for cubes and right prisms, 519–524
    multi-step problems with, 545–550
    for right prisms, 525–530
  Angle-Angle (AA) Similarity Postulate, 364–370, 382, 383
  angles
    adjacent complementary, 353
    adjacent supplementary, 353
    alternate exterior, 372–378
    alternate interior, 372–378, 379
    complementary, 216, 218, 223, 353
    congruent, 359, 363–370, 371–380, 383
    corresponding, 268, 360, 363–378, 440
    exterior, 357–362, 379
    interior, 356–362, 379
    non-adjacent complementary, 353
    non-adjacent supplementary, 353
    parallel line cut by transversal, 371–378
    relationship between, 354
    remote interior, 357–358, 360, 362, 372–378, 379
    same-side exterior, 372
    same-side interior, 372
    supplementary, 216, 219, 221, 223, 360–361, 371–380
    in triangles, 355–362
    vertical, 216, 219, 223, 353
  area
    of circles, 498, 531
    of composite figures, 503–508, 518
    of cross sections, 516
    of parallelograms, 490, 508
    of squares, 421
  circles
    deriving and applying formula for area of, 497–502
    deriving and applying formula for circumference of, 491–496
    diameter of, 296–300, 321, 492–496, 499, 500, 502, 509
    inscribing triangles in, 296–299
    pi (π) and, 416, 492
    radius of, 296–300, 321, 492, 493, 500, 509
  composite figures, 509, 610
    area of, 503–508, 518
  cones
    right, 537
    slant height of, 539
    volume of, 537–544
  congruent angles, 359, 363–370, 371–380, 383
  coordinate plane
    applying the Pythagorean Theorem in the, 453–460
    enlargements in the, 329
    ordered pairs in the, 4, 324, 336
    polygons in the, 252, 293, 294, 324, 335–340, 343–348
    reductions in the, 327–332
    transformations in the, 324, 332, 343–348, 384, 386, 388
  cross sections
    analyzing, 513–518
    area of, 516
  cubes
    deriving and applying formula for surface area of, 519–524
    edge length of, 422, 436, 467
    perfect, 424–428
    volume of, 422, 467
  cylindrical containers, 546
    volume of, 546
  decagons, 178, 299
  drawing and analyzing
    circles, 295–300
    shapes in problem solving, 315–320
    triangles, 293–322
    two-dimensional figures, 293–322
  equilateral triangles, 176, 359
  heptagons, 300
  hexagonal prisms, 522, 547
    height of, 527
    surface area of, 524, 547
    volume of, 527, 529, 547
  hexagonal pyramids, 515, 517
  hexagons, 276, 297, 300
  octagonal prisms, volume of, 530
  octagons, 181
  ordered pairs
    on the coordinate plane, 4, 324, 336
    graphing, 28, 34
  parallelograms, 194, 256, 270, 293
    area of, 490, 508
    in finding area of circles, 498
  pentagonal prisms, 515–516, 528, 530, 545
  pentagonal pyramids, 517
  pentagons, 178, 180, 331
  perimeter, 190, 192, 195, 208
  polygons
    in the coordinate plane, 252, 293, 294, 324, 335–340, 343–348
    inscribing, in circles, 296–299
  prisms, 511
    base of, 514
    deriving and applying formulas for surface area of, 519–524
    deriving and applying formulas for volume of right, 525–530
    hexagonal, 522, 524, 527, 529, 547
    octagonal, 530
    pentagonal, 515–516, 528, 530, 545
    rectangular, 512, 514, 523–524, 529, 545
    surface area of, 512, 521, 522, 524, 546
    trapezoidal, 547
    triangular, 515, 517, 522–524, 527–530, 546, 648
    volume of rectangular, 525–530, 531, 545, 610
    volume of triangular, 527–530, 546
  pyramids
    hexagonal, 515, 517
    pentagonal, 517
    triangular, 514
  quadrilaterals, 175, 257, 294, 298, 299, 350
    constructing given side lengths of, 303, 305, 307
  rectangles
    area of, 490
    perimeter of, 180
  rectangular prisms, 512, 514, 523–524, 529, 545
    volume of, 525–530, 531, 545, 610
  rhombus, 194
  right angles, 220
  right prisms
    deriving and applying formula for surface area of, 519–524
    surface area of, 521
  slope with similar triangles, 383–388
  solids, describing and analyzing cross sections of, 513–518
  spheres, volume of, 537–544
  square pyramids, 516
  squares, 293, 339, 346, 489, 490
  transformations
    describing, 259–266
    dilations as, 342–348, 349
    images in, 260–266, 268–271, 273
    investigating, 253–258
    mapping notation, 261–265, 280, 285, 336, 337, 345–347
    preimages in, 260–266, 268–271, 273, 275–282
    prime notation, 261–262
    reflections as, 267–274
    rotations as, 275–282, 324, 345, 348, 349
  trapezoidal prisms, 547
  trapezoids, 293, 348
  triangles, 293, 294, 321–322
    angles in, 340, 355–362
    area of, 490
    drawing and constructing given angle measures of, 309–314, 318
    drawing and constructing given side lengths of, 301–308, 318
    equilateral, 176, 359
    hypotenuse, 384, 440–444, 446, 447, 453–460
    inscribing, in circles, 296–299
    isosceles, 190, 437, 522
    legs, 384, 440–444, 453–454
    right, 296–300, 316, 439–444, 453–460, 546

rise, visualizing with, 384
run, visualizing with, 384
similar, 341–348, 349, 364–370, 378, 379, 382, 383–388
slope, explaining with similar, 383–388
using a ruler and protractor to draw, 354, 355
vertices of, 281, 285, 290, 346, 348
triangular prisms, 515, 517, 522–524, 527–530, 546, 648
triangular pyramids, 514
vertical angles, 216, 219, 223, 353
volume
  of cones, 537–544
  of cubes, 422, 467
  of cylinders, 531–536
  exploring, 512
  of rectangular prisms, 525–530, 531, 545, 610
  solving multi-step problems with surface area and, 545–550
  of spheres, 537–544, 548–549

Glossary, G2–G34
graphic organizers, 247
graphs. *See also under* **represent**
  dashed lines in, 29
  equivalent ratios in, 382
  origin in, 27–34
  proportional relationships in, 27–34
  solid lines in, 28, 29
gratuities, using equations to determine, 67–72, 86
greatest common factor (GCF), 177, 178, 180, 417

H

health and fitness, 23, 193, 213, 494, 568, 573
heptagons, 300
hexagonal prisms, 522
  height of, 527
  surface area of, 524, 547
  volume of, 527, 529, 547
hexagonal pyramids, 515, 517
hexagons, 276, 297, 300
history, 431
hypotenuse, 384, 440–444, 446, 447, 453–460

I

Identity Property of Multiplication, 138, 161
images, 326
  of a dilation, 349
inequalities
  interpreting, writing, and graphing, 226, 308
  problem solving using, 225–248
    one-step, 227–234
    two-step, 235–246
  solutions of, 228, 236, 247
inferences
  from random samples, 563–570
  repeated, 571–576
infinitely many solutions, linear equations with, 209–214, 224, 362
integers, division of, 141–148
interest, proportional reasoning in calculating simple, 79–84
interior angles, 356–362, 379
  alternate, 372–378
  same-side, 372–378
interquartile range, 579, 580, 587–592, 600
inverse operations, 107, 135
Inverse Property of Multiplication, 161
irrational numbers, 415–420, 423, 428, 429, 435–436
  comparing, 430–432
isolating the variable, 202
isosceles triangles, 190, 437, 522

L

layers, 526
Learning Mindset
  challenge-seeking, 250, 256, 264, 272, 280, 288, 298, 306, 312, 330, 338, 346, 352, 360, 368, 376, 386, 392, 398, 602, 608, 616, 624, 642
  perseverance, 2, 8, 16, 24, 32, 488, 494, 500, 516, 522, 528, 534
  resilience, 186, 192, 198, 206, 212, 232, 238, 412, 418, 426, 442, 450, 468, 554, 560, 568
  strategic help-seeking, 88, 94, 102, 110, 122, 130, 138, 146, 152
legs, 384, 440–444, 453–454
like terms, 190, 204
linear equations
  applying, 195–200, 215–222
  deriving, 389–394, 395–400
  with no solutions, one solution, or infinitely many solutions, 209–214
linear expressions
  adding, subtracting, and factoring, with rational coefficients, 175–182
  operations with, 354
linear relationships, 381–410
  explaining slope with similar triangles, 383–388
line of reflection, 268

lines
  parallel, 371, 379
    cut by a transversal, 371–378
  perpendicular, 321
  of symmetry, 257, 321
line symmetry, 257
lower quartile, 588

M

MAD. *See* **mean absolute deviation (MAD)**
manipulatives and materials
  algebra tiles, 201, 209
  balance scale, 187
  calculators, 475, 480
  compasses, 295–297, 301–308, 315–320, 491, 497, 498
  counters, 5, 11, 133
  fraction bars, 5, 19, 141
  grid paper, 27, 141, 255, 389, 439, 443, 445, 446, 497, 503, 506, 507, 513, 519, 525, 529
  number cubes, 601, 606–609, 614, 615, 617, 618, 620, 622, 623, 625, 626, 640, 641, 650–652, 655–658, 666
  number lines, 91, 117, 125, 133, 141, 195, 227, 235
  protractors, 253–255, 268, 275–277, 309–311, 315–320, 325, 326, 328, 330, 331, 333, 341, 342, 354, 355, 363, 364, 372, 383, 421
  rulers, 253, 254, 267, 275–277, 283, 297, 301–308, 325, 326, 328, 330, 331, 333, 341, 354, 363, 383, 421, 439, 445, 491, 513, 519
  spinners, 98, 99, 613, 616, 624, 636, 638, 642, 644, 645, 647, 650–652, 653, 655, 661, 664, 666
  straight edges, 453
  tracing paper, 289, 342, 354
  unit cubes, 525, 526
  x, y tables, 5, 11, 19, 27, 209, 395, 463, 557, 563, 619
mapping notation, 261–265, 280, 285, 336, 337, 345–347
maps, 455–457, 585
markdowns, proportional reasoning in calculating, 61–66, 85
markups
  as constant of proportionality, 63
  equations, 61–66
  proportional reasoning in calculating, 61–66
Mathematical Practices and Processes
  1. *make sense of problems and persevere in solving them,* occurs throughout. Some examples are 25, 38, 67, 236, 303

Index

Mathematical Practices and Processes (continued)
  2. *reason abstractly and quantitatively*, in some lessons. Some examples are 8, 9, 15, 23, 25, 57, 63, 69, 71, 75, 94, 95, 109, 122, 129, 153, 163, 179, 181, 205, 207, 256, 289, 319, 329, 339, 367–369, 375–377, 392, 404, 407, 425, 431, 432, 442, 469, 474, 476, 482, 494, 500, 516, 547, 548, 560, 575, 589, 596, 608, 609, 615, 625, 641, 643, 650, 662
  3. *construct viable arguments and critique the reasoning of others*, in some lessons. Some examples are 33, 76, 102, 111, 138, 139, 171, 172, 206, 212, 213, 232, 239, 263, 265, 273, 287, 306, 307, 313, 347, 359, 361, 418, 419, 456, 482, 500, 540, 542, 549, 560, 583, 590, 616, 623, 656
  4. *model with mathematics*, in some lessons. Some examples are 15, 17, 31, 38, 39, 41, 48, 49, 63, 64, 69, 70, 81, 82, 123, 137, 139, 165, 178, 180, 181, 192, 193, 198, 199, 220, 231, 232, 233, 238, 239, 244, 245, 263, 264, 265, 272, 279, 281, 337, 367, 377, 387, 392, 398, 542, 623, 629, 631, 648, 656, 657
  5. *use appropriate tools strategically*, in some lessons. Some examples are 94, 101, 103, 109, 111, 138, 173, 298, 299, 312, 313, 317, 319, 330, 339, 457, 475, 481, 507, 615, 617, 624, 662
  6. *attend to precision*, in some lessons. Some examples are 58, 59, 64, 65, 76, 164, 172, 198, 199, 221, 232, 243, 244, 257, 264, 272, 279, 280, 386, 393, 399, 433, 455, 474, 483, 506, 534, 540, 547, 548, 574, 595, 629, 630
  7. *look for and make use of structure*, in some lessons. Some examples are 46, 57, 70, 77, 82, 83, 123, 139, 145, 162, 231, 443, 481, 495, 501, 516, 528, 547, 548, 549, 569, 573, 583, 584, 589, 591, 596, 641, 642, 648, 650
  8. *look for and express regularity in repeated reasoning*, in some lessons. Some examples are 145, 147, 162, 346, 426, 468

Math on the Spot videos. *See* student and parent resources on Ed: Your Friend in Learning

mean, 580, 581, 583, 585, 593–600

mean absolute deviation (MAD), 593–600

measurement, constant of proportionality and, 16

median, 579–592, 598, 599

mixed numbers
  division of, 116
  division of fractions and, 4
  writing rational numbers as, 417–419

model. *See* represent

Module Opening Task, 3, 53, 89, 115, 157, 187, 225, 251, 293, 323, 353, 381, 413, 437, 461, 489, 511, 555, 579, 603, 635

Module Review, 51–52, 85–86, 113–114, 155–156, 183–184, 223–224, 247–248, 291–292, 321–322, 349–350, 379–380, 409–410, 435–436, 459–460, 485–486, 509–510, 551–552, 577–578, 599–600, 633–634, 665–666

multiplication
  Associative Property of, 161, 164, 188
  Commutative Property of, 134, 161, 164
  of decimals, 54, 116
  division as inverse operation of, 161
  to eliminate decimals, 203
  in equations, 191–194
  Identity Property of, 138, 161
  Inverse Property of, 161
  multi-step problems, applying properties to, 159–166
  Property of Equality, 384
  Property of Zero, 138
  of rational numbers, 133–140, 149–154
  with scientific notation, 480–486

multi-step problems
  applying properties to, 159–166
  proportional relationship in solving, 35–42
  solving linear, 189–194, 201–208, 462
  solving with rational numbers, 167–174
  solving with surface area and volume, 545–550

music, 239

N

negative integers
  addition of, 97–104, 113–114
  subtraction of, 97–104, 113–114

negative numbers
  addition of, 92–95, 117–124
  division of, 133–140
  multiplication of, 133–140
  on number lines, 92–95
  subtraction of, 92–95, 125–132

nets, surface area and, 512, 520

non-adjacent complementary angles, 353

non-adjacent supplementary angles, 353

nonlinear relationships, 401–408

nonproportional relationships, 30, 32–33

no solutions, linear equations with, 209–214, 224

number cubes, 601, 606–609, 614, 615, 617, 618, 620, 622, 623, 625, 626, 640, 641, 650–652, 655–658, 666

number lines, 42. *See also under* represent
  addition on, 91–96, 97–104, 105–112, 113–114, 118–119
  add or subtract positive integers on, 91–96
  comparisons on, 429–434
  double, 37, 141, 149
  fractions on, 115
  inequalities on, 225, 228–234, 241–245, 247
  negative integers on, 97–104
  negative numbers on, 92–95
  plotting expressions on, 432, 433
  plotting rational numbers on, 84, 89, 90, 91–96, 98–104, 105–112, 113–114, 118–119, 124, 126, 127, 140, 148, 155, 414
  plotting roots on, 436
  probability, 606
  showing absolute value on, 42
  subtraction on, 91–96, 97–104, 105–112, 113–114, 126–127
  thermometers as, 92–93, 95, 108, 109

numbers. *See also* mixed numbers; rational numbers
  investigating roots of, 421–428
  irrational, 415–420, 423, 428, 429, 430, 435–436
  ordering, 429–436
  positive root of, 423–435
  rational, 115–156, 414, 415–420, 424, 429, 435–436
  real, 413–436
  in scientific notation, 471–486
  standard or decimal form of, 471, 485, 486

number systems and operations, 87–184

numerator, 152
  greatest common factor of, and denominator, 417

numerical expressions. *See also* expressions
  writing and interpreting, 116, 158

Index

O

obtuse angles, 359
octagons, perimeter of, 181
octagonal prisms, volume of, 530
one solution, linear equations with, 209–214, 224
one-step equations, 490
   solving, 4, 188, 414
one-step inequalities, applying properties in solving, 227–234
open-ended problems, 23, 31, 33, 49, 65, 77, 102, 110, 111, 138, 146, 151, 172, 199, 212, 218, 238, 239, 244, 256, 287, 289, 305, 318, 319, 346, 360, 361, 387, 398, 407, 426, 433, 443, 449, 468, 477, 482, 507, 529, 534, 542, 561, 575, 590, 596, 608, 609, 615, 624, 631, 650, 661
operations
   inverse, 161
   with linear expressions, 354
   order of, 158, 438, 462
opposites, 126
   absolute value and, 90, 155
   Addition Property of, 107
   subtracting rational numbers by adding the, 128
ordered pairs
   on the coordinate plane, 4, 324, 336
   graphing, 28, 34
order of operations, 158, 438, 462
origin
   center of rotations, 277–282
   in graphs, 28, 33
outcome, 605, 607, 612, 665

P

parallel cross sections, 513–518
parallel lines, 371, 379
   exploring when cut by transversal, 371–378
   segments of, 260
parallelograms, 194, 256, 270, 293
   area of, 490, 508
   in finding area of circles, 498
parallel sides, 254–258
patterns
   in ratios, 3
   in tables, 6, 7
pentagons, 331
   perimeter of, 178, 180
pentagonal prisms, 515–516, 528, 530, 545
pentagonal pyramids, 517
Pentagon building, 331, 515

percent
   change, proportional reasoning and, 55–60
   decrease, 55–60
   equations, change in, 55–60
   error, 58
   finding, 54
   fractions written as, 604
   increase, 55–60
   in making predictions, 627–632
   proportional reasoning with, 53–86
   writing probability as, 639, 643, 647
perfect cubes, 424, 425, 427, 428, 429
perfect squares, 423, 426, 429
perimeter, 190, 192, 195, 208
perpendicular cross sections, 513–518
perpendicular lines, 321
perseverance, 2, 8, 16, 24, 32, 488, 494, 500, 516, 522, 528, 534
pi (π), 416, 492
   approximation for, 532
   in computing volume of cones and spheres, 537–544
   in computing volume of cylinders, 531–536
polygons
   in the coordinate plane, 252, 293, 294, 324, 335–340, 343–348
   drawing, 255
   exterior angles of, 357
   inscribing in circles, 296–299
   interior angles of, 357
population, 558, 565
positive numbers
   addition or subtraction of, on a number line, 113, 114
   cube root of, 424
   square root of, 423
Postulate, Angle-Angle (AA) Similarity, 364–370, 382, 383, 440
Power of Powers Law, 465, 466, 468
predictions
   experimental probability and proportional reasoning in making, 627–632
   making, based on simulation, 614, 622, 659–664
   proportional relationships in making, 11
   theoretical probability and proportional reasoning in making, 653–658
preimages, 327, 334
   of reductions, 349
   of reflections, 268–271, 273
   rotations of, 275–282
   translations of, 260–266
   vertex of, 261
prerequisite skills. *See also* Are You Ready?

add and subtract fractions and decimals, 90
add fractions and decimals, 116
angle relationships, 354
apply properties of operations, 158, 188
area of circles, 512
area of quadrilaterals and triangles, 490
box plots, 580
compare rational numbers, 226
convert fractions to decimals, 414
decimals, fractions written as, 604
divide fractions and mixed numbers, 4, 116
dot plots, 580
draw shapes with given conditions, 252, 438
evaluate algebraic expressions, 490
experimental probability, 636
explore volume, 512
find a percent or a whole, 54
fractions, decimals, and percents, 604
identify proportional relationships, 382
interpret, write, and graph inequalities, 226
mean, 580
more likely, less likely, equally likely, 636
multiply decimals by whole numbers, 54
multiply with decimals, 116
nets and surface area, 512
operations with linear expressions, 354
opposites and absolute value, 90
ordered pairs on the coordinate plane, 4
order of operations, 158, 438, 462
percents, fractions written as, 604
polygons in the coordinate plane, 252, 294, 324
quadrilaterals, 294
ratio language, 4
rational numbers on a number line, 90, 414
reflections, 324
representing equivalent ratios, 556
rotations, 324
scale drawings, 324
similar figures, 354
similar triangles, 382
solve equations with roots, 438
solve multi-step problems, 462
solve one-step equations, 4, 188, 414, 490
statistical data collection, 556, 604
tables and graphs of equivalent ratios, 382
translations, reflections, and rotations, 324
use ratio and rate reasoning, 54, 556, 604

Index **IN7**

Index

prerequisite skills (continued)
   use roots to solve equations, 438
   write and interpret numerical expressions, 116, 158
prices, retail, 61
prime notation, 261–262
principal, simple interest and, 79, 85
principal square root, 423
prisms
   base of, 514
   deriving and applying formulas for surface area of right, 519–524
   deriving and applying formulas for volume of right, 525–530
   hexagonal, 522, 524, 527, 529, 547
   octagonal, 530
   pentagonal, 515–516, 528, 530, 545
   rectangular, 512, 514, 523–524, 529, 545
      volume of, 525–530, 531, 545, 610
   surface area of, 522–524, 530, 545, 546
   trapezoidal, 547
   triangular, 515, 517, 522–524, 527–530, 546, 648
   volume of, 527–530, 545, 546
probability, 601–666
   conducting simulations, 614–618, 659–664
   experimental, 603–634, 635, 636, 665
      of compound events, 619–626
      of an event, 605–610
      proportional reasoning in making predictions, 627–632
      of simple events, 611–618
   theoretical, 635–666
      of compound events, 645–652
      proportional reasoning in making predictions, 653–658
      of simple events, 637–644
   understanding, 605–610
   writing as fraction, decimal, or percent, 639, 643, 647
problem solving
   adding, subtracting, and factoring, with rational coefficients, 175–182
   drawing and analyzing shapes in, 315–320
   linear equations, 215–222
   of multi-step problems, 167–174, 462
      with surface area and volume, 545–550
   proportional relationships in rate problems, 35–42
   ratios and rates in, 54
   two-step inequalities in, 235–246
   using inequalities in, 225–248
      one-step, 227–234
      two-step, 235–246
Product of Powers Law, 464–469
products
   finding, 116

   of rational numbers, 133–140
properties of exponents, 464
properties of operations, 157–184
   Addition Property of Equality, 138
   Addition Property of Opposites, 107
   applying, 158, 188
   Associative Property of Addition, 138, 157, 159, 160, 165, 175, 176, 177, 188
   Associative Property of Multiplication, 161, 164, 188
   Commutative Property of Addition, 120, 157, 158, 160, 165, 175–177, 188
   Commutative Property of Multiplication, 134, 161, 164
   Distributive Property, 134, 138, 157, 164, 167, 177, 178, 188, 197, 204, 208, 223, 479
   Division Property of Equality, 197
   of exponents, 465, 468, 485
   Identity Property of Multiplication, 138, 161
   Inverse Property of Multiplication, 161
   Multiplication Property of Equality, 384
   Multiplication Property of Zero, 138
   Power of Powers, 465, 466, 468
   Product of Powers, 464–469
   Quotient of Powers, 464–469
   Subtraction Property of Equality, 197
Property of Equality
   addition, 138
   division, 197
   multiplication, 384
   subtraction, 197
proportionality, constant of, 11–18, 22, 30–34, 51
proportional reasoning, 555–578
   in calculating markups and markdowns, 61–66, 85
   in determining commissions and fees, 73–78
   experimental probability and, in making predictions, 627–632
   making inferences from random samples, 563–570, 571–576
   percents in, 55–60
   representative samples and, 557–562
   scale drawings in, 43–50, 324
   simple interest, 79–84
   theoretical probability and, in making predictions, 653–658
   in writing equivalent ratios, 604
proportional relationships, 1–86, 321
   comparing, 36–37, 39–41
   computing unit rates involving complex fractions in, 19–26
   equations for, 12–18, 29, 35–42, 43, 44
   exploring, 5–10
   in graphs, 27–34
   identifying, 382

   in multi-step problems, 35–42
   percent in, 53–86
   in rate problems, 3–52
   in tables, 11–18
   in triangles, 383–388
proportions, in making predictions, 627–632
protractors. *See* manipulatives and materials
pyramids
   hexagonal, 515, 517
   pentagonal, 517
   triangular, 514
Pythagorean Theorem
   applying, 445–452, 453–460
   converse of, 439–444
      proving, 439–444
   in the coordinate plane, 453–460
   proving, 439–444
   uses of, 446–448
Pythagorean triple, 440, 441, 444

Q

quadrant, 270
quadrilaterals, 175, 294, 299, 350
   area of, 490
   constructing given side lengths of, 303, 305, 307
   drawing, 298
   measuring angles of, 254
   measuring sides of, 254
   parallel sides in, 254, 257
quantities, comparison of, 5–10
Quotient of Powers Law, 464–469
quotients. *See also* division
   finding, 116, 152
   of rational numbers, 133–140

R

radical symbol, 423
radius, 296–300, 321, 492, 493, 500, 509
random numbers, calculators in generating trials of, 660, 664
random samples, 559
   making inferences from, 563–570
   making inferences from repeated, 571–576
range, 579, 580, 581–592
rate of change, 228
rates
   comparing, 20
   constant, 7–10, 12, 19, 20, 22, 34, 38, 42
   markdowns, 61–66, 85
   markups, 61–66

Index

proportional relationships and, 3–52
reasoning on, 54, 556, 604
unit, 5–10, 12, 19–26, 34, 35–42, 47, 48, 51

rational numbers, 115–156, 414, 415–420, 424, 429, 435–436
addition of, 89–114, 117–124
fractions, 90, 116
comparing, 226, 430
division of, 133–140, 141–148, 149–154
multiplication of, 133–140, 149–154
plotting on a number line, 84, 89, 90, 91–96, 98–104, 105–112, 113–114, 118–119, 124, 126, 127, 140, 148, 155, 414
solving multi-step problems with, 167–174
subtraction of, 89–114, 125–132
fractions, 90
writing as decimals, 141–148

ratio notation, 419
ratio reasoning, 556, 604
ratios, 47, 51, 334, 370
of the circumference to the diameter, 492
constant, 30–34
in describing scale models, 1
equivalent, 3, 11–18, 23, 556
expressing in words, 3
patterns in, 3
proportional reasoning in writing equivalent, 604
rate reasoning, 54, 556, 604
in recipes, 5, 21, 23
simplifying, 45
writing, 19, 20

real numbers, 413–436
investigating roots and, 421–428
ordering, 429–436
understanding rational and irrational numbers, 415–420

real-world situations, applying linear equations to, 195–200

reasoning. See proportional reasoning

recipes
ratios in, 5, 21, 23
unit rates in, 28, 51

reciprocals, in finding unit rate, 21

rectangles
area of, 490
perimeter of, 180

rectangular prisms, 512, 514, 523–524, 529, 545
volume of, 525–530, 531, 545, 610

reductions, 326, 349
on a coordinate grid, 327–332
investigating, 325–332
preimage of, 349
thumbnails as, 326

reflections, 324, 345
exploring, 267–274
line of, 268
preimage of, 268–271, 273

relationships, exploring, 5–10. See also proportional relationships

remote interior angles, 357–358, 360, 362, 372–378, 379

repeated sampling
comparing means using mean absolute deviation and, 593–600
making inferences from random, 571–576

repeating decimals, 416–420, 435

represent
bar graphs, 569
bar models, 3, 19, 35, 38, 40, 53
box plots, 566, 568, 576, 580, 587–592, 598, 600
cubes, 526
diagrams, 6, 9, 35, 37, 40, 43–47, 61–65, 69–71, 73, 74, 80–83, 98, 99, 105, 138, 145, 147, 150, 155, 158, 161, 163, 164, 168–171, 176, 178, 180, 181, 187, 190–193, 199, 201, 203, 205, 216–220, 223, 227, 229, 230, 232–234, 238, 240, 259, 260, 264–268, 271, 275, 276, 281–284, 288–292, 294, 296–300, 302–304, 307, 309–313, 315–319, 328–330, 332, 337, 339, 345, 348–350, 363–377, 379, 380, 387, 388, 406, 418–422, 427, 429, 431, 433, 434, 437, 440–443, 446–451, 459, 464, 466, 467, 468, 473, 477, 478, 481, 483, 489, 490, 492–496, 498–500, 503–518, 520–547, 549–551, 607, 613, 616, 619, 620, 624, 635–639, 641, 642, 644–647, 649–654, 661, 666
dot plots, 567, 570, 572–575, 578, 580–586, 592, 594, 595, 596, 597, 599, 600, 604
double number lines, 37, 141, 149
equations, 12–18, 22, 24, 26, 29, 31, 33, 35–44, 46, 48, 49, 52, 67–74, 79–82, 161, 189, 196, 205, 206, 215–222, 396, 418, 469, 542
graphic organizers, 247
graphs, 4, 27–34, 36, 38, 39, 41, 42, 50, 52, 251, 293, 401–408, 564, 570
grids, 44, 45, 48, 261–265, 269, 270, 277–282, 285–292, 294, 297–300, 314, 318, 319, 321–324, 327–332, 335–340, 344–350, 363, 383–389, 391, 393–399, 410, 453–456, 458, 503, 505–508, 551
maps, 455–457, 585
number lines, 42, 84, 89–115, 118, 119, 124, 126, 127, 133, 140, 148, 154, 155, 225, 226, 228–234, 241–245, 247, 414, 430, 432, 433, 436, 606
pie charts, 317, 318
proportions, 3–86, 627–632, 653–658
scale drawings, 43–50
tables, 3, 4, 6–19, 24, 27–34, 36–41, 43, 46, 50, 52, 66, 81, 85–86, 90, 98, 99, 101, 113, 134, 135, 145, 157, 162, 168, 170, 197, 210, 211, 214, 222, 224, 259, 261, 262, 266, 269, 270, 276–278, 286, 291, 318, 322, 334, 350, 381, 390–393, 400, 409, 415, 422, 426, 435, 444, 449, 454, 464, 467, 468, 472, 474, 475, 483–485, 492, 542, 551, 556, 572–576, 579, 580, 583, 587, 589, 593, 595, 596, 603, 607, 611–618, 620–623, 625, 626, 631, 632, 634–636, 640, 641, 643–645, 648, 651, 659–661, 664–666
tree diagrams, 646, 649, 651
unit cubes, 525, 526

representative samples, 557–562
resilience, 186, 192, 198, 206, 212, 232, 238, 412, 418, 426, 442, 450, 468, 554, 560, 568
retail prices, 61
Review and Test
Are You Ready? appears in every module. 4, 54, 90, 116, 158, 188, 226, 252, 294, 324, 354, 382, 414, 438, 462, 490, 512, 556, 580, 604, 636
Module Review, appears in every module. 51–52, 85–86, 113–114, 155–156, 183–184, 223–224, 247–248, 291–292, 321–322, 349–350, 379–380, 409–410, 435–436, 459–460, 485–486, 509–510, 551–552, 577–578, 599–600, 633–634, 665–666

rhombus, 194
right angles, 220
right cones, 537
right prisms
deriving and applying formulas for surface areas of, 519–524
surface area of, 521

right triangles, 444
converse of the Pythagorean Theorem and, 439–444
determining slope with, 383
hypotenuse of, 384, 440–444, 446, 447, 453–460
Pythagorean Theorem and, 439–444, 445–452, 453–460

rise, 384
roots, 421–428
cube, 424–428, 429–436
square, 423–428, 429–436, 441
using to solve equations, 438

Index **IN9**

Index

rotations, 324, 345, 348, 349
   exploring, 275–282
rulers, 297, 301–308, 333, 354
   in measuring sides of quadrilaterals, 254
run, 384

S

sales tax, 67, 85
same-side exterior angles, 372
same-side interior angles, 372
sample data, 593–600
samples
   bias of, 558
   making inferences from, 563–570
   making inferences from repeated, 571–576
   random, 559
   representative, 557–562
sample space, 607, 620, 645–652
sampling, comparing means using mean absolute deviation and repeated, 593–600
scale, 43, 44, 45, 46, 50
scale drawings
   dimensions, 45
   proportional reasoning with, 43–50, 324
scale factors, 334–340, 344–348, 349–350, 370
scientific notation, 471–486
   computing with, 479–486
   division in, 480–486
   multiplication in, 480–486
segments, 260
sequence of transformations, 341–348
shapes, drawing, with given conditions, 252, 438
sides
   corresponding, 363
   parallel, 254–258
signs. *See* symbols
similar figures, 354
   understanding and recognizing, 341–348
similarity
   angle-angle, 363–370, 440
   dilations and, 333–340
   reductions and enlargements and, 325–332
   similar figures and, 341–348
   transformations and, 323–350
similar triangles, 341–348, 349, 364–370, 378, 379, 382, 383–388
simple events
   experimental probability of, 611–618
   theoretical probability of, 637–644
simple interest, proportional reasoning in calculating, 79–84, 86

simulations, 614, 622
   making predictions based on, 614, 659–664
slant height, of cones, 539
slope
   of a line, 389–394, 395–400
   similar triangles, explaining with, 383–388
slope-intercept form, 395–400
social studies, 257, 406, 476, 547, 630
solids, describing and analyzing cross sections of, 513–518
solution of an equation, 196–200
solution of an inequality, 228, 236, 247
spheres
   diameter of, 467, 537–544
   height of, 537–544
   radius of, 537–544
   volume of, 537–544, 548–549
      formula for, 537–544
spinners, 613, 616, 624, 636, 638, 642, 644, 645, 647, 650–653, 655, 661, 664, 666
spread of data
   comparing center and, when displayed
      in box plots, 587–592
      in dot plots, 581–586
square pyramids, 516
square roots, 423–428, 429–436, 441
   symbol for ($\sqrt{}$), 423
   of zero, 426
squares, 293, 339, 346, 489, 490
   area of, 421
   perfect, 423, 426, 429
statistical data collection, 556, 604
STEM Task, 1, 87, 185, 249, 351, 411, 487, 553, 601
strategic help-seeking, 88, 94, 102, 110, 122, 130, 138, 146, 152
substitute, 210
subtraction
   absolute value (||), 119, 131
   of exponents, 464–470
   of fractions, 90
   of negative integers on a number line, 97–104
   Property of Equality, 197
   of rational numbers, 89–114, 125–132
   with scientific notation, 479–486
   of temperature, 92–93, 95
sum, 90, 116, 121. *See also* addition
   absolute value (||), 118–120
supplementary angles, 216, 219, 221, 223, 360–361, 371–380
surface area
   deriving and applying formulas for cubes and right prisms, 519–524
   nets and, 512, 520

   solving multi-step problems with volume and, 545–550
surveys, 558
symbols, M2
   cube root ($\sqrt[3]{}$), 424
   greater than (>), 226, 228–234, 304, 306
   greater than or equal to (≥), 228–234
   less than (<), 226, 228–234, 304, 306
   less than or equal to (≤), 228–234
   pi (π), 416, 492
   radical, 423
   square root ($\sqrt{}$), 423
symmetry, lines of, 257, 321

T

Table of Measures, M1–M2
tables. *See also under* represent
   fraction and decimal conversions, 145
   graphs of equivalent ratios and, 382
   products of rational numbers, 134
   proportional relationships in, 11–18
   quotients of rational numbers, 135
   rational and irrational numbers, 415
   relationships in, 6–10
   representing inverse operations, 135
taxes
   equations in determining, 67–72
   sales, 67, 85
technology and digital resources.
   See Ed: Your Friend in Learning for interactive instruction, interactive practice, and videos
temperature
   addition expression for, 119
   nonlinear relationships, 403, 407
   plotting on a thermometer, 92–93, 95, 108–109
   subtraction expression for, 131
terminating decimals, 416–419
theorems
   Exterior Angle, 358
   Pythagorean, 437–460
      applying, 445–452, 453–460
      converse of, 439–444
      proving, 439–444
      proving the converse of, 439–444
      uses of, 446–448
   Triangle Sum, 356–357, 359, 365, 374
theoretical probability, 635–666
   of compound events, 645–652
   proportional reasoning in making predictions, 653–658
   of simple events, 637–644
thermometers, as number lines, 92–93, 95, 108, 109
time, nonlinear relationships, 403

tips, using equations to determine, 67–72, 86. *See also* gratuities
tools. *See* calculators; manipulatives and materials
transformation, 324, 332, 343–348, 384, 386, 388
transformational geometry
   congruence and, 251–292, 349
   dilations in, 342–348, 349
   images in, 260–266, 325, 327, 328
   mapping notation, 261–265, 280, 285, 336, 337, 345–347
   preimage in, 260–266, 268–271, 273, 275–282
   prime notation, 261–262
   reductions and enlargements in, 325–332
   reflections in, 267–274
   rotations in, 275–282
   sequence of, 283–290
   similarity and, 323–350
translations, 259–266, 324
transversals, 379, 387
   exploring parallel lines cut by, 371–378
trapezoidal prisms, 547
trapezoids, 293, 348
tree diagrams, 646, 649, 651
trials, 607
triangles, 293, 294, 321–322
   angle relationships for, 340, 355–362
   drawing and constructing
     given angle measures, 309–314, 318
     given side lengths, 301–308, 318
   drawing with ruler and protractor, 354, 355
   equilateral, 176, 359
   hypotenuse of, 384, 440–444, 446, 447, 453–460
   inscribing, in circles, 296–299
   isosceles, 190, 437, 522
   right, 296, 316, 439–444, 453–460, 546
   legs of, 384, 440–444, 453–454
   similar, 341–348, 349, 364–370, 378, 379, 382, 383–388
   slope, explaining with similar, 383–388
   vertices of, 281, 285, 290, 346, 348
Triangle Sum Theorem, 356–357, 359, 365, 374

triangular prisms, 515, 517, 522–524, 527–530, 546, 648
triangular pyramids, 514
triple, Pythagorean, 440, 441, 444
two-dimensional figures
   drawing and analyzing, 293–322
     circles and other figures, 295–300
     shapes in problem solving, 315–320
     triangles given angle measures, 309–314
     triangles given side lengths, 301–308
two-step inequalities
   in problem solving, 241–246
   writing, 235–240

U

unit openers, 1–2, 87–88, 185–186, 249–250, 351–352, 411–412, 487–488, 553–554, 601–602
unit rates, 5–10, 12, 34, 35–42, 47, 48
   computing, involving complex fractions, 19–26
   density as, 25
   division in finding, 21
   in recipes, 28, 51
   reciprocals in finding, 21
   triangles, 385
upper quartile, 588, 599

V

variables, isolating, 202
vertex. *See* vertices
vertical angles, 216, 219, 223, 353
vertices, 261
   coordinates of, 270, 281
   of triangles, 281
volume
   of composite figures, 546
   of cones, 537–544
   of cubes, 422, 467
   of cylinders, 531–536
   exploring, 512
   of rectangular prisms, 525–530, 531, 545, 610
   of spheres, 537–544, 548–549

W

whiskers of box plots, 587
whole numbers, multiplication of decimals by, 54
words, expressing ratios in, 3

X

***x*-axis**
   reflections over, 269–273
   sides of right triangles, 383
***x*-coordinates,** run, 384

Y

***y*-axis,** reflections over, 269–273
***y*-coordinates,** rise, 384
***y*-intercept,** 396–400

Z

zero
   cube root of, 426
   square root of, 426

Tables of Measures, Symbols, and Formulas

SYMBOLS

$=$	is equal to	10^2	ten squared
$\neq$	is not equal to	10^3	ten cubed
$\approx$	is approximately equal to	2^4	the fourth power of 2
$>$	is greater than	$|-4|$	the absolute value of -4
$<$	is less than	%	percent
$\geq$	is greater than or equal to	(2, 3)	ordered pair (x, y)
$\leq$	is less than or equal to	°	degree

FORMULAS

Perimeter and Circumference

Polygon	$P =$ sum of the lengths of sides
Rectangle	$P = 2\ell + 2w$
Square	$P = 4s$
Circle	$C = \pi d$ or $C = 2\pi r$

Area

Rectangle	$A = \ell w$
Parallelogram	$A = bh$
Triangle	$A = \frac{1}{2}bh$
Trapezoid	$A = \frac{1}{2}h(b_1 + b_2)$
Square	$A = s^2$
Circle	$A = \pi r^2$

Volume

Right Prism	$V = \ell wh$ or $V = Bh$
Cube	$V = s^3$
Pyramid	$V = \frac{1}{3}Bh$
Cylinder	$V = \pi r^2 h$
Cone	$V = \frac{1}{3}\pi r^2 h$
Sphere	$V = \frac{4}{3}\pi r^3$

Surface Area

Right Prism	$S = Ph + 2B$
Cube	$S = 6s^2$
Square Pyramid	$S = \frac{1}{2}P\ell + B$

Pythagorean Theorem

$a^2 + b^2 = c^2$

Tables of Measures, Symbols, and Formulas

LENGTH

1 meter (m) = 1,000 millimeters (mm)
1 meter = 100 centimeters (cm)
1 meter ≈ 39.37 inches
1 kilometer (km) = 1,000 meters
1 kilometer ≈ 0.62 mile

1 inch = 2.54 centimeters
1 foot (ft) = 12 inches (in.)
1 yard (yd) = 3 feet
1 mile (mi) = 1,760 yards
1 mile = 5,280 feet
1 mile ≈ 1.609 kilometers

CAPACITY

1 liter (L) = 1,000 milliliters (mL)
1 liter = 1,000 cubic centimeters
1 liter ≈ 0.264 gallon
1 kiloliter (kL) = 1,000 liters

1 cup (c) = 8 fluid ounces (fl oz)
1 pint (pt) = 2 cups
1 quart (qt) = 2 pints
1 gallon (gal) = 4 quarts
1 gallon ≈ 3.785 liters

MASS/WEIGHT

1 gram (g) = 1,000 milligrams (mg)
1 kilogram (kg) = 1,000 grams
1 kilogram ≈ 2.2 pounds

1 pound (lb) = 16 ounces (oz)
1 pound ≈ 0.454 kilogram
1 ton = 2,000 pounds

TIME

1 minute (min) = 60 seconds (s)
1 hour (h) = 60 minutes
1 day = 24 hours
1 week = 7 days

1 year (yr) = about 52 weeks
1 year = 12 months (mo)
1 year = 365 days
1 decade = 10 years